EDUCATIONAL PSYCHOLOGY 96/97

Eleventh Edition

Editor

Kathleen M. Cauley
Virginia Commonwealth University

Kathleen M. Cauley received her Ph.D. in educational studies/human development from the University of Delaware in 1985. Her research interests center on applying cognitive developmental research to school learning. Currently, she is studying children's mathematical understanding in classrooms that are implementing the National Council of Teachers of Mathematics Standards for Mathematics.

Editor

Fredric Linder
Virginia Commonwealth University

Fredric Linder received an A.B. in American civilization from the University of Miami, Florida, a M.A. in psychology from the New School for Social Research, and a Ph.D. in educational psychology from the State University of New York at Buffalo. His research and publications focus on the values, locus of control, and cognitive learning styles of students.

Editor

James H. McMillan
Virginia Commonwealth University

James H. McMillan received his bachelor's degree from Albion College in 1970, his M.A. from Michigan State University in 1972, and his Ph.D. from Northwestern University in 1976. He has reviewed and written extensively on many topics in educational psychology. His current interests are classroom assessment and school report cards.

A Library of Information from the Public Press

Cover illustration by Mike Eagle

**Dushkin Publishing Group/
Brown & Benchmark Publishers**
Sluice Dock, Guilford, Connecticut 06437

The Annual Editions Series

Annual Editions is a series of over 65 volumes designed to provide the reader with convenient, low-cost access to a wide range of current, carefully selected articles from some of the most important magazines, newspapers, and journals published today. Annual Editions are updated on an annual basis through a continuous monitoring of over 300 periodical sources. All Annual Editions have a number of features designed to make them particularly useful, including topic guides, annotated tables of contents, unit overviews, and indexes. For the teacher using Annual Editions in the classroom, an Instructor's Resource Guide with test questions is available for each volume.

VOLUMES AVAILABLE

Abnormal Psychology
Africa
Aging
American Foreign Policy
American Government
American History, Pre-Civil War
American History, Post-Civil War
American Public Policy
Anthropology
Archaeology
Biopsychology
Business Ethics
Child Growth and Development
China
Comparative Politics
Computers in Education
Computers in Society
Criminal Justice
Developing World
Deviant Behavior
Drugs, Society, and Behavior
Dying, Death, and Bereavement
Early Childhood Education
Economics
Educating Exceptional Children
Education
Educational Psychology
Environment
Geography
Global Issues
Health
Human Development
Human Resources
Human Sexuality

India and South Asia
International Business
Japan and the Pacific Rim
Latin America
Life Management
Macroeconomics
Management
Marketing
Marriage and Family
Mass Media
Microeconomics
Middle East and the Islamic World
Multicultural Education
Nutrition
Personal Growth and Behavior
Physical Anthropology
Psychology
Public Administration
Race and Ethnic Relations
Russia, the Eurasian Republics, and Central/Eastern Europe
Social Problems
Sociology
State and Local Government
Urban Society
Western Civilization, Pre-Reformation
Western Civilization, Post-Reformation
Western Europe
World History, Pre-Modern
World History, Modern
World Politics

Cataloging in Publication Data
Main entry under title: Annual Editions: Educational Psychology. 1996/97.
    1. Educational psychology—Periodicals. 2. Teaching—Periodicals. I. Cauley, Kathleen M., *comp.*; Linder, Fredric, *comp.*; McMillan, James H., *comp.* II. Title: Educational psychology.
ISBN 0–697–31555–X   370.15′05   82–640517

Eleventh Edition

Printed in the United States of America

Printed on Recycled Paper

Editors/ Advisory Board

EDITORS

Kathleen M. Cauley
Virginia Commonwealth University

Fredric Linder
Virginia Commonwealth University

James H. McMillan
Virginia Commonwealth University

Members of the Advisory Board are instrumental in the final selection of articles for each edition of Annual Editions. Their review of articles for content, level, currentness, and appropriateness provides critical direction to the editor and staff. We think you'll find their careful consideration well reflected in this volume.

ADVISORY BOARD

Roberta Ahlquist
San Jose State University

Thomas L. Bennett
Bowling Green State University

Edward J. Caropreso
Clarion University

Karen G. Duffy
SUNY College, Geneseo

Godfrey Franklin
University of West Florida

Albert H. Gardner
University of Maryland
College Park

Christian Gerhard
George Washington University

William L. Goodwin
University of Colorado
Denver

William M. Gray
University of Toledo

Cheryl Greenberg
University of North Carolina
Greensboro

Elaine C. Koffman
Northeastern Illinois University

Kelton F. Lustig
Bethel College

Golam Mannan
Indiana University–
Purdue University

Laura J. Massey
Montana State University

Donald H. Saklofske
University of Saskatchewan

Fred Schultz
University of Akron

Thomas J. Shuell
University of Buffalo

Sandra M. Stokes
University of Wisconsin
Green Bay

Harvey N. Switzky
Northern Illinois University

Lani M. Van Dusen
Utah State University

STAFF

To the Reader

In publishing ANNUAL EDITIONS we recognize the enormous role played by the magazines, newspapers, and journals of the *public press* in providing current, first-rate educational information in a broad spectrum of interest areas. Within the articles, the best scientists, practitioners, researchers, and commentators draw issues into new perspective as accepted theories and viewpoints are called into account by new events, recent discoveries change old facts, and fresh debate breaks out over important controversies.

Many of the articles resulting from this enormous editorial effort are appropriate for students, researchers, and professionals seeking accurate, current material to help bridge the gap between principles and theories and the real world. These articles, however, become more useful for study when those of lasting value are carefully *collected, organized, indexed,* and *reproduced* in a *low-cost format,* which provides easy and permanent access when the material is needed. That is the role played by ANNUAL EDITIONS. Under the direction of each volume's *Editor,* who is an expert in the subject area, and with the guidance of an *Advisory Board,* we seek each year to provide in each ANNUAL EDITION a current, well-balanced, carefully selected collection of the best of the public press for your study and enjoyment. We think you'll find this volume useful, and we hope you'll take a moment to let us know what you think.

Educational psychology is an interdisciplinary subject that includes human development, learning, intelligence, motivation, assessment, instructional strategies, and classroom management. The articles in this volume give special attention to the application of this knowledge to teaching.

Annual Editions: Educational Psychology 96/97 is presented in six units. An overview precedes each unit, explaining how the articles in the unit are related to the broader issues within educational psychology. The first unit presents issues central to the teaching role. The authors discuss the challenges of responding to calls for educational reform and the role of research in meeting those challenges.

The second unit, concerned with child and adolescent development, covers the cognitive, social, and emotional components of development. The articles in this unit examine the developmental implications for teachers of early childhood programs, the social forces affecting children and adolescents, and the personal and social skills needed to cope with school learning and developmental tasks.

The third unit, concerning exceptional and culturally diverse students, focuses on the learning disabled, the gifted, and the minority student. All of these students are different in some way and require an individualized approach to education. The articles in this unit review the characteristics of these children and suggest programs and strategies to meet their needs.

The fourth unit includes articles about theories of learning and instructional strategies. The different views of learning, such as information processing, behaviorism, and constructivist learning, represent the accumulation of years of research on the way humans change in thinking or behavior due to experience. The principles generated by each approach have important implications for teaching. These implications are addressed in a section on instructional strategies, covering such topics as instructional methods, authentic instruction, computer-aided teaching, learning styles, and discovery methods.

The topic of motivation is perhaps one of the most important aspects of school learning. Effective teachers need to motivate their students both to learn and to behave responsibly. How to manage children and what forms of discipline to use are issues that concern parents as well as teachers and administrators. The articles in the fifth unit present a variety of perspectives on motivating students and discuss approaches to managing student behavior.

The articles in unit six review assessment approaches that can be used to diagnose learning and improve instruction. The focus is on grading practices and appropriate uses of standardized tests. Performance based assessment is introduced as a promising new approach to classroom measurement.

This 11th edition of *Annual Editions: Educational Psychology* has been revised so as to present articles that are current and useful. Your responses to the selection and organization of materials are appreciated. Please fill out and return the postage-paid *article rating form* on the last page of the book.

Kathleen M. Cauley

Fredric Linder

James H. McMillan
Editors

Contents

The concepts in bold italics are developed in the article. For further expansion please refer to the Topic Guide and the Index.

Unit 3

Exceptional and Culturally Diverse Students

Seven articles look at the problems and positive effects of educational programs for learning disabled, gifted, and culturally diverse children.

The concepts in bold italics are developed in the article. For further expansion please refer to the Topic Guide and the Index.

Unit 4

Learning and Instruction

Eleven selections explore the important types of student/teacher interaction.

The concepts in bold italics are developed in the article. For further expansion please refer to the Topic Guide and the Index.

Unit 5

Motivation and Classroom Management

Seven selections discuss student control and motivation in the classroom.

The concepts in bold italics are developed in the article. For further expansion please refer to the Topic Guide and the Index.

Unit 6

Assessment

Six articles discuss the implications of educational measurement for the classroom decision-making process and for the teaching profession.

The concepts in bold italics are developed in the article. For further expansion please refer to the Topic Guide and the Index.

Topic Guide

This topic guide suggests how the selections in this book relate to topics of traditional concern to educational psychology students and professionals. It is useful for locating articles that relate to each other for reading and research. The guide is arranged alphabetically according to topic. Articles may, of course, treat topics that do not appear in the topic guide. In turn, entries in the topic guide do not necessarily constitute a comprehensive listing of all the contents of each selection.

TOPIC AREA	TREATED IN	TOPIC AREA	TREATED IN
Action Research	3. Using Action Research to Assess Instruction	Discipline	28. Choices for Children 33. Why Violence Prevention Programs Don't Work 34. Corporal Punishment
Advance Organizer	24. About Instruction	Diverse Students	15. "All Kids Can Learn" 16. Student Diversity
At-Risk Students	9. At-Risk Students and Resiliency	Early Childhood	4. Learning through "Play" 6. Young Children's Understanding of Everyday Emotions 7. Encouraging Positive Social Development in Young Children
Authentic Assessment	37. Creating Tests Worth Taking 38. Performance Assessment		
Behaviorism	19. Rewards of Learning 20. Rewards versus Learning 21. Sticking Up for Rewards	Educational Reform	2. Six National Goals 37. Creating Tests Worth Taking
Character Development	23. Beyond the Pendulum	Effective Teaching	24. About Instruction
Child/Adolescent Development	4. Learning through "Play" 5. Helping Children Develop Self-Control 6. Young Children's Understanding of Everyday Emotions 7. Encouraging Positive Social Development in Young Children 8. Caring for Others and Being Cared For 9. At-Risk Students and Resiliency	Family Structure	5. Helping Children Develop Self-Control 9. At-Risk Students and Resiliency
		Gifted Children and Youth	12. Ability Grouping 13. Meeting the Needs of Your High-Ability Students
		Grouping Students	12. Ability Grouping
Classroom Management	31. From Negation to Negotiation 32. Images of Management for Learner-Centered Classrooms	Humanistic Education	22. Tyranny of Self-Oriented Self-Esteem 23. Beyond the Pendulum
Cognitive Development	4. Learning through "Play" 5. Helping Children Develop Self-Control	Individual Differences	24. About Instruction 26. Allowing for Thinking Styles
Cognitive Learning	17. Remembering the Forgotten Art of Memory 18. Mind's Journey from Novice to Expert 24. About Instruction 25. Problem Based Learning	Information Processing	17. Remembering the Forgotten Art of Memory 18. Mind's Journey from Novice to Expert
		Instruction	24. About Instruction
Computer-Assisted Instruction	27. How K–12 Teachers Are Using Computer Networks	Learning Centered	30. Using Motivational Theory with At-Risk Children 32. Images of Management for Learner-Centered Classrooms
Constructivism	2. Six National Goals 25. Problem Based Learning 28. Choices for Children		
		Learning Styles/Strategies	24. About Instruction 26. Allowing for Thinking Styles 39. Planning for Classroom Portfolio Assessment
Criterion Referenced	36. Making the Grade 37. Creating Tests Worth Taking		
Critical Thinking	25. Problem Based Learning	Mainstreaming	11. Courtside
Disabilities	10. When Your Child Is Special 11. Courtside	Memory	17. Remembering the Forgotten Art of Memory
		Metacognition	25. Problem Based Learning

Perspectives on Teaching

The teaching-learning process in school is enormously complex. Many factors influence pupil learning—such as family background, developmental level, prior knowledge, motivation, and, of course, effective teachers. Educational psychology investigates these factors to better understand and explain student learning. We begin our exploration of the teaching-learning process by considering the teaching role.

In the first article, Jeffrey Aceto describes the teacher's role through the eyes of a first-time substitute teacher. He leaves his first day with a renewed admiration for the many talents required of full-time teachers.

Aceto, however, only sees the surface features of a school day. As the selection by Constance Kamii, Faye Clark, and Ann Dominick suggests, our philosophy of teaching can have an enormous influence over the way we conceive of the teaching role. These authors expound a constructivist perspective on the goals in *America 2000*. They argue that developing both moral and intellectual autonomy in children ought to be our overarching goal. If we adopt the goal of autonomy, then classroom practices will change in significant ways.

Another less obvious aspect of the teaching role is the systematic effort to improve. Engaging in action is rapidly becoming a new role for teachers to assume as they conduct systematic inquiry—or research—to improve teaching and learning. As the professional development schools envisioned by the Holmes group and others are established, teacher research will become more widespread. In the next selection, the authors illustrate that teachers should conduct an action research project to improve the classroom learning environment. Carole Schulte Johnson and Inga Kromann-Kelly describe five basic questions to guide the development of action research projects. The five questions determine (1) the main question to pursue; (2) data that are relevant; (3) how to collect the data; (4) analyzing the data; and (5) what data implicate.

Educational psychology is a resource for teachers that emphasizes disciplined inquiry, a systematic and objective analysis of information, and a scientific attitude toward decision making. The field provides information for decisions that are based on quantitative and qualitative studies of learning and teaching rather than on intuition, tradition, authority, or subjective feelings. It is our hope that this aspect of educational psychology is communicated throughout these readings, and that as a student you will adopt the analytic, probing attitude that is part of the discipline.

While educational psychologists have helped to establish a knowledge base about teaching and learning, the unpredictable, spontaneous, evolving nature of teaching suggests that the best they will ever do is to provide concepts and skills that teachers can adapt for use in their classrooms. The issues raised in these articles about the impact of the reform movement on teachers help us understand the teaching role and its demands. As you read articles in other chapters, consider the demands they place on the teaching role as well.

Looking Ahead: Challenge Questions

Describe several of the roles teachers are expected to perform.

As educational reform progresses, what new demands will it place on teachers?

How does research, either teacher research or formal educational research, improve teaching?

A Piece of Cake

Mr. Aceto describes his first day as a substitute teacher in an elementary school. Would he do it again? Absolutely! Would he consider doing it for a living? Not a chance!

Jeffrey T. Aceto

JEFFREY T. ACETO is a civil engineer with DeLuca Hoffman Associates, Inc., consulting engineers, in South Portland, Me.

RECENTLY I found myself nearing 30 and an unemployed college graduate. So when a friend urged me to try substitute teaching, I thought, Why not? How could it possibly be difficult? I'm a mature, well-adjusted adult, and they'd only be little kids. Besides, the day would be a short seven hours. It would be a piece of cake!

Arriving at school on a crisp autumn morning, I find the scene reminiscent of my own youth. School buses unloading kids in colorful jackets who clutch homework, books, and lunch boxes. My own lunch is the sole content of my briefcase, and it occurs to me that after 20 years I've only traded my metal lunch box for a leather one.

The assistant principal greets me warmly and assures me the day will go smoothly. "Just follow your instructions, and everything will be fine," she says. Sure, I think. Piece of cake.

I find my classroom spotless and orderly, with clean chalkboards and the

Illustration by Brenda Grannan

desks and chairs lined up neatly. Student work and seasonal displays adorn the walls. A paper turkey with necktie feathers watches me warily from the back wall. Not a bad room, I think, although the teacher I'm replacing has spelled *calendar* wrong. That's a bad sign, I think, but I shrug it off.

The children begin to flood into the room. At least, I assume that these are my students. I realize that I'm largely at their mercy with regard to who is supposed to be where and when. As they shrug off their child-sized backpacks, they turn fresh little faces toward me. It is a scene a grandparent would love. At first they are reluctant to speak to me, but soon I am bombarded with questions and comments: "Where is Mrs. Smith? Are you Mr. Smith? How long will you be here?"

I can see the realization dawning on them that what they have here is a rare bird, indeed: a substitute teacher — and a man, to boot. This guy is fresh meat. The class quickly reaches a silent consensus: today is a good day for raising some hell.

"Just" follow the instructions, and everything will be okay, the assistant principal had said. Here, Christian, "just" go in there and take on those lions. Hail, Caesar, we who are about to die salute thee! Let the games begin. I confidently announce that it is time for math and ask them to take out their books. Immediately there is a flurry of activity that Federal Express would admire.

Have you ever tried to wrestle an octopus? One boy is fighting with another, and a girl is writing on the chalkboard. Someone has just gone out the door, and half a dozen girls are crooning over a troll catalogue.

Names are the first minor crisis. I have no idea who is who. I look up to the turkey for assistance, but its facial expression clearly says, "You're on your own, pal."

Great. Four years of college, and I've been reduced to babysitting on a large scale. My vocabulary for the day swiftly degenerates into versions of a few set phrases: Please sit down. Do your own work. Leave her alone. Raise your hand if you want to speak. Stay in line. I quickly discover that fact is stranger and more complicated than fiction; Schwarzenegger had it easy in *Kindergarten Cop*.

I find myself frantically scanning the instructions every five minutes or so. Are we doing what we're supposed to be doing? Is everyone in the right place? Are we falling behind or running ahead of the schedule? These instructions are my lifeline, and I tape them up — out of the students' reach — with great reverence.

An unbidden rush of thoughts cascades through my brain. Why did I wear a tie? It just gives them something to get a grip on. I've heard less noise at a University of Maine hockey game. Are fishing vessels lost at sea homing in on the roar emanating from this classroom? Are the other teachers shaking their heads in disgust at a rookie who can't control the students?

"Quiet, please" is like whistling in the wind. "Let's keep it quiet" has all the impact of a popgun on an elephant. It's time to go ballistic. "I need quiet right now or someone's going to the office!" That's better. Good job, Jeff, practice "teaching by terrorism." I'm not surprised that threats work — after all, I'm a little bit afraid of the office myself. But threats work for only about five minutes.

Soon, snack time arrives. Everything so far has been just a warm-up for the main event, as the little darlings go into a sugar-crazed frenzy. I see candy, donuts, chips, and soda; fruit, vegetables, and juice are scarcely to be found. What a great idea this is: fill them up with sugar-laden snacks; then ask them to sit quietly and read.

WE MOVE steadily through the day. There is a toothache, an earache, a nosebleed, a lost pair of glasses. Two of the worst offenders are dispatched to the office; one student has to take anti-nervousness drugs. I am assured by the veteran teachers that this qualifies as a typical day.

Recess duty is the longest 20 minutes of my life. Now I know how Custer felt. I'm surrounded by 200 little wingnuts running into, over, and through each other. "Suzie hit me!" "Johnny kissed me!" "I can't find my watch!" I resist the strong urge to seek a hiding place instead of the missing watch.

With the incessant din of children's sounds, I find myself yearning for adult companionship. I pass fellow teachers in the halls; as if we're members of a secret society, we salute one another with weary, harried looks.

The teachers' lounge has all the warmth of an unemployment office. The chairs are wooden, hard, and too heavy for most of us to move by ourselves. The teachers share the room with mimeograph machines and cast-off office equipment. Ragged notices from the union compete for bulletin board space with news of bake sales and Tupperware parties. Talk in the lounge revolves around kids with head lice, kids who aren't toilet trained, abused kids, and kids who, it is conjectured, need psychological evaluation. I've felt more relaxed during dental surgery.

The children are the centerpiece of this confusing circus, of course, and no one can spend even one day with them without encountering a few special moments. A girl whom I coax through a reading passage breaks into a broad smile when I tell her she did a great job. A few children who are clearly ignored by their parents and starved for attention give me big hugs at the end of the day. I notice a chubby, plain girl who is ignored by the rest of the children. She reads aloud a story she has written. "Once-upon-a-time stories are stories of beautiful places where you will never go," she reads. It's the saddest thing I've ever heard; she's 8 years old, and already she's decided that she can never go to beautiful places.

I realize that this teaching stuff is more than babysitting. Trying to encourage youngsters like her is truly an important, even noble, cause.

"You're the best teacher in the world! Are you coming back tomorrow?" All day long they've been running through the halls, talking out in class, and using the restricted art supplies. They're pulling fast ones on me, but it doesn't matter. My sole goal is to end the day with the same number of warm, breathing bodies with which it began.

The end of the day arrives at last. A bus number is garbled over the intercom, there's a final rush to the door, and, suddenly, the quiet and stillness are deafening. The room looks as if it has been visited by a division of Patton's tanks. Desks and chairs are strewn about; the wastebaskets are overflowing. The carpeted floor is a collage of paper, candy wrappers, crayons, a half-eaten donut, an escaped earring, and one blue sock. That last item troubles me a bit. The turkey droops from the wall and appears to be laughing at me. One of the paper decorations hanging from the ceiling suddenly comes unglued and drifts to the floor.

It's time to put the day into perspective, I think. This was a class of "normal" kids. I didn't have those with fetal alcohol syndrome or those who have been abused. Everything was in my favor. There will be janitors to clean up after us, and there were other teachers to take charge of music, physical education, library, and special needs. I had a detailed plan and a schedule of what to do. The buses ran on time, and no gangs stalked the halls. I didn't have to deal with any parents or committees. And yet I feel as if I have just run a marathon.

The insignificant events of this, my first day in elementary education, are just a sampling of business as usual. I am now doubly impressed by the commitment and talents required of full-time teachers. I no longer condemn Mrs. Smith for her spelling error. I'm so tired that I have trouble finding my car after just one brief, seven-hour day.

Would I do it again? Absolutely. Piece of cake. Would I consider doing this for a living? Not a chance!

The Six National Goals

A Road to Disappointment

The people who set goals for education seldom take into account scientific knowledge about how children acquire knowledge and moral values — and the six national goals formulated in 1990 are no exception, these authors charge.

CONSTANCE KAMII,
FAYE B. CLARK, AND
ANN DOMINICK

CONSTANCE KAMII is a professor in the Department of Curriculum and Instruction at the University of Alabama, Birmingham; FAYE B. CLARK is an assistant professor in the School of Education, Samford University, Birmingham; and ANN DOMINICK is a fourth-grade teacher at Shades Cahaba Elementary School, Homewood, Ala.

Illustration by Mario Noche

MANY FACTORS can be cited to explain the meager results of the reform efforts of the past decade. The quick-fix approach to accountability that led only to attempts to raise test scores and increase graduation requirements and a variety of other reasons have been mentioned in recent years. Many people are calling for bolder, fundamental, systemic changes, especially changes that bring true innovation into the classroom. A factor seldom mentioned is the need for coherent goals that are based on the best scientific theory available today about how human beings acquire knowledge and moral values. Such goals are of the utmost importance in education reform because, if our objectives are poorly conceived, the rest of our efforts will be misdirected.

Goals in education are usually defined by groups of people who have the power to decide what outcomes are desirable. The people who set these goals seldom take into account scientific knowledge about how children acquire knowledge and moral values. They usually formulate goals based on tradition and on their own values and priorities. The six national goals that were formulated by President Bush and the National Governors' Association are no exception.[1]

In contrast to our political leaders, Jean Piaget started out by conceptualizing only one broad aim for education — the development of autonomy.[2] Our purpose here is to argue that, unless we have a set of goals coherently formulated with autonomy as the overall aim, the results of the second decade of reform will once again be disappointing. Piaget's conception of autonomy as the aim of education was a result of his application of his theory, constructivism, which is a scientific theory supported by 60 years of research all over the world.[3]

Since autonomy in the Piagetian sense means something different from what we often understand by the term, we will first explain what Piaget meant by autonomy. Then we will discuss autonomy as the aim of education — and the drastic changes in classroom practices that this goal entails. We will also point out the inadequacies of the six national goals.

PIAGET AND AUTONOMY

In common parlance, autonomy means the *right* of an individual or group to be self-governing. When we speak of Palestinian autonomy, we are referring to this kind of political right. In Piaget's theory, however, autonomy refers not to the right but to the *ability* of an individual to be self-governing — in the moral as well as in the intellectual realm. Autonomy is the ability to think for oneself and to decide between right and wrong in the moral realm and between truth and untruth in the intellectual realm by taking all relevant factors into account, independently of rewards or punishments. The opposite of autonomy in the Piagetian sense is heteronomy. Heteronomous people are governed by someone else because they are unable to think for themselves.

Moral autonomy. An extreme example of moral autonomy is the struggle of Martin Luther King, Jr., to obtain civil rights for African Americans and others. King was autonomous enough to take relevant factors into account and to conclude that the laws discriminating against African Americans were unjust and immoral. Convinced of the need to make justice a reality, he fought to end the discriminatory laws in spite of the police, jails, dogs, fire hoses, and threats of assassination. Morally autonomous people are not governed by rewards and punishments.

An extreme example of moral heteronomy is the affair of the Watergate cover-up. The perpetrators went along with what they knew to be morally wrong to reap the rewards that President Nixon could bestow on those who helped in the cover-up.

In *The Moral Judgment of the Child*, Piaget cited more commonplace examples of autonomy and heteronomy.[4] He interviewed children between the ages of 6 and 14 and asked them, for example, why it is bad to tell lies. Young heteronomous children replied, "Because you get punished when you tell lies." Piaget asked, "Would it be okay to tell lies if you were not punished for them?" The young children answered yes. Their judgment of matters of right and wrong was obviously governed by others.

Piaget also made up many pairs of stories and asked children which one of the two children in the stories was the worse. The following is an example of such a pair.

> A little boy . . . goes for a walk in the street and meets a big dog who frightens him very much. So then he goes home and tells his mother he has seen a dog that was as big as a cow.
> A child comes home from school and tells his mother that the teacher had given him good marks, but it was not true; the teacher had given him no marks at all, either good or bad. Then his mother was very pleased and rewarded him.[5]

Young children systematically manifested the morality of heteronomy by saying that it was worse to say, "I saw a dog as big as a cow." Why was it worse? Because dogs are never as big as cows, and adults do not believe such stories. Older, more autonomous children, however, tended to say that it was worse to say, "The teacher gave me good marks" *because* this lie is more believable. For more autonomous children, a believable lie is worse than one that is so outlandish that people will not be deceived.

All babies are born helpless and neither autonomous nor heteronomous. But young children are initially dependent on adults and, therefore, become heteronomous. Ideally, they become increasingly autonomous as they grow older. As they become more autonomous, they become less heteronomous. In other words, to the extent that children become able to govern themselves, they are governed less by other people.

In reality, however, human development does not happen in this ideal way. Most people do not attain their potential, and many stop developing at a low level. This observation can easily be confirmed in our daily lives. Newspapers are filled with stories about corruption in government and dishonesty in business practices, as well as with items dealing with drug trafficking, theft, assault, and murder.

The important question for parents and teachers is, What causes certain children to become more autonomous than others? Piaget's answer to this question was that adults reinforce children's heteronomy when they use rewards and punishments, thereby hindering the development of autonomy. By refraining from using rewards and punishments and by instead exchanging points of view with children, we can foster the development of autonomy, he said.

For example, if a child tells a lie, an adult could punish the child by saying, "No dessert tonight." Alternatively, the adult could look the child straight in the eye, with both affection and skepticism, and say, "I *really* can't believe what you are saying because . . . (state the reason). And when you tell me something next time, I am not sure I'll be able to believe you. . . . I want you to go to your room (or seat) and think about what you might do to be believed next time." Children want to be trusted, and, when they are confronted with this kind of statement, they are likely, over time, to come to the conclusion that it is best for people to deal honestly with each other.

In general, punishment leads to three possible outcomes. The first outcome is a weighing of risks. Children who are punished will learn to calculate their chances of getting caught the next time and to weigh the price they might have to pay against their chances of getting caught. The second possible outcome is, interestingly, the opposite of the first one: blind obedience. Sensitive children will do anything to avoid being punished. Thus by completely conforming to the rules, they give the impression that punishment works. The third outcome of punishment derives from the second: revolt. Many "model" children surprise everyone by beginning to cut classes, to take drugs, and to engage in other acts that characterize delinquency. Their reason for switching to these behaviors is that they are tired of living for their parents and teachers and think that the time has come for them to start living for themselves.

Piaget was realistic enough to say that it is sometimes necessary to impose restrictions on children. However, he made an important distinction between *punishment* and *sanctions by reciprocity*. Depriving the child of dessert for telling a lie is an example of a punishment, because the relationship between the lie and dessert is completely arbitrary. Telling children that we cannot believe what they said and sending them away to think about how they can be believed next time is an example of a sanction by reciprocity. Sanctions by reciprocity are directly related to the act that we want to discourage and to the adult's point of view. They have the effect of motivating the child to construct rules of conduct from within, through the coordination of viewpoints. Other examples of sanctions by reciprocity — such as excluding the child from the group, depriving the child of the thing he or she has misused, and having the child make restitution — can be found in *The Moral Judgment of the Child* and in *Young Children Reinvent Arithmetic*.[6]

Piaget's theory about how children acquire moral values is fundamentally different from traditional theories and from common sense. In the traditional view, the child is believed to acquire moral rules and values by *internalizing* them from the environment. According to Piaget, children acquire moral convictions not by absorbing them directly from the environment but by *constructing* them from the inside, through the exchange of points of view with people who are close and important to them. For example, no child is taught that it is okay to tell lies if one is not punished for them. Yet young children construct this belief as they try to make sense out of what adults say and do. Fortunately, they continue to construct other relationships, and many children ultimately conclude that

lies are bad even if one is not punished for them.

The exchange of viewpoints between adults and children fosters the development of autonomy by enabling the children to consider relevant factors, such as other perspectives. When children can take relevant factors into account, especially other people's rights and feelings, they construct from within the rule of treating others as they wish to be treated by them. A person who has constructed this conviction from within cannot lie in situations like the Watergate affair — no matter what reward may be offered.

Many behaviorists and others believe that punishment is bad because it is negative and that rewards are positive and good. However, rewards do not make children any more autonomous than punishment. Children who help their parents only to get money and those who fill out worksheets only to get stickers are governed by someone else, just as much as those who behave well only to avoid being punished.

Money, candy, and stickers are rewards because they are attractive objects used to manipulate or control children. By contrast, honest praise and expressions of appreciation are part of human relationships involving the exchange of points of view. Just as it is necessary to express disbelief when a child is not telling the truth, it is desirable to communicate our pleasure and appreciation when children behave in especially praiseworthy ways. Praise is thus different from rewards, such as money and stickers, but it too can be used in insincere, manipulative ways. Praise can thus degenerate into a reward, just as an expression of disbelief can turn into an angry, punitive act.

Autonomy is often confused with adopting a laissez-faire attitude. However, when one takes such relevant factors into account as the rights and feelings of other people, one is not free to break promises, tell lies, or act inconsiderately or irresponsibly.

Intellectual autonomy. In the intellectual realm, too, autonomy means the ability to govern oneself by being able to take relevant factors into account in deciding what is true or untrue. Copernicus provides an extreme example of intellectual autonomy. (The same applies to inventors of any other revolutionary theory.) Copernicus invented the heliocentric theory when nearly everybody else believed that the sun revolved around the earth. He was ridiculed off the stage but was

autonomous enough to remain convinced of his own idea. An intellectually heteronomous person, by contrast, believes unquestioningly what he or she is told, including illogical conclusions, slogans, and propaganda.

A more common example of intellectual autonomy is the case of a child who used to believe in Santa Claus. When she was about 6, she surprised her mother by asking, "How come Santa Claus uses the same wrapping paper as we do?" Her mother's explanation satisfied her for a few minutes, but she soon came up with the next question: "How come Santa Claus has the same handwriting as Daddy?" This child had her own way of thinking, which was different from what she had been taught.

According to Piaget, the child acquires knowledge in a way similar to the way a child acquires moral values: by *constructing* knowledge from within, rather than by internalizing knowledge directly from the environment. Children may accept what they are told for a time, but they are not passive vessels that merely hold what is poured into their heads. Children construct knowledge by creating and coordinating relationships. When the child described above put Santa Claus into a relationship with everything else she knew, she began to feel that something was wrong somewhere. When children are not convinced by what they are told, they rack their brains to make sense of these "facts."

Unfortunately, children are not encouraged to think autonomously in school. Teachers use rewards and punishments in the intellectual realm to get children to give "correct" responses. An example of this practice is the use of worksheets. For example, in first-grade arithmetic, if a child writes "4 + 4 = 7 ," most teachers mark this answer wrong. The result of this kind of teaching is that children become convinced that only the teacher (or someone else) knows which answers are correct. Furthermore, when we walk around a first-grade classroom while children are working on worksheets and stop to ask individual children how they arrived at particular answers, they typically react by grabbing their erasers — even when their answers are perfectly correct! Already many children have learned to distrust their own thinking. Children who are thus discouraged from thinking critically and autonomously will construct less knowledge than those who are confident and do their own thinking.

If a child says that 4 + 4 = 7, a better reaction is to refrain from correcting him or her and inquire instead, "How did you get 7?" Children often correct themselves as they try to explain their reasoning to someone else. The child who tries to explain his or her reasoning has to decenter in order to make sense to the other person. Trying to coordinate his or her point of view with that of another person makes the child think critically, and this often leads to a higher level of thinking.

Another way of dealing with a child's correct or incorrect answer to 4 + 4 is to ask the class, "Does everybody agree?" The exchange of points of view among peers stimulates critical thinking, which leads to a higher level of reasoning. In

Figure 1. Autonomy Versus Traditional Goals

the following section, we argue that we must replace the conformity and obedience that are now valued in schools with an education that emphasizes the honest, critical exchange of viewpoints.

AUTONOMY AS THE AIM OF EDUCATION

Figure 1 is our interpretation of the relationship of autonomy, the goal Piaget set for education, to the goals of most educators and the public. In the circle on the right, labeled "goals of most educators and the general public," we would put those goals that resulted in our memorizing words and their definitions just to pass one test after another. All of us who succeeded in school achieved this success by memorizing an enormous number of words without necessarily understanding them or caring about them. The

shaded part also includes the moral heteronomy that schools generally reinforce by using rewards and punishments.

A more accurate label for the circle on the right would have been "heteronomy." However, we did not use that label because today's educators do not consciously set out to foster children's heteronomy. Indeed, most educators (to say nothing of the general public) have not even heard of autonomy and heteronomy. Nevertheless, they unwittingly manipulate children with rewards and punishments, thereby reinforcing children's heteronomy.

In the intersection with the circle labeled "autonomy," we put those things we learned in school but did not forget after the test. The ability to read and write, to do basic arithmetic, to read maps and charts, and to situate events in history are examples of what we learned in school that we did not forget after cramming for tests. The little bit of moral autonomy we have managed to build came mostly from our homes, but schools have also made a contribution to this development. *When fostering moral and intellectual autonomy becomes our aim, educators will work hard to increase the area of overlap between the two circles.*

The six national education goals for the year 2000 were conceived within the circle on the right in Figure 1. There is nothing new in these six goals. Everybody agrees on the values they endorse. However, because they are not guided by an overall goal based on scientific theory, the six goals are fragmentary, some-

times contradictory, and conspicuous in their lacunae.

Goal 2 — increasing the graduation rate to 90% — would be easily fulfilled if autonomy were the aim of education and if schools were better adapted to today's students. All adolescents want to become competent and socially respectable, but they drop out of school when classes seem irrelevant and coercive. If high school curricula were relevant and interesting to students, we would find it unnecessary to preach the value of a high school diploma.

The aims of Goal 3 — demonstrating competency in challenging subject matter and being prepared for responsible citizenship — are already included within the idea of autonomy as the aim of education, but they are conceptualized differently. A teacher whose aim is to foster autonomy does not teach English, mathematics, science, history, and so on merely to prepare students for "responsible citizenship, further learning, and productive employment in our modern economy." Intellectual pursuits should enable individuals to make sense of the world and to become competent human beings. Of course, competent individuals are likely to be good citizens and good workers, and educators need to pay closer attention to what sense individuals are making of the world during each hour in every subject.

Goal 4 — to be first in the world in math and science — would be eliminated because mathematics and science are already included in Goal 3, and being first in the world is not a valid goal for education. Our goal should be to turn out young people who can make sense of mathematics and science and who like these subjects. Another reason for eliminating Goal 4 is that it contradicts Goal 2. If 90% of the students stayed in high school, it would certainly not be possible to be "first in the world in mathematics and science achievement" by the year 2000.

Goal 5 — dealing with adult literacy and lifelong learning — would be eliminated, too, because literacy and "knowledge and skills" are already included in Goal 3. Goal 5 makes us wonder whether the governors viewed it as a special goal for the part of the student population that traditionally consists of low achievers.

Goal 6 — that schools be safe, orderly, and free of drugs and violence — would also be eliminated if autonomy were the aim of education because individuals who can take relevant factors into account do not take drugs or resort to violence. The statement that every school in America "will offer a disciplined environment" also reveals a traditional way of thinking. Schools cannot *offer* a disciplined environment. A disciplined environment has to be *created from within* by students and teachers — together.

The lacunae in the six national goals are conspicuous. Nowhere in the formulation of these goals is any attention paid to young people's sense of self, to their relationships with other human beings, to their making sense of the world, or to their mastering of their environment by becoming creative problem solvers.

The social and moral qualities necessary for successful employment, such as dependability, initiative, and a sense of responsibility, are totally absent from the six national goals. These qualities are part of autonomy, which is prevented from developing in most schools and in many homes today. Since heteronomous parents raise heteronomous children, public schools must assume a major role in breaking the cycle of heteronomy.

In a multicultural society, autonomy as the aim of education has the special advantage of not specifying the particular values that we want youngsters to have. We cannot predict, for example, whether an autonomous child will have the values and priorities associated with an environmentalist or those that characterize an industrialist. While we cannot predict what specific virtues and aspirations the child will have, we can be sure of two things about all autonomous people: 1) they will have thought deeply about the factors relevant to any decision, and 2) through exchanging viewpoints, they will have constructed certain basic values, such as taking the rights and feelings of others into account, negotiating solutions in situations of conflict, and basing decisions on what is morally right rather than on anticipated rewards or punishments.

AUTONOMY IN CLASSROOM LIFE

Classrooms today are all too often heteronomous environments in which teachers control children and push them through uninspiring textbooks. Below we specify and illustrate three practices that can be observed throughout the day when the teacher's aim is to develop autonomy in children.

1. *Encouraging children to make decisions and to enforce their own rules.* The traditional role of the teacher is to control children by telling them what to do and by giving them ready-made rules. But children who are always controlled by others can only learn to be controlled. If we want children to be able to make their own decisions and to feel responsible for those decisions, it is best to allow them to make decisions from an early age. For example, a third-grade teacher asked her class to decide how many minutes each student should be allotted to give an oral book report. The children initially decided on 10-minute reports. Then they considered relevant factors, such as the fact that this would take a total of three hours and 40 minutes for the 22 students in the class. Deciding that this was much too long, they next considered five minutes and finally settled on three-minute reports. Having to make such a decision also made for an excellent math lesson, motivated by a genuine need to know.

Children often make exactly the same rules and decisions that the teacher would have made. However, the fact that children have made a rule or decision makes an enormous difference in their commitment to it. Children tend to understand and respect the rules they make. In the course of making a rule, they also come to know that *their* opinions are respected, and they are then more likely to respect the opinions of others, including adults.

To cite another example, teachers often announce that they will give a lower grade or a zero to a paper that is turned in late. By contrast, a teacher whose aim is the development of children's autonomy presents the problem to the class and asks for suggestions about the best way to deal with the problem. The group may make the same rule as the teacher, but this rule will have been constructed by the group out of a personally felt need of its members. Someone may even ask the person whose paper was late, "Do you want me to call you in the evening to make sure you're doing your homework?" The very fact of participating in such a discussion helps children take relevant factors into account as they learn how to make good decisions. Whole-class discussions are much more powerful in motivating students from within than the rewards and punishments teachers usually use.

2. *Fostering intrinsic motivation.* Traditional teaching tries to transmit knowledge through well-organized, "objective," and uninspiring textbooks, with assistance from tests, grades, and other forms of rewards and punishments. The result is that most of us remember such terms as cosine and neutron and such names as the Second Continental Congress. However, we may have only the vaguest notion of what these words mean.

Constructivism, a scientific theory, coupled with the development of autonomy as the aim of education, recognizes that human beings have an intrinsic desire to make sense of the world and that they learn best when they are personally curious, deeply involved, or in a social situation that requires them to take and defend a position. As Piaget pointed out, children work hard when they have intriguing questions to answer and problems to solve. If teaching truly appealed to the human desire to make sense of things, the memorization and the rewards and punishments used today would become outdated. Nor would we forget most of what we "learned" in school.

To take an example from the teaching of American history, a teacher whose goal is children's development of autonomy might ask students to prepare for a debate. With respect to the Second Continental Congress, for instance, a good debate might be between a position in sympathy with the loyalists (loyal to the British Crown) and a position opposing them. Students would have to be extremely well-informed, logical, and critical to participate in such a debate. They might, for example, read biographies of such figures as John Adams, Joseph Galloway, and Thomas Jefferson and come to know the uncertainties and agonies each individual faced as well as the façades and strategies each employed under various circumstances. Having to coordinate subjective perspectives in a debate makes history much more alive and unforgettable than does the "objective," dull textbook. If children are allowed to change sides in the middle of a debate, this especially motivates them to understand both sides of an issue.

3. *Encouraging children to exchange viewpoints.* An essential part of Piaget's theory is the importance of social interaction for the construction of knowledge and moral values. In fact, Piaget pointed out that science has been constructed over the centuries through the exchange

of points of view among scientists. Science is a social enterprise.[7]

Let us return to the example given above of 4 + 4. If in response to the answer "8" the teacher refrains from saying, "That's right," but asks instead, "Does everybody agree?" the class has to come to its own conclusion through the exchange of ideas. If a child says that 4 + 4 = 7, the teacher should also ask if everybody agrees and encourage the subsequent debate. Children *will* arrive at the truth in mathematics if they debate long enough, because nothing is arbitrary in mathematics. In traditional classrooms, the teacher's role is to reinforce correct answers and to correct wrong ones. But children stop thinking and debating when the teacher assumes the responsibility of judging which answer is correct.

If the reader asks any fourth-grader why he or she works from left to right in long division but not in addition, subtraction, and multiplication, the answer is likely to be: "That's the way the teacher told us to do it." In most elementary schools today, mathematics is taught with intellectual heteronomy as the unintended goal of education. If long division were taught through honest, critical debate about each step, there would be no need for all the repetition and worksheets that are now endlessly imposed on children.[8]

A similar situation exists in the social/moral realm. In the case of a conflict between two children in class, traditional teachers tell the parties to "stop it" and to pay attention to the lesson. The result is often that the conflict continues when the teacher's back is turned. A teacher whose aim is autonomy is likely to tell the students to step away from the group to negotiate a solution. If negotiation (the exchange of viewpoints) is encouraged from an early age, children become surprisingly good about settling their disputes.

If two kindergartners are fighting over a toy, for example, traditional teachers preach the virtue of sharing and specify how the toy will be shared. A teacher who fosters the development of autonomy, however, may say to the children, "I don't know what to do, but what I do know how to do is to keep the toy for you until *you* decide on a fair way to solve this problem." As noted earlier, children often decide that neither of them should get the toy. This outcome may be the same as the adult's taking the toy away because they "don't know how to play nicely with it." From the standpoint of the development of the children's autonomy, however, there is a world of difference between their making the decision and an adult's imposition of the same decision.

Most educators and most of the public today think that the hour for English is only for English, that the hour for math is only for math, and so on. They also view the drug problem, AIDS, teenage pregnancies, and violence as separate issues, to be dealt with apart from academic subjects. However, drug abuse, unsafe sex, and violence are all symptoms of heteronomy. As noted earlier, children who can take relevant factors into account do not take drugs or resort to violence to settle conflicts. In the classroom, students develop or are prevented from developing intellectually as well as socially and morally. And the intellectual and social/moral domains are inseparable. A classroom cannot foster the development of autonomy in the intellectual realm while suppressing it in the social and moral realms.

Traditional education begins with a list of desired outcomes and seeks to produce results through the use of pep talks and the promise or threat of rewards or punishments. Piaget's theory, constructivism, coupled with the idea of autonomy as the aim of education, reflects the belief that the education of human beings requires a much deeper, longer-range perspective that is different from the mindset necessary to produce quality cars.

Education that aims to produce autonomy is better suited for life in a democracy than traditional education, which fosters conformity. A long-lasting, successful democracy requires informed, autonomous citizens who consider relevant factors in voting for laws and representatives who make those laws. Autonomy goes far beyond equipping youngsters with "the knowledge and skills necessary to compete in a global economy." If all the public schools in the United States educated children for autonomy during every hour of the 13 years the children are in school, the nation's prisons would be less crowded, the federal deficit and the drug problem would be more amenable to control, and we would be working more positively to solve many of our human and social problems.

1. *America 2000: An Education Strategy* (Washington, D.C.: U.S. Government Printing Office, 1991), pp. 62-66.

2. Jean Piaget, *To Understand Is to Invent* (1948; reprint, New York: Viking, 1973).

3. For example, the experiments described in Jean Piaget and Alina Szeminska, *The Child's Conception of Number* (1941; reprint, London: Routledge and Kegan Paul, 1952) have been replicated in Africa, Asia, Australia, North America, and South America.

4. Jean Piaget, *The Moral Judgment of the Child* (1932; reprint, New York: Free Press, 1965).

5. Ibid., p. 148.

6. Ibid.; and Constance Kamii, *Young Children Reinvent Arithmetic* (New York: Teachers College Press, 1985).

7. Jean Piaget and Rolando Garcia, *Psychogenesis and the History of Science* (1983; reprint, New York: Columbia University Press, 1989).

8. For further detail on a constructivist approach to primary arithmetic within the context of autonomy as the overall goal, readers should refer to the following books and videotapes by Constance Kamii, published by Teachers College Press, New York, N.Y.: *Young Children Reinvent Arithmetic* (1985); *Young Children Continue to Reinvent Arithmetic, 2nd Grade* (1989); *Young Children Continue to Reinvent Arithmetic, 3rd Grade* (in press); *Double-Column Addition: A Teacher Uses Piaget's Theory* (videotape, 1989); *Multiplication of Two-Digit Numbers: Two Teachers Using Piaget's Theory* (videotape, 1990); and *Multidigit Division: Two Teachers Using Piaget's Theory* (videotape, 1990).

Using Action Research To Assess Instruction

Carole Schulte Johnson and Inga Kromann-Kelly

Carole Schulte Johnson is a faculty member in the Department of Elementary and Secondary Education, at Washington State University, in Pullman, Washington. Inga Kromann-Kelly is a faculty member in the Department of Teaching and Learning, at Washington State University, in Pullman, Washington.

For years teachers have used self assessment as one way to improve the learning environment in their classrooms. Such assessment, however, tended to be of a private, nonsystematic nature and often was not clearly focused on a central question. Today more and more teachers are developing and experiencing an organized approach to classroom inquiry, known as action research, a concept which has evolved over the past several years. This approach entails stepping back from the immediate concern in order to gain a broader perspective on a problem; then collecting, analyzing, and interpreting data on the basis of a defined plan, and often sharing the results with professional colleagues.

Rather than formulating complex research procedures, perhaps best left to experts, we recommend beginning action research by answering these five basic questions: 1) What is the main question I am interested in pursuing? 2) What data are relevant? 3) What specific data will be collected, and how? 4) How will the data be analyzed? 5) What interpretations or implications can be drawn from the data?

THE QUESTION

Teachers often have several questions they wish to explore; however, in order to keep the research manageable you as a teacher embarking on action research need to decide your basic or most important question. Limited questions related to what you are doing in your classroom, such as "Are my students learning from this strategy?" or "What strategies do students use most successfully in perform-

ing some particular task?" work well for action research. For example, suppose we are interested in learning more about our students' attitude toward reading. We realize that various elements of the literacy program probably affect those attitudes so our basic question could be "How do the students feel about the different methods and materials used in the literacy program?"

COLLECTING DATA

Data can be gathered from transactions/interactions, products and cued or structured responses. Figure 1, while not all inclusive, suggests various sources of data within each category.

Triangulation of data (using at least three different data sources) is recommended. The value of using triangulation is in analyzing the question from several different viewpoints. For instance, one data set could be from each of the three categories on the chart or from two of the three categories. If only three data sources are used, it is recommended that no more than one cued or structured response source be included since these data usually are collected only at specific points of time, thus limiting the information to the context of those times.

When the different data sources are congruent, the acceptance of the results is strengthened. Conflicting data raise questions such as: Should other types of data sets have been used? Should some data sources carry more weight—for example, were the cued responses too structured or answered to please the teacher? Would it be valuable to refine or do additional research on this question?

We make decisions regarding the specific data to collect on the basis of its importance in seeking answers to the question and also the feasibility of collecting and analyzing it. In general, quantifiable data take less time to collect and analyze; however, meaningful data are not always readily quantifiable. While importance and feasibility are basic, other aspects are considered. Using excessive class, student and/or teacher time is avoided by collecting data from ongoing class activities such as journals and portfo-

From *Reading Horizons*, Vol. 35, No. 3, 1995, pp. 199-208. © 1995 by Western Michigan University, Kalamazoo, MI. Reprinted by permission.

Figure 1
Data Sources

	From Teacher	*From Students*
Transactions/ Interactions	Field/observation/anecdotal notes	Video/audio tapes
	Video/audio tapes	
Products		Written products
		Artifacts
		Open-ended interviews
		Open-ended conferences
Cued/Structured Responses	Ratings	Tests
	Checklists	Questionnaires
	Tally of behaviors	Attitude measures
		Structured interviews
		Structured conferences
		Writing/work samples
		Checklists
		Ratings
		Logs

lios, the taping of class or small group activities as well as from brief cued or structured responses.

Unless individual conferences are part of the ongoing program and the data to be collected a normal part of the conferences, they may not be a feasible source of information. However, if a second person is available or only a small subset of students is involved, individual conferences become a possibility.

Another consideration is that students may tell teachers what they think the teacher wants to hear when cued or structured responses are obtained face-to-face. Responses on paper may be similarly biased, but such data-gathering instruments are generally viewed as providing a degree of anonymity.

When teacher observations are used, consideration is given to how structured and systematic they will be. Ways to provide structure include using a checklist of behaviors (e.g., answering, volunteering, getting out of seat) and keeping a tally of the number of times a behavior occurs, or by describing behavior at set time intervals. Audio/videotaping of an on-going class activity is an example of an unstructured observation. Systematic observations are made on a regular basis such as daily or weekly. The data can be taped; however, if teacher notes

are used, it is recommended they be written daily. Less systematic observations are those noted occasionally, when the teacher has time or when something strikes the teacher as important to note.

When writing notes, we need to remind ourselves that we see what we expect, so there is danger of bias. For example, as teachers, we know that certain of our students love to read while others do not. Thus, in examining attitudes, we are more inclined to note student behaviors which confirm what we already believe than those which conflict with our expectations.

Each source of data requires decisions on the part of the teacher. With materials such as journals, portfolios, or tapes, you decide what data to include and then structure the class or group so it can be collected. When a checklist or questionnaire is involved, you decide its content and how students (or teacher) will respond. Among the possibilities for such instruments are open ended questions or statements, items for the respondent to check off, or some type of rating system.

If you use a rating scale, you need to decide whether it will be an even numbered scale, thus avoiding a neutral position, or an odd numbered one which includes it. A two or three point scale is simpler for students in the primary grades; a five to seven point scale is common in upper grades and has the advantage of identifying subtle differences. Common terms for labeling points on a scale are *agree/disagree, like most/like least,* or 1 *(very low)* to 5 *(highest).*

A simple format is helpful. Present the ratings at the top of the page; then list the items below with a blank for the number rating in front of each item. With instruments such as this, it is important to remind the students that you really want to know what they think so their opinions can be considered in making decisions about materials or procedures. From whom will student data be collected—the entire class, a small group or groups of students, individuals or some combination? For our research on student attitudes, we prefer information from the class rather than from selected representative students. The latter may well provide the spectrum of attitudes regarding reading, but not its strength related to specific methods or materials.

In examining student attitudes toward reading, the feelings of students constitute important and relevant data. To collect such information, we might use informal teacher observations, preferably collected on a regular basis, and student records of books and pages read daily and brief comments or reactions to what they have read. All of these items are easily obtained as a normal part of classroom activity.

Additionally, we would include a questionnaire asking students to rate what they think about each of the different literacy materials and activities used in the program. If many items are included, the questionnaire can be divided into several parts. Class discussion of the results would provide a useful source of additional information. Neither activity would take an inordinate amount of time and the findings could result in an improved curriculum. Our questionnaire requires limited teacher preparation time since it only involves developing a list of the materials and activities used, deciding their order as well as the kind of rating scale to use, and formatting the instrument.

ANALYZING AND INTERPRETING DATA

When analyzing data, teachers may want information about the class as a whole, about individual children, or about certain subgroups. Subgroups might include students at certain achievement levels, such as above grade level, at grade level, students with special needs, boys at different achievement levels, or girls at different ones. When data are kept for each student, teachers can decide at any time what individuals or subgroups they may wish to study.

Some of the data teachers gather are quantifiable and can be analyzed without the use of statistics. Under some circumstances, statistical analyses show significance with only small differences in raw data, and such results may not be particularly useful. For example, knowing the percent of the class rating an item *very low* or *highest* may be more important for your consideration in curriculum change. Again, it is the teacher who must interpret the data and decide what is meaningful. What do the results mean in your classroom? How do they answer your original question? Were they what you expected? Any surprises? What was successful or not successful?

Our questionnaire regarding student opinion about materials and activities can best be summarized with tables for the class and for each subgroup. We would list the materials and activities in a column with the ratings listed across the top. Then for each item, the percent choosing the rating is listed.

To interpret the tables, we would consider the class or group distribution across the continuum: Were responses concentrated at one end of the continuum? Were there gross differences such as a large group at each end of the continuum, or was there a fairly even distribution across it? If the distribution is mainly at one end, we would decide what percent of the class or group to consider significant in our decision making: it might be 40 percent, $\frac{1}{3}$, $\frac{1}{4}$ or whatever we feel is appropriate. For example, if 40 percent of students rate something *very low* while few or no students rate it *highest,* or the reverse, that clearly is important information.

Data which are not readily quantifiable, such as that from logs, journals, informal observations, conferences or tapes of class activities, are usually reviewed by teachers so they can pull out what appear to be trends, major ideas, or important elements related to the question at hand. If these data are collected over a period of time, or if the material is extensive, it will need to be reviewed periodically, and preferably over a time frame which allows for reflection. This is an important and valuable process because it often leads to further insights and refinements. In general, for non-quantified data, we would review all the categories and subcategories and draw conclusions related to the original question. The conclusions may be firm or tentative. In either case, it is important to consider whether data from other sources agree with it. Informal observations, anecdotal notes, and class discussion of results are used to confirm, disconfirm or raise questions about findings from the rest of the data.

In the case of our question about students' attitudes, we would review teacher observations and anecdotal notes as well as student logs for indication of feelings about reading, positive, negative, or general reactions indicating that students are or are not involved with their reading. While we would start with categories such as *positive* and *negative,* as the data collection grows we would expect subcategories to develop. For example, we might subcategorize aspects related to writing, to self-selected reading, to assigned reading, or to informational reading. Categories are flexible and can change as we continue to review the data. Which categories make sense and help answer the question? How do these data fit with the results of the questionnaire?

Finally, we would review the data as a whole. What is supported by all data sources? What is partially supported? Is anything not supported? What conclusions do you draw?

We piloted a questionnaire in a fourth grade class which used both trade books and children's literature. The results indicated that boys and girls were quite similar in their high and low ratings, as were the readers who were mature, on-grade level or special needs readers. However, when we looked at the groups of items rated *high* or *low,* we noticed those rated *low* tended to be the type of activities associated with the basal while those rated *high* were those traditionally considered enrichment activities. In terms of materials, with the exception of the special needs readers, all rated using literature books higher than using basals. The students in the class willingly informed us why they responded as they did. In general, the special needs readers felt they could handle the grade level basal but with literature books they had trouble keeping pace with others in their groups, and in some cases with the vocabulary as well.

Since there was nothing in teacher notes or student logs to contradict this, we would use literature books as the core of the literacy program, avoiding "basalizing" them by incorporating writing and enrichment activities similar to those suggested by Yopp and Yopp (1992). In selecting and gathering books related to themes or units, we would seek to include books special needs readers would feel successful in using. Then while implementing this program, we'd probably start a new action research project concentrating on the special needs readers.

CONSIDERATIONS FOR INVOLVEMENT IN ACTION RESEARCH

There are four important factors to consider in planning action research. First, action research requires additional planning time. However, useful and successful projects can be accomplished without consuming an inordinate amount of additional time. Second, action research is improved when teachers discuss the five questions with colleagues because the interaction provides a supportive environment which helps clarify and solidify thinking regarding the project. Sharing ideas and suggestions, whether for the same question or different ones, can be valuable. Colleagues not involved in action research also can provide helpful insights.

Third, teachers undertaking action research should be aware that expectations affect what we see and how we interpret data. Triangulation of data is helpful as are our awareness of this effect, discussion with others as the research evolves, and an effort on our part to be open to alternative explanations as well as to surprises in the data. Finally, teachers can use the results of action research in their classrooms. Action research can improve the teaching/learning process in classrooms by reinforcing, modifying and/or changing perceptions based solely on more informal techniques such as non-systematic observations.

REFERENCES

Yopp, R. H., & Yopp, H. K. (1992). *Literature-based reading activities.* Boston: Allyn and Bacon.

Development

- Childhood (Articles 4–7)
- Adolescence (Articles 8 and 9)

The study of human development provides us with knowledge of how children and adolescents mature and learn within the family, community, and school environments. Educational psychology focuses on description and explanation of the developmental processes that make it possible for children to become intelligent and socially competent adults. Psychologists and educators are presently studying the idea that biology as well as the environment influence cognitive, personal, social, and emotional development and involves predictable patterns of behavior.

Jean Piaget's theory regarding the cognitive development of children and adolescents is perhaps the best known and most comprehensive. According to this theory, the perceptions and thoughts that young children have about the world are often prelogical and premoral. When compared to adolescents and adults, children think about moral and social issues in a unique way. Children need to acquire cognitive, moral, and social skills in order to interact effectively with parents, teachers, and peers. If human intelligence encompasses all of these above skills, then Piaget may have been correct in saying that human development is the child's intelligent adaptation to the environment.

Today the cognitive, moral, social, and emotional development of children takes place in a rapidly changing society. A child must develop a sense of self-worth and autonomy within the family as well as at school in order to cope with the changes and become a competent and socially responsible adult. In "Learning through 'Play' as Well as 'Work' in the Primary Grades," Jane Perlmutter

with Louise Burrell present ways teachers can provide children with appropriate experiences that enhance their development, while the articles by Judith Schickedanz, Janet Kuebli, and Donna Wittmer and Alice Honig discuss the social and emotional needs of children. Adolescence brings with it the ability to think abstractly and hypothetically and to see the world from many perspectives. Adolescents strive to form goals and achieve a sense of identity, but they often become frustrated and feel alienated from the adult world. Their ideas about the kinds of adults they want to become and the ideals they want to believe in sometimes lead to conflicts with parents and teachers. Adolescents are also sensitive about espoused adult values versus adult behavior. The essays in this unit discuss the social and personal problems that confront adolescents and also suggest ways in which the family and school can help meet the needs of adolescents.

Looking Ahead: Challenge Questions

What social pressures and risks do children face in growing up? How can parents and teachers help children to develop a sense of competence and self-esteem?

How can teachers provide children and adolescents with experiences that promote their cognitive, moral, social, and emotional development?

Describe the societal and personal problems adolescents face. What is meant by *resiliency*?

What can adolescents tell us about their perceptions of caring?

Learning through "Play" As Well As "Work" in the Primary Grades

Jane C. Perlmutter with Louise Burrell

Jane C. Perlmutter, *Ed.D., is an associate professor of early childhood education at Western Carolina University in Cullowhee, North Carolina. She has worked collaboratively with Louise Burrell for many years in Louise's primary classrooms.*

Louise Burrell, *M.A. Ed., is now a second-grade teacher at Cullowhee Valley Elementary School. She has been teaching for more than 30 years.*

A visitor to Mrs. Burrell's class is struck by the level of purposeful activity as kindergarten and first- and second-grade children all share work and play in a room full of learning materials. While a first-grade child is in the woodworking center building a small bed to be used for book sharing, a second grader saws purposefully. Across the room a 5-year-old and a 7-year-old are engrossed in a computer game. Several children shop in the creative play center. Another child working on "investigations" estimates and then checks his classmate's weight, using bathroom scales. Other children write in their journals or on planning pads. The teacher and the assistant confer with individual children and check their reading progress. In such a busy, exciting place where children can be observed both playing and working, the lines between work and play become blurred.

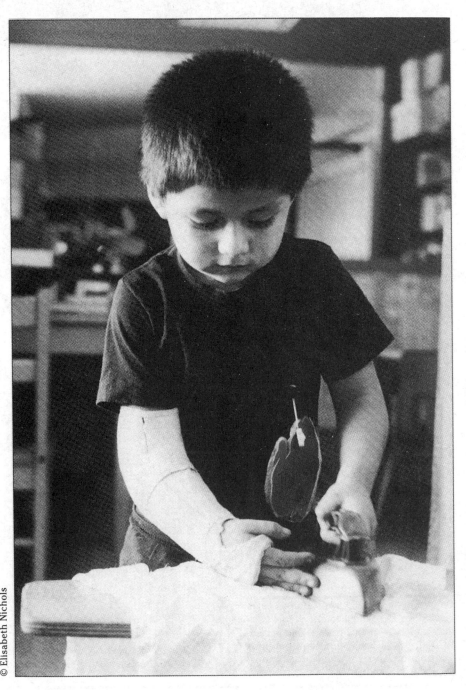

© Elisabeth Nichols

From *Young Children,* July 1995, pp. 14-21. © 1995 by the National Association for the Education of Young Children. Reprinted by permission.

Mrs. Burrell's class is unusual because there are few primary classrooms where one may observe kindergarten, first-, and second-grade children in one class *or* in groups playing and making choices of activities (King 1987). In many primary classrooms, recess is the only officially sanctioned, voluntary play left for children.

The relationship of children's play to various aspects of children's development has been studied intensively, especially over the last several decades (Rubin, Fein, & Vandenberg 1983). Most of the research on children's play has focused on preschool populations (Bergen 1987) and provides evidence that play is related to the development of preschool children's language, social competence, creativity, and problem-solving abilities (Athey 1987; Rogers & Sawyer 1988).

Children's perceptions of the differences between work and play change as they move from kindergarten into elementary school (King 1987). King asked kindergarten and elementary children about play and work in school. She found that kindergarten children call what the teacher tells them to do "work" and what they choose to do "play." Older elementary children will call a teacher-directed activity "play" if it is "fun." All children designate outside recess time as "playtime."

Currently, there is considerable debate in the field of early childhood education about developmentally appropriate practices for young children. In the primary grades, many people call for a return to a child-sensitive approach to teaching and learning (Morrison 1991). Play is part of this approach (Fromberg 1987). The debate deals with the balance between child-chosen activity and teacher-assigned ac-

We Studied Play in a Mixed-Age Primary Class

Mrs. Burrell's class is a combination kindergarten, first, and second grade in a K–8 school in Cullowhee, North Carolina. The school, adjacent to the campus of Western Carolina University, is one of five elementary schools in the Jackson County school district. The surrounding area is primarily rural, the people strongly rooted in the mountain Appalachian heritage. Students in Mrs. Burrell's class come from families associated with the university, as well as from families who have lived in the area for generations.

For the past four years, I have been participating in and observing Mrs. Burrell's classroom, while children are at work and play. The field data for this study were collected throughout the school year. Most of the observational data on children's play were collected in the fall of the year. I visited the classroom once or twice a week usually during the morning work period. A graduate student also spent approximately 20 hours a week as a participant–observer in the class. Interviews with the children about their perceptions of work and play were conducted during the spring semester.

We wanted to see what happens to play past preschool and how play fits with developmentally appropriate practice in primary grades. We wanted to describe the classroom organization in order to see how opportunities for play affect the academic climate. We were also interested in finding out how children in this type of setting perceive their work and play. A variety of types of data were collected, including the following:

• field notes on children's play and on interactions between children and teachers;

• notes taken during large-group times for planning and sharing;

• records of conferences between children and teachers;

• informal interviews with children as they did their work;

• notes about our helping out as children measured sand and water, sawed through big pieces of wood, wrote stories, sewed designs, made birthday cards, and all the other things children were busy doing; and

• individual interviews with the children about their perceptions of the classroom, the activities they did, and the differences between work and play.

tivity or, as some children might see it, between play and work.

Do first and second graders still play? Our observations confirm what most parents of primary school children know, that primary children are still accomplished pretenders and builders. Their play is creative and full of drama. Wars fought in the sand table reflected conflicts happen-

ing in the Middle East. Children shopped, took care of babies, became animals, and flew airplanes. What from a distance appeared to be a water-measuring activity was also two girls making a magic potion. Obviously, creative play and building with blocks are not just for kindergarten children.

Does the play of primary children differ from that of preschool children? With older children even more than with younger children, the play is often difficult to assign to neat categories. For example, building may overlap with games played with rules. The play of two children with an inclined plane and cars in the block center illustrates the difficulty of categorization. The children were conducting "slow" races to see which car could be pushed down the ramp most slowly. They recorded scores and pretended to be driving. They were building with the blocks, pretending, making up and playing a game. This was also a response to the day's math assignment, which was to make up and record a game with rules.

Observing children's play allowed us to peek into their private worlds of fantasy. In dramatic play, particularly in the sand, water, and blocks centers, the stories the children created as they played often seemed to be internalized. Two children playing side by side interacted frequently. Words were exchanged, little figures moved about, but each child seemed to

Many people are calling for a return to child-sensitive teaching and learning in the primary grades. Play is part of this approach.

be constructing a private story. Pretending may be becoming more of a private fantasizing. This parallels Vygotsky's notion of *inner speech* (1978) and the changes in inner speech from "out loud" to "private" that occur as children move from preschool to primary school.

Play of primary-grade children is more precise and focused than the play of most younger children. Second graders playing in sand want to have areas clearly marked and want a purpose for all of the materials. Buildings become more complex and intricate as children's abilities expand. In dramatic play a group of the same children may maintain a complex story line over several weeks.

The additional experiences that two more years of living have furnished are evident in the

play of primary children compared to younger children, as seen in the transition from dramatic play to the dramatization of plays and puppet shows. Older primary children are also likely to create more detail and accessories to accompany their plays than are kindergarten children. Plays and puppet shows are more carefully planned when older children produce them. The beauty of a multi-age class is that younger children observe older children and want to do what they are doing. Older children can help the younger ones out of difficulties. Peer tutoring happens naturally and on an as-needed basis.

How is the classroom organized? There are three different layers in the classroom. The first layer is the environment of play and learning materials, the second is the work layer or the daily assignments, and the third layer is composed of the applications to real life in projects and businesses. The layers are linked informally and most activity flows comfortably from one to the next. These layers form a learning web that supports integrated learning, formal and informal.

The classroom environment itself constitutes the first layer. The room is full of raw materials for children's learning. Sand, water, clay, woodworking, junk materials for art, blocks, books, empty food containers, a cash register, dressup clothes, many kinds of writing materials, tapes with books to listen to, puppets and puppet theater—all have educational purposes. In linking

© The Growth Program

play with academics, educational materials like containers for measuring volume are placed next to small plastic figures for dramatic play. For example, playing with water and containers that hold water builds knowledge about how liquids flow and what things sink or float and what air pressure does to containers when they are turned over in the water. As another example, a displacement vessel is available for playing in the water center. The juxtaposition of play and learning materials encourages hands-on explorations that prepare children for more formal investigations and projects. This exploration leads to intuitive understandings of mathematical concepts of comparative size, volume, length, height, shapes, and patterns.

The classroom environment encourages dramatic play, which provides the context for all kinds of learning. In the Creative Play area, children play "store" and "house" and in the process count money and classify by attributes. When setting the table, a child uses one-to-one correspondence to have enough for everyone. In the store children read labels, write notes, and make grocery lists. As children construct buildings with blocks, they are adding and subtracting with concrete objects. Building means measuring and balancing. Using unit blocks, children gain intuitive understanding of fractions and division.

Out of children's spontaneous play comes the need for solving real-life problems. When a building collapses the builders must revise their thinking and solve the problem. Trying another way builds persistence and a willingness to revise and try again. Writers also must develop the same persistence and patience with the need for revision. The joy of constructive play is in the infinite possibilities of creating new things.

Play and language are intimately linked. Cooperative play

What Do the Children Call "Work" or "Play"?

We asked, "What kinds of things in your classroom are for playing and what things are for working?" The children tended to categorize the activities that they chose in the classroom environment as "play." As Laura said, "Centers are for playing, but actually everything in our class is work." The children most often identified creative play, blocks, and sand as "for play," although the blocks that stick together are to be counted and measured and thus are for work. Books, cooking, clay, and the computer were also mentioned as "play." One child said that sand is "sort of workish but fun, too." How a material is categorized appears to depend on what the child is doing with the material. This may be why several children said that blocks and sand are for working and playing. If the child measures the sand, that child is working, but if the child has a war in the sand table, he is probably playing. In the teacher's mind, in each case, the child is gaining valuable concrete experiences with raw materials.

Cooking was called "work" by some children and "play" by others. One child said, "Then there's one center that you pretty much have to work in or you'll be thrown out of . . . that would be cooking. 'Cause you can't be messing around with the stove and messing around with food." Woodworking has work in the title, so it must be work. Joshua got very specific about the work and play possibilities in woodworking. "Woodworking is kinda like a hobby. Woodworking would be like a beginner's thing for carpenters. And we work with wood, we measure, we do stuff like that, and then it can be play 'cause sometimes you nail stuff together and . . . don't measure." Dates on the calendar, writing, and reading were labeled "work." "When you read," described another child, "it'd be working 'cause you have to record it."

provides constant opportunities for oral language to develop. Two children building a fort or playing store must discuss and organize their efforts with words as well as actions. Puppet shows and other dramatic productions challenge children to plan and organize. Writing a script gives real reasons for writing. If a child wants friends to take part in a puppet show, she must write clearly enough to be understood.

The arrangement of materials in the various centers and the daily need to put things in order create real-life sorting and classifying problems. The children are responsible for maintaining the environment. Guided practice in classification happens every day when blocks are organized by size or science materials by function.

What kinds of work do these children do? The second layer in the classroom is composed of the daily assignments. Although the teacher respects the children's need for self-directed play activity, she also sets high standards for work the children must do. The children are responsible for completing certain work tasks every day. Even though there is a great deal of child choice in deciding how to accomplish the tasks and children help plan the parameters of each assignment, the tasks are still determined by the teacher. When the children are asked to tell about the work in the classroom, they talk about their journals, planning pads, investigations, and reading logs. All of these are done in blank books with open-ended assignments. All of the children are given a topic, but each child handles it differently and often uses different materials. Most of the children show a strong sense of responsibility for getting their work done. Many mention "getting all of their work done" as a source of pride.

According to Erikson (1963), a central task of primary children is to develop a sense of industry. Most 5-, 6-, and 7-year-olds want to work and to feel successful in their work. Big kids who ride on the bus, and big brothers and sisters, all go to school and work all day and have homework all night. Being a big kid means to have plenty of work to do. Completed work can be a badge of honor and brings with it the feeling of self-fulfillment and accomplishment.

How does Mrs. Burrell help the children integrate their work and play? Mrs. Burrell thinks children learn when they play, as do many theorists and play researchers. She tries to help children use their play in their work. One example of the integration of work and play is found in the formal mathematics activities for the class, called "investigations." Children help develop challenges to find ways to measure, graph, add, or record in a variety of situations. Often investigations are tied to activities and materials normally termed "play." For example, Mrs. Burrell tells the children, "Construct something in the block area and record what you've used in your construction." This open-ended assignment could be completed by listing the sizes and shapes of the blocks used.

Some children use tally marks, while others make a chart. Other investigations might involve going to the water center and finding out how many measured cups are in different containers. Students plan solutions, try them out, and record in writing what they have done. During sharing time, they report on their activities. One person's ideas often spark others to consider the problem from a different angle. "That's wonderful! How else could you try it?" is frequently heard.

Through recording and sharing, children become more self-aware of the learning processes involved in building with blocks and playing in sand or water. Having to plan for, record, and report on play activities ties play to academic learning. Children have real-life subject matter to write about and read to others. Not all play must be recorded by any means. But the frequent challenge to find a way to record what you have built or created ties naturally occurring constructive play to academic demands and gives purpose to reading, writing, and arithmetic.

How do these children learn responsibility? Play provides content and context for academic work. It also provides motivation for "getting your work done" so you will still have time to play. This is a worthy goal for children and adults. Balanced lives are happy lives. The children in Mrs. Burrell's class learn to balance the demands of work and play.

They must plan responsibly. This classroom would not work without clear expectations and requirements for academic work. Mrs. Burrell makes these expectations clear each morning in group time. Due dates for larger projects are marked on large calendars. Sharing times are posted. Children know what they must accomplish in the course of each day and week. This is not a laissez-faire environment. If a child does not complete the "givens," Mrs. Burrell may worry out loud that the child is tired and needs to rest in order to be able to get the work done. Usually, after a few minutes of "rest," the child asks for his work.

Key words for this class are dependability, responsibility, caring, and persistence. Mrs. Burrell relates class work to real-world responsibilities. Grownups have to go to work each day. They have to pay their light bills, or they will have no power. All through life, responsibility accompanies freedom. In this class, freedom to explore in centers is tied to completing the tasks for which you are responsible.

Accepting responsibility and organizing time for accomplishing tasks are vital skills that develop as children are allowed to decide what to do first, then next, and next, and then last. One day during a morning sharing time, Tim admitted that he had not completed his investigations from the day before. The other

The current debate about what is or is not developmentally appropriate in the primary grades deals, in part, with the balance between child-chosen activity and teacher-assigned activity.

children were asked what should be done if work was not completed. They answered in unison, "Do it the next day!" Mrs. Burrell assured him that she would remember to call on him first during the afternoon sharing time so he would have a chance to finish his work. Friendly, respectful accountability encourages children to complete their assignments on time. Children are taught not to make excuses and not to blame others for things that happen. They learn to reach into themselves to find the solutions to problems. Forgetting to do a task one day means finding a way to solve the problem of completing double assignments the next day.

How does children's work and play relate to the real world of grownups and work? The link of classroom responsibility to real-world responsibility is part of the third and final layer in the classroom, which Mrs. Burrell calls "applications." Projects that the children plan and execute are a part of this level. Through projects children pull together the skills learned in daily play and work (levels one and two) and apply them to topics that interest them. Children work alone or together on subjects they choose. For example, a second-grade girl and a kindergarten boy decided to find out about dolphins. They began by writing down what they knew and what they wanted to find out. They found books, read about dolphins, made models with various art materials, and wrote about what they learned. They also presented their project to the whole class.

Cooking in the classroom, selling the food, keeping track of the money, saving for classroom needs are other real-life applications. Through these activities dramatic play becomes simulation of real-world businesses. Children work and play at being producers and consumers. Since

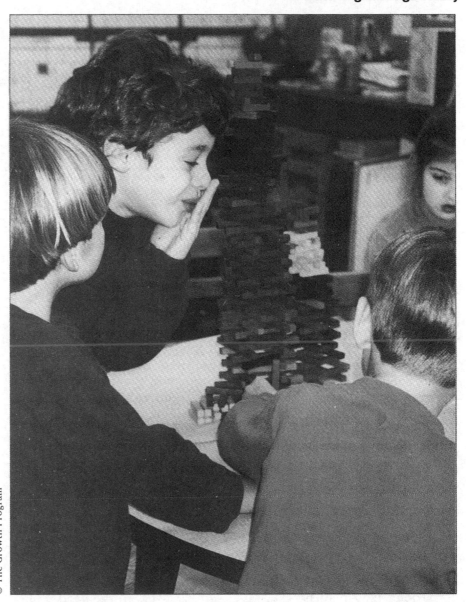

© The Growth Program

part of the real world is holding a job, in this class the children apply for positions, such as cleaning up a center, writing for the newsletter, or handling money for the bank. The dramatic play we see in kindergarten becomes more serious and more closely approximates adult roles when second graders are in charge.

How does play relate to motivation and management? Motivation and apathy are two central issues that plague educators today. Many teachers use grades, stickers, or other forms of external reinforcement to induce children to complete work and to do

the best they can. In this classroom, children's work is treated with respect and receives honest and constructive feedback. Both in individual conferences and in group sharing times, work is scrutinized. Work that shows thought and creativity is appreciated. Areas in which changes would help the finished product are pointed out. When work is done in blank books, there are few wrong answers. Children are encouraged to evaluate their own work rather than to wait for others to sit in judgment. Through work that is tied to play, children's love of learning is fostered. They learn to reach out

The additional experiences that two more years of living have furnished are evident in the play of primary children compared to younger children, as seen in the transition from dramatic play to the dramatization of plays and puppet shows. Older primary children are also likely to create more detail and accessories to accompany their plays than are kindergarten children.

for more knowledge. Through an emphasis on persistence, they learn not to give up quickly.

Ironically, many teachers fear a classroom in which children move around and select activities because they assume chaos will ensue. King (1987) categorizes elementary school play as instrumental (games and fun activities with specific academic focus), recreational (recess), or illicit (fooling around, acting up). Illicit play often happens when the teacher's back is turned. Children use illicit play as a way to make contact with friends or to keep from doing work tasks that they may regard as irrelevant. According to King, illicit play provides children a sense of control and autonomy in a teacher-dominated situation. Thus, in a traditional classroom, play may be seen as the enemy. In Mrs. Burrell's child-sensitive class, play is an accepted part of children's lives and is assumed to help carry the academic agenda forward.

True discipline comes from within. In order to learn self-control and self-discipline, children must be allowed to be in charge of themselves. Learning to be a self-disciplined person is a long-term project, but helping children develop independent thought in a community of learners removes many discipline problems common to more teacher-controlled situations.

From a teacher's point of view, plenty of play opportunities means that little time is wasted

in trying to keep small bodies unnaturally still in seats. For many children, having to sit still for long periods of time takes so much concentration that they can not attend to the academic work tasks at hand. Active playtimes allow for increased concentration during work times. The children in this class find comfortable individual rhythms for their work and play. After the morning group discussions, the children are told to go to work. Having been well trained in the purposes of courtesy, they get up in an orderly fashion and disperse quickly to all parts of the classroom. The attentive listener often hears comments from some children, for instance, "I'm going to do all my work first so I'll be able to play this afternoon." Other children start with the sand table or the blocks before settling down to journal writing or investigations.

The smooth transitions from group time to individual work are the result of careful planning, training, and monitoring of the work that is accomplished. At the beginning of the year, the children go on "field trips" around the room to discuss appropriate behaviors in each area. The children themselves generate guidelines for working and playing together in the small space that is their classroom. All guidelines spell out clear purposes. The overriding principle is that of consideration for other people. Caring, respect, and courtesy make the class into a very functional family group.

How does play provide a context for assessing children's progress? In grades one and two, the North Carolina educational system uses a checklist format for continuous teacher monitoring of children's progress through observation of their performance. Mrs. Burrell finds the children's play, as well as their work, an excellent context for evaluating the development of their concepts and skills. The children are often unaware that the teacher or the assistant is making note of what they are doing. Watching several children playing with Cuisenaire rods, Mrs. Burrell is able to check their use of patterns and symmetry. Listening to children pretending allows teachers to assess oral language skills. Thus, play is a context in which the teacher can see what a child can do.

Summary

Children do continue to play in primary school when the opportunity is provided. Their play is rich, creative, and more complex than that of younger children. Work and play intertwine throughout the layers of the classroom. Children learn while playing and play while learning, and the combination helps them learn to manage time responsibility. One clear message comes through in talking to these children: the reason school is a pleasure rather than a pain is the choices involved and the play opportunities available.

What do primary children learn when they work and play in school in a child-sensitive classroom? They learn responsibility, organization, how to enjoy themselves and still be task oriented. As they play together, oral language skills are honed in ways that would not be possible through traditional classroom talk. Play for primary children, like play for preschool children and play for adults, is about possibilities. Playful people are risk takers whose thinking is open ended and whose minds are creative.

What are the teaching implications of tying play and work together? Teachers anxious to maintain developmentally appropriate classrooms would do well to provide plenty of time and materials for a class full of work and play. Having children responsible for organizing their time "to get everything done and still play in centers" helps train them for future organizing of life, work, and leisure. Giving children choices at 5, 6, and 7 prepares them for major choices at 15, 16, and 17—and 27. A child who learns at 7 to say, "No, I can't play right now, I have to finish my journal," may be the child who can manage time well as a first-year college student. Children need to learn that their actions have consequences. Children need to be able to balance the demands of responsibilities and relaxation. We all need healthy doses of work and play.

References

Athey, I. 1987. The relationship of play to cognitive, language and moral development. In *Play as a medium for learning and development: A handbook of theory and practice,* ed. D. Bergen, 81–101. Portsmouth, NH: Heinemann.

Bergen, D. 1987. Stages of play development. In *Play as a medium for learning and development: A handbook of theory and practice,* ed. D. Bergen, 49–66. Portsmouth, NH: Heinemann.

Erikson, E. 1963. *Childhood and society.* New York: Norton.

Fromberg, D.P. 1987. Play. In *The early childhood curriculum: A review of current research,* ed. C. Seefeldt, 35–74. New York: Teachers College Press.

King, N.R. 1987. Elementary school play: Theory and research. In *School play: A source book,* eds. J.H. Block & N.R. King, 143–65. New York: Garland.

Morrison, G.S. 1991. *Early childhood education today.* 3rd ed. New York: Merrill.

Rogers, C.S., & J.K. Sawyer. 1988. *Play in the lives of children.* Washington, DC: NAEYC.

Rubin, K.N., G.G. Fein, & B. Vandenberg. 1983. Play. In *Handbook of child psychology. Vol. 4, Socialization, personality and social development,* eds. E.M. Hetherington & P.H. Mussen, 698–774. New York: Wiley.

Vygotsky, L.S. 1978. *Mind in society: The development of higher psychological processes,* eds. M. Cole, V. Dan-Steiner, S. Scribner, & E. Souberman. Cambridge, MA: Harvard University Press.

Helping Children Develop Self-Control

Judith A. Schickedanz

Judith A. Schickedanz is a Professor in the School of Education, Boston University.

The apparent causes of children's violent behavior are well known. Children are often witnesses of violence committed by one adult against another, and are themselves frequent victims of abuse or neglect. Gunfire has become commonplace in cities. Gangs and drugs are other destructive forces. During the times when not directly affected by real violence, many children watch violent television programs. Finally, child socialization, both within the family and at school, seems weaker today than in years past, and many adults seem incapable of making sacrifices for the sake of their own or someone else's children.

It is no wonder that today's children create difficult challenges for their teachers, or that teachers feel physically and emotionally exhausted at day's end. For many years, I have worked with urban preschool and kindergarten teachers, sometimes spending two or three days a week in their classrooms. I know firsthand about teachers' exhaustion. And I understand what they mean when they say, "Children today are violent and lack self-control." But I also think that some of the difficulties in classrooms emerge because teachers themselves are unaware of children's potential for developing social competence, including self-regulation.

A cognitive-developmental view of social development has dominated early childhood teachers' thinking about children's social and moral development for several decades. Therefore, teachers sometimes have been less effective in promoting self-regulation in children than they might have been. Teachers cannot, and must not, be blamed for the larger societal forces that play havoc with children's lives. They cannot be expected to work miracles. But neither can we ignore the potential good that teachers can achieve; in fact, teachers should be considered an important element in the effort to improve children's self-control.

Child Socialization: Theory, Research and Practice

Beginning in the 1960s, ideas about child socialization were influenced dramatically by Piaget's cognitive-developmental theories. According to this theory, moral development is necessarily a late occurrence because it depends on, and emerges from, well-developed capacities for logical reasoning and social role-taking (Piaget, 1977). Also, skill in social role-taking—the adoption of different perspectives—depends on interaction with people of equal status (Piaget, 1977).

Piaget used several tasks to gauge moral development by probing children's reasoning. To study children's understanding of rules, he observed them as they played marbles, asked them to teach him

to play and questioned them about the origin of the rules (Piaget, 1977). He examined children's understandings of intentions by telling stories and then asking the children to make and explain judgments about them (Piaget, 1977). Kohlberg, a follower of Piaget, also asked children to make judgments and explain their reasoning about moral dilemmas (Kohlberg, 1969).

Logical reasoning, however, is not the young child's strength. Requiring children to reveal their social understanding through verbal explanations puts them at a big disadvantage in demonstrating their budding competence. Not surprisingly, young children, especially preschoolers, perform poorly on most of these tasks (Piaget, 1977).

Another requirement for moral development, beyond building children's capacity to engage in logical reasoning, is developing skills in social perspective-taking. Cognitive-developmentalists believe development of this skill requires social interaction in situations of "mutual respect" (i.e., among peers or with adults who don't "pull rank"). Piaget stated that "the sense of justice, though naturally capable of being reinforced by the precepts and the practical example of the adult, is largely independent of these influences, and requires nothing more for its development than the mutual respect and solidarity ... among children themselves" (Piaget 1977, p. 190). Young children's poor grasp of the rules of marbles was, he believed, a result of their "unilateral respect" for the older children and adults who taught them the rules. Because the younger children had not participated in rule formation, they viewed the rules as external and, therefore, did not understand or abide by them.

Kohlberg (1969) expressed similar views: "Family participation is not unique or critically necessary for moral development . . . other primary groups stimulate more development" (p. 399). Given children's "unilateral respect" for their parents, Kohlberg found parent-child interaction was not ideal for mutual role-taking. Kohlberg recommended "intense peer group interaction, supervised by a group leader." He observed high levels of moral reasoning among adolescents living in an Israeli kibbutz where they had "low interaction with parents" (1976, p. 400). The kibbutz leaders included the adolescents in decisions about many daily activities.

Considerable research has been conducted on peer interaction since the early 1970s, perhaps because of its primary importance in cognitive-developmental theory. Many researchers have wondered how social behavior differs among children who have been judged by peers to be popular, neglected or outcast. Results from many studies show that rejected children tend to be aggressive and self-centered. They also are more likely to infer hostility from their peers' behavior even when this may not be the case (Hudley & Graham, 1993).

Social skills researchers, like cognitive developmentalists, have focused on reasoning—children's understanding of others' views and intentions. While some of these researchers recognize anger, they attribute its cause to perceptions of the social situation. To reduce anger and the resulting aggression, children are trained to interpret situations differently (Hudley & Graham, 1993) and to improve their participation, cooperation and communication skills (Oden & Asher, 1977).

The Impact of Cognitive-Developmental Theory

Early childhood educators are continually told that children's interaction with peers is very important, while interaction with adults is less important. After hearing that "obedience is not enough" (Kamii, 1984), educators may wonder if it is desirable at all. They have been cautioned that "unless handled positively, discipline of any kind may be perceived by the child as punishment . . . children of 3 to 8 years of age are still just beginning to learn the advanced skills of seeing things from another person's perspective" (Gartrell, 1987, p. 55).

Furthermore, professionals have been encouraged not to get too involved in children's conflicts. Oken-Wright (1992) encourages teachers to use a "teacher behavior continuum" (TBC) developed by Wolfgang and Glickman (1980). Oken-Wright urges teachers to intervene initially in children's conflicts in a way that gives children complete control. If this fails, the teacher intervenes in ever-increasing amounts, finally taking complete control only if necessary. As an example, a child excluded from a school sandbox reported her mistreatment to the teacher, who asked, "What do you suppose you could do if you want to play there?" The child said that she could ask the other child. The teacher and child returned to the sandbox, whereupon the first child "invited" the second child to play. According to the author, this invitation was extended while a "non-judgmental" adult looked on (Oken-Wright, 1992, p. 18).

In this case, however, it is inaccurate to say that the adult was "non-judgmental." When the teacher asked the child what she could do to play in the sandbox, the teacher implied her belief that the child had the right to play in the sandbox and that the other child had been wrong to exclude her. The adult made the moral decision, while the child was responsible only for finding a solution to the specific conflict.

Many authors explicitly tell teachers not to make moral decisions. For example, Hitz and Driscoll (1988) note their agreement with Kamii's (1984) view that praise is a reward and "like other forms of reward [it] discourages children from judging for themselves what is right or wrong" (p. 9). They imply that moral decisions should be left to the children. Ironically, to give praise, sometimes teachers first must make a decision about what behavior is right or desirable. Instead of telling a child that he is nice because he shared with a classmate, Hitz and Driscoll advise teachers to say, "José, I noticed that you shared today with Alice," leaving José to decide if he was "nice" (p. 12).

Because teachers cannot determine easily the child's intent in many situations, it is wise to describe the child's desirable behavior and leave it at that. In addition, young children can become overly concerned about what the teacher thinks of them, rather than their behavior. Whatever the approach used to praise children, teachers first must make a moral judgment. A teacher wouldn't comment on sharing if she did not consider sharing to be more desirable than not sharing. Because such comments usually are accompanied by smiles and a pleasant tone of voice, most young children probably know that the teacher holds sharing in high regard.

Because researchers recommend that teachers allow children to make their own moral judgments, the teachers often conclude that they should remove themselves completely from children's conflicts. Even in situations where a teacher knows a child has been wronged, the teacher might not intervene in order to provide the child with crucial experience in making moral judgments and solving conflicts. Often the child continues to complain to the teacher about the transgression and may start whining, crying or throwing a tantrum. The teacher does not realize, perhaps, that his own reluctance to take a stand in the situation confuses and undermines the child, making it difficult for the child to act.

It is true that children's skills in handling conflicts can be limited if adults think of all the solutions, or completely intercede to solve a dispute. But research (and human experience) does not show any benefits to children when adults remove themselves completely from children's conflicts or refuse to take a stand on what is right or wrong.

Evidence That Moral Development Begins Early

Cognitive-developmental theorists, as we have seen, assume that social understandings, especially the development of awareness about other people's feelings and thoughts, emerge late in development. Dunn (1988) questioned this assumption:

Do we conclude that for a child the crucial development—the understanding that other people have feelings and minds like his or her own, yet also different—is extremely slow? Children develop their powers of communication, understanding and thought, their emotional security and their sense of themselves, within a complex social framework: do they nevertheless fail to grasp the nature of the moods, interests and relationships of others who share that world, or the ground rules of that world, until they are 5 or 7 years old? (p. 3)

Children only 2 years old will attempt to comfort a parent in distress (Dunn, 1988; Zahn-Waxler & Radke-Yarrow, 1982). At first, they use simple strategies, such as offering their own comfort objects to the parent or patting the parent. As they develop, they find another person to help and they locate objects or materials they have seen used when people are hurt (i.e., first aid items).

Very young children's other behaviors also indicate social competence, including judgments about violations of a standard and awareness that others make social judgments and hold opinions. In Dunn's study (1988), children not yet 3 years old called their mother's attention to a sibling's wrongdoing. A study by Zahn-Waxler, Radke-Yarrow, Wagner and Chapman (1992) demonstrated that 2-year-olds responded differently in situations where they caused someone's distress as opposed to situations where they witnessed but did not cause distress. In other studies, babies as young as 8 or 9 months used a "social reference"—perhaps by reading their mothers' social signals—to ascertain their reaction to a stranger or a novel toy (Klinnert, 1981; Walden & Baxter, 1989).

When rejecting parents express negative emotion, their children do not absorb moral lessons or internalize standards.

Other researchers have also documented the abilities that very young children bring to social situations. Kagan (1981) noted some advances in relevant cognitive abilities during the last half of children's second year. At this stage, the child becomes able to "infer the cause of an event" and begins to "expect events to have antecedents." As a result, the child "automatically generates cognitive hypotheses as to causes" (p. 124). The 2-year-old is also "self-aware," and can judge his or her "competence to attain a goal defined by a standard" (p. 129). In addition, the child is able "to generate ideas of goals and to hold them in awareness . . . He becomes aware of the fact that he can initiate, cease, and monitor his actions" (p. 135).

Zahn-Waxler, et al. (1992), summarized the abilities of the very young child. They concluded that the very young child has "a) the cognitive capacity to interpret the physical and psychological states of others, b) the emotional capacity to affectively experience the other's state and c) the behavioral repertoire that permits the possibility of trying to alleviate discomfort in others" (p. 127).

Although the skills of young children do not match those of older children, their competence is substantial enough to provide a substratum upon which moral development can take hold. Researchers working outside of the cognitive-developmental tradition think reason is not the basic starting point of moral development. In their view, emotion is the key.

Emotion and Moral Development

Those emphasizing the role of emotion in moral development consider conscience to be of central importance. Conscience, the internalization of standards, is what causes the child to "restrain antisocial or destructive impulses, even in the absence of surveillance" (Kochanska, 1993, p. 325). Kochanska summarizes the origins of moral development from this point of view:

The foundations of the moral self derive from repeated early interactions with consistently available—not threatening, as suggested by early psychoanalysis—caregivers. During the continual, early affective exchanges, a young child develops a sense of connectedness and the ability to read others' emotions and to react with distress, empathy and prosocial activity to others' distress. . . . Simultaneously . . . an older infant and toddler begins to internalize first prohibitions. Parents communicate their prohibitions by expressing anger, disapproval or warning during the process of affective communications. Because the child has established a bond . . . with the parent . . . such emotional signals function as inhibitors of forbidden acts—first, when the parent is physically present and can be referenced, and later . . . when the parent is absent. Thus, the roots of internalization are in the process of the early affective communication between parents and the child—transgressions become highly affectively charged events due to the parents' subtle affective signals. Caregivers endow the act of wrong-doing with affective significance because they express negative emotion. . . . (p. 326)

Research provides some support for this view. In virtually all of the attachment studies, parents who score high on measures of warmth and nurturance have children who are securely attached (Ainsworth, Blehar, Waters & Wall, 1978). Furthermore, these children later show the most skill in peer interactions and comply easily with parental and teacher requests (Matas, et al., 1978; Sroufe, 1982; Stayton, Hogan & Ainsworth, 1971). These behaviors are early indices of later self-regulation, which is a good predictor of mature conscience (Kochanska, 1991).

In other studies, Hoffman (1988) and Baumrind (1968) found that the affective climate of parenting influences children's subsequent social and moral behavior. Baumrind identified two kinds of parents who exerted control over their children. The authoritative parent "exerts firm control at points of parent-child divergence. . . . She uses reason as well as power to achieve her objectives. She does not base her decisions on group consensus or the individual child's desires; but also, does not regard herself as infallible" (Baumrind, 1968, p. 261). An authoritarian parent, in contrast, "favors punitive, forceful measures to curb self-will at points where the child's actions or beliefs conflict with what she thinks is right conduct" (Baumrind, 1968, p. 261). Authoritarian parents "value obedience as a virtue" (p. 261), forgetting that compliance shown only in the face of authority is not the final goal. When parents focus only on obedience, their discipline is harsh and they often convey a message of rejection.

When rejecting parents express negative emotion, their children do not absorb moral lessons or internalize standards. Authoritative parents, on the other hand, are effective because they express negative emotions in a larger context of overall acceptance of their children (Baumrind, 1972). Kochanska (1993) stresses that caregivers must be "consistently available and non-threatening," but that "caregivers endow the act of wrong-doing with affective significance because they express negative emotion." In other words, parents must create an affective climate in which children are certain of the parent's love and unwavering acceptance.

Research on temperament provides further evidence of the central role of emotion in social and moral development. Kagan, Reznick and Gibbons (1989) have documented biological differences among children in their tendencies to be inhibited or uninhibited. Other researchers (Dienstbier, 1984) have wondered if these emotional tendencies lead to different responses to parents' socialization. For example, they asked if inhibited children fare better under low power-assertion parenting conditions because they respond to subtler cues, and because too much power will divert their attention away from internal feelings of distress toward external controls. Conversely, will uninhibited children be less sensitive to low power-assertion because it fails to induce enough emotional distress to cause the child to attend to a parent's reasoning about prohibitions? Recent research suggests that the answer is yes. In one study (Kochanska, 1991), uninhibited children whose parents exerted little authority had a more poorly developed conscience at ages 8 to 10 than did inhibited children with the same socialization history.

One study examined preschool children to learn how well their understanding of moral rules ver-

sus appropriate moral emotions predicts actual moral behavior. Differences in moral rule understanding predicted poorly, while differences in the attribution of appropriate moral emotions predicted well (Asendorpf & Nunner-Winkler, 1992). Children's knowledge of how one would *feel* seems to play a more important role in children's moral behavior than the knowledge of how one should *behave* in certain situations.

Summary and Implications for Practice

Research and theory from outside the cognitive-developmental tradition can broaden the early childhood teacher's view of young children's capacity for social and moral learning. The research is compelling in demonstrating: a) the central role adults play in children's social and moral learning; b) the early emergence of the basic language and cognitive underpinnings necessary for social and moral learning, and of aspects of social and moral learning itself and c) the importance of emotion in early social and moral development.

1. Think carefully about your place in children's conflicts. Do not hesitate to let children know when you think certain behavior is right or wrong, but incorporate their ideas to right a wrong.

2. Emphasize the effects on others of children's appropriate and inappropriate behavior. Adults must, at times, express negative emotions when prohibitions and standards are violated. It is never excusable or effective, however, to belittle children, be punitive or hold a grudge.

3. Use enough authority-assertion to get a child's attention in a situation where a prohibition or a standard has been violated. Deal with individual children in private as much as possible, adapting levels of authority-assertion to individual needs.

4. Provide interesting activities. Prevent unnecessary conflicts by

providing adequate materials. The ability to share materials and wait for a turn does not develop well in children accustomed to deprivation.

5. Avoid the trap of thinking that you cannot begin implementing your curriculum until children's social and emotional behavior is under control. Kounin's (1970) research with kindergartners indicated that a challenging and interesting program is an excellent way to solve children's behavior problems.

6. Use tactics that make compliance easier for young children. Keep rules to a few basic, necessary and understandable ones. Organize the classroom to make cleaning up easy. Give children some choice, while enforcing expectations. Enable children to predict events and expectations by being consistent and following a daily routine.

7. Give reasons for your prohibitions, but do not wait for their agreement as a condition for following through. Baumrind's (1968) effective, authoritative parent "does not base her decisions on group consensus or the individual child's desires," although this parent does "share with the child the reasoning behind her policy" (p. 168).

8. Interact with children as they play. Adult interaction increases children's learning. In addition, it is essential to the development of teacher-child affective bonds (Moss, 1992).

9. Ask yourself how you teach children to keep promises. This is an effective means of thinking about the nature of good conscience.

References

Ainsworth, M. D. S., Blehar, M. D., Waters, E., & Wall, S. (1978). *Patterns of attachment.* Hillsdale, NJ: Lawrence Erlbaum.

Asendorpf, J. B., & Nunner-Winkler, G. (1992). Children's moral motive strength and temperamental inhibition reduce their immoral behavior in real moral conflicts. *Child Development, 63,* 1223-1235.

Baumrind, D. (1968). Authoritarian vs. authoritative parental control. *Adolescence, 3,* 255-272.

Baumrind, D. (1972). Socialization and instrumental competence. In W. W. Hartup (Ed.), *The young child: Reviews of research (Vol. 2)* (pp. 202-204). Washington, DC.: National Association for the Education of Young Children.

Dienstbier, R. A. (1984). The role of emotion in moral socialization. In C. Izard, J. Kagan & R. B. Zajonc (Eds.), *Emotions, cognitions and behaviors.* New York: Cambridge University Press.

Dunn, J. (1988). *The beginnings of social understanding.* Cambridge: Harvard University Press.

Gartrell, D. (1987). Punishment or guidance? *Young Children, 42,* 55-61.

Hitz, R., & Driscoll, A. (1988). Praise or encouragement? *Young Children, 43,* 6-13.

Hoffman, M. L. (1988). Moral development. In M. H. Bornstein & M. E. Lamb (Eds.), *Developmental psychology: An advanced textbook* (2nd ed.). Hillsdale, NJ: Lawrence Erlbaum.

Hudley, C., & Graham, S. (1993). An attributional intervention to reduce peer-directed aggression among African American boys. *Child Development, 64,* 124-138.

Kagan, J. (1981). *The second year: The emergence of self-awareness.* Cambridge, MA: Harvard University Press.

Kagan, J., Reznick, J. S., & Gibbons, J. (1989). Inhibited and uninhibited types of children. *Child Development, 60,* 838-845.

Kamii, C. (1984). Viewpoint: Obedience is not enough. *Young Children, 39,* 11-14.

Klinnert, M. (1981). *The regulation of infant behavior by maternal facial expression.* Unpublished doctoral dissertation, University of Denver, Denver, CO.

Kochanska, G. (1991). Socialization and temperament in the development of guilt and conscience. *Child Development, 62,* 1379-1392.

Kochanska, G. (1993). Toward a synthesis of parental socialization and child temperament in early development of conscience. *Child Development, 64,* 325-347.

Kohlberg, L. (1969). Stage and sequence: The cognitive-developmental approach to socialization. In D. A. Goslin (Ed.), *Handbook of socialization: Theory and research* (pp. 347-480). Chicago: Rand McNally.

Kohlberg, L. (1976). Moral stages and moralization. In T. Lickona (Ed.), *Moral development and behavior: Theory, research, and social issues* (pp. 31-53). New York: Holt, Rinehart & Winston.

Kounin, J. (1970). *Discipline and group management in classrooms.* New York: Holt, Rinehart & Winston.

Matas, L., Arend, R. A., & Sroufe, L. A. (1978). Continuity of adaptation in the second year of life: The relationship between quality of attachment and later competence. *Child Development, 49,* 547-556.

Moss, E. (1992). The socio/affective context of joint cognitive activity. In L. T. Winegar & J. Valsiner (Eds.), *Children's development within social context (Vol. 2)* (pp. 117-154). Hillsdale, NJ: Lawrence Erlbaum.

Oden, S., & Asher, S. (1977). Coaching children in social skills for friendship making. *Child Development, 48,* 495-506.

Oken-Wright, P. (1992). From tug of war to "let's make a deal": The teacher's role. *Young Children, 48,* 15-20.

Piaget, J. (1977). *The moral judgment of the child.* (M. Gabain, trans.). Harmondsworth, England: Penguin. (Original work published in 1932.)

Sroufe, L. A. (1982). Attachment and the roots of competence. In H. E. Fitzgerald & T. H. Carr (Eds.), *Human development: Annual Editions,* Guilford, CT: Dushkin.

Stayton, D., Hogan, R., & Ainsworth, M. D. (1971). Infant obedience and maternal behavior: The origins of socialization reconsidered. *Child Development, 42,* 1057-1069.

Walden, T. A., & Baxter, A. (1989). The effect of context and age on social referencing. *Child Development, 60*(6), 1511-1518.

Wolfgang, C., & Glickman, C. (1980). *Solving discipline problems: Strategies for classroom teachers.* Boston: Allyn & Bacon.

Zahn-Waxler, C., & Radke-Yarrow, M. (1982). The development of altruism: Alternative research strategies. In N. Eisenberg (Ed.), *The development of prosocial behavior* (pp. 109-137). New York: Academic Press.

Zahn-Waxler, C., Radke-Yarrow, M., Wagner, E., & Chapman, M. (1992). Development of concern for others. *Developmental Psychology, 28,* 126-136.

Young Children's Understanding of Everyday Emotions

Janet Kuebli

Janet Kuebli, M.S., is a doctoral student in the Department of Psychology at Emory University in Atlanta, Georgia, where she is studying parent–child narratives about children's emotional experiences.

*This is one of a regular series of Research in Review columns. This column was edited by **Laura E. Berk**, Ph.D., professor of psychology at Illinois State University.*

W hat young children understand about emotion states and behaviors is of importance to early childhood educators who deal with children's feelings every day. Children, like adults, experience many emotions in the course of each day. Strong emotions arising from their own experiences may be very confusing for children. Children also have to make sense of other people's emotional reactions or feelings; therefore, we often try to help children talk about their own and others' feelings. We think of this especially when children encounter traumatic life events, such as when a child's parents divorce or someone in the family is very sick or dies.

Children may also need help in understanding everyday emotions. Teachers and parents may, for example, suggest ways that children can cope with feelings of distress, fear, or shyness on the first day of school or explain how it is possible to feel sad and happy at the same time about moving to a new school. Sometimes we urge children to talk about their anger or sadness as a way of handling minor daily conflicts and disappointments. By helping children to understand emotions, we hope to help them channel their feelings in self-enhancing ways and also prepare them to deal with similar experiences in the future.

As children mature, we also expect them to master their emotions to some extent. Learning to express some feelings and how to mask others are common everyday lessons in children's lives. Hochschild (1983) calls this learning how to do "emotion work." Getting along with others often means handling feelings in a socially acceptable fashion. Children who get mad because they have to wait their turn or who laugh at a crying child who has taken a fall and skinned a knee sometimes are encouraged to think about how others feel. A child who overexuberantly boasts about being a winner may be urged to remember how it also feels to be the loser. In some cases the ability to regulate and manage emotions tells us that a child is ready for new challenges.

Over the last decade, researchers have shown keen interest in the nature of children's understanding of emotion, especially as it relates to social–cognitive development. Much of this work has concerned school-age children. Results from these studies suggest, not sur-

At the heart of the studies with younger children are two related issues. The first concerns identifying links between early developments in emotion understanding and language.

prisingly, that emotion understanding becomes more complex and sophisticated during elementary school. At these ages, for example, children begin to appreciate the fact that they can experience more than one emotion at a time (Carroll & Steward, 1984; Donaldson & Westerman, 1986; Harter & Buddin, 1987; Wintre, Polivy, & Murray, 1990). They also begin to take into greater account the situations that cause emotional reactions (Barden, Zelko, Duncan, & Masters, 1980; Strayer, 1986; Brody & Harrison, 1987; Camras & Allison, 1989). At this time children's skill in hiding their feelings also shows considerable improvement (Saarni, 1984, 1985; Davis, 1992), as does their understanding of emotions that involve self-evaluations, such as pride, guilt, and shame (Graham, Doubleday, & Guarino, 1984; Graham, 1988; Harter & Whitesell, 1989).

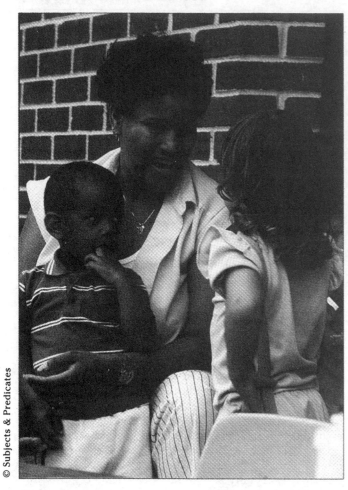

while not exhaustive of the work in this area, provide a selective overview of what is known about emotion understanding in young children. Finally, I suggest ways that teachers can use these findings to facilitate children's understanding of their own and others' feelings.

Emotional experience

According to Lewis (Lewis & Michalson, 1983; Lewis, 1992), it's useful to think of emotional behavior as consisting of a variety of components. One of these components, *emotional experience,* refers to how individuals interpret and evaluate their emotions. Other components include (a) emotion states and (b) their expressions, which may be conveyed either verbally or through nonverbal changes in facial expressions, physical posture, or movement. The componential model of

---

One major conclusion derived from these studies is that conversations about feelings are an important context for learning about emotions and how to manage them.

---

emotion proposes that our emotional experiences, states, and expressions do not always correspond to each other. On some occasions we may be unaware of our emotions or simply unable to name the particular feelings we are having. At other times we might intentionally express one emotion while experiencing a different feeling, or we might recognize our feelings but lack insight into the reasons for having them.

Among these various emotion components, emotional experience is considered the most cognitive (Lewis & Saarni, 1985) because it relies upon basic mental processes of attention, perception, and memory. We cannot begin, thus, to understand our feelings until we pay attention to them. Emotional experience further entails arriving at cognitive judgments and insights about our own emotion states and expressions. Emotional experience, in effect, depends upon being able to introspect or reflect upon ourselves (Lewis, 1992). Cognitive processes that underlie emotional experience essentially bring our emotions into consciousness and provide the basis for our having emotional experiences.

The developmental timetable for the emergence of various emotion states and expressions has already been well documented (e.g. Campos, Barrett, Lamb, Goldsmith, & Stenberg, 1983). Newborns, for example, display joy, interest, disgust, and distress; around eight months most babies show surprise, anger, fear, and sadness (Stenberg, Campos, & Emde, 1983; Izard & Malatesta, 1987). Embarrassment, empathy, pride, shame, and guilt only begin to appear at the end of infancy, usually after the age of 18 months. Much less is

Emotion-understanding studies with younger children are by comparison less common. New research, however, has begun to yield information both about what younger children know about emotions and how this understanding may develop. At the heart of the studies with younger children are two related issues. The first concerns identifying links between early developments in emotion understanding and language. The second issue centers on how children's emotion understanding is socialized in the course of children's interactions with others. One major conclusion derived from these studies is that conversations about feelings are an important context for learning about emotions and how to manage them.

This article considers the general nature of emotional experience first. The focus turns next to several studies

---

The second issue centers on how children's emotion understanding is socialized in the course of children's interactions with others.

---

on children's early emotion vocabulary and concepts, followed by research on how emotions are discussed by young children with others. The studies described here,

Some Characteristics of Young Children's Emotion Language and Understanding

Approximate age of child	Description
Birth to 18 months	display emotions and respond to emotions in others at preverbal stage
	use emotion cues of others to guide own responses to new or ambiguous situations
	do not produce or comprehend emotion terms with a few exceptions
18 to 20 months	use first emotion words in vocabulary (e.g. cry, happy)
	begin to discuss emotions spontaneously in conversations with others
2 to 3 years	increase emotion vocabulary most rapidly
	correctly label simple emotions in self and others, and talk about past, present, and future emotions
	talk about the causes and consequences of some emotions and identify emotions associated with certain situations
	use emotion language in pretend play
4 to 5 years	show increased capacity to verbally reflect on emotions and to consider more complex relations between emotions and situations
	understand that the same event may call forth different feelings in different people and that feelings sometimes persist long after the events that caused them
	demonstrate growing awareness about controlling and managing emotions in accord with social standards
6 to 11 years	exhibit conceptual advances in their understanding of complex emotions (e.g. pride and shame) and of mixed or multiple emotions
	show marked improvements in the ability to suppress or conceal negative emotional reactions and in the use of self-initiated strategies for redirecting feelings
	take into fuller account the events leading to emotional reactions

known about the developmental course of emotional experience and understanding. The components model of emotion, however, suggests that it is not necessary for emotional states, expressions, and experience to develop in lock-step fashion all together. This model may explain why children have emotions and express them before they are able to reflect upon and understand their feelings (Michalson & Lewis, 1983; Lewis, 1992).

Researchers hypothesize that a fundamental prerequisite underlying emotional experience is having a *self-concept;* that is, children need a sense of an "I" who owns and knows her or his own emotion states and expressions in order to experience them. Even prior to forming a self-concept, however, children acquire several important cognitive skills related to self-understanding, which may also underlie their capacity for emotional experience. Collectively these skills are known as self-referential behaviors. They are first evident at ages between 15 and 24 months and include acquiring (a) an awareness of oneself as separate from others, (b) knowledge that objects independent of oneself have a permanent exist-

ence, (c) a sense of oneself as a causal agent, and (d) the ability to visually recognize oneself (Bertenthal & Fisher, 1978; Lewis & Brooks-Gunn, 1979; Sroufe, 1979; Kagan, 1981; Harter, 1983; Lewis, Sullivan, Stanger, & Weiss, 1989). Harter (1983) refers to these developments as contributing to the formation of an "existential self." Existential awareness of self forms the foundation for the child's initial self-concept. Together, these cognitive abilities enable children to make themselves objects of thought. Thereafter, emotional experience probably develops gradually, most likely in concert with changes in children's self-concepts. Emotions are, thus, integral to children's sense of who they are, helping them to form their own personal views of the world around them.

Learning words and concepts for emotions

Emotion theorists suspect that learning to talk is another critical factor in the development of emotional experience; acquiring word labels for emotions is re-

---

We cannot begin to understand our feelings until we pay attention to them.

garded as particularly important for developments in children's understandings of emotions. Certainly, parents refer to emotions in conversations with their children, almost from birth. Emotion communication enables others to draw attention to children's expressions of emotion. No doubt, this communication accelerates the development of emotional experience and understanding (Izard & Malatesta, 1987). Children's emotional self-understanding may start with being able to name emotion states and behaviors. From maternal reports, diary studies, and direct observations, we know that children begin to use emotion terms around the ages of 20 to 24 months (see Bretherton, Fritz, Zahn-Waxler, & Ridgeway, 1986 for a review of research on how children learn to talk about emotions). By 36 months children use emotion words to talk about both themselves and others, and in reference to events in the present, past, and future (Bretherton & Beeghly, 1982).

To learn about children's first emotion words, Bretherton and Beeghly (1982) gave mothers of 28-month-olds a list of terms for emotions as well as for mental states (e.g. knowing, remembering, dreaming), physiological states (e.g. hunger, fatigue), and perceptual states (e.g. seeing, hearing, tasting). Mothers indicated which words on the list their children used. At this age about 75% of the children had acquired the emotion words *mad* and *scared*, and well over half used *happy* and *sad*. Nearly all of the children used the emotion-behavior term *cry;* however, *surprise,* apparently a late acquisition, was reported for only 13% of the children. Additionally, children used emotion words to refer to both self and others, rather than only to self or only to others. This suggests that children's early emotional understanding of themselves and others may be closely related rather than developing separately. Finally, emotion terms were more common than mental-state words but less frequent than words for perceptual or physiological states. Notably, however, children talked about causes for emotions more often than causes for other kinds of states of being. This finding underscores the importance of emotional understanding as central to how children make sense of what happens to them.

In several experimental studies, researchers have looked at preschoolers' ability to label facial expressions. Michalson and Lewis (1985), for example, asked two- to five-year-olds "What kind of face" another child was making in a series of snapshots. They found that children knew the labels for *happiness* and *sadness* at earlier ages than they knew the terms for *anger, surprise, disgust,* or *fear*. In fact, children did not produce many verbal labels at all until after age three, and even by five years of age children had difficulty naming the surprise, disgust, and fear expressions. When asked to point to the face that matched the emotion label given by the experimenter, however, children as young as two demonstrated they knew something about the situations in which certain facial expressions were likely. Seventy percent of two-year-olds matched the happy face with a birthday-party drawing. These results tell us that children's early knowledge of some emotional situations may considerably outpace their ability to talk about those emotions. Less than half of the two- and

three-year-olds, however, matched the sad and disgust faces with the correct pictures; whereas, the majority of the four- and five-year-olds made the correct match. This more gradual development trend in understanding negative emotions has also been observed in several other studies (e.g. Borke, 1971; Glasberg & Aboud, 1982; Reichenbach & Masters, 1983).

Clearly, preschoolers become more adept at talking about their own and others' emotions. The largest and most rapid increase in the number of terms children have for emotions occurs between the ages of two and three (Ridgeway, Waters, & Kuczaj, 1985), but children continue to acquire new emotion words after this time. During the preschool period, caregivers also increasingly urge children to "use words" rather than act out their feelings. Research shows that young children are learning more than just an emotion vocabulary. Specifically, children learn more about the nature of emotional processes, including new insights about the causes and consequences of feelings.

Denham and Zoller (1993) were particularly interested in what preschoolers think causes various emotions. The two researchers showed children puppets with happy, sad, fearful, or angry faces and then asked them to think of what would make the puppets "feel that way." Results showed that the children more often associated

---

Emotional experience further entails arriving at cognitive judgments and insights about our own emotion states and expressions.

---

happiness with nonsocial causes (e.g. playing or going somewhere without reference to being with others) than with social ones. By contrast, the reasons children gave for sadness and anger were mostly social in nature. Children said that being hurt or left by others caused sadness, for example; their reasons for anger included being punished, fighting, or not liking someone else. Interestingly, neither social nor nonsocial reasons were given for feeling fearful; instead, children said fear was caused by make-believe creatures, such as monsters or ghosts. One notable gender difference in the responses was that girls gave more reasons for sadness than did boys. This outcome is intriguing in light of research with adults and adolescents in which females report thinking about sadness in relation to themselves and experiencing depression more often than do males (Brody, 1984; Conway, Giannopoulos, & Stiefenhofer, 1990).

Some preschoolers also have begun to recognize that a single event sometimes causes different feelings in different people. In one study (Gove & Keating, 1979) three- and five-year-olds heard a short story in which only one of two characters won a game. All of the older children, but only two thirds of the younger ones, judged that the victor would feel happy, while the loser would be sad in this social situation. This result is somewhat at odds

Emotional experience, in effect, depends upon being able to introspect or reflect upon ourselves.

with what Denham and Zoller found, but the differences may be products of the methods used in the two studies. In addition, although preschoolers demonstrate an increasing ability to reason about the causes and consequences of single emotions, few children prior to the age of five grasp the concept of mixed or conflicting feelings. That is, while preschoolers may say that one feeling can follow another one sequentially, they tend to deny that two different emotions can be experienced simultaneously (Harter & Buddin, 1987). Even after short training about mixed emotions, four- and five-year-olds have shown little improvement in their understanding of mixed emotions (Peng, Johnson, Pollock, Glasspool, & Harris, 1992). Younger children's greater difficulty with multiple feelings may be tied to their limitations in the cognitive skills necessary for integrating opposing emotions.

Socialization of emotion understanding

Studies on children's emotion concepts have sought to document at what ages children demonstrate higher levels of understanding about emotions. Other research has focused on identifying experiences in children's lives that influence the particular forms emotion understandings can take. A key assumption is that children's insights into their own emotions are socially shaped in important ways (e.g. Lutz, 1985; Gordon, 1989). Whereas research on the content of emotion concepts has concentrated on older children, studies examining how emotions are socialized have usually been conducted with younger children.

The goal of emotion socialization is usually to redirect or change the way children spontaneously express their emotions to conform more closely with social rules or conventions. Sometimes this means substituting one feeling for a different one, as when we smile after receiving a disappointing gift (Saarni, 1984) or look on the bright side of things that worry or sadden us. Saarni (1985; Saarni & Crowley, 1990) outlines three general classes of processes by which emotions may be socialized. First, *direct* socialization refers to occasions when others chide or praise children's immediately prior emotional behaviors. In this case an adult's behavior reinforces the child's expression of emotions. Reinforcement, either reward or punishment, gives children explicit information about the way certain emotions are valued by others. Didactic teaching is another direct form of socialization often used with children to convey social conventions for expressing emotions. A child may be told, for example, that "girls don't brag" about their successes or that "boys don't cry" about their failures. Emotions are also socialized *indirectly*. A classic example is when a child imitates someone else's emotional reactions, such as one child's fearful reluctance to try

something new being copied by another child who only moments before was a willing and eager participant. We can view this situation, in part, as a case in which one person's emotional reactions are "catching." There are times when uncontrolled laughter seizes a group of children in this way or sadness sweeps through a classroom. Adults also provide ready models, of course, for children's emotional reactions. Research shows that children faced with a situation in which they do not know how to react will scan a caregiver's face in search of cues for the appropriate emotional response. This behavior, known as social referencing, has been studied extensively with infants. One study, for example, showed that eight-month-olds' reactions to a stranger were influenced by their mothers' immediately prior emotional reactions toward that person (Feinman & Lewis, 1983). Although fewer studies have considered this phenomena among preschoolers, the notion in all cases is that children learn about emotion states, expressions, and events by watching others and imitating their emotional behaviors.

A third channel for emotion socialization involves *expectancy communication*. For Saarni and Crowley (1990) emotion expectancies are beliefs about how emotions should. be felt and expressed that are conveyed to children, verbally or nonverbally, in advance of particular events in which children's own emotional reactions are called forth. Saarni and Crowley liken the process to hypnosis, in which adults, first, plant "suggestions" in children's minds about how to respond in certain situations. If children subsequently encounter the same or similar situations, they may use this information to guide their own emotional responses. In this way children remember and act upon at later points in time the information previously acquired about emotions. So, when we tell young children, for example, about how we felt afraid (or excited) at their age, going on a ferris wheel ride or sleeping away from home the first time, these verbal suggestions may be internalized as expectancies upon which children subsequently rely. By such means, Saarni and Crowley (1990) contend, strategies for managing emotions initiated "outside" the child are imported into children's own private, emotional lives.

A general, theoretical framework for studies on emotion socialization is found in the works of Cooley (1902), Mead (1956), and Vygotsky (1978), who each discussed links between emotion, self, and cognition. These writers proposed that (a) we become conscious of ourselves through how others know us and (b) consciousness is forged, in large part, through social activity and discourse. Mead, for example argued that self-consciousness only arises when we take on the attitudes of others toward ourselves. He wrote

> the child can think about his conduct as good or bad only as he reacts to his own acts in the remembered words of his parents. (1913, p. 146)

The imagined judgments of others "drawn from the communicative life" (1902, p. 179) were also essential to Cooley's *looking-glass self:*

> in imagination we perceive in another's mind some thought of our appearance, manners, aims, deeds,

© Blendi Reynolds

© Cleo Photography

character . . . and are variously affected by it. (1902, p. 184)

Although Vygotsky did not explicitly write about emotion development, he believed that children became self-conscious by using

the same forms of behavior in relation to themselves that others initially used in relation to them. (1981, p. 157)

In particular, Vygotsky stressed the role that everyday social speech plays in children's development.

Contemporary researchers speculate that asking about emotions provides children with "reflective distance" from feeling states themselves (Stern, 1985; Bretherton et al., 1986; Dunn, Brown, & Beardsall, 1991). Discussing emotions is thought to distance children from the rush and immediacy of affective responses. Distancing gives children space in which to interpret and evaluate their feelings and to reflect upon causes and consequences.

Emotion discourse may further allow adults and children to work out socially acceptable meanings of feeling states. Especially significant may be the way adults attribute meaning to children's own emotional behavior and development (Lutz, 1983). The way we talk about emotions with children, thus, has the potential to uniquely organize and transform their emotional lives.

Researchers also assume that preschoolers begin to formulate emotion concepts specific to their own culture or subculture (Lutz, 1983; Lutz & White, 1986; Miller & Sperry, 1987). From this perspective emotion concepts are viewed as embedded in broader cultural knowledge about situations and social relationships. How children come to understand emotions will presumably depend on the particular cultural vocabulary and meaning systems available to children for talking about emotions (Levy, 1984; Lutz & White, 1986; Gordon, 1989) and on existing social norms about ways emotions should be felt and expressed.

Cognitive processes that underlie emotional experience essentially bring our emotions into consciousness and provide the basis for our having emotional experiences.

Both psychologists and anthropologists have studied how emotions are variously viewed and talked about in different cultures. There is evidence that emotions downplayed or left undefined in some cultures are central to how other cultures make sense of experiences. Cross-cultural comparisons indicate that Americans and Chinese, for example, identify different types of causes for pride (Stipek, Weiner, & Li, 1989), and Japanese culture emphasizes shame more than other groups do (Lewis, 1992). Americans also report experiencing emotions longer and more intensely than do Japanese sub-

Children use emotion words to refer to both self and others, rather than only to self or only to others. This suggests that children's early emotional understanding of themselves and others may be closely related, rather than developing separately.

jects (Matsumoto, Kudoh, Scherer, & Wallbott, 1988). In contrast to the Western culture's sense of sadness as an emotion, Tahitians classify sadness as a physical illness or body state (Levy, 1984). How adults approach childrearing, moreover, is thought to be related to their knowledge and beliefs about emotions (Lutz & White, 1986; Miller & Sperry, 1987; Markus & Kitayama, 1991). Yet, until recently, few researchers have directly observed adult–child conversations about emotions. The few studies so far have, not surprisingly, focused mostly on how mothers talk with young children.

Miller and Sperry (1987), for example, interviewed three working-class mothers of two-and-one-half-year-old daughters and observed how they socialized anger and aggression. Notably, the mothers led lives in which violence and aggression were all too commonplace; they typically discussed these events in their daughters' presence but usually while talking to other family members or friends. It is striking that at least one child's own stories about anger and aggression were closely patterned after her mother's recollections. In this way what children overhear others relating about emotional events may be one context for learning about emotions. Miller and Sperry observed a second important context—episodes of anger between mothers and daughters. Mothers sometimes intentionally provoked their daughters' anger by teasing or trading insults with them as a way of teaching the girls how to stand up for themselves. Miller and Sperry also found that, rather than talking explicitly about the emotional state of anger itself, families referred to those emotion behaviors that only indirectly expressed anger (e.g. *fight, hit, punch*).

Children's interactions with their mothers and a sibling have been examined by Dunn and her associates. Their analyses of these three-way interactions included tracking how the amount and kind of emotion talk that

Some preschoolers have begun to recognize that a single event sometimes causes different feelings in different people.

occurs in the home changes as young children grow older. One study's home observations conducted when younger siblings were 18 and 24 months old revealed that family members' references to emotion states and to their causes and consequences increased over time (Dunn, Bretherton, & Munn, 1987). Mothers' comments during these interactions usually served to guide or explain children's feelings rather than simply to bring attention to children's emotions. This suggests that mothers, consciously or not, actively worked at shaping their children's emotional experiences, much like the mothers in the Miller and Sperry study. Moreover, the more frequently mothers and older siblings referred to feeling states at the 18-month visit, the more often the younger child talked about emotions at the 24-month visit. In other research Dunn and Kendrick (1982) found that two- and three-year-olds whose mothers commented more often about a new baby's feelings were more likely to have friendly interactions with that sibling one year later.

Dunn has also examined sibling conflicts as contexts for emotion socialization. Between the ages of 14 and 36 months, younger siblings' ability to tease and upset their older siblings appears to increase significantly (Dunn & Munn, 1985; Dunn, Brown, & Beardsall, 1991). This finding demonstrates how young children are learning to anticipate and influence others' feelings. Dunn et al. (1991) further found that mothers and children who

The way we talk about emotions with children has the potential to uniquely organize and transform their emotional lives.

engaged in more frequent emotion talk were more apt to also discuss the causes and consequences of siblings' disputes. Finally, three-year-olds from families with more emotion talk showed a better understanding of others' emotions three years later at age six. These results provide additional support for the contention that emotion talk provides an important context for learning about feelings.

Together, these studies indicate that exposure to different types and amounts of emotion talk may be related to individual differences in children's emotion understanding (Gordon, 1989). Especially intriguing in this regard are reports of differences in how mothers talk about emotions with daughters and sons. In the

Applications for Early Childhood Educators

For educators and parents, it is certainly not earthshaking to find that children learn about emotions from us; but, emotions are sometimes so "close to the skin" and fleeting that it is easy for feelings to slip out of one's conscious awareness. Becoming conscious of the roles we play in children's emotion socialization empowers us to provide children with better opportunities in their daily lives for understanding themselves and others. Teachers have some unique occasions for structuring children's activities in ways that can encourage children to talk about their own and others' emotions. Consider the following recommendations for meeting this objective.

1. Evaluate whether the emotional climate of the classroom itself is conducive to expressing emotions. In other words, caregivers need to legitimate children's feelings in order for children to feel it is acceptable to talk about and reflect upon their emotions. Leavitt and Power (1989) contend that we give meaning to children's emotions when we recognize and respond to their feelings. Essentially this means entering into authentic emotional relationships with children and regarding them as "emotional associates" (Leavitt & Power, 1989, p. 37) who are capable of interpreting and understanding their own and others' emotions.

2. Consider the physical environments in which children may learn about feelings. Play centers no doubt vary in the opportunities they afford for emotional engagement and reflection. Family-living or dramatic-play sections, for example, may encourage children to act out social interactions into which emotions figure. Well-stocked play centers can also provide sources of suggestions to children's imaginations for reworking earlier emotional altercations or experiences. Either from the sidelines or as players ourselves, adults can observe the way individual children play out emotion scripts dramatically. Introduce themes and ask questions that prompt children to vicariously explore the causes and consequences of emotions. Similarly, puppets and dolls are excellent vehicles for emotion play.

3. The arts center provides another valuable context for emotion conversation. Encourage children to make pictures that tell about personal events in their lives. This idea, borrowed from therapists who work with disturbed children, adapts well for children whose "troubles" are within the typical range of life experiences. Children might be encouraged to "draw about the time when . . ." they were upset with another child, afraid of something new, and so forth. Engaging children in conversations about their pictures, either as they are being created or afterwards, can give children chances to reflect upon their emotions. Children can also dictate the stories and feelings that go with their pictures. Older children may want to construct longer picture stories, several pages in length. Sometimes, children will enjoy "reading" back their picture stories to someone else, either during group times or on their own to other children and teachers.

4. Stories written for children are yet another readily available resource for talking about emotions. Books can be selected that show other children being emotional and dealing with their feelings (some titles well suited to this activity are suggested at the end of this article). Children and teachers can discuss the causes and consequences of story characters' emotions and then link them with children's own experiences. Certainly, other media (e.g. TV, movies, plays, children's magazines) provide similar options.

5. Tape recorders and video equipment can be used advantageously as well. Children might audiotape or videotape each other telling stories in which they recreate emotions. Subsequent viewing of these mini productions can serve as a springboard for later discussion about choices children have in responding to their own or others' emotions. Audiovisual projects can also be sources of collaborative production and pride. We show children that we value their emotions if we put the emotion work they do in projects of this sort on display for others to see and share. Invite parents or other classes for a film showing, or put on loan children's story tapes for other children's listening.

6. Dealing with children's quarrels and disputes offers a final classroom context in which children can develop their understanding of emotions. Fighting children learn more about anger and aggression if we do more than simply separate them. Ask each child to "tell what happened" from his or her perspective without interruption by the other participant(s). Teachers can convey back what the child says, asking for any corrections or clarifications before calling on the other child to tell her or his part in the altercation. All children should be urged to examine their personal contributions to the conflict. Teachers can also ask children to talk about how the events made them feel and how they think the other child feels, along with what they each could do differently next time. In this way teachers can help children to manage their feelings rather than simply to suppress or deny them; by doing so, Leavitt and Power (1989) claim that we enhance children's ability to develop authentic emotional understandings and relationships.

study by Dunn et al. (1987), for example, references to emotions were more frequent in mother–daughter, than mother–son, conversations at both 18 and 24 months; and by 24 months girls also talked about feeling states more often than boys did. Gender differences have also

expression of emotions, and to report experiencing a variety of emotions (Allen & Hamsher, 1974; Allen & Haccoun, 1976; Balswick & Avertt, 1977; Fitzpatrick & Indvik, 1982).

How children come to understand emotions will presumably depend on the particular cultural vocabulary and meaning systems available to children for talking about emotions.

---

been reported by Fivush (1989; 1991). Reasoning that conversations about past emotions might provide even more reflective distance, Fivush asked mothers to talk with children about specific events in their child's past. In one study with 30- to 35-month-olds, Fivush (1989) found that mothers attributed more talk about sadness to daughters and more talk about anger to sons. Mother–daughter conversations also focused more on feelings, whereas mother–son pairs were more apt to discuss causes and consequences for emotions.

When fathers talk about the past with young children, they, too, seem to talk differently about emotions with daughters than with sons. Kuebli and Fivush (1992) found that both mothers and fathers of 40-month-olds talked about a greater number and variety of emotions with daughters than they did with sons; again, sadness was more often a topic in conversations with girls. At the age of 40 months, differences were not yet apparent in how boys and girls talked about emotions. Mother–child interviews conducted just before the children started kindergarten, however, revealed that the number of girls' references to emotions nearly quadrupled over this time, whereas boys' references had remained about the same (Kuebli & Fivush, 1993). These results suggest that girls' and boys' emotional lives may be socialized in somewhat different ways. In related research, moreover, adult women were found to be more likely than men to say they are emotional, to value the

Conclusion

Research on young children's emotion understanding and socialization is still very new. Based on what we know so far, however, we can expect that children will show individual differences in the kinds of emotion understandings they possess. Differences will be apparent among children of different ages and even in the rate at which age-mates gain new insights into emotions; moreover, children's family backgrounds and histories are likely to translate into different ways of conceptualizing and using emotions. Cross-cultural evidence on emotion understanding should make teachers particularly sensitive to multicultural variation in the ways emotions figure in children's lives. Despite the differences, however, research also suggests that the basic processes by which children learn about emotions are similar, although much more needs to be learned about the nature of these mechanisms. What is, perhaps, fundamentally important is realizing that a great deal of what young children understand about feelings is apparently learned in the informal curriculum provided by their social interactions with others. Emotions frequently are at the heart of these interactions, and children may greatly benefit when we direct their attention to talking about these experiences.

Between the ages of 14 and 36 months, younger siblings' ability to tease and upset their older siblings appears to increase significantly. This finding demonstrates how young children are learning to anticipate and influence others' feelings.

Four processes by which emotions are socialized are
(1) chiding or praising children's immediately prior emotional behaviors;
(2) giving direct instruction regarding social conventions for expressing emotion ("girls don't brag about their successes");
(3) modeling emotion states, expressions, and events—children watch and imitate; and
(4) communicating expectancies, verbally or nonverbally, directly to the child or within his hearing ("when I was your age I was afraid the first time I slept away from home").

Books About Emotions for Young Children

Many books for young children afford opportunities for adults and children to talk about emotions. The following titles are good examples of books in which emotional themes are central to the story.

Carle, E. (1977). *The grouchy ladybug*. New York: Harper & Row.

Carlson, N. (1988). *I like me!* New York: Viking Kestrel.

Clarke, G. (1991). *. . . along came Eric*. New York: Lothrop, Lee, & Shepard.

Cole, J. (1990). *Don't call me names!* New York: Random House.

Engel, D. (1989). *Josephina hates her name*. New York: Morrow Junior.

Godwin, P. (1993). *I feel orange today*. New York: Firefly.

Gretz, S. (1981). *Teddy bears' moving day*. New York: Four Winds.

Havill, J. (1989). *Jamaica tag-along*. Boston: Houghton Mifflin.

Hazen, B.S. (1981). *Even if I did something awful*. New York: Atheneum.

Lakin, P. (1985). *Don't touch my room*. Boston: Little, Brown.

Macdonald, M. (1990). *Little hippo starts school*. New York: Dial.

Mayer, M. (1983). *I was so mad*. Racine, WI: Western Publishing.

Noll, S. (1991). *That bothered Kate*. New York: Puffin.

Sharmat, M.J. (1983). *Frizzy the fearful*. New York: Holiday House.

Stevenson, J. (1983). *What's under my bed?* New York: Greenwillow.

Viorst, J. (1972). *Alexander and the terrible, horrible, no good, very bad day*. New York: Atheneum.

Waber, B. (1972). *Ira sleeps over*. Boston: Houghton Mifflin.

Wells, R. (1988). *Shy Charles*. New York: Dial.

Wilhelm, H. (1990). *A cool kid—like me!* New York: Crown.

References

Allen, J.G., & Haccoun, D.M. (1976). Sex differences in emotionality: A multidimensional approach. *Human Relations, 29*(8), 711–722.

Allen, J.G., & Hamsher, J.H. (1974). The development and validation of a test of emotional styles. *Journal of Consulting and Clinical Psychology, 42*(5), 663–668.

Balswick, H., & Avertt, C.P. (1977). Differences in expressiveness: Gender, interpersonal orientation, and perceived parental expressiveness as contributing factors. *Journal of Marriage and the Family, 39*(1), 121–127.

Barden, R.C., Zelko, F., Duncan, S.W., & Masters, J.C. (1980). Children's consensual knowledge about the experiential determinants of emotion. *Journal of Personality and Social Psychology, 39*(5), 968–976.

Bertenthal, B.I., & Fisher, K.W. (1978). Development of self-recognition in the infant. *Developmental Psychology, 14*(1), 44–50.

Borke, H. (1971). Interpersonal perception of young children: Egocentricism or empathy. *Developmental Psychology, 5*(2), 263–269.

Bretherton, I., & Beeghly, M. (1982). Talking about internal states: The acquisition of an explicit theory of mind. *Developmental Psychology, 18*(6), 906–921.

Bretherton, I., Fritz, J., Zahn-Waxler, C., & Ridgeway, D. (1986). Learning to talk about emotions: A functionalist perspective. *Child Development, 57*(3), 529–548.

Brody, L.R. (1984). Sex and age variations in the quality and intensity of children's emotional attributions to hypothetical situations. *Sex Roles, 11*(1/2), 51–59.

Brody, L.R., & Harrison, R.H. (1987). Development changes in children's abilities to match and label emotionally laden situations. *Motivation and Emotion, 11*(4), 347–365.

Campos, J.J., Barrett, K.C., Lamb, M.E., Goldsmith, H.H., & Stenberg, C. (1983). Socioemotional development. In M. Haith & J.J. Campos (Eds.), *Handbook of child psychology: Vol. 2. Infancy and developmental psychobiology* (pp. 783–915). New York: Wiley.

Camras, L.A., & Allison, K. (1989). Children's and adults' beliefs about emotion elicitation. *Motivation and Emotion, 13*(1), 53–70.

Carroll, J.J., & Steward, M.S. (1984). The role of cognitive development in children's understanding of their own feelings. *Child Development, 55*(4), 1486–1492.

Conway, M., Giannopoulos, C., & Stiefenhofer, K. (1990). Response styles to sadness are related to sex and sex-role orientation. *Sex Roles, 22*(9/10), 579–587.

Cooley, C.H. (1902). *Human nature and the social order*. New York: Scribner's.

Davis, T.L. (1992, April). *Sex differences in the masking of children's negative emotions: Ability or motivation?* Paper presented at the Human Development Conference, Atlanta, GA.

Denham, S.A., & Zoller, D. (1993). *"When mommy's angry. I feel sad": Preschoolers' causal understanding of emotion and its socialization*. Manuscript submitted for publication.

Donaldson, S.K., & Westerman, M.A. (1986). Development of children's understanding of ambivalence and causal theories of emotions. *Developmental Psychology, 22*(5), 655–662.

Dunn, J., Bretherton, I., & Munn, P. (1987). Conversations about feeling states between mothers and their young children. *Developmental Psychology, 23*(1), 132–139.

Dunn, J., Brown, J., & Beardsall, L. (1991). Family talk about feeling states and children's later understanding of others' emotions. *Developmental Psychology, 27*(3), 448–455.

Dunn, J., & Kendrick, C. (1982). *Siblings: Love, envy and understanding*. Cambridge, MA: Harvard University Press.

Dunn, J., & Munn, P. (1985). Becoming a family member: Family conflict and the development of social understanding in the second year. *Child Development, 56*(2), 480–492.

Feinman, S., & Lewis, M. (1983). Social referencing at ten-months: A second-order effect on infants' responses to strangers. *Child Development, 54*(4), 878–887.

Fitzpatrick, M.A., & Indvik, J. (1982). The instrumental and expressive domains of marital communication. *Human Communications Research, 8*(3), 195–213.

Fivush, R. (1989). Exploring sex differences in the emotional content of mother–child conversations about the past. *Sex Roles, 20*(11/12), 675–691.

Fivush, R. (1991). Gender and emotion in mother–child conversations about the past. *Journal of Narrative and Life History, 1*(4), 325–341.

Glasberg, R., & Aboud, F. (1982). Keeping one's distance from sadness: Children's self-reports of emotional experience. *Development Psychology, 18*(2), 287–293.

Gordon, S.L. (1989). The socialization of children's emotions: Emotional competence, culture, and exposure. In C. Saarni & P.L. Harris (Eds.), *Children's understanding of emotion* (pp. 319–349). New York: Cambridge University Press.

Gove, F.L., & Keating, D.P. (1979). Empathic role-taking precursors. *Developmental Psychology, 15*(6), 594–600.

Graham, S. (1988). Children's developing understanding of the motivational role of affect: An attributional analysis. *Cognitive Development, 3*(2), 71–88.

Graham, S., Doubleday, C., & Guarino, P.A. (1984). The development of relations between perceived controllability and the emotions of pity, anger, and guilt. *Child Development, 55*(2), 561–565.

Harter, S. (1983). Developmental perspectives on the self-system. In E.M. Hetherington (Ed.), *Socialization, personality and social* development, Vol IV, Handbook of Child Psychology (pp. 275–385). New York: Wiley.

Harter, S., & Buddin, B.J. (1987). Children's understanding of the simultaneity of two emotions: A five-stage development acquisition sequence. Developmental Psychology, 23(3), 388–399.

Harter, S., & Whitesell, N.R. (1989). Developmental changes in children's understanding of single, multiple, and blended emotion concepts. In C. Saarni & P.L. Harris (Eds.), Children's understanding of emotion (pp. 81–116.). Cambridge, England: Cambridge University Press.

Hochschild, A.R. (1983). The managed heart: Commercialization of human feelings. Berkeley: University of California Press.

Izard, C.E., & Malatesta, C.A. (1987). Perspectives on emotional development I: Differential emotions theory of early emotional development. In J.D. Osofsky (Ed.), Handbook of infant development (2nd ed.), (pp. 494–554.) New York: Wiley.

Kagan, J. (1981). The second year: The emergence of self-awareness. Cambridge, MA: Harvard University Press.

Kuebli, J., & Fivush, R. (1992). Gender differences in parent–child conversations about past emotions. Sex Roles, 27(11/12), 683–698.

Kuebli, J., & Fivush, R. (1993, March). Children's developing understanding of emotion and mind. Paper presented at the biennial meetings of the Society for Research in Child Development, New Orleans, LA.

Leavitt, R.L., & Power, M.B. (1989). Emotional socialization in the postmodern era: Children in day care. Social Psychology Quarterly, 52(1), 35–43.

Levy, R.I. (1984). Emotion, knowing, and culture. In R.A. Shweder & R.A. LeVine (Eds.), Culture theory: Essays on mind, self, and emotion (pp. 214–237). Cambridge, England: Cambridge University Press.

Lewis, M. (1992). Shame: The exposed self. New York: The Free Press.

Lewis, M., & Brooks-Gunn, J. (1979). Social cognition and acquisition of self. New York: Plenum.

Lewis, M., & Michalson, L. (1983). Children's emotions and moods. New York: Plenum.

Lewis, M., & Saarni, C. (1985). Culture and emotions. In M. Lewis & C. Saarni (Eds.), The socialization of emotions (pp. 1–17). New York: Plenum.

Lewis, M., Sullivan, M.W., Stanger, C., & Weiss, M. (1989). Self-development and self-conscious emotions. Child Development, 60(1), 146–156.

Lutz, C. (1983). Parental goals, ethnopsychology, and the development of emotional meaning. Ethos, 11(4), 246–262.

Lutz, C. (1985). Cultural patterns and individual differences in the child's emotional meaning system. In M. Lewis & C. Saarni (Eds.), The socialization of emotions (pp. 37–53). New York: Plenum.

Lutz, C., & White, G.M. (1986). The anthropology of emotions. Annual Review of Anthropology, 15, 405–436.

Markus, H.R., & Kitayama, S. (1991). Culture and the self: Implications for cognition, emotion, and motivation. Psychological Review, 98(2), 224–253.

Matsumoto, D., Kudoh, T., Scherer, K., & Wallbott, H. (1988). Antecedents of and reactions to emotions in the United States and Japan. Journal of Cross-Cultural Psychology, 19(3), 267–286.

Mead, G.H. (1913). The social self. In A.J. Reck (Ed.), Selected writings: George Herbert Mead (pp. 142–149). Chicago: Chicago University Press.

Mead, G.H. (1956). On social psychology: Selected papers. Chicago: The University of Chicago Press.

Michalson, L., & Lewis, M. (1985). What do children know about emotions and when do they know it? In M. Lewis & C. Saarni (Eds.), The socialization of emotions (pp. 117–139). New York: Plenum.

Miller, P., & Sperry, L.L. (1987). The socialization of anger and aggression. Merrill-Palmer Quarterly, 33(1), 1–31.

Peng, M., Johnson, C., Pollock, J., Glasspool, R., & Harris, P. (1992). Training young children to acknowledge mixed emotions. Cognition and Emotion, 6(5), 387–401.

Reichenbach, L., & Masters, J.C. (1983). Children's use of expressive and contextual cues in judgments of emotion. Child Development, 54(4), 992–1004.

Ridgeway, D., Waters, E., & Kuczaj, S.A. (1985). Acquisition of emotion-descriptive language: Receptive and productive vocabulary norms for ages 18 months to 6 years. Developmental Psychology, 21(5), 901–908.

Saarni, C. (1984). An observational study of children's attempts to monitor their expressive behavior. Child Development, 55(4), 1504–1513.

Saarni, C. (1985). Indirect processes in affect socialization. In M. Lewis & C. Saarni (Eds.), The socialization of emotions (pp. 187–209). New York: Plenum.

Saarni, C., & Crowley, M. (1990). The development of emotion regulation: Effects on emotional state and expression. In E.A. Blechman (Ed.), Emotions and the family: For better or for worse (pp. 53–73). Hillsdale, NJ: Erlbaum.

Sroufe, L.A. (1979). Socioemotional development. In J.D. Osofsky (Ed.), Handbook of infant development (pp. 462–516). New York: Wiley.

Stenberg, C., Campos, J., & Emde, R. (1983). The facial expression of anger in seven-month-old infants. Child Development, 54(1), 178–184.

Stern, D. (1985). The interpersonal world of the infant. New York: Basic.

Stipek, D., Weiner, B., & Li, K. (1989). Testing some attribution-emotion relations in the People's Republic of China. Journal of Personality and Social Psychology, 56(1), 109–116.

Strayer, J. (1986). Children's attributions regarding the situational determinants of emotion in self and others. Developmental Psychology, 22(5), 649–654.

Vygotsky, L.S. (1978). Mind in society: The development of higher psychological processes. Cambridge, MA: Harvard University Press.

Vygotsky, L.S. (1981). The genesis of higher mental functions. In J.V. Wertsch (Ed.), The concept of activity in Soviet psychology. Armonk, NY: M.E. Sharpe.

Wintre, M.G., Polivy, J., & Murray, M.A. (1990). Self-predictions of emotional-response patterns: Age, sex, and situational determinants. Child Development, 61(4), 1124–1133.

For further reading

Berk, L.E. (1985). Research in review. Why children talk to themselves. Young Children, 40(5), 46–52.

Frieman, B.B. (1993). Separation and divorce: Children want their teachers to know—meeting the emotional needs of preschool and primary school children. Young Children, 48(6), 58–63.

Kemple, K.M. (1991). Research in review. Preschool children's peer acceptance and social interaction. Young Children, 46(5), 47–54.

Pellegrini, A.D., & Glickman, C.D. (1990). Measuring kindergartners' social competence. Young Children, 45(4), 40–44.

Rogers, D.L., & Ross, D.D. (1986). Encouraging positive social interaction among young children. Young Children, 41(3), 12–17.

Rousso, J. (1988). Talking with young children about their dreams: How to listen and what to listen for. Young Children, 43(5), 70–74.

Solter, A. (1992). Understanding tears and tantrums. Young Children, 47(4), 64–68.

Warren, R.M. (1977). Caring: Supporting children's growth. Washington, DC: NAEYC.

Zavitkovsky, D., Baker, K.R., Berlfein, J.R., & Almy, M. (1986). Listen to the children. Washington, DC: NAEYC.

Encouraging Positive Social Development in Young Children

Donna Sasse Wittmer and Alice Sterling Honig

Donna Sasse Wittmer, Ph.D., is assistant professor in early childhood education at the University of Colorado in Denver. She has had extensive experience directing, training in, and conducting research in early childhood care and education programs.

Alice Sterling Honig, Ph.D., professor of child development at Syracuse University in Syracuse, New York, was program director for the Family Development Research Program and has authored numerous books, including Parent Involvement in Early Childhood Education *and* Playtime Learning Games for Young Children. *She directs the annual Syracuse Quality Infant/ Toddler Caregiving Workshop.*

Editor's note: *This two-part review presents techniques for teachers and parents, schools and communities, to promote young children's social development. Supportive research findings are often cited to back up the techniques suggested. In Part 1, suggestions refer to interpersonal interactions of caregivers with individual children or small groups of children. Techniques in Part 2 (. . . published in a subsequent issue of* Young Children*) target entire classrooms as well as broader systems, such as centers, schools, families, and communities.*

An earlier version of this article was presented at NAEYC's Annual Conference in Denver, Colorado, in November 1991. Portions of this article have been adapted from Prosocial Development in Children: Caring, Sharing, & Cooperating: A Bibliographic Resource Guide *by Alice Sterling Honig and Donna Sasse Wittmer (1992).*

A toddler, reaching for a toy, got his finger pinched in the hinge on the door of a toy shelf in his child care classroom. He cried loudly; his pacifier fell from his mouth. Another toddler, obviously distressed by the sounds of pain coming from his playmate, picked up the pacifier and held it in the crying toddler's mouth in an apparent attempt to help and comfort the injured toddler.

This example, shared by a child care provider, is one of many exciting prosocial events that have been observed in young toddlers, preschoolers, and primary-age children as they interact together in group settings. Caregivers of young children notice events such as the one above as they live and work with very young children. If adults implement curriculum that promotes interpersonal consideration and cooperation in children, we see even more of these behaviors.

Social development was seen as the core of the curriculum in nursery schools and kindergartens until a cognitive emphasis was brought into the field in the late 1960s; social development has recently been getting renewed attention by early childhood education leaders. Skilled teachers of young children implement prosocial goals for young children as they attempt to facilitate children's positive social interactions. Prosocial goals that teachers emphasize include

• showing sympathy and kindness,
• helping,
• giving,
• accepting food or toys,
• sharing,
• showing positive verbal and physical contact,
• comforting another person in distress,
• donating to others who are less fortunate,
• showing concern
• responding to bereaved peers,
• taking the perspective of another person,
• showing affection, and
• cooperating with others in play or to complete a task.

The adults in children's lives play an important role in helping children develop these prosocial attitudes and behaviors.

Not surprisingly, if caregivers and teachers take time to encourage, facilitate, and teach prosocial behaviors, children's prosocial interactions increase and aggression decreases (Honig 1982). In an interesting study, children who attended, from 3 months to kindergarten, an experimental child care program that focused on intellectual growth were rated by their kindergarten teachers as more aggressive than a control group of children who attended community child care programs during their preschool years for less amount of time (Haskins 1985). But when a prosocial curriculum entitled "My Friends and Me" was implemented, the next groups of child care graduates did not differ in aggression rates from control-group children. Emphasizing and encouraging prosocial behaviors made a difference in how children learned to interact and play with each other. A number of other intriguing research studies concerning teacher educators and curriculum intended to enhance positive social development in young children are described in our book *Prosocial Development in Children: Caring, Sharing, & Cooperating.*

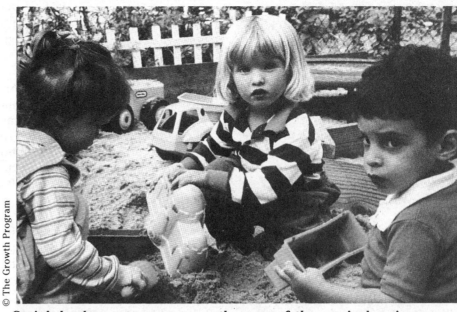

Social development was seen as the core of the curriculum in nursery schools and kindergartens until a cognitive emphasis was brought into the field in the late 1960s; social development has recently been getting renewed attention by early childhood education leaders.

Focus on prosocial behaviors: Value, model, and acknowledge

Need it be said? What the adults who are important in children's lives value, model, and encourage in children influences them. What values do we value and encourage?

Value and emphasize consideration for others' needs. Children become aware at an early age of what aspects of life their special adults admire and value. Research on toddlers (Yarrow & Waxler 1976) and boys with learning disabilities (Elardo & Freund 1981) shows that when parents encourage their children to have concern for others, the children behave more prosocially.

As every experienced teacher knows, emphasizing the importance of children helping others whenever possible results in children undertaking more helping activities (Grusec, Saas-Kortsaak, & Simultis 1978). Children whose parents esteem altruism highly are more frequently considered

by peers as highly prosocial (Rutherford & Mussen 1968).

Model prosocial behaviors. "Practice what you preach," "Do as I say, not as I do," and "Monkey see, monkey do" are tried-and-true sayings that remind us that children model many behaviors that we do—and do not!—want them to imitate. Adults who model prosocial behaviors influence children's willingness to behave prosocially (Bandura 1986). A teacher who patiently tied his toddlers' shoelaces day after day observed that toddlers who saw a peer tripping over laces would bend down and try to twist their

friend's sneaker laces in an attempt to help. Bryan (1977) stresses that children imitate helping activities whether the models are living people or fictional characters. Over the years, modeling has proven more powerful than preaching. Traditionally we have called it *setting a good example.* How caregivers and parents act—kind, considerate, and compassionate, or cruel, thoughtless, and uncaring—influences young children to imitate them.

Children who frequently observe and are influenced by family members and teachers who behave prosocially will imitate those special adults. "Mama," ob-

---

If adults implement curriculum that promotes interpersonal consideration and cooperation in children, we see even more of these behaviors.

served 3-year-old Dana, "that was a very good job you did buckling my seat belt." How often Mama had used just such encouraging words with her preschooler!

Label and identify prosocial and antisocial behaviors. We all love it when our positive deeds are acknowledged. Notice the positive interactions, however small, that occur between children and encourage them through your comments. When adults label behaviors, such as "considerate toward peers" and "cooperative with classmates," children's dialogues and role-taking abilities increase (Vorrath 1985). Rather than just saying "That's good" or "That's nice" to a child, be specific in identifying prosocial behaviors and actions for children. Saying "You are being helpful" or "You gave him a tissue, he really needed it to wipe his nose" will be most helpful to children.

Attribute positive social behaviors to each child. Attributing positive intentions, such as "You shared because you like to help others" or "You're the kind of person who likes to help others whenever you can," results in children donating more generously to people in need (Grusec, Kuczynski, Rushton, & Simultis 1978; Grusec & Redler 1980).

After 8-year-olds had shared their winnings from a game with "poor" children, the children who were given positive attributions (e.g., "You're the kind of person who likes to help others whenever you can"), as opposed to social reinforcers (just being told that it was good to share with others), were more likely to share at a later time (Grusec & Redler 1980).

Skilled teachers personalize attributions so that each child feels special. Say such things as "You are a very helpful person," "You are the kind of person who likes to stick up for a child who is being bothered," and "You really try to be a buddy to a new child in our class who is shy at first in finding a friend."

Children from punitive homes may need help understanding how to make attributions that are true rather than assuming that others have evil intentions. For example, you might ask, "Did your classmate step on your homework paper in the school-yard to be mean or to keep it from blowing away?" Focus children's thinking on attributes and intentions of others' actions as a way to prevent children from unthinkingly lashing out at others in angry response.

Notice and positively encourage prosocial behaviors, but do not overuse external rewards. In research by Rushton and Teachman (1978), social reinforcement for sharing increased sharing among young children even when the experimenter was no longer present. Goffin (1987) recommends that teachers notice when children share mutual goals, ideas, and materials, as well as when they negotiate and bargain in decision making and accomplishing goals. When caregivers and parents use external reinforcement too much, however, children's prosocial behaviors may decrease. Fabes, Fultz, Eisenberg, May-Plumlee, and Christopher (1989) reported that mothers who like using rewards may undermine their children's internalized *desire* to behave prosocially by increasing the salience of external rather than internal rewards.

Teachers have reported that offering stickers for prosocial be-

© The Growth Program

As every experienced teacher knows, emphasizing the importance of children helping others whenever possible results in children undertaking more helping activities. Children whose parents esteem altruism highly are more frequently considered by peers as highly prosocial.

haviors to one child in a classroom often backfires when other children become upset that they didn't also get stickers. A kindergarten child went home from school one day and told his grandmother, "I've got it figured out now. First you have to be bad, and then good, and then you get a sticker." Commenting on positive behaviors and attributing positive characteristics to children rather than using external rewards help young children internalize prosocial responses.

Encourage understanding of children's own and others' feelings and perspectives

Skilled teachers understand how to do these things:

Acknowledge and encourage understanding and expression of children's feelings. The ability to empathize with a peer who is experiencing sadness, anger, or distress may depend on a child having had a prior similar experience with those feelings (Barnett 1984). Children from ages 3 to 8 are becoming aware of *happy* feelings (3½ years), *fear* (3½ to 4 years), and *anger and sadness* (3 to 8 years) (Borke 1971).

Caregivers need to help children put feelings into words and to understand their feelings. Teachers can acknowledge and reflect children's feelings by making comments such as "It seems as if you are feeling so sad" or "You look like you are feeling angry. You want my attention *now*. As soon as I change

Luanne's diaper, I can read to you." This calm observation by a child care provider wiped the thunder off a toddler's face. He looked amazed that his teacher had understood his feelings. He relaxed when she reassured him with a promise to come back in a few minutes and read with him.

Facilitate perspective- and role-taking skills and understanding others' feelings. Helping young children notice and respond to the feelings of others can be quite effective in teaching them to be considerate of others. A preschool teacher kneeled to be at eye level with a child who had just socked another child during a struggle for a bike. The teacher pointed out the feelings of the other child: "He's very sad and hurt. What can you do to make him feel better?" The aggressor paused, observed the other child's face, and offered the bike to the crying child.

A child's ability to identify accurately the emotional state of another, as well as the empathic ability to experience the feelings of another, contribute to prosocial behavior. Children who are altruistic and more willing to help others display more empathy and perspective-taking skills (a cognitive measure) (Chalmers & Townsend 1990).

Feshbach (1975) reported that two training techniques that promoted understanding in children of other children's feelings were *role playing* and *maximizing the perceived similarity* between the observer and the stimulus person. The latter is what antibias education is about.

Encourage children to act out stories dramatically. Children who act out different stories become aware of how the characters feel. Switching roles gives children a different perspective on the feelings and motives of each character. Acting out roles, as in "The Three Billy Goats Gruff" or "Goldilocks and the Three Bears" gives children a chance to understand each story character's point of view (Krogh & Lamme 1983). A first- or second-grade class may want to write a letter of apology from Goldilocks to the Bear family!

Trovato (1987) created the puppets "Hattie Helper," "Carl Defender," "Robert Rescuer," "Debra Defender," "Kevin Comforter," and "Sharon Sharer" for adults to use to help young children learn prosocial behaviors with other children. Crary (1984) also promotes the use of puppets for teachers and children to use in role playing different social situations that may arise in the classroom.

Perspective taking is not enough to ensure children's development of prosocial behaviors. Children who are low in empathy but high in perspective taking may demonstrate Machiavellianism (a tendency to take advantage in a negative way of knowledge concerning another person's feelings and thoughts) (Barnett & Thompson 1985). Although Howes and Farber's (1987) research with toddlers ages 16 to 33 months of in child care showed that 93% of toddlers responded prosocially to peers who showed distress, George and Main (1979) reported that abused toddlers looked on impassively or reacted with anger when a playmate was hurt or distressed. Vulnerable children urgently need help understanding and acknowledging their range of often very strong feelings and empathizing with other people's feelings.

Helping young children notice and respond to the feelings of others can be quite effective in teaching them to be considerate of others.

Use victim-centered discipline and reparation: Emphasize consequences. Other-oriented techniques focus a child on the effects of hurtful and antisocial behaviors, such as hitting or pinching. Results of a study of how children learned altruism at home revealed that parents of the most prosocial toddlers had emphasized the negative consequences of their toddlers' aggressive acts on other children (Pines 1979). Point out the consequences of the child's behavior. Emphasize to the aggressor the results of hurtful actions upon another person. Choose statements such as "Look—that hurt him!" "He is crying" and "I cannot let you hurt another child, and I do not want anyone to make you hurt; we need to help each other feel happy and safe in this class."

Help children become assertive concerning prosocial matters. If a child has high-perspective-taking skills and is assertive, then the child is likely to be prosocial. In contrast, if a child has high-perspective-taking skills and is timid, then the child is less likely to be prosocial (Barrett & Yarrow 1977). In the book *Listen to the Children* (Zavitkovsky, Baker, Berlfein, & Almy 1986, 42), the authors shared a true story about two young girls, Dolores and Monica, who were washing their hands before lunch. Eric was waiting for his turn to wash his hands. Out of the blue, he shouted crossly into Monica's face, "You're not pretty." The author and observer reported that out of the stillness came Dolores's firm voice, "Yes, she is. She looks just right for her." Dolores was demonstrating both perspective-taking skills—knowing that Monica's feelings were hurt—and prosocial defending skills. As teachers notice and acknowledge prosocial behaviors, children's self-confidence concerning prosocial interactions will increase.

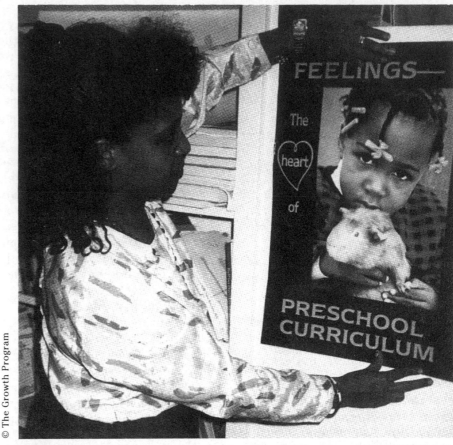

© The Growth Program

Acknowledge and encourage understanding and expression of children's feelings. Facilitate perspective- and role-taking skills and understanding others' feelings.

Encourage problem solving and planfulness for prosocial behaviors

You have heard this before, but it takes time, effort, and planfulness to *do* it.

Encourage means–ends and alternative-solution thinking in conflict situations. Help children think through, step-by-step, their reasoning about how to respond when they are having a social problem with a peer. What are the steps by which they figure out how to get from the conflict situation they are in to peaceful, friendly cooperation or a courteous live-and-let-live situation?

Shure (1992) provides daily lessons for teachers to help children discover when their feelings and wishes are the *same* or *different* from other children's, or whether *some* or *all* of the children want to play the game that *one* prefers. Teachers who use these daily lesson plans with emphasis on encouraging children to think of alternative solutions to their social conflicts and to imagine the consequences of each behavior or strategy they think of can help aggressive and shy children become more positively social within three months. Increased positive social functioning is associated with children's ability to think of more strategies rather than with the quality of the social solutions they devise (Shure & Spivak 1978).

Use Socratic questions to elicit prosocial planfulness and recognition of responsibility. When a child is misbehaving in such a way as to disturb his own or class progress, quietly ask, "How does that help you?" This technique, recommended by Fugitt (1983), can be expanded to encourage group awareness by asking the child, "How is that helping the group?" or "How is that helping your neighbor?" This strategy is designed to help children recognize and take responsibility for their own behaviors.

Show pictured scenes of altruism, and ask children to create verbal scenarios. Show children pictured scenes of children being helpful, cooperative, generous, charitable, patient, courteous, sharing, and kind. Working with a small group of children, call on each child to make up a scenario or story about the child or children in the picture. Ask, "What do you think is happening here?" Be sure to help children become aware of how the child being helped feels and how the child who has been helpful or generous will feel about herself or himself.

Provide specific behavioral training in social skills. Cartledge and Milburn (1980) recommend defining skills to be taught in behavioral terms assessing children's level of competence. Then teach the skills that are lacking, evaluate the results of teaching, and provide opportunities for children to practice and generalize the transfer of these new social skills to other situations.

McGinnis and Goldstein use structured "skillstreaming" strategies to teach prosocial skills to preschool (1990) and elementary

© The Growth Program

Encourage means–ends and alternative-solution thinking in conflict situations. Help children think through, step-by-step, their reasoning about how to respond when they are having a social problem with a peer. What are the steps by which they figure out how to get from the conflict situation they are in to peaceful, friendly cooperation or a courteous live-and-let-live situation?

school (1984) children. Skills such as listening, using nice talk, using brave talk, saying thank you, asking for help, greeting others, reading others, waiting one's turn, sharing, offering help, asking someone to play, and playing a game are a few of the "beginning social skills" and "friendship making skills." Other skills help children deal with feelings and provide them with alternatives to aggression. Preschool

children who received training and were encouraged to (1) use politeness words, (2) listen to who is talking, (3) participate with a peer in an activity, (4) share, (5) take turns, and (6) help another person have fun were more sociable in the training classroom and at follow-up (Factor & Schilmoeller 1983).

Teaching concern for others is a familiar idea to teachers of children from infancy through 8 years!

Place a child who is experiencing social problems with a friendly, socially skilled playmate, preferably a younger one, to increase the social isolate's positive peer interactions.

Use positive discipline for promoting prosocial behaviors and less aggression

We have to educate children about socially desirable behaviors, as about many other things.

Use positive discipline strategies, such as induction and authoritative methods. When teachers use positive discipline techniques—such as reasoning, use of positive reinforcement, and empathic listening—and *authoritative* strategies (Baumrind 1977)—loving, positive commitment to the child plus use of firm, clear rules and explanations—children are more likely to behave prosocially. The more nonauthoritarian and nonpunitive the parent, the higher the child's level of reasoning (Eisenberg, Lennon, & Roth 1983). Discipline that is *emotionally intense but nonpunitive* is effective with toddlers (Yarrow & Waxler 1976).

Positive discipline: A protection against media violence. As one might guess, a relationship has been found between parents' positive discipline techniques and the effects of prosocial and antisocial television programs on children. Using Hoffman's terms to describe parenting styles, Abelman (1986) reported that parents who are most *inductive* (who use reasoning) and who rarely use love withdrawal or power assertion have children who are *most* affected by prosocial and *least* affected by antisocial television. The reverse is also true. Positive discipline, then, is a powerful buffer against the negative effects of antisocial media materials.

Respond to and provide alternatives to aggressive behaviors. This has been a basic principle of nursery and kindergarten education since their beginning. Writing much more recently, Caldwell (1977) advises caregivers not to ignore aggression or permit aggression to be expressed and assume that this venting will "discharge the tension." For example, bullying that is ignored does not disappear. Caldwell writes, "In order to control aggression, we must strengthen altruism" (1977, 9). Teach children what they can do to help others feel good.

Redirect antisocial actions to more acceptable actions. A child who is throwing a ball at someone may be redirected to throw a beanbag back and forth with another child.

Teach angry, acting-out children to *use words* to express feelings. When children are feeling aggrieved, tell them, "Use your words" instead of hurtful actions. Help children learn "I" statements to express their feelings or wishes and to express how they perceive a situation of distress or conflict (Gordon 1970). Give children words and phrases to use, such as "I feel upset when our game is interrupted," "I cannot finish my building if you take away these blocks," or "I was using that Magic Marker first. I still need it to finish my picture."

Ask children to restate classroom rules about not hitting or hurting others (Honig 1985). Preschool children, however, may interpret the rules from an egocentric viewpoint and not always understand the reasons for rules. Deanna, a preschooler, went home from school and told her mother, "Matthew pinched me." After talking about the classroom rule, "Don't pinch or hit back," Deanna's mother tried to get Deanna to problem-solve other solutions to the problem, such as telling Matthew that it hurt when he pinched. The next day, when her mom picked her up from school, Deanna reported angrily, "Matthew pinched me back." When asked why she pinched him, Deanna restated the classroom rule, "That doesn't matter; he's not supposed to pinch me back."

Offer children choices. This is another "basic" of professional work with young children. Toddlers and preschoolers struggling to assert newly emergent autonomy cooperate more easily with caregiver requests if they feel empowered to make choices. Adults can decide on the choices to be offered. For the toddler having trouble settling at naptime, the offer "Would you like to sleep with your head at this end of your cot or the other end?" may empower him enough to decide cheerfully just how he wants to lie down for naptime. Gilligan observed that "The essence of the moral decision is the exercise of choice and the willingness to accept responsibility for that choice" (1982, 58). Often adults forget that if they carefully craft choices, children may more readily cooperate in the home and in the classroom. During snacktime adults can offer a choice of "darker or lighter toast," "apple or orange juice" to the finicky eater who generally resists food simply set down without her being allowed some choice. When children want to practice throwing a small basketball into a preschooler-size net, discuss the need for a turn-taking rule and offer a choice: "Do you want to take two or three throws for your turn?" Later, comment on how the children followed the rule. Ask them how they think the rule helped their game go more peaceably.

Provide opportunities for social interactions through play—pair "social isolates" with sociable children

Place a child who is experiencing social problems with a friendly, socially skilled playmate, preferably a younger one, to increase the social isolate's positive peer interactions (Furman, Rahe, & Hartup 1978). Pair an assertive, gregarious, but gentle child (who is the recipient of many prosocial overtures and is likely to offer help and friendliness) with a very shy child.

Create good adult–child relationships

Children learn to enjoy being with other people when they experience adults who are positive, caring, loving, and responsive. When adults respond to a child in affectionate, kind, empathetic ways, the child learns how to be a communicative partner who knows how to take turns, listen, negotiate, and help others; common sense tells us that this is logical. Park and Waters (1989)

found that two children who had experienced affirmative first relationships with their mothers engaged in more harmonious, less controlling, more responsive, and happier play together than did children who had not experienced positive first relationships.

Provide body relaxation activities

Create a relaxed classroom climate to further harmonious interactions. Relaxation exercises can restore harmony when children are fussy or tense. Back rubs help. Sand play and water play promote relaxation in some children who have a difficult time acting peaceably.

Children may lie down on mats and wiggle each limb separately, in turn, to relax and ease body tension. Many classical music pieces, such as the Brahms *Lullaby* or Debussy's *Reverie*, can be useful in helping children imagine peaceful scenes. Focused imagery activities can reduce tensions. Have children close their eyes and imagine being in a quiet forest glade, listening to a stream flow nearby and feeling the warm sunshine on their faces.

Group movement to music adds another dimension of relaxation. Dancing partners need to tune in to each other's motions and rhythmic swaying as they hold hands or take turns imitating each other's gestures.

Use technology to promote prosocial behaviors

Unlike most of the familiar principles for promoting social development reviewed in this article, *this* idea will be new to many teachers. Videotape children who are behaving prosocially to facilitate sharing. A video camera in the classroom can help promote altruism. Third-grade children viewed videotapes of themselves and models in situations involving sharing. This technique was effective in increasing sharing immediately following training and one week later (Devoe & Sherman 1978). Maybe some teachers who like trying new things will try this idea with *younger* children.

© The Growth Program

Offer children choices. This is another "basic" of professional work with young children. Toddlers and preschoolers struggling to assert newly emergent autonomy cooperate more easily with caregiver requests if they feel empowered to make choices. Adults can decide on the choices to be offered.

Conclusion

As teachers focus on and facilitate prosocial behaviors, the whole ambience of a classroom may change. As teachers model kindness and respect, express appreciation for prosocial actions, promote cooperation, teach children how their behaviors affect others, point out each child's prosocial behaviors with admiration to the other children, and encourage children to help each other, prosocial deeds and attitudes will increase. Adults' interactions with young children make a powerful difference in the atmosphere and climate of the classroom.

References

Abelman, R. 1986. Children's awareness of television's prosocial fare: Parental discipline as an antecedent. *Journal of Family Issues* 7: 51–66.

Bandura, A. 1986. *The social foundation of thought and action: A social cognitive theory.* Englewood Cliffs, NJ: Prentice Hall.

Barnett, M. 1984. Similarity of experience and empathy in preschoolers. *The Journal of Genetic Psychology* 145: 241–50.

Barnett, M., & S. Thompson. 1985. The role of perspective-taking and empathy in children's Machiavellianism, prosocial behavior, and motive for helping. *The Journal of Genetic Psychology* 146: 295–305.

Barrett, D.E., & M.R. Yarrow. 1977. Prosocial behavior, social inferential ability, and assertiveness in young children. *Child Development* 48: 475–81.

Baumrind, D. 1977. Some thoughts about childrearing. In S. Cohen & T.J. Comiskey (Eds.), *Child development: Contemporary perspectives.* Itasca, IL: F.E. Peacock.

Borke, H. 1971. Interpersonal perception of young children: Egocentrism or empathy? *Developmental Psychology* 5: 263–9.

Bryan, J.H. 1977. Prosocial behavior. In H.L. Hom, Jr., & P.A. Robinson, eds. *Psychological processes in early education.* New York: Academic.

Caldwell, B. 1977. Aggression and hostility in young children. *Young Children* 32 (2): 4–14.

Cartledge, G., & J.F. Milburn, eds. 1980. *Teaching social skills to children.* New York: Pergamon.

Chalmers, J., & M. Townsend. 1990. The effects of training in social perspective taking on socially maladjusted girls. *Child Development* 61: 178–90.

Crary, E. 1984. *Kids can cooperate: A practical guide to teaching problem solving.* Seattle, WA: Parenting Press.

Devoe, M., & T. Sherman. 1978. A microtechnology for teaching prosocial behavior to children. *Child Study Journal* 8 (2): 83–92.

Eisenberg, N., R. Lennon, & K. Roth. 1983. Prosocial development: A longitudinal study. *Developmental Psychology* 19: 846–55.

Elardo, R., & J.J. Freund. 1981. Maternal childrearing styles and the social skills of learning disabled boys: A preliminary investigation. *Contemporary Educational Psychology* 6: 86–94.

Fabes, R.A., J. Fultz, N. Eisenberg, T. May-Plumlee, & F.S. Christopher. 1989. Effect of rewards on children's prosocial motivation: A socialization study. *Developmental Psychology* 25: 509–15.

Factor, D., & G.L. Schilmoeller. 1983. Social skill training of preschool children. *Child Study Journal* 13 (1): 41–56.

Feshbach, N. 1975. Empathy in children: Some theoretical and empirical considerations. *The Counseling Psychologist* 5: 25–30.

Fugitt, E. 1983. *"He hit me back first!" Creative visualization activities for parenting and teaching.* Rolling Hills Estates, CA: Jalmar.

Furman, W., D.F. Rahe, & W.W. Hartup. 1978. Rehabilitation of low-interactive preschool children through mixed-age and same-age socialization. In H. McGurk, ed., *Issues in childhood social development.* Cambridge: Methuen.

George, C., & M. Main. 1979. Social interactions of young abused children: Approach, avoidance, and aggression. *Child Development* 50: 306–18.

Gilligan, C. 1982. *In a different voice.* Cambridge, MA: Harvard University Press.

Goffin, S.G. 1987. Cooperative behaviors: They need our support. *Young Children* 42 (2): 75–81.

Gordon, T. 1970. *Parent effectiveness training.* New York: Wyden.

Grusec, J.E., & E. Redler. 1980. Attribution, reinforcement, and altruism. *Developmental Psychology* 16: 525–34.

Grusec, J., P. Saas-Kortsaak, & Z. Simultis. 1978. The role of example and moral exhortation in the training of altruism. *Child Development* 49: 920–3.

Grusec, J., J. Kuczynski, P. Rushton, & Z. Simultis. 1978. Modeling, direct instruction, and attributions: Effects on altruism. *Developmental Psychology* 14: 51–7.

Haskins, R. 1985. Public school aggression among children with varying day care experience. *Child Development* 56: 689–703.

Honig, A.S. 1982. Research in review. Prosocial development in children. *Young Children* 37 (5): 51–62.

Honig, A.S. 1985. Research in review. Compliance, control, and discipline. Part 1. *Young Children* 40 (2): 50–8.

Honig, A.S., & D.S. Wittmer. 1992. *Prosocial development in children: Caring, sharing, & cooperating: A bibliographic resource guide.* New York: Garland.

Howes, C., & J. Farber. 1987. Toddlers' responses to the distress of their peers. *Journal of Applied Developmental Psychology* 8: 441–52.

Krogh, S., & L. Lamme. 1983 (January–February). Learning to share: How literature can help. *Childhood Education* 59 (3): 188–92.

McGinnis, E., & A. Goldstein. 1984. *Skillstreaming the elementary school child: A guide to prosocial skills.* Champaign, IL: Research Press.

McGinnis, E., & A. Goldstein. 1990. *Skillstreaming in early childhood. Teaching prosocial skills to the preschool and kindergarten child.* Champaign, IL: Research Press.

Park, K., & E. Waters. 1989. Security of attachment and preschool friendships. *Child Development* 60: 1076–81.

Pines, M. 1979. Good Samaritans at age two? *Psychology Today* 13: 66–77.

Rushton, J.P., & G. Teachman. 1978. The effects of positive reinforcement, attributions, and punishment on model induced altruism in children. *Personality and Social Psychology Bulletin* 4: 322–5.

Rutherford, E., & P. Mussen. 1968. Generosity in nursery school boys. *Child Development* 39: 755–65.

Shure, M.B. 1992. *I can problem solve: An interpersonal cognitive problem-solving program.* Champaign, IL: Research Press.

Shure, M., & G. Spivack. 1978. *Problem-solving techniques in childrearing.* San Francisco: Jossey-Bass.

Trovato, C. 1987. Teaching today's kids to get along. *Early Childhood Teacher* 34: 43.

Vorrath, H. 1985. *Positive peer culture.* New York: Aldine.

Yarrow, M.R., & C.Z. Waxler. 1976. Dimensions and correlates of prosocial behavior in young children. *Child Development* 47: 118–25.

Zavitkovsky, D., K.R. Baker, J.R. Berlfein, & M. Almy. 1986. *Listen to the children.* Washington, DC: NAEYC.

Caring for Others And Being Cared For
Students Talk Caring in School

What can adolescents themselves tell us about their perceptions of caring? Ms. Bosworth — who was co-director of a study team that spent a year in two middle schools, exploring the indicators of caring in young adolescents — draws some answers from that experience.

Kris Bosworth

KRIS BOSWORTH is director of the Center for Adolescent Studies, Indiana University, Bloomington. She wishes to thank Gerald Smith, Maria Ferriera, Darren Smith, and Chris Jaffe for their contributions.

Illustration by Loren Long

RECENTLY, IN one mid-sized city in the Midwest, two teenagers, ages 18 and 15, fired a single shot from a stolen gun into the head of a cab driver. Following the incident, a juvenile probation officer lamented, "We're seeing an increase in kids who just don't care."

Often adults see negative, disrespectful, or violent behavior as evidence that teens simply do not care. They tend to react to adolescents as if their noncaring behavior were the norm, as if caring attitudes and behaviors were as foreign to young people as neural surgery. Thus the first approach many adults take to dealing with teens is to focus on changing the be-

haviors seen as "uncaring." In fact, strategies dealing with negative behavior dominate most schools. Programs or strategies that enhance caring values, attitudes, and behaviors by providing students with opportunities to discuss caring, to demonstrate caring to others, and to participate thoughtfully in caring relationships with peers and adults are scarce.

If adults tend to think that many young people don't care, what can adolescents themselves tell us about their perceptions of caring? In discussions of how caring manifests itself in schools and other institutions that serve young people, their opinions are often missing. What do ado-

lescents say about caring, about how they demonstrate caring, and about how they identify caring in others, particularly in their teachers? Understanding how young people view caring provides a place to begin in developing formal programs that promote and encourage caring, as well as in showing how the behaviors of adults who work with teens might support and encourage caring.

Does what adolescents say about caring have any relationship to how they behave? Although values and attitudes are important contributors to behavior, they are certainly not the only influences that determine whether a teen demonstrates caring behavior. However, valuing caring and having a positive attitude toward it are certainly steps toward exhibiting caring behavior. What values, attitudes, and understandings do teens have about caring? How can these be used to enhance the qualities of caring in school relationships?

Teachers are the brokers of caring in schools. They provide the bridge between the school and the individual. Understanding what adolescents see as caring behavior can facilitate communication between teachers and students and can help teachers model caring behavior. Hearing student voices can provide educators with a clearer understanding of approaches to enhance caring.

Before talking to teens, though, we should explore several assumptions that may influence our expectations. The first concerns gender issues. Are female adolescents better able to articulate what caring is? Are girls able to provide more sophisticated definitions of what it means to care? Such an expectation comes both from the common perception of females in this society as nurturing and caring and from some studies of adolescent girls. A finding of gender differences or lack thereof would be important in designing any programs or interventions to enhance caring in schools.

One might also expect that adolescents would be so self-absorbed (often described as "egocentric") that altruism and caring would be totally out of character for any of them, regardless of gender. Adults often describe adolescents' behavior in ways that suggest that young people scarcely recognize that anyone else exists, let alone has feelings, wants, and needs. Caring implies relationship. Indeed, some have described the relationship between the giver and the recipient of caring as reciprocal or mutual. To what extent do teens find caring to be mutual with other students or with adults?

Recently, Gerald Smith and I led a study team that spent a year in two middle schools, exploring the indicators of caring in young adolescents. One school, serving a population of 800 students, was located in the heart of a large industrial city in the Midwest. The other was located about 10 miles from that urban area and drew its student body (1,200 students) from suburban subdivisions, poor rural areas, and the inner city (as a result of a desegregation plan). In our exploration we observed about 300 classrooms over four months. We interviewed more than

100 students in the sixth, seventh, and eighth grades in the two schools.

To select students who would represent a range of caring and uncaring behavior, we asked teachers to identify their five most caring and their five most uncaring students. Although the goal in collecting these data was to identify students for the interviews, the teachers' reports can serve as crude indicators of caring behavior. The students we interviewed represented a range of early adolescents from rural, suburban, and urban areas and from low-income and middle-class families. About one-third of the adolescents interviewed were nonwhite, mostly African American.

Definition of Caring

What does it mean to care? All but four of the adolescents interviewed could clearly articulate a definition of caring and identify specific behaviors that indicated caring. A few definitions were simple synonyms, such as "loving" or "helping," but most included two or more dimensions or characteristics of caring. The teens sometimes discussed caring in terms of single acts (e.g., helping someone with schoolwork), but more often they saw caring as an integral part of relationships within their circle of intimate friends and family members, as well as in their school, their community, and the rest of the world. When asked what came to mind when they heard the word "caring," most students gave responses like these:

> *Bob*: Doing something for somebody when they can't do it, like helping them, giving them their needs and watching over them.

Bob's definition of caring includes both specific acts, "doing something for somebody," and the more general attitude, "watching over them." Most students, regardless of grade, gender, or race, agreed with Bob that caring involved helping of some kind.

> *Alicia*: I think of loving. Maybe appreciating the fact that somebody's different than you. If you care for them, no matter what they are or what they do wrong, then you still care for them. You appreciate who they are.

Alicia begins her explanation with a synonym, "loving," but she goes on to explain that this includes the concept of appreciating differences and a belief that caring is constant.

> *William*: To be sure somebody knows how you feel, to have sympathy for somebody, to have feelings for somebody, to be interested about somebody.

Like many of the middle schoolers with whom we spoke, William's definition has a strong relationship component. To let someone know how you feel, communication needs to be clear and probably reciprocal. The kind of caring relationship William describes is most likely not casual, as indicated by the other ways he describes the relationship: having sympathy, having feelings, and being interested.

> *Tara*: The way one person feels toward another person about their feelings. Like if I was injured or something and you were to come by, you wouldn't sit there and laugh at me. You'd want to try to help.

Tara elaborates on the theme of helping as part of caring. For Tara, feelings play an important role in explaining caring. She also understands what caring is not: laughing at adversity or making fun of someone.

The responses of Bob, Alicia, William, and Tara suggest the range of responses students made to our general question about what caring means. Most students identified more than one dimension or attribute when discussing what caring is. In looking at what all the students said, five themes were dominant: helping, feelings, relationships, personal values, and activities.

Helping. The most common theme to emerge from students' discussions of the concept of caring was that caring involves helping. Nearly 30% of the responses described helping of some kind. For a few students, the phrase "to help" was synonymous with "to care." When discussing caring in terms of helping, some students used concrete or specific situations. For example, friends and classmates were described as the recipients of help with schoolwork. "If a friend is having a problem with schoolwork," said one female eighth-grader, "I show them the way to do it and do an example for them or something." Similarly, a male seventh-grader said, "In class, I usually go back and explain work to them [classmates and friends], because sometimes the teacher is up front, and there's noise, and they don't understand. So I'll just go and help them out."

Besides helping classmates and friends with schoolwork, some adolescents mentioned helping in other ways. "I help them [friends and family members]: when there is something that I can do that they cannot do, I do it for them," said one eighth-grade female. To another student, helping went beyond the intimate circle of friends and family: "If somebody is elderly or if somebody is just having a rough time and needs something done, all you're able to do is help them out." This suggests that there is more to caring than the mere act itself. A kind of sensitivity should guide a person's act of caring. One sixth-grade male took this helping a step further. He would "ask them what the problem is, and try to help them solve it."

Students who talked about taking care of someone or something usually referred to a concrete situation. Saying "give them their needs" or "to be cared for while you are sick" gives the impression that the relationship between the caregiver and the receiver is richer than a relationship based just on one person physically providing for another. There is a certain warmth that transcends the physical act of caring.

Providing guidance was another specific kind of helping that students identified. Thus "giving advice" becomes part of the process of trying to help someone with a problem. But giving advice must be done in a caring manner. In the words of an eighth-grade male, "When you're with somebody and they're doing something wrong, . . . you don't just go out and yell at them."

Helping a specific person with a specific task is an activity that may be easy for an adolescent to identify as caring because it is visible and because the person being cared for is easily identified. A less direct indicator of caring — such as doing a conscientious job of mowing the school lawn so that the school looks nice or attending a workshop to learn a new teaching technique — would be harder to identify. Such activities are not aimed toward a specific person and may not be evident to the student for some time after they have taken place. When asked what they do to care for others, students themselves did not identify the more subtle caring acts, such as paying attention when others speak in class or not littering, as acts of caring.

Feelings. The theme that came in second, mentioned by about one-fourth of the students, was that caring concerns feelings. An important component of feelings is empathy or "knowing how someone else feels," and the flip side of empathy is

being able to "tell someone how you feel."

"Love" or "loving" was the feeling most commonly mentioned as a part of caring. Some students just offered the word "love," while others identified the recipients of love as parents or friends. A number of students, however, mentioned "loving other people." As one female seventh-grader put it, "When somebody really cares for you, they love you."

Other feelings mentioned include comforting someone by "picking them up when they are down." It could involve cheering them up by "making them laugh, making funny faces, or something." These responses reflected a one-sided relationship in which there was a caregiver and a receiver of care. Other students described a more reciprocal connection between those involved: "Let them lean on you, just like you lean on them." This is akin to having an unconditional acceptance and appreciation for another person.

Relationships. A sizable number of student responses explicitly mentioned relationships with self, family, friends, or simply "others." The relationship in and of itself was a definition of caring. For example, to a seventh-grader, caring meant simply "caring about yourself," whereas to a sixth-grade male it meant "having respect for what you have" and "taking care of what you do."

Some students associated caring with family members. "I think about my parents," said an eighth-grade female. She went on to acknowledge that they gave her a home, clothes, and shelter. This student seemed to understand the fact that her parents had chosen to care for her by taking care of her needs.

Friendship was also a synonym for caring. Although some students mentioned their particular friends, others felt that caring meant "being a friend to everybody." Interestingly, although friends play an important developmental role in the lives of young adolescents, the concept of friends and friendship was not mentioned as often as family or the more general "others."

Although early adolescence is often seen as an egocentric period, nearly one in four of the adolescents we interviewed said that caring involved a relationship with others, and many of them did not limit that relationship to those closest to them. In the words of a sixth-grader, "If more people cared, there wouldn't be that much crime on the streets."

Values. Students identified three per-

sonal values related to the concept of caring: kindness, respect, and faithfulness. When speaking of kindness as a value related to caring, most students simply said that caring involves "being nice to people" or "being kind." Those who identified respect as an important component of caring gave such examples as "not calling people names" and "not talking about other people." Because of the realities of peer relationships typical in middle schools, these simple statements describe an attitude of tolerance and consideration toward others that seems to run counter to some peer-group norms. In the words of a sixth-grade female, one respects others by "appreciating the fact that somebody's different than you."

Faithfulness is another value to live by in a caring relationship. To the students we surveyed, this meant that "someone won't just one minute be your friend and, if something better comes along, they won't just leave you behind." These students sense that real caring involves a bond that survives, as one student said, "the good and the bad times."

Activities. The theme mentioned least often as a component of caring had to do with activities; only 10% of the total number of responses mentioned activities. Three activities garnered a similar number of responses: spending time with someone, sharing, and listening. Some of these activities are single events, but most students described general activities that suggest that a caring relationship is more than one isolated instance.

For one sixth-grader, caring related to someone "spending time with you" and "taking you to places"; to another, it meant being with someone "to get to know you better." One of the assumptions underlying these responses is that each individual is content with spending time in the company of another, without the draw of entertainment or a holiday or celebration.

Sharing implies a sort of equivalence in the context of a relationship. In sharing activities it is not at all clear who is the caregiver and who is the receiver. Sharing differs from lending in that lending may be an isolated event in which no relationship outside the event is implied. Interestingly, lending school materials was never identified by students as an act of caring. "Sharing things" and "sharing with them" were the most common responses in the sharing category. One very pragmatic student equated sharing with letting others "play with my Nintendo."

Listening implied different degrees of involvement. To one sixth-grader, caring meant "somebody who listens to what you've got to say," whereas, to one seventh-grader, a caring person is "wanting to listen." To an eighth-grade female, listening is an important component in her relationships with her friends: "When they are having problems, you just sit there and listen to them."

In its simplest form, any definition of caring involves at least two people who are engaged in some sort of activity in which one person gives while the other receives, and the roles of the giver and receiver may be interchangeable at any point in a relationship or at any moment in time. When the students described what they meant by caring, however, they indicated that something more than a particular, isolated event or activity bonds two persons. "To think about people around you" and "to be interested about someone" indicate that the relationship between the caregiver and the receiver is richer than just a relationship based on helping someone with an isolated homework problem. For the adolescents we surveyed, caring arose from relationships that involved a commitment on the part of both parties.

While about 90% of the young adolescents with whom we spoke gave complex, multidimensional definitions of caring, there appeared to be some differences in the nature of those definitions. Although 69% of the females identified "helping" as a characteristic of caring, an even larger proportion of males (87%) gave responses related to the helping theme. A similar pattern occurred with the theme of "feelings": 83% of the males and 62% of the females made responses that fell into this category. There was a smaller difference in the "relationships" theme: 65% of males gave responses that fell into this category, as opposed to 56% of females. Females provided slightly more responses related to activities (31% to 24%). And similar proportions of males and females gave responses related to "personal values." These findings suggest that males and females share similar conceptions of caring. In fact, the adolescent boys with whom we spoke attributed helping and feelings to caring more often than did the girls.

When we examined each theme in relation to racial groups, we found some differences. Proportionally more nonwhite students provided responses under the themes of "relationships" and "activities," whereas a greater number of white stu-

Our observations indicated that most interactions between students or between students and their teachers were neutral.

dents provided responses under "feelings" and "personal values." We did not find differences with regard to the theme of "helping."

It appears that, for many nonwhite students, caring is more concrete and is translated through such activities as "spending time with someone," "sharing," and "listening when someone has a problem." In addition, when discussing caring, nonwhite students tended to talk about specific people. "To think about someone you really dearly care about, like your friends," said an eighth-grade female. In contrast, many white students discussed caring more abstractly and included emotions or values. "Showing respect," responded a sixth-grade female. "The way a person feels towards another person" reflects a caring attitude, replied another.

While we did notice some differences, they should not detract from the voices of most of the middle school students, who give evidence that — regardless of age, race, or gender — there is a rich and multidimensional understanding of what caring is. This understanding can serve as a basis for engaging young adolescents in activities that will enhance their comprehension of caring and help turn it into positive action.

Given the rich understanding that young adolescents have of the concept of caring, how did this understanding manifest itself in the classroom? What did teachers do to support or nurture caring in their students? Our observations indicated that most interactions between students or between students and their teachers were neutral. Each went about his or her busi-

ness without engaging in overt acts of caring or uncaring. Mostly they were pleasant and polite to one another, but the structure of the school day left little space or time for interpersonal interaction.

During class time teachers were clearly in charge, and the majority of time was devoted to traditional types of learning (lectures, workbook exercises, silent reading, viewing videos, and so on) in which caring interactions are not encouraged. In both schools we studied, there was pressure to improve scores on standardized tests administered statewide. While the teachers were not "teaching to the test," a clear goal was to improve academic performance. This goal may have influenced teachers to use the traditional learning strategies that left little time for personal interactions.

Some teachers took advantage of the times before and after school to be in the halls and to interact with students. But many teachers simply played the role of disciplinarian during these times.

Themes of caring were rarely discussed, even though course content — such as study of the Holocaust — could have reasonably generated such discussion. Even such a clearly caring/helping activity as donating cans of food for the needy did not become a springboard for a discussion of caring. The focus was more on ways to increase the number of cans collected than on why the school was involved in the activity.

We saw only a few instances in which students were given the opportunity to help other students. In one case, a boy was asked to orient a new student (also a boy) to the classroom. The other cases involved free time at the end of a class. Teachers asked students who had received good grades on their tests or quizzes to help those who were studying for the retest.

Outside of the classroom, time constraints (students had less than five minutes to change classes) and structure (students had to line up to move from class to class) offered few opportunities for caring or helping. Since most students rode buses to school, they did not "hang around" after school. Thus, although these middle school students had the prerequisite understanding of what caring is, they had few chances to demonstrate it within the structure of the school day. When teachers did provide opportunities to demonstrate caring, those opportunities often favored students who were academically stronger. This tendency could lead teachers to see a false correlation between caring behavior and academic proficiency.

Caring Teachers

Although a typical school day does not offer students much opportunity to demonstrate caring, what did the students identify as caring from their teachers? When asked to describe what they would see in the classroom of a caring teacher, most students gave descriptions similar to this one from an eighth-grade male: "Everyone would be in their seats, doing work. The teacher would go around the room talking to everybody to see how they were doing [and] to answer questions. Sometimes she'd just say, 'Good job.'" In this scenario, the teacher is involved with each student, meeting the needs of each student for specific help with an academic problem or offering positive reinforcement and encouragement.

Most students had little difficulty articulating characteristics of caring teachers. Their responses can be grouped into three large categories: the most frequently identified characteristic (140 responses) had to do with classroom or teaching practices; the second most frequently mentioned category (81 responses) was nonclassroom activities, such as after-school help and guidance; and the final category (49 responses) was personal characteristics.

Teaching Practices

While some of the caring things teachers did in classrooms could be described as "good teaching" (helping with schoolwork, explaining work, and checking for understanding), others represent such personal traits as valuing individuality, showing respect, encouraging students, and being tolerant. The following paragraphs discuss these characteristics and behaviors in rank order, by the number of times students mentioned them.

Helping with schoolwork. Student descriptions of caring teachers were consistent across grades, race, and gender. A caring teacher would help students under the following conditions: "if you are stuck on a problem," "when you need it," "if you don't understand something," "when you ask a question," and "even if you don't need it." Helping students with schoolwork was the highest-ranking category for both males and females, for whites, and for all grades. It ranked second for nonwhite students. Clearly, simply helping with

schoolwork is seen as a strong indicator that a teacher cares.

Valuing individuality. Teachers who saw students as individuals in the classroom were perceived to be caring teachers by many students. The caring teachers noticed and inquired about changes in behavior; they recognized different learning styles and speeds; they sought to know students as unique human beings. Valuing individuality ranked highest among seventh- and eighth-graders and among males.

As one seventh-grade female put it, "[A caring teacher] doesn't see you as a unit; she sees each person as an individual." Another seventh-grade female said, "If you were the only person in the classroom who didn't understand it and everybody did, then he or she wouldn't doubt you for not understanding it." An eighth-grade male explained it this way: "[Caring teachers] can see problems in your schoolwork and help you with them." Or, as another seventh-grade male said, "They ask you questions about how you are doing with all your classes." One eighth-grade male said, "She wants to know what type of person you are."

Showing respect. Showing respect has several dimensions for middle schoolers. In regular classroom practice, teachers who show respect will call on students when they raise their hands and listen to what the students have to say. As one seventh-grade male said, "They treat you the way you want to be treated."

Many students described the actions of respectful, caring teachers in situations where students had made a mistake or broken a rule. For example, one sixth-grade female said, "She won't yell at you or anything like that." Another aspect of respect was "talking in a quiet voice or talking to you in private or alone" when a reprimand was needed.

Being tolerant. According to students, tolerant teachers give students second chances to make up work, to improve their behavior, or to get the right answer. One seventh-grade female eloquently described this characteristic of tolerance and equity: "Somebody who no matter what the student is, what their past was, would start off with a clean slate, just come in, make them feel good about themselves, saying, 'You're going to be one of my best students, and you will succeed in this class.' Making them know from the start that they can do it." A sixth-grade male said that this characteristic is shown by a teacher who "pays attention, not just to

one person, but to all." Another sixth-grade male said, "Let's say there's an uncaring student. A caring teacher has to care about that student, too."

Explaining work. Students report that a caring teacher does a good job of explaining the content area, particularly with regard to assignments that students must do. This category differs from helping with work in that it requires of a teacher the specific skill of making sure that all students understand rather than simply helping with specific problems of an individual student.

According to one seventh-grade female, a caring teacher "wouldn't just say, 'Do it the way you think you do it, and see if you get it right.'" Instead, a caring teacher would "explain your assignments before you do them, would explain an assignment thoroughly, would show you how to do the work before you take it home." This characteristic was identified more frequently by older students.

Checking for understanding. Teachers who display this trait are very active in the classroom. They do more than help only when a hand is raised. They interact with students and seek out students who need clarification or additional explanation. One eighth-grade male described such a teacher as "someone who walks around making sure you're understanding your work."

Encouraging. Actively encouraging students to improve is another dimension of teaching practice that a caring teacher would exhibit. Some students talked about the encouragement as a material reward, such as candy, but most students focused on the verbal encouragement that caring teachers gave. One sixth-grade female said, "She sticks up for you when she knows you did something right." A sixth-grade male said, "When you get bad grades, she says, 'You can do better than this.'"

Planning fun activities. A few students mentioned that a caring teacher provided an enjoyable classroom atmosphere and would take students on field trips and plan fun activities for them. Some students also mentioned that a caring teacher was considerate about the amount of homework given.

Nonclassroom Activities

Eighty-one responses focused on things that teachers did outside of their classroom teaching responsibilities. These responses fell clearly into three categories:

helping with personal problems, providing guidance, and going the extra mile.

Helping with personal problems. Most responses were fairly general in identifying the types of problems a caring teacher helps with or in specifying what a caring teacher does to help. For some students, just listening was sufficient. Others found that a caring teacher was much more active in problem solving. One seventh-grade female said, "If you were mad at one of your friends and you were really upset and were crying, they would probably help you guys work it out." Another seventh-grade female said, "A lot of times they can help you with problems at home or anything." An eighth-grade male mentioned that a caring teacher would help students with family problems and with problems between friends.

Looking at the distribution of these responses, it is interesting to note that males were somewhat more likely to mention help with personal problems than females. One might think of asking for and getting help with personal problems as more characteristic of females than of males, but our data show that males ranked this an important indicator of a caring teacher.

Providing guidance. The guidance category was the second most frequently mentioned topic. In this category were responses that indicated that teachers took a full, active role in providing direction, goal-setting activities, and advice. Viewed from a distance, these actions might often be seen as uncaring, for they include such things as talking to parents if a student has been disruptive. However, a high percentage of responses testified to the role that caring teachers play in providing direction and correction to students. A seventh-grade female said, "A caring teacher wants to make sure you don't get in trouble." Another seventh-grade female said, "A caring teacher doesn't let students get by with everything." An eighth-grade female described a caring teacher as one "who is always helping me decide what I want to do and where I'm going to go to college." An eighth-grade male said, "Sometimes they can be a little rough or angry with us when trying to look out for our well-being."

The frequency with which students mentioned the guidance offered by caring teachers indicated that they were perceptive about those teachers who had the best interests of students at heart — even if they took actions that could be seen by students as firm, if not actually harsh. It is significant that a large number of minor-

ity students emphasized this category of caring behavior. Indeed, it was the highest-ranked category for nonwhite students.

Going the extra mile. Students said that caring teachers would extend themselves in ways that went beyond the job description. A major caring behavior in this category was staying after school to help students with their work or to talk to them about their problems. Considering the number of students who mentioned this action, it appears that extending the school day was seen in a positive light. Although the majority of statements in this category were as vague as "Teachers that really go out of their way to make you happy" or "They're there for you to listen," a few students offered specific examples. One seventh-grade female said, "They'll take you out on their own time to help you with schoolwork and privately tutor you after school." An eighth-grade female said, "She always is available if we need help." An eighth-grade male said, "Stops fights and stuff." Another eighth-grade male reported, "She comes to every sport I play."

Personal Attributes

Forty-eight students listed personal attributes or descriptions of caring teachers that did not involve their teaching strategies or out-of-classroom activities. These attributes fell into four categories: being nice or polite, liking to help students, being success-oriented, and being involved.

Being nice/polite. Ten students representing both schools, both genders, and all grades simply said that caring teachers are "nice." Three students framed their comments negatively, saying that caring teachers are not rude or mean. Three students gave behavioral descriptions of what they meant by "nice." One seventh-grade female said that caring teachers "are always smiling and stuff." Another seventh-grade female said, "They always greet you with a smile."

Liking to help students. Willingness to assist students was seen as an important personal attribute of caring teachers. One sixth-grade female said, "They put forth a lot of effort." An eighth-grade male said, "[They are] devoted to helping you." This category is different from the previous categories of helping, in that there was no actual activity to which the students could point. The impression that teachers were willing to help was the personal attribute discussed by many student respondents.

Being success-oriented. A number of students identified caring teachers as being success-oriented. That is, they believed in their students' capabilities and wanted them to do their best and to succeed.

Being involved. Students identified being involved with students as an attribute of caring teachers. Many simply said that such teachers "are involved." Others focused on friendship. For example, a seventh-grade female said, "A caring teacher is not only a teacher but your friend, too." Other examples of involvement included setting a good example for students, trusting students, telling the truth, and "just liking kids."

Overall, students were able to identify specific behaviors and — to a lesser extent — attitudes of caring teachers. Many of these were similar to those that they identified in defining the concept of caring. However, in describing their teachers' behaviors, students depicted one-way relationships — the teacher did something (e.g., helping or listening) for the student. Students did not describe these activities as mutual or reciprocal.

Except for a few students who saw caring related to fun activities in the classroom, most students did not attribute caring to content or to curricular matters. A

> *For all groups, helping with schoolwork was the most frequently mentioned characteristic of a caring teacher.*

good lesson, an interesting unit, or bringing in an outside speaker were never offered as examples of caring on the part of a teacher. It was through personal actions and attitudes that teachers demonstrated that they cared, both in and out of the classroom. Broadly interpreted, these data say that a "caring teacher" is an interpreter or guide to learning.

Although the disparities were small, there were some differences in responses between grades, genders, and races that bear further investigation. For nonwhite students, 56% ranked guidance as an indicator of caring. Although this guiding role was identified by a considerable number of white students (23%), the difference between racial groups was clear. Teachers should be aware that students value and appreciate a teacher who has standards for student performance and is willing to play a role in guiding students.

For all groups, helping with schoolwork was the most frequently mentioned characteristic of a caring teacher. This is more important to females (58%) than to males (41%). Regardless of grade or race, males see what teachers do outside the classroom as more closely related to caring than do females. Thirty-nine percent of the males versus 20% of the females saw "help with problems" as an important characteristic.

Observations

Clearly, young adolescents from a variety of backgrounds have a clear understanding of the complexity of the concept of caring. Almost all of them are able to articulate a multidimensional description of what caring means to them and to list a variety of activities in which they engage that constitute caring. Moreover, most of the caring activities have a positive orientation: most teens will tell you what they do that demonstrates caring (e.g., helping others with schoolwork), rather than mention activities that they avoid because such activities (e.g., spreading rumors) are not caring activities.

These young adolescents see caring demonstrated within the context of personal relationships. Caring behaviors are almost exclusively described in the context of an ongoing relationship rather than as a single generous act, such as helping a stranger who has fallen down in the hallway or on the street. Moreover, within these ongoing relationships, very few young adolescents mentioned material forms of caring, such as giving gifts. What they reported as demonstrations of caring involved giving time and sharing of themselves.

Helping was the dominant theme in all our discussions with these teens about car-

ing. The central focus of both their definition of caring and their description of activities that demonstrate caring is helping — with schoolwork and with personal problems. The closeness of the relationship between caring and helping is expressed by all genders, grades, and races.

Where teachers are concerned, caring is often a one-way affair; few students report some reciprocal caring. Caring teachers are seen as teachers who help students and treat them as individuals.

These observations lead us to offer several suggestions for educators who wish to nurture caring in students. Our finding that young adolescents see caring as grounded in relationships and find it more difficult to discuss caring for others outside their immediate circle of friends and family suggests that more people need to be included in an adolescent's circle of relationships. Creating caring communities by actively promoting activities and attitudes that help develop relationships is essential. The students we interviewed came from large schools. Large schools tend to be impersonal — and even the strategy of breaking the student body into smaller teams or houses, which the schools we studied employed, could be further exploited to build stronger caring communities.

Young adolescents also need the opportunity to demonstrate caring. In our months of observations, we found that the schools offered little opportunity for most students to practice caring or to be recognized or rewarded for it. Nearly all the events and activities in each school were organized and directed by adults. Both schools had community service organizations, but they were either very small or required a specific grade-point average of participants. The most common way students were asked to show caring was for the teacher to ask the better students to help others who were having academic difficulties. This happened rarely during our observations, and when it did, very few of the eligible students responded.

One-time acts of caring, such as food drives or neighborhood clean-up activities, are important, but they are not sufficient for the development of caring in

young adolescents. All students need multiple opportunities to engage in caring activities in caring educational communities.

Students' perceptions of what a caring teacher does indicate a style of teaching that takes into consideration the needs of individual learners. The caring teacher first provides good explanations and then seeks to clarify misunderstandings. Although some students also appreciate a teacher who will help with specific problems, this is less important to students than the role of teacher as learning guide or coach.

Even within a highly structured school day, we saw numerous "missed opportunities" for the demonstration of caring. We observed too many classes in which teachers rarely smiled, said anything positive to a student, or used a student's name other than for a reprimand. Changes in these behaviors might go a long way toward promoting caring and need not detract from the pursuit of academic goals. In a number of classes, students would seek help with a lesson or assignment only from the teacher. Often students had to wait their turn for the teacher to have time to answer their questions. Because the adolescents in this study identified helping as a key component of caring, schools that wish to provide opportunities for adolescents to demonstrate caring should work to expand the pool of people who can help with schoolwork.

The school can take action to facilitate teachers' demonstration of caring to students as well. Reducing the size of schools and classrooms would allow teachers to get to know their students individually, to help them more with their work, to become involved with their extracurricular activities, and to interact with families. All of these are activities that students recognize as caring. With institutional support teachers can heed the words of their young adolescent students and model caring behaviors, offer students opportunities to practice caring, support a widening circle of relationships in which caring is more likely to be meaningful, and regularly reward and affirm caring behaviors.

At-Risk Students and Resiliency: Factors Contributing to Academic Success

JAMES H. McMILLAN and DAISY F. REED

James H. McMillan is a professor and Daisy F. Reed is an associate professor—both at the School of Education, Virginia Commonwealth University, Richmond, Virginia. Funds to support this research were received from the Metropolitan Educational Research Consortium. The views expressed are those of the authors and do not represent opinions or beliefs of the members of the consortium.

The increasingly high number of at-risk middle and high school students—those in danger of dropping out of school because of academic failure or other problems—is a major concern in education today. At-risk students show persistent patterns of under-achievement and of social maladjustment in school, leading to their failure to finish high school. Indeed, the national dropout rate averages about 25 percent (Sklarz 1989), and for minorities, that rate is higher, with an average of 30 percent leaving school before they graduate (Liontos 1991). In Texas, the dropout rate for Hispanic Americans is 45 percent. Additionally, students in urban schools have much higher dropout rates than those in other areas: in Boston, Chicago, Los Angeles, Detroit, and other major cities, dropout rates range from 40 percent to 60 percent of the total school population (Hahn 1987).

An interesting approach to helping at-risk students succeed is to examine the notion of "resilience." Despite incredible hardships and the presence of at-risk factors, some students have developed characteristics and coping skills that enable them to succeed. They appear to develop stable, healthy personas and are able to recover from or adapt to life's stresses and problems. These students can be termed *resilient* (Winfield 1991).

In one recent large-scale study, approximately 19 percent of students who could be classified as at-risk became individuals who had success in school, with positive goals and plans for the future (Peng, Lee, Wang, and Walberg 1992). What enables these resilient students to succeed

academically? What can educators and other concerned citizens do to foster these qualities in the 81 percent of at-risk students who do not succeed in school? We believe that much can be learned from studying students who may be classified as at-risk but are resilient, that is, doing well in school despite the odds against them. In this article, we integrate existing literature with our own research that examines resiliency, and then suggest a model to explain resiliency that can be used to better understand why these students have been successful and what can be done to help other at-risk students.

The factors that seem to be related to resiliency can be organized into four categories: individual attributes, positive use of time, family, and school (Peng et al. 1992; McMillan and Reed 1993).

Elements of Resiliency

Individual Attributes

Resilient at-risk students possess temperamental characteristics that elicit positive responses from individuals around them. These personality traits begin in early childhood and are manifested in adolescence as students seek out new experiences and become self-reliant. This begins a cycle of positive reciprocity that enables these students to reach out to other people and expect help. Their positive attitudes are usually rewarded with helpful reactions from those around them. Thus, they come to see the world as a positive place in spite of the difficult issues with which they have to deal. Their positive attitudes include respecting others, coming to class prepared, volunteering for in- and out-of-class assignments, and knowing how to play the school game.

High intrinsic motivation and internal locus of control seem to enable resilient at-risk students to succeed. In their study of 17,000 tenth graders from low-income families, Peng et al. (1992) found that locus of control was a significant predictor of academic success—students with higher academic achievement tended to have a more in-

From *The Clearing House*, January/February 1994, pp. 137-140. © 1994 by the Helen Dwight Reid Educational Foundation.
Reprinted by permission of Heldref Publications, 1319 Eighteenth Street, NW, Washington, DC 20036-1802.

ternal locus of control. They also found that successful students had higher educational aspirations than non-resilient students. In a qualitative study of the perceptions of academically successful at-risk students, many students spoke of satisfaction gained from experiencing success in self-fulfilling activities (McMillan and Reed 1993). These students were motivated by a desire to succeed, to be self-starting, and to be personally responsible for their achievements. They attributed poor performance to internal factors such as a lack of effort, not caring, not trying, not studying as much as they needed to, goofing off, and playing around; most respondents thought that poor performing students could do better if they put in more work and got serious about school. A strong sense of self-efficacy is important; students see themselves as being successful because they have chosen to be so and give much credit to themselves.

Resilient students have clear, realistic goals and are optimistic about the future. They have hope, despite all the negative circumstances in their lives, and confidence that they can achieve their long-range goals. For some students a particularly difficult experience, either direct or vicarious, reinforces the importance of getting an education. These might be called "reality checks" because they seem to motivate students toward positive goals (McMillan and Reed 1993). The reality check may have been dropping out of school, becoming pregnant, being in drug rehabilitation, or some other event or circumstance that showed them that without an education their opportunities would be limited. As a result, these resilient students tend to be very mature in their explanations and goals.

Resilient students do not believe that the school, neighborhood, or family is critical in either their successes or failures. They acknowledge that a poor home environment can make things difficult, but they do not blame their performance on these factors.

Positive Use of Time

In the qualitative study conducted by McMillan and Reed (1993), resilient students were asked about their hobbies, activities, and participation in clubs, church, or other organizations and about how they spend their time. It was clear that they used their time positively and were meaningfully involved in school and other activities. With some exceptions, this involvement was not in a special program or group for at-risk students or students with specific problems. This positive involvement did not leave these students with much spare time. Active involvement in extracurricular events at school and in other areas seems to provide a refuge for resilient students. Hobbies, creative interests, and sports help promote the growth of self-esteem. Being recognized and supported for special talents is also important. In addition, simply being involved in an activity considered special appears to increase self-esteem and a belief in one's ability to succeed (Geary 1988; Werner 1984; Coburn and

Nelson 1989; McMillan and Reed 1993). Such involvement may provide an important social-psychological support system by connecting the students to others in meaningful ways. Success in these activities may be important in enhancing self-esteem by providing recognition and a sense of accomplishment.

Involvement in "required helpfulness" seems to be a factor in resilient students' experiences. Required helpfulness may mean volunteer work in the community, tutoring or buddying at school, or taking care of siblings or otherwise helping at home. These activities seem to lend purpose to the difficult life of an at-risk student and serve to increase their caring about others. They realize there are people that even they can help (Werner 1984; Philliber 1986).

Family Factors

Most resilient at-risk students have had the opportunity to establish a close bond with at least one caregiver who gives them needed attention and support. A sense of trust is developed that is very important in interactions with teachers and peers. This support may be from people other than parents, such as siblings, aunts, uncles, or grandparents who become positive role models. Resilient children seem to be adept at finding these substitute caregivers, much as they are adept at eliciting positive responses from many people around them (Werner 1984).

Family support seems to be an attribute of successful at-risk students. Parents of resilient students have higher expectations for their children's education. Such expectations exert pressure on the children to remain engaged in school and work toward high achievement. These students are more likely to interact with parents, to have more learning materials in the home, and to be involved in out-of-school educational activities than are non-resilient at-risk students (Peng et al. 1992).

Interestingly, family composition seems to have no significant relationship to at-risk students' success or failure (Peng et al. 1992). Students living with both parents do not necessarily have a higher level of resiliency than students in single-parent families or other configurations. Instead, good parent-child relationships and supportive attachments appear to act as protective factors from the environment. Parents who are committed to their children provide informal counseling, support, and help in achieving success. This parental commitment lends a feeling of coherence to the family unit. Werner (1984) maintains that these strong family ties help at-risk students to believe that life makes sense and that they have some control over their own lives. This sense of meaning becomes a powerful motivation for many resilient at-risk students.

Finally, the educational background of parents is related to student resiliency. Peng et al. (1992) found that less than 11 percent of students whose parents had less than a high school education were classified as resilient students as compared with 23 percent of students whose parents had a high school education or beyond.

School Factors

Resilient students seem to find support outside of the home environment, usually in school. They like school, in general, or at least put up with it. Most attempt to involve themselves in classroom discussions and activities. School is more than academics for these students. Most are involved in at least one extracurricular event that becomes an informal source of support. The extracurricular event not only increases involvement, belonging, and self-esteem, it also provides a network of people who have a common bond and work in cooperation with each other (Werner 1984; Coburn and Nelson 1989). Extracurricular events at school, especially sports, seem to mitigate the powerful and widespread peer pressure not to do well. Many resilient students seem to feel they must be involved with a nonacademic activity in order to "fit in" with the majority of students. This involvement maintains the resilient at-risk student's positive engagement in school (Geary 1988).

Teachers play an important role in the success of resilient students. In three qualitative studies, resilient at-risk students mentioned school staff who had taken a personal interest in them as being important to their success (Geary 1988; Coburn and Nelson 1989; McMillan and Reed 1993). Both interpersonal relations and professional competence are important to at-risk students. They cite the following interpersonal qualities of a teacher as important: being caring, having respect for them as persons and as learners, being able to get along with them, listening without being intrusive, taking them seriously, being available and understanding, helping and providing encouragement, and laughing with them. Professional behavior and competence are also important. Resilient at-risk students look for these qualities: the ability to represent and further the goals of the system and the school, a willingness to listen to the motivations behind inappropriate behavior before they discipline, fairness in grading and instruction, praise and encouragement that they can succeed, high expectations, and a willingness to get to know the students personally as well as academically (Werner 1984). Students feel that they can talk to "good" teachers and counselors about almost anything and that the teacher or counselor will listen without judging the student. These counselors and teachers "push" the students and at the same time are very supportive.

Profile of the Resilient Student

Resilient at-risk students have a set of personality characteristics, dispositions, and beliefs that promote their academic success regardless of their backgrounds or current circumstances. They have an internal locus of control and healthy internal attributions, taking personal responsibility for their successes and failures and showing a strong sense of self-efficacy. They feel that they have been successful because they have *chosen* to be successful and have put forth needed effort. Even though they welcome and appreciate the efforts of the significant adults in their lives, they do not see these people as being responsible for their success or failure. They credit themselves. They have positive expectations about their abilities and the future, an optimistic perspective with realistic long-range goals. This strong sense of hope is accompanied by a belief that doing well in school is necessary to doing well in life. These students are very mature in their outlook and attitudes and tend to make positive choices about how to use their time.

To develop these characteristics, resilient students have a psychological support system that provides a safety net and encouragement. This system is evident in the way the students are meaningfully connected to others, in or out of school. They are actively involved in positive activities that provide a sense of support, success, and recognition. Activities such as hobbies give these students a reason to feel proud and provide a solace when other aspects of their lives are troubling. Involvement in both academic and extracurricular activities maintains resilient students' positive engagement in school.

Resilient students have adults—usually a parent (more often mother than father) and someone from the school—with whom they have trusting relationships. These adults have high expectations and provide support and encouragement with firmness. Students respect these adults because they obviously care about their welfare.

Thus, there are important environmental factors that contribute to the strong, resilient personalities and beliefs that are critical to these students. These factors are illustrated with the conceptual model in figure 1. The model shows how significant relationships with adults and positive use of time provide encouragement, high expectations, a psychological support system, and recognition and accomplishment. These environmental factors influence these students so that they develop self-efficacy, goals, personal responsibility, and so forth. It is these traits that make students resilient. The challenge to schools is to provide the relationships and involvement that can foster this development.

Implications for School Personnel

The model suggests several implications for school personnel. First, instructional strategies and techniques, as well as other dimensions of the school environment, must be developed to promote a sense of internal locus of control, self-efficacy, optimism, and a sense of personal responsibility. Teachers should establish reference points where achievement will be identified, and they must continually relate success to effort and ability. Goal setting is also important, particularly setting long-range goals that demonstrate the need to focus beyond one's immediate interests and activities.

Second, teachers, administrators, and counselors need to be trained and encouraged to provide classroom activities and classroom environments that stress high academic achievement while also building students' self-es-

FIGURE 1
A Conceptual Model of Factors Influencing Resilient At-Risk Students

teem and self-confidence. The classroom environment should facilitate time-on-task, student interaction, student success, and positive reinforcement for desired classroom behaviors. Teachers need to be aware of the difference between high expectations and high standards. High expectations involve beliefs about what students are capable of doing and achieving, while high standards do not necessarily suggest that students can reach them. Positive experiences in school help provide students a sense of belonging, bonding, and encouragement.

In addition, extracurricular activities need to be expanded and promoted in schools where there are large populations of at-risk students. As previously mentioned, these activities increase involvement in school. However, many at-risk students will not voluntarily participate in activities because of their general feelings of disconnectedness. Teachers and administrators should develop needed programs and systematically issue personal invitations for at-risk students to join. These programs should include the usual school clubs such as drama, choir, "Future Teachers," "Future Farmers," and others, as well as support groups for various concerns such as adolescent mothers, victims of abuse, children of alcoholic parents, and children of incarcerated parents.

Third, teachers need to be provided with training and encouragement to develop relationships that benefit at-risk children. These students need teachers who are respectful, caring, honest, patient, open-minded, and firm. They also need teachers who understand learning styles, expect positive results, and recognize cultural norms and differences. Perhaps teacher education programs for preservice and inservice teachers need to offer special seminars or classes on working with at-risk populations.

Resilient students give us hope and encouragement, for it is clear that despite unfavorable odds, they have succeeded. We need to learn from them and put into practice what we have learned.

REFERENCES

Coburn, J., and S. Nelson. 1989. *Teachers do make a difference: What Indian graduates say about their school experience* (Report No. RC-017-103). Washington, D.C.: Office of Educational Research and Improvement. (ERIC Document Reproduction Service No. ED 306 071)

Geary, P. A. 1988. *"Defying the odds?": Academic success among at-risk minority teenagers in an urban high school* (Report No. UD-026-258). Paper presented at the annual meeting of the American Educational Research Association, New Orleans, La. (ERIC Document Reproduction Service No. ED 296 055)

Hahn, A. 1987. Reaching out to America's dropouts: What to do? *Phi Delta Kappan* 69(4): 256-63.

Liontos, L. B. 1991. *Trends and issues: Involving families of at-risk youth in the educational process.* ERIC Clearinghouse on Educational Management. Eugene, Oregon: College of Education, University of Oregon. ED 328946

McMillan, J. H., and D. F. Reed. 1993. A qualitative study of resilient at-risk students. Paper presented at the 1993 annual meeting of the American Educational Research Association, Atlanta.

Peng, S. S., R. M. Lee, M. C. Wang, and H. J. Walberg. 1992. Resilient students in urban settings. Paper presented at the 1992 annual meeting of the American Educational Research Association, San Francisco.

Philliber, S. 1986. *Teen outreach: Data from the second year of a national replication.* Paper presented at the 1986 annual national conference of the Children's Defense Fund, Washington, D. C.

Sklarz, D. P. 1989. Keep at-risk students in school by keeping them up to grade level. *The American School Board Journal* 176(9): 33-34.

Werner, E. E. 1984. Resilient children. *Young Children* 40(1): 68-72.

Winfield, L. A. 1991. Resilience, schooling, and development in African-American youth: A conceptual framework. *Education and Urban Society* 24(1): 5-14.

Exceptional and Culturally Diverse Students

- **Educationally Disabled (Articles 10 and 11)**
- **Gifted and Talented (Articles 12 and 13)**
- **Culturally and Academically Diverse (Articles 14–16)**

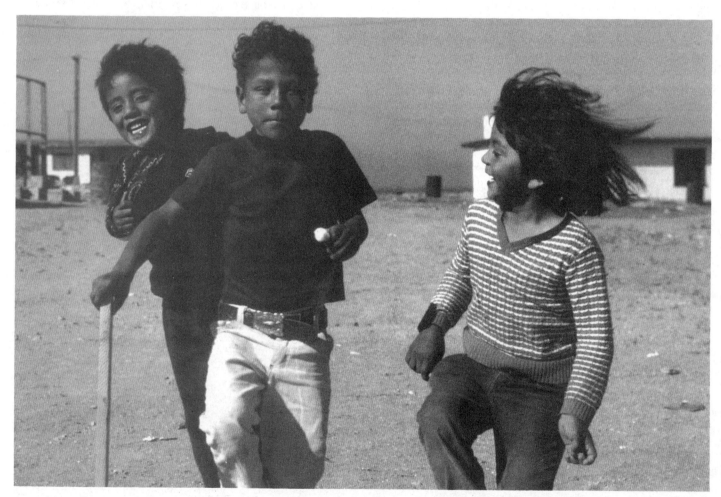

The Equal Educational Opportunity Act for All Handicapped Children (Public Law 94-142) gives disabled children the right to an education in the least-restrictive environment, due process, and an individualized educational program that is specifically designed to meet their needs. Professionals and parents of exceptional children are responsible for developing and implementing an appropriate educational program for each child. The application of these ideas to classrooms across the nation at first caused great concern among educators and parents. Classroom teachers whose training did not prepare them for working with the exceptional child expressed negative attitudes about mainstreaming. Special resource teachers also expressed concern that mainstreaming would mitigate the effectiveness of special programs for the disabled and would force cuts in services. Parents feared that their children would not receive the special services they required because of governmental red tape and delays in proper diagnosis and placement.

It has been two decades since the implementation of the act, which was amended by the Individuals with Disabilities Education Act (IDEA) in 1991. Many of the above concerns have been studied by psychologists and educators, and their findings have often influenced policy. For example, research has indicated that mainstreaming is more effective when regular classroom teachers and special resource teachers work cooperatively with disabled children.

The articles concerning the educationally disabled confront many of these issues. Elaine Wilmore, in "When Your Child Is Special," describes her personal and professional experiences with exceptional children. The next essay by Perry Zirkel discusses the components of the Individuals with Disabilities Education Act (IDEA) as it applies to a specific case.

Other exceptional children are the gifted and talented. These children are rapid learners who can absorb, organize, and apply concepts more effectively than the average child. They often have IQs of 140 or more and are convergent thinkers (i.e., they give the correct answer to teacher or test questions). Convergent thinkers are usually models of good behavior and academic performance, and they respond to instruction easily; teachers generally value such children and often nominate them for gifted programs. There are other children, however, who do not score well on standardized tests of intelligence because their thinking is more divergent (i.e., they can imagine more than one answer to teacher or test questions). These gifted divergent thinkers may not respond to traditional instruction. They may become bored, respond to questions in unique and disturbing ways, and appear uncooperative and disruptive. Many teachers do not understand these unconventional thinkers and fail to identify them as gifted. In fact, such chil-

dren are sometimes labeled as emotionally disturbed or mentally retarded because of the negative impressions they make on their teachers. Because of the differences between these types of students, a great deal of controversy surrounds programs for the gifted. Such programs should enhance the self-esteem of all gifted and talented children, motivate and challenge them, and help them realize their creative potential. The two articles in this unit on gifted and talented children consider the characteristics of giftedness, and they explain how to identify gifted students and provide them with an appropriate education.

The third subsection of this unit concerns student diversity. Just as labeling may adversely affect the disabled child, it may can also affect the child who comes from a minority ethnic background where the language and values are quite different from those of the mainstream culture. The term "disadvantaged" is often used to describe these children, but it is negative, stereotypical, and apt to result in a self-fulfilling prophecy whereby teachers perceive such children as incapable of learning. Teachers should provide academically and culturally diverse children with experiences that they might have missed in the restricted environment of their homes and neighborhoods. The reports in this section address these individual differences and suggest strategies for teaching these diverse children.

Looking Ahead: Challenge Questions

What are some issues regarding the P.L. 94-142 provision called "least restrictive environment"? What is meant by "full inclusion"? What are the pros and cons?

Who are the gifted and talented? How can knowledge of their characteristics and learning needs help to provide them with an appropriate education?

What cultural differences exist in our society? How can teacher expectations affect the culturally diverse child? How would multicultural education help teachers deal more effectively with these differences?

When Your Child Is Special

Decisions about where to enroll a child should come down to this: What would I do to ensure success if this were my child?

Elaine L. Wilmore

Elaine L. Wilmore is a Professor, Center for Professional Teacher Education, University of Texas at Arlington, Box 19227, Arlington, TX 76019-0227.

Everywhere you go in education today *inclusion* is the new buzzword, the new save-the-world concept. Everyone seems to have not only an opinion, but a strong opinion about allowing any physically, emotionally, or academically handicapped child, regardless of the severity, to return to the regular classroom, preferably with support.

Social reformers zealously seek to change society through the schools. In order to provide the handicapped more accessibility, they seek to abandon the traditional resource room and, teachers fear, revert to many practices commonly used prior to passage of the *Individuals with Disabilities Education Act* (P.L. 94-142 amended) in 1991. Teachers publicly protest and sign petitions.

Proponents of full inclusion, alluding to a P.L. 94-142 provision, argue that the regular classroom is the only true "least restrictive environment." They contend that all children

do better academically and socially when exposed to higher performing students, and that "normal" children need to learn how to live in a society with handicapped people. Many parents of handicapped children want their offspring in an age-appropriate educational environment for many of these same reasons.

Then there is me. I am a former classroom teacher, counselor, and principal. I am now a professor and still teach Sunday school. I am also

the mother of a handicapped child. Where does that leave me? Somewhere in between, in Peter Pan's Never-Never Land.

Brooke

Why do so many people push for inclusion?

I have a 12-year-old daughter named Brooke. Her middle name is Elaine, after me, her mom. She has long blonde hair almost to her waist. She has beautiful blue eyes and braces

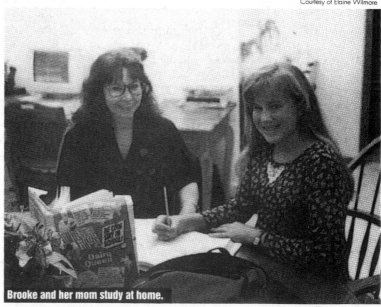

Courtesy of Elaine Wilmore

Brooke and her mom study at home.

on her teeth. She has a smile from ear to ear and loves to have a friend over to spend the night. She likes to sing in the front yard while she jumps rope. She is a nice, well-behaved child who earns "Excellent" in Conduct on her report cards. She also has a great big learning disability.

School is hard for Brooke. She is academically and developmentally delayed. She was slower than her peers in learning to talk. She had difficulty learning to read. We still haven't mastered two-place long division. Fractions elicit blank stares. Even attempting much work on her grade level is a major event. Every teacher Brooke has had has been loving, cooperative, and helpful. It's not their fault Brooke is a slow learner. Her father and I work with her every night of her life just to help keep her afloat.

The Teacher's Perspective

Many mainstream educators argue that they lack the time, training, and inclination to teach handicapped students. They see it as modified baby-sitting at the expense of the rest of the class, and often feel that slow, sometimes *very* slow learners will hold back the rest of the class. In many cases, they see the presence of severely handicapped or emotionally disturbed children as a distraction at best, a major disruption at worst, impinging on the rights of the other children to a calm and safe environment.

As a former teacher, I can sympathize with teachers' typical anxieties. I prided myself in having a well-organized, structured, efficient learning environment. I also enjoyed being creative with my class, and taught the love of language and reading as life skills. I was proud that my classes were disciplined but fun, that my students scored well on standardized tests, and that parents often requested that their children be placed in my classes. I was into lots of hugs, kisses, and warm fuzzies for my students.

So how would I have reacted to having a severely handicapped child in my class? I would have to answer that

with a firm "it depends." If the child was physically able to maintain himself or herself in my room, was cooperative, and, most important, able to behave so as not to distract or threaten the safety of my other students, then great. Send that child in. I would not mind modifying, or using a totally different curriculum for the child. On the other hand, if the student's behavior negatively affected or harmed the other children, I would have a problem; that, I firmly believe, is where that person's rights end. It would be time to have another Admission, Review, or Dismissal meeting and either modify the situation or change it totally.

The Principal's Perspective

As a principal, my philosophy was the same. I was responsible for the total learning situation for our campus. Because of that, it would not have been fair to come out for or against inclusion. I was for all children having every opportunity to succeed to the best of his or her ability in a positive, supportive environment.

These decisions must be made on an individual basis. No school district should say, "We are going to full inclusion; we are getting rid of our resource rooms." Phooey! No one learning situation is perfect for *all* children. Recommendations on inclusion or anything else should be made for individual children by everyone involved in their education.

I believe parents' views should be strongly and compassionately considered. Some parents of severely or multiply handicapped children do not want their child removed from the security of the resource classroom. They feel their child is physically safe with more people who have been trained to work with his or her disabilities. Regardless of the philosophy of the district, the campus, or the special education department, those parents' wishes should be honored. Not listening to parents has been a major factor in public education's bad rap.

Of course, other parents are equally adamant that their handicapped children be placed in a regular classroom,

with support as needed. Common reasons are the desire to expose their children to good behavior and higher academic standards. Still other parents point out that the world is not segregated. They feel their children will make greater strides if they are in the mainstream. But then what?

Again, if it is possible to honor the parents' wishes and write an Individualized Education Program to make the situation work, go for it. Be reasonable with it. Write in behavioral as well as academic objectives. Allow for classroom modifications. Try from the outset to set the child up for success and a happy day. Don't expect more from a child than that child can possibly give.

I'd also try my best to provide the child with a cooperative classroom teacher who is open-minded and really wants to try to make the situation work. Teachers need to *want* the child in their room. I would never consider putting a child into a classroom in which I did not think he or she stood a reasonable chance of success.

We all want our child to be one of the rest of the kids, to have a happy, successful life.

Brooke's Challenge

For the last three years, my daughter Brooke has received assistance with math and language. Her resource teacher has become a surrogate mother to her. She sincerely loves Brooke, and Brooke returns her love. Every child with a learning disability should have a teacher as fine, efficient, and caring as Helen Nelson. And still Brooke struggles.

Next school year Brooke will be entering intermediate school. We will attempt to place her in the regular classroom and attempt content mastery. Do you know how I feel as her mother? Scared to death. What if she can't do it? What if changing classes and having so many teachers is more than she can handle? She may be 12, but maturationally she is behind. What if she can't keep up with her assignments? What if in her anxiety to bring home her math, she completely forgets her language arts and science?

What if the teachers and principal don't take good care of Brooke? What if no one looks out for my little girl? In elementary school her classroom teachers and Mrs. Nelson worked together to keep her on track and somewhat organized. Now, we won't be there as her safety net, even though we have worked hard to make her independent. She knows she is as responsible for herself, her work, and her conduct as any other student. Behavior is not a problem for Brooke. Learning is.

Reality

As a former principal, I believe teacher attitudes and perceptions are critical to successful inclusion for any child, regardless of how minor the handicap. Some teachers will welcome a handicapped child with open arms; many others will pitch a screaming fit, especially if the child placed in their classroom is emotionally

disturbed or has a behavior disorder. Selling inclusion to this group will be a formidable task.

Many teachers feel overwhelmed just keeping up with their daily routine and their regular children, let alone teaching a handicapped child. They do not feel educationally, emotionally, or, sometimes, philosophically prepared to handle handicapped children in their classrooms. Even the strongest of inclusion advocates believe in providing training and support for regular education teachers. But reality intrudes. Where will the money come from? Where's the available time? Most local school districts are strapped for both. Few special education departments or district instructional specialists have the staff or expertise to provide the training classroom teachers so desperately need.

When Brooke goes off to her new school next year, I, like all the other inclusion parents, will worry, bite my fingernails, and pray a whole lot. Her father and I want Brooke to succeed so much. We'd give anything to make learning easier for her. I understand how the parents of more severely handicapped children feel. They want their children to be normal. We all want our child to be one of the rest of

the kids, to experience all the joys of childhood, to have a happy, successful life. In a perfect world we wouldn't have these worries. But we don't live in a perfect world.

Which brings us back to the concept of inclusion. Is it good, or is it bad? It's both. Under the best of circumstances, it can be very, very good. With too little funding, training, or development, it can be a disaster. Like anything else, it is what we make it. One secret is in selecting the right children to use it. And that decision ultimately comes down to the child's Admission, Review, or Dismissal Committee.

Every committee must think, What if this child were my child? Think about the child's tomorrows. Think about what we do now that will affect those tomorrows. We can't afford to make mistakes.

Author's note: Since this article was written, Brooke successfully completed the 6th grade, returning to the resource classroom for math only. She is happily enjoying the 7th grade and passing all her subjects—so far! She has Content Mastery assistance when needed, which is often. I am now a professor and seek daily to teach preservice teachers the importance of opening their hearts as well as their minds in their classrooms.

Courtside

W(h)ither Full Inclusion?

Perry A. Zirkel

PERRY A. ZIRKEL is University Professor of Education and Law at Lehigh University, Bethlehem, Pa.

DURING THE 1991-92 school year, Ryan K., a student with Attention Deficit Hyperactivity Disorder (ADHD) and Tourette's Syndrome, was 15 years old. Identified years earlier as a special education student, he received assistance in a resource room while he attended "mainstream" classes at Ballou Junior High School, which is located in Puyallup, Washington.

In January 1992 Ryan's behavioral problems began to escalate dramatically. He frequently disrupted class by taunting other students with name-calling and profanity, insulting teachers with vulgar comments, directing sexually explicit remarks at female students, refusing to follow directions, and kicking classroom furniture.

He also engaged in several violent confrontations. For example, on January 27 he received a one-day suspension for punching a fellow student in the face. On February 10 he received a second suspension after pushing another student's head into a door. Finally, on March 12, after he assaulted a staff member, he was removed from school, pursuant to a temporary emergency expulsion order.[1] Ryan's par-

ents acquiesced to the school officials' insistence that it was no longer safe for Ryan to remain at Ballou.

Immediately thereafter, the school's multidisciplinary team convened. Although Ryan's doctors had attributed the boy's behavior to his disability, the team reached the opposite conclusion. After discussing available alternatives, they further concluded that the goals and objectives in his individualized education program (IEP) could be met satisfactorily at an off-campus, self-contained program called STARS, for "Students Temporarily Away from the Regular School."

On March 17 school officials notified Ryan's parents of the recommendation that Ryan be placed in the STARS program on an interim basis while the IEP team developed a plan to safely reintegrate him into the mainstream setting.

Although Ryan's parents initially agreed with the school's proposed change of placement, they had second thoughts. On March 27 they requested a due process hearing, formally refusing to put him in the STARS program until a new IEP had been drafted. The other members of the IEP team subsequently met with Ryan's parents on more than one occasion, but the matter was not resolved. At the third meeting, on May 1, on finding that the parents' repeated requests for Ryan's teachers to be on the team had been denied once again, the parents' attorney abruptly end-

ed the meeting, declaring that further negotiations would be pointless. Further, on the next school day, which was May 4, he had Ryan return to Ballou Junior High for the rest of the school year.

During the summer of 1992 the parents and the school district participated in a 10-session due process hearing. On September 14 the impartial hearing officer issued her decision, ruling that the school district had complied with the Individuals with Disabilities Education Act (IDEA). Among her findings was that Ryan's behaviors were volitional rather than tics stemming from Tourette's Syndrome. She ordered Ryan's placement in the STARS program, pending further developments.

The parents agreed to Ryan's placement but only on an interim basis while the federal district court reviewed the case. On March 23, after hearing additional testimony and reviewing the record of the due process hearing, the court affirmed the hearing officer's order. Although finding, contrary to the hearing officer, that Ryan's behavior problems did stem from his disability, the court agreed with her bottom-line conclusion that STARS, not Ballou, was the appropriate placement.

The parents then appealed to the Ninth Circuit Court of Appeals, the same court that had issued the well-publicized "full inclusion" ruling in favor of Rachel H. and against the Sacramento Unified

School District.[2] On 13 September 1994 the Ninth Circuit issued its decision in favor of the Puyallup School District.[3] The appeals court addressed the parents' three contentions in sequence.

First, the parents had argued that the burden of proof was on the school district, regardless of who had prevailed at the lower levels, based on the Third Circuit's ruling in the other major "full inclusion" decision, *Oberti* v. *Board of Education*.[4] The Ninth Circuit disagreed with the *Oberti* court, concluding that, in the absence of a clear statutory directive, the general rule applies that the burden of proof belongs to the party challenging the administrative ruling. Thus, inasmuch as the school district had prevailed at the due process hearing, the burden was on the parents to persuade the court that the hearing officer was wrong.

Second, the parents alleged various procedural violations of the IDEA. For example, they argued that the school violated the IDEA's procedural requirements by failing to draft a new IEP before placing Ryan in STARS. The appeals court rejected this argument, concluding that the parents had agreed with the multidisciplinary team's determination that Ryan's current IEP could be met at STARS. Similarly, the court rejected their arguments centering on whether Ballou or STARS was the "then current educational placement," which the IDEA required to "stay put" during the dispute. Deferring to the factual findings of the trial court, the Ninth Circuit pointed out that the parents had consented to his placement in the STARS program. Thus STARS was Ryan's stay-put placement when the parents invoked the IDEA's formal dispute resolution process. "That Ryan's parents later withdrew their consent [when they pursued administrative remedies]," the court concluded, "doesn't change this reality."

Finally, and most important, the court considered the parents' argument that Ryan's placement in regular classes at Ballou, with the specialized interventions of the special education resource room teacher, was the least restrictive environment if the school would also provide a personal classroom aide to assist him. Applying the four factors that it identified in its *Rachel H.* decision, the Ninth Circuit concluded that STARS was the least restrictive environment for Ryan.

The first factor to be considered is the academic benefits of placement in a mainstream setting with appropriate supplementary aids and services. Citing an actual decline in Ryan's achievement test scores during the 1991-92 school year, the court concluded that, at the time of his escalating behavior problems, Ryan was no longer receiving any academic benefits from his Ballou placement. Similarly citing the "maximum support" he received from the resource room teacher and the behavior intervention specialist and the dramatic level that his behavioral problems reached, the court concluded, "nor is it likely . . . that a personal aide would have made a meaningful difference."

Similarly, the court gave short shrift to the second factor, the nonacademic benefits of a mainstream placement. In addition to the lack of evidence of effective role modeling, the court pointed to the findings of Ryan's doctors that he was "socially isolated at Ballou, had few friends, and suffered a great deal of stress from the teasing he was subjected to by other students."

The third factor, the effects of the student on the teacher and the other students, was, in the court's words, "overwhelmingly negative." His behavior had become dangerous to other students and disruptive to the teaching/learning process. Moreover, reflecting an intersecting legal development, the court pointed out that Ryan's sexually explicit remarks to female students posed the possibility that school officials could incur liability for "failing to remedy peer sexual harassment that exposes female students to a hostile educational environment."

The fourth factor, the comparative cost, was deemed irrelevant in this case. The cost of hiring a classroom aide for Ryan was, in the court's view, immaterial in light of the finding that an aide would not have notably improved his ability to benefit from the mainstream placement.

Weighing the four factors together, the court concluded that "STARS was Ryan's least restrictive environment." In what was effectively a postscript, the court characterized the case as "a poignant reminder that everyone's interests are better served when parents and school officials resolve their differences through cooperation and compromise rather than litigation." Adding that, "when combat lines are firmly drawn, the child's interests are often damaged in the ensuing struggle," the court recognized litigation as "simply too slow and too costly to deal adequately with the rapidly changing needs of children" and remarked that it "tends to poison relationships, destroying channels for constructive dialogue."

In support of this anticlimactic lesson, the court pointed out that Ryan had spent two years in a self-contained program originally intended to serve as a short-term interim placement, that the fees for the school district's attorney alone were over $100,000, and that "the lawyers would have better served their clients — and the interests of society — had they concentrated their efforts on being healers and negotiators rather than warriors."

THE APPEALS court was primarily pointing its finger at one of the parent's attorneys for his "hardball tactics" in breaking off the negotiations at the May 1 meeting. In any event, blaming — like running to — lawyers is the American pastime. The problem here is that the dispute resolution system under the IDEA promotes adversariness and litigation.[5]

The related but more particular lesson of this case is that the recent trend toward "full inclusion"[6] has its limits. At this point, the concept represents a pedagogical philosophy, not a legal requirement. The standard in the IDEA, and in Section 504 of the Rehabilitation Act, is "least restrictive environment," a slippery phrase.

Although recent prior court decisions, such as *Rachel H.*, have shown that this slippery slope steeply favors placements — with appropriate supplementary aides and services — in the regular classroom for the major portion of the school day,[7] this decision demonstrates that, depending on the relevant facts of the case, such placements are not always the least restrictive environment. It was not a coincidence that the leading prior cases arose in the early grades and had to do with disabilities that were not so egregiously disruptive. What is more surprising is how dramatically the same Ninth Circuit moved from a relatively rigorous to a rather cursory application of the relevant factors.

Whether the full inclusion interpretation of least restrictive environment is swept away by or weathers the storms of controversy will largely depend on the attitudes of politicians, parents, and professionals, as well as the individual needs of each student with disabilities. To the extent that we allocate a greater amount and proportion of resources to classrooms rather than to courtrooms, practicing the art of compromise rather than confrontation, the better off Rachel H., Ryan K., and we all will be. In any event, demonstrating the ad hoc rather than the absolute or permanent nature of least restrictive environment, Ryan K. is currently attending his neighborhood high school, assigned to a combination of resource room and regular classrooms.[8]

1. Although not the focus of this case, the applicable boundaries for such discipline under the IDEA were established in *Honig* v. *Doe*, 484 U.S. 305 (1988). See Perry A. Zirkel, "Disciplining Handicapped Students: Jack and John Went up the Hill," *Phi Delta Kappan*, June 1988, pp. 771-72.

2. *Sacramento Unified Sch. Dist.* v. *Rachel H.*, 14 F.3d 1398 (9th Cir. 1994), *cert. denied*, 62 U.S.L.W. 3825 (1994).

3. *Clyde K.* v. *Puyallup Sch. Dist.*, 21 IDELR 664 (9th Cir. 1994). I obtained supplementary information via telephone interviews in late October 1994 with Charles Williams, co-counsel for the parents, and Joni Kerr, attorney for the school district.

4. 995 F.2d 1204 (3d Cir. 1993). Subsequently, the Ninth Circuit had not found it necessary to determine the burden of proof in *Rachel H.*

5. See, for example, Perry A. Zirkel, "Over-Due Process Revisions for the Individuals with Disabilities Education Act," *Montana Law Review*, Summer 1994, pp. 403-14.

6. See, for example, Lynn Schnaiberg, "E.D. Report Documents 'Full Inclusion' Trend," *Education Week*, 19 October 1994, p. 17.

7. See Perry A. Zirkel, "A Least Restrictive Environment Checklist," *The Special Educator*, 14 December 1994, pp. 134-35.

8. Ryan stayed in the STARS program until April 1994, when the parties finally agreed, on an interim basis, to an IEP that enabled Ryan to make a transition to three regular education classes at his new neighborhood junior high school. In the summer of 1994 they agreed to an IEP for a combination resource room and regular program at the high school for 1994-95.

Ability Grouping: Geared for the Gifted

The anti-tracking movement has given ability grouping a bad name. The two are not the same.

Ellen D. Fiedler, Richard E. Lange, and Susan Winebrenner
From *Roeper Review*

Ellen D. Fiedler is Associate Professor, Gifted/ Talented Masters Degree Program, Northeastern Illinois University, Chicago. Richard E. Lange is Director of Gifted Education, Staff Development, and Assessment, Prospect Heights Public Schools, and Adjunct Faculty Member, College of Education, National-Louis University, Evanston, both in Illinois. Susan Winebrenner is an independent consultant in staff development.

IN the 1990s, the anti-tracking movement has suddenly become anti*ability grouping*, side effects ranging from the Regular Education Initiative for students with learning handicaps to attempts to eliminate programs for highly able or gifted students. The concern is about negative effects of locking certain students into unchallenging classes and locking them out of educational situations that stretch their minds. But, all of the relevant research and its ramifications have not been considered.

There are six common myths about appropriate educational programs for all students, including the gifted:

Myth 1:
Tracking and ability grouping are the same.
Reality:

Tracking separates students into class-size groups using their perceived ability or prior achievement. It results in students being assigned full-time to instructional groups based on a variety of criteria, including presumed ability derived from achievement test scores and teacher observations of classroom performance.

This often means a high-ability group for Teacher A, a middle-ability group for Teacher B, and a low-ability group for Teacher C. Once students are in a track, there is little movement between tracks during a school year or from one school year to another. Consistent placement in the low track leads students to disenfranchisement in a class system where there are clear differences between the "haves" and "have-nots."

Ability grouping is re-grouping students to provide curriculum aimed at a common instructional level. Elementary teachers create more homogeneous reading or math groups while teaching heterogeneous groups for most other subjects. Secondary students may be assigned to high-ability groups in areas of their strengths and to average- or low-ability groups in other subjects. Ability grouping does not imply permanently locking students out of settings that are appropriately challenging; it means placing them with others with similar learning needs for whatever length of time works best.

Myth 2:
Ability grouping is elitist.
Reality:

Most gifted educators work to develop an understanding of giftedness in the context of individual differences rather than superiority—consistent with newly emerging approaches

From *The Education Digest*, January 1994, pp. 52-55. Condensed from *Roeper Review*, 16 (September 1993), pp. 4-7.

that consider cognitive and affective development as equally important.

Keeping one or two highly gifted students in a classroom of mixed abilities may create snobbery. Scattering gifted students through all classrooms may lead them to feel far superior to classmates and promote arrogance. Unless gifted students can be challenged by intellectual peers, the possibilities that they will develop an elitist attitude might increase.

However, when gifted students are grouped together for instruction, studying with intellectual peers may actually lower self-esteem somewhat. There is nothing so humbling as discovering other students in the group equally capable or more knowledgeable. If one goal of education is to help all students develop a realistic appraisal of their own ability, students need to measure themselves with appropriate yardsticks. Comparisons are more likely to be accurate when made with others of similar abilities.

Interestingly, educators have no qualms about identifying outstanding athletes and providing specialized programs for them. If this is not considered elitist, why should intellectual giftedness be given short shrift?

Myth 3:
Ability grouping inevitably discriminates against racial and ethnic minorities.
Reality:

Gifted educators have made great progress in refining identification methods. Widespread efforts are being made to overcome inequities of over-reliance on standardized test scores and assumptions that too often have been made about students who, although gifted, may not fit the stereotype of high achievers with positive attitudes toward school.

The direction is toward approaches that include studying student behaviors for indicators of gifted potential, with attention on training teachers to do this. Also, behavioral descriptors are used to identify other underserved populations. Preschool and kindergarten children, creative thinkers, nonproductive gifted students, and gifted students with learning disabilities and other handicaps are being screened more accurately.

Eliminating ability grouping because of inequitable identification is throwing out the baby with the bath water. Furthermore, singling out racial and ethnic minorities as the only disenfranchised group is misleading. The intent of gifted programs has not been to exclude certain populations. But identification procedures needed revision, and improved methodologies are already being implemented.

Myth 4:
Gifted students will make it on their own; grouping them by ability does not improve their learning or achievement.
Reality:

Studies confirm what gifted educators have known for years: Gifted students benefit cognitively and affectively from working with other gifted students.

Some studies indicate no increase in achievement test scores for high-ability students grouped together, but they omit gifted students. Robert Slavin's research that recommended heterogeneous grouping for all ability groups systematically omitted data from students in the top 5 percent. Such omissions can lead to dangerous overgeneralizations by interpreters.

Also consider ceiling effects: Grade-level achievement tests fail to reveal growth for students who already perform in the top percentile ranks because they have reached the ceiling of the test—the highest scores attainable for that age group. Only with instruments designed for older students can actual achievement gains be determined for students in the extreme upper range.

Another critical issue involves the goals of the gifted program and whether its purposes are actually focused on increasing academic achievement. What gifted students learn should be measured by far more comprehensive criteria than increased achievement test scores. Equally important are the development of socialization and leadership skills, experience with complex concepts and challenging learning, and opportunities to pursue topics in great depth. If such a program is more concerned with helping gifted students work together to grapple with global concerns that are complex and substan-

tive, increases in achievement test scores in specific subject areas are not appropriate for measuring success.

Myth 5:
Heterogeneously grouped cooperative learning is most effective for serving all students, including the gifted.
Reality:

The students who may learn the least in a given class are the gifted. So much of what they are asked to learn they may have already mastered. Teachers may then be tempted to use them as classroom helpers or to teach others, robbing the gifted of consistent opportunities to learn through real struggle. This can have a negative impact on them in many ways, including lowered self-esteem. Without regular encounters with challenging material, the gifted fail to learn how to learn and have problems developing study skills for future academic pursuits.

Cooperative learning is designed to be used with either homogeneous or heterogeneous groups. It seems reasonable to allow teachers the flexibility to determine which lessons lend themselves to heterogeneous cooperative learning groups and which to homogeneous cooperative learning groups and make professional decisions to place students accordingly.

Myth 6:
Having gifted students in all classrooms provides positive role models and will automatically improve the classroom climate.
Reality:

The notion that gifted students in low-ability classrooms will automatically benefit students performing at lower levels rests on questionable assumptions: that the performance discrepancies will be perceived as alterable by the less capable students; that gifted students are consistently highly-motivated high achievers who will inspire others to similar accomplishments; and that gifted students placed in low-ability or heterogeneous classrooms will continue to perform at their peak even when they lack regular opportunities to interact with intellectual peers who can stimulate their thinking. Research indicates that students model their behavior on that of others who are of similar ability and are coping well in school.

Furthermore, heterogeneous grouping may have negative side-effects on both the gifted and others. Gifted students who are a minority of one or who have only one or two classmates whose ability level approaches their own feel either odd or arrogant. If all the other students watch from the sidelines while the smart one provides all the answers,

their perceptions of themselves as competent, capable learners suffer.

Equality in education does not require that all students have exactly the same experiences. Rather, education in a democracy promises that everyone will have an equal opportunity to actualize their potential, to learn as much as they can.

Education in a free society should not be a choice between equity and excellence. Providing for formerly disenfranchised groups need not take away appropriate programs from any

other group. As the research clearly indicates, gifted students benefit from working together. Therefore, ability grouping for the gifted must continue. While the educational community moves toward heterogeneity for students who benefit more from working in mixed ability groups, it should not deny gifted students the right to educational arrangements that maximize their learning. The goal of an appropriate education must be to create optimal learning experiences for all.

Meeting the Needs of Your High-Ability Students

Strategies every teacher can use

SUSAN WINEBRENNER

Do you feel you could be doing more to help your gifted and talented students achieve their potential? The four strategies described here will help you engage your most advanced students and develop the abilities of every child.

1. FIND HIDDEN ABILITIES
Student Scenario: Elizabeth

Sixth grader Elizabeth had difficulty reading and writing because of a learning disability, and didn't appear to be gifted. But when I introduced a unit on map skills, Elizabeth approached me after class and said, "You know, Mrs. Winebrenner, I know a lot about maps."

"You do? How did that happen?" I asked.

"I don't know. I just love maps."

"What do you like to do with this love of maps?"

"Well, when my family goes on a vacation, I plan our trip on the map."

"No kidding! Where did you go last year?"

"Yellowstone National Park."

"And how did you get there?"

Elizabeth proceeded to do something I'm not sure I could do—she told me how she had navigated her family to Yellowstone: highway by highway, county by county, state by state. I was amazed.

"Pretty impressive," I said. "I bet the prospect of doing a unit on map skills is not very appealing to you."

"I've thought about that."

"I'll tell you what. I'll give you the end-of-unit test

From *Instructor*, September 1994, pp. 60-65. Adapted from *Teaching Gifted Kids in the Regular Classroom: Strategies and Techniques Every Teacher Can Use to Meet the Academic Need of the Gifted and Talented* by Susan Winebrenner. © 1992 by Free Spirit Publishing. To order the book, call 800-735-7323.

tomorrow, and if you pass it with an A, you'll be able to spend your social studies time on a different activity of your choice." Elizabeth was thrilled.

Next, I offered the same deal to everyone in the class. This is something I've learned to do routinely, so that every student has the opportunity to shine.

Sixteen of my twenty-seven students volunteered to take the pretest. The pretesters knew beforehand that if they did not earn an A, their tests would not count. Two passed with A's—Elizabeth was one of them.

While the class honed their map skills, Elizabeth worked independently, creating a papier-mâché relief map of an imaginary country. Because her learning disability prevented her from writing well, I encouraged her to simply flag the population centers, the natural resources, the manufacturing centers, and so on. When she'd finished her project, she gave an interesting talk about her country that fascinated the class.

Did other students ask to do a project like Elizabeth's? Yes! And I let everyone do one as a culminating activity for the map unit, while Elizabeth acted as a consultant. Imagine the boost to Elizabeth's self-esteem when her classmates turned to her for advice.

CUSTOM-MADE LEARNING

What does Elizabeth's story tell us? It's up to teachers to determine what competencies certain students have, and give them full credit for what they already know. Then we need to decide how to modify the curriculum so that these students will learn something new. Dr. Joseph S. Renzulli of The National Research Center on the Gifted and Talented in Storrs, Connecticut, calls this process "curriculum compacting." Dr. Renzulli, author of *Schools for Talent*

Development: A Practical Plan for Total School Improvement, and Linda H. Smith developed the form that follows. Use it to record all the modifications you make for your students.

2. APPOINT RESIDENT EXPERTS
Student Scenario: Joey

Joey, a student in my fifth-grade class, was exceptional in every subject area, but his actual classroom performance left a lot to be desired. He spent most of his time daydreaming, and he seldom completed his homework, yet he always aced the tests. Joey behaved rudely during class discussions, often remarking under his breath to amuse other students.

When Joey's class was about to begin a Civil War unit, I gave him and other students whom I felt could tackle the text on their own a chance to do an independent project on the Civil War during social studies.

I dubbed them "resident experts" and told them they would be responsible for presenting a report on their topic to the class. I gave them each a list of project ideas, but they were free to choose a topic of their own. I also assured all my students that they could do an independent project at the end of the unit.

I asked each resident expert to sign an independent study contract that included the major Civil War concepts I expected them to know, activities related to these ideas, and a timetable of all class quizzes and discussions to assess their progress. (Resident experts take the quizzes and/or participate in discussions along with the other students. Those who do not earn a B or higher, or who display problematic behavior, must rejoin the class until the next quiz. If they achieve a B or higher on the next quiz, they may return to their project. If they don't, they can finish their project when the rest of the class gets school time to work on independent projects.)

You can modify these contracts to include detailed expectations about the quality of the projects you would like students to produce. A contract I designed especially for Joey is shown below.

Unlike the independent study method I used with Elizabeth, the resident-expert strategy is not based on the results of a pretest given to all students willing to give it a try. Instead, teachers use their own judgment, selecting students they feel are capable of developing an in-depth talk, performance, or display of their investigation.

THE COMPACTOR		
Joseph Renzulli & Linda H. Smith		
Student's Name: _____		
Areas of Strength	Methods used to document student's mastery of a skill, competency, chapter, concept, or unit	Activities student will be engaged in as an alternative to the regular class activities

EVALUATION CONTRACT
Civil War Project

For a grade of "B," use information gathered from other sources. Choose from the ideas below, or design your own with my approval:

1. Research the different types of trains and locomotives that would have been used during the Civil War era. Draw them to scale.
2. Discover the details about the lives of two famous generals, one Union and one Confederate. Comment on at least two similarities you find.
3. Learn several Civil War songs from both sides. Teach one song from each side to the class. Lead the class in a discussion of similarities and differences in the songs.

For a grade of "A," create a unique product that requires high levels of thinking. Choose from the ideas below, or design your own with my approval:

1. Draw the trains of the Civil War era on routes between the major manufacturing centers and four famous battlefields: two in the North and two in the South. Be prepared to discuss how the proximity of the battlefields to the manufacturing centers may have affected the outcome of the war.
2. Create an interview with a famous Civil War general. Include some information that was probably unknown to the general public at the time of the Civil War. Prepare a live interview where you and a friend impersonate the general and the interviewer. Come in appropriate costume.
3. Discover the role that music has played to create and maintain patriotic feelings during wartime. Illustrate your presentation with musical excerpts.

Use this space to describe your project:

#1

I am contracting for a grade of: A

Student's signature: Joey

3. PROVIDE A VENUE TO SHOWCASE TALENTS
Student Scenario: Alvin

Alvin was passionate about reading and writing poetry, and he had the talent to match it. But he was reluctant to share his poetry with me or his peers, and kept his work at home. In school, Alvin preferred to work alone, wary of group activities. I needed to showcase Alvin's poetic talent in a way that would make him feel more comfortable with his peers.

One Monday, I announced that Friday would be the first of many Great Friday Afternoon Events and explained how the events would work (see chart, **on next page**). **I asked Alvin if he would like to be captain of the poetry team.** "I guess so," he replied, nervously.

Within a couple of days, Alvin seemed at ease with the other team members, and the poem the team recited had lots of Alvin-like language and images. The Great Friday Afternoon Events became an effective way to have Alvin and other high-ability students work productively in heterogeneous groups, and gave all students a chance to showcase their talents.

WHO'S GIFTED?
CHARACTERISTICS TO LOOK FOR

Whom teachers consider gifted is changing as we use new tools to measure children's talents and consider a broader range of "gifts," from visual intelligence to affective abilities. (For more about evolving definitions of **giftedness, see next page.**) Nevertheless, the partial list of indicators below, which is organized into three different categories, will help you recognize the high-ability students in your classroom. Gifted students may exhibit many but not all of these qualities.

General
- Has an advanced vocabulary
- Possesses an outstanding memory
- Is curious about many things; asks lots of questions
- Has many interests and hobbies
- Is intense; gets totally absorbed in activities and thoughts
- Operates on higher levels of thinking than his or her age peers
- Perceives subtle cause-and-effect relationships
- Catches on quickly, then resists doing work, or works in a sloppy, careless manner
- Is sensitive to beauty and other people's feelings and emotions
- Possesses an advanced sense of justice
- Sees connections between apparently unconnected ideas and activities
- May prefer to work alone; resists cooperative learning
- May be street-smart while not doing well on school tasks

Creative Thinking
- Displays original ideas
- Is fluent in idea generation and development
- Is able to elaborate on ideas
- Values nonconformity in appearance, thought, etc.

Perfectionism
- Believes he is valued for what he can do rather than who he is
- May cry easily in frustration that her work at school can never be perfect
- Procrastinates to the point that work never even gets started
- Asks for lots of help and reassurance from the teacher

New Ways to Think About Giftedness

Carolyn Callahan, a researcher and teacher at the University of Virginia's Curry School of Education and president-elect of the National Association for Gifted Children, talks with Instructor's Senior Associate Editor Wendy Murray about giftedness and what teachers can do to encourage the special abilities of every child.

How has our society's conception of giftedness changed over the years?

In the past, the traditional gifted child was one who possessed exceptional reading and writing skills—a giftedness that everyone could see. This usually meant children who scored well on standardized tests, which was problematic because the tests don't accommodate children's different learning styles. New definitions of intelligence have stretched our definition of giftedness and talent. Now we know we must consider many ways of assessing how children perform, interact with their learning, and problem-solve, beyond just reading and writing, to find out who's gifted.

How can teachers unveil their students' talents?

We need to give children the opportunity to show their strengths in a variety of ways. Can students fix a toy pump? Tell a story dramatically? Create a song? Construct a model of a mathematical principle? We have to combine tests with portfolios, observations, and other performance-based assessments.

What is the most important thing a teacher can do to meet the needs of gifted students?

Differentiate the curriculum! For example, say you're planning a unit on community. Think to yourself, I have some chidren who need to learn what a community is; I have others who already know. What activities will challenge each group? While one group might explore the community of their family or the local community, the other can compare world communities.

What other strategies should teachers use?

Teach in an interdisciplinary manner, weaving math, literature, science, social studies, and so on, into whatever it is your students are exploring. Ask yourself, How can I structure this unit so that children think about and solve real-world problems?

Here's my favorite example of bringing the real world into school: One kindergarten teacher I know was teaching her class about germs—viruses and bacteria—in all sorts of interesting ways. Still, there was one child who went ten steps further. He wanted to figure out how to stop the spread of flu at school. He designed an experiment where he put up paper cups at the drinking fountain for a certain number of days and noted student absences from school during that period. Then he took the cups away, tracked the absences, and put the data on a graph that showed drinking cups cut down on the number of students absent due to colds and flus. Then he went to the PTA and got it to pay for cups! Never underestimate the learner!

THE GREAT FRIDAY AFTERNOON EVENT

Students, in four teams, present a program to class.
Teams stay intact for four weeks.
Each week, each team has a different task.
Tasks rotate until each team has done each task.

	POETRY	DECLAMATION	PLAY	NEWSCAST
	Students read or recite a poem of their choice or creation.	(Readers' Theater) Students present a dramatic reading.	Students present Readers' Theater or dramatic play.	Students broadcast a 5–10 minute radio or video show.
WEEK 1	A	B	C	D
WEEK 2	B	C	D	A
WEEK 3	C	D	A	B
WEEK 4	D	A	B	C

Teachers Who Are Good with the Gifted

A team of researchers at the National Research Center on the Gifted and Talented and I recently examined ten U.S. schools that had a reputation for meeting the needs of capable students in regular classrooms. Among other things, we wanted to find out what these successful teachers were doing right. Here's what we found.

In addition to using methods such as curriculum compacting, independent study projects, and hetero-geneous-group activities requiring critical thinking, teachers who were most successful with high-ability students possessed these attributes:

● **Trust.** At a northeastern school, we observed a teacher as she showed a group of capable math students how to use protractors to measure degrees in angles. Afterward, she said, "Go through the first four pages of the next chapter. Along the way, *you* decide which problems you need to do to help you understand measurement of triangles."

● **Spontaneity.** In an urban school, a student approached her teacher, a Shakespearean play in hand.

"I know Shakespeare is not very popular at this time, but I really feel he will be appreciated again soon," she said, before asking whether she could share the play with another student. The teacher didn't miss a beat; she told her it was a great idea. This same teacher once put aside what she had planned, to take advantage of a snowstorm. When we walked into her room, students were busy determining the volume of snow that had to be plowed from the school's driveway.

● **Rapport.** One of the most memorable things we observed was watching teachers who clearly enjoy swapping ideas with colleagues. At one school, four teachers of the same grade level meet for dinner at a Mexican restaurant once a week. They refer to these evenings as Ol' Mexico night, and during these dinners they plan their unique "Enrichment Wednesdays," during which they teach special classes designed to address their students' interests. ■

—*Karen L. Westberg, Ph.D., The National Center on the Gifted and Talented, Storrs, Connecticut.*

4. REDIRECT LEADERSHIP QUALITIES

Student Scenario: Lucy

Twelve-year-old Lucy had unusual leadership abilities. She could think on her feet, persuade others to see her point of view, and inspire classmates to work as a team—when she applied herself. But too often she took the shortcut, dominating discussions and bossing other students around. She needed more structured opportunities to hone her gift for persuasion.

With Lucy in mind, I built an array of group activities into the curriculum, setting aside every Wednesday afternoon to engage in these events. Groups of kids held mock trials (we even invited in a lawyer, who ended up being a great mentor for the children),

worked together to simulate running a business, and planned a city of the future, to mention just a few.

By posing open-ended questions to groups of students (such as: If you were sent to live on a planet, what five people would you need to have along to survive?) every student gets to stretch intellectually, and students like Lucy positively blossom. Lucy relished the intellectual challenge, and her peers enjoyed the chance to make her back up her opinions with facts.

The self-assessment involved in these activities is also valuable for children of every ability who lack confidence. Students assess their own ideas and those of the group, and come to see that these evaluations are as valid as yours.

What We Can Learn from Multicultural Education Research

Educators will be more successful if they understand five variables that matter in working with a diverse student population.

Gloria Ladson-Billings

Gloria Ladson-Billings is an Assistant Professor at the University of Wisconsin–Madison, Department of Curriculum and Instruction, 225 N. Mills St., Madison, WI 53706.

Many findings from multicultural education research can be applied in the everyday world of teachers and administrators. This observation holds regardless of whether the educators work with many students of color or with only a few.

The research shows that five areas matter a great deal in the education of a multicultural population: teachers' beliefs about students, curriculum content and materials, instructional approaches, educational settings, and teacher education. One other area—whether the race and ethnicity of teachers affects student learning—remains unclear.

Beliefs About Students Matter

To begin to see how teacher beliefs affect student achievement, imagine two

> How teachers think about education and students makes a pronounced difference in student performance and achievement.

new teachers. Don Wilson and Margie Stewart are starting their first year of teaching.

Don Wilson. After his first weeks of teaching in an urban school, Wilson is exhausted and uncertain about whether he chose the right profession. His class of 28 fourth graders are African Americans and Latinos. Wilson knows

that they have not had many advantages, so he doesn't push them too hard. He wants his students to have fun learning. He worries, though, because many of them don't seem to be having fun or learning. Many are one or more achievement levels below national averages, and some attend school sporadically, fail to complete homework assignments, and seem unmotivated in the classroom. Although Wilson has sent several notes home expressing concern, parents have not responded. Wilson doubts that he makes any difference in the lives of his students.

Margie Stewart. The first weeks of teaching in a suburban school have been exhausting for Stewart, too, but she is enjoying herself. Of Stewart's 28 third graders, 23 are white, upper-middle-class children. Three of the remaining five are African American, and two are Mexican American (one speaks limited English). In general, the students test at or above grade level on standardized tests, but the students of color lag behind the others. Stewart is also concerned about José. Because José's English is limited, Stewart must explain everything to him four or five times, and she can seldom work with him one-on-one. She fears that he is a special needs student. Perhaps she will ask the school psychologist to test José.

The research literature suggests that how teachers like Wilson and Stewart think about education and students makes a pronounced difference in student performance and achievement (Apple 1990, Cooper 1979). Winfield (1986) found that teachers expect more from white students than from African-American students, and they expect more from middle-class students than from working- and lower-class students. Teachers often perceive African-American students from working- or lower-class backgrounds as incapable of high-quality academic work. Both Wilson and Stewart are entertaining such thoughts. They are not attributing their problems with students of color to ineffective teaching approaches.

Sometimes, unrecognized or outright racism causes teachers to hold negative beliefs about students of color. A dramatic example from a first-year teacher's journal entry:

> I hate [African-American students'] ethnic attitude and their lingo. I hate to categorize it but ... I am more comfortable with black students who act white (Birrell 1993).

Such negative attitudes toward students of color lower expectations for achievement, which lowers achievement (King and Ladson-Billings 1990, Lipman 1993).

Content and Materials Matter

Teachers who are sincerely committed to multicultural education cannot be satisfied with superficial celebrations of heroes and holidays. This approach to content trivializes multicultural education and conveys the idea that diversity issues come into play only during celebratory moments with foods, fun, and festivals.

In the multicultural festival model, teachers, students, and parents typi-cally spend lots of time and energy preparing for an all-school activity. Students may do background research about a culture, prepare maps, and help create indigenous costumes. Parents may help to prepare various ethnic foods. On the day of the festival, members of the school community go from class to class, visiting the various cultures, sampling the foods, and enjoying dances, songs, and arts and crafts. At the end of the day, everyone agrees that the annual event has been a great success. Then teachers and students go back to their real work.

In the transformative model, on the other hand, multicultural education is not a separate, isolated, once-a-year activity. Instead, the regular curriculum includes a range of cultural perspectives, as in the following two classroom scenarios.

In a primary classroom, the teacher reads several versions of the Cinderella story. One is the familiar European tale by the Brothers Grimm, but other versions are Chinese, Egyptian, and Zimbabwean. The teacher helps students compare the different versions. Similarities include story structure, plot development, moral and ethical dilemmas, and the use of magic. Differences include standards of beauty, settings, use of language, and specific characters. The students absorb the importance of understanding cultural differences and similarities.

In an intermediate history class, students study the African slave trade, but not solely from the perspective of the European traders. They also read a range of primary documents, like the slave narrative called *The Interesting Life of Olaudah Equiano* (it compares slavery in Africa with slavery in the Americas). In addition, the teacher introduces information about the European feudal system. The students compare the lives of enslaved people in Africa, the Americas, and medieval Europe. Finally, they generate analytical questions, such as, What is the relationship between slavery and racism? How could a nation striving for equality and justice permit slavery? Why did some people in Africa participate in the slave trade? And how does the textbook's treatment of slavery compare to primary source material?

The teacher in this class plans to do similar in-depth study when the class studies the displacement of Native Americans, the Spanish mission system, European immigration of the 1890s, and Japanese internment. Although the transformative approach requires redesigning the curriculum, searching for additional materials, and limiting the number of topics taught, the teacher thinks the outcome is worth the effort. Students learn more content and develop a real ability to ask and answer critical questions.

The materials used in classrooms have important effects, too. As Banks' comprehensive literature review (1993a) points out, children are aware of their race and ethnicity at an early age. "If realistic images of ethnic and racial groups are included in teaching materials in a consistent, natural, and integrated fashion," Banks (1993b) concludes, all children "can be helped to develop more positive racial attitudes." Similar results are reported on gender issues (Scott and Schau 1985).

If classrooms use materials that do not portray diverse groups realistically, students are likely to develop, maintain, and strengthen the stereotypes and distortions in the traditional curriculum. Text analysis (a common form of multicultural research) indicates that textbook images and representations exclude, distort, and marginalize women, people of color, and people from lower socioeconomic echelons. A growing proportion of textbooks do include diversity, but their images and representations tend to be superficial and incorrect (Swartz 1992).

Instructional Approaches Matter

Changes to make curriculum content more equitable must be accompanied by changes that make pedagogy even-handed. To ensure "equitable pedagogy," Banks says, teachers must modify instruction to "facilitate academic achievement among students from diverse groups."

For some teachers, providing more equitable pedagogy may be as simple as using more cooperative learning strategies.

To some teachers, simultaneously dealing with the flood of new materials and modifying instructional approaches seems like an overwhelming task. These teachers think that it is all they can do to teach the new material in old ways. In other classrooms, however, teachers have asked themselves, what one move can I make to ensure that all students have opportunities for success?

For some teachers, providing more equitable pedagogy may be as simple as using more cooperative learning strategies in class. After all, cooperative learning was first developed as a way to create more equitable classroom environments (Cohen and Benton 1988, Slavin 1987).

For other teachers, equitable pedagogy will demand that they use the language and understandings that children bring to school to bridge the gap between what students know and what they need to learn (Au and Jordan 1981, Erickson and Mohatt 1982, Jordan 1985, Vogt et al. 1987). In addition, the total school context must come to accept whatever students have learned and experienced as legitimate knowledge (Irvine 1990, Ladson-Billings 1992, in press). Teachers can further these ends if they spend time in their students' community and apply in the classroom what they learned in students' homes.

Teachers may also profit by learning their students' language. A teacher who knows how to ask and answer basic questions in a second language can often make the classroom a welcoming and psychologically safe environment for speakers of that language. If a teacher becomes sufficiently fluent to teach academic content in English and a student's home language, the teacher tacitly promotes bilingualism and biliteracy (Hornberger 1988).

Educational Settings Matter

Forty years ago, the Supreme Court handed down a landmark decision, *Brown v. Board of Education,* which declared separate schools inherently unequal. Yet now, after years of hard-fought battles to desegregate the nation's schools, most students of color still attend segregated schools (Orfield 1989). Even when students go to desegregated schools, they are resegregated within the school via tracking and ability grouping (Oakes 1985).

For students of color, perhaps more devastating is the lack of access to high-quality education (Kozol 1991). Clearly, as a society, our care and concern for student learning is differentiated along racial, class, and ethnic lines.

To grasp the impact of these inequities, imagine that our new teachers, Wilson and Stewart, were to participate in a school exchange program. Wilson's students would visit Stewart's class. Then Stewart's class would visit Wilson's. What will each setting informally teach the children?

When Wilson's students arrive at Stewart's school, they are struck by its physical beauty and space. Well-kept grounds have ample playground equipment. Inside the school, the halls gleam, and a lively buzz emanates from the various classrooms. Each brightly lighted classroom has at least one computer. The school library has several computers, CD-ROM, laser disks, and an extensive library of videotapes. The school has many special rooms: a gymnasium, a multi-purpose room, vocal and instrumental music rooms, an art room, and a room for enrichment activities. In each of the rooms is a teacher who regularly works with Stewart's students, freeing her for 45 minutes each day. She uses the time to plan, read, hold parent conferences, and do research.

When Stewart's class visits Wilson's school, they enter an old structure built in the 1920s. Its concrete yard is littered with broken glass, graffiti cover the walls, and the only piece of playground equipment is a netless basketball hoop. Inside the building, the dark halls are eerily silent, since room doors are closed and locked from the inside. There is a room where books are stored, but they are not catalogued because there is no librarian. The entire school shares one VCR and monitor. One of the two 16 mm film projectors is broken. A few filmstrips hide in various closets. The one room that does have computers, listening centers, and film loop machines is the Chapter One lab.

Here, students with literacy and mathematics deficits receive small-group instruction and skill practice for 30 to 45 minutes each day. In a corner of the multipurpose room, 12 gifted students in grades 3 to 5 meet one morning a week with a visiting gifted and talented education teacher. Classroom teachers are responsible for all other instruction, so they rarely have time to plan or confer.

What Stewart's students learn from their encounter is that Wilson's students are underprivileged, and perhaps, undeserving. The students will probably come to see inequities as normal and to equate African Americans and Latinos with poverty.

Meanwhile, Wilson's students learn that material advantages go with being white. Since Stewart's and Wilson's students are all about the same age with similar interests and abilities, the major difference that Wilson's students can see is skin color.

The few students of color in Stewart's class learn that they are very lucky. Under other circumstances, they could be at Wilson's school. Even though they may do poorly in a predominantly white school, they regard being there as a privilege.

Teacher Education Matters

If Wilson's and Stewart's students derive naive conceptions from their exchange visits, the teachers themselves also have trouble making sense of the differences. Neither teacher learned much about cultural variation during preservice preparation (Zeichner 1992, Ladson-Billings, in press).

Wilson took an ESL course, but Stewart did not, and she has José. Both Wilson and Stewart took a required human relations course, but although it presented some historical information about Native Americans, African Americans, Asian Americans, and Latinos, it was silent on European-American cultures and the role of culture in learning and achievement. Both Wilson and Stewart believed, further, that the course was designed to make them feel guilty. As a result, they silently resisted the material, and its impact on their eventual practice was sharply reduced.

As inservice teachers, Wilson and Stewart have had some opportunities to learn about multicultural education, but these have taken the form of fleeting, one-time workshops. The experiences had little or no follow-up, and no one attempted to ensure that teachers applied the new information (Sleeter 1992).

Fortunately, one of Wilson's colleagues is a graduate student who has taken several courses dealing with race, class, and gender issues. He has learned from the experiences of two teachers like Vivian Paley (1979) and Jane Elliot (Peters 1987). Wilson's colleague is impressive because he seems to manage his classes easily, and his students achieve well on tasks that go beyond worksheets and drills. Wilson plans to enroll in a multicultural education course next semester. He hopes to learn something that will help him succeed with students of color.

While Wilson is motivated to change, Stewart is not. Because she is successful with most of her students, she thinks her lack of success with students of color stems from their deficiencies. Stewart's colleagues and the parents of her white students reinforce this belief.

Does the Race and Ethnicity of Teachers Matter?

Whether teachers' race and ethnicity affect student achievement remains an open question. We know that most teachers in the United States are white and that the next largest group, African Americans, comprise less than 5 percent of all public school teachers. We also know that the majority of students in the 25 largest public school systems are students of color.

No empirical evidence, however, indicates that students of color learn better when taught by teachers of color. The most recent review of the literature on African-American teachers (King 1993) finds no connection between teacher race/ethnicity and student achievement. The positive aspect of this finding is that it makes all teachers accountable for teaching all students.

If current demographic trends hold, our student population will become more diverse, while the teaching population remains predominantly white. The implication is that if teachers are to be effective, they will need to be prepared to teach children who are not white. If we are lucky, more teachers will follow Wilson's lead. They will know that the multicultural education research literature can help them understand themselves, their culture, and the cultures of others, and be more successful with all students.

References

Apple, M. (1990). *Ideology and Curriculum*. 2nd ed. New York: Routledge.

Au, K., and C. Jordan. (1981). "Teaching Reading to Hawaiian Children: Finding a Culturally Appropriate Solution." In *Culture and the Bilingual Classroom: Studies in Classroom Ethnography*, edited by H. Trueba, G. Guthrie, and K. Au. Rowley, Mass.: Newbury House.

Banks, J. A. (1993a). "Multicultural Education for Young Children: Racial and Ethnic Attitudes and Their Modification." In *Handbook of Research on the Education of Young Children*, edited by B. Spodek. New York: Macmillan.

Banks, J. A. (1993b). "Multicultural Education: Development, Dimensions, and Challenges." *Phi Delta Kappan* 75: 22-28.

Birrell, J. (February 1993). "A Case Study of the Influence of Ethnic Encapsulation on a Beginning Secondary School Teacher." Paper presented at the annual meeting of the Association of Teacher Educators, Los Angeles.

Cohen, E., and J. Benton. (Fall 1988). "Making Groupwork Work." *American Educator*: 10-17, 45-46.

Cooper, H. (1979). "Pygmalion Grows Up: A Model for Teacher Expectation Communication and Performance Influence." *Review of Educational Research* 49: 389-410.

Erickson, F., and G. Mohatt. (1982). "Cultural Organization and Participation Structures in Two Classrooms of Indian Students." In *Doing the Ethnography of Schooling*, edited by G. Spindler. New York: Holt, Rinehart and Winston.

Hornberger, N. (1988). "Iman Chay?: Quechua Children in Peru's Schools." In *School and Society: Teaching Content Through Culture*, edited by H. Trueba and C. Delgado-Gaitan. New York: Praeger.

Irvine, J. (1990). *Black Students and School Failure*. Westport, Conn.: Greenwood Press.

Jordan, C. (1985). "Translating Culture: From Ethnographic Information to Educational Program." *Anthropology and Education Quarterly* 16: 105-123.

King, J., and G. Ladson-Billings. (1990). "The Teacher Education Challenge in Elite University Settings: Developing Critical Perspectives for Teaching in Democratic and Multicultural Societies." *European Journal of Intercultural Education* 1: 15-20.

King, S. H. (1993). "The Limited Presence of African-American Teachers." *Review of Educational Research* 63: 115-149.

Kozol, J. (1991). *Savage Inequalities*. New York: Crown Publishers.

Ladson-Billings, G. (1992). "Reading Between the Lines And Pages: A Culturally Relevant Approach to Literacy Teaching." *Theory into Practice* 31: 312-320.

Ladson-Billings, G. (In press). "Multicultural Teacher Education: Research, Practice, and Policy." In *Handbook of Research in Multicultural Education*, edited by J. A. Banks and C. M. Banks. New York: Macmillan.

Lipman, P. (1993). "Teacher Ideology Toward African-American Students in Restructured Schools." Doctoral diss., University of Wisconsin-Madison.

Oakes, J. (1985). *Keeping Track: How Schools Structure Inequality*. New Haven, Conn.: Yale University Press.

Orfield, G. (1989). *Status of School Deseg-regation 1968- 1986.* (Report of Urban Boards of Education and the National School Desegregation Research Project). Washington, D.C.: National School Boards Association.

Paley, V. (1979). *White Teacher.* Cambridge, Mass.: Harvard University Press.

Peters, W. (1987). *A Class Divided: Then and Now.* New Haven, Conn.: Yale University Press.

Scott, K. P., and C. G. Schau. (1985). "Sex Equity and Sex Bias Instructional Mate-rials." In *Handbook for Achieving Sex Equity Through Education,* edited by S. S. Klein. Baltimore: Johns Hopkins University Press.

Slavin, R. (November 1987). "Cooperative Learning and the Cooperative School." *Educational Leadership* 45, 3: 7-13.

Sleeter, C., and C. Grant. (1988). "An Analysis of Multicultural Education in the United States." *Harvard Educational Review* 57: 421-444.

Swartz, E. (1992). "Multicultural Educa-tion: from a Compensatory to a Scholarly Foundation." In *Research and Multicultural Education: From the Margins to the Mainstream,* edited by C. Grant. London: Falmer Press.

Vogt, L., C. Jordan, and R. Tharp. (1987). "Explaining School Failure, Producing School Success: Two Cases." *Anthro-pology and Education Quarterly* 18: 276-286.

Winfield, L. (1986). "Teacher Beliefs Toward At-Risk Students in Inner-Urban Schools." *The Urban Review* 18: 253-267.

Zeichner, K. (1992). *Educating Teachers for Cultural Diversity.* East Lansing, Mich.: National Center for Research on Teacher Learning.

"All Kids Can Learn": Masking Diversity in Middle School

CAROL ANN TOMLINSON

Carol Ann Tomlinson is an assistant professor of educational studies, Curry School of Education, The University of Virginia, Charlottesville.

In the Northwest Territories of Canada, the aboriginal peoples build giant figures roughly in the shape of a human by piling stone upon stone. The primitive-looking shapes, called *inukshuks*, serve a dual purpose. In the heavy snows and ice fogs, they serve as guides to people trying to find their way home. In better weather, they serve as decoys to fool bears and other prey. The inukshuk is placed near a location where a bear may go for food or water. Seeing the looming, human-like form, the bear believes it to be a man and turns away from the inukshuk toward a blind where a hunter hides, waiting for the bear to be frightened and to retreat in the hunter's direction. It is an interesting paradox that inukshuks serve as both guideposts and traps.

We build educational inukshuks too. We construct them to offer us guidance in making critical decisions. Sometimes, however, we become the bear, and the inukshuk becomes our trap. One example of guide-turned-snare is our current buzz-phrase, "All kids can learn." It is particularly pervasive in educational settings, such as middle schools, which promote "educational equity."

Like all clichés, this one reflects some reality. It is invoked as a way of telling teachers not to give up on students whom we might assume to be struggling, at risk, or remedial. The cliché is problematic, however, because rather than pointing middle school educators homeward, it lures us into the dangerous assumption that what benefits one child educationally is bound to benefit others in the same way. At a time in our educational history when middle school learners are more diverse, both culturally and academically, than at any other time in the past, it validates educational practices that mask the diversity. The real problem has never been so much that middle school teachers believe that some kids *can't* learn. The real problem is that, as middle school educators, we've exhibited for decades a belief that all kids can learn the same things, in the same way, over the same time span.

Cases in Point: A Tale of Two Learners

Early in my career as a middle school teacher, I taught Golden and Jonathan during third period English. Eyes downcast and hand over his mouth, Golden whispered to me on the first day of school that he could not read. He was correct. At fifteen, he was a seventh grader who did not know the alphabet well and took a long time to grasp simple meanings, even when ideas were delivered orally or in pictures. He was a gentle boy, beautiful and persistent, and resilient in a quiet sort of way. I spent much of my time that year looking inside myself and learning from Golden how to teach reading to a fifteen-year-old and still have him feel fifteen. I was not trained to teach Golden, and I don't know that I did brilliantly with him academically, but I tried, and we cared for each other, and we both made progress in our learning.

Later that year, I discovered Jonathan. He'd been in the class all along—at the table with Golden, actually. It wasn't that I had been unaware of his physical presence. I knew he was there, interacted with him in the sort of way that's invited by the presence of 150 young bodies passing through the door each day. It was April when I discovered Jonathan's mental presence. It happened one day when Jonathan responded with a sigh to my query about whether anyone could explain what a symbol is in literature. He waited until it was clear no one else was going to answer. Then, sighing not with impatience so much as with resignation, Jonathan explained, "A symbol is a concrete representation of an abstract entity." He was right too. And it's as good a definition as I've ever read or heard. I wasn't trained to teach Jonathan either—or even to notice him. He made good grades. He was no trouble. I was grateful. In April, I discovered that my magical seventh-grade English class was as poorly suited to Jonathan as to Golden.

I concluded that year of teaching with my own two symbols clearly in mental view. They were concrete representations of the abstract reality that middle school stu-

From *The Clearing House*, January/February 1995, pp. 163-166. © 1995 by the Helen Dwight Reid Educational Foundation. Reprinted by permission of Heldref Publications, 1319 Eighteenth Street, NW, Washington, DC 20036-1802.

dents differ immensely and that my previous notion of developing a single lesson plan that would reach them all was unrealistic. I always believed that both Jonathan and Golden could learn. Like most other teachers, I could not have continued to show up at school without that conviction. I would be a better teacher for Golden and Jonathan if I had the opportunity to teach them today, not because I have been a recent convert to believing "all kids can learn," but because I have spent a sizable portion of my career learning to respond to the reality that students have *different* learning needs.

Neglecting Golden

I have also spent a great deal of my career as a middle school educator being dismayed at our inability at this level to embrace Jonathan and Golden simultaneously and in ways appropriate for their individual needs. For at least a decade, students like Golden have drifted through junior high or middle school compensatory classes where they were taught to read in the same standard ways that proved unsuccessful during the previous year. As teachers, we weren't hostile to these students; we just accepted them as "limited." We understood little about how school must look to them. We certainly underestimated the impact of poverty and culturally different homes—or maybe we just didn't look outside the schoolhouse door often or long enough. Nature and nurture challenged Golden's learning, and a traditional, single lens view of students and schooling aggravated the problem.

Golden is not only a symbol for me as a teacher. He is a three-dimensional case for the urgency of addressing the needs of at-risk learners in American middle schools. Powerful cases for increasing attention to at-risk learners have been made by many sensitive and convincing writers (e.g., Kozol 1991; Freedman 1990; McLaren 1989). It is clear that schooling as it is typically structured still falls short of addressing the immense needs of many of America's young who are like Golden.

Points to Ponder on Golden's Behalf

Of course there is a need for educational improvement for at-risk learners, for "educational equity." The guidepost of equity becomes a trap, however, if we assume that equity for Golden means that all middle school students must learn the same things, in the same way, over the same time span. We need to think carefully about at least three propositions in Golden's behalf as we plan for his years in middle school:

Golden's educational challenges are real. Some students like Golden contend with specific physiological impairments in the intake or the processing of information. Many like him come to middle school lacking food or affection or security. Many come to middle school with communication patterns or views of time or ways of relating to peers and adults that differ in meaningful ways from those of the majority of educators who will

work with them. The list of challenges can be long and varied. Each item on the list can affect learning in powerful ways.

Ignoring Golden's differences is damaging. Traditional school practices seldom serve Golden well. Many educators make compelling arguments for movement away from traditional schooling for *all* children. The strengths of those arguments notwithstanding, many children have at least survived traditional schooling with functional skills in place. That has not often been the case for students like Golden. It may be that the ways in which we have most poorly served previous Goldens have stemmed from our assumptions that the culture that reflects the worldview of many children accurately reflects Golden's as well, and that the ways in which many children successfully take in and process information will yield success for Golden also. Those educators who have been triumphant with students like Golden have deeply understood the students' differences and have made powerful adjustments in their responses to those differences.

Most educational generalists are currently unprepared to respond appropriately to Golden's needs. Why can't Golden read at fifteen? How do we motivate him to try again for one more year? What if his peers reject schooling as well? What can we do to make his effort worth the risk? Why doesn't he follow directions that seem clear enough to other students? How do we contend with our curriculum when Golden can't read the basic vocabulary list in the rear of the text? What do we do if his anger causes him to boil over in the classroom? Why doesn't he look us in the eye when we talk with him? Why does he seem unconcerned at turning in assignments late? How do we keep him hopeful when we also operate in the tradition of keeping a gradebook? Our understandings of educational handicaps are shallow. Our understandings of cultural diversity are sparse. Our definitions of instruction are narrow. Our sense of fairness hangs on norms. We know how to teach groups better than individuals. In middle school, regular classroom teachers may (or may not) be prepared to work on Golden's self-concept. We currently know of little to do for his sense of self-efficacy.

Rejecting Jonathan

At least in our rhetoric, middle school education in recent years has embraced Golden. The irony is that, in doing so, we seem to feel it necessary to reject Jonathan.

I happened upon a colleague in an airport recently. She is an enthusiastic educator and an effective staff developer for teachers of middle school students. As we walked down a corridor, she said she had been puzzling about the tensions that exist between middle school and gifted education and that she had discussed it with a nationally known middle school educator and leader. "I think I understand now," she said. "In middle school, we are for the underdog. Gifted kids are so far ahead.

What we are interested in is making sure the other kids catch up. Gifted kids are just so privileged. They don't need us like at-risk learners do."

Another nationally respected educator with deep middle school roots said to me recently, "Gifted education just isn't interesting. It's not important."

In a recent issue of the *Washington Post* (Denny 1994), a staff editorialist called for the abolition of special programs for gifted learners, advocating that all students be exposed to "the same challenging curriculum."

Middle school students mirror our adult rejection of high-end achievement. In our schools, notes the president of the Educational Testing Service (Anrig 1992), we apply derogatory names to our brightest students. These days, they are *nerds* or *dweebs*. Students like Jonathan understand the messages. In a recent study, such adolescents indicated that they wanted to do well in school but not exceptionally well. To do too well is to be rejected by the "in crowd." To be perceived as "a brain" is to be banished.

Points to Ponder on Jonathan's Behalf

It is not acceptable for middle school educators to deny or dismiss students like Jonathan, any more than it is to turn our interest away from Golden. There are at least three propositions that middle school educators need to consider in determining a course of action for Jonathan and his tribe:

High-end talent is a reality. Some kids learn faster than others and with a greater depth of understanding. At twelve, Greg understood the physics of black holes and of time. Ray could discuss the imagery and symbolism of Poe. Theresa was more than conversant with calculus. These youngsters once again give evidence that while it is true that all kids can learn, they learn in different ways, at different rates, with differing facility and insight. Advanced talent is not everything, but it is real. It is an important human resource.

It is okay to have talent as a learner. It is not elitist to be an advanced learner any more than it is elitist to be taller than average or a better-than-average soccer player. It is the way some kids are. Middle schools need to be in the talent development business, eager to latch onto and develop talent whenever it surfaces—and to help it surface when it does not do so on its own. If middle school does not celebrate and extend the talent of high-end learners, it is at risk as an institution. No organization grows that does not accept the challenge of those of its members who push against its ceilings and cause them to rise.

Highly talented kids need teacher assistance in developing their potential. In part, the learning capacity of students like Golden is compromised by parents, neighborhoods, teachers, or adults in society at large who fail to become mentors and advocates. Jonathan may or may not have been failed by home or neighborhood or society at large.

There are Jonathans in the most impoverished settings. Even a Jonathan from a supportive home, however, needs teachers. It is the teacher who is the keeper of knowledge, a gadfly for persistence, an encourager when the risk seems too great. Twelve-year-old Kathleen understood when she wrote a poem to her teacher:

> Push me. See how far I go.
> Work me 'til I drop. Then pick me up.
> Open a door, and make me run to it before it closes.
> Teach me so that I might learn.
> But then show me the Tunnel of Experience and let me
>   walk through it alone.
> And when, near the end, I look back, and I see you in
>   the opening with another,
> I shall smile.

Points to Ponder for Both Golden and Jonathan

If middle schools are going to be good places for Jonathan and Golden, and if middle school educators are going to move past slogans to action, we must consider several propositions:

There is no time for a linear approach to student needs. We have a pattern in American schools of focusing on high-end learners to the exclusion of troubled learners for a period of time—then turning our rhetoric and practice in the direction of troubled learners, to the exclusion of advanced learners. All the while, we lament that attention to learning needs of those groups robs the "average" student. In middle school, we have been prone to embrace the at-risk learner and to alternate between irritation at, and denial of, the high-end learner. So long as schools take a sort of one-at-a-time approach to its clients, schools will fail many more children than necessary. A given child has only one passage through the middle school years. If it is not Jonathan's "turn" to be attended to and valued, or Golden's, or any other student's, we have a moral obligation to inform his parents that he is not currently "in vogue" and therefore not a priority for talent development.

"The same challenging curriculum" is a myth. The science curriculum that intrigued Greg would have stupefied most other preadolescents. Golden could not have understood *oral* renditions of Poe in seventh grade, let alone *print* versions. It seems virtually impossible that he could have understood the tapestry of symbols in Poe's works that year. Do we make "the same challenging math curriculum" one that Golden can master? One that more typical seventh graders can master? Or do we accept the calculus curriculum that challenged eleven-year-old Theresa and attempt to challenge *all* seventh graders with it? Embracing diversity is our challenge in education, not pretending singularity.

One-size-fits-all instruction is not an acceptable option. Jonathan and Golden differ significantly from each other and from many of their age-mates. If we advocate instructional arrangements in which middle schoolers are treated largely or wholly alike, we will, in the long run, be as unfair to Golden as we were in the days when we overlooked him or when we subscribed to the notion of remediation. We will also continue to assume, by comparison with the norm, that Jonathan is fine and producing high quality work. Middle school students will become discouraged or disenchanted. Middle school teachers will become weary and weighted with the guilt they carry when it is evident that they are losing students. In the end, we will, as we have in the past, revert to separate classes within a very few years.

We need to teach teachers to adjust for student differences, not trick them into doing so. Much of the argument for heterogeneity is that teachers lower expectations for students in homogeneous remedial classes. If teachers receive all students en masse, the logic goes, they automatically raise expectations for struggling learners because of the greater mass of comparatively more advanced learners. There are problems with that theory. First, such a plan will as likely *lower* expectations for students like Jonathan who were in advanced classes as it will raise them for students who were in slower-paced classes. Second, it perpetuates the idea that a single level of expectations will somehow be appropriate for all students. It skirts the more significant reality that in an increasingly diverse classroom, teachers will need to identify individual needs and respond in various ways to those needs. It is also insulting in its implications that (*a*) teachers cannot learn to adjust expectations proactively, and, therefore, (*b*) students must be moved about in ways that cause reactive teacher response.

Differentiated classrooms are a rarity. If we intend to recognize and address individual differences and needs within heterogeneous settings, we have a long way to go. Most teachers are like I was—stymied by the presence of Golden and unaware that Jonathan had any real problems. National studies indicate that little appropriate differentiation of instruction for academically diverse learners currently takes place in classrooms (Tomlinson et al., 1994; Archambault, Westberg, Brown, Hallmark, Zhang, and Emmons 1993; McIntosh, Vaughn, Schumm, Haager, and Lee 1993; Tomlinson In press). The paucity of differentiation has a multitude of causes: our own long histories as students in one-size-fits-all classrooms, our own experiences as practitioners of one-size-fits-all instruction, our general lack of preservice and inservice preparation in teaching academically diverse learners, teach-to-the-test mandates that cause us to drag all learners through the same content, over-dependence on text-driven curricula, discouraging student-teacher ratios,

choppy time blocks that invite dealing with students as a herd, and lack of administrative and policy support for the long-term change process that is required to alter habitual teaching behaviors. There is little guidance in the middle school literature that exhorts us to differentiate instruction or that offers us concrete guidance in how to do so.

Truth or Trap

Golden and Jonathan are real. Most middle school teachers have taught them. Odds are, most of us have taught them less well than they deserve because we taught them as though they were alike. We have to move beyond intoning the belief that both can learn. We know that. It's why we became teachers—why we stayed on. Rather, we need to confront the harder truths: that middle schoolers differ greatly in the ways they learn and in their learning needs; that middle school educators have to be serious students of learner differences and have to respond effectively to those differences; that single-size instruction is going to be a misfit for many middle schoolers; and that we cannot be truly effective so long as we pretend that Golden and Jonathan can flourish in a learning environment that offers them both "the same challenging curriculum."

The inukshuk is out there, stone piled upon stone. Jonathan and Golden need middle school educators who will make it a guidepost rather than a trap.

REFERENCES

Anrig, G. 1992. What we can learn from the Second International Assessment of Educational Progress. Prepared remarks for press conference. Washington, D.C. (5 February).

Archambault, F., K. Westberg, S. Brown, B. Hallmark, W. Zhang, and C. Emmons. 1993. Classroom practices used with gifted third and fourth grade students. *Journal for the Education of the Gifted* 16(2): 103–19.

Denny, S. 1994. How Fairfax fails the "normal" student. *Washington Post* (14 August): C-10.

Freedman, S. 1990. *Small victories: The real world of a teacher, her students and their high school.* New York: Harper and Row.

Kozol, J. 1991. *Savage inequalities: Children in America's schools.* New York: Crown.

McIntosh, R., S. Vaughn, J. Shumm, D. Haager, and O. Lee. 1993. Observations of students with learning disabilities in general education classrooms. *Exceptional Children* 60(3): 249–61.

McLaren, P. 1989. *Life in schools: An introduction to critical pedagogy in the foundations of education.* New York: Longman.

Tomlinson, C. In press. Deciding to differentiate instruction in middle school: One school's journey.

Tomlinson, C., E. Tomchin, C. Callahan, C. Adams, P. Pizzat-Tinnin, C. Cunningham, B. Moore, L. Lutz, C. Roberson, N. Eiss, M. Landrum, S. Hunsaker, and M. Imbeau. 1994. Practices of preservice teachers related to gifted and other academically diverse learners. *Gifted Child Quarterly* 38(3): 106–14.

Student Diversity: Implications for Classroom Teachers

Daniel D. Drake

Daniel D. Drake is an associate professor in the Department of Educational Leadership at Cleveland State University and a former principal and community superintendent.

America's call for excellence and equity cannot be answered except in a diverse and culturally rich environment. The changing demographics for students in public schools, especially within metropolitan areas, demand a revised approach to the education process. Harold Hodgkinson's (1986) examination of population trends projected between 1980 and 2000 notes that "these population dynamics can already be seen in many schools. Fully 27 percent of all school students in the United States represent minorities, and each of the nation's 24 largest city school systems has a minority majority."

All classrooms today are becoming more reflective of America's multiracial and multiethnic society. According to Hodgkinson,

The schools of tomorrow may have to be more sensitive to minority differences. Many blacks resent being lumped into a single racial grouping without regard for social and economic status. Similarly, Puerto Ricans do not necessarily enjoy being labeled with Cubans and Mexicans as Hispanics. It is clear that Asian immigrants from Japan, Korea, and Vietnam are very different. All of these groups and subgroups want to retain as much of their culture as possible, which is one reason California provides instructions for connecting a gas stove in English, Spanish, Chinese, Korean, and Vietnamese.

Teachers today work with students from every continent. Such a mixture of students is sure to generate challenges related to diversity. These challenges should be addressed in a way that promotes cooperation and understanding between people of all cultures.

In an article entitled "Multicultural Education: For Freedom's Sake," James Banks (1991/1992) states that "education within a pluralistic society should affirm and help students understand their home and community cultures. However, it should also help free them from their cultural boundaries." Although parents, administrators, and other school support staff serve an important role in helping students to have a meaningful school experience, it is the teachers who are the key to successful learning and character formation. All across America, teachers create the climate for learning within the classroom. Therefore, their awareness and knowledge of the cultural differences of students in the nation's classrooms are critical factors in the educative process. In this article, I will provide suggestions for what teachers can do on Monday morning to enhance the benefits of student diversity.

Creating the most favorable climate for learning is a challenge to teachers because of the numerous variables that are involved, such as interpersonal relationships, the attitudes of students, and the development of the teachers' own abilities to interact with people from different cultures. However, teachers should settle for nothing less than a classroom environment that nurtures and values cultural differences. Valuing language differences, ethnic hairstyles, styles of dress, and attitudes toward authority are all links to addressing cultural diversity in a supportive and understanding manner. An example of attitudes toward authority would be female teachers giving directives to male students who are from a cultural orientation where women are not regarded as authority figures. The challenge is how these teachers can show sensitivity to the students' cultural orientation while using a strategy to elicit the cooperation of the students. Teachers can achieve the goal of developing an excellent learning climate by working creatively in three areas: infusing the curriculum, making instruction

From *The Clearing House*, May/June 1993, pp. 264-266. © 1993 by the Helen Dwight Reid Educational Foundation. Reprinted by permission of Heldref Publications, 1319 Eighteenth Street, NW, Washington, DC 20036-1802.

relevant, and implementing meaningful programs. Activities and use of supplemental materials in these areas can be initiated by teachers without policies from outside the classroom.

Infusing the Curriculum

Teachers need to ensure that their curricula are flexible, bias-free, and relevant. For instance, course materials should encompass references to males, females, and people from different ethnic and cultural groups, and teachers should address the concerns and issues of these student populations. In a recent article, Asa Hilliard III (1991/1992) indicates that "the primary goal of a pluralistic curriculum process is to present a truthful and meaningful rendition of the whole human experience." In this frame of reference, teachers should ask themselves this question: Are the study materials reflective of individuals from different cultural groups engaging in similar occupations and social roles? Unless teachers examine the materials with this concern in mind, they could miss the fact that the materials may present an overall impression that promotes a stereotypical bias. Materials on Mexico, for example, may feature what appears to be a harmless illustration of a man in a sombrero and serape dozing against the stucco wall of an adobe hut. But would this be a fair image of Mexicans? What kind of a statement does such a picture make about the people of a land that is steeped in ancient history and rich culture?

J. B. Boyer (1990) and others make a valid point when they say that if the teachers' supplemental curriculum materials ignore the existence of a student's ethnic profile, the learner gets the message that people in that ethnic group have made no contribution to the development of America. Therefore, when teachers select supplemental materials, they should include some ethnic-specific magazines, music, and audiovisuals. Examples would be *Ebony* magazine, rap mu-

sic, and films with Spanish-speaking characters. Teachers can easily work these kinds of materials into any curriculum to establish the fact that they want to develop and maintain a diverse ethnic environment within the classroom.

One way that teachers can receive assistance with their effort to address diversity in the classroom is to consult with advisory committee members and parents. Ask them to discuss aspects of the curriculum that they feel are positive with respect to diversity as well as those that are negative. Teachers should carefully analyze and use the committee's recommendations. Further preparations for working with culturally and ethnically different students include reading literature on their cultural heritage and political and economic development and being familiar with the present day successes and problems of minority groups. Teachers should openly discuss these issues with their students in order to establish a better rapport with them. Such discussions should help in making the students more receptive for learning about different cultures.

Making Instruction Relevant

Teachers need to be aware of their personal attitudes toward culturally diverse students. It is necessary to have this awareness because one's attitudes will be reflected in the instructional process. In her book, Frances Kendall (1983) indicates that teachers pass their own values and attitudes on to students both intentionally and unintentionally during the teaching and learning process. One way teachers can check on their own attitudes and values is to ask themselves a series of questions: Do I respect diversity in American society? Do I accept differences in individuals? Have I ever rejected a student's answer because I did not understand her or his frame of reference? Did I assume that the answer given by a student who used slang was wrong?

Teachers need to develop a mindset that allows them to be accepting of student differences. For instance, teachers should make sure to use examples of minority persons or groups that highlight their successes or respected positions in the community. Such practices have been identified as "culturally relevant teaching." In a recent article, Gloria Ladson-Billings (1990) describes it in this way: "It is the kind of teaching that uses the students' culture to help them achieve success. The teachers work within three important dimensions: their conception of themselves and others, their knowledge, and their classrooms' social structure."

In the development of an ideal classroom, teachers need to solicit the views of students and other advisers who are sensitive to cultural differences. A helpful exercise is to have students identify information that is culturally specific. For example, a social studies class might discuss the issue of a bilingual education program to address the needs of some Hispanics. Then, within the instructional process, put that information in the context of that community of people and have the students respond to it in ways that are meaningful to that culture. The bilingual education issue would be examined by the students in class; they would identify the barriers that could cause problems for Hispanics who are unable to speak or understand English. Because all minority persons do not have the same kinds of concerns or problems, it is unrealistic for teachers to assume that it is possible to address the needs of every student with a single approach. Teachers do not have to be experts on different cultures, but they must be sensitive to the fact that cultural differences must be respected.

Teachers should also provide opportunities for critical-thinking and problem-solving activities where no answers are labeled as incorrect. This allows students to build self-confidence. To the extent possible, teachers should use open-ended statements in their evaluations or case studies that make reference to different groups of students. Teachers' questioning techniques should personally involve the students. This practice will permit the students to respond differently, reflecting their cultural diversity for their fellow students to see and understand. Whenever possible, teachers should use resource persons from the community who are representative of the ethnic make-up of the student population. Teachers should also make sure that bulletin board displays reflect the demographic mix of the community.

A positive relationship between teachers' expectations and students' academic progress will have a positive effect on learning. Research substantiates the fact that if teachers believe that a student cannot learn or improve, then that student will not make progress. This is especially significant in the case of minority students. Therefore, teachers need to guard against giving up on a student because it appears that the student is not capable of understanding. Unconsciously the teacher may be reflecting a bias that believes that "these kinds" of kids will never learn. Teachers who have this fatalistic attitude about the amount of progress minority students can make may not go that extra step to foster school success.

Implementing Meaningful Programs

Students need to see teachers as role models who accept and value diversity. Some things that can affect their perceptions are the tone of a teacher's voice when he or she responds to certain students and the eye contact that the teacher does or does not make with students. The teacher's own belief about the value of cultural differences is reflected in such verbal and nonverbal communications. Kendall (1983) indicates that teachers are indeed role models

for students, and, therefore, they should show respect and concern for all people.

Teachers need to be honest and sincere with their students. Students will sense it. This does not mean trying to become a buddy by using their vernacular and attempting to imitate their behaviors. There should always be a social distance between teachers and students. Teachers must remember that it is far better to respect students' differences than to try to become part of the group.

A concerted effort must be made to avoid segregating students by cultural groups or allowing the students to separate themselves in this manner. Such student groupings can defeat everything else that teachers do to promote a diverse classroom. Seating should be arranged so as to encourage students to interact with one another and accept one another's differences. Role playing, in situations where students can reflect their personal perceptions of a problem and use their cultural outlook to apply a solution, is a viable way to promote the understanding of differences. Such an activity will go a long way toward developing an atmosphere conducive to educating all students.

When evaluating students, teachers need to select student assessment methods that are appropriate for the diverse student population. For instance, teachers should make sure that the language of assessment instruments is free of ethnic or cultural biases, omissions, and stereotypes. Teachers should consider and employ, when possible, multiple approaches to assessing students.

Conclusion

There is no one approach that will allow teachers to meet the needs of all students. Understanding cultural differences is part of a life-long learning process. Teachers must continue to seek opportunities that will help

them to be effective. Further, they should work to become more knowledgeable about their own attitudes toward cultural differences. As professionals, teachers cannot use the excuse of being ignorant about the problems and cultures of African Americans, Asian Americans, Spanish Americans, native Americans, and other minorities. The ethnic texture of our student population is growing more diverse, and teachers must be ready to deal with the challenges that it brings. This means that teachers will need to lean on their support systems (family, administrators, community members) as they engage in proactive ventures that are directed toward developing an ideal classroom for the students and themselves.

The best learning climate will be productive for all students, not just for minority students. In these excellent classrooms, teachers can generate experiences that promote diversity, respect, and acceptance of others while at the same time providing students with the opportunities to learn about the benefits of diversity. American school systems can no longer afford to produce citizens who are unable to value a culturally diverse world and to interact effectively in it.

REFERENCES

Banks, J. A. 1991/1992. Multicultural education: For freedom's sake. *Educational Leadership* (Dec./Jan.): 32–34.

Boyer, J. B. 1990. *Curriculum materials for ethnic diversity.* Lawrence, Kan.: University of Kansas Press.

Hilliard III, Asa G. 1991/1992. Why we must pluralize the curriculum. *Educational Leadership* (Dec./Jan.): 12–14.

Hodgkinson, H. L. 1986. What's ahead for education. *Principal* (Jan.): 6–11.

Ladson-Billings, G. 1990. Culturally relevant teaching: Effective instruction for black students. *College Board Review* (155): 2025.

Kendall, F. E. 1983. *Diversity in the classroom: A multicultural approach to the education of young children.* New York: Teachers College Press, Columbia University.

Learning and Instruction

- **Information Processing/Cognitive Learning (Articles 17 and 18)**
- **Behavioristic Learning (Articles 19–21)**
- **Humanistic/Social Psychological Learning (Articles 22 and 23)**
- **Instructional Strategies (Articles 24–27)**

Learning can be broadly defined as a relatively permanent change in behavior or thinking due to experience. Learning is not a result of change due to maturation. Changes in behavior and thinking of students result from complex interactions between their individual characteristics and environmental factors. A continuing challenge in education is understanding these interactions so that learning can be enhanced. This unit focuses on approaches within educational psychology that represent different ways of viewing the learning process and related instructional strategies. Each approach to learning emphasizes a different set of personal and environmental factors that influence certain behaviors. While no one approach can fully explain learning, each is a valuable contribution to our knowledge about the process.

The discussion of each learning approach includes suggestions for specific techniques and methods of teaching to guide teachers in understanding student behavior and in making decisions about how to teach. The articles in this section reflect a recent emphasis on applied research conducted in schools and on constructivist theories. The relatively large number of articles on information processing/cognitive learning and instruction, as opposed to behaviorism, also reflects a change in emphasis. Behaviorism, however, remains important in our understanding of learning and instruction.

Researchers have recently made significant advances in understanding the way our minds work. Information processing refers to the way that the mind receives sensory information, stores it as memory, and recalls it for later use. This procedure is basic to all learning, no matter what teaching approach is taken, and we know that the method used in processing information determines to some extent how much and what we remember. The essays in the first subsection present some of the fundamental principles of information processing.

In cognitive learning, new knowledge is obtained as existing knowledge is reorganized, altered, and expanded. This process is often stimulated when we are presented with information that disagrees or is incompatible with knowledge we already possess. Cognitive learning of this sort is practiced continually by children as they learning about their world; they make discoveries by perceiving things that pique their curiosity or raise questions in their minds.

For years, behaviorism was the best-known approach to learning. Most practicing and prospective teachers are familiar with concepts such as classical conditioning, reinforcement, and punishment, and there is no question that behaviorism has made significant contributions to understanding learning. But behaviorism has also been subject to much misinterpretation, in part because it seems so simple. In fact, the effective use of behavioristic principles is complex and demanding, as debate presented in the articles in the second subsection point out.

Humanistic/social psychological learning emphasizes the affective, social, moral, and personal development of students. Humanistic learning involves acceptance of the uniqueness of each individual, stressing character, feelings, values, and self-worth. To the humanist, learning is not simply a change in behavior or thinking; learning is also the discovery of the personal meaning of information. Social psychology is the study of the nature of interpersonal relationships in social situations. In education, this approach looks at teacher-pupil relationships and group processes to derive principles of interaction that affect learning. The two articles in the third section examine self-esteem and the emerging issue of caring.

Instructional strategies are the teacher behaviors and methods of conveying information that affect learning. Teaching methods or techniques can vary greatly, depending on objectives, group size, types of students, and personality of the teacher. For example, discussion classes are generally more effective for enhancing thinking skills than are individualized sessions or lectures. For the final subsection, major instructional strategies to illustrate a variety of approaches have been selected. The first subsection article, "About Instruction: Powerful New Strategies Worth Knowing," shows how appropriate teaching techniques can be based on the findings from cognitive science. This is followed by John Savery and Thomas Duffy's article that describes a problem-based approach to teaching. Different thinking and learning styles of students are reviewed in the next article, while the final subsection article examines the growing importance of technology in the classroom.

Looking Ahead: Challenge Questions

Compare and contrast the different approaches to learning. What approach do you think is best, and why? What factors are important to your answer (e.g., objectives, types of students, setting, personality of the teacher)?

What teaching strategies could you use to promote greater student retention of material? What are good ways to attract and keep students' attention? Must a teacher be an "entertainer"? Why or why not?

How can a teacher promote positive self-esteem, values, character, and attitudes? How are they related to cognitive learning? How much emphasis should be put on cultivating character or positive student interactions? How would you create a "caring" classroom? Discuss whether or not this would interfere with achievement of cognitive learning targets. Is cooperative learning feasible in the grade level and subject in which you will teach? Why or why not?

What are learning styles, and how can teachers use them to enhance teaching effectiveness?

How can technology be used productively in the classroom? What learning theories should be used as a basis for instruction that utilizes technology?

REMEMBERING THE FORGOTTEN ART OF MEMORY

THOMAS E. SCRUGGS AND MARGO A. MASTROPIERI

Thomas E. Scruggs and Margo A. Mastropieri are professors of special education at Purdue University. Their book on memory techniques is entitled Teaching Students Ways To Remember: Strategies for Learning Mnemonically, *published in 1991 by Brookline Books, Cambridge, Massachusetts.*

IN THE fifth century B.C., the Greek poet Simonides narrowly escaped death, and in so doing provided the birth of memory strategies. Reciting a poem at a banquet, Simonides was called out of the house for a message. While he was out, the building collapsed, and the diners within were crushed beyond recognition. Asked to help identify the bodies, Simonides noted that he was able to do so by remembering an image of the diners' positions at the table. This inspiration gave birth to the *Method of Loci,* the most ancient of mnemonic techniques.

Ancient Greeks and Romans placed great value on the development of memory skills, partly because the relative lack of printed materials required individuals to commit many things to memory. Throughout the Middle Ages, complex memory strategies took on religious aspects, and sometimes became associated with individuals who dabbled in magic and the occult, such as Giordano Bruno and his secret of "Shadows."

With the development of the printing press, memory skills received less and less emphasis; nonetheless, knowledge of many of these techniques survived, such as those described in 1890 by William James in his *Principles of Psychology.* For a time in American schools, memorization and recitation of inspirational passages and quotations were considered important in developing well-trained minds. Unfortunately, the act of memorizing *per se* is not usually helpful in intellectual development; further, many of the things American schoolchildren were compelled to memorize were decontextualized and therefore of little meaning in themselves. As a result, "memorizing" began to become regarded as a pointless waste of time, as it no doubt was in many cases. Further, "progressive" educators such as John Dewey began rightly to promote the facilitation of "higher-order" thinking skills over the mindless repeti-

tion of facts and passages. With the recent renewal of interest in constructivist perspectives and the rise of technological advances in information storage and retrieval, the decline of interest in memory skills has apparently become nearly complete.

With this decline in interest in memory skills, students' memory for important school content also has declined. A recent national report documented the sad fact that American students have become deficient at recall of even the most basic information about history and literature. For example, only one out of three American seventeen-year-olds could place the Civil War within the correct half-century or correctly identify the Reformation or the Magna Carta.

In this article, we wish to provide a different perspective on memory. We define memory skills as techniques for increasing the initial learning and long-term retention of important information. We argue that good memory skills are as important now as they were in Simonides' day; that memory strategy instruction has a very impor-

> *American Students have become deficient at recall of even the most basic information about history and literature.*

tant place in schools, yet unrealized; and that good instruction in memory strategies enhances, rather than detracts from, the facilitation of "higher-order" skills such as comprehension and critical thinking. Indeed, while there are many important things to learn and do in school, and learning and retaining factual information is only one component of the entire school experience, it is our contention that a strong declarative knowledge base is an absolutely critical first step to "higher-level" skills.

We also provide brief descriptions of nine strategies for promoting strong memory skills.

W E BECAME aware of the critical importance of good memory skills during the course of our work with students with learning disabilities. Many learning-disabled students have some difficulty with semantic memory, or memory for verbally presented information. Clearly, such students face enormous challenges in courses that require vast amounts of verbal information to be "memorized," such as traditionally taught social studies and science courses. In addition, learning-disabled students usually perform poorly on tests of verbal reasoning or higher-order thinking skills. One explanation why these students with average intelligence may do so poorly on verbal reasoning tasks is that they can remember little verbal information to help them on the task. And, it has been well established that content knowledge is one of the best predictors of performance on reasoning tasks. When we trained students in powerful mnemonic strategies to facilitate memory of the core content, we noticed dramatic improvements in their ability not only to remember content information but also to participate actively in classroom discussions that required thinking actively about the subject.

The relation between knowledge and thinking can be further explained by an example. In a recent national educational performance test, one item presented outlines of four birds and asked students to identify the one that probably lives close to water. Students who make effective use of their reasoning abilities could consider the characteristics of such environments, observe the four bird outlines, and correctly conclude that the long-legged bird, physically equipped for wading, was the most likely choice. However, students who remembered important information about birds and their environments could easily recognize one of the birds as a heron and immediately answer the question. Thus, what is a higher-order thinking task to a student lacking background knowledge is a simple recall task to a student possessing the relevant information. As can be seen, the "reasoning" deck is stacked against the student who has not learned, or cannot remember, critical information.

Memory is not only helpful for facilitating thought about academic subjects. One of us remembers the great difficulties he had learning to sail, until he began to master the highly specialized vocabulary associated with sailing. When terms such as *sheet, jib, starboard,* and *boom-vang* became automatic, he began to make rapid progress in sailing. Likewise, we found that students began to make greater progress in vocational skills when they began to learn and remember the specialized vocabulary associated with such areas as rough construction and electricity. Why does verbal knowledge seem to facilitate procedural knowledge, such as sailing and construction? Since we are accustomed to thinking in language, we find it difficult to reflect and elaborate on new information until the relevant language associated with this information has been acquired and remembered. So, it can be seen that a well-established verbal knowledge base is a prerequisite for critical or reflective thinking.

Although memory and attention are not the same thing, it is true that things are not likely to be remembered if they are not attended to in the first place.

Nor can computer data bases take the place of a broad background of knowledge committed to memory. We often here the refrain, "In a few years, all of this will be unnecessary. Students will wear on their arms a computer no larger than a wristwatch but powerful enough to contain all the information known to mankind." The problem with this line of thinking is that one needs a sufficient knowledge base to know *what* to call forth from the computer, to give form to the endless ocean of information. Research has shown that students who have the most firmly established knowledge base are the ones who can most easily assimilate and apply new information.

Unfortunately, it is not only students with learning disabilities who may find themselves weak in prior knowledge. Students from less-privileged economic backgrounds may come to school not having had the same background experiences as other students. Students for whom English is a second language may have more difficulty expressing their knowledge in English. Finally, if recent national reports are considered, many "ordinary" students exhibit a surprising lack of memory for basic information in school subjects. It seems, therefore, that the argument should not be *whether* to teach memory skills, but *how* memory skills can be best taught. Some recommendations are given in the section that follows.

O UR RESEARCH and experience have shown us that there are at least nine ways that teachers can greatly improve the ability of their students to remember. We will summarize these recommendations in order of complexity. The ninth method, promoting mnemonic strategy use, is the most complicated and will require the most explanation.

1. Promote Attention

Although memory and attention are not the same thing, it is true that things are not likely to be remembered if they are not attended to in the first place. This makes attention an important prerequisite to memory.

There are several methods for improving attention. The simplest include direct appeals ("Please pay attention to what I'm about to say") and follow-up ("What did I say was the assignment for tomorrow?"), and physical proximity to students who are likely not to pay attention. Other strategies for promoting attention include intensifying instruction, with enthusiastic teaching, use of high-intensity visual aids, and providing relevant activi-

> *Teachers who are expert in certain content areas may forget how difficult it is to acquire new speech sounds to represent new concepts or facts.*

ties for students, rather than simple listening and note-taking. Teaching is more easily intensified by focusing on a smaller number of critical concepts than by covering a wide range of less important information.

Provide positive feedback for students when they exhibit good attending skills. For more persistent attending problems, teach self-recording of attending, e.g., by having an egg timer go off at random intervals and hav-

ACROSTICS AT HARVARD

SOURED, PERHAPS, by memories of the multiplication tables, college students hate the annual ritual of memorizing the geological time scale in introductory courses on the history of life. We professors insist, claiming this venerable sequence as our alphabet. The entries are cumbersome—Cambrian, Ordovician, Silurian—and refer to such arcana as Roman names for Wales and threefold divisions of strata in Germany. We use little tricks and enticements to encourage compliance. For years, I held a mnemonics contest for the best entry to replace the traditional and insipid "Campbell's ordinary soup does make Peter pale . . ." or the underground salacious versions that I would blush to record, even here. During political upheavals of the early seventies, my winner for epochs of the Tertiary (see table) read: "Proletarian efforts off many pig police. Right on!" The all-time champion reviewed a porno movie called *Cheap Meat*—with perfect rhyme and scansion and only one necessary neologism, easily interpreted, at the end of the third line. This entry proceeds in unconventional order, from latest to earliest, and lists all the eras first, then all the periods:

> *Cheap Meat* performs passably,
> Quenching the celibate's jejune thirst,
> Portraiture, presented massably,
> Drowning sorrow, oneness cursed.

The winner also provided an epilogue, for the epochs of the Cenozoic era:

> Rare pornography, purchased meekly
> O Erogeny, Paleobscene.*

When such blandishments fail, I always say, try an honest intellectual argument: If these names were arbitrary divisions in a smooth continuum of events unfolding through time, I would have some sympathy for the opposition—for then we might take the history of modern multicellular life, about 600 million years, and divide this time into even and arbitrary units easily remembered as 1-12 or A-L, at 50 million years per unit.

But the earth scorns our simplifications and becomes much more interesting in its derision. The

---

*There are two in jokes in this line: *orogeny* is standard geological jargon for mountain building; *Paleobscene* is awfully close to the epoch's actual name—Paleocene.

GEOLOGIC ERAS			
Era	Period	Epoch	Approximate number of years ago (millions of years)
Cenozoic	Quaternary	Holocene (Recent) Pleistocene	
	Tertiary	Pliocene Miocene Oligocene Eocene Paleocene	
Mesozoic	Cretaceous Jurassic Triassic		65
Paleozoic	Permian Carboniferous (Pennsylvanian and Mississippian) Devonian Silurian Ordovician Cambrian		225
Precambrian			570

The geological time scale.

history of life is not a continuum of development, but a record punctuated by brief, sometimes geologically instantaneous, episodes of mass extinction and subsequent diversification. The geological time scale maps this history, for fossils provide our chief criterion in fixing the temporal order of rocks. The divisions of the time scale are set at these major punctuations because extinctions and rapid diversifications leave such clear signatures in the fossil record. Hence, the time scale is not a devil's ploy for torturing students, but a chronicle of key moments in life's history. By memorizing those infernal names, you learn the major episodes of earthly time. I make no apologies for the central importance of such knowledge.

Excerpted with permission from Wonderful Life: The Burgess Shale and the Nature of History, *by Stephen Jay Gould (W. W. Norton & Company, 1989).*

ing students indicate whether or not they were paying attention at that moment.

William James argued, "My experience is what I agree to attend to." Promoting attending will not guarantee improvement in memory, but it is a great place to start.

2. Promote External Memory

One very simple way for students to remember things better is to learn to write them down and refer back when necessary. This is one method of "external memory," which refers to the use of any device outside the student's own mind used to enhance memory. External memory devices include writing things in notebooks, appointment books, or on cards; placing things to be remembered (e.g., books, notes, self-reminders) in prominent places where they will be noticed; and using physical prompts (e.g., a string on the finger, a watch placed on the opposite wrist), which remind students to think of or do some particular thing. One drawback to external memory is that it is not a substitute for truly remembered information, especially in test situations, in which use of such systems is usually considered cheating.

3. Increase Meaningfulness

Students remember familiar and meaningful information much more readily than non-meaningful information; and students often surprise us by what is not meaningful to them. The most usual way of increasing meaningfulness is to develop experiences with the things being learned and to relate new information in some way to things that are already known. For instance, in describing the components of levers, use see-saws, oars, rakes, and wheelbarrows as examples. Tie examples of abstractions, such as "torque," to everyday things the student already understands.

4. Use of Pictures or Imagery

Most information is more easily remembered when it is pictured. Pictures make concepts more concrete, and, therefore, more easily remembered. Pictures allow students to more easily employ their mental imagery, which also facilitates remembering. Pictures can be shown to all students simultaneously on the overhead or opaque projector. If information is only presented verbally, it is less likely to be stored in students' memories as images, and, therefore, may be more difficult for them to retrieve. If it is not possible to show pictures, describe the information clearly and concretely, and encourage students to make pictures in their minds. If they can draw their images clearly, they are more likely to remember them.

5. Minimize Interfering Information

Highlight the most important information and reduce the number of unnecessary digressions. Provide only the most highly relevant examples. Unfortunately, some textbooks present what appears to be an endless string of facts, concepts, and vocabulary for students to memorize; it has been reported that some science textbooks

Research has consistently indicated that mnemonic techniques help students perform better on comprehension tasks.

contain more vocabulary words than are found in foreign language texts! If you do rely on textbooks to cover important class information, prioritize the terminology, facts, and concepts to include those that you consider most important and provide special emphasis on this information.

6. Encourage Active Participation

Concepts are better remembered if students actively manipulate or otherwise act out instances or manifestations of these concepts. For instance, in science, students are more likely to remember about series and parallel circuits if they have actively created these circuits. In social studies, students are more likely to remember information if they assume roles in debating historical issues, such as the U.S. recognition of the Republic of Texas, or current events, such as United Nations policy in the Sudan. Students can also assume roles in historical problem solving, such as problems in pioneer bridge building.

7. Promote Active Learning

Encourage students to reason actively through new information. Promote deductive reasoning when appropriate. Ask students to draw conclusions for themselves rather than simply telling them the information. For example, rather than explaining to students why earthworms are found on the ground after a rainfall, or why the full moon rises shortly after sunset, ask questions intended to lead students to draw the correct conclusions for themselves.

8. Increase Practice and Review

Many teachers require information to be remembered for a weekly or unit test (e.g., spelling, science) but rarely monitor recall of that information after it has been tested. To promote long-term recall of previously learned information, isolate the most critical content and provide brief but regular reviews over a longer time period. Students can review this information individually, question each other with flash cards, ask questions from books, or review with the teacher as a whole class activity. Although finding even small amounts of additional time for such activities may seem unlikely, look for occasions for brief reviews before or after transitions (lunch, recess, assemblies) or while students are standing in line or doing other activities that take minimal mental energy.

9. Use Mnemonic Techniques

Mnemonics are systematic techniques designed to enhance memory, particularly memory for new vocabu-

OKAY, WHO REMEMBERS THE FIVE MAJOR DIVISIONS OF VERTEBRATES?

SCIENCE IS an area in which many students experience frustration and disappointment. There are many causes for this. Although science itself is a fascinating subject, many students may fail to become interested because they fail to learn and remember key concepts and vocabulary. Without this foundation, more advanced learning and meaningful applications are impossible. In other cases, the content may be too complex or abstract for some students to readily grasp. Many advocates of science education have stressed the importance of experiment and discovery in science learning. Nevertheless, many key concepts and vocabulary must first be learned to make later experiment and discovery meaningful.

Mnemonic techniques can be very effective in science teaching, since they help make complex content simpler, abstractions more concrete, and seemingly meaningless information more meaningful.

For example, life science, as typically taught, has much to do with the classification, organization, and description of living things. Therefore, much instruction in life science has to do with learning characteristics and taxonomies. This type of learning easily lends itself to mnemonic instruction.

Vertebrates. The study of vertebrates is a relatively easy unit in life science because students usually are familiar with many of the relevant concepts. In fact, most students are familiar with what a "backbone" is, although they may not know the meaning of the word "vertebrate." In this case, a keyword strategy is helpful in teaching this verbal label for an already-familiar concept.

"Dirt" can be used as a keyword for "vertebrate" because it sounds like the first syllable of vertebrate and can be pictured (e.g., a dirt pile). A picture then can show a backbone (or a vertebrate animal with an obvious backbone) sticking out of a pile of dirt, to help students remember this definition of vertebrate.

There are five major divisions of vertebrates: amphibians, fish, reptiles, birds, and mammals. Two of the five, fish and birds, are almost certainly familiar to students. Therefore, fish and birds can be shown in *mimetic* or representational pictures, and important concrete attributes, such as scales, fins, and feathers, can be portrayed within these mimetic pictures.

Reptiles are also familiar to many students. However, many other students may not know what reptiles are, or they may not know all the different types of reptiles, such as snakes, lizards, turtles, and crocodilians. If reptiles are as familiar to students as birds and fish, they can be presented in a mimetic picture. If they are less familiar, a keyword elaboration will be helpful. In this case, the word "tiles" could be a good keyword for reptiles, because it sounds like the second syllable for reptiles, and can be pictured. A picture depicting reptiles in some relationship to tiles, e.g., a picture of snakes, lizards, turtles, and crocodilians sitting on tiles, or with tiles for scales, or both, could be effective.

Possible keywords could be "bib" for amphibian (*amplifier* may also be good) and "camel" for mammal. "Bib" is an acceptable keyword because, although a short keyword for a long word, bib sounds very much like the accent-ed second syllable of amphibian. Camel is a particularly good keyword because a camel *is* a mammal.

Organization. Much of life science instruction involves teaching which of several types of plants or animals go together. With respect to the *vertebrates* examples, above, students may be required to "have the five types committed to memory." Once the names of these animals have become familiar, a first-letter strategy is appropriate. The first letters of the five vertebrates cannot be combined to make a "real" word, but together they do form the acronym (suggested by Roy Halleran) "FARM-B." Now, FARM-B does not convey any particular meaning to us, other than, say, an unusual name for a farm; nevertheless, with a little practice this can become a very effective mnemonic for retrieving *f*ish, *a*mphibian, *r*eptile, *m*ammal, *b*ird. To integrate this idea with the concept "vertebrate," place a picture of each animal on a pile of *dirt* (keyword for vertebrate). Also, to reinforce the keywords in the acoustically transformed animal names, show the amphibian with a *bib,* the reptile on *tiles,* and a camel for the *mammal.*

———

Excerpted from Teaching Students Ways To Remember: Strategies for Learning Mnemonically.

Types of Vertebrates = Fish, Amphibians (bib), Reptiles (tiles), Mammals (camel), Birds (FARM-B)

lary or terminology, facts, and concepts. They are most effective, and most appropriate, when used to facilitate memory of things that cannot be deduced or otherwise constructed by students. Examples include remembering the seemingly arbitrary speech sounds in new vocabulary or terminology, human conventions, or basic facts such as the number and names of continents or planets.

Teachers who are expert in certain content areas may forget how difficult it is to acquire new speech sounds to represent new concepts or facts. Mnemonics often work by impacting on retrieval of the *acoustic properties,* or sounds, of unfamiliar words. A retrieval route is constructed between the sound of the word and the underlying meaning or conceptualization. Mnemonic techniques have been studied empirically over the past two decades and have been shown to be remarkably facilitative in promoting memory objectives.

In our recent book, *Teaching Students Ways to Remember: Strategies for Learning Mnemonically* (Cambridge, MA: Brookline Books), we describe a variety of effective mnemonic techniques and provide examples of how they can be applied in classroom settings. We will provide here some examples of *keyword, pegword,* and *letter* mnemonic strategies.

Keyword strategies. Keyword strategies are employed by creating an acoustically similar proxy (the keyword) for a new vocabulary word, proper name, fact or concept, and linking the keyword to the relevant associated information through an interactive picture or image. For instance, to help students remember that ranid (rā'nid) refers to the family of typical frogs, create a keyword for ranid that sounds like ranid and is easily pictured, e.g., *rain.* Then, show the rain and the frog interacting in a picture, e.g., a *frog* in the *rain.* Then remind students, when they hear the word ranid, think of the keyword, rain, think of the picture with rain in it, think what else was in the picture, and retrieve the response, *frog.* Have students practice until they can retrieve the information backwards, i.e., frog = ranid. For another example, to help students remember that *olfactory* refers to *sense of smell,* create a keyword for olfactory, e.g., "oil factory," and show or prompt imagery of a *smelly oil factory.* Verbal elaboration is also helpful. In this case, a person could be pictured walking past a smelly oil factory, holding his nose, and commenting, "That *oil factory* is bothering my *olfactory* sense!" When students hear the word olfactory, they can think of the keyword, oil factory, think of the picture of the smelly oil factory, and remember that olfactory referred to sense of smell. Keywords can also be used to promote foreign vocabulary learning and to help remember the names of important people and places in history. In a recent investigation, we found that pictured keywords for place names (e.g., Ticonderoga = Tiger) on maps promoted better recall of historical locations than the place names alone.

Pegwords. Pegwords are rhyming proxies (one is *bun,* two is *shoe,* three is *tree,* etc.) for numbers and are used in remembering numbered or ordered information.

For example, to help students remember that a *rake* is an example of a third-class lever, show a picture of a rake leaning against a *tree* (pegword for three). To help them remember that a wheelbarrow is an example of a second-class lever, show a picture of a wheelbarrow on a *shoe* (pegword for two).

Letter strategies. Letter strategies, particularly acronyms, are the strategies most commonly used by adults to remember things in clusters or series. Most everyone knows the HOMES strategy for remembering the names of the Great Lakes or that the name ROY G. BIV can help retrieve the colors of the spectrum. Acronyms can also be combined with keywords and pegwords. For example, you can help students remember the names of countries in the World War I Central Powers Alliance by using the acronym TAG (T = Turkey, A = Austria-Hungary, G = Germany). This acronym can be linked to the Central Powers by depicting children playing TAG in Central Park (keyword for Central Powers). To remember freedoms guaranteed by the First Amendment to the Constitution, have students think of a contemporary singer who RAPS (R = religion, A = assembly and petition, P = press, S = speech). To effectively tie these freedoms to the First Amendment, portray a singer who RAPS about *buns* (pegword for one).

In addition to acronyms are acrostics, which expand rather than condense representations. One example is *My Very Educated Mother Just Served Us Nine Pizzas,"* to represent the planets in order from the Sun: Mercury, Venus, Earth, Mars, Jupiter, Saturn, Uranus, Neptune, Pluto. Another is "King Phillip's Class Ordered a Family of Gentle Spaniels," to remember the classifications Kingdom, Phylum, Class, Order, Family, Genus, and Species, in order. Letter strategies are helpful whenever information can be clustered and when the information itself is relatively familiar.

IN SPITE of their success in facilitating memory, mnemonic techniques have often been criticized for promoting simple recall at the expense of conceptual understanding. However, research has consistently indicated that mnemonic techniques do not inhibit comprehension and actually help students perform better on comprehension tasks, probably because students employing these techniques can use more information in answering questions. Of course, it is possible to remember information that is not comprehended, and it is advisable to ensure that all information to be remembered is meaningful to students and that coursework is not overloaded with excessive amounts of facts and vocabulary to be memorized. On the other hand, it is not possible to comprehend or use information that is not remembered. To address this potential problem, memory strategies are appropriate.

Good memory skills have benefited humanity for thousands of years, and no doubt will continue to do so for thousands more. Although memory objectives can certainly be overemphasized in school settings, it is time to place appropriate emphasis on the importance of memory in school learning, as well as the skills that allow us to remember effectively.

THE MIND'S JOURNEY FROM NOVICE TO EXPERT

*If We Know the Route,
We Can Help Students
Negotiate Their Way*

JOHN T. BRUER

*John T. Bruer is president of the James S. McDonnell
Foundation, St. Louis, Missouri.*

CHARLES IS in the seventh grade. He has an IQ of 70 and reads at the third-grade level. He has had several years of remedial reading instruction in a public school, but seems to make little progress. Charles has sufficient decoding skills to read aloud, but has almost no comprehension of what he reads. He is representative of many students who will fail—students whom our educational system can't reach.

Teachers report that they often see students who are unable to comprehend written language. What is odd is that these children can tell stories and often have no trouble understanding spoken language. This suggests they do have language comprehension skills and at least some background knowledge about the world, but cannot bring these skills and knowledge to bear on written language. Sometimes they can even read aloud, but still have difficulty understanding what they have read. Obviously, standard reading instruction has failed these students in a fundamental way.

On the first day of a new remedial reading program, the teacher asked Charles to read a short passage about reptiles. To see if he understood the passage, the teacher asked him to formulate a question based on the passage, a question that might appear on a test. Although he tried, he couldn't think of a question and gave up. He had not understood and retained enough of what he had just read to frame a question about it.

After 15 days in the new remedial program, the teacher and Charles repeated this exercise. After Charles had read a passage about Antarctic research, he immediately offered the question "Why do scientists come to the South Pole to study?" By this time he also had raised his comprehension scores on the reading passages from 40 to 75 percent, an average performance level for a seventh-grader. On comprehension tests given in his regular classroom, he improved from the 25th to the 78th percentile in social science and from the 5th to the 69th percentile in science. At the end of the 20-day program he had gained 20 months on standardized reading comprehension tests, and he maintained this improvement long after his remedial instruction ended.

Charles was the beneficiary of *reciprocal teaching,* a method that applies results of cognitive research to reading instruction. To understand what lies behind this method, we have to go back more than three decades to the beginning of what has come to be called the cognitive science revolution.

In 1956, a group of psychologists, linguists, and computer scientists met at the Massachusetts Institute of Technology for a symposium on information science (Gardner 1985). This three-day meeting was the beginning of the cognitive revolution in psychology, a revolution that eventually replaced behaviorist psychology with a science of the mind. In essence, the revolutionaries claimed that human minds and computers are sufficiently similar that a single theory—the theory of computation—could guide research in both psychology and computer science. "The basic point of view inhabiting our work," wrote two of the participants, "has been that the programmed computer and human problem solver are both species belonging to the genus IPS" (Newell and Simon 1972, p. 870). Both are species of the genus *information-processing system;* both are devices that process symbols.

That scientific revolution became a movement, and eventually a discipline, called cognitive science. Cognitive scientists study how our minds work—how we think, remember, and learn. Their studies have profound implications for restructuring schools and improving learning environments. Cognitive science—the science of mind—can give us an applied science of learning and instruction. Teaching methods based on this research—methods that result in some sixth-graders' having a better understanding of Newtonian physics than most high school students, or that, as recounted above, help remedial students raise their reading comprehension scores four grade levels after 20 days of instruction—are the educational equivalents of polio vaccine and penicillin. Yet few outside the educational research community are aware of these breakthroughs or understand the research that makes them possible.

Certainly cognitive science, or even educational research in general, isn't the sole answer to all our educational problems. Yet it has to be part of any attempt to improve educational practice and to restructure our schools. The science of mind can guide educational practice in much the same way that biology guides medical practice. There is more to medicine than biology, but basic medical science drives progress and helps doctors make decisions that promote their patients' physical well-being. Similarly, there is more to education than cognition, but cognitive science can drive progress and help teachers make decisions that promote their students' educational well-being.

In the years following the MIT symposium, cognitive scientists worked to exploit the similarities between thinking and information processing. Allen Newell and Herbert Simon developed the first working artificial intelligence computer program, called the Logic Theorist. It could prove logical theorems using methods a human expert might use. Besides logic, Newell and Simon studied problem solving in other areas, ranging from tic-tac-toe to arithmetic puzzles to chess. Problem solving in each of these areas depends on learning facts, skills, and strategies that are unique to the area. As cognitive scientists say, expertise in each area requires mastery of a distinct knowledge *domain.* Cognitive research began to have relevance for education as scientists gradually started to study knowledge domains that are included in school instruction—math, science, reading, and writing.

In their 1972 book *Human Problem Solving,* Newell and Simon summarized the results of this early research program and established a theoretical outlook and research methods that would guide much of the work that now has educational significance. Newell and Simon argued that if we want to understand learning in a domain, we have to start with a detailed analysis of how people solve problems in that domain. The first step is to try to discover the mental processes, or programs, that individuals use to solve a problem. To do this, cognitive scientists give a person a problem and observe everything the subject does and says while attempting a solution. Newell and Simon prompted their subjects to "think aloud"—to say everything that passed through their minds as they worked on the problems. Cognitive psychologists call these "think-aloud" data *protocols.* Analysis of the protocols allows cognitive scientists to form hypotheses about what program an individual uses to solve a problem. Cognitive scientists can test their hypotheses by writing computer programs based on their hypotheses to simulate the subject's problem-solving performance. If the scientists' analysis is correct, the computer simulation should perform the same way the human did on the problem. If the simulation fails, the scientists revise their hypotheses accordingly and try again. After studying and simulating performances from a variety of subjects, Newell and Simon could trace individual differences in problem-solving performance to specific differences in the mental programs the subjects used.

To be sure they could find clear-cut differences among individual programs, Newell and Simon initially compared the problem-solving performances of experts and novices—which were almost certain to be different—in a variety of domains. In such studies (now a mainstay of the discipline), cognitive scientists consider any individual who is highly skilled or knowledgeable in a given domain to be an "expert" in that domain. The domains can be ordinary and commonplace; they don't have to be arcane and esoteric. In the cognitive scientists' sense of the word, there are experts at tic-tac-toe, third-grade arithmetic, and high school physics. Comparing experts with novices makes it possible to specify how experts and novices differ in understanding, storing, recalling, and manipulating knowledge during problem solving.

Of course Newell and Simon knew that experts in a

domain would be better at solving problems in that domain than novices, but it was not always obvious how experts and novices actually differed in their problem-solving behavior. In one early expert-novice study, Simon and Chase (1973) looked at chess players. One thing we do when playing chess is to choose our next move by trying to anticipate what our opponent's countermove might be, how we might respond to that move, how the opponent might counter, and so on. That is, we try to plan several moves ahead. One might think that experts and novices differ in how far ahead they plan: a novice might look ahead two or three moves, an expert ten or twelve. Surprisingly, Simon and Chase found that experts and novices both look ahead only two or three moves. The difference is that experts consider and choose from among vastly superior moves. When expert chess players look at a board, they see configurations and familiar patterns of pieces; they see "chunks" of relevant information. Novices, in contrast, see individual pieces. The experts' more effective, more information-rich chunks allow them to see superior possible moves and choose the best of these. Chunking, rather than planning farther ahead, accounts for the experts' superiority. Experts process more and better information about the next few moves than novices.

Newell and Simon's emphasis on problem-solving performance and expert-novice differences was a first step toward a new understanding of learning. In short, learning is the process by which novices become experts. As one learns chess, math, or physics, one's problem-solving performance in the domain improves as the programs one uses to solve problems improve. If we know what programs a person first uses to solve problems in a domain, and if we can compare them with the programs the person eventually constructs, we have a measure and a description of what the person learned. We can study learning by tracing changes in the mental processes students use as they progress from novice to higher levels of proficiency. If we have detailed knowledge of these processes, such as the computer simulations give us, we can know not only that learning has occurred but also *how* it has occurred.

Other investigators joined in the program that Newell and Simon had outlined, and the research developed and expanded along two dimensions.

First, the kinds of problems and tasks the scientists studied became more complex. To play games and solve puzzles, even in logic and chess, one has to know a few rules, but one doesn't need much factual knowledge about the world. As cognitive scientists honed their methods on puzzle problems and accumulated insights into how people solve them, they became more ambitious and began applying their methods to more knowledge-rich domains. They started to study problem solving in physics, mathematics, and medical diagnosis. They began to study language skills, such as reading and writing, and how students use these skills to acquire more knowledge. Extending their research into these domains made it applicable to understanding expert and novice performance in school subjects.

Second, the research evolved from merely comparing novices against experts to studying the process by which

novices *become* experts. Psychologists began to develop intermediate models of problem-solving performance in a variety of domains. The intermediate models describe how domain expertise *develops* over time and with experience. If learning is the process by which novices become experts, a sequence of intermediate models in a domain traces the learning process in that domain. The intermediate models describe the stages through which students progress in school.

By the mid 1970s, cognitive scientists were studying school tasks over a range of competencies—from novice to expert, from pre-school through college. In many subject areas, our knowledge of students' cognitive processes is now sufficiently detailed that we can begin to describe their performance at every level of competence, from novice to expert. We can describe the normal trajectory of learning in these subject areas. If we understand the mental processes that underlie expert performance in school subjects, we can ask and answer other questions that are important for education. How do students acquire these processes? Do certain instructional methods help students acquire these processes more quickly or more easily? Can we help students learn better? Answers to these questions can guide educational practice and school reform. For example, research in science learning shows that novices—and all beginning students are novices—hold naive theories about how the physical world works. These theories so influence how the students interpret school instruction that the instruction is often ineffective. Curricula based on cognitive research that build from and correct these naive theories can overcome this problem.

Later in this article, we will see how researchers and teachers are applying the new learning theory to create classroom environments in which students are successfully moving along the path from novice to expert. But first let's look at how cognitive scientists work and how their results can contribute to better instructional methods.

II.

Balance-Scale Problems:
A Classic Study of
Novice-to-Expert Performance

Research on how children learn to solve balance-scale problems illustrates the main ideas, methods, and instructional applications of cognitive science.

Try to solve the balance-scale problem shown in Figure 1. Assume the scale's arm is locked so that it can't rotate around the fulcrum. If I were to unlock the arm, what would happen? Would the scale tip left, tip right, or balance?

This is a tricky problem. Rule IV in Figure 1 gives a set of rules one might use to solve it. Each rule has an IF clause that states the conditions under which the rule is applicable and a THEN clause that states what to do under those conditions. To use these rules, find the rule whose conditions fit the pattern of weights and distances in the problem. You find that P4 is the only rule whose IF clause fits the problem. Its THEN clause tells you to compute torques for each side; that is, for each side, multiply the number of weights by their distance from the fulcrum. Doing that gives $t_1 = 5 \times 3 = 15$ for the left side and $t_2 = 4 \times 4 = 16$ for the right. These new data satisfy the condition for P7; executing its THEN clause gives the correct answer, "Right side down." Some readers might remember the THEN clause in P4 from high school physics as a version of the law of torques: Multiply weight by distance on each arm to find the torque, or rotational force; the side with the larger torque goes down. This simple law solves all balance-scale problems.

The set of rules is an English-language version of a computer program for solving balance-scale problems. It takes as input data about the weight on each side of the scale and the distance of the weight from the fulcrum. The output is the answer for a balance-scale problem: tip left, tip right, or balance. The program is a series of IF-THEN rules. Computer scientists call the IF clauses *conditions,* the THEN clauses *actions,* and the entire IF-THEN statement a *production rule.* They call computer programs written using only production rules *production systems.* Computing devices that execute production systems efficiently have a specific internal structure (or *architecture,* as computer scientists say).

Cognitive scientists claim that the human mind can be described as a computing device that builds and executes production-system programs. In fact, rule IV is a production system an expert would use to solve balance-scale problems. Robert Siegler, a cognitive psychologist, showed that production systems can simulate human performance on such problems (Siegler 1976; Klahr and Siegler 1978; Siegler and Klahr 1982). He also showed that a series of increasingly complex production systems can model the way in which children gradually develop expertise on balance-scale problems from ages 5 through 17. Children learn, says Siegler, by adding better rules to their production systems. Proper instruction, he goes on to show, can help children acquire these better rules.

The beauty of the balance-scale task for developmental psychology is that it is complex enough to be interesting but simple enough for exhaustive task analysis. Two variables are relevant: the amount of weight on each arm and the distance of the weight from the fulcrum. There are three discrete outcomes: tip left, tip right, and balance. There is a simple law, the law of torques, that solves all balance-scale problems, though few of us discover this law on our own. If weight and distance are the only two relevant variables and if the scale either tips or balances, there are only six possible kinds of balance-scale problems:

■ balance problems—equal weight on each side and the weights at equal distances from the fulcrum;

■ weight problems—unequal weight on each side and the weights at equal distance from the fulcrum;

■ distance problems—equal weight on each side and the weights at unequal distances from the fulcrum;

■ conflict-weight—one side has more weight, the other side has its weight at a greater distance from the fulcrum, and the side with greater weight goes down;

■ conflict-distance—one side has more weight, the other side has its weight at a greater distance from the fulcrum, and the side with greater distance goes down;

■ conflict-balance—one side has more weight, the other side has its weight at a greater distance from the fulcrum, and the scale balances.

Siegler called the last three types "conflict" problems, because when one side has more weight but the other side has its weight farther from the fulcrum one can have conflicting intuitions about which variable dominates. (The problem illustrated in Figure 1 is a conflict-distance problem: there is more weight on the left side, the weight is farther from the fulcrum on the right side, and the right side goes down.)

These six possibilities cover all possible cases for how weight and distance influence the action of the scale. The six cases provide a complete theory, or task analysis, of the balance scale. Notice that the six problem types place varying demands on the solver. For a balance problem or a weight problem, a solver need only consider weight. For the conflict problems, a solver has to pay attention to weight, distance, and the ways in which weight and distance interact.

Siegler formulated some psychological hypotheses about how people might solve balance-scale problems. Using the information from the task analysis, he could test his hypotheses by giving subjects problems and observing their performance. Siegler called his hypotheses "rules" and formulated them as four production-system programs (see Figure 1).

The rules make different assumptions about how and when people use weight or distance information to solve the problems. Rule I considers only weight. Rule II considers distance, but only when the weights on the two sides are equal (P3). Rule III attempts to integrate weight and distance information (P4 and P5). Rule IV introduces the law of torques (P4) when one side has more weight but less distance.

If children use Siegler's rules, then the pattern of a child's responses to a set of balance-scale problems that contains all six types will reveal what rule that child uses. Children's responses will tell us what they know about the balance-scale task, including what information—weight, distance, or both—they use to solve the problem. Siegler tested his hypotheses and predictions by giving a battery of 30 balance-scale problems (five of each of the six kinds) to a group of 40 children that included equal numbers of 5-year-olds, 9-year-olds, 13-year-olds, and 17-year-olds. He showed each child a balance scale that had weights placed on it and asked the child to predict what the scale would do. As soon as the child made a prediction, Siegler rearranged the weights for the next problem. He did not let the children see if their predictions were correct, because he wanted to find out what they knew initially. He wanted to avoid giving the students feedback on their performance so he could be sure they weren't learning about the task during the experiment. He wanted to look at their learning, but only after he assessed their initial understanding.

The children's performance confirmed Siegler's hypotheses. Ninety percent of them made predictions that followed the pattern associated with one of the four rules.

WILL THE SCALE TIP LEFT, TIP RIGHT, OR BALANCE?

The 5-year-old—who considers only weight—says the left side will go down. The 13-year-old—who understands there's a conflict here but doesn't know how to figure it out—makes an educated guess. The expert, invoking the law of torques, says the right side will go down.

This is a classic example of novice-to-expert progression. Young children develop simple rules that will work with simple problems. Some children modify those rules when they encounter problems their current rules can't solve. Other children don't. By knowing in some detail what stages children typically pass through on their mental journeys from novice to expert—including the roadblocks and deadends—we can help them progress along the path.

RULE I

P1   **IF** weight is the same
     THEN say "balance."

P2   **IF** side X has more weight
     THEN say "X down."

This is the rule that 5-year-olds most often use—for *all* problems. They only consider weight; they don't really notice the distance the weight is from the fulcrum.

RULE II

P1   **IF** weight is the same
     THEN say "balance."

P2   **IF** side X has more weight
     THEN say "X down."

P3   **IF** weight is the same **AND** side X has more distance
     THEN say "X down."

As children progress, they begin to consider distance, but only when the weights on the two sides are equal.

RULE III

P1   **IF** weight is the same
     THEN say "balance."

P2   **IF** side X has more weight
     THEN say "X down."

P3   **IF** weight is the same **AND** side X has more distance
     THEN say "X down."

P4   **IF** side X has more weight **AND** side X has less distance
     THEN make an educated guess.

P5   **IF** side X has more weight **AND** side X has more distance
     THEN say "X down."

By age 13, almost all are using this rule, and—with the proper kind of instruction—5 and 8-year olds can be taught to use it. Notice in P4 that the Rule III user can only make an educated guess when it comes to solving problems where one side has more weight but less distance.

RULE IV

P1   **IF** weight is the same
     THEN say "balance."

P2   **IF** side X has more weight
     THEN say "X down."

P3   **IF** weight is the same **AND** side X has more distance
     THEN say "X down."

P4   **IF** side X has more weight **AND** side X has less distance
     THEN compute torques: $t_1 = w_1 \times d_1$; $t_2 = w_2 \times d_2$.

P5   **IF** side X has more weight **AND** side X has more distance
     THEN say "X down."

P6   **IF** the torques are equal
     THEN say "balance."

P7   **IF** side X has more torque
     THEN say "X down."

This is the set of rules an expert might use. Now P4 has progressed from an educated guess to the law of torques: Multiply weight by distance on each arm to find the torque; the side with the larger torque goes down. The expert doesn't always use P4; only when the easier rules won't suffice. Almost no one progresses to Rule IV spontaneously, that is, without being taught.

Figure 1

Siegler's rules I-IV for the balance-scale task. (From Siegler and Klahr 1982, p. 198. Used with permission of Lawrence Erlbaum Associates.) Commentary by John T. Bruer.

There was also a strong developmental trend. The 5-year-olds most often used rule I. The 9-year-olds used rule II or rule III. The 13- and 17-year-olds used rule III. Only two children, a 9-year-old and a 17-year-old, used rule IV.

Taken together, Siegler's four rules constitute a developmental theory that explains development in terms of changes in children's knowledge structures and how they initially encode, or as cognitive psychologists say, *represent* problems. By age 5, most children are using rule I. By age 13, almost all are using rule III. Few children spontaneously progress to rule IV, the expert-level rule for the balance scale. Thus, the rules chart a course of normal development on the task, from novice to expert performance.

Siegler's rules also tell us what cognitive changes underlie the transition from novice to expert. On tasks like the balance scale, children progress through a series of partial understandings that gradually approach mastery. Performance improves, or learning occurs, when children add more effective production rules to the theories they have stored in their long-term memories. If we know what the developmental stages are and how they differ at the level of detail provided by a cognitive theory, we ought to be able to design instruction to help children advance from one stage to the next.

To investigate how children learn about the balance scale, Siegler conducted a training study. Working with 5-year-olds and 8-year-olds, all of whom used rule I, he had each child make predictions for 16 problems. After each prediction, Siegler released the lock on the balance scale and let the child see if his or her prediction was correct. This feedback experience gave the children an opportunity to learn about the balance scale. Two days later, the children had a retest with no feedback to see if they had learned anything from the training.

In this experiment, there were three training groups. One group of 5- and 8-year-olds served as a control group. Their training session consisted only of balance and weight problems—problems they could solve using rule I. A second group had training on distance problems, where rule II, but not rule I, would work. A third group had training on conflict problems, which require at least rule III for performance even at chance levels. With this training, would the children learn anything? Would they progress from rule I to a more advanced rule?

As expected, the children in the control group made no progress. They learned nothing from training on problems they already knew how to solve. The children in the second group, both 5- and 8-year-olds trained on distance problems, did learn something. Feedback from 16 problems was enough for these children to advance from rule I to rule II. The surprise came with the third group, the children who had training on conflict problems. The 8-year-olds in this group advanced two levels in their mastery of the balance scale, from rule I to rule III. *The 5-year-olds in this group either stayed at rule I or became so confused and erratic that it appeared they were no longer using a rule.*

To find out why the 8-year-olds learned and the 5-year-olds didn't, Siegler and his collaborators selected several children between 5 and 10 years old for in-depth study (Klahr and Siegler 1978). Each child had a training ses-

sion with the balance scale that included conflict problems. In the training session the child was asked to make a prediction for each problem and to state his or her reasons for the prediction. The experimenter then unlocked the scale's arm and the child observed the result. If the prediction was not borne out, the experimenter asked "Why do you think that happened?" The researchers videotaped the entire session with each child and transcribed all the children's verbal responses, which provided data for protocol analysis.

Lisa, a typical 5-year-old, took 30 minutes to do 16 problems. Protocols like Lisa's suggested that the younger children were not encoding or representing distance in their initial interpretations of balance-scale problems. For example, when Lisa was given a distance problem (on the left side, one weight on peg 3; on the right side, one weight on peg 1), she predicted the scale would balance—"They would both stay up," she said. Asked why she thought this she answered "'Cause they are both the same." When she saw the left side tip down, she was genuinely puzzled: "Well, why are they both the same thing and one's up and one's down?" Lisa did not see any difference between the two sides. She was not including distance information in her initial representation of the problem. She simply did not notice and encode distance information.

An 8-year-old's protocol gave very different data. Jan was given a conflict-distance problem: on the left side, three weights on the first peg; on the right side, two weights on the third peg. She predicted incorrectly that the left side would go down. When shown what really happens (right side down) and asked for an explanation, she gave one involving both weight and distance. For her, pegs 1 and 2 on each side were "near" the fulcrum and pegs 3 and 4 were "far" from the fulcrum. She stated a rule: "If far pegs have weights, then that side will go down." She then pointed out that in this problem the far pegs on the right side had weights but the far pegs on the left had none, so the right side would go down. Jan's is not a perfect explanation, nor is her rule always true. Her protocol shows, though, that she, unlike Lisa, had noticed and encoded both weight and distance information in her representation of the problem.

On the basis of the protocols, the difference between 5-year-olds and 8-year-olds seemed to be that the younger children saw the problems in terms of weight only, whereas the older children could see the problems in terms of weight at a distance from the fulcrum. If the younger children were not encoding distance, they could not learn from training on conflict problems that differences in distance sometimes overcome differences in weight. They could not develop the concepts or—similar to the chess expert—build the chunks they needed for the conditions of P4 and P5 in rule III. On the other hand, the older children, even if they were using rule I, appeared to encode distance. They could learn from training on conflict problems how to use that information to build new productions and progress to rule III.

Can 5-year-olds learn to encode both weight and distance, or is it beyond their level of cognitive development? Siegler found that giving 5-year-olds more time to study the configurations or giving them more explicit instructions ("See how the weights are on the pegs? See how many are on each side and how far they are from the center on each side?") made no difference in their ability to reproduce the configurations from memory.

Only one intervention seemed to work. *The 5-year-olds had to be told explicitly what to encode and how to encode it.* The instructor had to tell them what was important and teach them a strategy for remembering it. The instructor taught the children to count the disks on the left side, count the pegs on the left side, and then rehearse the result (i.e., say aloud "three weights on peg 4"); to repeat this process for the right side; and then to rehearse both results together ("three weights on peg 4 and two weights on peg 3"). The instructor then told the children to try to reproduce the pattern their statement described. The instructor guided each child through this strategy on seven problems. With each problem, the children took more responsibility for executing the strategy.

After this training, the 5-year-olds' performance on reconstructing distance information from memory improved. They now correctly reproduced weight information 52 percent of the time, and distance information 51 percent of the time. Although they now apparently encoded the information, they, like the 8-year-old rule I users, did not spontaneously start using it. They continued to use rule I. However, when these 5-year-olds were given training on conflict problems, they too progressed from rule I to rule III. They had to be taught explicitly what representation, or encoding, to use in order to learn from the training experience.

The results of this study exemplify features of learning that are common to almost all school subjects. Students learn by modifying long-term memory structures, here called production systems. They modify their structures when they encounter problems their current rules can't solve. Some children modify their structures spontaneously; that is how children normally develop through Siegler's four rules. But by giving appropriate training we can facilitate children's development. For some children, presenting anomalous problems is enough. Like the 8-year-olds confronted with conflict problems, some children can build better rules when challenged with hard problems. Other children can't. Some children have inadequate initial representations of the problem. Children have to notice the information they need and encode it if they are to build better rules.

Poor readers executed a 'once-over, desperate, nonfocused read.'

Students who can't learn spontaneously from new experiences need direct instruction about the relevant facts *and* about the strategies to use. Teaching just facts or teaching strategies in isolation from the facts won't work. To know when and how to intervene, we have to understand, in some detail, what stages children pass through on their mental journeys from novice to expert. Cognitive science tells us how we can then help children progress from relative naivete through a series of partial understandings to eventual subject mastery.

The difficulties children have in learning about the balance scale are highly similar to the difficulties they encounter in learning mathematics, science, and literacy skills. The tasks, representations, and production systems will become more complex—the progression from novice to expert can't be captured by four rules in every domain. However, our innate cognitive architecture remains the same no matter what domain we try to master, and the methods of cognitive science yield detailed information about how we think and learn. The lessons learned on the simple balance scale apply across the curriculum.

III.

What Does Expertise Consist Of?

Imagine that a small, peaceful country is being threatened by a large, belligerent neighbor. The small country is unprepared historically, temperamentally, and militarily to defend itself; however, it has among its citizens the world's reigning chess champion. The prime minister decides that his country's only chance is to outwit its aggressive neighbor. Reasoning that the chess champion is a formidable strategic thinker and a deft tactician—a highly intelligent, highly skilled problem solver—the prime minister asks him to assume responsibility for defending the country. Can the chess champion save his country from invasion?

This scenario is not a plot from a Franz Lehar operetta, but a thought experiment devised by David Perkins and Gavriel Salomon (1989). As they point out, our predictions about the chess champion's performance as national security chief depend on what we believe intelligence and expertise are. If the goal of education is to develop our children into intelligent subject-matter experts, our predictions about the chess champion, based on what we believe about intelligence and expertise, have implications for what we should do in our schools.

Since the mid 1950s cognitive science has contributed to the formulation and evolution of theories of intelligence, and so to our understanding of what causes skilled cognitive performance and what should be taught in schools. In this section, we will review how our understanding of intelligence and expertise has evolved over the past two decades and see how these theories have influenced educational policy and practice.

Four theories will figure in this story.

The oldest theory maintains that a student builds up his or her intellect by mastering formal disciplines, such as Latin, Greek, logic, and maybe chess. These subjects build minds as barbells build muscles. On this theory the chess champion might succeed in the national security field. If this theory is correct, these formal disciplines should figure centrally in school instruction.

At the turn of the twentieth century, when Edward Thorndike did his work, this was the prevailing view. Thorndike, however, noted that no one had presented scientific evidence to support this view. Thorndike reasoned that if learning Latin strengthens general mental functioning, then students who had learned Latin should be able to learn other subjects more quickly. He found no evidence of this. Having learned one formal discipline did not result in more efficient learning in other domains. Mental "strength" in one domain didn't transfer to mental strength in others. Thorndike's results contributed to the demise of this ancient theory of intelligence and to a decline in the teaching of formal disciplines as mental calisthenics.

In the early years of the cognitive revolution, it appeared that general skills and reasoning abilities might be at the heart of human intelligence and skilled performance. If this is so, again the chess champion might succeed, and schools should teach these general thinking and problem-solving skills—maybe even in separate critical-thinking and study-skills classes.

But by the mid 1970s, cognitive research suggested that general domain-independent skills couldn't adequately account for human expertise. Research shows that either the teaching of traditional study skills has no impact on learning or else the skills fail to transfer from the learning context to other situations. Either way, teaching these general skills is not the path to expertise and enhanced academic performance.

A wide variety of books and commercially available courses attempt to teach general cognitive and thinking skills. (For reviews and evaluations see Nickerson et al. 1985, Segal et al. 1985, and Chipman et al. 1985.) Analysis and evaluation of these programs again fail to support the belief that the teaching of general skills enhances students' overall performance.

Most of these programs teach general skills in stand-alone courses, separate from subject-matter instruction. The assumption is that students would find it too difficult to learn how to think and to learn subject content simultaneously. Like the early artificial intelligence and cognitive science that inspire them, the courses contain many formal problems, logical puzzles, and games. The assumption is that the general methods that work on these problems will work on problems in all subject domains.

A few of these programs, such as the Productive Thinking Program (Covington 1985) and Instrumental Enrichment (Feuerstein et al. 1985), have undergone extensive evaluation. The evaluations consistently report that students improve on problems like those contained in the course materials but show only limited improvement on novel problems or problems unlike those in the materials (Mansfield et al. 1978; Savell et al. 1986). The programs provide extensive practice on the specific kinds of problems that their designers want children to master. Children do improve on those problems, but this is different from developing *general* cognitive skills. After reviewing the effectiveness of several thinking-skills programs, one group of psychologists concluded that "there is no strong evidence that students in any of these thinking-skills programs improved in tasks that were dissimilar to those already explicitly practiced" (Bransford et al. 1985, p. 202). Students in the programs don't become more intelligent generally; the general problem-solving

and thinking skills they learn do not transfer to novel problems. Rather, the programs help students become experts in the domain of puzzle problems.

Researchers then began to think that the key to intelligence in a domain was extensive experience with and knowledge about that domain.

One of the most influential experiments supporting this theory was William Chase and Herb Simon's (1973) study of novice and expert chess players, which followed on earlier work by A.D. De Groot (1965). Chase and Simon showed positions from *actual* chess games to subjects for 5 to 10 seconds and asked the subjects to reproduce the positions from memory. Each position contained 25 chess pieces. Expert players could accurately place 90 percent of the pieces, novices only 20 percent. Chase and Simon then had the subjects repeat the experiment, but this time the "positions" consisted of 25 pieces placed randomly on the board. These were generally not positions that would occur in an actual game. The experts were no better than the novices at reproducing the random positions: both experts and novices could place only five or six pieces correctly.

Other researchers replicated the Chase-Simon experiment in a variety of domains, using children, college students, and adults. The results were always the same: Experts had better memories for items in their area of expertise, but not for items in general. This shows, first, that mastering a mentally demanding game does not improve mental strength in general. The improved memory performance is domain specific. Chess isn't analogous to a barbell for the mind. Second, it shows that if memory *strategies* account for the expert's improved memory capacity, the strategies aren't general strategies applicable across all problem-solving domains. Chess experts have better memories for genuine chess positions, but not for random patterns of chess pieces or for strings of words or digits. Thus, experts aren't using some general memory strategy that transfers from chess positions to random patterns of pieces or to digit strings.

From long experience at the game, chess experts have developed an extensive knowledge base of perceptual patterns, or chunks. Cognitive scientists estimate that chess experts learn about 50,000 chunks, and that it takes about 10 years to learn them. Chunking explains the difference between novice and expert performance. When doing this task, novices see the chessboard in terms of individual pieces. They can store only the positions of five or six pieces in their short-term, or working, memory—numbers close to what research has shown our working memory spans to be. Experts see "chunks," or patterns, of several pieces. If each chunk contains four or five pieces and if the expert can hold five such chunks in working memory, then the expert can reproduce accurately the positions of 20 to 25 individual pieces. Chase and Simon even found that when experts reproduced the positions on the board, they did it in chunks. They rapidly placed four or five pieces, then paused before reproducing the next chunk.

Expertise, these studies suggest, depends on highly organized, domain-specific knowledge that can arise only after extensive experience and practice in the domain. Strategies can help us process knowledge, but first we have to have the knowledge to process. This suggested that our chess expert might be doomed to failure, and that schools should teach the knowledge, skills, and representations needed to solve problems within specific domains.

In the early 1980s researchers turned their attention to other apparent features of expert performance. They noticed that there were intelligent novices—people who learned new fields and solved novel problems more expertly than most, regardless of how much domain-specific knowledge they possessed. Among other things, intelligent novices seemed to control and monitor their thought processes. This suggested that there was more to expert performance than just domain-specific knowledge and skills.

Cognitive scientists called this new element of expert performance *metacognition*—the ability to think about thinking, to be consciously aware of oneself as a problem solver, and to monitor and control one's mental processing.

As part of an experiment to see which metacognitive skills might be most helpful when learning something new, John Bransford, an expert cognitive psychologist, tried to learn physics from a textbook with the help of an expert physicist. He kept a diary of his learning experiences and recorded the skills and strategies most useful to him (Brown et al. 1983). Among the things he listed were (1) awareness of the difference between understanding and memorizing material and knowledge of which mental strategies to use in each case; (2) ability to recognize which parts of the text were difficult, which dictated where to start reading and how much time to spend; (3) awareness of the need to take problems and examples from the text, order them randomly, and then try to solve them; (4) knowing when he didn't understand, so he could seek help from the expert; and (5) knowing when the expert's explanations solved his immediate learning problem. These are all metacognitive skills; they all involve awareness and control of the learning problem that Bransford was trying to solve. Bransford might have learned these skills originally in one domain (cognitive psychology), but he could apply them as a novice when trying to learn a second domain (physics).

This self-experiment led Bransford and his colleagues to examine in a more controlled way the differences between expert and less-skilled learners. They found that the behavior of intelligent novices contrasted markedly with that of the less skilled. Intelligent novices used many of the same strategies Bransford had used to learn physics. Less-skilled learners used few, if any, of them. The less-skilled did not always appreciate the difference between memorization and comprehension and seemed to be unaware that different learning strategies should be used in each case (Bransford et al. 1986; Bransford and Stein 1984). These students were less likely to notice whether texts were easy or difficult, and thus were less able to adjust their strategies and their study time accordingly (Bransford et al. 1982). Less-able learners were unlikely to use self-tests and self-questioning as sources of feedback to correct misconceptions and inappropriate learning strategies (Brown et al. 1983; Stein et al. 1982).

The importance of metacognition for education is that a child is, in effect, a universal novice, constantly confronted with novel learning tasks. In such a situation it would be most beneficial to be an intelligent novice. What is encouraging is that the research also shows that it is possible to teach children metacognitive skills and when to use them. If we can do this, we will be able to help children become intelligent novices; we will be able to teach them how to learn.

We are just beginning to see what this new understanding of expertise and intelligence might mean for educational practice. The most important implication of the theory is that how we teach is as important as what we teach. Domain-specific knowledge and skills are essential to expertise; however, school instruction must also be metacognitively aware, informed, and explicit. In the next section, we will see a vivid example of this in the teaching of reading comprehension.

IV.

Reading Comprehension: Teaching Children the Strategies Experts Use

Reciprocal teaching, the method mentioned in the introduction to this article, improved Charles' classroom reading comprehension by four grade levels in 20 days. This method illustrates how instruction designed on cognitive principles can help children to apply language-comprehension skills in their reading and to acquire the metacognitive strategies essential to skilled reading.

Reciprocal teaching also shows how researchers, administrators, and teachers can collaborate to apply the results of research in the classroom. Annemarie Palincsar, Ann Brown, and Kathryn Ransom—a graduate student, a professor, and a school administrator—shared the belief that cognitive research could improve classroom practice and that classroom practice can improve research.

After five years working as a special education teacher and administrator, Palincsar returned to the University of Illinois as a doctoral student. She felt her previous training in psychodiagnostics—training based on a medical model of learning disabilities—was not meeting the needs of her students. She decided to broaden her academic background and to study how sociocultural factors might influence students' experience in school.

The cognitive revolution was spreading through academic circles, but had not yet reached teacher-practitioners. Palincsar's classroom experience influenced her choice of a thesis project. In her words: "As a teacher, one of the situations I found most baffling was having children who were fairly strong decoders but had little comprehension or recall of what they had read." She was baffled by students like Charles, students who can adequately comprehend spoken, but not written, language.

At first, Palincsar was interested in how self-verbalization might be used to help children regulate their cognitive processing. Donald Meichenbaum (1985) had developed techniques based on self-verbalization to help impulsive children—children who mentally fail to stop, look, and listen—pace their actions and develop self-control. At the time, most of the work on self-verbalization had explored how it could be used to regulate social behavior. Palincsar wondered how it might be used to regulate *cognitive* behavior—specifically, how it might be used to improve reading comprehension. She wrote to Meichenbaum, who suggested that the application of his ideas to academic subjects might be strengthened by incorporating ideas from research on metacognition. He told Palincsar to discuss her idea with Ann Brown, an authority on metacognition who at that time was also at Illinois.

At their initial meeting, Palincsar showed Brown a design for the pilot study that was to evolve into reciprocal teaching. Brown offered her a quarter-time research appointment to do the study. When it proved successful (Brown and Palincsar 1982), Brown gave Palincsar a full-time research assistantship and supervised her thesis research.

Palincsar and Brown developed reciprocal teaching from the pilot study on a sound theoretical basis. (See Brown and Palincsar 1987). They analyzed the task's demands, developed a theory of task performance based on expert-novice studies, and formulated a theory of instruction that might improve task performance. This is the same sequence Bob Siegler followed with the balance-scale task. A major difference, of course, is that reading comprehension presents a more complex problem than the balance scale.

From their analysis and a review of previous research, Palincsar and Brown (1984) identified six functions that most researchers agreed were essential to expert reading comprehension: The competent reader *understands* that the goal in reading is to construct meaning, *activates* relevant background knowledge, *allocates* attention or cognitive resources to concentrate on major content ideas, *evaluates* the constructed meaning (the gist) for internal consistency and compatibility with prior knowledge and common sense, *draws* and *tests* inferences (including interpretations, predictions, and conclusions), and *monitors* all the above to see if comprehension is occurring.

Palincsar and Brown then identified four simple strategies that would together tap all six functions needed for comprehension: *summarizing, questioning, clarifying,* and *predicting.* They explained the relation between the four strategies and the six functions as follows (Palincsar and Brown 1986): Summarizing a passage requires that the reader recall and state the gist he or she has constructed. Thus, a reader who can summarize has activated background knowledge to integrate information appearing in the text, allocated attention to the main points, and evaluated the gist for consistency. Formulating a question about a text likewise depends on the gist and the functions needed for summarizing, but with the additional demand that the reader monitor the gist to pick out important points. When clarifying, a reader must allocate attention to difficult points and engage in critical evaluation of the gist. Making predictions involves drawing and testing inferences on the basis of

what is in the text together with activated background knowledge. A reader who self-consciously uses all four strategies would certainly appreciate that the goal of reading is to construct meaning.

Expert-novice studies supported the hypothesized connection between comprehension functions and strategies. After completing a comprehension task, expert readers reported that they spent a lot of time summarizing, questioning, clarifying, and predicting. Experts' "comprehend-aloud" protocols substantiated these self-reports. Poor readers did not report using the strategies and showed no evidence of using them in their comprehension protocols. As Palincsar and Brown characterize it, novices executed a "once-over, desperate, nonfocused read."

But can you teach the strategies to novices? And if you can, will it improve their comprehension? To answer these questions, Palincsar and Brown designed a prototype instructional intervention to teach nonexperts how to use the strategies. As with all instruction, the primary problem is transfer. How should one teach the strategies to get novices to use them spontaneously? Here Palincsar based her strategy instruction on Brown's work on teaching metacognitive skills. Brown's research had shown that successful strategy instruction must include practice on specific task-appropriate skills (the cognitive aspect), explicit instruction on how to supervise and monitor these skills (the metacognitive aspect), and explanations of why the skills work (the informed instruction aspect).

The research suggests what teachers should do to help students master strategies. First, teachers have to make the strategies overt, explicit and concrete. Teachers can best do this by modeling the strategies for the students.

Second, to ensure that students will spontaneously use the strategies where needed, teachers should link the strategies to the contexts in which they are to be used and teach the strategies as a functioning group, not in iso-

Strategies can help us process knowledge, but first we have to have the knowledge to process.

lation. This suggests that reading-strategy instruction should take place during reading-comprehension tasks, where the explicit goal is to construct meaning from written symbols.

Third, instruction must be informed. The students should be fully aware of why the strategies work and where they should use particular strategies. Thus, instruction should involve discussion of a text's content and students' understanding of why the strategies are useful in that situation.

Fourth, students have to realize the strategies work no matter what their current level of performance. Thus, instruction should include feedback from the teacher about the students' success relative to their individual abilities and encouragement to persist even if a student is not yet fully competent.

Finally, if students are to become spontaneous strategy users, responsibility for comprehension must be transferred from the teacher to the students gradually, but as soon as possible. This suggests that the teacher should slowly raise the demands made on the students and then fade into the background, becoming less an active modeler and more a sympathetic coach. Students should gradually take charge of their learning.

Palincsar designed reciprocal teaching to satisfy all five of these requirements. Reciprocal teaching takes the form of a dialogue. Dialogue is a language game children understand, and it is a game that allows control of a learning session to alternate between teacher and student. Most important, when engaged in dialogue students are *using* their language-comprehension skills and *sharing* any relevant background knowledge they have individually with the group. In reciprocal teaching, dialogue directs these skills and knowledge toward reading.

The dialogue becomes a form of cooperative learning, in which teachers model the strategies for the students and then give students guided practice in applying them to a group task of constructing a text's meaning. Teacher and students take turns leading a dialogue about the portion of text they are jointly trying to understand. The dialogue includes spontaneous discussion and argument emphasizing the four strategies.

In reciprocal teaching, the teacher assigns the reading group a portion of a text and designates one student to be the leader for that segment. Initially, the teacher might be the leader. The group reads the passage silently. Then the assigned leader summarizes the passage, formulates a question that might be asked on a test, discusses and clarifies difficult points, and finally makes a prediction about what might happen next in the story. The teacher provides help and feedback tailored to the needs and abilities of the current leader. The student-listeners act as supportive critics who encourage the leader to explain and clarify the text. Each student takes a turn as leader. The group's public goal is collaborative construction of the text's meaning. The teacher provides a model of expert performance. As the students improve, the teacher fades into the background.

In the first test of reciprocal teaching, Palincsar served as the teacher and worked with one student at a time. The students were seventh-graders in a remedial reading program who had adequate decoding skills but who were at least three grades behind in reading comprehension. At first, students found it difficult to be the leader, and Palincsar had to do a lot of modeling and prompting, but gradually the students' performance improved. In the initial sessions, over half the questions students formulated were inadequate. Only 11 percent of the questions addressed main ideas, and only 11 percent of the summaries captured the gist of the passage. After ten tutoring sessions, however, students could generate reasonably sophisticated questions and summaries. By the end of training, 96 percent of the students' questions were appropriate, 64 percent of the questions addressed main ideas, and 60 percent of their summaries captured the gists of the passages.

Students' reading comprehension improved along with their performance in reciprocal teaching. On daily comprehension tests, scores improved from 10 percent to 85 percent correct and stayed at this level for at least 6 months after reciprocal teaching ended. Back in the classroom, reciprocal-teaching students improved their performance on other reading tasks from the seventh percentile before reciprocal teaching to the fiftieth percentile after. Palincsar repeated the study working with two children simultaneously and obtained the same results. (Charles, mentioned above, was one of the students in this second study.)

Palincsar and Brown wanted to know if reciprocal teaching was the most efficient way to achieve these gains before they asked teachers to try it in classrooms. Reciprocal teaching demands a great deal of the teacher's time and requires intensive interaction with small groups of students. Both are valuable classroom commodities. Could the same results be achieved more efficiently by a different method? Reciprocal teaching turned out to be superior to all the alternatives tested (Brown and Palincsar 1987, 1989). In all the comparison studies, reciprocal teaching improved remedial seventh-graders' performance on comprehension tests from less than 40 percent before instruction to between 70 and 80 percent after instruction, a level typically achieved by average seventh-graders. The best of the alternative methods—explicit strategy instruction, where the teacher demonstrated and discussed each strategy and the students then completed worksheets on the strategies—raised scores from around 40 percent to between 55 and 60 percent (Brown and Palincsar 1987). These studies showed that the intense and prolonged student-teacher interaction characteristic of reciprocal teaching is crucial to its success (Palincsar et al. 1988). This is the investment teachers have to make to cash in on reciprocal teaching's dividends.

INTO THE CLASSROOM

Can reciprocal teaching work in a real classroom? Here Kathryn Ransom, Coordinator for Reading and Secondary Education in District 186, Springfield, Illinois, enters the story. Ransom—a former teacher—is a veteran professional educator. She makes it clear she has seen many trends come and go, and realizes that neither she nor the schools will please all the people all the time. Nonetheless, Ransom devotes time and effort to get new things happening in the Springfield schools. She has become adept at, as she puts it, "making deals" with research groups. "We can bring in people who have exciting ideas that need to become practical, and as the researchers work with Springfield teachers they can provide staff development experiences I never could."

Springfield's District 186 serves a population of 15,000 students, from kindergarten through high school. The system is 25 to 28 percent minority. On standardized tests, classes at all grade levels score at or above grade level in all subjects. This is a solid achievement, Ransom points out, because the majority of special education children in the district receive instruction in regular classrooms. When it was time for the classroom testing of reciprocal teaching, Palincsar approached Ransom. Ransom saw the potential of reciprocal teaching and recognized in Palincsar a researcher who could make cognitive science meaningful to administrators and teachers. The researcher and the administrator struck a deal advantageous to both.

Together, they decided to approach Springfield's middle school remedial reading teachers. These teachers worked daily with children who had adequate decoding skills but no functional comprehension skills. Ransom and Palincsar collaborated to design a staff development program that would encourage the teachers to think about instructional goals and methods and that would allow the researchers to introduce reciprocal teaching and the theory behind it. The teachers first watched videos of Palincsar conducting reciprocal teaching sessions. Later the teachers took part in reciprocal teaching sessions, playing the roles of teacher and student. Next a teacher and a researcher jointly conducted a reciprocal teaching lesson. The final training consisted of three formal sessions on the method over a three-day period.

In the first classroom study of reciprocal teaching, four volunteer remedial reading teachers used the method with their classes (Palincsar et al. 1988). Class size varied from four to seven students. Before reciprocal teaching, the baseline on daily reading-assessment tests for the students was 40 percent. After 20 days of reciprocal teaching their performance rose to between 70 and 80 percent, just as in Palincsar's initial laboratory studies. Students maintained this level of performance after reciprocal teaching and also improved their performance on other classroom comprehension tasks, including science and social studies reading. Reciprocal teaching worked in the classroom! Experienced volunteer teachers, after limited training, could replicate the laboratory results in classroom settings.

Palincsar and Ransom obtained similar results in a study that used conscripted teachers, who varied greatly in experience and expertise. The students also were more diverse in their reading deficiencies than the students in the first study. Class size varied from 7 to 15, with an average size of 12. Each teacher taught one reciprocal teaching group and one control group; the latter received standard reading-skills instruction. Again, after 20 days of reciprocal instruction, scores on daily comprehension tests improved to 72 percent for the reciprocal teaching group, versus 58 percent for the control group. Thus, average classroom teachers, working in less-than-ideal circumstances and teaching groups of seven or more students, replicated the original laboratory results. As the ultimate test, the Springfield team ran an experiment in which the strongest student in a remedial group served as the teacher. In this study, the student-teachers improved their scores on comprehension tests from 72 percent to 85 percent correct. The other students in the group improved their scores from 50 percent to 70 percent correct.

Since the study ended, in 1989, reciprocal teaching has become a mainstay in the Springfield schools. It is now used in all remedial reading classes, and its methods have been incorporated in some form into all regular classroom reading programs. Even more encouraging, Springfield teachers exposed to reciprocal teaching and to the importance of strategic thinking attempt to integrate these elements into their teaching of other subjects.

One benefit of reciprocal teaching, and of similar projects in the Springfield system, has been the teachers' participation in extended applied research. This was part of Ransom's original agenda. A project running over 5 years, as reciprocal teaching did, provides a powerful way to change teachers' behavior. Most in-service training for teachers lasts only a day or two and at best can have only a minor impact on their thinking and their performance. Ransom sees collaboration in classroom research as a way for teachers and researchers to interact in a dignified, mutually beneficial way. The teachers gain meaningful in-service experience that is intellectually satisfying. Working closely with fellow teachers and other education professionals helps them overcome the isolation of seven-hour days as the only adult in the classroom. The research team also gains, as the reciprocal teaching researchers will attest. The teachers initially helped refine reciprocal teaching for classroom use, providing important insights into how to make an instructional prototype work in a school. Later, they helped identify new research questions and helped the researchers design ways to test the method's classroom effectiveness. Because of her Springfield experience, Palincsar decided that all her subsequent educational research would be done in close collaboration with classroom professionals.

Interest in reciprocal teaching continues within District 186 through instructional chaining. A network has developed in which teachers who have used reciprocal teaching conduct in-service sessions for other teachers. By the 1987-88 school year, 150 teachers in 23 buildings had taken part in these sessions. Teachers formed peer support groups so they could discuss progress and problems associated with daily use of reciprocal teaching and other strategy instruction. The remedial teachers also helped the district design new reading tests to assess students' use of comprehension strategies. The Springfield experience contributed to ongoing efforts at the state level to revamp reading instruction and to develop reading tests that can measure the skills that methods such as reciprocal teaching try to impart. Veterans of the Springfield experiment now work in other schools and with national educational organizations to improve reading instruction.

In the Springfield schools and in others that have used reciprocal teaching, teachers have a better understanding of what reading is about. As Palincsar and Brown (1986, p. 770) observe, "There was a time not long ago when successful reading was thought to be execution of a series of component subskills." To teach reading one taught the subskills, from word recognition through finding the main idea, often in isolation and in a fixed sequence. Charles and the approximately 60 percent of American 17-year-olds who fail to reach the fourth reading proficiency level of the National Assessment of Educational Progress—who fail to become adept readers (Mullis and Jenkins 1990)—show the inadequacy of this approach. Reciprocal teaching works. The strategies it teaches enable students to apply their language-comprehension skills to reading so that they can read for meaning. Reading is more than decoding and more than the mastery of a series of small, isolated subskills.

V.

High School Physics: Confronting the Misconceptions of Novices

One of the best places to see a cognitive science approach to teaching is in Jim Minstrell's physics classes at Mercer Island High School. (See Minstrell 1989; Minstrell 1984; Minstrell and Stimpson 1990.)

Mercer Island is an upper-middle-class suburb of Seattle. The high school serves just over 1,000 students in four grades. Jim Minstrell has been teaching there since 1962. He holds bachelors', master's, and doctoral degrees from the Universities of Washington and Pennsylvania, and during his career he has worked on several national programs to improve high school physics instruction. Although deeply committed to educational research, he prefers the classroom to a university department or a school of education. "I have one of the best laboratories in the world right here," he observes. He adopted what he calls "a cognitive orientation to teaching" for practical, not theoretical, reasons. The cognitive approach addresses a fundamental classroom problem that confronts science teachers: Students' preconceptions influence how they understand classroom material.

In the early 1970s, after a decade of outstanding teaching (as measured both by students' test scores and by supervisors' evaluations), Minstrell became concerned about his effectiveness. His students couldn't transfer their formal book and lecture learning to the physics of everyday situations, and they showed little understanding of basic physical concepts, such as force, motion, and gravity. At first he thought, following Jean Piaget's theory of cognitive development, that his students lacked logical, or formal operational, skills. However, when he tested this hypothesis, he found otherwise.

Minstrell describes a task of Piaget's in which students are given two clay balls of equal size. Students agree that the two balls weigh the same. But if one ball is then flattened into a pancake, many students will then say that the pancake weighs more than the ball. They reason that the pancake weighs more because it has a larger upper surface on which air can press down. This is not a logical error but a conceptual one. Students believe that air pressure contributes to an object's weight.

"Students were bringing content ideas to the situation, ideas that were greatly affecting their performance on questions that were supposed to be testing their reasoning," Minstrell recalls.

Minstrell became actively involved in research on students' misconceptions, and he tried to apply the research in his classroom. First he expanded his classroom agenda. A teacher's primary goals are to control the students and to provide explanations that allow the students to solve textbook problems. A third goal, in the current climate of accountability, is to prepare the students to pass standardized tests of low-level skills. Minstrell maintains the first two goals, minimizes the third, and adds two goals of his own, based on cognitive research: to establish explicit instructional targets for understanding and to help the students actively reconstruct their knowledge to reach that understanding.

Minstrell attempts to diagnose students' misconceptions and to remedy them by instruction. Most teachers aren't trained to recognize and fix misconceptions. How does Minstrell do it?

FACETS

Minstrell assumes from the first day of school that his students have some knowledge of physics and that they have adequate reasoning ability. Unlike expert scientists who want to explain phenomena with a minimum of assumptions and laws, students are not driven by a desire for conceptual economy. Their knowledge works well enough in daily life, but it is fragmentary and local. Minstrell calls pieces of knowledge that are used in physics reasoning *facets*. Facets are schemas and parts of schemas that are used to reason about the physical world.

Students typically choose and apply facets on the basis of the most striking *surface* features of a problem. They derive their naive facets from everyday experience. Such facets are useful in particular situations; however, they are most likely false in general, and for the most part they are only loosely interrelated. Thus, students can quickly fall into contradictions. Two facets Minstrell typically finds students using when reasoning about objects are (1) that larger objects exert more force than smaller objects and (2) that only moving objects exert force. The first facet explains why the smart money was on Goliath and not David; the second explains why a football can "force" its way through a window. But how do you explain what happens when you throw a ball against the side of a building? The first facet suggests that the wall must exert a larger force on the ball than the ball does on the wall, but the second facet says that only the ball can exert a force, not the wall. So how is it that the ball bounces off the wall? As Minstrell sees it, the trick is to identify the students' correct intuitions—their facets that are consistent with formal science—and then build on these. As Minstrell says, "Some facets are anchors for instruction; others are targets for change."

BENCHMARK LESSONS: WHAT ARE YOUR IDEAS RIGHT NOW?

At the outset, Minstrell's students are not different from other high school juniors and seniors. Early in each course unit he administers a diagnostic test to assess qualitative, not quantitative, physical reasoning.

Between 50 percent and 75 percent of the students believe that when a heavy object and a light object are dropped or thrown horizontally, the heavier one hits the ground first. As many as half believe that when two moving objects are at the same position they are traveling at the same speed; yet they all know that to pass a car on the highway the overtaking car must be going faster, even when the two cars are side by side. Nearly half believe that air pressure affects an object's weight. Almost all believe that a constant, unbalanced force causes constant velocity. The results of the diagnostic tests give Minstrell a profile of which facets are prevalent, which ones might be anchors, and which ones are targets for change.

Minstrell organizes his course into units, such as measurement, kinematics, gravity, and electromagnetism. Some lessons, usually presented early in a unit, are particularly important in helping students change their reasoning. Minstrell calls these *benchmark lessons*.

In a benchmark lesson, the teacher and the students dissect their qualitative reasoning about vivid, everyday physics problems into facets. They become aware of the limitations of each facet, and they identify which facets are useful for understanding a particular phenomenon. They can explore how appropriate facets can be combined into powerful explanations that can be used to solve other problems.

The benchmark lesson on gravity begins 6 weeks into the course. By this time Minstrell has established a rapport with his class. He has created an environment conducive to developing understanding, a climate where questioning and respect for diverse opinions prevail, a climate where the process of scientific reasoning can be made explicit and self-conscious. Even veteran teachers marvel at how uninhibited Minstrell's students are in expressing ideas, suggesting hypotheses, and arguing positions.

Minstrell explains to the students that the unit will begin with a three-problem diagnostic quiz, and that their answers will be the subject of discussion for the next two days. He reassures them that the quiz is not intended to embarrass them or show how little they know. He wants to find out what they already know, and he wants them to be aware of what they already know. (Two of the problems from the quiz are reproduced in Figure 2.)

As the students work, Minstrell moves among them and observes their answers and explanations. After 15 minutes he collects the quizzes and goes to the board at the front of the classroom. He reports that on the first question, the scale problem, he saw several answers, and he writes them on the board: 15-20 pounds, a little over 10 pounds, exactly 10 pounds, a little less than 10 pounds, and about 0 pounds. "Now let's hold off on attacking these answers. Rather, let's defend one or more of them," he suggests.

Ethan explains why he thinks the object in the vacuum weighs nothing: "I felt it was zero, because when you're in space you float. It would be related to that." Minstrell helps fill in the argument: "When you're in space things seem weightless. Space is essentially an airless environment, so the object would weigh nothing."

A few students argue that the object weighs the same in the vacuum as in air. One says that when air is present the air above and the air below the scale balance out; some air pushes down and some pushes up, with no net effect. Chris, baseball cap on the back of his head and arms crossed, offers: "Ten pounds. The vacuum inside only has a relation to air pressure, not a relation to mass."

Two students argue that the object in a vacuum weighs slightly more than 10 pounds, because under normal conditions air helps hold up the scale. When you remove the air, the object will weigh more because there is no air supporting the scale.

The most popular student response is that the scale would read slightly less than 10 pounds. These arguments invoke facets involving density and buoyancy. John presents the rationale: "It's gonna be a little less than 10. You remember Bob Beamon. He set a world record in the long jump at the Mexico City Olympics. He jumped really far there because there is less air and it is lighter and so everything weighs less."

In the class period devoted to discussion, over half the students offer explanations for one of the answers. Minstrell is strictly a facilitator, offering no facts, opinions, or arguments himself. He then encourages students to present counterarguments. When the counterarguments and the responses have run their course, Minstrell signals the start of the next lesson segment: "Sounds like there are some pretty good arguments here across the spectrum. So what do we do?" The students urge him to run an experiment. He says, "Luckily, I happen to have a scale, a bell jar, and a vacuum pump here."

Minstrell calls two students to the front to help conduct the crucial experiment. Such demonstrations are dramatic and exciting for the students and allow them to

---

Problem 1. Under normal atmospheric conditions, an object is placed on a scale and the scale reads 10 pounds. If the scale and the object were placed under a glass dome and all the air were removed from under the dome, what would the scale read?

Problem 2. An object weighing 1 kilogram in normal air takes 1 second to fall a distance *d*. How long will it take an object the same size but weighing 5 kilograms to fall the same distance?

Figure 2
(From Jim Minstrell's diagnostic quiz. Used with his permission.)

see which prediction is correct. Research also suggests that such experiences have an important cognitive role in inducing conceptual change. They provide an initial experience that places naive and expert theories in conflict. As the students try to resolve the conflict, the dramatic demonstration serves as an organizing structure in long-term memory (an anchor) around which schemas can be changed and reorganized (Hunt 1993).

The first student reports that the object on the scale weighs 1.2 newtons under normal circumstances. Minstrell starts the vacuum pump, and the students watch the gauge as the pressure drops inside the bell jar. The pump stops when the pressure gauge reads nearly zero.

"Did the weight go to zero?" Minstrell asks. Somewhat amazed, the students respond that the weight stayed the same. Minstrell suggests that they see what happens when the air rushes back into the jar. He opens the valve and the air whistles in. A student exclaims, "Air or no air in there, there's not much difference either way!"

Minstrell asks "What does this tell us about gravity and air pressure?" "Air pressure doesn't affect weight," the students respond. They have started to correct a major misconception. Other experiences in the unit and throughout the course reinforce this benchmark discovery that air pressure and gravity are distinct physical phenomena.

DON'T FEEL DUMB!

A few days later, Minstrell and the class analyze their reasoning about the time it would take a 1-kilogram and a 5-kilogram object to fall the same distance (problem 2 above). They run the crucial experiment—a miniature replay of Galileo's apocryphal experiment at Pisa. After both balls hit the floor simultaneously, Minstrell returns to the board where he had written the quiz answers. "Some of you were probably feeling pretty dumb with these kinds of answers. Don't feel dumb," he counsels. "Let's see what's valuable about each of these answers, because each one is valuable. Why would you think that heavier things fall faster?"

A student suggests that heavy things (such as barbells) are harder to pull up, so it seems they would fall back to the ground more quickly too. "Right," Minstrell says. "When you lift something heavy, that sucker is heavy. Gravity is really pulling down. 'Aha,' you think, 'big effect there.' A useful rule of daily life is the more of X, the more of Z."

Why would anyone think a heavier object falls more slowly? A student argues that heavier objects are harder to push horizontally than light ones, and that because they are harder to push, one moves them more slowly; thus, when a heavier object is dropped, it must fall more slowly. Minstrell reinforces what is correct about this intuition. He points out that the first argument uses the facet of direct proportional reasoning and the second argument the facet of indirect proportional reasoning. Minstrell and the class will revisit these facets when they grapple with Newton's Second Law, $F = ma$ (i.e., when a force acts on an object the acceleration is directly proportional to the force and inversely proportional to the object's mass).

Minstrell concludes: "So, there are some good rationales behind these answers. Part of what I'm saying is that the rationales you have—the physics you've cooked up in the past 16 to 19 years of living—are valuable. But they are valuable only in certain contexts." The trick to becoming a competent physicist is knowing when to use which facet. It's not just a matter of having the pieces of knowledge; what counts is knowing when to use them—linking *conditions* of applicability to cognitive *actions*.

The unit on gravity continues with students doing experiments in the classroom and around the school building. It ends with seven problems, all taken from standard high school texts, which allow the students to assess their mastery of the unit's central facets and concepts.

Throughout the unit, Minstrell has not lectured, expounded, or "taught" in the traditional sense. He has identified students' initial intuitions, made their reasoning explicit by eliciting and debating their positions, provided vivid benchmark experiences to help trigger conceptual change, and encouraged them to reason about these views and experiences. He has taught physics from a cognitive perspective.

DOES IT WORK? WHY?

In 1986 Minstrell initiated a collaboration with Earl Hunt, a cognitive psychologist at the University of Washington, to assess and refine his classroom method. Hunt, a "basic" cognitive scientist who has developed an interest in an applied science of learning, describes himself as the "wet blanket" of the project. "I'm the professional skeptic who must be convinced that it is the cognitive approach and not just Minstrell that accounts for the effects," he says.

A comparison of students' scores on pretests and posttests makes it clear that Minstrell's method works. The students learn physics. But why does it work?

One concern is whether the method's success depends entirely on Jim Minstrell's pedagogical talents. This was the first issue Hunt and Minstrell investigated. Could someone other than Minstrell use the method successfully?

Minstrell trained Virginia Stimpson and Dorothy Simpson, two math teachers at Mercer Island High who had never taught physics, to use his method. At Mercer Island, as at most high schools, which students end up in which physics sections is due more to scheduling than to student choice or teacher selection. Thus, students of varying abilities are likely to end up in each section. This allowed Minstrell and Hunt to make reliable comparisons between the performances of Minstrell's students and the performances of Stimpson's and Simpson's. Gini's and Dottie's students did at least as well as Jim's, so the effect (at least at Mercer Island High) is not due to Minstrell himself.

Is Minstrell's method better than other instructional methods currently in use? Minstrell himself has shown at Mercer Island High that his method is superior to traditional methods. His students have fewer misconceptions at course's end than do students taught traditionally. For example, on the pretest 3 percent of Minstrell's students showed correct understanding of both Newton's First and Second Laws. When he used the traditional methods and curriculum, Minstrell observed that after instruction 36 percent understood the First Law and 62 percent the Second Law. When he used his cognitive approach, 95 percent of the students ended up with a correct understanding of the First Law and 81 percent with a correct understanding of the Second Law (Minstrell 1984).

Minstrell and Hunt compared Mercer Island students with students at a neighboring, comparable high school that Hunt calls "Twin Peaks." The physics instructor there also uses a conceptual, non-quantitative approach in his course. Performance on standardized math tests is the best predictor of high school physics performance. On this measure, Mercer Island and Twin Peaks students were not significantly different. So, in physics one would expect similar outcomes at the two schools. However, on the same final exam in mechanics, taken after 3 months of studying that topic, the Mercer Island students scored about 20 percent higher than the Twin Peaks students across the entire range of math scores. "This is an important result," skeptic Hunt emphasizes, "because it shows that the method does not selectively appeal to brighter students as measured by math achievement."

For good measure, Minstrell and Hunt also compared Mercer Island students with students in a "nationally known experimental, physics teaching, research and development program." The Mercer Island students consistently outperformed the other experimental group on all topics tested. Hunt adds: "We regard these data as particularly important because the questions we used in this comparison were developed by the other experimental group."

These results have allayed some of Hunt's initial skepticism, but Hunt and Minstrell realize that much remains to be done. The success of Minstrell's theory-based curriculum vindicates the cognitive approach, but for Hunt success raises further theoretical questions. He has begun a research program back in his laboratory to refine the theory underlying Minstrell's method. Why are benchmark lessons so important? How does transfer occur? How do students develop deep representations and make appropriate generalizations? Minstrell's classroom is a good laboratory, but a teacher who is responsible for seeing that his students learn physics is limited in the experiments he can conduct. No doubt, in a few years results from Hunt's basic research will feed back into Minstrell's applied research at Mercer Island High.

The next challenge for Minstrell and Hunt will be to test the method elsewhere. What will happen when teachers who are not under the innovators' direct supervision try to use the method? Instructional materials, including videotapes of benchmark lessons for each unit, will soon be ready for dissemination. The next step will be to assemble an implementation network and conduct applied research in a variety of classroom situations.

TEACHING FOR UNDERSTANDING

Jim Minstrell's students end up with a better understanding of physics, in part, because they learn more expert-like representations and concepts, as well as how

to reason with them. There is a price to pay for this deeper understanding. As Earl Hunt points out, "From a traditional perspective one might argue that Minstrell's classes fail, because often students don't get through the standard curriculum. Last year, they did not complete electricity, and atomic physics and waves were barely mentioned." Hunt thinks that changes in curricular time and course coverage will be crucial in making science instruction more effective. Hunt is quick to add that in other countries curricula sometimes allow two to three years to teach what we cram into one.

The applied work of Minstrell and others shows that we can teach in such a way as to make a significant impact on students' scientific understanding. All who have attempted to teach for understanding, though, emphasize that doing so takes time. Minstrell spends over a week developing Newton's laws, not one or two days as in most traditional courses. Reflecting on his classroom experiences, Minstrell (1989, p. 147) advises: "We must provide the time students need for mental restructuring. Hurrying on to the next lesson or the next topic does not allow for sufficient reflection on the implications of the present lesson."

Results from cognitive research indicate that if we want more students to understand science, the instruction should start early in school, and that throughout the curriculum instruction should build on students' correct intuitions and prior understanding. We should try to teach experts' conceptual understandings, not just formulas and equations, and along with this content we should teach students how to reason scientifically. Better science instruction along these lines may require a "less is more" (or at least a "longer is better") approach to the science curriculum.

Conclusion

Learning is the process whereby novices become more expert. Teaching is the profession dedicated to helping students learn, helping them become more expert. Cognitive research has matured to where it can now tell us what is involved in the mental journey from novice to expert not just in reading and physics, but across a variety of school subject domains. The research can now describe these journeys in sufficient detail—recall Siegler's exacting, fine-grained analysis of learning the balance scale—that it can serve as a map and guide for improved learning and teaching. We have at our disposal the basis for an applied science of learning that can inform the design of new materials, teaching methods and curricula. These are the tools students and teachers must have, if, as a nation, we are serious about becoming more productive and helping all students develop their intelligence as fully as possible.

Developing these tools and restructuring our schools to use them won't be easy. We will have to start in the classroom, where teachers interact with students. We will need teachers who can create and maintain learning environments where students have the smoothest possible journey from novice to expert and where they can learn to become intelligent novices. To do this, we will have to rethink, or at least re-evaluate, much of our received wisdom about educational policy, classroom practices, national standards, and teacher training.

Admittedly, there is much we still don't know about how our minds work, how children best learn, and how to design better schools. On the other hand, we already know a great deal that we can apply to improve our schools and our children's futures.

REFERENCES

Bransford, J.D., Sherwood, R., Vye, N., and Rieser, J. 1986. Teaching thinking and problem solving. *American Psychologist* 41(10): 1078-1089.

Bransford, J.D., and Stein, B.S. 1984. *The IDEAL problem solver.* Freeman.

Bransford, J.D., Stein, B.S., Arbitman-Smith, R., and Vye, N.J. 1985. Improved thinking and learning skills: An analysis of three approaches. In J.W. Segal, S.F. Chipman, and R. Glaser, eds., *Thinking and Learning Skills,* volume 1: *Relating Instruction to Research.* Erlbaum.

Bransford, J.D., Stein, B.S., Vye, N.J., Franks, J.J., Auble, P.M., Mezynski, K.J., and Perfetto, G.A. 1982. Differences in approaches to learning: An overview. *Journal of Experimental Psychology: General* 111: 390-398.

Brown, A.L., Bransford, J.D., Ferrara, R.A., and Campione, J.C. 1983. Learning, remembering, and understanding. In P.H. Mussen, ed., *Handbook of Child Psychology,* volume 3: *Cognitive Development.* Wiley.

Brown, A.L., and Palincsar, A.S. 1982. Inducing strategic learning from text by means of informed, self-control training. *Topics in Learning and Learning Disabilities* 2: 1-17.

Brown, A.L., and Palincsar, A.S. 1987. Reciprocal teaching of comprehension strategies: A natural history of one program for enhancing learning. In J.D. Day and J.G. Borkowski, eds., *Intelligence and Exceptionality: New Directions for Theory, Assessment, and Instructional Practices.* Ablex.

Brown, A.L., and Palincsar, A.S. 1989: Guided, cooperative learning and individual knowledge acquisition. In L.B. Resnick, ed., *Knowing, Learning, and Instruction: Essays in Honor of Robert Glaser.* Erlbaum.

Chase, W.G., and Simon, H.A. 1973. Perception in chess. *Cognitive Psychology* 4: 55-81.

Chipman, S.F., Segal, J.W., and Glaser, R. 1985. *Thinking and Learning Skills,* volume 2: *Research and Open Questions.* Erlbaum.

Covington, M.V. 1985. Strategic thinking and the fear of failure. In J.W. Segal, S.F. Chipman, and R. Glaser, eds., *Thinking and Learning Skills,* volume 1: *Relating Instruction to Research.* Erlbaum.

De Groot, A.D. 1965. *Thought and Choice in Chess.* Mouton.

Feuerstein, R., Hoffman, M.B., Jensen, M.R., and Rand, Y. 1985. Instrumental enrichment, an intervention program for structural cognitive modifiability: Theory and practice. In J.W. Segal, S.F. Chipman, and R. Glaser, eds., *Thinking and Learning Skills,* volume 1: *Relating Instruction to Research.* Erlbaum.

Gardner, H. 1985. *The Mind's New Science.* Basic Books.

Hunt, E. 1993. *Thoughts on Thought: An Analysis of Formal Models of Cognition.* Erlbaum.

Klahr, D., and Siegler, R.S. 1978. The representation of children's knowledge. In H. Reese and L.P. Lipsett, eds., *Advances in Child Development and Behavior,* volume 12. Academic Press.

Mansfield, R.S., Busse, T.V., and Krepelka, E.J. 1978. The effectiveness of creativity training. *Review of Educational Research* 48(4): 517-536.

Meichenbaum, D. 1985. Teaching thinking: A cognitive-behavioral perspective. In S. F. Chipman, J. W. Segal, and R. Glaser, eds., *Thinking and Learning Skills,* volume 2: *Research and Open Questions.* Erlbaum.

Minstrell, J. 1984. Teaching for the development of understanding of ideas: Forces on moving objects. In *Observing Classrooms: Perspectives from Research and Practice.* Ohio State University.

Minstrell, J. 1989. Teaching science for understanding. In L.B. Resnick and L.E. Klopfer, eds., *Toward the Thinking Curriculum.* Association for Supervision and Curriculum Development.

Minstrell, J., and Stimpson, V.C. 1990. A teaching system for diagnosing student conceptions and prescribing relevant instruction. Paper prepared for AERA session "Classroom Perspectives on Conceptual Change Teaching," Boston.

Mullis, I.V.S., and Jenkins, L.B. 1990. *The Reading Report Card, 1971-88: Trends from the Nation's Report Card.* Office of Educational Research and Improvement, U.S. Department of Education.

Newell, A., and Simon, H.A. 1972. *Human Problem Solving.* Prentice-Hall.

Nickerson, R.S., Perkins, D.N., and Smith, E.E. 1985. *The Teaching of Thinking.* Erlbaum.

Palincsar, A.S., and Brown, A.L. 1984. Reciprocal teaching of comprehension-fostering and comprehension-monitoring activities. *Cognition and Instruction* 1(2): 117-175.

Palincsar, A.S., and Brown, A.L. 1986. Interactive teaching to promote independent learning from text. *Reading Teacher* 39: 771-777.

Palincsar, A.S., Ransom, K., and Derber, S. 1988. Collaborative research and the development of reciprocal teaching. *Educational Leadership* 46: 37-40.

Perkins, D.N., and Salomon, G. 1989. Are cognitive skills context-bound? *Educational Researcher* 18: 16-25.

Savell, J.M., Wohig, P.T., and Rachford, D.L. 1986. Empirical status of Feuerstein's "Instrumental Enrichment" (FIE) technique as a method of teaching thinking skills. *Review of Educational Research* 56(4): 381-409.

Segal, J.W., Chipman, S.F., and Glaser, R. 1985. *Thinking and Learning Skills,* volume 1: *Relating Instruction to Research.* Erlbaum.

Siegler, R.S. 1976. Three aspects of cognitive development. *Cognitive Psychology* 8: 481-520.

Siegler, R.S., and Klahr, D. 1982. When do children learn? The relationship between existing knowledge and the acquisition of new knowledge. In R. Glaser, ed., *Advances in Instructional Psychology*, volume 2. Erlbaum.

Simon, H. A., and Chase, W. G. 1973. Skill in chess. *American Scientist* 61:394-403.

Stein, B.S., Bransford, J.D., Franks, J.J., Vye, N.J., and Perfetto, G.A. 1982. Differences in judgments of learning difficulty. *Journal of Experimental Psychology (General)* 111: 406-413.

The Rewards of Learning

To teach without using extrinsic rewards is analogous to asking our students to learn to draw with their eyes closed, Mr. Chance maintains. Before we do that, we should open our own eyes.

Paul Chance

Paul Chance (Eastern Shore Maryland Chapter) is a psychologist, writer, and teacher. He is the author of Thinking in the Classroom *(Teachers College Press, 1986) and teaches at James H. Groves Adult High School in Georgetown, Del.*

A man is seated at a desk. Before him lie a pencil and a large stack of blank paper. He picks up the pencil, closes his eyes, and attempts to draw a four-inch line. He makes a second attempt, a third, a fourth, and so on, until he has made well over a hundred attempts at drawing a four-inch line, all without ever opening his eyes. He repeats the exercise for several days, until he has drawn some 3,000 lines, all with his eyes closed. On the last day, he examines his work. The question is, How much improvement has there been in his ability to draw a four-inch line? How much has he learned from his effort?

E. L. Thorndike, the founder of educational psychology and a major figure in the scientific analysis of learning, performed this experiment years ago, using himself as subject.[1] He found no evidence of learning. His ability to draw a four-inch line was no better on the last day than it had been on the first.

The outcome of this experiment may seem obvious to us today, but it was an effective way of challenging a belief widely held earlier in this century, a belief that formed the very foundation of education at the time: the idea that "practice makes perfect."

It was this blind faith in practice that justified countless hours of rote drill as a standard teaching technique. Thorndike's experiment demonstrated that practice in and of itself is not sufficient for learning. Based on this and other, more formal studies, Thorndike concluded that practice is important only insofar as it provides the opportunity for reinforcement.

To reinforce means to strengthen, and among learning researchers *reinforcement* refers to a procedure for strengthening behavior (that is, making it likely to be repeated) by providing certain kinds of consequences.[2] These consequences, called *reinforcers,* are usually events or things a person willingly seeks out. For instance, we might teach a person to draw a four-inch line with his eyes closed merely by saying "good" each time the effort is within half an inch of the goal. Most people like to succeed, so this positive feedback should be an effective way of reinforcing the appropriate behavior.

Hundreds of experimental studies have demonstrated that systematic use of reinforcement can improve both classroom conduct and the rate of learning. Yet the systematic use of reinforcement has never been widespread in American schools. In *A Place Called School*, John Goodlad reports that, in the elementary grades, an average of only 2% of class time is devoted to reinforcement; in the high schools, the figure falls to 1%.[3]

THE COSTS OF REWARD

There are probably many reasons for our failure to make the most of reinforcement. For one thing, few schools of education provide more than cursory instruction in its use. Given Thorndike's finding about the role of practice in learning, it is ironic that many teachers actually use the term *reinforcement* as a synonym for *practice.* ("We assign workbook exercises for reinforcement.") If schools of education do not teach future teachers the nature of reinforcement and how to use it effectively, teachers can hardly be blamed for not using it.

The unwanted effects of misused reinforcement have led some teachers to shy away from it. The teacher who sometimes lets a noisy class go to recess early will find the class getting noisier before recess. If high praise is reserved for long-winded essays, students will develop wordy and redundant writing styles. And it should surprise no one if students are seldom original in classrooms where only conventional work is admired or if they are uncooperative in classrooms where one can earn recognition only through competition. Reinforcement is powerful stuff, and its misuse can cause problems.

Another difficulty is that the optimal use of reinforcement would mean teaching in a new way. Some studies suggest that maximum learning in elementary and middle schools might require very high rates of reinforcement, perhaps with teachers praising someone in the class an average of once every 15 seconds.[4] Such a requirement is clearly incompatible with traditional teaching practices.

Systematic reinforcement can also mean more work for the teacher. Reinforcing behavior once every 15 seconds means 200 reinforcements in a 50-minute period — 1,000 reinforcements in a typical school day. It also implies that, in order to spot behavior to reinforce, the teacher must be moving about the room, not sitting at a desk marking papers. That may be too much to ask. Some studies have found that teachers who have been taught how to make good use of reinforcement often revert to their old style of teaching. This is so even though the teachers acknowledge that increased use of reinforcement means fewer discipline problems and a much faster rate of learning.[5]

Reinforcement also runs counter to our Puritan traditions. Most Americans have

---

From *Phi Delta Kappan*, November 1992, pp. 200-207. © 1992 by Phi Delta Kappa, Inc. Reprinted by permission.

always assumed — occasional protestations to the contrary notwithstanding — that learning should be hard work and at least slightly unpleasant. Often the object of education seems to be not so much to teach academic and social skills as to "build character" through exposure to adversity. When teachers reinforce students at a high rate, the students experience a minimum of adversity and actually enjoy learning. Thus some people think that reinforcement is bad for character development.

All of these arguments against reinforcement can be countered effectively. Schools of education do not provide much instruction in the practical use of reinforcement, but there is no reason why they cannot do so. Reinforcement can be used incorrectly and with disastrous results, but the same might be said of other powerful tools. Systematic use of reinforcement means teaching in a new way, but teachers can learn to do so.[6] A great deal of reinforcement is needed for optimum learning, but not all of the reinforcement needs to come from the teacher. (Reinforcement can be provided by computers and other teaching devices, by teacher aides, by parents, and by students during peer teaching and cooperative learning.) No doubt people do sometimes benefit from adversity, but the case for the character-building properties of adversity is very weak.[7]

However, there is one argument against reinforcement that cannot be dismissed so readily. For some 20 years, the claim has been made that systematic reinforcement actually undermines student learning. Those few teachers who make extensive use of reinforcement, it is claimed, do their students a disservice because reinforcement reduces interest in the reinforced activity.

Not all forms of reinforcement are considered detrimental. A distinction is made between reinforcement involving intrinsic reinforcers — or rewards, as they are often called — and reinforcement involving extrinsic rewards.[8] Only extrinsic rewards are said to be harmful. An *intrinsic reward* is ordinarily the natural consequence of behavior, hence the name. We learn to throw darts by seeing how close the dart is to the target; learn to type by seeing the right letters appear on the computer screen; learn to cook from the pleasant sights, fragrances, and flavors that result from our culinary efforts; learn to read from the understanding we get from the printed word; and

learn to solve puzzles by finding solutions. The Japanese say, "The bow teaches the archer." They are talking about intrinsic rewards, and they are right.

Extrinsic rewards come from an outside source, such as a teacher. Probably the most ubiquitous extrinsic reward (and one of the most effective) is praise. The teacher reinforces behavior by saying "good," "right," "correct," or "excellent" when the desired behavior occurs. Other extrinsic rewards involve nonverbal behavior such as smiles, winks, thumbs-up signs, hugs, congratulatory handshakes, pats on the back, or applause. Gold stars, certificates, candy, prizes, and even money have been used as rewards, but they are usually less important in teaching — and even in the maintenance of good discipline — than those mentioned earlier.

The distinction between intrinsic and extrinsic rewards is somewhat artificial. Consider the following example. You put money into a vending machine and retrieve a candy bar. The behavior of inserting money into a vending machine has been reinforced, as has the more general behavior of interacting with machines. But is the food you receive an intrinsic or an extrinsic reward? On the one hand, the food is the automatic consequence of inserting money and pressing buttons, so it would appear to be an intrinsic reward. On the other hand, the food is a consequence that was arranged by the designer of the machine, so it would seem to be an extrinsic reward.[9]

Though somewhat contrived, the distinction between intrinsic and extrinsic rewards has been maintained partly because extrinsic rewards are said to be damaging.[10] Are they? First, let us be clear about the charge. The idea is that — if teachers smile, praise, congratulate, say "thank you" or "right," shake hands, hug, give a pat on the back, applaud, provide a certificate of achievement or attendance, *or in any way provide a positive consequence (a reward) for student behavior* — the student will be less inclined to engage in that behavior when the reward is no longer available.

For example, teachers who offer prizes to students for reading books will, it is said, make the children less likely to read when prizes are no longer available. The teacher who reads a student's story aloud to the class as an example of excellent story writing actually makes the student less likely to write stories in the future, when such public approval is not forth-

coming. When teachers (and students) applaud a youngster who has given an excellent talk, they make that student disinclined to give talks in the future. The teacher who comments favorably on the originality of a painting steers the young artist away from painting. And so on. This is the charge against extrinsic rewards.

No one disputes the effectiveness of extrinsic rewards in teaching or in maintaining good discipline. Some might therefore argue that extrinsic rewards should be used, even if they reduce interest in learning. Better to have students who read only when required to do so, some might say, than to have students who cannot read at all.

But if rewards do reduce interest, that fact is of tremendous importance. "The teacher may count himself successful," wrote B. F. Skinner, "when his students become engrossed in his field, study conscientiously, and do more than is required of them, but *the important thing is what they do when they are no longer being taught*" (emphasis added).[11] It is not enough for students to learn the three R's and a little science and geography; they must be prepared for a lifetime of learning. To reduce their interest in learning would be a terrible thing — even if it were done in the interest of teaching them effectively.

The question of whether rewards adversely affect motivation is not, then, of merely academic or theoretical importance. It is of great practical importance to the classroom teacher.

Extrinsic rewards are said to be damaging. Are they? First, let us be clear about the charge.

More than 100 studies have examined this question.[12] In a typical experiment, Mark Lepper and his colleagues observed 3- to 5-year-old nursery school children playing with various kinds of toys.[13] The toys available included felt tip pens of various colors and paper to draw on. The researchers noted the children's inclination to draw during this period. Next the researchers took the children aside and asked them to draw with the felt tip pens. The researchers promised some children a "Good Player Award" for drawing. Other children drew pictures without receiving an award.

Two weeks later, the researchers returned to the school, provided felt tip pens and paper, and observed the children's inclination to draw. They found that children who had been promised an award spent only half as much time drawing as they had originally. Those students who had received no award showed no such decline in interest.

Most studies in this area follow the same general outline: 1) students are given the opportunity to participate in an activity without rewards; 2) they are given extrinsic rewards for participating in the activity; and 3) they are again given the opportunity to participate in the activity without rewards.

The outcomes of the studies are also fairly consistent. Not surprisingly, there is usually a substantial increase in the activity during the second stage, when extrinsic rewards are available. And, as expected, participation in the activity declines sharply when rewards are no longer available. However, interest sometimes falls below the initial level, so that students are less interested in the activity than they had been before receiving rewards. It is this net loss of motivation that is of concern.

Researchers have studied this decline in motivation and found that it occurs only under certain circumstances. For example, the effect is most likely to occur when the initial interest in the activity is very high, when the rewards used are *not* reinforcers, and when the rewards are held out in advance as incentives.[14]

But perhaps the best predictor of negative effects is the nature of the "reward contingency" involved. (The term *reward contingency* has to do with the nature of the relationship between behavior and its reward.) Alyce Dickinson reviewed the research literature in this area and identified three kinds of reward contingency:[15]

Task-contingent rewards are available for merely participating in an activity, without regard to any standard of performance. Most studies that find a decline in interest in a rewarded activity involve task-contingent rewards. In the Lepper study described above, for instance, children received an award for drawing *regardless of how they drew*. The reward was task-contingent.

Performance-contingent rewards are available only when the student achieves a certain standard. Performance-contingent rewards sometimes produce negative results. For instance, Edward Deci offered college students money for solving puzzles, $1 for each puzzle solved. The rewarded students were later less inclined to work on the puzzles than were students who had not been paid. Unfortunately, these results are difficult to interpret because the students sometimes failed to meet the reward standard, and failure itself is known to reduce interest in an activity.[16]

Success-contingent rewards are given for good performance and might reflect either success or progress toward a goal. Success-contingent rewards do not have negative effects; in fact, they typically *increase* interest in the rewarded activity. For example, Ross Vasta and Louise Stirpe awarded gold stars to third- and fourth-graders each time they completed a kind of math exercise they enjoyed. After seven days of awards, the gold stars stopped. Not only was there no evidence of a loss in interest, but time spent on the math activity actually increased. Nor was there any decline in the quality of the work produced.[17]

Dickinson concludes that the danger of undermining student motivation stems not from extrinsic rewards, but from the use of inappropriate reward contingencies. Rewards reduce motivation when they are given without regard to performance or when the performance standard is so high that students frequently fail. When students have a high rate of success and when those successes are rewarded, the rewards *do not have negative effects*. Indeed, success-contingent rewards tend to increase interest in the activity. This finding, writes Dickinson, "is robust and consistent." She adds that "even strong opponents of contingent rewards recognize that success-based rewards do not have harmful effects."[18]

The evidence, then, shows that extrinsic rewards can either enhance or reduce interest in an activity, depending on how they are used. Still, it might be argued that, because extrinsic rewards *sometimes* cause problems, we might be wise to avoid their use altogether. The decision not to use extrinsic rewards amounts to a decision to rely on alternatives. What are those alternatives? And are they better than extrinsic rewards?

ALTERNATIVES TO REWARDS

Punishment and the threat of punishment are — and probably always have been — the most popular alternatives to extrinsic rewards. Not so long ago, lessons were "taught to the tune of a hickory stick," but the tune was not merely tapped on a desk. Students who did not learn their lessons were not only beaten; they were also humiliated: they sat on a stool (up high, so everyone could see) and wore a silly hat.

Gradually, more subtle forms of punishment were used. "The child at his desk," wrote Skinner, "filling in his workbook, is behaving primarily to escape from the threat of a series of minor aversive events — the teacher's displeasure, the criticism or ridicule of his classmates, an ignominious showing in a competition, low marks, a trip to the office 'to be talked to' by the principal, or a word to the parent who may still resort to the birch rod."[19] Skinner spent a lifetime inveighing against the use of such "aversives," but his efforts were largely ineffective. While extrinsic rewards have been condemned, punishment and the threat of punishment are widely sanctioned.

Punishment is popular because, in the short run at least, it gets results. This is illustrated by an experiment in which Deci and Wayne Cascio told students that, if they did not solve problems correctly within a time limit, they would be exposed to a loud, unpleasant sound. The threat worked: all the students solved all the problems within the time limit, so the threat never had to be fulfilled. Students who were merely rewarded for correct solutions did not do nearly as well.[20]

But there are serious drawbacks to the use of punishment. For one thing, although punishment motivates students to learn, it does not teach them. Or, rather, it teaches them only what *not* to do, not what *to* do. "We do not teach [a student] to learn quickly," Skinner observed, "by punishing him when he learns slowly, or to recall what he has learned by punishing him when he forgets, or to

119

think logically by punishing him when he is illogical."[21]

Punishment also has certain undesirable side effects.[22] To the extent that punishment works, it works by making students anxious. Students get nervous before a test because they fear a poor grade, and they are relieved or anxious when they receive their report card depending on whether or not the grades received will result in punishment from their parents.[23] Students can and do avoid the anxiety caused by such punishment by cutting classes and dropping out of school. We do the same thing when we cancel or "forget" a dental appointment.

Another response to punishment is aggression. Students who do not learn easily — and who therefore cannot readily avoid punishment — are especially apt to become aggressive. Their aggression often takes the form of lying, cheating, stealing, and refusing to cooperate. Students also act out by cursing, by being rude and insulting, by destroying property, and by hitting people. Increasingly, teachers are the objects of these aggressive acts.

Finally, it should be noted that punishment has the same negative impact on intrinsic motivation as extrinsic rewards are alleged to have. In the Deci and Cascio study just described, for example, when students were given the chance to work on puzzles with the threat of punishment removed, they were less likely to do so than were students who had never worked under the threat of punishment.[24] Punishment in the form of criticism of performance also reduces interest in an activity.[25]

Punishment is not the only alternative to the use of extrinsic rewards. Teachers can also encourage students. Encouragement consists of various forms of behavior intended to induce students to perform. We encourage students when we urge them to try, express confidence in their ability to do assignments, and recite such platitudes as "A winner never quits and a quitter never wins."[26]

In encouraging students, we are not merely urging them to perform, however; we are implicitly suggesting a relationship between continued performance and certain consequences. "Come on, Billy — you can do it" means, "If you persist at this task, you will be rewarded with success." The power of encouragement is ultimately dependent on the occurrence of the implied consequences. If the teacher tells Billy he can do it and if he tries

and fails, future urging by the teacher will be less effective.

Another problem with encouragement is that, like punishment, it motivates but does not teach. The student who is urged to perform a task is not thereby taught how to perform it. Encouragement is a safer procedure than punishment, since it is less likely to provoke anxiety or aggression. Students who are repeatedly urged to do things at which they ultimately fail do, however, come to distrust the judgment of the teacher. They also come to believe that they cannot live up to the expectations of teachers — and therefore must be hopelessly stupid.

Intrinsic rewards present the most promising alternative to extrinsic rewards. Experts on reinforcement, including defenders of extrinsic rewards, universally sing the praises of intrinsic rewards. Unlike punishment and encouragement, intrinsic rewards actually teach. Students who can see that they have solved a problem correctly know how to solve other problems of that sort. And, unlike extrinsic rewards, intrinsic rewards do not depend on the teacher or some other person.

But there are problems with intrinsic rewards, just as there are with extrinsic ones. Sometimes students lack the necessary skills to obtain intrinsic rewards. Knowledge, understanding, and the aesthetic pleasures of language are all intrinsic rewards for reading, but they are not available to those for whom reading is a difficult and painful activity.

Often, intrinsic rewards are too remote to be effective. If a student is asked to add 3 + 7, what is the intrinsic reward for answering correctly? The student who learns to add will one day experience the satisfaction of checking the accuracy of a restaurant bill, but this future reward is of no value to the youngster just learning to add. Though important in maintaining what has been learned, intrinsic rewards are often too remote to be effective reinforcers in the early stages of learning.

One problem that often goes unnoticed is that the intrinsic rewards for academic work are often weaker than the rewards available for other behavior. Students are rewarded for looking out the window, daydreaming, reading comic books, taking things from other students, passing notes, telling and listening to jokes, moving about the room, fighting, talking back to the teacher, and for all sorts of activities that are incompatible

with academic learning. Getting the right answer to a grammar question might be intrinsically rewarding, but for many students it is considerably less rewarding than the laughter of one's peers in response to a witty remark.

While intrinsic rewards are important, then, they are insufficient for efficient learning.[27] Nor will encouragement and punishment fill the gap. The teacher must supplement intrinsic rewards with extrinsic rewards. This means not only telling the student when he or she has succeeded, but also praising, complimenting, applauding, and providing other forms of recognition for good work. Some students may need even stronger reinforcers, such as special privileges, certificates, and prizes.

REWARD GUIDELINES

Yet we cannot ignore the fact that extrinsic rewards can have adverse effects on student motivation. While there seems to be little chance of serious harm, it behooves us to use care. Various experts have suggested guidelines to follow in using extrinsic rewards.[28] Here is a digest of their recommendations:

1. Use the weakest reward required to strengthen a behavior. Don't use money if a piece of candy will do; don't use candy if praise will do. The good effects of reinforcement come not so much from the reward itself as from the reward contingency: the relationship between the reward and the behavior.

2. When possible, avoid using rewards as incentives. For example, don't say, "If you do X, I'll give you Y." Instead, ask the student to perform a task and then provide a reward for having completed it. In most cases, rewards work best if they are pleasant surprises.

3. Reward at a high rate in the early stages of learning, and reduce the frequency of rewards as learning progresses. Once students have the alphabet down pat, there is no need to compliment them each time they print a letter correctly. Nor is there much need to reward behavior that is already occurring at a high rate.

4. Reward only the behavior you want repeated. If students who whine and complain get their way, expect to see a lot of whining and complaining. Similarly, if you provide gold stars only for the three best papers in the class, you are rewarding competition and should not be surprised if students do not cooperate

with one another. And if "spelling doesn't count," don't expect to see excellent spelling.

5. Remember that what is an effective reward for one student may not work well with another. Some students respond rapidly to teacher attention; others do not. Some work well for gold stars; others don't. Effective rewards are ordinarily things that students seek — positive feedback, praise, approval, recognition, toys — but ultimately a reward's value is to be judged by its effect on behavior.

6. Reward success, and set standards so that success is within the student's grasp. In today's heterogeneous classrooms, that means setting standards for each student. A good way to do this is to reward improvement or progress toward a goal. Avoid rewarding students merely for participating in an activity, without regard for the quality of their performance.

7. Bring attention to the rewards (both intrinsic and extrinsic) that are available for behavior from sources *other than the teacher*. Point out, for example, the fun to be had from the word play in poetry or from sharing a poem with another person. Show students who are learning computer programming the pleasure in "making the computer do things." Let students know that it's okay to applaud those who make good presentations so that they can enjoy the approval of their peers for a job well done. Ask parents to talk with their children about school and to praise them for learning. The goal is to shift the emphasis from rewards provided by the teacher to those that will occur even when the teacher is not present.[29]

Following these rules is harder in practice than it might seem, and most teachers will need training in their implementation. But reinforcement is probably the most powerful tool available to teachers, and extrinsic rewards are powerful reinforcers. To teach without using extrinsic rewards is analogous to asking our students to learn to draw with their eyes closed. Before we do that, we should open our own eyes.

1. The study is described in E. L. Thorndike, *Human Learning* (1931; reprint ed., Cambridge, Mass.: MIT Press, 1966).

2. There are various theories (cognitive, neurological, and psychosocial) about why certain consequences reinforce or strengthen behavior. The important thing for our purposes is that they do.

3. John I. Goodlad, *A Place Called School: Prospects for the Future* (New York: McGraw-Hill, 1984). Goodlad complains about the "paucity of praise" in schools. In doing so, he echoes B. F. Skinner, who wrote that "perhaps the most serious criticism of the current classroom is the relative infrequency of reinforcement." See B. F. Skinner, *The Technology of Teaching* (Englewood Cliffs, N.J.: Prentice-Hall, 1968), p. 17.

4. Bill L. Hopkins and R. J. Conard, "Putting It All Together: Superschool," in Norris G. Haring and Richard L. Schiefelbusch, eds., *Teaching Special Children* (New York: McGraw-Hill, 1975), pp. 342-85. Skinner suggests that mastering the first four years of arithmetic instruction efficiently would require something on the order of 25,000 reinforcements. See Skinner, op. cit.

5. See, for example, Bill L. Hopkins, "Comments on the Future of Applied Behavior Analysis," *Journal of Applied Behavior Analysis*, vol. 20, 1987, pp. 339-46. In some studies, students learned at double the normal rate, yet most teachers did not continue reinforcing behavior at high rates after the study ended.

6. See, for example, Hopkins and Conard, op. cit.

7. For example, Mihaly Csikszentmihalyi found that adults who are successful and happy tend to have had happy childhoods. See Tina Adler, "Support and Challenge: Both Key for Smart Kids," *APA Monitor*, September 1991, pp. 10-11.

8. The terms *reinforcer* and *reward* are often used interchangeably, but they are not really synonyms. A reinforcer is defined by its effects: an event that strengthens the behavior it follows is a reinforcer, regardless of what it was intended to do. A reward is defined by social convention as something desirable; it may or may not strengthen the behavior it follows. The distinction is important since some studies that show negative effects from extrinsic rewards use rewards that are *not* reinforcers. See Alyce M. Dickinson, "The Detrimental Effects of Extrinsic Reinforcement on 'Intrinsic Motivation,' " *The Behavior Analyst*, vol. 12, 1989, pp. 1-15.

9. John Dewey distrusted the distinction between extrinsic and intrinsic rewards. He wrote that "what others do to us when we act is as natural a consequence of our action as what the fire does to us when we plunge our hands in it." Quoted in Samuel M. Deitz, "What Is Unnatural About 'Extrinsic Reinforcement'?," *The Behavior Analyst*, vol. 12, 1989, p. 255.

10. Dickinson writes that "several individuals have demanded that schools abandon reinforcement procedures for fear that they may permanently destroy a child's 'love of learning.' " See Alyce M. Dickinson, "Exploring New Vistas," *Performance Management Magazine*, vol. 9, 1991, p. 28. It is interesting to note that no one worries that earning a school letter will destroy a student's interest in sports. Nor does there seem to be much fear that people who win teaching awards will suddenly become poor teachers. For the most part, only the academic work of students is said to be put at risk by extrinsic rewards.

11. Skinner, p. 162.

12. For reviews of this literature, see Edward L. Deci and Richard M. Ryan, *Intrinsic Motivation and Self-Determination in Human Behavior* (New York: Plenum, 1985); Dickinson, "The Detrimental Effects"; and Mark R. Lepper and David Greene, eds., *The Hidden Costs of Reward: New Perspectives on the Psychology of Human Motivation* (Hillsdale, N.J.: Erlbaum, 1978).

13. Mark R. Lepper, David Greene, and Richard E. Nisbett, "Undermining Children's Intrinsic Interest with Extrinsic Rewards," *Journal of Personality and Social Psychology*, vol. 28, 1973, pp. 129-37.

14. See, for example, Dickinson, "The Detrimental Effects"; and Mark Morgan, "Reward-Induced Decrements and Increments in Intrinsic Motivation," *Review of Educational Research*, vol. 54, 1984, pp. 5-30. Dickinson notes that studies producing negative effects are often hard to interpret since other variables (failure, deadlines, competition, and so on) could account for the findings. By way of example, she cites a study in which researchers offered a $5 reward to top performers. The study was thus contaminated by the effects of competition, yet the negative results were attributed to extrinsic rewards.

15. Dickinson, "The Detrimental Effects."

16. Edward L. Deci, "Effects of Externally Mediated Rewards on Intrinsic Motivation," *Journal of Personality and Social Psychology*, vol. 18, 1971, pp. 105-15.

17. Ross Vasta and Louise A. Stirpe, "Reinforcement Effects on Three Measures of Children's Interest in Math," *Behavior Modification*, vol. 3, 1979, pp. 223-44.

18. Dickinson, "The Detrimental Effects," p. 9. See also Morgan, op. cit.

19. Skinner, p. 15.

20. Edward L. Deci and Wayne F. Cascio, "Changes in Intrinsic Motivation as a Function of Negative Feedback and Threats," paper presented at the annual meeting of the Eastern Psychological Association, Boston, May 1972. This paper is summarized in Edward L. Deci and Joseph Porac, "Cognitive Evaluation Theory and the Study of Human Motivation," in Lepper and Greene, pp. 149-76.

21. Skinner, p. 149.

22. For more on the problems associated with punishment, see Murray Sidman, *Coercion and Its Fallout* (Boston: Authors Cooperative, Inc., 1989).

23. Grades are often referred to as rewards, but they are more often punishments. Students study not so much to receive high grades as to avoid receiving low ones.

24. Deci and Cascio, op. cit.

25. See, for example, Edward L. Deci, Wayne F. Cascio, and Judy Krusell, "Sex Differences, Positive Feedback, and Intrinsic Motivation," paper presented at the annual meeting of the Eastern Psychological Association, Washington, D.C., May 1973. This paper is summarized in Deci and Porac, op. cit.

26. It should be noted that encouragement often closely resembles reinforcement in form. One teacher may say, "I know you can do it, Mary," as Mary struggles to answer a question; another teacher may say, "I knew you could do it, Mary!" when Mary answers the question correctly. The first teacher is encouraging; the second is reinforcing. The difference is subtle but important.

27. Intrinsic rewards are more important to the maintenance of skills once learned. An adult's skill at addition and subtraction is not ordinarily maintained by the approval of peers but by the satisfaction that comes from balancing a checkbook.

28. See, for example, Jere Brophy, "Teacher Praise: A Functional Analysis," *Review of Educational Research*, vol. 51, 1981, pp. 5-32; Hopkins and Conard, op. cit.; and Dickinson, "The Detrimental Effects."

29. "Instructional contingencies," writes Skinner, "are usually contrived and should always be temporary. If instruction is to have any point, the behavior it generates will be taken over and maintained by contingencies in the world at large." See Skinner, p. 144.

Rewards Versus Learning:
A Response to Paul Chance

Mr. Kohn raises some questions about Paul Chance's article in the November 1992 Kappan *and suggests that an engaging curriculum — not manipulating children with artificial incentives — offers a genuine alternative to boredom in school and to diminished motivation when school lets out.*

....

ALFIE KOHN

ALFIE KOHN is an independent scholar living in Cambridge, Mass., who writes and lectures widely on human behavior and education. His newest book is Punished by Rewards: The Trouble with Gold Stars, Incentive Plans, A's, Praise, and Other Bribes *(Houghton Mifflin, October 1993). ©1993, Alfie Kohn.*

I N THE COURSE of offering some suggestions for how educators can help children become more generous and empathic ("Caring Kids: The Role of the Schools," March 1991), I argued that manipulating student behavior with either punishments or rewards is not only unnecessary but counterproductive. Paul Chance, taking exception to this passage, wrote to defend the use of rewards (Backtalk, June 1991). Now, following the publication of his longer brief for behaviorism ("The Rewards of Learning," November 1992), it is my turn to raise some questions — and to continue what I hope is a constructive

dialogue between us (not to mention a long overdue examination of classroom practices too often taken for granted).

To begin, I should mention two points where our perspectives converge. Neither of us favors the use of punishment, and both of us think that rewards, like other strategies, must be judged by their long-term effects, including what they do for (or to) children's motivation. Chance and I disagree, however, on the nature of those effects.

Rewards, like punishments, can usually get people to do what we want for a while. In that sense, they "work." But my reading of the research, corroborated by real-world observation, is that rewards can never buy us anything more than short-term compliance. Moreover, we — or, more accurately, the people we are rewarding — pay a steep price over time for our reliance on extrinsic motivators.

REWARDS ARE INHERENTLY CONTROLLING

Applied behaviorism, which amounts to saying, "Do this and you'll get that," is essentially a technique for controlling people. In the classroom, it is a way of doing things *to* children rather than working *with* them. Chance focuses on the empirical effects of rewards, but I feel obliged to pause at least long enough to stress that moral issues are involved here regardless of whether we ultimately endorse or oppose the use of rewards.

By now it is not news that reinforcement strategies were developed and refined through experiments on laboratory animals. Many readers also realize that underlying the practice of reinforcement is a theory — specifically, the assumption that humans, like all organisms, are

basically inert beings whose behavior must be elicited by external motivation in the form of carrots or sticks. For example, Alyce Dickinson, the author Chance cites six times and from whom he borrows the gist of his defense of rewards, plainly acknowledges the central premise of the perspective she and Chance share, which is that "all behavior is ultimately initiated by the external environment."[1] Anyone who recoils from this theoretical foundation ought to take a fresh look at the real-world practices that rest on it.

I am troubled by a model of human relationship or learning that is defined by control rather than, say, persuasion or mutual problem solving. Because the reinforcements themselves are desired by their recipients, it is easy to miss the fact that using them is simply a matter of "control[ling] through seduction rather than force."[2] Rewards and punishments (bribes and threats, positive reinforcements and "consequences" — call them what you will) are not really opposites at all. They are two sides of the same coin. The good news is that our options are not limited to variations on the theme of behavioral manipulation.[3]

REWARDS ARE INEFFECTIVE

The question of how well rewards *work*, apart from what they do to children's long-term motivation, is dispatched by Chance in a single sentence: "No one disputes the effectiveness of extrinsic rewards in teaching or in maintaining good discipline" (p. 203). I found myself rereading the paragraph in which this extraordinary claim appears, searching for signs that Chance was being ironic.

In point of fact, the evidence over-

From *Phi Delta Kappan*, June 1993, pp. 783-787. © 1993 by Alfie Kohn. Reprinted by permission of the author.

whelmingly demonstrates that extrinsic rewards are ineffective at producing lasting change in attitudes or even behaviors. Moreover, they typically do not enhance — and often actually impede — performance on tasks that are any more complex than pressing a bar. This evidence, which I have been sorting through recently for a book-length treatment of these issues (*Punished by Rewards*, scheduled for publication this fall), is piled so high on my desk that I fear it will topple over. I cannot review all of it here; a few samples will have to do.

Consider first the matter of behavior change. Even behaviorists have had to concede that the token economy, a form of behavior modification once (but, mercifully, no longer) popular for controlling people in institutions, doesn't work. When the goodies stop, people go right back to acting the way they did before the program began.[4] Studies have found that rewarding people for losing weight,[5] quitting smoking,[6] or using seat belts[7] is typically less effective than using other strategies — and often proves worse than doing nothing at all.

Children whose parents make frequent use of rewards or praise are likely to be less generous than their peers.[8] On reflection, this makes perfect sense: a child promised a treat for acting responsibly has been given no reason to keep behaving that way when there is no longer a reward to be gained for doing so. The implications for behavioristic classroom management programs such as Assertive Discipline, in which children are essentially bribed or threatened to conform to rules that the teacher alone devises, are painfully clear.

Rewards (like punishments) can get people to do what we want in the short term: buckle up, share a toy, read a book. In that sense, Chance is right that their effectiveness is indisputable. But they rarely produce effects that survive the rewards themselves, which is why behaviorists are placed in the position of having to argue that we need to keep the goodies coming or replace one kind of reward with another (e.g., candy bars with grades). The fact is that extrinsic motivators do not alter the attitudes that underlie our behaviors. They do not create an enduring *commitment* to a set of values or to learning; they merely, and temporarily, change what we do. If, like Skinner, you think there is nothing to humans other than what we do, then this criticism will not trouble you. If, on the

> The good news is that our options are not limited to variations on the theme of behavioral manipulation.

other hand, you think that our actions reflect and emerge from who we *are* (what we think and feel, expect and will), then you have no reason to expect interventions that merely control actions to work in the long run.

As for the effect on performance, I know of at least two dozen studies showing that people expecting to receive a reward for completing a task (or for doing it successfully) don't perform as well as those who expect nothing. The effect is robust for young children, older children, and adults; for males and females; for rewards of all kinds (including money, grades, toys, food, and special privileges). The tasks in these studies range from memorizing facts to engaging in creative problem solving, from discriminating between similar drawings to designing collages. In general, the more cognitive sophistication and open-ended thinking required, the worse people do when they are working for a reward.[9]

At first researchers didn't know what to make of these findings. (A good sign that one has stumbled onto something important is the phrase "contrary to hypothesis" in a research report.) "The clear inferiority of the reward groups was an unexpected result, unaccountable for by theory or previous empirical evidence," a pair of experimenters confessed in 1961.[10] Rewards "have effects that interfere with performance in ways that we are only beginning to understand," said Janet Spence (later president of the American Psychological Association) in 1971.[11] Since then, most researchers — with the exception of a small cadre of un-

reconstructed behaviorists — have gotten the message that, on most tasks, a Skinnerian strategy is worse than useless: it is counterproductive.

REWARDS MAKE LEARNING LESS APPEALING

Even more research indicates that rewards also undermine *interest* — a finding with obvious and disturbing implications for the use of grades, stickers, and even praise. Here Chance concedes there may be a problem but, borrowing Dickinson's analysis, assures us that the damage is limited. Dickinson grants that motivation tends to decline when people are rewarded just for engaging in a task and also when they receive performance-contingent rewards — those "based on performance standards" (Dickinson) or "available only when the student achieves a certain standard" (Chance).

But Dickinson then proceeds to invent a new category, "success-contingent" rewards, and calls these innocuous. The term means that, when rewards are given out, "subjects are told they have received the rewards because of good performance." For Chance, though, a "success-contingent" reward is "given for good performance and might reflect either success or progress toward a goal" — a definition that appears to diverge from Dickinson's and that sounds quite similar to what is meant by "performance-contingent." As near as I can figure, the claim both Dickinson and Chance are making is that, when people come away thinking that they have done well, a reward for what they have achieved doesn't hurt. On this single claim rests the entire defense against the devastating charge that by rewarding students for their achievement we are leading them to see learning as a chore. But what does the research really say?

Someone who simply glances at the list of studies Dickinson offers to support her assertion might come away impressed. Someone who takes the time to read those studies will come away with a renewed sense of the importance of going straight to the primary source. It turns out that two of the studies don't even deal with rewards for successful performance.[12] Another one actually *disproves* the contention that success-contingent rewards are harmless: it finds that this kind of reward not only undermines intrinsic motivation but is more destructive than rewards given just for engaging in the task![13]

The rest of the studies cited by Dickinson indicate that some subjects in laboratory experiments who receive success-contingent rewards are neither more nor less interested in the task than those who get nothing at all. But Dickinson curiously omits a number of *other* studies that are also set up so that some subjects succeed (or think they succeed) at a task and are presented with a reward. These studies have found that such rewards *do* reduce interest.[14]

Such a result really shouldn't be surprising. As Edward Deci and his colleagues have been pointing out for years, adults and children alike chafe at being deprived of a sense of self-determination. Rewards usually feel controlling, and rewards contingent on performance ("If you do a good job, here's what I'll give you") are the most controlling of all. Even the good feeling produced by doing well often isn't enough to overcome that fact. To the extent that information about how well we have done *is* interest-enhancing, this is not an argument for Skinnerian tactics. In fact, when researchers have specifically compared the effects of straight-forward performance feedback ("Here's how you did") and performance-contingent rewards ("Here's a goody for doing well"), the latter undermined intrinsic motivation more than the former.[15]

Finally, even if all the research really did show what Dickinson and Chance claim it does, remember that outside of the laboratory people often fail. That result is more likely to be de-motivating when it means losing out on a reward, such as an A or a bonus. This Chance implicitly concedes, although the force of the point gets lost: students do not turn off from failing per se but from failing when a reward is at stake. In learning contexts free of extrinsic motivators, students are more likely to persist at a task and to remain interested in it even when they don't do it well.

All of this means that getting children to think about learning as a way to receive a sticker, a gold star, or a grade — or, even worse, to get money or a toy *for* a grade, which amounts to an extrinsic motivator for an extrinsic motivator — is likely to turn learning from an end into a means. Learning becomes something that must be gotten through in order to receive the reward. Take the depressingly pervasive program by which children receive certificates for free pizza when they

have read a certain number of books. John Nicholls of the University of Illinois comments, only half in jest, that the likely consequence of this program is "a lot of fat kids who don't like to read."

Educational psychologists such as Nicholls, Carol Dweck, and Carole Ames keep finding that when children are led to concentrate on their performance, on how well they are doing — an inevitable consequence of the use of rewards or punishments — they become less interested in *what* they are doing. ("Do we have to know this? Will it be on the test?") I am convinced that one of the primary obligations of educators and parents who want to promote a lasting commitment to learning is to do everything in their power to help students forget that grades exist.

REWARDS IGNORE CURRICULAR QUESTIONS

One last point. Chance's defense of the Skinnerian status quo might more properly have been titled "The Rewards *for* Learning." My interest is in the rewards *of* learning, a concern that requires us to ask whether we are teaching something *worth* learning. This is a question that behaviorists do not need to ask; it is enough to devise an efficient technique to reinforce the acquisition of whatever happens to be in someone's lesson plan.

Chance addresses the matter of intrinsic motivation just long enough to dismiss it as "too remote to be effective." He sets up a false dichotomy, with an abstract math problem on one side (Why would a child be motivated to learn that $7 + 3 = 10$? he wants to know) and reinforcements (the solution to this problem) on the other. Indeed, if children are required to fill in an endless series of blanks on worksheets or to memorize meaningless, disconnected facts, they may *have* to be bribed to do so. But Chance seems oblivious to exciting developments in the field of education: the whole-language movement, the emphasis on "learner-centered" learning, and the entire constructivist tradition (in which teaching takes its cue from the way each child actively constructs meaning and makes sense of the world rather than treating students as passive responders to environmental stimuli).

I invite Chance to join the campaign for an engaging curriculum that is connected to children's lives and interests, for an approach to pedagogy in which students

are given real choices about their studies, and for classrooms in which they are allowed and helped to work with one another. Pursuing these approaches, not manipulating children with artificial incentives, offers a *real* alternative to boredom in school and to diminished motivation when school lets out.

1. Alyce M. Dickinson, "The Detrimental Effects of Extrinsic Reinforcement on 'Intrinsic Motivation,' " *The Behavior Analyst*, vol. 12, 1989, p. 12. Notice the quotation marks around "intrinsic motivation," as if to question the very existence of the phenomenon — a telltale sign of Skinnerian orthodoxy.

2. Edward L. Deci and Richard M. Ryan, *Intrinsic Motivation and Self-Determination in Human Behavior* (New York: Plenum, 1985), p. 70.

3. Behaviorists are apt to rejoin that control is an unavoidable feature of all relationships. In response I would point out that there is an enormous difference between saying that even subtle reinforcements can be controlling and asserting that all human interaction is best described as an exercise in control. The latter takes on faith that selfhood and choice are illusions and that we do only what we have been reinforced for doing. A far more defensible position, it seems to me, is that some forms of human interaction are controlling and some are not. The line might not be easy to draw in practice, but the distinction is still meaningful and important.

4. "Generally, removal of token reinforcement results in decrements in desirable responses and a return to baseline or near-baseline levels of performance," as the first major review of token economies concluded. In fact, not only does the behavior fail "to generalize to conditions in which [reinforcements] are not in effect" — such as the world outside the hospital — but reinforcement programs used each morning generally don't even have much effect on patients' behavior during the afternoon! See Alan E. Kazdin and Richard R. Bootzin, "The Token Economy: An Evaluative Review," *Journal of Applied Behavior Analysis*, vol. 5, 1972, pp. 359-60. Ten years later, one of these authors — an enthusiastic proponent of behavior modification, incidentally — checked back to see if anything had changed. "As a general rule," he wrote, with an almost audible sigh, "it is still prudent to assume that behavioral gains are likely to be lost in varying degrees once the client leaves the program." See Alan E. Kazdin, "The Token Economy: A Decade Later," *Journal of Applied Behavior Analysis*, vol. 15, 1982, pp. 435-37. Others reviewing the research on token economies have come to more or less the same conclusion.

5. The only two studies I am aware of that looked at weight loss programs to see what happened when people were paid for getting slimmer found that the incentives either had no effect or were actually counterproductive. See Richard A. Dienstbier and Gary K. Leak, "Overjustification and Weight Loss: The Effects of Monetary Reward," paper presented at the annual meeting of the American Psychological Association, Washington, D.C., September 1976; and F. Matthew Kramer et al., "Maintenance of Successful Weight Loss Over 1 Year: Effects of Financial Contracts for Weight Maintenance or Participation in Skills Training," *Behavior Therapy*, vol. 17, 1986, pp. 295-301.

6. A very large study, published in 1991, recruited subjects for a self-help program designed to help people quit smoking. Three months later, those who had been offered a prize for turning in weekly prog-

ress reports were lighting up again more often than were those who had received a no-reward treatment — and even more than those who didn't take part in any program at all. In fact, for people who received both treatments, "the financial incentive somehow diminished the positive impact of the personalized feedback." See Susan J. Curry et al., "Evaluation of Intrinsic and Extrinsic Motivation Interventions with a Self-Help Smoking Cessation Program," *Journal of Consulting and Clinical Psychology*, vol. 59, 1991, p. 323.

7. A committed behaviorist and his colleagues reviewed the effects of 28 programs used by nine different companies to get their employees to use seat belts. Nearly half a million vehicle observations were made over six years in the course of this research. The result: programs that rewarded people for wearing their seat belts were the least effective over the long haul. The author had to confess that "the greater impact of the no-reward strategies from both an immediate and [a] long-term perspective . . . [was] not predicted and [is] inconsistent with basic reinforcement theory." See E. Scott Geller et al., "Employer-Based Programs to Motivate Safety Belt Use: A Review of Short-Term and Long-Term Effects," *Journal of Safety Research*, vol. 18, 1987, pp. 1-17.

8. Richard A. Fabes et al., "Effects of Rewards on Children's Prosocial Motivation: A Socialization Study," *Developmental Psychology*, vol. 25, 1989, pp. 509-15. Praise appears to have a similar detrimental effect; see Joan E. Grusec, "Socializing Concern for Others in the Home," *Developmental Psychology*, vol. 27, 1991, pp. 338-42. See also the studies reviewed in Alfie Kohn, *The Brighter Side of Human Nature: Altruism and Empathy in Everyday Life* (New York: Basic Books, 1990), pp. 201-4.

9. A complete bibliography will be available in my forthcoming book, *Punished by Rewards*. Readers unwilling to wait might wish to begin by reading Mark R. Lepper and David Greene, eds., *The Hidden Costs of Rewards* (Hillsdale, N.J.: Erlbaum, 1978), and some of Teresa Amabile's work from the 1980s documenting how rewards kill creativity.

10. Louise Brightwell Miller and Betsy Worth Estes, "Monetary Reward and Motivation in Discrimination Learning," *Journal of Experimental Psychology*, vol. 61, 1961, p. 503.

11. Janet Taylor Spence, "Do Material Rewards Enhance the Performance of Lower-Class Children?," *Child Development*, vol. 42, 1971, p. 1469.

12. In one of the studies, either money or an award was given to children just for taking part in the experiment — and both caused interest in the task to decline. See Rosemarie Anderson et al., "The Undermining and Enhancing of Intrinsic Motivation in Preschool Children," *Journal of Personality and Social Psychology*, vol. 34, 1976, pp. 915-22. In the other, a total of three children were simply praised ("good," "nice going") whenever they engaged in a task; no mention was made of how well they were performing. See Jerry A. Martin, "Effects of Positive and Negative Adult-Child Interactions on Children's Task Performance and Task Preferences," *Journal of Experimental Child Psychology*, vol. 23, 1977, pp. 493-502.

13. Michael Jay Weiner and Anthony M. Mander, "The Effects of Reward and Perception of Competency upon Intrinsic Motivation," *Motivation and Emotion*, vol. 2, 1978, pp. 67-73.

14. Chance doesn't like Deci's 1971 study, but there are plenty of others. In David Greene and Mark R. Lepper, "Effects of Extrinsic Rewards on Children's Subsequent Intrinsic Interest," *Child Development*, vol. 45, 1974, pp. 1141-45, children who were promised a reward if they drew very good pictures — and then did receive the reward, along with a reminder of the accomplishment it represented — were less interested in drawing later than were children who got nothing. See also James Garbarino, "The Impact of Anticipated Reward upon Cross-Age Tutoring," *Journal of Personality and Social Psychology*, vol. 32, 1975, pp. 421-28; Terry D. Orlick and Richard Mosher, "Extrinsic Awards and Participant Motivation in a Sport Related Task," *International Journal of Sport Psychology*, vol. 9, 1978, pp. 27-39; Judith M. Harackiewicz, "The Effects of Reward Contingency and Performance Feedback on Intrinsic Motivation," *Journal of Personality and Social Psychology*, vol. 37, 1979, pp. 1352-63; and Richard A. Fabes, "Effects of Reward Contexts on Young Children's Task Interest," *Journal of Psychology*, vol. 121, 1987, pp. 5-19. See too the studies cited in, and conclusions offered by, Kenneth O. McGraw, "The Detrimental Effects of Reward on Performance: A Literature Review and a Prediction Model," in Lepper and Greene, eds., p. 40; Mark R. Lepper, "Extrinsic Reward and Intrinsic Motivation," in John M. Levine and Margaret C. Wang, eds., *Teacher and Student Perceptions: Implications for Learning* (Hillsdale, N.J.: Erlbaum, 1983), pp. 304-5; and Deci and Ryan, p. 78.

15. Richard M. Ryan et al., "Relation of Reward Contingency and Interpersonal Context to Intrinsic Motivation: A Review and Test Using Cognitive Evaluation Theory," *Journal of Personality and Social Psychology*, vol. 45, 1983, pp. 736-50. "Rewards in general appear to have a controlling significance to some extent and thus in general run the risk of undermining intrinsic motivation," the authors wrote (p. 748).

Sticking Up for Rewards

It is ironic that honest feedback or a straightforward contingency between work and rewards should be called manipulative, while "persuasion" and "mutual problem solving" should not, Mr. Chance retorts.

. . . .

PAUL CHANCE

PAUL CHANCE (Eastern Shore Maryland Chapter) is a psychologist, writer, and former teacher. He is the author of Thinking in the Classroom *(Teachers College Press, 1986).*

I T IS DIFFICULT to know how to respond to Alfie Kohn's critique.* It is so disjointed and so full of misrepresentations of fact and theory that it is like a greased pig: one can scarcely get a grip on it, let alone wrestle it to the ground. I will illustrate what I mean with a few examples and then reply to what I believe to be Kohn's major objections.

Item: To reward, Kohn says, is to say to a student, "Do this and you'll get that." But this is only one kind of reward — and one that I specifically advised readers to avoid when possible. It is these "contractual rewards" (or incentives) that are apt to be problematic.[1] My article focused on rewards that provide feedback about performance. Such "informational rewards" reflect effort or the quality of performance (e.g., "Good try, Janet"; "Great job, Billy"). As we shall see, even researchers who criticize contractual rewards do not normally object to informational rewards.

[*See *Annual Editions* Article 20. Ed.]

Item: Kohn says that I ask, Why would a child be motivated to learn that 7 + 3 = 10? But my question was, *How* can a child learn that 7 + 3 = 10 without some sort of response from the environment? A teacher, a peer tutor, or a computer program may provide the necessary feedback, but the natural environment rarely does. This was the point of E. L. Thorndike's line experiment, described in my article.

Item: Kohn suggests that the use of rewards is manipulative and controlling. It is ironic that honest feedback or a straightforward contingency between work and rewards should be called manipulative, while "persuasion" and "mutual problem solving" should not. Students, I suspect, know the truth of the matter. As for control: a parent rewards a baby's crying when he or she offers a bottle, and the baby rewards the parent's action by ceasing to cry. Each controls the other. Students and teachers exert the same sort of reciprocal control in the classroom.[2]

Item: Nowhere do I suggest that students must "fill in an endless series of blanks on worksheets or memorize meaningless, disconnected facts," nor is there any reason to assume that the use of rewards implies such practices. The truth is that rewards are useful whether the student is memorizing dates, mastering algebra word problems, or learning to think.[3] Some sort of extrinsic reinforcement (informational reward) is usually necessary, in the early stages at least, for learning to occur efficiently.

Item: Kohn refers to "practices too often taken for granted." Evidently he believes the mythology that rewards are widely used in our schools. Yet I noted in my article that John Goodlad found that only 2% of class time is devoted to reinforcement in elementary school — and only 1% in high school.[4] Other research consistently shows that reinforcement is notable by its absence. Harold Stevenson, for example, compared elementary classrooms in America and Asia. He found pronounced differences in the activities of teachers when students were engaged in seatwork. In half of the classes observed in the Chicago area, the teachers provided no feedback about student performance; this seldom happened in Taiwan and almost never happened in Japan.[5]

Item: I do not assume, as suggested, that "humans, like all organisms, are basically inert beings." Nor do I know any psychologist who would embrace this view. Behavioral psychologists in particular emphasize that we learn by *acting on* our environment. As B. F. Skinner put it: "[People] act on the world, and change it, and are changed in turn by the consequences of their actions."[6] Skinner, unlike Kohn, understood that people learn best in a responsive environment. Teachers who praise or otherwise reward student performance provide such an environment.

Item: Kohn implies that I consider grades a reward. In fact, I noted (as Skinner and others had before me) that grades are more often a form of punishment. Incidentally, F. S. Keller, a behaviorist, proposed a system of education that could eliminate grades. In the Keller plan, students are required to demonstrate mastery of each skill before moving to the next. Mastery of each unit in the curriculum is recorded, so grades become superfluous.[7]

Item: Kohn says that "moral issues are involved." The implication is that I and other teachers who use rewards are immoral. If it is immoral to let students know they have answered questions correctly, to pat a student on the back for a good effort, to show joy at a student's understanding of a concept, or to recognize the achievement of a goal by providing a gold star or a certificate — if this is immoral, then count me a sinner.

From *Phi Delta Kappan*, June 1993, pp. 787-790. © 1993 by Phi Delta Kappa, Inc. Reprinted by permission.

The above points illustrate, I think, the slippery nature of Kohn's critique and may lead the reader to question his scholarship and his motives for writing. I now turn to what seem to be his major criticisms of rewards.

■ Kohn insists that rewards undermine interest in rewarded activities.[8] Notice that Kohn does not argue that *some* rewards — or *some uses of* rewards — undermine interest. There is, in his view, no such thing as a good reward. Simple feedback, praise, smiles, hugs, pats on the back, gold stars, applause, certificates of completion, public and private commendations, prizes, special privileges, money, informational rewards, and contractual rewards — they are all one to Kohn, and they are all bad.

The best-known researchers who have found rewards sometimes troublesome are Edward Deci, Richard Ryan, Mark Lepper, and David Greene. Kohn cites all four in making his case. What he does not tell us (though he must surely know it) is that all of these researchers reject his view.[9]

Deci and Ryan believe that rewards can undermine motivation if used in a controlling way. But they add, "When used to convey to people a sense of appreciation for work well done, [rewards] will tend to be experienced informationally and will *maintain or enhance intrinsic motivation*" (emphasis added).[10]

Lepper and Greene take a similar stand. They note, "If rewards provide [a student] with new information about his ability at a particular task, this may *bolster his feelings of competence and his desire to engage in that task for its own sake*" (emphasis added).[11] They add, "If a child does not possess the basic skills to discover the intrinsic satisfaction of complex activities such as reading, the use of extrinsic rewards may be required to equip him with these skills."[12]

The position taken by Deci, Ryan, Lepper, and Greene reflects the consensus among researchers who are concerned about the possible negative effects of rewards. Mark Morgan, for example, reviewed the research and wrote that "the central finding emerging from the present review is that rewards can have either undermining or enhancing effects depending on circumstances."[13] He concludes that "the evidence seems to support strongly the hypothesis that rewards that emphasize success or competence on a task enhance intrinsic motivation."[14]

■ Kohn claims that rewards do not work. It is true that not all rewards are

> Certain rewards (e.g., attention, positive feedback, praise) are almost always effective reinforcers when used properly.

reinforcing. Teachers must not assume that a reward will strengthen behavior merely because that is the teacher's intention. What is reinforcing for one student may not be for another. But there is overwhelming evidence that certain rewards (e.g., attention, positive feedback, praise) are almost always effective reinforcers when used properly.

In a study by Bill Hopkins and R. J. Conard, cited in my article, teachers who provided frequent feedback, praise, and other rewards saw much faster learning.[15] Students in these classes advanced at the normal rate in spelling, at nearly twice the normal rate in mathematics, and at more than double the usual rate in reading.[16] Studies showing similar gains, due at least partly to frequent use of rewards (especially feedback and praise), are easily found by those who seek them.[17]

Even contractual rewards may be useful in some circumstances. In one program, high-risk, low-income adolescents and young adults in Lafayette Parish, Louisiana, were paid $3.40 an hour to participate in a summer program of academic instruction and job training. Students gained an average of 1.2 grade levels in reading and 1.5 grade levels in math in just eight weeks.[18]

It may be the case that the Lafayette Parish students stopped reading when money was no longer available. It probably cannot be said, however, that they read less than they did before participating in the program. If students show little or no interest in an activity, it is silly to refuse to provide rewards for fear of undermining their interest in the activity — a point made by Greene and Lepper.[19]

Kohn ignores such evidence and instead cites studies on the use of contractual rewards in weight control, smoking, and seat belt programs.[20] I am (understandably, I think) reluctant to take Kohn's assessment of these programs at face value.[21] But let us assume for the sake of argument that he is right. Note that none of these programs has anything to do with the value of rewards in classroom learning. Kohn's logic is, "If rewards do not help people stop smoking, they cannot help students learn to write." By the same logic, we would have to conclude that since aspirin is of no use in treating cancer, it must not be effective in treating headache. It is a bizarre logic.

■ The benefits of rewards, says Kohn, are only temporary. Obviously this is not true if we are speaking of academic learning: the child who learns the Pythagorean theorem at the hands of a teacher who provides frequent feedback and praise does not suddenly forget Pythagoras because his next teacher no longer pays attention to his efforts. Nor is there any reason to think that students who are paid to read become illiterate when the money runs out.

But perhaps Kohn has other kinds of learning in mind. Teachers who praise and attend to students when they are on-task will find those students spending less time staring out the window or doodling in their notebooks.[22] If the teacher abruptly stops rewarding on-task behavior, the rate of window staring and doodling will return to its previous level.[23] To conclude from this that teachers should not reward behavior is ridiculous. It is like saying that regular exercise is pointless because your muscles get flabby again when you stop exercising. The point is not to stop.

It should be noted, moreover, that one of the things we can strengthen with rewards is persistence. Once our students are on-task for short periods, we can then begin rewarding longer periods of on-task behavior. We must be careful not to raise the standard too quickly, but we can *gradually* require more from our students. Persistence at other kinds of activities can also be built up by systematically providing rewards (especially praise) for meeting successively higher standards. Many teachers do this over the course of a school year, often without realizing it.

When behavior is rewarded intermittently in this way, it tends to become stronger. That is, it becomes *less* likely to fall off when rewards are no longer available. This is a well-established phenomenon called the partial reinforcement effect (PRE). The PRE reflects the fact that, in an uncertain world, persistence often pays off.

ONE FINAL comment: I realize that this reply to Kohn's remarks will have little impact on most readers. Kohn is selling what educators want to buy — and what many of them have been buying for several decades. It is the philosophy of education that says that students must teach themselves, that the teacher's job is to let students explore and discover on their own, and that teachers can, at most, "facilitate learning."[24]

This philosophy renders the teacher essentially impotent and leads ultimately to the conclusion that, when students fail, it is their own fault.[25] If students do not learn, it is because of some deficiency in them: lack of ability, lack of motivation, hyperactivity, attention deficit disorder — we have lots of choices. The failure is never due to inadequate teaching. Learning depends, after all, on things inside the student, well out of the teacher's reach.

I reject this view. I believe that a fair reading of the research on classroom learning points to a better way. That better way includes a teacher who is actively engaged in the educational process. Such a teacher recognizes the importance of, among other things, providing students with opportunities to perform and providing consequences for that performance. Those consequences include feedback, praise, smiles, and other forms of informational reward. In certain circumstances, they may include contractual rewards. This view of education places responsibility for learning squarely on the teacher's shoulders. Perhaps that is why there is so much opposition to it.

1. B. F. Skinner was not fond of contractual rewards himself, but he agreed that they may sometimes be necessary. See B. F. Skinner, "The Contrived Reinforcer," *The Behavior Analyst*, Spring 1982, pp. 3-8.

2. In an *Industry Week* survey, about one in three employees complained about a lack of praise for their work, a fact reported in Randall Poe and Carol L. Courter, "Fast Forward," *Across the Board*, September 1991, p. 5. Would workers want more praise if they considered it manipulative and controlling?

3. For instance. students can learn to find logical errors in a text by reading texts containing such errors and receiving feedback and praise for their efforts. See Kent R. Johnson and T. V. Joe Layng, "Breaking the Structuralist Barrier: Literacy and Numeracy with Fluency," *American Psychologist*, vol. 47, 1992, pp. 1475-90. For more on the use of rewards to teach thinking, see Paul Chance, *Thinking in the Classroom* (New York: Teachers College Press, 1986), Ch. 9.

4. John I. Goodlad, *A Place Called School: Prospects for the Future* (New York: McGraw-Hill, 1984), p. 112. Goodlad argues that teachers should be taught the skills of "providing students with knowledge of their performance, and giving praise for good work" (p. 127). For the most part they are not taught these skills. Ernest Vargas notes that, "with the exception of a stray course here or there," the 1,200 colleges of education in this country offer little instruction in reinforcement and related techniques. See Ernest A. Vargas, "Teachers in the Classroom: Behaviorological Science and an Effective Instructional Technology," *Youth Policy*, July/August 1988, p. 35.

5. Harold W. Stevenson, "Learning from Asian Schools," *Scientific American*, December 1992, pp. 70-76. Stevenson suggests that the American preference for seatwork and the failure to provide feedback may be due partly to the fact that Americans teach longer hours than their Asian counterparts.

6. Quoted in James G. Holland, "B. F. Skinner (1904-1990)," *American Psychologist*, vol. 47, 1992, p. 667.

7. F. S. Keller, "Goodbye, Teacher . . . ," *Journal of Applied Behavior Analysis*, Spring 1968, pp. 79-89. See also Paul Chance, "The Revolutionary Gentleman," *Psychology Today*, September 1984, pp. 42-48.

8. Studies reporting a loss of interest following rewards typically involve 1) contractual rewards and 2) behavior that is already occurring at a high rate. This is, of course, a misuse of contractual rewards, since the purpose of such rewards is to boost the rate of behavior that occurs *infrequently*.

9. In my article, I provided guidelines for the effective use of rewards. These guidelines were drawn, in part, from the recommendations of Deci, Ryan, Lepper, and Greene.

10. Edward L. Deci and Richard M. Ryan, *Intrinsic Motivation and Self-Determination in Human Behavior* (New York: Plenum, 1985), p. 300.

11. David Greene and Mark R. Lepper, "Intrinsic Motivation: How to Turn Play into Work," *Psychology Today*, September 1974, p. 54. Elsewhere they write that "the effects of rewards depend upon the manner and context in which they are delivered." See Mark R. Lepper and David Greene, "Divergent Approaches," in idem, eds., *The Hidden Costs of Reward* (New York: Erlbaum, 1978), p. 208.

12. Greene and Lepper, p. 54.

13. Mark Morgan, "Reward-Induced Decrements and Increments in Intrinsic Motivation," *Review of Educational Research*, Spring 1984, p. 13.

14. Ibid., p. 9. Another of Kohn's sources, Teresa Amabile, also specifically defends the use of informational rewards. See Teresa Amabile, "Cashing in on Good Grades," *Psychology Today*, October 1989, p. 80. See also idem, *The Social Psychology of Creativity* (New York: Springer-Verlag, 1983).

15. Bill L. Hopkins and R. J. Conard, "Putting It All Together: Superschool," in Norris G. Haring and Richard L. Schiefelbusch, eds., *Teaching Special Children* (New York: McGraw-Hill, 1975), pp. 342-85.

16. The students also enjoyed school more and were better behaved.

17. See, for example, Charles R. Greenwood et al., "Out of the Laboratory and into the Community," *American Psychologist*, vol. 47, 1992, pp. 1464-74; R. Douglas Greer, "L'Enfant Terrible Meets the Educational Crisis," *Journal of Applied Behavior Analysis*, Spring 1992, pp. 65-69; and Johnson and Layng, op. cit.

18. Steven Hotard and Marion J. Cortez, "Evaluation of Lafayette Parish Job Training Summer Remedial Program: Report Presented to the Lafayette Parish School Board and Lafayette Parish Job Training Department of Lafayette Parish Government," August 1987. Note that this research may not represent the best use of contractual rewards, since payment was only loosely contingent on performance.

19. "Clearly," they write, "if a child begins with no intrinsic interest in an activity, there will be no intrinsic motivation to lose." See Greene and Lepper, p. 54.

20. Note that Kohn cites no evidence that his own preferred techniques — persuasion and mutual problem solving — are effective in helping people lose weight, quit smoking, or use seat belts. Indeed, reward programs have been used to treat these problems precisely because persuasion and education have proved ineffective.

21. For instance, in the study on smoking that Kohn cites, the researchers note that "the incentive was not linked directly to smoking cessation." See Susan J. Curry et al., "Evaluation of Intrinsic and Extrinsic Motivation Interventions with a Self-Help Smoking Cessation Program," *Journal of Consulting and Clinical Psychology*, vol. 59, 1991, p. 309. The researchers rewarded participants for completing progress reports, *not* for refraining from smoking.

22. Teacher attention can be an effective reward for on-task behavior. See R. Vance Hall, Diane Lund, and Deloris Jackson, "Effects of Teacher Attention on Study Behavior," *Journal of Applied Behavior Analysis*, Spring 1968, pp. 1-12.

23. Some might argue that we should merely provide students with more interesting (i.e., intrinsically rewarding) material. While interesting learning materials are certainly desirable, it is probably unrealistic to expect that students will always have interesting material with which to work. It may therefore be desirable for them to learn to concentrate on work even when it is not particularly agreeable.

24. The roots of today's constructivist "revolution" are described in Lawrence A. Cremin, "The Free School Movement," *Today's Education*, September/October 1974, pp. 71-74; and in B. F. Skinner, "The Free and Happy Student," *New York University Education Quarterly*, Winter 1973, pp. 2-6.

25. This is apparently the prevailing view. Galen Alessi has found that school psychologists, for instance, rarely consider poor instruction the source of a student's difficulties. Instead, the student and, in a few cases, the student's parents are said to be at fault. Galen Alessi, "Diagnosis Diagnosed: A Systematic Reaction," *Professional School Psychology*, vol. 3, 1988, pp. 145-51.

THE TYRANNY OF SELF-ORIENTED SELF-ESTEEM

Many modern self-esteem programs emphasize a self-focus, although a focus directed on external-to-self goals may be more productive.

James H. McMillan, Judy Singh, and Leo G. Simonetta

JAMES H. McMILLAN, Ph.D., is a professor of educational studies at Virginia Commonwealth University in Richmond, Virginia. JUDY SINGH is a doctoral student in education at Virginia Commonwealth University. LEO G. SIMONETTA is an assistant professor and social psychologist at the Center for Urban Policy Research at Georgia State University in Atlanta.

In Ryann's second-grade classroom there was a poster on one wall to celebrate each individual student. For one week during the year each student was the "special child" of the class, and the space on the poster indicated unique and valued things about the child, such as a favorite color, hobbies, or family. Students put up pictures and other items to announce publicly what they thought was good about themselves. (Ryann, daughter of one of the authors, liked being a "special child" for a week, but the parent was not as enthusiastic.)

Activities of this type are common in elementary schools, all seeking to boost the self-esteem of the students. They assume that self-esteem is the key to achievement, and in fact much evidence, both anecdotal and research-based, shows that students achieve more with self-esteem. Teachers also seem to accept self-esteem as critical for intellectual development and necessary for students to excel or even achieve needed competence in academic tasks. According to Barbara Lerner, "Teachers generally seem to accept the modern dogma that self-esteem is the critical variable for intellectual development—the master key to learning. Children . . . cannot achieve excellence, or even competence, until their self-esteem is raised."[1]

Linking self-esteem to success and overall well-being is so well accepted that there are many institutes, foundations, task forces, and centers dedicated to promoting self-esteem programs. For example, there is the California Task Force to Promote Self-Esteem and Personal and Social Responsibility, the Center for Self-Esteem, the National Council for Self-Esteem, and the Foundation for Self-Esteem.[2] In addition, an increasing number of books, monographs, audio- and videocassettes stress developing self-esteem, as well as "how to" programs for teachers at all levels. The fundamental idea is that once educators focus on improving students' self-esteem, not only will behavior and achievement improve, but students also will be more satisfied, better adjusted, and happier. The assumption is that concentrating on enhancing self-esteem will produce these positive outcomes.

But is it possible, with the best of intentions, to overemphasize self-esteem with self-oriented activities? What are we teaching our children by encouraging and reinforcing a self-focus, and what are its long-term consequences? Since the mid-'60s, psychology has transformed our way of thinking about explanations for people's behaviors, shifting from out-

What are we teaching our children by encouraging and reinforcing a self-focus, and what are its long-term consequences?

side the self (behaviorism) to within the self. The psychologist Martin Seligman terms our current culture one of "maximal selfs," in which the individual should be gratified, fulfilled, self-actualized, and in control.[3] Seligman argues that this revolutionary change has caused increased depression, hopelessness, and other personal difficulties because of the dual burden of high expectations and self-control. Since the focus is on ourselves as being responsible, and on an expectation that we will be most content and happy if we concentrate on what is best for us, coping with failure to reach our expectations becomes difficult. If Seligman is correct, many facets of current self-esteem programs may be based on fundamentally flawed and misdirected theory. In this article the theory of self-oriented self-esteem programs will be reviewed, with illustrations of suggested practices based on this theory and the results that can be expected from this approach. An alternative theory will be recommended, with suggested practices.

Self-oriented Self-esteem

Many self-esteem programs fundamentally encourage students to think more about themselves, to be more introspective and self-oriented. The idea is that the self can be enhanced by focusing on it positively. Barbara Lerner refers to this as "feel-good-now self-esteem."[4] Jack Canfield, a well-known advocate of self-esteem

enhancement, has suggested several strategies for the classroom that emphasize introspection: 1) assume an attitude of 100 percent responsibility by getting students to think about what they are saying to themselves; 2) focus on the positive—"I spend a lot of my time having students recall, write about, draw, and share their past experiences"; 3) learn to monitor your self-talk by replacing negative thoughts with positive—"I can learn to do anything I want, I am smart, I love and accept myself the way I am"; and 4) identify your strengths and weaknesses.[5]

A popular self-esteem book for educators suggests enhancing self-esteem with one or more of the following: improving self-evaluation skills; developing a sense of personal worth; reflecting on self-esteem; thinking of oneself in positive terms; discovering reasons the individual is unhappy; or examining sources of and influences on self-esteem. Their emphasis is on enhancing students' positive self-perceptions.[6] Such ideas are often implemented in classroom activities that teach students introspective thinking: for example, keeping a journal about themselves and indicating "what I like best about myself";[7] teaching a unit entitled "I Am Great" that emphasizes their individuality through self-portraits, silhouettes of themselves, "who am I," and "coat of arms" exercises;[8] and programs such as Developing Understanding of Self and Others (DUSO), Toward Affective Development, and Dimensions of Personality. Some less-complex programs simply encourage student self-talk with phrases such as "I'm terrific" or "I'm great." All these activities or programs are designed to promote self-acceptance and self-awareness, to help students become aware of their unique characteristics, and to "put children in touch with themselves."[9]

Although these are well-intentioned programs, their encouragement of self-introspection may distort a normal, healthy perspective about oneself into self-importance, self-gratification, and ultimately selfishness. If

the message is that "me" is most important, will selfishness be viewed as normal and expected? Are we making a virtue of self-preoccupation? If so, such "selfism" may have negative consequences. As William Damon points out, "A young mind might too readily interpret a blanket incantation toward self-esteem as a lure toward self-centeredness."[10] Damon believes that placing the child at the center of the universe is psychologically dangerous because "...it draws the child's attention away from the social realities to which the child must adapt for proper character development."[11] Children taught to place themselves first care most for their own personal experiences, and in doing so they do not learn how to develop respect for others. According to Lerner, the feel-good-now variety of self-esteem eventually leads to unhappiness, restlessness, and dissatisfaction.[12] Finally, Seligman argues that our obsession with self is responsible for an alarming increase in depression and other mental difficulties,[13] and it is well-documented that such problems result from rumination and obsessive thinking about oneself.[14]

There are other negative consequences of overemphasizing self-oriented self-esteem. For most students, and surely young children, the idea of self-esteem is abstract and hard to understand. Generalized statements such as "you're valued," or "you're great," or "you're special" have no objective reality. They are simply holistic messages that, untied to something tangible and real, have little meaning.[15] Teachers making such statements will lose credibility because children are adept at discerning valid feedback from such vague generalizations. Students may develop a skepticism toward and distrust of adults, or even worse may learn to tune them out entirely, as the teacher "shades the truth . . . [with] . . . empty rhetoric, transparent flattery, bland distortions of reality."[16] By trying to bolster self-esteem with messages that are not "entirely" true, teachers inadvertently undermine the trust of the child. For students who already have a low self-esteem, such statements reinforce a noncaring attitude from adults. From the perspective of children, caring adults "tell it like it is" and don't hide the truth—they don't cover up or make things up that aren't true.

In contrast, there is ample evidence that our mental health improves as we forget ourselves and focus on activities that are not self-oriented. Often we are most happy when we are so involved in outside pursuits that we don't think about ourselves. This leads us to an alternative theoretical foundation for self-esteem: the notion that healthy self-esteem results not from self-preoccupation and analysis but just the opposite—from **not** being self-oriented but being occupied by interests and pursuits external to self. Indeed, many self-esteem enhancement programs appear to be based on this idea.

Accomplishment and External-to-Self-oriented Self-esteem

As an alternative to the self-orientation approach, we suggest that a healthy esteem results not from self-preoccupation and analysis but from activities that result in meaningful accomplishment or have an external-to-self orientation. Accomplishment means that self-esteem is enhanced as children work hard to meet externally set, reasonable standards of achievement. Lerner calls this "earned" self-esteem: "Earned self-esteem is based on success in meeting the tests of reality—measuring up to standards—at home and in school. It is necessarily hard-won, and develops slowly, but is stable and long-lasting, and provides a secure foundation for further growth and development. It is not a precondition for learning but a product of it."[17]

Achieving meaningful success in schoolwork enhances self-esteem after many years of meeting standards and demands. A foundation for self-esteem based on tangible evidence is internalized by students because it makes sense to them in their social environment. Internally meaningful

Accomplishment means that self-esteem is enhanced as children work hard to meet externally set, reasonable standards of achievement.

performance and accomplishment can be attributed to ability and effort. Such internal attributions underlie a sense of self-efficacy so that the child becomes confident in being a capable learner. Striving for achievement also directs children's thinking off themselves and on something external to themselves. This change in thinking orientation determines self-esteem programs that theoretically are diametrically opposed to self-oriented programs.

Recently there have been signs that psychologists may be changing their views about the emphasis on selfism to enhance self-esteem. Seligman maintains that many have lost a sense of commitment to larger entities outside themselves—country, church, community, family, God, or a purpose that transcends themselves. Without these connections people are left to find meaning and fulfillment in themselves.[18] The negative consequences of de-emphasizing other people, groups, community, and the larger society include vandalism, violence, racial tensions, high divorce rates, and drug abuse. Some psychologists attribute the growth of the "me" generation and selfish behavior to the emphasis on individuality and related themes.[19] Others argue that schools should promote selflessness by emphasizing group welfare over individuals, involvement rather than iso-

lation, and self-denial rather than self-centeredness.

These authors suggest that student well-being is best enhanced by pursuits that take attention away from self, in which one gets "lost." Such pursuits could include a hobby; a concern for helping others; having a purpose or cause bigger than oneself; submitting to duty or to a role in community; or academic success following meaningful effort. The hypothesis is that self-esteem is a by-product of successful external-to-self experiences. The more success a student has in such activities, the stronger his or her own self-esteem will be.

From a social-psychological perspective, participating constructively with others is necessary for positive self-esteem. As stated by Damon:

> Growing up in large part means learning to participate constructively in the social world. This in turn means developing real skills, getting along with others, acquiring respect for social rules and legitimate authority, caring about those in need, and assuming social responsibility in a host of ways. All of these efforts necessarily bring children out of themselves. They require children to orient themselves toward other people and other people's standards.[21]

By focusing outside themselves children learn respect for others and an objective reference for acquiring a stable and meaningful sense of themselves. It is the outward focus that forms the foundation for self-esteem.

Some examples of self-esteem programs appear to be based on this external-to-self hypothesis. One is a successful program in which students are involved in an art project structured to enhance a feeling of belonging and accomplishment. Self-esteem is improved by involving students in meaningful group activity, not by self-introspection.[22] Another program reports that children acquire self-esteem from successful experiences and appropriate feedback in motor skill development.[23] Several other programs also stress successful achievement in affecting self-esteem.[24] In each case the program involves students in some meaningful activity, rather than focusing on themselves.

Conclusion

Clearly, educators need to concentrate their efforts on improving students' self-esteem. The important question is: How should this be done? We have suggested that approaches emphasizing meaningful achievement and external-to-self pursuits will result in more healthy self-esteem than programs that are self-oriented. Teachers and administrators need to design programs directing student attention away from the self, not toward it. Paradoxically, positive self-esteem develops as students forget about self-esteem, focus on external pursuits, and obtain positive feedback following meaningful involvement and effort

Teachers and administrators need to design programs directing student attention away from the self, not toward it.

1. Barbara Lerner, "Self-esteem and Excellence: The Choice and the Paradox," *American Educator* 9 (1985): 10-16.

2. Jack Canfield, "Improving Students' Self-esteem," *Educational Leadership* 48 (1990): 48-50.

3. Martin E. P. Seligman, "Boomer Blues: With Too Great Expectations, the Baby-Boomers Are Sliding into Individualistic Melancholy," *Psychology Today* 22 (1988): 50-55.

4. Lerner, "Self-esteem and Excellence."

5. Canfield, "Improving Students' Self-esteem."

6. James A. Beane and Richard P. Lipka, *Self-concept, Self-esteem, and the Curriculum* (Boston: Allyn and Bacon, 1984).

7. Anne E. Gottsdanker-Willenkens and Patricia Y. Leonard, "All about Me: Language Arts Strategies to Enhance Self-Concept," *Reading Teacher* 37 (1984): 801-802.

8. Richard L. Papenfuss, John D. Curtis, Barbara J. Beier, and Joseph D. Menze, "Teaching Positive Self-concepts in the Classroom," *Journal of School Health* 53 (1983): 618-620.

9. Frederic J. Medway and Robert C. Smith, Jr., "An Examination of Contemporary Elementary School Affective Education Programs," *Psychology in the Schools* 15 (1978): 266.

10. William Damon, "Putting Substance into Self-Esteem: A Focus on Academic and Moral Values," *educational HORIZONS* (fall 1991):13.

11. Ibid., 17.

12. Lerner, "Self-esteem and Excellence."

13. Seligman, "Boomer Blues."

14. Thomas J. Lasley and John Bregenzer, "Toward Selflessness," *Journal of Human Behavior and Learning* 3 (1986): 20-27.

15. Damon, "Putting Substance into Self-esteem."

16. Ibid., 15.

17. Lerner, "Self-esteem and Excellence," 13.

18. Martin E. P. Seligman, *Learned Optimism: The Skill to Conquer Life's Obstacles, Large & Small* (New York: Random House, 1990).

19. Sami I. Boulos, "The Anatomy of the 'Me' Generation," *Education* 102 (1982): 238-242.

20. Lasley and Bregenzer, "Toward Selflessness."

21. William Damon, "Putting Substance into Self-esteem," 16-17.

22. Marilee M. Cowan and Faith M. Clover, "Enhancement of Self-concept through Disciplined-based Art Education," *Art Education* 44 (1991): 38-45.

23. Linda K. Bunker, "The Role of Play and Motor Skill Development in Building Children's Self-confidence and Self-esteem," *Elementary School Journal* 91 (1991): 467-471.

24. David L. Silvernail, *Developing Positive Student Self-concept* (Washington, D.C.: National Education Association, 1987).

Beyond the Pendulum
Creating Challenging and Caring Schools

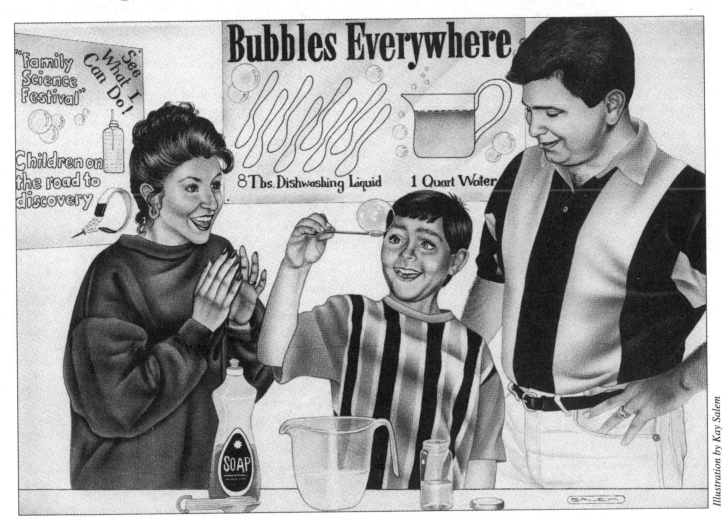

Illustration by Kay Salem

In the history of American education, the pendulum has swung back and forth between concern with intellectual rigor and concern with students' social adjustment. If our country is to move beyond this pattern, these authors suggest, schools must attend simultaneously to children's intellectual, social, and ethical development.

....

Catherine C. Lewis, Eric Schaps, and Marilyn Watson

For me, a turning point came at a science fair a few years back. We were videotaping the award winners as they were announced. Somehow I found myself watching the faces of the children who hadn't won awards. Kids aren't good at hiding their disappointment. They looked so sad and empty. The room was dead silent, as if a bomb had been dropped. We faculty members had knocked ourselves out working on the science fair, and yet we had turned off many of the kids.

— *An elementary teacher*

LAST YEAR, the teachers at El Rio Elementary School redesigned their school science fair.[1] Traditionally, the science fair had been a time for upper-grade students to make projects and compete for schoolwide awards. This year's "family science festival" transformed the school, for one evening, into a hands-on science museum. Students and a record number of family members explored the mysteries of bubbles, magnets, and kitchen chemistry in a series of activities planned and hosted by each class.

As staff members at El Rio worked to redesign the science fair, three goals guided their efforts. First, these teachers wanted to meet in constructive ways children's needs for friendship, participation, and belonging and thereby to create a school that would be more appealing than the local gangs. Rather than pit children against one another, the new science fair would unite the children in a shared and meaningful pursuit: the planning and organization of an interesting, informative science festival. Every child could gain, academically and socially, from contributing to this effort. There would be no "losers."

Second, El Rio staff members had been seeking ways to make the families of their students feel more welcome at school — including the 50% of parents whose first language was one other than English. Because families play a critical role in children's development, the teachers were eager to provide an inviting and inclusive experience for as many family members as possible. The competitive science fair had sent a confusing message: When did family help become "cheating"? It had also created winners and losers and had painfully reminded some parents of their own failures in school. By contrast, the new format clearly welcomed families. As others have noted, "Nobody flunks museum."[2]

Finally, the staff at El Rio had become uncomfortable about the use of awards to motivate science learning. Teachers had noticed that students were more interested in the awards than in the scientific content of their projects. Spurred on by research on the negative impact of rewards, the faculty chose to emphasize the inherent interest and challenge of designing hands-on science exhibits.

As El Rio's teachers redesigned the science fair, they carefully considered the students' bonds to one another and to the school, their science learning and motivation, and their relationships with family members. In other words, they considered the students' ethical, social, and intellectual development. Many school improvement efforts, by contrast, focus on a single outcome. Today, schools are being asked to promote everything from the prevention of drug abuse to the development of computer literacy, and it is tempt-

> *Adults want children to become able, motivated learners and principled, caring human beings.*

ing to choose a single, narrow goal for school improvement. Yet well-meaning efforts to boost academic achievement can actually damage children's social and ethical development, if they are not based on sound models of children's learning and development.[3] Schools cannot perform a surgical strike on children's intellects.

In the history of American education, the pendulum has swung back and forth between concern with intellectual rigor and concern with students' social adjustment. The process has served neither goal well. If our country is to move beyond the pattern of this swinging pendulum, schools must attend simultaneously to children's intellectual, social, and ethical development.

However, we think that most U.S. schools are *not* organized in ways that enable them to foster all three facets of development, despite widespread consensus that all three are central to the mission of education. More than two decades have passed since James Comer pointed out the interdependence of children's social, ethical, and intellectual development,[4] but many school improvement efforts still fail to grapple with all three facets of development and thereby risk compromising children's development in one or more domains.

Goals of Elementary Education

As they began to redesign the science fair, teachers at El Rio Elementary also elected to participate in the Child Development Project (CDP), a school change effort that targets children's social, ethical, *and* intellectual development. The

CDP program supports educators as they rethink every facet of elementary school life: how children learn, what they learn, what motivates them, what bonds they form with peers and adults. Supported by 30 days of staff development spread over three years, by curriculum materials, and by on-site support, educators in CDP schools strive to bring their practices into line with their long-term goals for children: that they become good learners *and* good people. Longitudinal research conducted in CDP schools and matched comparison schools suggests that the project does indeed foster children's development both as learners and as caring, principled human beings.[5]

For many years, our colleagues at the Child Development Project have asked groups of teachers, administrators, and parents to imagine what they would like their elementary school students to be like as adults. What qualities would they like these students to have 20 years from now? Across diverse American communities — rich and poor, urban and rural — the responses are remarkably similar. Adults want children to become able, motivated learners and principled, caring human beings. The American media obsessively hold up test scores as the sole gauge of the success of education, yet the American public overwhelmingly sees the teaching of moral values as an appropriate role for the public schools.[6] American business leaders view responsible attitudes toward work and a capacity to work with others as critical outcomes of schooling — often even more critical than specific academic skills.[7]

Students are shaped by myriad values expressed or implied in what is taught, how it is taught, and how students and teachers treat one another.[8] Do students have an opportunity to help shape classroom rules? Or do they see these rules as arbitrarily imposed from above? Do they have a chance to know their classmates as human beings or only as competitors to be bested in the quest for grades and honors? How schools answer these questions will profoundly shape children's social and ethical development. So the issue is not *whether* schools will influence children's ethical development, but *how* they will do so: thoughtfully or inadvertently.

To promote students' ethical, social, and intellectual development simultaneously, schools must establish three core conditions: important, engaging curriculum and pedagogy; intrinsic motivation; and a caring community.

Curriculum and Pedagogy: Important and Engaging?

Four second-graders are dividing 41 chocolate candies among themselves. They are brainstorming to come up with as many ways as they can to divide the candies evenly and suggesting things they might do with the leftover candy: divide it into four parts, leave it in the center of the table, and so on. The activity gives meaning to later class discussions about different ways to express division remainders.[9]

Students in another elementary class built a planter box for a class vegetable garden. Using small, measured blocks, they next figured the volume of the planter and then, after much trial, discussion, and debate, they derived a general formula for volume. Through these efforts, they were able to calculate how much soil to purchase for the planter.

Contrast the experience of children in these two classes with an experience that is probably far more common: being taught that division with remainders and volume calculation are simply procedures to be memorized. The difference between learning as arbitrary facts and procedures to be memorized or as truths to be discovered lies at the heart of what we mean by an "engaging" curriculum and pedagogy. Engaging lessons contain their own answers to the question "Why would I want to know this?"

To be engaging, curriculum and pedagogy must respond to three central qualities of children's development. First, children must be treated as whole people with many needs (social, physical, aesthetic, ethical, and intellectual) and many ways to learn. Curriculum and pedagogy that emphasize a narrow range of cognitive skills, that have students sitting down wielding pencil and paper most of the day, and that give them few opportunities to work collaboratively will lose many children. In contrast, a curriculum rich in drama, music, art, mechanical and hands-on activity, and social interaction can engage a wide range of children — including those whose strong suit may not be paper-and-pencil seatwork.

Second, children must be treated as seekers of meaning. Engaging curriculum and pedagogy allow students to see the purpose of what they are learning. They solve problems that interest them and explore issues that are meaningful to them — sometimes because the problems and issues are "naturally" compelling, but of-

ten because teachers have taken pains to help children see how the lessons relate to what they want to know and do. Facts and skills are learned in the context of meaningful activities. For example, students learn to write by writing something that they wish to communicate, or they learn mathematics by using it to understand the world around them. They see what they can do — now or in the future — with what they are learning.

Education that emphasizes memorization and drill and neglects understanding may account for many of the well-publicized failures of American students. For example, in 1984 half of California eighth-graders could not figure 100% of 32, though many of these students could correctly answer other percentage problems.[10] (Apparently, they had memorized an algorithm for computing percentages without really understanding what they were doing.) Likewise, a substantial number of children are able to read but choose not to do so; critiques of reading instruction argue that the barren language and shallow ideas found in basal readers offer little reason to read. "How can mental skills be developed except through exercise on materials that are challenging and substantial?" asks *American Memory*, a report on the humanities in American public schools.[11]

That a simplified, easily mastered curriculum actually does a disservice to students by limiting opportunities for real engagement is a tenet underlying much recent research in education.[12] In the words of Eleanor Duckworth, "Just as the poet seeks to present his thoughts and feelings in all their complexity, and in so doing opens a multiplicity of paths into his meaning, likewise a teacher who presents a subject matter in all its complexity makes it more accessible by opening a multiplicity of paths into it."[13]

Finally, an engaging pedagogy recognizes and fosters children's own efforts to make sense of the world. A great deal of research demonstrates that children "construct" knowledge: that they are young scientists who continuously devise theories (physical, social, ethical) about how the world works and who accept or reject information about the world based on these powerful intuitive theories. The child who believes that 378 is closer to 300 than to 400 "because it is in the 300s" may cling tenaciously to this idea. A teacher who simply presents correct information is unlikely to reach this child. Rather, instruction must elicit the child's thinking

and help the child reflect critically on it. And the teacher's role changes accordingly. The teacher is not so much a purveyor of knowledge as an architect and catalyst who helps students persistently engage important concepts.

When is a concept part of an "important" curriculum? Jere Brophy and Janet Alleman note that "curriculum development should be driven by major long-term goals, not just short-term coverage concerns" and that content should be "organized into networks structured around important ideas."[14] On both national and state levels, educators regularly debate about what content is important in various subject areas. In a world that is diverse and changing, we should not expect that an "important" curriculum will be universal and unchanging. Hence, it becomes important to have a sound, ongoing *process* for defining what children should learn — a continuing, thoughtful discussion that drives the curriculum. This discussion should focus on such basic questions as "What skills, knowledge, and dispositions are essential if children are to sustain a productive, democratic society and contribute responsibly to international society?"

In sharp contrast to such a goal-focused process of curriculum development, most curriculum in U.S. schools is determined by default — by textbook publishers and standardized tests that create a de facto national curriculum of isolated facts and subskills. The dispositions that are so central to the survival of a democratic, productive society — such personal qualities as fairness, a desire to contribute to society's betterment, a capacity to relate to diverse others, a willingness to work hard, a desire to learn — are noticeably absent from this curriculum, despite the widespread recognition of their importance.

Motivation to Learn

In times of rapid technological change, knowledge changes quickly. Hence students must be able and eager to continue learning throughout life.[15] What kind of schooling produces eager, lifelong learners? We cannot do justice here to the large literature on motivation to learn, but we will note several points. First, extrinsic rewards (prizes, honors, grades, and so forth) can actually *undermine* children's interest in learning if they lead children to see learning as something done "for the reward."[16] To minimize the use of extrinsic rewards, educators need a curriculum that is intrinsically worth learning and a pedagogy that helps students see why it is worth learning. Children motivated by the intrinsic challenge and interest of subject matter or by the desire to contribute something to the world are likely to find that their motivation endures long after the children motivated by prizes and praise have given up.

Second, encouraging children to learn for extrinsic rewards can enhance their focus on themselves and undermine the development of concern for others and for society.[17] Finally, some outcomes of greatest concern to educators — such as creativity and persistence — are linked to an orientation to learn for its own sake, which can be undermined by competition and extrinsic rewards.[18] Awarding prizes for creating science projects, reading books, running laps, or a host of other worthwhile activities can diminish interest in the activity itself — and, in turn, diminish creativity and persistence. Unfortunately, accounts of American teaching suggest that grades, recognition, and other external rewards are emphasized much more heavily than the intrinsic satisfactions of learning — a situation that is likely to undermine students' commitment to lifelong learning.[19]

A Caring Community in the Classroom and School

We call schools and classrooms in which every child feels connected to others, involved in decision making, and valued as an individual "caring communities." Rather than see one another primarily as competitors, students know one another and feel a shared sense of purpose. Like the family science festival at El Rio, activities are designed so that all children — whatever their academic skills — can make valued contributions.

In a caring community, students help shape the rules and norms they live by. Students ask, "What kind of class do we want to be?" and "How do we want to treat one another?" Their answers become some of the guiding principles for the classroom. Values of fairness, kindness, and responsibility are not simply abstract, adult-imposed dicta, but real, living ideas that help children get along. When problems arise, students work to solve them, motivated by a commitment to one another and to the rules and norms that they have helped to shape.

Three bodies of theory and research

suggest that a caring community, as we have defined it, fosters children's ethical and social development. First, research suggests that children have a need for belonging — for forming trusting and mutually satisfying relationships with others. Students are likely to internalize the values and expectations of the groups that meet this need, be they schools or gangs. Students within a school develop a sense of belonging when they have many opportunities to get to know one another as people and to work with a shared sense of purpose. Classroom and schoolwide activities — such as cooperative academic work, school beautification projects, and local service projects — provide opportunities for *all* community members to make valued contributions.

Schools that see belonging as a central need of students find ways to promote stable connections between students and between students and adults. For example, classes can be kept together with the same teacher for more than one year, regular times can be set aside for community-building activities, and school traditions can be designed to emphasize effort, participation, and the unique contributions of all individuals, rather than competition. These schools also minimize practices that are likely to undermine a sense of community, such as tracking, pull-out programs, "departmentalization," and other approaches that stratify or fragment a school or create an ever-changing cast of classroom members.

A second reason for the importance of developing a "caring community" is that children are constructive learners in the social and ethical domains, as well as in the intellectual domain.[20] Children need many opportunities to discuss and apply in daily life such values as responsibility and fairness; to talk about them as they come up in literature, history, or other contexts; and to hear others' perspectives and experiences. In the words of one teacher, "We expect that children beginning to dress themselves will often put together outfits that clash. So why should we expect them to learn something much more difficult — like fairness or responsibility — without many opportunities to make mistakes?"

In watching videotapes of class meetings and class discussions of literature, as part of their Child Development Project learning, teachers often remark on how passionately students discuss ethical and social issues, such as what is "fair" or what it means to be a friend. Students' in-

nate drive to understand the social and ethical world around them is apparent in these discussions. Teachers also remark on the power of opportunities for students to hear their classmates' perspectives and to learn about their needs. To recognize that a classmate was upset by a prank you thought was harmless or that a fellow reader found sympathetic traits in a character you dismissed can be an important catalyst for growth.

Finally, research on intrinsic motivation suggests that children will be most likely to develop a personal commitment to such values as responsibility and kindness when they understand that these values are not the result of arbitrary decisions by adults, but are necessary for the well-being of the group and each of its members. Schools can help children develop a personal commitment to these values by providing opportunities to discuss the ethical and social problems that occur in school life, to hear the needs and perspectives of others, and to devise solutions. Schools can emphasize problem-solving activities in which students have the chance to voice their concerns, hear the concerns of others, and work toward a mutually acceptable solution — rather than expect students to adapt to mechanical, adult-imposed rules and consequences. Schools can avoid the use of extrinsic rewards and punishments that may distract children's attention from the real reasons to behave responsibly: their own rights and needs and those of others.

These qualities of a caring community are interdependent. When students share a common goal (such as designing a class exhibit for the science fair), they will tend to value one another's contributions. When students feel like valued members of the school community, they will be strongly motivated to maintain that community and to learn how to solve problems that arise. When fairness and kindness become norms within the school, it opens arenas for *all* children to achieve in ways that are genuinely valued.

The idea of a caring community may seem like motherhood and apple pie — something so good that everyone would support it. Yet many common educational practices in American schools directly undermine it. Consider, for example, classroom and school discipline. Discipline systems based on teacher-imposed rewards and punishments — "assertive discipline," token economies, point systems, and so on — pervade American education.

We understand the appeal of such systems. Schools *do* have an obligation to maintain order so that children can learn — a basic obligation that can be difficult to meet when students arrive at school with a history of troubled relationships or neglect. Yet adult-imposed rewards and "consequences" undermine a caring community in several ways. With their emphasis on recognition and rewards, they distract children's attention from shared values as the *real* reason to behave responsibly. They make students reliant on adult surveillance, and they stigmatize poorly behaved children, further undermining their sense of belonging and their potential bonds with adults and peers.

Turning away from such systems once they have become the norm is very difficult. Listen to these elementary teachers talk about their struggles to adopt such practices as class meetings and mutual problem solving, the building blocks of a caring community:

> Discipline is the most difficult and frustrating thing to change because your gut reaction has to change. As a teacher, I am so used to fixing situations. I want to get the situation fixed and move on. But the point of developmental discipline is to help students learn to make decisions themselves. I always have to think before I speak.

* * *

> For years I have approached discipline [by asking]: What did you do? Is that against the rules? What can you do about it? But this isn't enough anymore — in fact, it really misses the point in a big way. It leaves out values entirely. . . . I want the template for making decisions to be values, *not* rules.

Connecting Elements of the Model

Although we can draw neat boxes around the three components we have just discussed — curriculum, motivation, and community — the real connections between them are numerous and messy. More than a decade ago, the Child Development Project began as an effort to help schools promote "prosocial" development — the development by students of such positive qualities as responsibility, helpfulness, fairness, and kindness.

Early on, we saw the need to reshape the whole culture of the school: its goals, governance, human relations, discipline, and climate. Yet we were surprised by how extensively we needed to reshape the *curriculum* in order to foster students' prosocial development. How could we create a caring community in the classroom when children's own needs — to make sense of the world, to be known and liked by others, to influence the environment — were being ignored by a skill-and-drill curriculum? A curriculum that holds little intrinsic interest for children forces teachers to use "motivators," "consequences," and competition to keep children on-task, thereby undermining community and demonstrating that some children are more valued than others.

Faced with such a curriculum, many children who are less well-prepared educationally may reduce their efforts in order to preserve their self-esteem and so come to be stigmatized as poor learners.[21] They may also withdraw psychologically from the classroom or school community, leaving school powerless to influence their social, ethical, or intellectual development. Research suggests that a competitive classroom atmosphere may be especially alienating for children from ethnic groups that experience competition as a violation of strong cultural values of friendship and community.[22]

It is important for educators to recognize the connection between the classroom community and a challenging curriculum. Indeed, it is unlikely that any child will experience school as a caring community if that child finds the *academic* curriculum unrewarding. Because children come to school with diverse skills, interests, and experiences, the curriculum must be rich, flexible, and sophisticated enough to engage all children. When students are immersed in complex, challenging tasks — such as revising a story to more effectively reach classmates, designing a science activity to interest families, or exploring how class members' families came to the U.S. — the usual indicators of comparative achievement (recall questions, short-answer tests, speed drills, and so on) become unimportant, and students can focus their attention on the inherent interest of the task.

Reciprocally, a caring community enhances the academic experience of students. For example, recent research suggests that caring, responsive classroom communities foster more than students' social and ethical development; such communities may also enhance students' academic development.[23] Students work harder, achieve more, and attribute more importance to schoolwork in classes in which they feel liked, accepted, and respected by the teacher and fellow students. The caring classroom is not one that avoids criticism, challenge, or mistakes. Rather, like a good family, it provides every member with a sense of being valued and important. This sense of belonging allows for lively, critical discussions and intellectual risk-taking. It provides an important source of motivation to do one's best.

How Can We Use the Model?

We hope that the model developed in the preceding pages will be useful to readers in several ways.

1. *Bringing education's long-term goals into sharper focus.* As we noted above, Americans give remarkably similar answers when asked to describe the people they want today's students to become: thoughtful, eager to learn, honest, kind, responsible, self-motivated. Yet, when asked their goals for the same children during the upcoming school year, these adults will often mention specific academic skills (e.g., "learn his numbers and letters") and rudimentary behavior (e.g., "be able to sit still"). Will years of focus on specific academic and behavioral skills produce honest, kind people who are also eager and capable learners? A good model should help us forge stronger connections between daily practice and long-term goals.

2. *Stimulating discussion, debate, and long-range planning.* We share the constructivist tenet that discussion — even controversy — can deepen thinking. Thus we hope that our model will stimulate discussion and provoke constructive questions. What is missing from the model as constituted? How do its elements connect? Must some components be achieved before others? Students of educational change have argued that, if school change efforts are to be successful, educators must be aware of a gap between what is and what should be.[24] So discussing what should be is an important first step.

3. *Serving as a gauge to evaluate prospective innovations.* Many teachers feel burdened, even overwhelmed, by the expectation that they will parcel out instructional time for "everything" — from computer education to the prevention of drug abuse. A proliferation of special programs, many of which pull students out of the classroom, fragments the lives of teachers and students. Sometimes the myriad special programs even contradict one another, as when teachers are asked

to foster students' assertiveness as part of the prevention of drug abuse but are simultaneously trained to use behaviorist disciplinary approaches that reinforce compliance. Teachers need to follow guiding principles — such as intrinsic motivation, caring community, engaging and important curriculum — to help evaluate what they do.

Narrowly focused innovations can lead to disappointing or even counterproductive results. As we noted above, a "surgical strike" on children's academic achievement can end up promoting antisocial behavior. We hope that the model we have laid out will allow parents and educators to step back and survey the overall strengths and weaknesses of education in their school or district.

4. *Serving as the starting point for self-assessment.* How should we be assessing our schools? Frameworks for schools — such as California's language arts and social studies frameworks — often focus on the civic and the social, as well as the academic, missions of schooling. Yet qualities beyond academic achievement are rarely "inspected" or "expected."[25] Broadly conceived assessments of education for early childhood programs and for the middle grades have been developed and may well be helping to improve education for those age groups.[26] For elementary education, too, assessment needs to be aligned with our long-term goals. It could begin with questions about children's learning, motivation, and sense of community. Consider these possible questions about learning:

• Do students understand the purpose of their learning? Do they learn skills and procedures in a meaningful and important context?

• Do students bring their prior knowledge and concepts to bear upon lessons, and do they develop a habit of critically examining their own thinking?

• As part of daily classroom life, do students have sustained discussions in which they elicit and respond to one another's ideas? Are these discussions "thoughtful," in terms of both the reasoning and the interpersonal consideration children show?

Or consider these questions about motivation:

• Do students actively and spontaneously apply what is learned in school? For example, do they read for pleasure and spontaneously apply mathematics to problems of daily life? Do students show

eagerness and persistence in their learning?

• Is student learning motivated primarily by extrinsic incentives — grades, praise, competition — or by interest in the learning itself?

• Do students feel personally committed to school rules and norms? Do they spontaneously apply them to new situations?

Or consider these questions about a sense of community:

• Do students work well with one another?

• Do students see fellow students primarily as collaborators or primarily as obstacles to their own success?

• Do students believe that their teachers value them and are working to help them succeed in life?

• Do all members of the school community — students, parents, teachers, and other staff members — develop strong positive bonds with one another? Is the school viewed as an important and valued place by all its members?

What It Will Take to Change

We think that relatively few American schools have managed to sustain a simultaneous focus on students' social, ethical, and intellectual development. What will it take to achieve on a much broader scale the conditions and goals outlined above?

First, it will take changes in thinking. The agenda we have proposed runs counter to much conventional wisdom in education today. It is often assumed, particularly for low-achieving children, that learning should be simplified, failure-free, presented in predetermined steps, and extrinsically rewarded. Such thinking about children's learning and development cannot be expected to change quickly or easily, because we adults are constructive learners ourselves.

Second, we need to place every school improvement effort in a larger context. It is not enough to ask whether a new curriculum increases students' subject-matter knowledge. We must also ask whether it fosters their intrinsic interest in learning and builds bonds with fellow students. But this means that educators who have traditionally worked in isolation — specialists in subject matter, pedagogy, school climate, motivation — must all see the big picture. In the history of American education, the pendulum has swung back and forth between concern with intellectual rigor and concern with social devel-

opment. Schools like El Rio show that we can move beyond the pendulum.

At El Rio's family science festival this year, as students helped friends and family members estimate the fat content of their diets, analyze water samples from three local rivers, and build simple electrical circuits, the video camera documented the emotions apparent on many faces: happiness, puzzlement, pride, absorption, surprise. None of the faces were "sad and empty." One teacher summed up the change: "This year we had to shove people out the doors at the end of the evening. Everyone was laughing; they were all smiles. We brought in parents who would never have stepped into the school for a science fair. And they'll come back."

1. The names of schools have been changed to maintain confidentiality.

2. Frank Oppenheimer, founder of the San Francisco Exploratorium, quoted in Howard Gardner, *The Unschooled Mind* (New York: Basic Books, 1991), p. 201.

3. Denise Daniels, "Didactic Versus Child-Centered Program Effects on Children's Achievement, Perceived Competence, and Emotions," paper presented at a symposium of the American Educational Research Association, San Francisco, April 1992; Rheta DeVries, Halcyon Reese-Learned, and Pamela Morgan, "Sociomoral Development in Children from Direct-Instruction, Constructivist, and Eclectic Kindergarten Programs," *Early Childhood Research Quarterly,* vol. 6, 1991, pp. 473-517; and Lawrence J. Schweinhart, David P. Weikart, and Mary B. Larner, "Consequences of Three Curriculum Models Through Age 15," *Early Childhood Research Quarterly*, vol. 1, 1986, pp. 15-54.

4. See James P. Comer, "Educating Poor Minority Children," *Scientific American*, November 1988, pp. 42-48.

5. Developed and studied in two California school districts over the past 11 years, the Child Development Project is now being extended to six additional school districts across the country. Descriptions of CDP's program and longitudinal study in California can be found in Daniel Solomon et al., "Cooperative Learning as Part of a Comprehensive Classroom Program Designed to Promote Prosocial Development," in Shlomo Sharan, ed., *Cooperative Learning: Theory and Research* (New York: Praeger, 1992), pp. 231-60; and Daniel Solomon, "Enhancing Children's Prosocial Behavior in the Classroom," *American Educational Research Journal*, vol. 25, 1988, pp. 527-54. Descriptions of the dissemination of the CDP and the results can be obtained from the Developmental Studies Center, 2000 Embarcadero, Suite 305, Oakland, CA 94606-5300.

6. Stanley M. Elam, "The Second Gallup/Phi Delta Kappa Poll of Teachers' Attitudes Toward the Public Schools," *Phi Delta Kappan*, June 1989, p. 794; and Stanley M. Elam, Lowell C. Rose, and Alec M. Gallup, "The 25th Annual Phi Delta Kappa/Gallup Poll of the Public's Attitudes Toward the Public Schools," *Phi Delta Kappan*, October 1993, p. 145.

7. *A Michigan Employability Profile: Report to the Governor's Commission on Jobs and Development* (Lansing: Employability Skills Task Force, April 1988).

8. Philip W. Jackson, Robert E. Boostrom, and David T. Hansen, *The Moral Life of Schools* (San Francisco: Jossey-Bass, 1993).

9. We are indebted to the Cooperative Mathematics Project for this example. Further information about this approach to mathematics and social development can be found in Laurel Robertson et al., *Number Power* (Menlo Park, Calif.: Addison-Wesley, 1993), or by writing to the Cooperative Mathematics Project, 2000 Embarcadero, Suite 305, Oakland, CA 94606-5300.

10. *California Assessment Program Annual Report, 1983-1984* (Sacramento: California State Department of Education, 1984).

11. Lynne V. Cheney, *American Memory: A Report on the Humanities in the Nation's Public Schools* (Washington, D.C.: National Endowment for the Humanities, 30 August 1987).

12. See, for example, Wendy Hopfenberg, Henry Levin, and Associates, *The Accelerated Schools Resource Guide* (San Francisco: Jossey-Bass, 1993).

13. Eleanor Duckworth, "Twenty-four, Forty-two, and I Love You: Keeping It Complex," *Harvard Educational Review*, vol. 61, pp. 1-24.

14. Jere Brophy and Janet Alleman, "Activities as Instructional Tools: A Framework for Analysis and Evaluation," *Educational Researcher*, May 1991, pp. 9-23.

15. Jere Brophy, "Socializing Students' Motivation to Learn," *Advances in Motivation and Achievement: Enhancing Motivation*, vol. 5, 1987, pp. 181-210.

16. Alfie Kohn, *Punished by Rewards* (Boston: Houghton-Mifflin, 1993); and Mark R. Lepper and David Greene, *The Hidden Costs of Reward: New Perspectives on the Psychology of Human Motivation* (Hillsdale, N.J.: Erlbaum, 1978).

17. John G. Nicholls, *The Competitive Ethos and Democratic Education* (Cambridge, Mass.: Harvard University Press, 1989).

18. Teresa Amabile, "Effects of External Evaluation on Artistic Creativity," *Journal of Personality and Social Psychology*, vol. 37, 1979, pp. 221-33; and Nicholls, op. cit.

19. Philip W. Jackson, *Life in Classrooms* (1968; reprint, New York: Teachers College Press, 1990); and Deborah Stipek, and Denise H. Daniels, "Declining Perceptions of Competence: A Consequence of Changes in the Child or in the Educational Environment?," *Journal of Educational Psychology*, vol. 80, 1988, pp. 352-56.

20. Marilyn Watson et al., "The Child Development Project: Combining Traditional and Developmental Approaches to Values Education," in Larry Nucci, ed., *Moral Development and Character Education: A Dialogue* (Berkeley, Calif.: McCutchan, 1989), pp. 51-92.

21. Nicholls, op. cit.

22. Ann Davidson, Hanh Cao, and Patricia Phelan, "The Flow of Ethnicity: Voices of Diverse High School Youth," paper presented at the annual meeting of the American Educational Research Association, Chicago, 1991; and Roland Tharp, "Psychocultural Variables and Constants: Effects on Teaching and Learning in Schools," *American Psychologist*, February 1989, pp. 349-59.

23. Daniel Solomon et al., "Educational Practices That Promote Children's Prosocial Development," in Fritz Oser, Andreas Dick, and Jean-Luc Patry, eds., *Effective and Responsible Teaching: The New Synthesis* (San Francisco: Jossey-Bass, 1992), pp. 383-96.

24. Michael Fullan, *The Meaning of Educational Change* (New York: Teachers College Press, 1982).

25. Phillip C. Schlechty, *Schools for the 21st Century* (San Francisco: Jossey-Bass, 1990).

26. Sue Bredekamp, *Regulating Child Care Quality: Evidence from NAEYC's Accreditation System* (Washington, D.C.: National Association for the Education of Young Children, #754, 1989); and Gayle Dorman, *Middle Grades Assessment Program* (Carrboro, N.C.: Center for Early Adolescence, University of North Carolina, 1985).

CATHERINE C. LEWIS is director of formative research at the Developmental Studies Center, Oakland, Calif., where ERIC SCHAPS is president and MARILYN WATSON is director of programs. The research and thinking on which this article is based were supported by the William and Flora Hewlett Foundation, the U.S. Center for Substance Abuse Prevention, the DeWitt Wallace-Reader's Digest Fund, the Annenberg Foundation, the Robert Wood Johnson Foundation, the Pew Charitable Trusts, the Stuart Foundations, the John D. and Catherine T. MacArthur Foundation, the Louise and Claude Rosenberg Foundation, the Danforth Foundation, and the San Francisco Foundation. The authors also wish to thank Daniel Solomon, Victor Battistich, and Sylvia Kendzior and the educators in the eight school districts that have collaborated in the development of the Child Development Project program. ©1995, Developmental Studies Center.

About Instruction: *Powerful New Strategies Worth Knowing*

Preston D. Feden

Preston D. Feden, Ed.D., is Associate Professor of Education at La Salle University in Philadelphia. A former special education teacher, he also consults widely with school districts on instructional practices.

Teaching involves many elements, and factors and conditions within schools have a significant effect upon teachers and learners. Teachers routinely deal with administrators who vary in leadership style and ability. Teachers also assume a wide range of non-instructional roles as they carry out school procedures and policies. Teachers must skillfully employ effective communication skills as they work with pupils and their parents. Nevertheless, *instruction* is central to the teaching process, and it is essential for teachers to refine their instructional skills continually. Even in the worst of situations, no teacher is in a position where he or she cannot apply, to some degree, powerful strategies that have recently emerged from cognitive science.

KERRY HALEY

Ten years later, despite exciting new research findings, Howard Gardner laments that what we know about learning is still not reflected in current teaching practice.

Advances in the knowledge base for teaching and learning now require a fundamental reconceptualization of the type of instruction provided to students at all levels of American education. A decade ago, when the knowledge base had already become sophisticated, John Goodlad's extensive study of schools found that teachers used a limited repertoire of pedagogical approaches. Strategies consisted mostly of their own talk and monitoring seatwork.[1] Ten years later, despite exciting new research findings, Howard Gardner laments that what we know about learning is still not reflected in current teaching practice.[2] And he is not alone. There is a clear need for teachers to know and understand newly emerging knowledge, and to base their practice on it.

This "contemporary" knowledge base, firmly rooted in cognitive science and substantiated by empirical data, stands in sharp contrast to "traditional" views of learning and teaching. Traditional views reflect the factory model of production in American society. This model "provided fertile soil for the behavioral approach to learning, which has dominated educational practices for the past fifty years."[3] The techniques that emanate from the contemporary knowledge base and its associated research have the potential to transform our classrooms and to empower the pupils who will compose the next generation of American citizenry. As John Bruer claims: "Teaching methods based on [research in cognitive science] . . . are the educational equivalents of polio vaccine and penicillin. Yet few outside the educational research community are aware of these breakthroughs or understand the research that makes them possible."[4]

Others who apply research in cognitive science to instruction support this dramatic claim. For example, a synthesis of research on models of teaching from Bruce Joyce, Beverly Showers, and Carol Rolheiser-Bennett lists information processing theory and cooperative learning as producing moderate to substantial effects upon student achievement.[5] Both models are derived from cognitivist research.

A research-supported, contemporary view of teaching and learning questions the assumptions underlying the traditional view, among them:

- that learning is the process of accumulating bits of information and isolated skills;
- that the teacher's primary responsibility is to transfer knowledge directly to students;
- that the process of learning and teaching focuses primarily on the interactions between the teacher and individual students.[6]

James Nolan and Pam Francis point out that ". . . for most educators [these views] have remained largely implicit and unexamined."[7]

In contrast, a contemporary view of teaching and learning based on research in cognitive science holds that, among other things:

- all learning, except for simple rote memorization, requires the learner to actively construct meaning;
- students' prior understandings and thoughts about a topic or concept before instruction exert a tremendous influence on what they learn during instruction;
- the teacher's primary goal is to generate a change in the learner's cognitive structure or way of viewing and organizing the world;
- learning in cooperation with others is an important source of motivation, support, modeling, and coaching.[8]

Implications

What, then, from this emerging, contemporary knowledge base is now worth knowing about instruction? What follows are key concepts gleaned from research and translated into practice. These procedures, based upon applied cognitive science, can help teachers in preparing and presenting better lessons to their students. They are meant to be neither formulaic nor mistaken for an attempt to oversimplify the very complex task of teaching. As Bruer points out, "There is more to medicine than biology, but basic medical science drives progress and helps doctors make decisions that promote their patients' physical well-being. Similarly, there is more to education than cognition, but cognitive science can drive progress and help teachers make decisions that promote their students' educational well-being."[9]

Focus on core concepts.

Teachers should focus on the core concepts of the subject or subjects that they teach. Much recent criticism of schools focuses on their tendency to promote and reward rote memorization rather than true understanding of academic content. David Perkins notes that students, although they may acquire fragmented knowledge and isolated skills, often do not truly understand the knowledge and cannot really use the skills they acquire. Perkins goes on to explain what he means by "understanding"—essentially, the ability to carry out various performances, such as making predictions, generalizing, explaining, analogizing, providing supporting evidence, and applying concepts. Further, he says that the more of these performances a pupil displays, the more confident we can feel that the student understands a topic or concept.[10]

Because truly useful understanding takes time to develop, it is usually not possible for teachers to "cover" as much curriculum, or as many topics, as they typically attempt. Using the principle that "less is more," teachers should cover less content. The point is to lead pupils to a *deep* understanding of what *is* covered. Lessons and units of instruction designed around core concepts are more likely to produce conceptual change that moves learners along from novice to expert in subject matter content.

Core concepts are generally agreed upon by experts as those that stand the test of time and that are capable of generating new knowledge for those pupils who master them. Lauren Resnick and Leopold Klopfer offer several examples of core concepts: in reading and writing, concepts such as text structures and genre; in history and government, the nature of representative government; in arithmetic, the decomposability of numbers. They observe that these key concepts and principles organize and structure much specific information.[11] Perkins offers samples of core concepts gathered from practicing teachers, which he believes are especially capable of generating new knowledge. They include: *What Is a Living Thing?; Civil Disobedience; Ratio and Proportion;* and *Whose History?* Each of these topics, he asserts, is a powerful conceptual system that can help learners generate new knowledge, while at the same

time connect information to realities in their own lives.[12]

Use advance organizers.

Teachers should begin each class with an advance organizer. These are statements, made by teachers just before presenting the day's lesson, that are usually presented at a higher level of abstraction than the content that will follow. Advance

> *The point is to lead pupils to a* deep *understanding of what* is *covered.*

organizers help pupils activate prior knowledge, and they also provide an anchor for later learning. Richard Arends gives an example of an advance organizer for a teacher about to present information about the Vietnam war:

I want to give you an idea that will help you understand why the United States became involved in the Vietnam war. *The idea is that most wars reflect conflict between peoples over one of the following: ideology, territory, or access to trade.* As I describe for you the United State's involvement in Southeast Asia between 1945 and 1965, I want you to look for examples of how conflict over ideology, territory, or access to trade may have influenced later decisions to fight in Vietnam.[13]

Recent research tells us that advance organizers are important because pupils need to locate themselves in the appropriate area of long-term memory to use prior knowledge effectively. Further, pu-

pils who connect new knowledge to prior knowledge are much more likely to retain the new knowledge in an organized fashion, or to reorganize existing knowledge in a more expert way. Teachers who launch a lecture or any other form of instruction without first helping pupils draw upon prior knowledge risk reducing these pupils to mindless note-taking, as they attempt to copy the teacher's knowledge rather than construct their own.

Teach pupils strategies for learning.

Contemporary research clearly outlines the importance of several powerful techniques for teaching pupils strategies for learning. Teachers can instruct pupils on using these strategies, and then encourage their application as the year progresses. One of these strategies is *elaboration*. Elaboration is the process of generating new ideas related to the ideas being received from external sources. When pupils add to information taught, discussed in class, or read, they engage in elaborative rehearsal. Research indicates elaboration is much more powerful than memorization in promoting retention of information.[14]

Teachers can employ many strategies to enhance elaboration among their pupils, including the use of drawings, metaphors, and analogies. Teachers can also have pupils summarize information in their own words.[15] Summarization is particularly useful in conjunction with note-taking. Teachers might also reexamine the types of questions they ask during lecture and discussion, to ensure that the questions encourage elaboration. Jay McTighe and Frank Lyman provide very practical examples of different types of questions, and a summary in the form of a bookmark for teachers to use while guiding discussions.[16]

Another technique that helps pupils learn strategies for learning is *imagery*. There is truth to the saying that "one picture is worth a thousand words." Current research reaffirms what many teachers have suspected—that things we can see or picture in our minds are generally easier to learn and remember than things we cannot see or picture. Information processing research suggests that this is because our working memories can hold only seven or so chunks of information before some information is forgotten. Images, which form a continuous representation of information, therefore take up less space than things we cannot imagine. Consequently, many items can be "chunked" together as one image, leaving much more space in working memory for additional information or thought.[17] Teachers should

Research indicates elaboration is much more powerful than memorization in promoting retention of information.

encourage children to form images or mental pictures whenever possible and appropriate. Furthermore, teachers should use abundant visual aids during lesson presentations.

Finally, *organization* can be a valuable aid in helping pupils to structure information and retain it. Recall the point above that learners can remember only about seven unrelated things at one time, because of limitations of working memory. But if material is "carefully divided into subsets, and the relations within and between subsets are noted,"[18] pupils can learn much information quickly and simulta-

neously increase their knowledge and understanding of that material. Teachers can assist pupils by instructing them in constructing and using traditional outlines or in concept mapping, an alternative using spatial organization of ideas.[19]

Teachers also need to carefully consider the organization of the content they plan to teach to their pupils. They cannot always rely upon textbooks to provide the organization scheme most appropriate for pupils. For example, history texts often organize events chronologically when core ideas or concepts might better relate to one another thematically.

Allow time and opportunity for practice.
Contemporary research indicates teachers should allow plentiful opportunities for their pupils to practice what they have been taught. Information processing researchers distinguish between two types of knowledge. Schools have typically devoted sufficient time to developing declarative knowledge—knowledge of facts, ideas, and concepts. Procedural knowledge is knowledge of how to do things. For example, knowing that a barometer and a thermometer are instruments used to predict weather is declarative knowledge; being able to actually read and interpret a barometer and thermometer is procedural knowledge. Schools typically do not devote ample time to the development of procedural knowledge.

Current research generally counsels resisting the temptation to move quickly through subject matter and to focus only on facts. When providing practice activities, teachers should not use activities that provide only rote practice. Rather, they should use activities that present problems or scenarios for pupils to analyze. Pupils should actually *do* the subject.[20] For example, during a unit on weather, pupils should try to predict the weather based upon instrument readings. Finally, research has made

clear that pupils learn procedural knowledge best through practice, followed by specific feedback from the teacher. Teachers can make it a point to provide frequent, specific feedback to pupils on their performances.

Schools typically do not devote ample time to the development of procedural knowledge.

Use cooperative learning strategies.
Many teachers are now beginning to use cooperative learning assignments in their classrooms, and contemporary research supports the use of this pedagogical strategy. Cooperative learning is useful while pupils are learning facts, and it is also appropriate while pupils practice applying facts and ideas. Cooperative learning is not just another name for group work; instead, it emphasizes mutual interdependence among learners and individual accountability for mastery of information.[21]

There are many ways to organize cooperative work groups. One popular technique is *jigsaw*, where pupils receive pieces of information on which they become experts. They then meet with others to share their expertise so that everybody learns the material by putting it together.

Cooperative learning is wholly consistent with recent cognitivist research on learning, because pupils become active learners and assist each other in constructing knowledge. That most children learn better when interacting with others is well established by empirical research. Teachers who use cooperative strategies are taking full advantage of a powerful technique that also teaches pupils a great deal about democratic living and the power of community.

Use interactive lecturing.

Contemporary research shows that unless teachers gain and maintain the pupils' attention, little if any learning can occur.[22] This finding might sound obvious to the point of humor, except for the common misperception that pupils who quietly listen to the teacher are attending to what the teacher is actually saying. While pupils do attend to *something* during waking hours, the lesson at hand might not be that something. Further, studies on attention span indicate that after about fifteen or twenty minutes a lecture loses its effectiveness for most learners.[23]

Therefore, teachers who feel that a lecture is the best approach for a topic should consider using alternative formats. These formats should be interactive in order to combat pupil boredom and focus attention on relevant information. For example, in the *participatory lecture* pupils brainstorm to generate ideas that the teacher then organizes into a rational and coherent pattern. Sivasailam Thiagarjan provides an example:

Janice has the members of her audience brainstorm a list of characteristics which make a seminar interesting. She writes down the audience inputs on a flipchart. After five minutes of brainstorming, she classifies the items into seven major categories. She then lectures on each category. Later, she adds two categories missed by the audience (but considered important by researchers). She reports the research data on effective seminars.[24]

Another example of an alternative format is the Assigned Reading Activity. In this format, reading is assigned as preparation for class. When class convenes, pupils are given roles such as *supporter, critic, observer,* and *discussion leader.*[25] Essentially, the supporter must defend the position of the author of the reading, and the critic must find flaws in the position. The discussion leader manages the session and the debate, and the observer decides whether the supporters or the critics were more convincing. This works best for controversial readings. There are many more alternatives available for those seeking a different approach.[26]

Keep learning styles in mind.

Children (and adults) differ in learning style preferences. The pioneering work of Howard Gardner has even suggested that humans actually possess multiple intelligences.[27] Teachers who present information in various ways are more likely to meet diverse learner needs.

An excellent system for helping teachers plan lessons that are both consistent with the contemporary cognitivist models and with learning styles theory is Bernice McCarthy's 4MAT System.[28] McCarthy's system incorporates left brain/right brain research into an instructional system that identifies four different learning styles: the "innovative" learners who need to be given a reason to learn; the "analytical" learners who need facts and information; the "common sense" learners who need to try things out to see how they work; and the "dynamic" learners who like to go beyond the information given and engage in self-discovery.

The 4MAT system fits cognitivist approaches beautifully, and it is especially well connected to information processing research. 4MAT moves instruction from catching the pupil's attention, to helping pupils gain declarative knowledge, to helping pupils attain procedural knowledge, to assisting pupils in making connections to their lives and among and between other ideas, facts, and concepts.

Practice some of the newer strategies.

There are many promising pedagogical practices now emerging from the practical literature that are consistent with contemporary research. Many of these come under the umbrella of authentic learning.[29] One of the most interesting, and potentially most powerful practices, is problem-based learning (PBL). This type of learning, which emerged from the literature on the education of physicians, is now influencing gifted education and teaching in mathematics and sciences.[30] William Stepien and Shelagh Gallagher are leading the way in applying PBL techniques in classroom settings.[31]

Essentially, PBL provides pupils the opportunity to understand and resolve ill-structured problems under the guidance, rather than direction, of the teacher. "Ill-structured problems" are those for which necessary solution procedures are not readily apparent and for which necessary solution information is not given up front. These problems may actually change course and become more complex as pupils tackle them.[32] Pupils work in small groups and take an active role in their learning. They must use knowledge and skills from the discipline, or from several disciplines, to work on the problems presented to them. In this way, they are learning content and skills in the context of the types of problems encountered in the "real world."[33]

The case method, although not as new, is consistent with recent research and cognitivist approaches. Like PBL, the case method also requires active participation on the part of the learner. The case method is an instructional technique that employs case studies to engage pupils in problem-solving activity. Case studies describe a decision or problem, and they are typically written from the perspective of the person who must make the decision. Cases are presented and then end with a problem or dilemma that needs to be resolved.[34] The case method differs from PBL in that cases tend to be more clearly structured; the case problems tend to be of shorter duration; and the cases allow pupils to practice knowledge they have attained, rather than to actually learn content.[35]

Summary

Will Rogers once said, "Schools aren't as good as they used to be, but then they never were." Only in the past decade or two have we had the tools to study human learning in more precise ways than ever before. The acceptance of cognitive psychology by American educators has loosened the grip of behavioral psychology, which has dominated educational practice during much of this century. Although cognitive science has provided the empirical studies for the contemporary knowledge base in teaching and learning, the application of cognitive science to school learning is clearly the domain and the responsibility of teachers. This application will allow teachers to transform classrooms into vital, interesting places where children truly move from novice to expert behavior in discipline-specific knowledge. And teachers can rest assured that the techniques they are using are supported by empirical data and are the most powerful currently available in our pedagogical arsenal. [eH]

1. John Goodlad, "A Study of Schooling: Some Findings and Hypotheses," *Phi Delta Kappan* 64 (March 1983): 467. See also John Goodlad, *A Place Called School* (New York: McGraw-Hill, 1984) for an in-depth study of 1,016 classrooms.

2. See Howard Gardner, *The Unschooled Mind: How Children Think and How Schools Should Teach* (New York: Basic Books, 1991), for an empirically-based treatise that merges cognitive science and education.

3. Renate Nummela Caine and Geoffrey Caine, *Making Connections: Teaching and the Human Brain* (Alexandria, Va.: Association for Supervision and Curriculum Development, 1991), 15.

4. John T. Bruer, "The Mind's Journey from Novice to Expert," *American Educator* 17 (Summer 1993): 7–8.

5. Bruce Joyce, Beverly Showers, and Carol Rolheiser-Bennett, "Staff Development and Student Learning: A Synthesis of Research on Models of Teaching," *Educational Leadership* 45 (October 1987): 11–23.

6. James Nolan and Pam Francis, "Changing Perspectives in Curriculum and Instruction," in *Supervision in Transition*, ed. Carl Glickman (Alexandria, Va.: Association of Supervision and Curriculum Development, 1992), 45.

7. Ibid., 45.

8. Ibid., 47–48.

9. Bruer, "The Mind's Journey," 8.

10. David Perkins, "Teaching for Understanding," *American Educator* 17 (Fall 1993): 28–35.

11. Lauren Resnick and Leopold Klopfer, eds., *Toward the Thinking Curriculum: Current Cognitive Research* (Alexandria, Va.: Association for Supervision and Curriculum Development, 1989), 207–208.

12. Perkins, "Teaching for," 33.

13. Richard Arends, *Learning to Teach*, 2nd edition (New York: McGraw-Hill, 1991), 243. It should be mentioned, however, that schema theorists believe that organizers containing concrete examples (such as drawings, etc.) are better than abstract organizers.

14. See Ellen Gagne, Carol Walker Yekovich, and Frank Yekovich, *The Cognitive Psychology of School Learning*, 2nd edition (New York: Harper-Collins, 1993), 127–135 for a solid treatment of studies supporting the use of elaboration.

15. Richard Hamilton and Elizabeth Ghatala, *Learning and Instruction* (New York: McGraw-Hill, 1994), 118.

16. Jay McTighe and Frank Lyman, Jr., "Cueing Thinking in the Classroom: The Promise of Theory-Embedded Tools," *Educational Leadership* 45 (April 1988): 21.

17. Gagne, Yekovich, and Yekovich, *Cognitive Psychology*, 70–71.

18. Hamilton and Ghatala, *Learning*, 119.

19. For examples, see McTighe and Lyman, "Cueing Thinking," 21.

20. For a more detailed treatise on declarative and procedural knowledge, and very practical classroom examples of activities to promote each one, see Robert Marzano, *A Different Kind of Classroom: Teaching with Dimensions of Learning* (Alexandria, Va.: Association of Supervision and Curriculum Development, 1992).

21. Much of the cooperative learning research has been pioneered by David and Roger Johnson at the University of Minnesota, Minneapolis, and by Robert Slavin at Johns Hopkins University in Baltimore, Maryland.

22. Anita Woolfolk, *Educational Psychology*, 5th edition (Massachusetts: Allyn and Bacon, 1993), 247.

23. Peter Frederick, "The Lively Lecture—8 Variations," *College Teaching* 34 (Spring 1986): 44.

24. Sivasailam Thiagarjan, "25 Ways to Improve Any Lecture," *Performance and Instruction Journal* 24 (December 1985/January 1986): 22.

25. Nina Buchanan, "Assigned Reading Activity: An Alternative to Lecture/Discussion," *College Teaching* 34 (Summer 1986): 111–113.

26. See Frederick and Thiagarjan for additional alternative formats.

27. Howard Gardner, *Frames of Mind: The Theory of Multiple Intelligences* (New York: Basic Books, 1983).

28. Bernice McCarthy, *The 4MAT System: Teaching to Learning Styles with Right/Left Mode Techniques* (Illinois: EXCEL, 1980). EXCEL has many additional materials that teachers might find useful in lesson preparation, and the company offers several levels of training in the 4MAT System for teachers and other school personnel.

29. For many classroom examples of authentic learning, readers are encouraged to consult *Educational Leadership* 50 (April 1993), which was devoted to this topic.

30. David Aspy, Cheryl Aspy, and Patricia Quinby, "What Doctors Can Teach Teachers about Problem-Based Learning," *Educational Leadership* 50 (April 1993): 22–24.

31. William Stepien and Shelagh Gallagher, "Problem-Based Learning: As Authentic as It Gets," *Educational Leadership* 50 (April 1993): 25–28. Teachers who would like to purchase units of instruction in PBL format may obtain a list of available topics and ordering information from the Center for Gifted Education, 232 Jamestown Road, Williamsburg, Va. 23185.

32. John O'Neil, "What Is Problem-Based Learning," *Update* 34 (August 1992): 4.

33. Stepien and Gallagher, "Problem-Based," 26.

34. Theodore Kowalski, Roy Weaver, and Kenneth Henson, *Case Studies on Teaching* (New York: Longman, 1990), ix.

35. O'Neil, "What Is Problem-Based," 4.

Problem Based Learning: An Instructional Model and Its Constructivist Framework

John R. Savery
Thomas M. Duffy

John R. Savery is a Ph.D. candidate in Instructional Systems Technology at Indiana University. His dissertation research is examining issues of learner ownership in a problem based, cooperative learning environment. He has recently joined the DLS Group in Denver, Colorado, as a senior instructional designer.

Thomas M. Duffy is Professor of Instructional Systems Technology and in Language Education at the School of Education, Indiana University, and director of the undergraduate Corporate and Community Education Program. His interests are in the design of learner-centered learning environments with particular design emphasis on technology supports and a research emphasis on the collaborative practical reasoning process.

It is said that there's nothing so practical as good theory. It may also be said that there's nothing so theoretically interesting as good practice.[1] This is particularly true of efforts to relate constructivism as a theory of learning to the practice of instruction. Our goal in this article is to provide a clear link between the theoretical principles of constructivism, the practice of instructional design, and the practice of teaching. We will begin with a basic characterization of constructivism, identifying what we believe to be the central principles in learning and understanding. We will then identify and elaborate on eight instructional principles for the design of a constructivist learning environment. Finally, we will examine what we consider to be one of the best exemplars of a constructivist learning environment—Problem Based Learning, as described by Barrows (1985, 1986, 1992).

[1]This succinct statement was noted in Gaffney & Anderson (1991).

Constructivism

Constructivism is a philosophical view on how we come to understand or know. It is, in our mind, most closely attuned to the pragmatic philosophy of Richard Rorty (1991). Space limitations for this article prevent an extensive discussion of this philosophical base, but we would commend to the interested reader the work of Rorty (1991) as well as vonGlasersfeld (1989). We will characterize the philosophical view in terms of three primary propositions:

1. Understanding is in our interactions with the environment. This is the core concept of constructivism. We cannot talk about what is learned separately from how it is learned, as if a variety of experiences all lead to the same understanding. Rather, what we understand is a function of the content, the context, the activity of the learner, and, perhaps most importantly, the goals of the learner. Since understanding is an individual construction, we cannot share understandings, but rather, we can test the degree to which our individual understandings are compatible. An implication of this proposition is that cognition is not just within the individual, but rather it is a part of the entire context, i.e., cognition is distributed.

2. Cognitive conflict or puzzlement is the stimulus for learning and determines the organization and nature of what is learned. When we are in a learning environment, there is some stimulus or goal for learning—the learner has a purpose for being there. That goal is not only the stimulus for learning, but it is a primary factor in determining what the

From *Educational Technology*, September/October 1995, pp. 31-38. © 1995 by Educational Technology Publications, Inc. Reprinted by permission.

learner attends to, what prior experience the learner brings to bear in constructing an understanding, and, basically, what understanding is eventually constructed. In Dewey's terms, it is the "problematic" that leads to and is the organizer for learning (Dewey, 1938; Roschelle, 1992). For Piaget it is the need for accommodation when current experience cannot be assimilated in existing schema (Piaget, 1977; vonGlasersfeld, 1989). We prefer to talk about the learner's "puzzlement" as being the stimulus and organizer for learning, since this more readily suggests both intellectual and pragmatic goals for learning. The important point, however, is that it is the goal of the learner that is central in considering what is learned.

3. Knowledge evolves through social negotiation and through the evaluation of the viability of individual understandings.
The social environment is critical to the development of our individual understanding as well as to the development of the body of propositions we call knowledge. At the first, or individual level, other individuals are a primary mechanism for testing our understanding. Collaborative groups are important because we can test our own understanding and examine the understanding of others as a mechanism for enriching, interweaving, and expanding our understanding of particular issues or phenomena. As vonGlasersfeld (1989) has noted, other people are the greatest source of alternative views to challenge our current views and hence to serve as the source of puzzlement that stimulates new learning. The second role of the social environment is to develop a set of propositions we call knowledge. We seek propositions that are compatible with our individual constructions or understanding of the world. Thus, facts are facts because there is widespread agreement, not because there is some ultimate truth to the fact. It was once a fact that the earth was flat and the sun revolved around the earth. More recently, it was fact that the smallest particles of matter were electrons, protons, and neutrons. These were facts because there was general agreement that the concepts and principles arising from these views provided the best interpretation of our world. The same search for viability holds in our daily life. In both cases, concepts that we call knowledge do not represent some ultimate truth, but are simply the most viable interpretation of our experiential world (see Resnick, 1987). The important consideration in this third proposition is that all views, or all constructions, are not equally viable. Constructivism is not a deconstructivist view in which all constructions are equal simply because they are personal experiences. Rather, we seek viability, and thus we must test understandings to determine how adequately they allow us to interpret and function in our world. Our social environment is primary in providing alternative views and additional information against which we can test the viability of our understanding and in building the set of propositions (knowledge) compatible with those understandings (Cunningham, Duffy, & Knuth, 1991). Hence we discuss social negotiation of meaning and understanding based on viability.

Instructional Principles

The constructivist propositions outlined above suggest a set of instructional principles that can guide the practice of teaching and the design of learning environments. All too often when we discuss principles of teaching we hear the retort, "But we already do that..." While that assertion may well be accurate, too often the claim is based on the principle in isolation rather than in the context of the overall framework. Indeed, everyone "does" collaborative groups; the real issue is what the goal is in using collaborative groups, since that determines the details of how they are used and how they are contextualized in the overall instructional framework.

We think Lebow (1993) has hit upon a strategy for summarizing the constructivist framework in a way that may help with the interpretation of the instructional strategies. He talks about the shift in values when one takes a constructivist perspective. He notes that:

> ...traditional educational technology values of replicability, reliability, communication, and control (Heinich, 1984) contrast sharply with the seven primary constructivist values of collaboration, personal autonomy, generativity, reflectivity, active engagement, personal relevance, and pluralism. (1993, p. 5)

We agree with Lebow and would propose that this value system serve to guide the reader's interpretation of our instructional principles as well as the interpretation of the problem based learning environment we will describe. The instructional principles deriving from constructivism are as follows:

1. Anchor all learning activities to a larger task or problem.
That is, learning must have a purpose beyond, "It is assigned." We learn in order to be able to function more effectively in our world. The purpose of any learning activity should be clear to the learner. Individual learning activities can be of any type—the important issue is that the learner clearly perceives and accepts the relevance of the specific learning activities in relation to the larger task complex (Cognition & Technology Group at Vanderbilt, 1992; Honebein, Duffy, & Fishman, 1993).

2. Support the learner in developing ownership for the overall problem or task. Instructional programs typically specify learning objectives and perhaps even engage the learner in a project, assuming that the learner will understand and buy into the relevance and value of the problem (Blumenfeld, Soloway, Marx, Krajcik, Guzdial, & Palincsar, 1991). Unfortunately, it is too often the case that the learners do not accept the goal of the instructional program, but rather simply focus on passing the test or putting in their time. No matter what we specify as the learning objective, the goals of the learner will largely determine what is learned. Hence, it is essential that the goals the learner brings to the environment are consistent with our instructional goals.

There are two ways of doing this. First, we may solicit problems from the learners and use those as the stimulus for learning activities. This is basically what happens in graduate schools when qualifying exams require the student to prepare publishable papers in each of several domains (Honebein et al., 1993). Scardamalia and Bereiter (1991) have shown that even elementary students can initiate questions (puzzlements) that can serve as the foundation of learning activities in traditional school subject matter. In essence, the strategy is to define a territory and then to work with the learner in developing meaningful problems or tasks in that domain. Alternatively, we can establish a problem in such a way that the learners will readily adopt the problem as their own. We see this strategy in the design of the Jasper series for teaching mathematics (Cognition & Technology Group at Vanderbilt, 1992) and in many simulation environments.[2] In either case, it is important to engage the learner in meaningful dialogue to help bring the problem or task home to that learner.

3. Design an authentic task. An authentic learning environment does *not* mean that the fourth grader should be placed in an authentic physics lab, nor that he or she should grapple with the same problems with which adult physicists deal. Rather, the learner should engage in scientific activities which present the same "type" of cognitive challenges. An authentic learning environment is one in which the cognitive demands, i.e., the thinking required, are consistent with the cognitive demands in the environment for which we are preparing the learner (Honebein et al., 1993). Thus, we do not want the learner to learn about history but rather to engage in the construction or use of history in ways that a historian or a good citizen would. Similarly, we do not want the learner to study science—

memorizing a text on science or executing scientific procedures as dictated—but rather to engage in scientific discourse and problem solving (see Bereiter, 1994; Duffy, in press; Honebein et al., 1993). Allowing the problem to be generated by the learner, an option discussed above, does not automatically assure authenticity. It may well require discussion and negotiation with the learner to develop a problem or task which is authentic in its cognitive demands and for which the learner can take ownership.

4. Design the task and the learning environment to reflect the complexity of the environment they should be able to function in at the end of learning. Rather than simplifying the environment for the learner, we seek to support the learner working in the complex environment. This is consistent with both cognitive apprenticeship (Collins, Brown, & Newman, 1989) and cognitive flexibility theory (Spiro et al., 1992) and reflects the importance of context in determining the understanding we have of any particular concept or principle.

5. Give the learner ownership of the process used to develop a solution. Learners must have ownership of the learning or problem-solving process as well as ownership of the problem itself. Frequently, teachers will give students ownership of the problem, but dictate the process for working on that problem. Thus, they may dictate that a particular problem solving or critical thinking methodology be used or that particular content domains be "learned." For example, in some problem based learning frameworks, the problem is presented along with the learning objectives and the assigned readings related to the problem. Thus, the student is told what to study and what to learn in relation to the problem. Clearly, with this pre-specification of activities, the students are not going to be engaged in authentic thinking and problem solving in that domain. Rather than being a stimulus for problem solving and self-directed learning, the problem serves merely as an example. The teacher's role should be to challenge the learner's thinking—not to dictate or attempt to proceduralize that thinking.

6. Design the learning environment to support and challenge the learner's thinking. While we advocate giving the learner ownership of the problem and the solution process, it is not the case that *any* activity or *any* solution is adequate. Indeed, the critical goal is to support the learner in becoming an effective worker/thinker in the particular domain. The teacher must assume the roles of consultant and coach. The most critical teaching activity is in the questions the teacher asks the learner in that consulting and coaching activity. It is essential that the teacher *value as well as*

---

[2]Let us hasten to add that many simulation environments are not designed to engage the learner in the problems they are addressing. This is a design issue, not a natural component of a particular instructional strategy.

challenge the learner's thinking. The teacher must not take over thinking for the learner by telling the learner what to do or how to think, but rather teaching should be done by inquiring at the "leading edge" of the learner's thinking (Fosnot, 1989). This is different from the widely used Socratic method wherein the teacher has the "right" answer and it is the student's task to guess/deduce through logical questioning that correct answer. The concept of a learning scaffold and the zone of proximal development, as described by Vygotsky (1978), is a more accurate representation of the learning exchange/interaction between the teacher and the student.

Learners use information resources (all media types) and instructional materials (all media types) as sources of information. The materials do not teach, but rather support the learners' inquiry or performance. This does not negate any kind of instructional resource—it only specifies the reason for using the resource. Thus, if domain specific problem solving is the skill to be learned, then a simulation which confronts the learner with problem situations within that domain might be appropriate. If proficient typing is required for some larger context, certainly a drill and practice program is one option that might be present.

7. Encourage testing ideas against alternative views and alternative contexts. Knowledge is socially negotiated. The quality or depth of one's understanding can only be determined in a social environment where we can see if our understanding can accommodate the issues and views of others and to see if there are points of view which we could usefully incorporate into our understanding. The importance of a learning community where ideas are discussed and understanding enriched is critical to the design of an effective learning environment. The use of collaborative learning groups as a part of the overall learning environment we have described provides one strategy for achieving this learning community (CTGV, 1994; Cunningham, Duffy, & Knuth, 1991; Scardamalia *et al.*, 1992). Other projects support collaboration by linking learners over electronic communication networks as they work on a common task; e.g., CoVis (Edelson & O'Neil, 1994), LabNet (Ruopp *et al.*, 1993), provide an alternative framework.

8. Provide opportunity for and support reflection on both the content learned and the learning process. An important goal of instruction is to develop skills of self-regulation—to become independent. Teachers should model reflective thinking throughout the learning process and support the learners in reflecting on the strategies for learning as well as what was learned (Clift, Houston, & Pugach, 1990; Schön, 1987).

In the next section we will explore how these eight instructional principles are realized in the problem-based learning approach.

Problem Based Learning

The instructional design principles, implemented within the framework of the values outlined by Lebow (1993), can lead to a wide variety of learning environments. A number of environments reflecting these principles are described in Duffy and Jonassen (1992) and Duffy, Lowyck, and Jonassen (1993). Further, the elaboration and application of these principles to specific contexts is described in Brooks and Brooks (1993), Duffy (in press), and Fosnot (1989). In our own examination of learning environments, however, we have found one application that seems to us to almost ideally capture the principles—the problem based learning model of Howard Barrows (1985, 1992).

Problem Based Learning (PBL), as a general model, was developed in medical education in the mid-1950's, and since that time it has been refined and implemented in over sixty medical schools. The most widespread application of the PBL approach has been in the first two years of medical science curricula, where it replaces the traditional lecture based approach to anatomy, pharmacology, physiology etc.. The model has been adopted in an increasing number of other areas, including business schools (Milter & Stinson, 1994), schools of education (Bridges & Hallinger, 1992; Duffy, 1994); architecture, law, engineering, social work (Boud & Feletti, 1991); and high school (Barrows & Myers, 1993).

As with any instructional model, there are many strategies for implementing PBL. Rather than attempting to provide a general characterization of PBL, we would like to focus on Barrows' model (Barrows, 1992) to provide a concrete sense of the implementation of this process in medical school. First we will present a general scenario, using the medical environment as the focus, and then examine some of the key elements in some detail.

When students enter medical school, typically they are divided into groups of five, and each group is assigned a facilitator. The students are then presented a problem in the form of a patient entering with presenting symptoms. The students' task is to diagnose the patient and to provide a rationale for that diagnosis and a recommended treatment. The process for working on the problem is outlined in Figure 1. The following paragraphs cover the highlights of that process.

The students begin the problem "cold"—they do not know what the problem will be until it is presented. They discuss the problem, generating hypotheses based on whatever experience or knowledge they have, identifying relevant facts in the case, and identifying learning issues. The learning issues are topics of any sort deemed of potential relevance to this problem and which the group members feel they do not understand as well as they should. A session is not complete until each student had an opportunity to verbally reflect on his or her current beliefs about the diagnosis (i.e., commit to a temporary position), and assume responsibility for particular learning issues that were identified. Note that there are no pre-specified objectives presented to the students. The students generate the learning issues (objectives) based on their analysis of the problem.

After the session, the students all engage in self-directed learning. There are no assigned texts. Rather, the students are totally responsible for gathering the information from the available medical library and computer database resources. Additionally, particular faculty are designated to be available as consultants (as they would be for any physician in the real world). The students may go to the consultants, seeking information.

After self-directed learning, the students meet again. They begin by evaluating resources—what was most useful and what was not so useful. They then begin working on the problem with this new level of understanding. Note that they do not simply tell what they learned. Rather, they use that learning in re-examining the problem. This cycle may repeat itself if new learning issues arise—problems in the medical school program last anywhere from a week to three weeks.

Milter and Stinson (1994) use a similar approach in an MBA program at Ohio University, and there the problems last between five and eight weeks (see also Stinson, 1994). In our own implementation, we are using one problem that lasts the entire semester. Of course, in the MBA program and in our own, the problems have multiple sub-problems that engage the students.

Assessment at the end of the process is in terms of peer- and self-evaluation. There are no tests in the medical school curriculum. The assessment includes evaluation (with suggestions for improvement) in three areas: self-directed learning, problem solving, and skills as a group member. While the students must pass the Medical Board exam after two years, this is outside of the curriculum structure.[3] However, tests as part of the PBL curriculum are not precluded. For example, one

---

[3]PBL students do as well as traditional students in a variety of discipline areas on standard or Board qualifying exams. The PBL students seem to retain their knowledge longer after the exam than students in traditional classes (Boud & Feletti, 1991; Bridges & Hallinger, 1992).

STARTING A NEW CLASS

1. **Introductions**
2. **Climate Setting** (including teacher / tutor role)

STARTING A NEW PROBLEM

1. **Set the problem.**
2. **Bring the problem home** (students internalize problem)
3. **Describe the product / performance required**
4. **Assign tasks** (Scribe 1 at the board, Scribe 2 copying from the board, and reference person)

IDEAS (Hypotheses)	FACTS	LEARNING ISSUES	ACTION PLAN
Students' conjectures regarding the problem--may involve causation, effect, possible resolutions, etc.	A growing synthesis of information obtained through inquiry, important to the hypotheses generated	Students' list of what they need to know or understand in order to complete the problem task	Things that need to be done in order to complete the problem task

5. **Reasoning through the problem**
   What you do with the columns on the board

IDEAS (Hypotheses)	FACTS	LEARNING ISSUES	ACTION PLAN
Expand / focus	Synthesize & re-synthesize	Identify / justify	Formulate plan

6. **Commitment as to probable outcome** (although much may need to be learned)
7. **Learning issue shaping/assignment**
8. **Resource identification**
9. **Schedule follow-up**

PROBLEM FOLLOW-UP

1. **Resources used and their critique**
2. **Reassess the problem**
   What you do with the columns on the board

IDEAS (Hypotheses)	FACTS	LEARNING ISSUES	ACTION PLAN
Revise	Apply new knowledge and re-synthesize	Identify new (if necessary)	Redesign decisions

PERFORMANCE PRESENTATION

AFTER CONCLUSION OF PROBLEM

1. **Knowledge abstraction and summary** (develop definitions, diagrams, lists, concepts, abstractions, principles)
2. **Self-evaluation** (followed by comments from the group)
   - reasoning through the problem
   - digging out information using good resources
   - assisting the group with its tasks
   - gaining or refining knowledge

Figure 1. The Problem Based Learning process.

Taken from Barrows and Myers (1993).

---

high school teacher we know who uses the PBL approach designs traditional tests based on what the students have identified as learning issues. Thus, rather than a pre-specification of what is to be learned, the assessment focuses on the issues the learners have identified.

That is an overview of the process in the medical school. Now we will comment on a few of the critical features.

Learning goals. The design of this environment is meant to simulate, and hence engage the learner in, the problem solving behavior that it is hoped a practicing physician would be engaged in. Nothing is simplified or pre-specified for the learner. The facilitator assumes a major role in modeling the metacognitive thinking associated with the problem solving process. Hence this is a cognitive apprenticeship environment with scaffolding designed to support the learner in developing the metacognitive skills.

Within the context of this cognitive apprenticeship environment, there are goals related to self-directed learning, content knowledge, and problem solving. To be successful, students must develop the self-directed learning skills needed in the medical field. They must be able to develop strategies for identifying learning issues and locating, evaluating, and learning from resources relevant to that issue. The entire problem solving process is designed to aid the students in developing the hypothetico-deductive problem solving model which centers around hypothesis generation and evaluation. Finally, there are specific content learning objectives associated with each problem. Since the students have responsibility for the problem, there is no guarantee that all of the content area objectives will be realized in a given problem. However, any given content objective occurs in several problems, and hence if it does not arise in one, it will almost certainly arise in one of the other problems.

Problem Generation. There are two guiding forces in developing problems. First, the problems must raise the concepts and principles relevant to the content domain. Thus, the process begins with first identifying the primary concepts or principles that a student must learn. Milter and Stinson working in the MBA program and Barrows working with medical education polled the faculty to identify the most important concepts or principles in their area. This, of course, generates considerable debate and discussion—it is not a matter of a simple survey. In developing high school PBL curricula, Myers and Barrows (personal communication) used the learning objectives identified by the state for grade and content domains.

Second, the problems must be "real." In the medical school, the patients are real patients. Indeed, Barrows worked with the presenting physician in gathering the details on the case. Milter and Stinson in the MBA program use problems such as "Should AT&T buy NCR?" These problems change each year so as to address current business issues. At the high school level, Myers and Barrows have developed problems such as:

- Do asteroids in space pose a problem, and if so, what should we be doing about it?
- What caused the flooding in the Midwest in 1993 and what should be done to prevent it in the future?

We are still developing problems and sub-problems for our Corporate and Community Education program. One of the problems currently being developed relates to the numerous PCB sites around Bloomington,

Indiana, and the general public apathy about cleaning up these sites. The problem is basically:

- What do citizens need to know about the PCB problem and how should that information be presented to encourage them to be active citizens in the discussion?

There are three reasons why the problems must address real issues. First, because the students are open to explore all dimension of the problem, there is real difficulty in creating a rich problem with a consistent set of information. Second, real problems tend to engage learners more—there is a larger context of familiarity with the problem. Finally, students want to know the outcome of the problem—what is being done about the flood, did AT&T buy NCR, what was the problem with the patient? These outcomes are not possible with artificial problems.

Problem Presentation. There are two critical issues involved in presenting the problem. First, if the students are to engage in authentic problem solving, then they must own the problem. We have been learners with the Asteroid Problem and we have been facilitators in two contexts: with a group of high school students and with a group of our peers who were attending a workshop to learn about constructivism. In all three cases, the learners were thoroughly engaged in the problem. Frankly, we were amazed at the generality across these disparate groups. In presenting this problem, we used a 10-minute video that described asteroids and showed the large number of sites on earth where they have hit and the kind of impact they can have (the diamond fields in South Africa, the possibility that an asteroid caused the extinction of dinosaurs, Crater Lake, etc.). We also talked about recent near misses—one in Alabama within the last year and one three years ago that could have hit Australia or Russia. Thus, the problem clearly has potential cataclysmic effects (we have past history) and it is a current real problem (we have had near misses quite recently).[4] This step in the PBL process of "bringing the problem home" is critical. The learners must perceive the problem as a real problem and one which has personal relevance. Of course, also central is the fact that the learners have ownership of the problem—they are not just trying to figure out what *we* want.

A second critical issue in presenting the problem is to be certain that the data presented do not highlight critical factors in the case. Too often when problems are presented, the only information that is provided is

---

[4]The potential value of real-world problems in terms of sustained learning and potential impact on interest in the news is illustrated in terms of the 1994 collisions of asteroids with Jupiter. Once having engaged in the asteroid "problem," news concerning asteroid events takes on considerably greater significance.

the key information relevant to the desired solution (end-of-chapter "problems" are notorious for this). Either the case must be richly presented or presented only as a basic question. For example, Honebein, Marrero, Kakos-Kraft, and Duffy (1994) present all of the medical notes on a patient, while Barrows (1985) provides answers generated by the presenting physician to any of 270 questions the learners might ask. In contrast, Milter and Stinson (1994) present only a four-word question and rely on natural resources to provide the full context.

Facilitator Role. In his discussion of the tutorial process, Barrows states:

> The ability of the tutor to use facilitory teaching skills during the small group learning process is the major determinant of the quality and the success of any educational method aimed at (1) developing students' thinking or reasoning skills (problem solving, metacognition, critical thinking) as they learn, and (2) helping them to become independent, self-directed learners (learning to learn, learning management). Tutoring is a teaching skill central to problem-based, self-directed learning. (1992, p. 12)

Throughout a session, the facilitator models higher order thinking by asking questions which probe students' knowledge deeply. To do this, the facilitator constantly asks "Why?" "What do you mean?" "How do you know that's true?" Barrows is adamant that the facilitators' interactions with the students be at a metacognitive level (except for housekeeping tasks) and that the facilitator avoid expressing an opinion or giving information to the students. The facilitator does not use his or her knowledge of the content to ask questions that will lead the learners to the "correct" answer.

A second tutor role is to challenge the learners' thinking. The facilitator (and hopefully the other students in this collaborative environment) will constantly ask: "Do you know what that means? What are the implications of that? Is there anything else?" Superficial thinking and vague notions do not go unchallenged. During his introduction of the Asteroid Problem, Barrows noted for the group that saying nothing about another member's facts or opinions was the same as saying "I agree." Similarly, the responsibility for a flawed medical diagnosis was shared by everyone in the group. During the first few PBL sessions, the facilitator challenges both the level of understanding and the relevance and completeness of the issues studied. Gradually, however, the students take over this role themselves as they become effective self-directed learners.

Conclusion

Our goal in this article was to present PBL as a detailed instructional model and to show how PBL is consistent with the principles of instruction arising from constructivism. We sought to provide a clear link between theory and practice. Some of the features of the PBL environment are that the learners are actively engaged in working at tasks and activities that are authentic to the environment in which they would be used. The focus is on learners as constructors of their own knowledge in a context similar to that in which they would apply that knowledge. Students are encouraged and expected to think both critically and creatively and to monitor their own understanding, i.e., function at a metacognitive level. Social negotiation of meaning is an important part of the problem-solving team structure and the facts of the case are only facts when the group decides they are.

PBL, as we have described it, contrasts with a variety of other problem or case based approaches. Most case based learning strategies (Williams, 1992) use cases as a means for testing one's understanding. The case is presented after the topic is covered in order to help test understanding and support synthesis. In contrast, in PBL, all of the learning arises out of consideration of the problem. From the start, the learning is synthesized and organized in the context of the problem.

Other case approaches simply use the case as a concrete reference point for learning. Learning objectives and resources are presented along with the case. These approaches use the case as an "example" and are not focused on developing the metacognitive skills associated with problem solving or with professional life. The contrast is perhaps that the PBL approach is a cognitive apprenticeship focusing on both the knowledge domain and the problem solving associated with that knowledge domain or profession. Other problem approaches present cases so that critical attributes are highlighted, thus emphasizing the content domain, but not engaging the learner in authentic problem solving in that domain.

Finally, this is not a Socratic process, nor is it a kind of limited discovery learning environment in which the goal for the learner is to "discover" the outcome the instructor *wants*. The learners have ownership of the problem. The facilitation is not knowledge driven; rather, it is focused on metacognitive processes.

References

Barrows, H. S. (1985). *How to design a problem based curriculum for the preclinical years.* New York: Springer Publishing Co.

Barrows, H. S. (1986). A taxonomy of problem based learning methods. *Medical Education, 20,* 481–486.

Barrows, H. S. (1992). *The tutorial process.* Springfield, IL: Southern Illinois University School of Medicine.

Barrows, H. S., & Myers, A. C. (1993). *Problem based learning in secondary schools.* Unpublished monograph.

Springfield, IL: Problem Based Learning Institute, Lanphier High School, and Southern Illinois University Medical School.

Bereiter, C. (1994). Implications of Postmodernism for science, or, science as progressive discourse. *Educational Psychologist, 29*, 3–12.

Blumenfeld, P. C., Soloway, E., Marx, R. W., Krajcik, J. S., Guzdial, M., & Palincsar, A. (1991). Motivating project-based learning: Sustaining the doing, supporting the learning. *Educational Psychologist, 26* (3&4), 369–398.

Boud, D., & Feletti, G. (Eds.) (1991). *The challenge of problem based learning.* New York: St. Martin's Press.

Bridges, E., & Hallinger, P. (1992). *Problem based learning for administrators.* ERIC Clearinghouse on Educational Management, University of Oregon.

Brooks, J. G., & Brooks, M. G. (1993). *In search of understanding: The case for constructivist classrooms.* Alexandria, VA: Association for Supervision and Curriculum Development.

Brown, J. S., Collins, A., & Duguid, P. (1989). Situated cognition and the culture of learning. *Educational Researcher, 18(1)*, 32–42.

Clift, R., Houston, W., & Pugach, M. (Eds.), (1990). *Encouraging reflective practice in education.* New York: Teachers College Press.

Cognition & Technology Group at Vanderbilt. (1992). Technology and the design of generative learning environments. In T. M. Duffy & D. H. Jonassen (Eds.), *Constructivism and the technology of instruction: A conversation.* Hillsdale, NJ: Lawrence Erlbaum Associates. Originally in *Educational Technology*, 1991, *31*(5).

Cognition & Technology Group at Vanderbilt. (1994). From visual word problems to learning communities: Changing conceptions of cognitive research. In K. McGilly (Ed.), *Classroom lessons: Integrating cognitive theory and classroom practice.* Cambridge, MA: MIT Press/Bradford Books.

Cohen, E. (1994). Restructuring the classroom: Conditions for productive small groups. *Review of Educational Research, 64*, 1–35.

Collins, A., Brown, J. S., & Newman, S. E. (1989). Cognitive apprenticeship: Teaching the crafts of reading, writing, and mathematics. In L.B. Resnick (Ed.), *Knowing, learning, and instruction: Essays in honor of Robert Glaser* (pp. 453–494). Hillsdale, NJ: Lawrence Erlbaum Associates.

Cunningham, D. J., Duffy, T. M., & Knuth, R. A. (1991). The textbook of the future. In C. McKnight, A. Dillon, & J. Richardson (Eds.), *Hypertext: A psychological perspective.* London: Horwood Publishing.

Dewey, J. (1938). *Logic: The theory of inquiry.* New York: Holt and Co.

Duffy, T. M. (1994). *Corporate and community education: Achieving success in the information society.* Unpublished paper. Bloomington, IN: Indiana University.

Duffy, T. M. (in press). *Strategic teaching frameworks: An instructional model for complex, interactive skills.* To appear in C. Dills & A. Romiszowski (Eds.), *Instructional development.* Englewood Cliffs, NJ: Educational Technology Publications.

Duffy, T. M., & Jonassen, D. H. (Eds.) (1992). *Constructivism and the technology of instruction: A conversation.* Hillsdale, NJ: Lawrence Erlbaum Associates.

Duffy, T. M., Lowyck, J., & Jonassen, D. H. (Eds.) (1993). *Designing environments for constructivist learning.* Berlin: Springer-Verlag.

Edelson, D., & O'Neil, K. (1994). *The CoVis collaboratory notebook: Computer support for scientific inquiry.* Paper presented at the annual meeting of the American Educational Research Association, New Orleans.

Fosnot, C. T. (1989). *Enquiring teachers, enquiring learners. A Constructivist approach to teaching.* New York: Teachers College Press.

Gaffney, J. S., & Anderson, R. C. (1991). Two-tiered scaffolding: Congruent processes of teaching and learning. In E. H. Hiebert (Ed.), *Literacy for a diverse society: Perspectives, practices, & policies.* New York: Teachers College Press.

Honebein, P., Duffy, T. M., & Fishman, B. (1993). Constructivism and the design of learning environments: Context and authentic activities for learning. In T. M. Duffy, J. Lowyck, & D. H. Jonassen (Eds.), *Designing environments for constructivist learning.* Berlin: Springer-Verlag.

Honebein, P., Marrero, D. G., Kakos-Kraft, S., & Duffy, T. M. (1994). *Improving medical students' skills in the clinical care of diabetes.* Paper presented at the annual meeting of the American Diabetes Association, New Orleans.

Johnson, D. W., & Johnson, R. T., (1990). Cooperative learning and achievement. In S. Sharan (Ed.), *Cooperative learning: Theory and practice.* New York: Praeger.

Kagan, S. (1992). *Cooperative learning.* San Juan Capistrano, CA: Kagan Cooperative Learning.

Lebow, D. (1993). Constructivist values for systems design: Five principles toward a new mindset. *Educational Technology Research and Development, 41*, 4–16.

MacDonald, P. J. (1991). Selection of health problems for a problem-based curriculum. In D. Boud & G. Feletti (Eds.), *The challenge of problem based learning.* New York: St. Martin's Press.

Milter, R. G., & Stinson, J. E. (1994). Educating leaders for the new competitive environment. In G. Gijselaers, S. Tempelaar, & S. Keizer S. (Eds.), *Educational innovation in economics and business administration: The case of problem-based learning.* London: Kluwer Academic Publishers.

Piaget, J. (1977). *The development of thought: Equilibrium of cognitive structures.* New York: Viking Press.

Resnick, L. B. (1987). Learning in school and out. *Educational Researcher, 16*, 13–20.

Rorty, R. (1991). *Objectivity, relativism, and truth.* Cambridge: Cambridge University Press.

Roschelle, J. (1992). *Reflections on Dewey and technology for situated learning.* Paper presented at annual meeting of the American Educational Research Association, San Francisco.

Ruopp, R., Gal, S., Drayton, B., & Pfister, M. (Eds.) (1993). *LabNet: Toward a community of practice.* Hillsdale, NJ: Lawrence Erlbaum Associates.

Scardamalia, M., & Bereiter, C. (1991). Higher levels of agency for children in knowledge building: A challenge for the design of new knowledge media. *The Journal of the Learning Sciences, 1*, 37–68.

Scardamalia, M., Bereiter, C., Brett, C., Burtis, P. J., Calhoun, & Lea, N. S. (1992). Educational applications of a networked communal database. *Interactive Learning Environments, 2*, 45–71.

Schön, D. A. (1987). *Educating the reflective practitioner.* San Francisco: Jossey-Bass.

Slavin, R. (1990). *Cooperative learning: Theory, research, and practice.* Boston: Allyn and Bacon.

Spiro, R. J., Feltovich, P. L., Jacobson, M. J., & Coulson, R. L. (1992). Cognitive flexibility, constructivism, and hypertext: Random access for advanced knowledge acquisition in ill-structured domains. In T. M. Duffy & D. H. Jonassen (Eds.), *Constructivism and the technology of instruction: A*

conversation. Hillsdale, NJ: Lawrence Erlbaum Associates. Originally in *Educational Technology,* 1991, *31*(5).

Stinson, J. E. (1994). *Can Digital Equipment survive?* Paper presented at the Sixth International Conference on Thinking, Boston, MA.

Williams, S. M., (1992) Putting case-based instruction into context: Examples from legal and medical education. *Journal of the Learning Sciences, 2*, 367– 427.

vonGlasersfeld, E. (1989). Cognition, construction of knowledge, and teaching. *Synthese, 80,* 121–140.

Vygotsky, L. S. (1978) *Mind in Society: The development of higher psychological processes.* Cambridge MA: Harvard University Press.

Allowing for Thinking Styles

Robert J. Sternberg

Robert J. Sternberg is IBM Professor of Psychology and Education, Department of Psychology, Yale University, P. O. Box 208205, New Haven, CT 06520-8205.

By keying teaching and assessment techniques to the diverse ways people think and learn, teachers will be surprised at how much smarter their students get.

When I received a *C* in my introductory psychology course, I concluded (and my teacher concurred) that I did not have the ability to pursue my true interest and intended major—psychology. I decided to switch to mathematics. But discovering that I had even less ability in that subject, I returned to psychology; three years later I was graduated summa cum laude with exceptional distinction in that field.

As a high school student I had a similar experience. My French teacher advised me that, while I did reasonably well in the subject, I lacked the natural ability to learn foreign languages and ought to take this fact into account in my future planning. I did, and proceeded to avoid all foreign language courses in college. Years later, as an assistant professor, I received a contract to develop a program to help Venezuelan schoolchildren enhance their thinking skills. I *had* to learn Spanish. I did so—rapidly—and today speak Spanish fluently. When I travel to Spain and Latin America, I have no problem presenting my talks in the native language.

These are the kinds of events in my own life—which are mirrored in almost everyone else's—that have interested me in styles of thinking and learning. In both psychology and foreign languages, the problem I faced was not a lack of ability, but a mismatch between the way a course was taught and the way I think and learn. My experiences illustrated the following:

■ Teachers almost invariably teach and assess students in ways that benefit those with certain styles of thinking and learning but place many others at a marked disadvantage.

■ Teachers and students alike confuse mismatches in styles of teaching and learning with lack of ability.

■ Teachers can easily and comfortably expand their ways of teaching and assessing students to accommodate virtually all thinking and learning styles. If they do, they will observe immediate and powerful increases in student performance.

What's My Style?

A *style* is a preferred way of using one's abilities. It is not in itself an ability but rather a preference. Hence, various styles are not good or bad, only different.

We all have a style profile, meaning we show varying amounts of each style, but we are not locked into any one profile. We can vary our styles to suit different tasks and situations. For example, the style you need to discern the meaning of a work of literature is not the same one you need to read detailed directions. The style you need to solve an algebra word problem is not the one you need to construct a geometric proof. Styles further vary over the course of a lifetime, and change as a result of the role models we emulate at different points in our lives. We do vary in our flexibility to shift styles, and in the strengths of our preferences. But while we have preferred styles, our styles are fluid, not fixed.

Many theories of styles have been proposed (for example, Gregorc 1985, Holland 1973, Renzulli and Smith 1978). All are attempts to describe how people think.

One such theory is known as *mental self-government*. The basic idea is that we must organize or govern ourselves, and the ways in which we do correspond to the kinds of governments and government branches that exist worldwide—legislative, executive, judicial; monarchic, hierarchic, oligarchic (see fig. 1). Note that there are 13 styles under five categories: functions, forms, levels, scope, and leanings.

Most of us tend toward one style within each category, although these preferences may vary with the task

> A style is not in itself an ability, but a preference. Hence, various styles are not good or bad, only different.

Figure 1

Styles of Mental Self-Government

Style	Characterization	Example
FUNCTIONS		
Legislative	Likes to create, invent, design, do things his or her own way, have little assigned structure.	Likes doing science projects, writing poetry, stories, or music, and creating original artworks.
Executive	Likes to follow directions, do what he or she is told, be given structure.	Likes to solve problems, write papers on assigned topics, do artwork from models, build from designs, learn assigned information.
Judicial	Likes to judge and evaluate people and things.	Likes to critique work of others, write critical essays, give feedback and advice.
FORMS		
Monarchic	Likes to do one thing at a time, devoting to it almost all energy and resources.	Likes to immerse self in a single project, whether art, science, history, business.
Hierarchic	Likes to do many things at once, setting priorities for which to do when and how much time and energy to devote to each.	Likes to budget time for doing homework so that more time and energy is devoted to important assignments.
Oligarchic	Likes to do many things at once, but has trouble setting priorities.	Likes to devote sufficient time to reading comprehension items, so may not finish standardized verbal-ability test.
Anarchic	Likes to take a random approach to problems; dislikes systems, guidelines, and practically all constraints.	Writes an essay in stream-of-consciousness form; in conversations, jumps from one point to another; starts things but doesn't finish them.
LEVELS		
Global	Likes to deal with big picture, generalities, abstractions.	Writes an essay on the global message and meaning of a work of art.
Local	Likes to deal with details, specifics, concrete examples.	Writes an essay describing the details of a work of art and how they interact.
SCOPE		
Internal	Likes to work alone, focus inward, be self-sufficient.	Prefers to do science or social studies project on his or her own.
External	Likes to work with others, focus outward, be interdependent.	Prefers to do science or social studies project with other members of a group.
LEANING		
Liberal	Likes to do things in new ways, defy conventions.	Prefers to figure out how to operate new equipment even if it is not the recommended way; prefers open-classroom setting.
Conservative	Likes to do things in tried and true ways, follow conventions.	Prefers to operate new equipment in traditional way; prefers traditional classroom setting.

and situation. For example, children who are liberal in science class (enjoy doing things in new ways) may be conservative in cooking class or in gym (prefer the familiar). Teachers who are legislative at work (preferring creation, invention) may be executive at home (following or giving directions, preferring structure), almost always taking the lead with the family.

We have devised a number of instruments to assess styles. One is based on self-reports of students or teachers, another on performance, and a third on evaluations by another person. One tool looks at teaching styles rather than learning styles (for example, whether a teacher fosters legislative or executive behavior in the classroom).

But these tests notwithstanding, teachers need no formal questionnaire or other measure to assess their own or their students' thinking styles. The most direct way is to analyze the types of instructional and assessment activities a person prefers. By doing this, you can make a difference to your students now! Figures 2–4 show you how. Figure 2 shows how different teaching methods favor students with different styles, Figure 3 shows the same for assessment methods, and Figure 4, for activity prompts.

Change Styles Often
One principle underlies all three approaches: Teachers must accommodate an array of thinking and learning styles, systematically varying teaching

Students receive higher grades and more favorable evaluations when their styles more closely match those of their teachers.

and assessment methods to reach every student. The key is variety and flexibility—using the full range of styles available to you. You probably know all these methods and have used them in the past, yet most teachers regularly use only a few.

As the figures show, the solution is not to replace traditional teaching and assessment methods with modern methods. Traditional methods (like multiple-choice tests) benefit children with an executive and conservative style, while modern methods (like performance assessment) benefit children with a legislative style. Neither method is uniquely correct. By changing from one to another, you'll merely benefit a different group of children. Again, the key is to vary your approach.

Note, too, that children with oligarchic and anarchic styles are almost always at a disadvantage: virtually nothing teachers do specifically benefits them. We therefore need to help students with an oligarchic style (they like to do many things at once) to become comfortable with setting priorities. And we need to help children with an anarchic style (who approach problems randomly and chafe at guidelines) learn to discipline themselves to direct their energies in an organized and focused way.

I'm Oligarchic, You're Oligarchic

Most teachers are best at teaching children who match their own styles of thinking and learning. We have found, however, that teachers tend to overes-

Figure 2

Mental Self-Government: Thinking Styles and Teaching Methods

Method of Instruction	Most Compatible Styles
Lecture	Executive/Hierarchical
Thought-Based Questioning	Judicial/Legislative
Cooperative Learning	External
Problem Solving of Given Problems	Executive
Projects	Legislative
Small-Group Recitation	External/Executive
Small-Group Discussion	External/Judicial
Reading	Internal/Hierarchical
For Details	Local/Executive
For Main Ideas	Global/Executive
For Analysis	Judicial
Memorization	Executive/Local/Conservative

Figure 3

Mental Self-Government: Thinking Styles and Assessment Methods

Forms of Assessment	Main Skills Tapped	Most Compatible Style(s)
Short Answer/ Multiple Choice	Memory	Executive/Local
	Analysis	Judicial/Local
	Time Allocation	Hierarchical
	Working by Self	Internal
Essay	Memory	Executive/Local
	Macroanalysis	Judicial/Global
	Microanalysis	Judicial/Local
	Creativity	Legislative
	Organization	Hierarchical
	Time Allocation	Hierarchical
	Acceptance of Teacher Viewpoint	Conservative
	Working by Self	Internal
Project/Portfolio	Analysis	Judicial
	Creativity	Legislative
	Teamwork	External
	Working by Self	Internal
	Organization	Hierarchical
	High Commitment	Monarchic
Interview	Social Ease	External

timate the extent to which their students share their own styles (Grigorenko and Sternberg in press, Sternberg 1994, Sternberg and Grigorenko 1993).

It's natural to think others are more like you than they really are. It

becomes a problem, though, when teachers underestimate the abilities and achievements of students simply because their styles are different. And the more students differ from the teacher culturally, ethnically, and socioeconomically, the more their styles are likely to differ; thus the more likely it is that these students will be undervalued and even appear to be stupid rather than mismatched.

Conversely, we have found that students do in fact receive higher grades and more favorable evaluations when their styles more closely match those of their teachers. Teachers therefore need to take special care not to undervalue students just because they are different. You don't have to match your students' learning styles, merely expand your methods. As you do, your students will expand their own styles of thinking and learning—the benefit will be mutual.

Our research further shows that students' styles, at least to some degree, come to match their teachers', just as teachers' styles come to match the predominant style profile at their school. In other words, we come to be like those we are with. As a role model, then, a teacher should exhibit a variety of styles in the classroom. If you want students to be flexible, you must be flexible yourself.

Teachers' styles not only differ across schools, but across grades and subject matter, demonstrating that the demands of the environment may mold the kinds of people we are. Teachers of younger students need to be more legislative and less executive than teachers of older students. In the upper grades, curriculums and requirements tend to be more rigidly specified because older students, and particularly those in high school, must take so many achievement tests for both college admissions and state and local requirements.

Of course, it is possible that the two groups of teachers also have dispositional differences. Both situational and dispositional differences may account, too, for our findings that science teachers tend to be more local (enjoy dealing with details, specifics) than humanities teachers, and that humanities teachers tend to be more liberal

Figure 4

Mental Self-Government: Thinking Styles and Activity Prompts

Teachers can reach more students by varying their activity prompts in teaching and assessment.

Executive Style	Judicial Style	Legislative Style
Who said?	Compare and contrast...	Create...
Summarize...	Analyze...	Invent...
Who did?	Evaluate...	If you...
When did?	In your judgment...	Imagine...
What did?	Why did?	Design...
How did?	What caused?	How would?
Repeat back...	What is assumed by?	Suppose...
Describe...	Critique...	Ideally?

than science teachers. We also have found that the longer teachers teach, the more executive, local, and conservative they become.

Groups of students differ as well. For example, the lower the socioeconomic level, the more likely the student will be judicial, oligarchic, local, and conservative (like to judge, do many things at once, deal with specifics and with the familiar). Later-borns are more likely to be legislative (preferring creation, invention) than first-borns.

Clearly, both students and teachers vary widely in their styles. In workshops I have held, teachers are often amazed to find that their peers, whom they previously viewed as a relatively homogeneous group, have a very diverse array of styles. If their own peer group is so diverse, imagine how diverse the student body must be!

They've Gotten Smarter!

I must confess that when I started teaching psychology, I did all the things that I have accused others of doing. I taught in a way that systematically benefited students with my own style profile (legislative, hierarchic, global, internal, liberal),

and tended to devalue the abilities and accomplishments of those who were unlike myself. I now systematically vary my instruction and assessment to meet the needs of more learners. In so doing, I have discovered that I have a lot more able learners than I realized. I suspect this is true of your students as well. They are there, waiting to be discovered and valued—waiting to learn.

References

Gregorc, A. F. (1985). *Inside Styles: Beyond the Basics*. Maynard, Mass.: Gabriel Systems.

Grigorenko, E. L., and R. J. Sternberg. (In press). "Thinking Styles." In *International Handbook of Personality and Intelligence*, edited by D. Saklosfske and M. Zeidner. New York: Plenum.

Holland, J. L. (1973). *Making Vocational Choices: A Theory of Careers*. Englewood Cliffs, N.J.: Prentice-Hall.

Renzulli, J. S., and L. H. Smith. (1978). *Learning Styles Inventory*. Storrs, Conn.: Creative Learning Press.

Sternberg, R. J. (1994). "Thinking Styles: Theory and Assessment at the Interface Between Intelligence and Personality." In *Intelligence and Personality*, edited by R. J. Sternberg and P. Ruzgis. New York: Cambridge University Press.

Sternberg, R. J. and E. L. Grigorenko. (1993). "Thinking Styles and the Gifted." *Roeper Review* 16, 2: 122–130.

How K–12 Teachers Are Using Computer Networks

[Internet Use in Schools: Observations and Issues]

Jon M. Peha

Jon M. Peha is Assistant Professor, Carnegie Mellon University, Department of Engineering and Public Policy, and Department of Electrical and Computer Engineering, Pittsburgh, PA 15213-3890 (http://www.ece.cmu.edu/afs/ece/usr/peha/peha.htm/)

A Carnegie Mellon University study, conducted in conjunction with the Pittsburgh Public Schools, looks at technology present and technology future.

[Proponents in both government and the telecommunications industry have fueled a growing interest in connecting schools to various regional, national, and international computer networks. Educators must now determine how these networks can be integrated into class room curricula, and how this affects school systems. Ultimately, we must also evaluate the potential benefits, and determine whether they justify the expense. While it is too soon to offer definitive answers to these difficult questions, this paper will present a few pieces of the puzzle. It will describe a wide range of promising classroom activities involving computer networks. Based on feedback from those involved and from direct observation, this paper will describe some of the apparent effects, including both potential benefits

and pitfalls to be avoided. It will also discuss how school systems might provide preparation and support for teachers.] By almost any measure, the world's largest computer network is the Internet. The Internet evolved from a U.S. Defense Department communications system to become an interconnected collection of more than 46,000 independent networks, public and private, around the world (National Science Foundation 1995). Now serving millions of users worldwide, its growth is rapid and exponential.

[Consequently, we focus on programs that bring Internet access to schools.] In 1993, the Pittsburgh Public Schools began such a program, in partnership with the Pittsburgh Supercomputer Center and the University of Pittsburgh, and with funding from the National Science Foundation. At that time, Carnegie Mellon University began a four-month project to aid the Pittsburgh Public Schools in their new endeavor, which was known as Common Knowledge Pittsburgh.

To observe the uses of the Internet in Pittsburgh, our research group surveyed and/or interviewed approximately 45 educators in various positions throughout the school system. Of that number, 24 teachers and 4 librarians from 4 schools attended a professional development workshop on Internet use in classrooms. Of the 28, 14 completed surveys about the effectiveness of that program. We also interviewed students.

In addition, we made numerous observations in one of the four schools participating in the first year of the project, an elementary school in a low-income area of Pittsburgh. A comparable number of schools have come online each subsequent year (Carnegie Mellon University 1994).

To catalog what other teachers outside of Pittsburgh were doing with the Internet, we compiled responses from a questionnaire addressed to educators who use the Internet via relevant newsgroups and e-mail distribution lists. We received 21 responses describing 34 distinct classroom activities. Given the small sample size and a method of distributing questionnaires that naturally favors frequent Internet users, our statistics are not terribly meaningful. Our questionnaire was deliberately unstructured, however, to enable recipients to elaborate on their experiences and to share insights about using the Internet. We also conducted unstructured interviews with educators who were using the Internet. To supplement these data, we studied descriptions from the printed literature of roughly 40 classroom activities.

How Students Are Using Computers

Before looking at what we found occurring in classrooms, let's define a few key terms. For many years, three types of traffic have dominated the Internet:

■ With *electronic mail*, the most popular tool at all grade levels, a user can quickly send a message to any other user or specified group of users. E-mail can also reach mass audiences when used in conjunction with:

— distribution lists, made up of e-mail addresses of people with shared interests (a list of educational distribution lists is available via anonymous FTP [see below] from nic.umass.edu); or

— newsgroups, also called electronic bulletin boards, where any user interested in a topic may read about it much the same way one reads personal e-mail.

■ *File transfers* (FTPs) allow a user to copy a file (which can contain text, software, pictures, and music) from, or to, another computer system. With a variation, anonymous FTP, a user can copy files without the need for password privileges.

■ *Telnet* allows a user to log onto a remote computer as if it were in the same room. For example, one might telnet onto a system because it has capabilities that the local system lacks.

A number of important tools have also developed in recent years that facilitate the search for information on the Internet, such as Gopher, Archie, Veronica, Mosaic, and, more recently, Netscape. Obviously, such tools are useful only if the network contains useful information. (There is no way to describe all of the resources available on the Internet; see Resources box for five examples.)

The classroom activities that we observed, that educators shared with us, or that we read about in the literature fall into the following broad categories that build on these capabilities.

1. Students send their work to some other party for evaluation or response. The network provides a high-tech postal service, but with no cost per letter, minimal hassle, and most important, a negligible time for the message to reach its destination, which enables meaningful interaction. With pen pal programs, younger students write e-mail messages about themselves and their interests to peers in distant places. There is strong mo-

The teachers who responded to our questionnaire offered several ways to overcome difficulties in introducing the Internet in a K–12 curriculum.

tivation for students to write good letters because, as one teacher put it, "A good letter writer generally receives good letters." Older students exchange more complex material like stories and artwork, sometimes critiquing one another's work.

Other programs provide a forum to learn about distant events and different ways of life. In one example, inner-city elementary school students corresponded with Native American peers who live on a reservation. E-mail is also sometimes written in a foreign language to both motivate and help students learning that language.

The Internet makes possible communication between students and older students or professionals as well. Some students send their writing samples to professional writers for feedback; others correspond with professional engineers for help with independent science projects. Still other activities link [disabled] students with big brothers and sisters, for example, or connect students from schools where few go on to college with their older counterparts who are in college.

2. Group projects enable students at different locations to collaborate on activities. For example, students can cooperate on tasks like taking temperature and barometric measurements for a weather project or surveying garbage around their schools for an environmental project. Because many of these projects are experimental in nature, students engage in meaningful exploratory science with a large body of data. They gather information locally, and then pool data from around the world. Although they spend a relatively small amount of time collecting their part of the data, students understand how all of the data were collected, and have a sense

of ownership. Other projects show students the value of working in groups, because each classroom is bound to produce ideas that improve the group's solution.

3. Students exploit remote data sources and processing capabilities on the network. Most often, the Internet serves as an enormous library with extraordinary search capabilities. With the growing popularity of new browsing tools, such activities are likely to become more common. The Internet's remote processing capabilities can also be valuable. For example, students can run computationally intensive scientific simulations on a powerful remote computer that cannot be run on the school's inexpensive equipment. Such simulations can also replace expensive (or dangerous) laboratory equipment in the school.

Many educators told us that the Internet allows them to tap information sources on their discipline or on teaching in general, and to correspond with other educators around the world with similar interests. As one teacher said, "When I get the information I'm seeking, I can incorporate some of the activities in my lessons, also advancing my own professionalism."

Figure 1 is a breakdown of activities described in responses to our questionnaire. Although these results are not statistically significant, they do dispel the myth that computers and networks are just for math and the sciences.

How the Internet Benefits the Classroom

Two-thirds of the respondents to our questionnaire said that a primary benefit of the Internet is making students aware that they are part of a global community. Others commented that the Internet gives students a wide variety of resources, stimulates thinking, and improves computer literacy.

From our many observations in the inner-city elementary school in Pittsburgh, an important benefit of using this technology is enthusiasm. Whenever the Internet teacher walked into the room, students appeared hopeful that it would be their turn to use the Internet. Teachers even threatened to revoke a student's computer privileges as a punishment for disruptive behavior. As for teachers, their enthusiasm was unmistakable in both direct interviews and survey responses.

The Internet and other information technology in the classroom, of course, do much more than boost enthusiasm or expand information resources. Internet use fundamentally alters the roles of teachers and students. For example, when students write to impress a pen pal or a distant expert, the teacher is no longer the sole judge of quality, and grades are less of a motivating factor than in traditional classrooms. In addition, many activities require students to work in teams. When students spend class time browsing the Internet rather than listening to a teacher's lecture, they encounter more diverse expert opinions, work more independently, and proceed at their own pace. In fact, we observed that students experiencing computer problems were more likely to consult peers than the teacher. Throughout this process, the teacher becomes more of a facilitator, helping students find information and, more important, figure out what to do with it.

There is also potential to change the role of parents with this technology. For example, during parents' nights, students may be able to teach their parents something new about computers or networks. Doing so can greatly boost a student's self-esteem. Because familiarity with information technology can lead to jobs, schools may also want to expand their efforts to train neighborhood adults after school hours.

When parents have access to this technology at home or at work, they can become more closely involved in

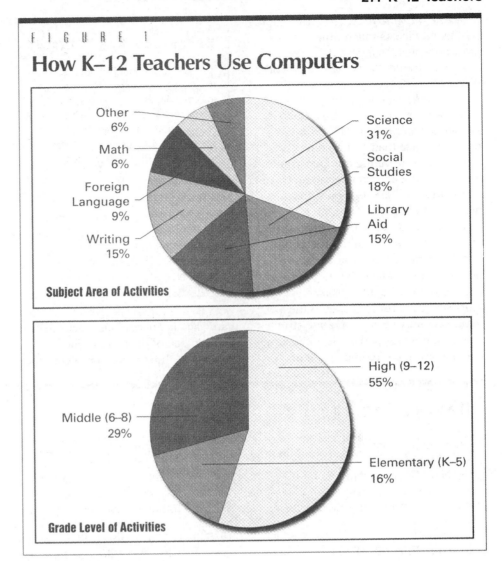

FIGURE 1

How K–12 Teachers Use Computers

Subject Area of Activities

- Other 6%
- Math 6%
- Foreign Language 9%
- Writing 15%
- Science 31%
- Social Studies 18%
- Library Aid 15%

Grade Level of Activities

- High (9–12) 55%
- Middle (6–8) 29%
- Elementary (K–5) 16%

their children's education. Many parents already have Internet access at work. Thirty-five percent of U.S. households now have computers, and those with children are more likely to have computers than those without, even families on a somewhat limited budget. Of households with children and total annual incomes under $30,000, 30 percent have computers. Given that consumer spending on home computers now exceeds spending on televisions, these percentages should continue to rise quickly (Negroponte 1995). All it takes is a telephone line and a modem to connect a home computer to the network. More important, because there will always be parents without home computers, some states and municipalities are bringing network capabilities to all of their citizens. In Seattle, for example, even

the homeless will be able to communicate over the network by getting an account from the city, using it in libraries and other public buildings.

How to Overcome Difficulties

The teachers who responded to our questionnaire offered several ways to overcome difficulties in introducing the Internet in a K–12 curriculum. Four suggestions in particular surfaced frequently:

1. Be specific about expectations and objectives. By providing deadlines for activities and for intermediate milestones, teachers can keep students moving in the right direction.

2. Search the Internet yourself before asking students to. As one teacher said, "Know what to look for in advance, so you and your students will not be disappointed."

3. Allow ample time. "Realize that it will take twice as much time as you have budgeted," suggested one teacher. Another offered, "Have students work in groups to speed up the process."

4. Establish a commitment with other parties involved in an activity. As one teacher urged, "There is nothing worse than getting a project organized or planning one into your lesson plans and then no mail arrives from your partners or people start dropping out."

Teachers also identified three difficulties not entirely within their control. First, 40- to 50-minute class periods limit students' ability to engage in unstructured tasks. Allowing time for longer activities, therefore, may require creative structuring of the school day. Second, some teachers must overcome a lack of hardware, telephone lines, or accounts. Finally, lack of time for teachers to explore the Internet is a problem. The Internet's resources are vast, and the tools change from year to year. Keeping up is not easy. Things will

---

Resources Available on the Internet: Some Examples

1. The Educational Resources Information Center (ERIC) provides information on curriculums, professional development, teaching methods, and educational materials. Telnet to acsnet.syr.edu, login: suvm, userid: suinfo. An ERIC gopher is also available.

2. The NASA Spacelink offers an interactive database with lesson plans, science activities, and NASA flight information. Telnet to spacelink.msfc.nasa.gov; username: newuser.

3. Digital images highlighting the photography of the Smithsonian Institution are available via anonymous FTP from photo1.si.edu.

4. Worldwide meteorological data (including forecasts, records, and storm warnings) are available. Telnet to hurricane.ncdc.noaa.gov, login: storm; password: research.

5. The Library of Congress Information System (LOCIS) contains more than 15 million catalog records. Telnet to locis.loc.gov; no password is necessary.

Navigating the Net

Looking for a handy reference to keep by your side as you cruise the Net? Choose from among these guides for an informative and pleasant voyage in cyberspace.

■ Braun, Eric. (1994). *The Internet Directory.* New York: Ballantine. $25.

The author calls this "the most complete hardcopy guide to the resources from around the world that are available via the Internet," and it probably is just that. The listings of usenet newsgoups, gopher servers, mailing lists, WAIS, FTP, and other resources are exhaustive. Each chapter begins with a description, hints on "netiquette," and brief comments on use. Some chapters offer so many alphabetic listings that you are left to browse until you find a resource of interest. Others include helpful annotations on content. Not for the timid.

■ Butler, Mark. (1994). *How to Use the Internet.* Emeryville, Calif.: Ziff-Davis. $17.95.

For the beginner who is just getting connected, this guide provides step-by-step directions on how to use the resources available on the Internet. Full-page illustrations make understanding Internet resources easy and visual; pictures from live-session screens show exactly what your own computer screen should look like; and numerous Tip Sheets explain trouble spots and offer practical advice.

■ Fraase, Michael. (1994). *The Mac Internet Tour Guide. The Windows Internet Tour Guide.* Chapel Hill, N. C.: Ventana Press. Includes disk. $24.95 (Windows). $27.95 (Mac).

In an informative yet conversational format, these *Tour Guides* help you with just about everything you need to know to connect to and use the Internet. From the chapter describing infrastructure to chapters explaining resources, you'll feel comfortable using these books for your voyages through cyberspace. Each chapter includes headings, diagrams, screen shots, and tips. The Windows disk includes *Chameleon*, a basic software package that allows you to access services on the Internet. The Macintosh disk includes *Eudora* software for e-mail and *Fetch* file transfer software to help you upload and download files at various archives on the Internet. Buyers are entitled to two free electronic updates and become members of Ventana's Visitor's Center on the Internet.

■ Harris, Judi. (1994). *Way of the Ferret—Finding Educational Resources on the Internet.* Eugene, Ore.: International Society for Technology in Education. $24.95.

Judi Harris's "Mining the Internet" column in *The Computing Teacher* inspired this book. In it, she shows educators how to locate primary source materials, free and inexpensive software, news and discussion groups, cooperative classroom projects, and opportunities for personal contacts. Carefully developed analogies help users grasp the basics of Internet tools and activities. In addition to the technical information you need to connect to and navigate the Net, the book provides tips on effective personal and practical classroom uses of its extensive resources. An excellent reference tool.

improve when more principals and others understand the value of the Internet, and the importance of teacher time spent exploring it.

To reduce installation costs, new schools should be wired for computers and networks when they are built, just as commercial office spaces are.

Probably the most disturbing problem came out in direct interviews with teachers who were not part of the Pittsburgh project. Not only are rewards for innovative teachers often small, but some principals and teachers actually discourage resourceful teachers from disrupting the status quo. The reasons for such opposition may include two fears: that benefits will be small and not worth the effort, and that benefits will be great, so other teachers will be expected to keep up. [Providing proper teacher incentives for innovation is critical, and may require some fundamental changes.]

Although our respondents did not mention the next problem, it has the potential to seriously disrupt efforts to bring the Internet to classrooms. Students using the Internet, like students wandering the Library of Congress, may look at something their parents would prefer they not see—for example, sexually explicit material. Topics like drugs, politics, religion, abortion, and homosexuality may also stir controversy.

In June 1995, the U.S. Senate attempted to address a part of this problem by approving an amendment to the telecommunications bill that would prohibit the flow of "indecent" material (not limited to pornography) on the Internet. Aside from the serious civil rights implications of such censorship, it would not even prevent the distribution of pornography on this network of millions of users around the world, any one of whom can provide such information.

■ Krol, Ed. (1994). *The Whole Internet User's Guide & Catalog.* Sebastopol, Calif.: O'Reilly & Associates. $24.95.

The best description for this reference tool comes from the author, who says it's aimed "at the 'garden variety' computer user: not the expert or the computer afficionado, just someone who has a job to get done." He provides thoughtful explanations of each of Internet's functions—perhaps too thoughtful for the nuts-and-bolts user—and provides screen diagrams along with step-by-step instructions. A thorough reference guide.

■ Kurshan, Barbara, and Deneen Frazier. (1994). *Internet (and More) for Kids.* Alameda, Calif.: Sybex. $16.95.

The authors take an enthusiastic look at the Internet for kids, teachers, and parents. Online activities include gathering information, sharing information with students around the world, communicating with experts, doing science experiments, participating in discussions and forums, playing online games, and more. Especially suited for middle and high school students. A basic understanding of the Internet and its tools is recommended.

■ Levine, John, and Margaret Levine Young. (1994). *The Internet for Dummies Quick Reference.* Boston: IDG Books. $8.95.

IDG's *Dummies* reference books for various electronic applications and services have gained a reputation for their friendly approach to otherwise confusing content. This guide to the Internet is no exception. With references to the expanded text, *The Internet for Dummies*, this companion guide is an excellent portable reference with helpful icons, screen diagrams, and plain-English headings. Each task is identified as easy, tricky, or very tricky to accomplish, and the content is suitable for beginning to advanced users.

■ Maxwell, Christine, and Czeslaw Jan Grycz. (1994). *The New Riders' Official Internet Yellow Pages.* Indianapolis: New Riders Publishing. $29.95.

This volume truly resembles the commerical phone directory from a large city. Open the yellow thumb-indexed pages, and you'll find alphabetized display "ads" listing each of the resources and services available on the Internet at the time of publication. After a brief introduction explaining how the Internet works and how to use the book, you are on your own with the listings. Each entry includes a one-line description, keywords, the intended audience, and names and e-mail addresses of contacts. If you are already comfortable using the Internet, this volume will lead you to its vast resources.

■ Pfaffenberger, Bryan. (1995). *World Wide Web Bible.* New York: MIS Press. Includes *Windows*-compatible disk. $27.95.

This book introduces the hypertext concepts, outlines in how to connect to the Web, and explains how to navigate a variety of Internet resources, including FTP, Gopher, WAIS, and USENET. By installing the software included on disk, you can learn how to use HTML, a document markup language, to build your own home page, create hypertext documents, and put these documents on the Web. For the user with lots of time to explore and learn.

Vicki Hancock is Regional Field Director, Northwest Region, for ASCD.

In April 1995, the Washington State legislature found a more drastic solution to protect minors from objectionable material: they made it illegal to give minors Internet access. (An even more effective solution would be to prohibit minors from learning to read.) The governor vetoed the bill.

Schools can take some precautions—for example, not carrying obviously troublesome newsgroups on local servers. And new information-filtering tools are coming. There is really no way, however, to prevent a bright, determined student from finding something he or she wants to see. Constant teacher supervision is one solution, but it is time-consuming and would deter curious exploration.

The best approach is to develop a written policy stating what does and does not constitute acceptable student usage of the Internet. In general, Internet usage should relate to coursework. Both students and parents must agree to this policy before gaining access. While such a strategy does not prevent abuse, it does make it easier to revoke the privileges of students who violate the policy, and it brings parents into the discussion from the beginning.

About Teacher Preparation and Support

Before adopting the Internet, a school system must determine how much preparation and ongoing support to provide. Two-thirds of the respondents to our questionnaire survived without any formal training, relying instead on printed literature and experimentation, or as one person described it, "blood, sweat, and tears."

Common Knowledge Pittsburgh developed a professional development workshop for teachers and librarians that participants generally found quite successful. The primary goal was to give them the problem-solving skills to become explorers of the Internet, rather than teaching them facts or rote methods. Because Internet tools and resources are constantly changing, teachers must have the ability to adapt—a view echoed by several respondents to our questionnaire.

The workshop, held in June 1993, provided 24 teachers and 4 librarians with 13 hours of instruction over two and a half days. Participants worked in pairs to promote brainstorming and to make the task less intimidating. They used a variety of tools ranging from newsgroups to Gopher, and explored resources that workshop organizers thought might be useful, like the NASA library (see Resources box). To test their newfound skills, they participated in a scavenger hunt for information on the Internet.

After this session, workshop organizers helped participants set up borrowed school computer equipment in their own homes to experiment during the summer. Finally, the workshop reconvened in August for 10 hours of additional instruction over a two-day period. In addition to learning more about the Internet, participants discussed possible lesson plans.

As noted earlier, 14 workshop participants responded to our survey. Every respondent agreed that the teaching methods were effective; only one person did not yet feel capable of teaching the Internet to students, with two people unsure. All found the workshop informative, and almost all would recommend it to a colleague.

Because a primary goal of this workshop was to encourage exploration, that issue deserves special consideration. After a few months into the school year, nearly half of the participants had done three or more Gopher searches in the week we surveyed them, but two people indicated that they were no longer exploring the Internet. Despite the popularity of the workshop, participants indicated that they learned only about half of the information on the Internet from workshop instructors. That finding would seem to corroborate the importance of independent exploration.

How would the Pittsburgh educators improve the workshop? They were about evenly split on the need for more step-by-step instruction time, but expressed a pressing need for more exploration time.

Because one can't afford to stop learning about the Internet, ongoing support may also be important. In answer to the questionnaire we sent to network users around the world, teachers indicated that Internet guides, newsgroups, and distribution lists are very helpful. Personal support is also needed at times.

In Pittsburgh, teachers turned to their fellow teachers most often, with the centralized support staff a close second. This finding is important because widescale adoption is possible only if teachers help one another; a centralized support staff can't be everywhere.

When asked [what] other kinds of ongoing technical assistance [would be helpful], teachers who responded to the questionnaire most often mentioned classroom visits by Internet instructors, monthly meetings of Internet users, and online support.

The Future

Teachers have only begun to exploit existing capabilities of network technology in schools. Indeed, the majority of classroom activities that we've observed use only Internet tools that are more than two decades old, like basic e-mail. As noted, tools such as Mosaic and Netscape greatly facilitate the process of finding information on the Internet.

People are also experimenting with more interactive applications. For example, the Internet has been used for person-to-person video teleconferences, and to broadcast part of a Rolling Stones concert live.

Moreover, new networks are coming based on ATM (asynchronous transfer mode) technology. Although such things are possible to a limited degree on the Internet, ATM networks are better able to support applications where intermittent disruptions are noticeable to the user, like using a telephone, playing interactive games with a distant player, or controlling a laboratory experiment at a remote site. ATM networks can also transmit data at a rapid rate, allowing users to watch broadcast-quality video or better on demand, to quickly retrieve a series of images from the space shuttle's telescope or the complete works of Shakespeare, or to use sophisticated visualization tools to watch changing weather patterns in the area. Recently, North Carolina deployed a statewide ATM network to which schools will have access. [Emerging wireless networks also offer many opportunities for education.]

Although the growth of Internet use in classrooms is encouraging, schools have not been keeping up with any of the commercial sectors in adopting new information technology—so it is not clear whether technical advances alone will be beneficial for learning. An obvious obstacle is money. However, 97 percent of American schools already have some computers (Wheland 1995), and adding a low-speed Internet connection is no more expensive than adding a telephone line. Still, many of these computers are not integrated into the curriculum in a meaningful way, other than one designed specifically to teach about

computers. While funding is certainly an issue—and more conclusive proof is needed that money spent on Internet access is more beneficial than money spent elsewhere—increased funding alone is unlikely to lead to productive use of information technology.

To truly exploit these advances, technology and innovation must permeate the culture of education. Teachers should be exposed to technology early in their careers, and should be actively encouraged to keep up on continual advances. To reduce installation costs, new schools should be wired for computers and networks when they are built, just as commercial office spaces are. Districts should hire staff who can help schools build and troubleshoot computer and network systems. Teachers must be given freedom and encouragement to experiment with technology.

Common Knowledge Pittsburgh, now operating in 14 schools, is currently funded through December

1997. The Pittsburgh Public Schools are showing that more teachers will choose to bring technology into the classroom when given both resources and encouragement.

References

Carnegie Mellon University. (1994). "The Internet in K–12 Education." Pittsburgh: Carnegie Mellon University.

National Science Foundation. (April 26, 1995). "NSF-MCI Background on the Internet/NSFnet." NSF Press Release.

Negroponte, N. (February 11, 1995). "homeless@info.hwy.net." *New York Times*, A15.

Wheland, R. (February 1995). U.S. Department of Education, personal communications.

Author's note: To order "The Internet in K–12 Education," send $12.40, or $16.60 from outside the U.S., to Department Receptionist, Department of Engineering and Public Policy, Carnegie Mellon University, Pittsburgh, PA 15213.

Motivation and Classroom Management

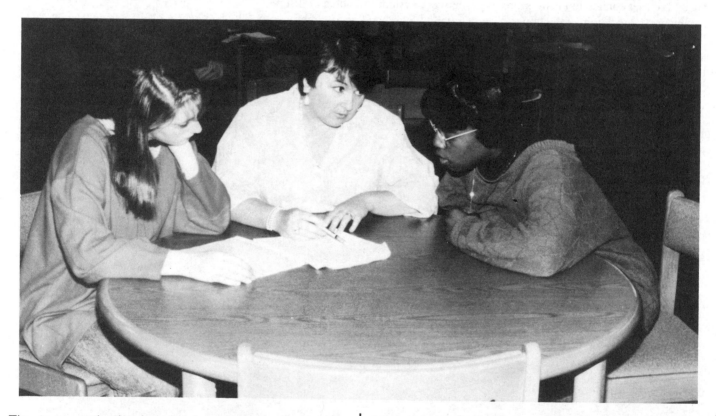

The term *motivation* is used by educators to describe the processes of initiating, directing, and sustaining goal-oriented behavior. Motivation is a complex phenomenon, involving many factors that affect an individual's choice of action and perseverance in completing tasks. Furthermore, the reasons why people engage in particular behaviors can only be inferred; motivation cannot be directly measured.

Several theories of motivation, each highlighting different reasons for sustained goal-oriented behavior, have been proposed. We will discuss three of them: behav-

ioral, humanistic, and cognitive. The behavioral theory of motivation suggests that an important reason for engaging in behavior is that reinforcement follows the action. If the reinforcement is controlled by someone else and is arbitrarily related to the behavior (such as money, a token, or a smile), then the motivation is extrinsic. In contrast, behavior may also be initiated and sustained for intrinsic reasons such as curiosity or mastery.

Humanistic approaches to motivation are concerned with the social and psychological needs of individuals. Humans are motivated to engage in behavior to meet these needs. Abraham Maslow, a founder of humanistic psychology, proposes that there is a hierarchy of needs that directs behavior, beginning with physiological and safety needs and progressing to self-actualization. Some other important needs that influence motivation are affiliation and belonging with others, love, self-esteem, influence with others, recognition, status, competence, achievement, and autonomy.

The dominant view of motivation in the educational psychology literature is the cognitive approach. This set of theories proposes that our beliefs about our success and failure affect our expectations and goals concerning future performance. Students who believe that their success is due to their ability and effort are motivated toward mastery of skills. Students who blame their failures on inadequate abilities have low self-efficacy and tend to set ability and performance goals that protect their self-image. Alfie Kohn, in the first subsection selection, argues that one important way to help eliminate student apathy is to allow students to make decisions about their own learning. His article provides a rationale for incorporating more opportunities for student choice in the classroom. Next, Deborah Stipek echoes the importance of allowing children to set their own goals. She also discusses other techniques to encourage more effort on academic tasks. Finally, Rachel Collopy and Theresa Green describe how one elementary school has changed in response to the dramatic findings of achievement goal theory. The school they created emphasizes learning rather than relative ability.

No matter how effectively students are motivated, teachers always need to exercise management of behavior in the classroom. Classroom management is more than controlling the behavior of students or disciplining them following misbehavior. Instead, teachers need to initiate and maintain a classroom environment that supports successful teaching and learning. The skills that effective teachers use include preplanning, deliberate introduction of rules and procedures, immediate assertiveness, continual monitoring, consistent feedback to students, and specific consequences.

The first two articles of the next subsection describe the most current thinking about the new forms of classroom management that will be required to meet the needs of learning-centered classrooms. H. James McLaughlin argues that management metaphors need to shift from obedience and responsibility to negotiation. In "Images of Management for Learner-Centered Classrooms," Catherine Randolph and Carolyn Evertson suggest that the management of instruction and the management of behavior become enmeshed in learning-centered classrooms. Their metaphor for classroom management is orchestration.

The last two selections in this unit address two disciplinary issues facing educators today: violence in schools and the use of corporal punishment. David Johnson and Roger Johnson argue that violence prevention needs to focus on helping students resolve conflicts in appropriate ways, such as using peer mediation. The adults in schools, too, need to model constructive ways to resolve conflicts by eliminating corporal punishment. Elizabeth Evans and Rita Richardson argue that despite its widespread use, corporal punishment is not only harmful to students, but it also teaches that violence is an effective way to solve problems.

Looking Ahead: Challenge Questions

Discuss several ways to motivate both at-risk and typical students. What difference is there?

How are motivation and classroom management related?

How are classroom management and discipline different? Discuss whether discipline can be developed within students, or whether it must be imposed by teachers, supporting your argument with data derived from your reading.

Choices for Children:

Why and How to Let Students Decide

The key to transforming student apathy into student engagement, Mr. Kohn suggests, may be as simple as allowing students to make decisions about their learning.

. . . .

ALFIE KOHN

ALFIE KOHN, who writes and lectures widely on education and human behavior, lives in Cambridge, Mass. His books include Punished by Rewards: The Trouble with Gold Stars, Incentive Plans, A's, Praise, and Other Bribes *(Houghton Mifflin, 1993), a newly revised edition of* No Contest: The Case Against Competition *(Houghton Mifflin, 1992), and* The Brighter Side of Human Nature *(Basic Books, 1990).*

The essence of the demand for freedom is the need of conditions which will enable an individual to make his own special contribution to a group interest, and to partake of its activities in such ways that social guidance shall be a matter of his own mental attitude, and not a mere authoritative dictation of his acts.

— John Dewey
Democracy and Education

EDUCATORS ARE painfully well acquainted with the phenomenon known as "burnout." Some days it seems that the bulbs have gone out in most faculty lounges and administration buildings. But what if, hypothetically speaking, this syndrome also affected students?

How would *they* talk and act? Teachers around the country to whom I have put this question immediately suggest such symptoms as disengagement and apathy — or, conversely, thoughtlessness and aggression. Either tuning out or acting out might signal that a student was burning out. In both cases, he or she would presumably just go through the motions of learning, handing in uninspired work and counting the minutes or days until freedom.

Of course, no sooner is this sketch of a hypothetical student begun than we recognize it as a depiction of real life. The fact is that students act this way every day. But now let us ask what we know from research and experience in the workplace about the cause of burnout. The best predictor, it turns out, is not too much work, too little time, or too little compensation. Rather, it is powerlessness — a lack of control over what one is doing.

Combine that fact with the premise that there is no minimum age for burnout, and the conclusion that emerges is this: much of what is disturbing about students' attitudes and behavior may be a function of the fact that they have little to say about

what happens to them all day. They are compelled to follow someone else's rules, study someone else's curriculum, and submit continually to someone else's evaluation. The mystery, really, is not that so many students are indifferent about what they have to do in school but that any of them are not.

To be sure, there is nothing new about the idea that students should be able to participate, individually and collectively, in making decisions. This conviction has long played a role in schools designated as progressive, democratic, open, free, experimental, or alternative; in educational philosophies called developmental, constructivist, holistic, or learner-centered; in specific innovations such as whole-language learning, discovery-based science, or authentic assessment; and in the daily practice of teachers whose natural instinct is to treat children with respect.

But if the concept is not exactly novel, neither do we usually take the time to tease this element out of various traditions and examine it in its own right. Why is it so important that children have a chance to make decisions about their learning? How might this opportunity be

 From *Phi Delta Kappan*, September 1993, pp. 8-20.

provided with regard to academic matters as well as other aspects of school life? What limits on students' right to choose are necessary, and what restrictions compromise the idea too deeply? Finally, what barriers might account for the fact that students so rarely feel a sense of self-determination today? A close inspection of these issues will reveal that the question of choice is both more complex and more compelling than many educators seem to assume.

SEVERAL years ago, a group of teachers from Florida traveled to what was then the USSR to exchange information and ideas with their Russian-speaking counterparts. What the Soviet teachers most wanted from their guests was guidance on setting up and running democratic schools. Their questions on this topic were based on the assumption that a country like the United States, so committed to the idea of democracy, surely must involve children in decision-making processes from their earliest years.

The irony is enough to make us wince. As one survey of American schools after another has confirmed, students are rarely invited to become active participants in their own education.[1] Schooling is typically about doing things *to* children, not working *with* them. An array of punishments and rewards is used to enforce compliance with an agenda that students rarely have any opportunity to influence.

Think about the rules posted on the wall of an elementary school classroom, or the "rights and responsibilities" pamphlet distributed in high schools, or the moral precepts that form the basis of a values or character education program. In each case, students are almost never involved in deliberating about such ideas; their job is basically to do as they are told.

Moreover, consider the conventional response when something goes wrong (as determined, of course, by the adults). Are two children creating a commotion instead of sitting quietly? Separate them. Have the desks become repositories for used chewing gum? Ban the stuff. Do students come to class without having done the reading? Hit them with a pop quiz. Again and again, the favorite motto of teachers and administrators seems to be "Reach for the coercion" rather than engaging children in a conversation about the underlying causes of what is happening and working together to negotiate a solution.

Earlier this year, the principal of a Brooklyn high school told a *New York Times* reporter that he lived by "a simple proposition: This is my house, I'm 46 years old. A 15-year-old is not going to dictate to me how this school is run."[2] But even educators who recoil from such a frank endorsement of autocracy may end up acting in accordance with the same basic principle. I have met many elementary teachers, for example, who make a point of assuring students that "this is *our* classroom" — but proceed to decide unilaterally on almost everything that goes on in it, from grading policy to room decor.

As for the content of instruction, the educators who shape the curriculum rarely bother to consult those who are to be educated. There is plenty of enthusiasm about reforms such as outcome-based education but little concern about bringing students into the process of formulating the outcomes. There is spirited debate about "school choice" — an arrangement in which districts are compelled to compete for the business of parent-consumers — but much less talk about how much choice students have concerning what happens in their classrooms. Indeed, spontaneous, animated conversations about topics of interest to children, when they are allowed to occur at all, are soon snuffed out in order that the class can return to the prescribed lesson plan.

THE RATIONALE

To talk about the destructive effects of keeping students powerless is to describe the benefits of having a sense of self-determination.[3] Five such benefits seem particularly compelling.

1. *Effects on general well-being.* Many different fields of research have converged on the finding that it is desirable for people to experience a sense of control over their lives. These benefits reach into every corner of human existence, starting with our physical health and survival. One series of studies has shown that people who rarely become ill despite having to deal with considerable stress tend to be those who feel more control over what happens to them.[4] In another well-known experiment, nursing home residents who were able to make decisions about their environment not only became happier and more active but were

> *Those who feel more control over what happens to them rarely become ill despite high levels of stress.*

also more likely to be alive a year and a half later than were other residents.[5]

The psychological benefits of control are, if anything, even more pronounced. All else being equal, emotional adjustment is better over time for people who experience a sense of self-determination; by contrast, few things lead more reliably to depression and other forms of psychological distress than a feeling of helplessness.[6] (One recent study showed this was true in an educational setting: distress was inversely related to how much influence and autonomy teachers said they had with respect to school policy.[7]) Whereas rewards and punishments are notably ineffective at maintaining behavior change,[8] people are likely to persist at doing constructive things, like exercising, quitting smoking, or fighting cavities, when they have some choice about the specifics of such programs.[9] Laboratory experiments have also shown that individuals are better able to tolerate unpleasant sensations like noise, cold, or electric shock when they know they have the power to end them.[10]

Children are no exception to these rules, the studies show. One-year-old infants had fun with a noisy mechanical toy if they could make it start; it was less interesting, and sometimes even frightening, if they had no control over its action.[11] Elementary students had higher self-esteem and a greater feeling of academic competence when their teachers bolstered their sense of self-determination in the classroom.[12]

2. *Effects on behavior and values.* One is repeatedly struck by the absurd spectacle of adults insisting that children need to become self-disciplined or lamenting

that "kids just don't take responsibility for their own behavior" — while spending their days ordering children around. The truth is that, if we want children to *take* responsibility for their own behavior, we must first *give* them responsibility, and plenty of it. The way a child learns how to make decisions is by making decisions, not by following directions. As Constance Kamii has written,

> We cannot expect children to accept ready-made values and truths all the way through school, and then suddenly make choices in adulthood. Likewise, we cannot expect them to be manipulated with reward and punishment in school, and to have the courage of a Martin Luther King in adulthood.[13]

In fact, an emphasis on following instructions, respecting authority (regardless of whether that respect has been earned), and obeying the rules (regardless of whether they are reasonable) teaches a disturbing lesson. Stanley Milgram's famous experiment, in which ordinary people gave what they thought were terribly painful shocks to hapless strangers merely because they were told to do so, is not just a comment about "society" or "human nature." It is a cautionary tale about certain ways of teaching children. Indeed, an emphasis on obedience, with all the trappings of control that must be used for enforcing it, typically fails even on its own terms: children are less likely to comply with a rule when they have had no role in inventing or even discussing it. And if our goals are more ambitious — if we want children to make good values their own over the long haul — then there is no substitute for giving them the chance to become actively involved in deciding what kind of people they want to be and what kind of classroom or school they want to have.

To talk about the importance of choice is also to talk about democracy. At present, as Shelley Berman of Educators for Social Responsibility has drily noted, "We teach reading, writing, and math by [having students do] them, but we teach democracy by lecture."[14] I believe it is time to call the bluff of every educator who claims to prize democratic principles. Anyone who truly values democracy ought to be thinking about preparing students to participate in a democratic culture — or to transform a culture *into* a democracy, as the case may be. The only way this can happen, the only way children can acquire both the skills of decision making and the inclination to use them, is if we maximize their experiences with choice and negotiation.[15]

Ultimately, even virtues that appear to be quite different from an orientation toward participation or a capacity to make intelligent decisions turn out to depend on these things. For example, like many others, I am concerned about how we can help children to become generous, caring people who see themselves as part of a community.[16] But these values simply cannot be successfully promoted in the absence of choice. A jarring reminder of that fact was provided by a man who recalled being "taught that my highest duty was to help those in need" but added that he learned this lesson in the context of how important it was to "obey promptly the wishes and commands of my parents, teachers, and priests, and indeed of all adults. . . . Whatever they said was always right." The man who said that was Rudolf Höss, the commandant of Auschwitz.[17] A commitment to helping is important, but if the environment in which such values are taught emphasizes obedience rather than autonomy, all may be lost.

3. *Effects on academic achievement.* Every teacher who is told what material to cover, when to cover it, and how to evaluate children's performance is a teacher who knows that enthusiasm for one's work quickly evaporates in the face of being controlled. Not every teacher, however, realizes that exactly the same thing holds true for students: deprive them of self-determination and you have likely deprived them of motivation. If learning is a matter of following orders, students simply will not take to it in the way they would if they had some say about what they were doing. Not long ago, in a 10th-grade geometry class whose teacher collaborates with students to decide about curriculum and grades, a student explained to me that being able to make such choices "leads to learning rather than just remembering."

The evidence to support that view is so compelling that it is frankly difficult to understand how anyone can talk about school reform without immediately addressing the question of how students can be given more say about what goes on in their classes. The classic Eight-Year Study, which should be required reading for everyone with an interest in education, provided data on this point more than half a century ago. After 30 high schools were encouraged to develop innovative programs whose "essential value was democracy,"[18] researchers found that the graduates of those schools did better in college than a matched comparison group from traditional schools. In fact, the students who were most successful tended to come from the schools that had departed most significantly from the conventional college-prep approach — the approach currently lauded by those calling for higher standards, more accountability, and getting back to basics.

Subsequent research has confirmed the conclusion:

• When second-graders in Pittsburgh were given some choice about their learning, including the chance to decide which tasks they would work on at any given moment, they tended to "complete more learning tasks in less time."[19]

• When high school seniors in Minneapolis worked on chemistry problems without clear-cut instructions — that is, with the opportunity to decide for themselves how to find solutions — they "consistently produced better write-ups of experiments" and remembered the material better than those who had been told exactly what to do. They put in more time than they had to, spending "extra laboratory periods checking results that could have been accepted without extra work." Some of the students initially resisted having to make decisions about how to proceed, but these grumblers later "took great pride in being able to carry through an experiment on their own."[20]

• When preschoolers in Massachusetts were allowed to select the materials they used for making a collage, their work was judged more creative than the work of children who used exactly the same materials but did not get to choose them.[21]

• When college students in New York State had the chance to decide which of several puzzles they wanted to work on and how to allot their time to each of them, they were a lot more interested in working on such puzzles later than were students who were told what to do.[22]

• When teachers of inner-city black children were trained in a program designed to promote a sense of self-determination, the students in these classes missed less school and scored better on a national test of basic skills than those in conventional classrooms.[23]

• When second-graders spent the year in a math classroom where textbooks and rewards were discarded in favor of an emphasis on "intellectual autonomy"

— that is, where children, working in groups, took an active role in figuring out their own solutions to problems and were free to move around the classroom on their own initiative to get the materials they needed — they developed more sophisticated reasoning skills without falling behind on basic conceptual tasks.[24]

The evidence goes on and on. At least one recent study has found that children given more "opportunity to participate in decisions about schoolwork" score higher on standardized tests;[25] other research shows that they are more likely than those deprived of autonomy to continue working even on relatively uninteresting tasks.[26] There is no question about it: even if our only criterion is academic performance, choice works.

In a way, this conclusion shouldn't be surprising. Putting aside the value of particular programs that give students more discretion about what they are doing, the irrefutable fact is that students always have a choice about whether they will learn. We may be able to force them to complete an assignment, but we can't compel them to learn effectively or to care about what they are doing. The bottom line is that "teaching requires the consent of students, and discontent will not be chased away by the exercise of power."[27] No wonder that expanding the realm in which the learner's consent is sought tends to enhance learning.

4. *Effects on teachers.* Despite attitudinal barriers to creating democratic classrooms and schools, which I will discuss later, educators who are willing to share power may well find that they benefit directly from doing so. One's job becomes a good deal more interesting when it involves collaborating with students to decide what is going to happen. As one fifth-grade teacher in upstate New York explained,

I've been teaching for more than 30 years, and I would have been burned out long ago but for the fact that I involve my kids in designing the curriculum. I'll say to them, "What's the *most* exciting way we could study this next unit?" If we decide their first suggestion isn't feasible, I'll say, "Okay, what's the *next* most exciting way we could study this?" They always come up with good proposals, they're motivated because I'm using their ideas, and I never do the unit in the same way twice.[28]

Teachers also benefit in other ways from allowing students to be active participants in their learning. In such a classroom, according to the researchers involved in the second-grade math project described above, the teacher is "freed from the chore of constantly monitoring and supervising the children's activity and [is] able to give her full attention to . . . interacting with the children" as they work.[29]

5. *Intrinsic value.* Finally, it needs to be said that allowing people to make decisions about what happens to them is inherently preferable to controlling them. It is more respectful and consistent with basic values to which most of us claim to subscribe. Apart from the skills that will be useful for students to have in the future, they ought to have a chance to choose in the present. Children, after all, are not just adults-in-the-making. They are people whose current needs and rights and experiences must be taken seriously. Put it this way: students should not only be trained to live in a democracy when they grow up; they should have the chance to live in one today.[30]

CHOOSING IN PRACTICE

Because quite a few programs and practices in which children can make meaningful choices have been described elsewhere, I will offer only a sampling of the ways this basic idea can be implemented. These suggestions can be grouped according to whether they are primarily concerned with academic decisions or with social and behavioral ones.

Academic issues. The four key realms in which students can make academic decisions are what, how, how well, and why they learn. *What* they learn is the most straightforward of these. Student participation here can range from choosing where in an assigned text to start reading to deciding what course to take. In between these examples is the question of what is to be read, not only by individual students but by the class as a whole. "Here are five books that the supply store has in stock," a fourth-grade teacher may say to the class. "Why don't you flip through them during your free time this week, and we'll decide together on Friday which one to read next." (Of course, if students are not reading stories at all but making their way through worksheets and workbooks, basals and primers and dittos, then their capacity to par-

ticipate in their education has been significantly curtailed from the start.)

Teachers may not always have the discretion to let students participate in deciding what topic to study. But even when compelled to teach a certain lesson, a teacher might open up a discussion in which members of the class try to figure out together why someone apparently thought the subject was important enough to be required. The next step would be to connect that topic to students' real-world concerns and interests. When teachers have themselves decided for one reason or another to exclude students from the selection of the subject matter, there is still room to give them choices about the specific questions within a general topic to be explored. A teacher might begin any unit, for example, by inviting children to discuss what they already know about the subject and what they would like to know.

The question of *how* students learn embraces a great many issues — beginning with whether to work alone, in small groups, or as a class — and including such incidental matters as where students will sit (or lie) while they work. (One teacher swears that achievement in her class improved markedly as soon as she gave students the right to find a favorite reading place and position.) And there are other choices as well: if a student has written a story, she ought to be able to decide whether or not to read it aloud and, if so, whether to answer her classmates' questions about it afterward and, if so, whom to call on.

> *Every day ought to include at least one block of time in which children can decide what to do.*

Every day ought to include at least one block of time in which children can decide individually what to do: get a head start on homework, write in one's journal, work on an art project, or read a library book. Creative writing assignments offer plenty of opportunity for decisions to be made by the writers themselves. In expressing an idea or responding to a lesson, children sometimes can be allowed to decide what medium or genre they will use — whether they want to write a poem, an essay, or a play or do a collage, painting, or sculpture. Mathematics lessons can be guided by quantitative issues of interest to students.

The entire constructivist tradition is predicated on the idea of student autonomy, which is to say, the chance for students to view learning as something "under their control rather than as disembodied, objectified, subject matter."[31] The same can be said about some (but not all) models of cooperative learning. One version, devised by Shlomo Sharan and his colleagues and known as Group Investigation, is based on the idea of active participation throughout the process. Students break a subject into specific questions, sort themselves into groups to explore these questions, plan and conduct an investigation, and figure out how to share what they have learned with the rest of the class.[32]

To talk about *how well* a student is doing is to raise the complicated issues of assessment and evaluation, the improvement of which has lately been of increasing concern to educators. But a key consideration in changing these systems, beyond whether judgments are based on sufficiently rich measures of student achievement, is the extent to which students themselves are involved in the process. Obviously, the chance to pick one of three possible essay questions for one's final paper does not begin to get at what is important here. Students ought to help determine the criteria by which their work will be judged and then play a role in weighing their work against those criteria. This achieves several things at once: it gives students more control over their education, it makes evaluation feel less punitive, and it provides an important learning experience in itself. Students can derive enormous intellectual benefits from thinking about what makes a story interesting, a mathematical proof elegant, or an argument convincing. More traditional approaches to testing can also be improved if students are consulted

about what the test ought to cover and when it ought to be given; there is no need for teachers to decide these things on their own.

Last, and most frequently overlooked, is the need to involve students in talking about *why* they are learning. Few aspects of education are more important than the "participation of the learner in the formation of the purposes which direct his activities in the learning process," as Dewey put it.[33] Children should be given a voice not only about the means of learning but also the ends, the why as well as the what. Even very young children are "curriculum theorists," according to John Nicholls, and there may be no better use of classroom time than a sustained conversation following someone's challenge: "Why do we gotta do this stuff?"[34]

Social and behavioral issues. School is about more than intellectual development; it is about learning to become a responsible, caring person who can make good choices and solve problems effectively. Thus educators must think about ways of helping students to take an active part in decisions that are only indirectly related to academics.

Is it necessary to raise one's hand before talking or to line up before walking through the school? How much noise is too much? How should the furniture be arranged in our room? Where might we take a field trip? These are the sorts of questions that children should be encouraged to ponder and argue about. In considering what kind of classroom or school each person wants to have, the point is to reach consensus on general guidelines or principles, not to formulate a list of rules. (Specific admonitions tend to invite legalistic thinking about their application and a preoccupation with enforcement that emphasizes punishment over problem solving.) Moreover, this process goes well beyond, and may even exclude, the practice of voting. What we want to promote are talking and listening, looking for alternatives and trying to reach agreement, solving problems together and making meaningful choices. Voting, which is an exercise in adversarial majoritarianism, often involves none of these acts. It may be the least objectionable method when a quarter of a billion people must govern themselves, but classroom teachers can do better.[35]

A structured opportunity for members of a class or school to meet and make decisions provides several advantages: it helps children feel respected by making

it clear that their opinions matter; it builds a sense of belongingness and community; and it contributes to the development of social and cognitive skills such as perspective taking (imagining how the world looks to someone else), conflict resolution, and rational analysis.[36] Few contrasts in education are as striking as that between students participating in such meetings, taking responsibility for deciding how they want their classroom to be, and students sitting in rows, having been bribed or threatened into complying with an adult's rules.

Thus, when problems develop, the adage for teachers to keep in mind is "Bring the kids in on it." This approach may call for a class meeting in the case of a conflict involving a number of students, or, when only one or two are directly concerned, it could mean a conversation just with them. If a child is daydreaming and failing to complete assignments, or if two children cannot seem to be anywhere near each other without becoming nasty, the most successful (and respectful)[37] solutions are those that emerge after the teacher asks, "What do you think we can do about this?"

REASONABLE LIMITS

A number of writers and teachers who resist giving children the chance to make decisions have justified their opposition by erecting an enormous straw man called "absolute freedom" and counterposing it to the status quo. Since most of us do not relish the idea of children spending their time at school doing anything they please, deprived of structure or adult guidance, we are encouraged to settle for the controlling practices that now exist.

Not only is this a classic false dichotomy, but virtually every influential proponent of choice for students — as well as the programs that have put the idea into effect — proceeds from the assumption that there are indeed limits on the capacity and right of children to decide. The scary specter of laissez-faire liberty that shows up in the rhetoric of traditionalists is not easy to locate in the real world. Nearly every essay on education by John Dewey, the father of progressive schooling, stresses the importance of adult guidance and derides the idea of "leaving a child to his own unguided fancies."[38] Even A. S. Neill, whose Summerhill school and philosophy lie at the outer edges of serious discussion about the issue, distinguished sharply between freedom and license, emphasizing repeatedly that "a child should not be permitted to violate the personal rights of others."[39] All reasonable adults, meanwhile, acknowledge that safety concerns will necessitate placing constraints on certain kinds of actions.

While agreement exists at a general level about the need to restrict students' choice, however, there is far less consensus about when and how to do so. The issues most frequently raised in support of such restrictions are not as simple as they first appear. Take the question of *age*. It goes without saying that a 16-year-old can approach a decision in a more sophisticated way than a 6-year-old and therefore can usually be entrusted with more responsibility. But this fact is sometimes used to justify preventing younger children from making choices that are well within their capabilities. Moreover, the idea that we must wait until children are mature enough to handle responsibilities may set up a vicious circle: after all, it is experience with decisions that helps children become capable of handling them.[40]

A second rationale for restricting choice is *time*: if students were entitled to make decisions about, and had to agree on, everything they did, there would be no time to do anything else. True enough, and yet the heuristic value of such discussions is often overlooked in the rush to get on with the "real" lesson. In class meetings, for example, teachers would do well to remember that, at least to some extent, *the process is the point*. The idea isn't just to make a choice, reach a decision, and move on.

Of course, it is still true that there won't be time to hash out every matter; sometimes a teacher will need to request that students just do something. But a democratic approach doesn't demand that everything *is* actively chosen, only that it *can* be. As Deborah Meier has said, what matters is not whether a given issue is discussed but that it is discussable. Unavoidable time constraints should not be used to rationalize avoidable authoritarian practices.

Third, the importance of choice is often weighed against the fact that children need some *structure or limits* for their behavior, if not for their learning. Once again, this point may be accurate but does not justify much of what educators actually do. "The critical question," as Thomas Gordon has put it, "is not *wheth-*

er limits and rules are needed . . . but rather *who* sets them: the adults alone or the adults and kids — together."[41] Before depriving children of choice, then, an educator is obliged to demonstrate not that they need some structure but that there is some reason to exclude them from helping to shape that structure. The crucial difference between structures and limits, on the one hand, and control and coercion, on the other, has generally gone unrecognized.[42]

Fourth, and possibly most compelling, is the caution that the right to choose must give way to the needs and preferences of *other people*. Even the minimalist sort of liberalism articulated by Neill (in which one's connection to others is limited to not violating their rights) implies that people cannot do whatever they want. A more ambitious commitment to the value of community would seem to restrict choice even more severely. While each child ought to have more opportunity to make decisions than is typically allowed in American classrooms, such decisions must take into account their impact on the other people in the room. This may not feel like a burdensome restriction once a child has internalized a concern about others' well-being — but, strictly speaking, one person's freedom to choose is always compromised by a set of obligations to others. At a recent town meeting of the long-standing experimental school-within-a-school program at Brookline (Massachusetts) High School, one student remarked that someone's choice to show up in class without having done the reading assignment adversely affects the quality of discussion for everyone. "It's not just 'You get out what you put into it,' " another girl added. "It's 'You get out what the class puts into it' " — and vice versa.

On closer examination, however, it seems clear that what must occasionally be restricted is not choice but *individual* choice. (It is an interesting reflection on our culture that we tend to see these as interchangeable.) To affirm the importance of community does not at all compromise the right to make decisions, per se, or the importance of involving everyone in a class or school in such a process. In fact, we might say that it is the integration of these two values, community and choice, that defines democracy.

I THINK we can conclude that, while some legitimate limits to the right to choose can be identified, the most commonly cited reasons for those

limits may not automatically justify restrictions. But this discussion also raises questions about a conventional response to the matter of appropriate limits. Many people, understandably impatient with an either/or choice in which the possibilities are limited to freedom and its absence, assert that we need to find a happy medium between these two poles. This seems facile. For one thing, such a pronouncement offers no guidance about where on that continuum we should set up camp. For another, it overlooks the fact that the sensible alternative to two extremes may not be an intermediate point but a different way of thinking about the issue altogether. The interesting question here, for example, is not how *much* adults should limit the power of children to make decisions, but *how* they should get involved.

In a broad sense, that involvement may consist of suggesting the tasks, teaching the skills, supplying the resources — in short, providing the conditions under which students can choose productively and learn effectively. The teacher's role is to be a facilitator, but, as Carolyn Edwards points out, this doesn't mean to " 'mak[e] smooth or easy,' but rather to 'stimulate' [learning] by making problems more complex, involving, and arousing."[43] Notice the implication here: a democratic classroom is not one where the teacher has less work to do. There is no zero-sum game in which more responsibility for the children means less for the adults. Helping students to participate effectively takes talent and patience and hard work. "I'm in control of putting students in control," one teacher told me — a responsibility that demands more of an educator than simply telling students what to do.

Notice also that this role for the teacher does not always amount to being a voice for moderation or mainstream values — a conservative counterweight to students' reckless impulses. If, for example, children have been raised to assume that anyone who does something wrong must be forced to suffer a punitive consequence, they will be likely, left to their own devices, to spend their time deciding what should be done to a rule breaker. Here, the teacher might intervene to guide the discussion away from "Which punishment?" and toward the more radical question of whether an entirely different response — "Something has gone wrong; how can we solve this problem?" — might be more productive.

On a range of issues, adults can participate — and circumscribe children's choices — in fundamentally different ways. To wit:

• The teacher and the students may take turns at deciding something, each choosing on alternate weeks, for example, which book to read next. Or the responsibility can rotate between individual students, cooperative learning groups, the whole class, and the teacher.

• The teacher may offer suggestions and guidance, questions and criticism, but leave the final choice to students. Thus I have heard a third-grade teacher advise her students that it might not be a good idea to go outside for recess on a day when there is slush on the ground but then make it clear that it is up to each child to make the final decision for him- or herself. A high school teacher, meanwhile, suggests that it might make sense for the whole class to talk about the homework together but offers them the option of discussing it in small groups if they prefer.

• The teacher can narrow the number of possibilities from which students are permitted to choose. He or she may want to do this to make sure that any material or text a student works with is likely to be of educational value and of approximately the right level of challenge. (On the other hand, neither of these goals always requires restricting children's choice.[44] And even when the teacher does decide to limit their options, she should explain her rationale for doing so and remain open to reasonable additions to her list. As a general rule, it is more important for children to have the chance to *generate* different possibilities than merely to select one possibility from among those that have been set before them.[45])

• The teacher may provide the parameters according to which decisions can be made, perhaps specifying the goal that has to be reached but inviting students to figure out how they want to get there. For example, "It's important to me that no one in here feels scared that other people will laugh at him for saying something stupid. How do you think we can prevent that from happening?" Or, "I need some way at the end of this unit to see how much you understand. Think of a way you might be able to demonstrate what you've learned."

• A decision does not have to be thought of as something that teachers either make or turn over to students. Instead, it can be negotiated together. The emphasis here is on shared responsibility for deciding what gets learned and how the learning takes place. This process can become a lesson in itself — an opportunity to make arguments, solve problems, anticipate consequences, and take other people's needs into account — as well as a powerful contribution to motivation.

WHILE well-meaning educators may offer very different prescriptions regarding the nature and scope of students' participation in decision making, I believe that certain ways of limiting participation are basically deceptive and best described as "pseudochoice." It is disturbing to find these tactics recommended not only by proponents of blatantly controlling classroom management programs, such as Assertive Discipline, but also by critics of such programs who purport to offer an enlightened alternative.

In the first version of pseudochoice, a student is offered a choice that is obviously loaded. "You can finish your math problems now or you can stay in during recess. Which would you prefer?" The problem here is not just that the number of options has been reduced to two, but that the second one is obviously something no student would select. The teacher is really saying, "Do what I tell you or you'll be punished," but he is attempting to camouflage this conventional use of coercion by pretending to offer the student a choice.

In a variation of this gambit, the student is punished after disobeying the teacher's command, but the punishment is presented as something the student asked for: "I see you've chosen to miss recess today." The appeal of this tactic is no mystery: it appears to relieve the teacher of responsibility for what she is about to do to the child. But it is a fundamentally dishonest attribution. Children may choose not to complete a math assignment,* but they certainly do not choose to miss recess; teachers do that *to* them. To the injury of punishment is added the insult of a kind of mind game whereby reality is redefined and children are told, in effect, that they chose to be punished. This gimmick uses the word *choice* as a bludgeon rather than giving children what they need, which is the opportunity to participate in making real decisions about what happens to them.[46]

Another kind of pseudochoice purports to let a student or a class make a decision even though there is only one choice that will be accepted. I recently heard a well-known educator and advocate for children reminisce about her experiences as a teacher. Recalling a student of hers who frequently and articulately challenged her authority, she commented with a smile, "I had to be a better negotiator than she was." This remark suggests that what had taken place was not negotiation at all but thinly disguised manipulation. As Nel Noddings has written, "We cannot enter into dialogue with children when we know that our decision is already made."[47]

If students are informed that they have made the "wrong" decision and must try again, they will realize they were not truly free to choose in the first place. But the last, and most insidious, variety of pseudochoice tries to prevent students from figuring this out by encouraging them to think they had a say when the game was actually rigged. The "engineering of consent," as it has been called, seems to offer autonomy while providing "the assurance of order and conformity — a most seductive combination. Yet its appearance and its means should be understood for what they really are: a method of securing and solidifying the interests of those in power."[48] This description by educator James Beane might have been inspired by the behavior of politicians, but it is no less applicable to what goes on in schools. If we want students to learn how to choose, they must have the opportunity to make *real* choices.

---

*Even this assumption needs to be questioned, since a young child may lack the capacity for rational decision making or impulse control that is implicit in the suggestion that he made a choice. If so, the child needs help in developing these faculties, not punishment accompanied by blame. I have heard some teachers reply to this point by insisting that, if students are permitted to make choices, they must "take responsibility" for making a bad one. This approach, however, assumes that "taking responsibility" for a poor decision means being made to suffer for it rather than being part of a nonpunitive problem-solving process.

BARRIERS

If we are to act on the arguments and evidence supporting the value of making students active participants in their education, we need to understand why more educators haven't already done so. I think the barriers to giving students more choice fall into three categories: structural impediments, resistance by teachers, and resistance by the students themselves.

Structural impediments. Classroom teachers frequently protest that they would love to open up the decision-making process but for the fact that a significant number of decisions are not theirs to give away or even to make themselves. Highly controlling schools and school districts may leave teachers very little discretion about either curricular or disciplinary issues. As Dewey noted, classrooms characterized by demands for "sheer obedience to the will of an adult" may sometimes imply a "situation [that] almost forced [that arrangement] upon the teacher," such as an absence of democracy or community among the educators themselves.[49] Even if controlling structures do not literally remove options from teachers, they may create a climate in which teachers do to children what is done to them. Often, teachers subject to rigid directives from above may find it easier not "to resist administrators but to increase controls on their students."[50]

Resistance by teachers. While structural constraints are sometimes very real, they can also be used as excuses to with-

> *Parting with power is not easy, if only because the results are less predictable without control.*

hold power from students that teachers in any case are not inclined to share. The traditional instructional model sees the teacher as the king or queen of the classroom, and the fact is that monarchs do not always abdicate gracefully. On the basis of my own years as a teacher as well as my conversations with scores of others in the profession, I would argue that there is a certain reassurance and satisfaction to be taken from making unilateral decisions. No wonder many teachers who express relief at having "a good class this year" use the word *good* as parents of a newborn might talk about having "a good

baby" — that is, one who is quiet, docile, and little trouble to manage.

Popular books about classroom life, as well as workshops and other forms of guidance offered to educators, typically take for granted that a teacher must secure control of the class. Hence the use of curricular materials, including basals and worksheets, that have the effect of keeping order.[51] And hence the popularity of manipulative measures such as punishments and rewards: their use can be traced back to the belief that there are exactly two possibilities: control or chaos. When students are allowed to make decisions, it is therefore only about matters that don't threaten the teacher's reign. More than once I have heard teachers pride themselves on letting students choose "when I don't really care what they end up with" — which is, of course, a far cry from a democratic process that helps students to become responsible decision makers.

If challenged, defenders of classroom autocracy may insist that a teacher must get control of the class *first* in order that students can be helped to become good learners and good people. Whether this is a sincerely held belief or just a rationalization for holding on to power, it is simply wrong. Control not only is unnecessary for fostering academic motivation; it undermines its development, substituting reluctant compliance for the excitement that comes from the experience of self-determination. Likewise for the nonacademic realm: as one group of social scientists put it, the emphasis on control "endanger[s] the long-term enterprise of socialization itself."[52]

This is no mere academic speculation. Watch what happens when a teacher concerned about maintaining control of his classroom walks away for a few minutes or is absent for a day: the class is likely to erupt, just as a child raised by parents who emphasize strict discipline is apt to misbehave when he is away from home. It is in classrooms (and families) where participation is valued above adult control that students have the chance to learn *self*-control — and are more likely to keep working when the teacher or parent isn't around.

There is nothing surprising about the fact that teachers resist being told what they can teach and how they must manage their classrooms. The astonishing fact is that so many of these teachers treat their students in exactly the way they themselves find so offensive. Whatever

the reason for this discrepancy, though, students must be permitted to make substantive decisions about learning and living together, and this will not happen until teachers and administrators understand that *control can't be the goal* — or even a technique. This recognition, in turn, may require reconsidering basic beliefs about human nature and motivation. A teacher convinced that children are egocentric little terrors who must be forced to attend to other people's needs is likely to prefer a model of tight control.[53] And control, in turn, produces exactly the sort of antisocial behavior that such a teacher expects, confirming the view that such tactics are needed.

Sometimes, however, the main barrier to giving children choices is a simple lack of gumption. Parting with power is not easy, if only because the results are less predictable than in a situation where we have control. Asking students to decide about even the simplest issues can be scary. An elementary teacher once told me how difficult it was for her to leave the classroom walls bare when her students showed up on the first day of school. If she had already decorated them, she realized, it was really *her* room they were entering. But it took several years before she found the courage to bring them into the process, a decision that ultimately made an enormous difference in how the children felt about coming to school — and also occasioned a natural and eagerly received lesson on fractions so that the students could measure and tack up the construction paper that they had chosen for *their* walls.

Student resistance. Finally, and most discouragingly, teachers sometimes find that their willingness to let students make decisions is met with an apparent reluctance on the part of the students. This is really not so surprising, given that most of them have been conditioned to accept a posture of passivity at school and sometimes at home. After a few years of being instructed to do what you're told, it is disconcerting to be invited — much less expected — to take responsibility for the way things are.[54]

This resistance takes three primary forms. The first is simply *refusing*: "That's your job to decide," students may protest. The second is *testing*: offering outrageous suggestions or responses to see if the teacher is really serious about the invitation to participate. The third is *parroting*: repeating what adults have said or guessing what this adult probably wants to hear. (Thus a fifth-grader asked to suggest a guideline for class conduct may recite, "We should keep our hands and feet to ourselves.")

The key question is how we respond to these maneuvers. It can be tempting to conclude that students are either unable to handle the responsibility of making decisions or unworthy of having it. But our challenge is to persevere. As Selma Wassermann has written,

> I have heard teachers give it up after a single attempt, saying, "Children cannot behave responsibly," then remove all further opportunity for students to practice and grow in their responsible behavior. I have also heard teachers say, "Children cannot think for themselves," and proceed thereafter to do children's thinking for them. But these same teachers would *never* say, "These children cannot read by themselves," and thereafter remove any opportunity for them to learn to read.[55]

Specifically, the comment "That's your job" provides a teachable moment, a chance to engage students in a conversation about their experiences with being controlled and about when they have found learning to be most exciting. Outlandish ideas can be met with a sense of humor but also taken seriously: a student who is asked how school could be improved and replies that all the books should be thrown away may be saying something about her experience of the curriculum that we ignore at our peril. Finally, in the case of parroting, it can be hard even to recognize this tactic as a form of resistance — or as something undesirable. Getting our ideas to come out of their mouths is a ventriloquist's trick, not a sign of successful participation and student autonomy. It represents an invitation to ask students about their experiences with saying what they knew would please an adult and how different that feels from taking the risk of making a suggestion that someone might not like — and then emphasizing that the latter is what we are looking for here.

Of course, whether the last point is true — whether we really are looking for students who take risks and make decisions — is the first question that each of us must answer. The structural and attitudinal barriers erected by educators often seem impregnable, with the result that students continue to feel powerless and, to that extent, burned out. For decades, prescriptions have been offered to en-

hance student motivation and achievement. But these ideas are unlikely to make much of a difference so long as students are controlled and silenced. It is not "utopian" or "naive" to think that learners can make responsible decisions about their own learning; those words best describe the belief that any group of people will do something effectively and enthusiastically when they are unable to make choices about what they are doing.

1. For example, see Charles E. Silberman, *Crisis in the Classroom: The Remaking of American Education* (New York: Random House, 1970); John I. Goodlad, *A Place Called School: Prospects for the Future* (New York: McGraw-Hill, 1984); Linda McNeil, *Contradictions of Control: School Structure and School Knowledge* (New York: Routledge and Kegan Paul, 1986); and the observations of William Glasser in much of his work.

2. Felicia R. Lee, "Disrespect Rules," *New York Times Education Life*, 4 April 1993, p. 16.

3. Strictly speaking, as such thinkers as Jean-Paul Sartre and Viktor Frankl have pointed out, people are never entirely powerless. Deborah Meier applies this observation to an education context: "Even devalued and disrespected people remain powerful, but they are forced to exercise their powers in odd, distorted, and limited ways. . . . Children have been exercising their powers for years, without the formal right to do so. Ditto for teachers . . . [who] sabotage reforms — the best and the worst — when they feel imposed upon and helpless." See "The Kindergarten Tradition in the High School," in Kathe Jervis and Carol Montag, eds., *Progressive Education for the 1990s: Transforming Practice* (New York: Teachers College Press, 1991), pp. 140-41.

4. Suzanne C. Kobasa and her colleagues found that control, together with a deeply felt commitment to one's activities and the tendency to perceive change as a positive challenge, contributed to a profile of "hardiness" that provides significant protection against illness. See, for example, "Stressful Life Events, Personality, and Health: An Inquiry into Hardiness," *Journal of Personality and Social Psychology*, vol. 37, 1979, pp. 1-10. See also Robert A. Karasek et al., "Job Characteristics in Relation to the Prevalence of Myocardial Infarction in the U.S. Health Examination Survey (HES) and the Health and Nutrition Examination Survey (HANES)," *American Journal of Public Health*, vol. 78, 1988, pp. 910-16.

5. Judith Rodin and Ellen J. Langer, "Long-Term Effects of a Control-Relevant Intervention with the Institutionalized Aged," *Journal of Personality and Social Psychology*, vol. 35, 1977, pp. 897-902. In another study, nursing home residents who were able to control (or at least predict) when a student would come visit them were not only happier and more hopeful but also physically healthier than those who received the same number of visits but on a random schedule. See Richard Schulz, "Effects of Control and Predictability on the Physical and Psychological Well-Being of the Institutionalized Aged," *Journal of Personality and Social Psychology*, vol. 33, 1976, pp. 563-73.

6. Martin Seligman's research on helplessness is central to this field of study. For a review of the relevant studies by him and others, see Shelley E. Taylor, *Positive Illusions: Creative Self-Deception and the Healthy Mind* (New York: Basic Books, 1989).

7. See Elizabeth Tuettemann and Keith F. Punch, "Teachers' Psychological Distress: The Ameliorating Effects of Control over the Work Environment," *Educational Review*, vol. 44, 1992, pp. 181-94.

8. See Alfie Kohn, *Punished by Rewards: The Trouble with Gold Stars, Incentive Plans, A's, Praise, and Other Bribes* (Boston: Houghton Mifflin, 1993).

9. Women who were told they could choose the particulars of an exercise program at a health club were more likely to continue attending over six weeks (and to declare their willingness to keep coming after that) than were women who were told their program was simply assigned to them — even though they, too, were actually assigned activities on the basis of the preferences they had expressed. See Carol E. Thompson and Leonard M. Wankel, "The Effects of Perceived Activity Choice upon Frequency of Exercise Behavior," *Journal of Applied Social Psychology*, vol. 10, 1980, pp. 436-43. A smoking cessation program that "focused attention on the individual's own efforts in smoking cessation" was more successful than one in which people followed a set of guidelines. See Judith M. Harackiewicz et al., "Attributional Processes in Behavior Change and Maintenance: Smoking Cessation and Continued Abstinence," *Journal of Consulting and Clinical Psychology*, vol. 55, 1987, pp. 372-78. Adolescent girls (but not boys) were more likely to continue using an anticavity fluoride rinse for nearly half a year when they were invited to make decisions about how the program was designed and monitored. See Joseph A. Burleson et al., "Effects of Decisional Control and Work Orientation on Persistence in Preventive Health Behavior," *Health Psychology*, vol. 9, 1990, pp. 1-17.

10. This research has been reviewed and evaluated by Suzanne C. Thompson, "Will It Hurt Less If I Can Control It? A Complex Answer to a Simple Question," *Psychological Bulletin*, vol. 90, 1981, pp. 89-101.

11. Megan R. Gunnar-Vongnechten, "Changing a Frightening Toy into a Pleasant Toy by Allowing the Infant to Control Its Actions," *Developmental Psychology*, vol. 14, 1978, pp. 157-62.

12. Richard M. Ryan and Wendy S. Grolnick, "Origins and Pawns in the Classroom: Self-Report and Projective Assessment of Individual Differences in Children's Perceptions," *Journal of Personality and Social Psychology*, vol. 50, 1986, pp. 550-58.

13. Constance Kamii, "Toward Autonomy: The Importance of Critical Thinking and Choice Making," *School Psychology Review*, vol. 20, 1991, p. 387. In fact, the lessons of conformity that Kamii finds troubling are those that concern academic activities (such as having to "learn mathematics through blind obedience"), not just behavior.

14. Shelley Berman, "The Real Ropes Course: The Development of Social Consciousness," *ESR Journal*, 1990, p. 2. The authors of a classic text on high school teaching comment wryly that the American motto could be: "Let's have education *for* democracy, but let's be careful about democracy *in* education!" See Jean Dresden Grambs and John C. Carr, *Modern Methods in Secondary Education*, 4th ed. (New York: Holt, Rinehart & Winston, 1979), p. 71.

15. Citing several sources, Joseph D'Amico concludes that "children who have experiences in a school where they participate in making decisions are more likely to be . . . motivated to make decisions both in and out of school." See "Reviving Student Participation," *Educational Leadership*, October 1980, pp. 44-46.

16. See Alfie Kohn, "Caring Kids: The Role of the Schools," *Phi Delta Kappan*, March 1991, pp. 496-506.

17. Höss is quoted in Alice Miller, *For Your Own Good: Hidden Cruelty in Child-Rearing and the*

Roots of Violence (New York: Farrar, Straus & Giroux, 1984), pp. 67-68.

18. Kathy Irwin, "The Eight Year Study," in Jervis and Montag, eds., p. 59. For a more comprehensive description of the study, see Wilford M. Aiken, *The Story of the Eight-Year Study* (New York: Harper, 1942); and Dean Chamberlin et al., *Did They Succeed in College?* (New York: Harper, 1942).

19. Margaret C. Wang and Billie Stiles, "An Investigation of Children's Concept of Self-Responsibility for Their School Learning," *American Educational Research Journal*, vol. 13, 1976, pp. 159-79. Unfortunately, task completion was the only outcome measured in this study.

20. Robert G. Rainey, "The Effects of Directed Versus Non-Directed Laboratory Work on High School Chemistry Achievement," *Journal of Research in Science Teaching*, vol. 3, 1965, pp. 286-92.

21. Teresa M. Amabile and Judith Gitomer, "Children's Artistic Creativity: Effects of Choice in Task Materials," *Personality and Social Psychology Bulletin*, vol. 10, 1984, pp. 209-15.

22. Miron Zuckerman et al., "On the Importance of Self-Determination for Intrinsically-Motivated Behavior," *Personality and Social Psychology Bulletin*, vol. 4, 1978, pp. 443-46. On the relation between choice and task involvement, see also John G. Nicholls, *The Competitive Ethos and Democratic Education* (Cambridge: Harvard University Press, 1989), p. 169.

23. Richard deCharms, "Personal Causation Training in the Schools," *Journal of Applied Social Psychology*, vol. 2, 1972, pp. 95-113.

24. For a description of the classroom structure in this yearlong experiment, see Erna Yackel et al., "Small-Group Interactions as a Source of Learning Opportunities in Second-Grade Mathematics," *Journal for Research in Mathematics Education*, vol. 22, 1991, pp. 390-408. For a discussion of the results, see Paul Cobb et al., "Assessment of a Problem-Centered Second-Grade Mathematics Project," *Journal for Research in Mathematics Education*, vol. 22, 1991, pp. 3-29.

25. Ann K. Boggiano et al., "Helplessness Deficits in Students: The Role of Motivational Orientation," *Motivation and Emotion*, vol. 16, 1992, pp. 278-80. Informal reports from other researchers suggest that a more typical result from an intervention of this sort is an enhancement of conceptual thinking skills (along with intrinsic motivation and other psychological and social benefits) but no change on standardized test scores, which probably is a reflection on how little these scores really mean. It should be sufficient to be able to show people who care about these scores that giving students more choice about their learning has no detrimental effect on their performance on machine-scored tests while bringing about a variety of other advantages.

26. Three studies to this effect are cited in John Condry, "Enemies of Exploration: Self-Initiated Versus Other-Initiated Learning," *Journal of Personality and Social Psychology*, vol. 35, 1977, p. 466.

27. John Nicholls and Susan P. Hazzard, *Education as Adventure: Lessons from the Second Grade* (New York: Teachers College Press, 1993), p. 76.

28. Richard Lauricella is quoted in Thomas Lickona, *Educating for Character: How Our Schools Can Teach Respect and Responsibility* (New York: Bantam, 1991), p. 148. Presumably he does not mean to suggest that every aspect of a unit must be taught differently from one year to the next, only that an element that is changed on the basis of students' suggestions within a predictable structure can be invigorating for a teacher.

29. Yackel et al., p. 401.

30. This point is made forcefully by David Char-

noff, "Democratic Schooling: Means or End?," *High School Journal*, vol. 64, 1981, pp. 170-75.

31. Paul Cobb et al., "Young Children's Emotional Acts While Engaged in Mathematical Problem Solving," in D. B. McLeod and V. M. Adams, eds., *Affect and Mathematical Problem Solving: A New Perspective* (New York: Springer-Verlag, 1989), p. 129.

32. See Yael Sharan and Shlomo Sharan, *Expanding Cooperative Learning Through Group Investigation* (New York: Teachers College Press, 1992). At its best, cooperative learning "gives students an active role in deciding about, planning, directing and controlling the content and pace of their learning activities. It changes the students' role from recipients of information to seekers, analyzers and synthesizers of information. It transforms pupils from listeners into talkers and doers, from powerless pawns into participant citizens empowered to influence decisions about what they must do in school." See Shlomo Sharan, "Cooperative Learning: Problems and Promise," *The International Association for the Study of Cooperation in Education Newsletter*, December 1986, p. 4.

33. John Dewey, *Experience and Education* (1938; reprint, New York: Collier, 1963), p. 67.

34. See Nicholls and Hazzard, esp. pp. 182-84.

35. Sometimes elementary school students are asked to put their heads down when they raise their hands to register a preference. This strikes me as an apt metaphor for the whole enterprise of voting. "Who thinks we should take our field trip to the museum? Who prefers the zoo? Okay, the zoo wins, 15 to 12." About the best that can be said for this exercise is that it didn't take very long. Children have learned precious little about how to solve a problem, accommodate other people's preferences, or rethink their initial inclinations. Moreover, 12 children are now unlikely to feel very excited about the upcoming field trip. The same analysis applies on a schoolwide basis. The usual student council apparatus is deficient on three counts: most students are excluded from direct participation in decision making, some students are turned into losers since the representatives are chosen in a contest, and the council has little real power in any case. Educators interested in democratic values will discourage voting whenever possible; as the political philosopher Benjamin Barber has cogently argued, it is "the least significant act of citizenship in a democracy." See *Strong Democracy: Participatory Politics for a New Age* (Berkeley: University of California Press, 1984), p. 187.

36. My own thinking on how class meetings might be structured has been influenced primarily by the work of the Child Development Project, whose writings on the topic have not been published. I would, however, recommend two other useful and very practical discussions of class meetings: William Glasser, *Schools Without Failure* (New York: Harper and Row, 1969), chaps. 10-12; and Lickona, chap. 8.

37. "Democracy in the classroom . . . begins simply: with respect for the child as a person, someone who has a point of view and a right and a need to express it." See Thomas Lickona and Muffy Paradise, "Democracy in the Elementary School," in Ralph Mosher, ed., *Moral Education: A First Generation of Research and Development* (New York: Praeger, 1980), p. 325.

38. The quotation is from Dewey's *The School and Society* (Chicago: University of Chicago Press, 1990), p. 130.

39. "In Summerhill, a child is *not* allowed to do as he pleases," Neill added. See *Summerhill* (New York: Hart, 1960), pp. 308, 348.

40. On this point, see Lickona and Paradise, p. 323.

41. Thomas Gordon, *Teaching Children Self-Discipline* (New York: Times Books, 1989), p. 9.

42. This distinction is offered frequently in the work

of Edward Deci and Richard Ryan. It seemed to be lost on several teachers at an alternative school program I visited recently who maintained that, because today's students come from less structured home environments or are more conservative, it is appropriate to give them fewer choices about their learning.

43. Carolyn Edwards, "Partner, Nurturer, and Guide," in Carolyn Edwards et al., eds., *The Hundred Languages of Children: The Reggio Emilia Approach to Early Childhood Education* (Norwood, N.J.: Ablex, 1993), p. 157.

44. Indeed, children whose curiosity has not been killed by the use of rewards or other extrinsic controls typically select tasks of the right difficulty level for themselves. This finding "suggests that at least part of the teacher's difficult problem of matching tasks to children can be solved by providing children with more choices than they are typically offered." See Fred W. Danner and Edward Lonky, "A Cognitive-Developmental Approach to the Effects of Rewards on Intrinsic Motivation," *Child Development*, vol. 52, 1981, p. 1050.

45. A related restriction on choice that may be employed excessively is the practice of preventing students from altering an activity once they have selected it. They can choose, in other words, only among tasks that must be performed in a rigidly prescribed manner. Some critics have argued that this is a weakness of the Montessori method.

46. A nice discussion of this misuse of the idea of choice can be found in Vincent Crockenberg, "Assertive Discipline: A Dissent," *California Journal of Teacher Education*, vol. 9, 1982, esp. pp. 65-70.

47. Nel Noddings, *The Challenge to Care in Schools* (New York: Teachers College Press, 1992), p. 23.

48. James A. Beane, *Affect in the Curriculum: Toward Democracy, Dignity, and Diversity* (New York: Teachers College Press, 1990), p. 35.

49. Dewey, *Experience and Education*, p. 55.

50. McNeil, p. 9. This phenomenon is not limited to schools, of course. There is evidence from the corporate world that the middle managers most likely to act in an autocratic fashion toward those below them in the hierarchy are those who are restricted and controlled themselves. See Rosabeth Moss Kanter, *Men and Women of the Corporation* (New York: Basic Books, 1977), pp. 189-90.

51. Despite the claim that discipline is "instrumental to mastering the content," the truth is often just the reverse: "many teachers . . . maintain discipline by the ways they present course content." The reduction of teaching to the transfer of disconnected facts and skills is the means; keeping a tight grip on student behavior is the end. See McNeil, pp. 157-58.

52. Phyllis C. Blumenfeld et al., "Teacher Talk and Student Thought," in John M. Levine and Margaret C. Wang, eds., *Teacher and Student Perceptions* (Hillsdale, N.J.: Erlbaum, 1983), p. 147.

53. A survey of more than 300 parents found that those who inclined toward a negative view of human nature were more likely to prefer an authoritarian approach to child rearing. See Lawrence O. Clayton, "The Impact upon Child-Rearing Attitudes of Parental Views of the Nature of Humankind," *Journal of Psychology and Christianity*, vol. 4, no. 3, 1985, pp. 49-55. For an argument that the data do not support this negative view of human nature, see Alfie Kohn, *The Brighter Side of Human Nature: Altruism and Empathy in Everyday Life* (New York: Basic Books, 1990).

54. On this point, see Seth Kreisberg, "Educating for Democracy and Community," *ESR Journal*, 1992, p. 72; and Rheta DeVries, *Programs of Early Education: The Constructivist View* (New York: Longman, 1987), p. 379.

55. Selma Wassermann, "Children Working in Groups? It Doesn't Work!," *Childhood Education*, Summer 1989, p. 204.

Motivating Underachievers:
Make them *want* to try

DEBORAH STIPEK

Deborah Stipek was an associate professor of education at UCLA when she wrote this article.

SOONER OR LATER, AN UNDER-achiever will challenge your teaching skill—and your patience—with unfinished assignments, complaints, and excuses. Maybe you'll try to coax the child into working harder. Maybe you'll enlist the aid of parents. Maybe you'll search for special projects to pique the child's interest. And maybe none of these tactics will succeed.

Laziness, boredom, and apathy don't explain the behavior of all underachieving students. For many smart kids who fail, *not* trying simply makes more sense than the alternative. Take Melanie and Jeff, for example.

Melanie, an intelligent 2nd grader, rarely hands in homework. And when given an in-class assignment, she invariably whines, "That's too hard" or "I can't do this" until her teacher comes to help. On tests, Melanie often "consults" her classmates' papers.

Jeff, on the other hand, would never cheat on a test or seek help from a teacher or classmate. But the 6th grader is often conspicuously inattentive in class. And "bad luck" keeps him from completing a surprising number of tasks, particularly ones dealing with new material. He leaves books necessary for doing homework at school. He loses assignments on the bus. Sometimes during a test his pen runs out of ink, and he wastes valuable time rummaging through his desk to find another.

Why try?
Both Jeff and Melanie pay a price for their lack of effort: bad grades, reprimands from their teachers, detentions. Yet both persist in their behavior. Why? The answer is deceptively simple: These kids see the benefits of not trying as outweighing the costs.

Melanie is sure she *can't* do the assigned work, regardless of how hard she tries. Since effort or apathy will lead to the same end—failure—putting forth the least effort possible is perfectly logical. So Melanie continues to rely on teachers and classmates to get her through.

Unlike Melanie, Jeff isn't convinced that he can't do his schoolwork. But he has serious doubts. Since Jeff desperately wants to believe that he's intelligent and competent, and wants others to believe this too, he's afraid to try hard and fail. So for Jeff also, *not* trying—and flaunting his lack of effort—makes sense. It allows him to hold on to a self-image of competence.

Stubborn beliefs
For students like Jeff and Melanie, beliefs about personal ability and the costs and benefits of

effort can be difficult to change. For example, when Melanie *does* do well on an assignment or test, she's likely to attribute her success to the teacher's help, an easy task, or good luck. So occasional successes won't necessarily bolster her self-confidence. What really needs to be changed is her belief that no amount of effort will improve her chances of succeeding. Similarly, Jeff needs to be persuaded that making mistakes isn't a sign of stupidity or incompetence, but a natural part of the learning process. Only then will trying make sense.

Encouraging effort

The following guidelines will help you make sure that the benefits of trying outweigh those of not trying—for *all* your students.

1. Make sure that assigned tasks are realistic, so that all students can complete them if they really try. When your class contains kids with vastly different skill levels, this isn't easy. But you can use such techniques as teaching in small, flexible groups; creating cooperative work groups or setting up a peer teaching program; and preparing different assignments for different skill levels. To alleviate the additional burden this places on you, have your students check some of their own or one anoth-

er's assignments. This also gives students a sense of responsibility for their own learning.

2. Focus students' attention on their own progress, not on their classmates' performance. When students measure their success by their peers' performance, those who don't do as well are bound to feel like failures. Base grades and rewards on mastery or improvement, not on relative performance. Reward the child who reduced his spelling errors from 50 percent to 20 percent just as enthusiastically as you reward the child who invariably gets all the words right. Put papers that show improvement, not just the best papers, on the bulletin board. Consider marking workbook exercises with a check mark if they're correct but making no mark if they're not. Have the student continue to work on the exercises until all have received a check mark. This allows kids many opportunities to improve their performance without any negative evaluation.

3. Reward effort, whatever the outcome. Tell your students that in learning, as in any endeavor, setbacks are inevitable. But effort and perseverance *do* pay off. Praise kids when they make progress, not just when they get everything right. If only success is praised, some students may become demoralized when their

efforts don't lead to immediate mastery—which is a likely outcome when they're studying new material. And when a student does immediately master a new skill, take care not to be overly enthusiastic. Otherwise, you'll risk sending the message that you really do value brilliance rather than diligence, and slower kids may become discouraged.

4. Give every student opportunities to demonstrate competence in class. Consider setting aside a few minutes each week for kids to demonstrate an unusual—and nonacademic—skill. For example, ask your teeny Houdini to show off some sleight of hand, or your fledgling "Bird" to play a saxophone solo. This way, even academically weak students will get a good dose of self-confidence.

5. Allow students to set their own goals. (Of course, you need to make sure that these goals are realistic but challenging.) For example, encourage a child who consistently fails the weekly math quiz to set a goal for next week's quiz (say, getting two more problems correct). Have the child record the goal and his actual performance on a chart. This will give the child a concrete picture of his own progress and will foster personal responsibility. It will also reinforce the importance of perseverance.

Using Motivational Theory with At-Risk Children

Rachel Buck Collopy
and Theresa Green

Rachel Buck Collopy is a doctoral student, Combined Program in Education and Psychology, 1400 School of Education, University of Michigan, Ann Arbor, MI 48109. **Theresa Green** is Principal, Rawsonville Elementary School, 3110 Grove Rd., Ypsilanti, MI 48198.

Rawsonville Elementary is a neighborhood school near Detroit, where the automotive industry is the major employer. Recent layoffs have affected many families in the area, and more than half of the school's 480 students receive reduced or free lunch. Of the district's six elementary schools, Rawsonville has been identified as most in need of Chapter 1 services. For years, the school improvement team had worked hard to improve student motivation and learning. Yet, something was still missing. The number of at-risk and underachieving students entering the school continued to increase.

At the same time, a group of researchers at the University of Michigan had been testing a theory of student motivation known as achievement goal theory (see Maehr and Midgley 1991, Maehr and Pintrich 1991). Their work confirmed what other studies had indicated: The goals that students pursue have a powerful influence on the quality of their learning. Schools, through their policies and practices, give strong messages to students about how success is defined within their walls. As collaborative partners, the faculty at Rawsonville Elementary and the researchers at the University of Michigan aimed to create a school where the emphasis was on learning rather than on relative ability.

Rawsonville Elementary used achievement goal theory to create a learner-centered school, where success is measured not by relative ability but by individual accomplishment.

Emphasizing Achievement, Not Ability

Often in schools where students adopt ability goals, students come to believe that success is defined in terms of how they do in comparison to others. Implicit in the comparative definition of success is the belief that some students are smart, some are average, and some are dumb. The goal becomes trying to look smart—or at least not to look dumb. Mistakes and failure, because they indicate lack of ability, are threats to a child's self-esteem (Covington 1984). Students who adopt ability goals are more likely to avoid challenging tasks and to give up in the face of difficulty (Elliott and Dweck 1988).

In contrast, learning goals define success in terms of developing skills, expanding knowledge, and gaining understanding. Success means being able to do something you could not do before. When students adopt learning goals, they take on more challenging tasks, persist longer, are less debilitated by mistakes and failure, and use higher-level thinking skills than when they focus on ability goals (See Ames 1992 for a review of research).

As partners in a three-year collaboration, we aimed to make Rawsonville a school where the emphasis was on learning rather than on relative ability. Achievement goal theory does not mandate policies and practices. Rather, practitioners use it as a framework to develop consistent, integrated policies and practices that are appropriate to the needs and strengths of their students, staffs, and communities. The issues of most urgent concern to teachers were our starting point.

Photos courtesy of Theresa Green

In cooperative groups, students learn spatial awareness using tangrams.

FIGURE 1

Rawsonville Elementary School's Principles of Recognition

1. Recognize individual student effort, accomplishment, and improvement.

2. Give all students opportunities to be recognized.

3. Give recognition privately whenever possible.

4. Avoid using "most" or "best" for recognizing or rewarding, as in "best project" or "most improved." These words usually convey comparisons with others.

5. Avoid recognizing on the basis of absence of mistakes. For example, avoid giving awards for students who get "fewer than five words wrong on a spelling test."

6. Avoid using the same criteria for all students. For example, avoid giving an award to "all students who get an *A* on the science test, or all students who do four out of five projects."

7. Recognize students for taking on challenging work or for stretching their own abilities (even if they make mistakes).

8. Recognize students for coming up with different and unusual ways to solve a problem or approach a task.

9. Try to involve students in the recognition process. What is of value to them? How much effort do they feel they put in? Where do they feel they need improvement? How do they know when they have reached their goals?

10. It's OK to recognize students in various domains (behavior, athletics, attendance), but every student should have the opportunity to be recognized *academically*.

11. Try to recognize the quality of students' work rather than the quantity. For example, recognizing students for reading a lot of books could encourage them to read easy books.

12. Avoid recognizing grades and test scores. This takes the emphasis away from learning and problem solving.

13. Recognition must be real. Do not recognize students for accomplishing something they have not really accomplished, for improving if they have not improved, or for trying hard if that is not the case.

Copyright © 1993 by Carol Midgley and Timothy Urdan, *Middle School Journal*. Reprinted with permission.

Creating Learning-Focused Classrooms

Having heard a lot about the long-term negative effects of retaining students, Rawsonville's teachers were eager to find alternatives to retention. Their early discussions focused on add-ons of financial, human, and material resources. Then, two teachers suggested fundamentally changing the structure of the classroom. If several grades were taught together, they proposed, children would focus on their own improvement and progress at their own developmental pace.

A flood of questions followed. More than just the ages of students would be different in these classrooms. All areas of schooling—from curriculum, materials, and scheduling to teaching methods, classroom management, and evaluation—needed to be reconsidered. Together, we gathered information from experts in other schools and universities. We discussed the obstacles to change. Most important, we confronted our assumptions about the way learning and schooling had to be conducted and began to dream about how it could be.

As the learning-focused, multi-age classrooms began to take shape, it became clear that high- as well as low-achieving students would benefit from the proposed changes:

■ Students would stay with the same teacher for at least two years.

■ The approach to instruction would be interdisciplinary and thematic.

■ Students would progress at their own speed—focusing on meeting learning objectives, not following a lockstep curriculum.

■ The learning-focused classrooms would take advantage of the variety of skill levels through peer tutoring, cooperative learning, and inter-age cooperation.

■ Report cards would reflect progress and mastery rather than emphasizing comparative performance with letter grades.

Four teachers decided to pilot the classrooms during 1990–91. At the beginning, they were understandably anxious about possible student failures. By the end of the first year, however, they reported that students were more willing to participate in learning activities, more enthusiastic about learning, and showed greater concern for the learning of classmates. Now, half of Rawsonville's classrooms contain children of two or three grade levels.

Developing a learning-focused environment for children did not stop at the doorway of multi-age classrooms. The theoretical framework of achievement goal theory can be used to redesign single-age classrooms, too. Since Rawsonville's self-renewal began five years ago, the teachers of single-age classrooms have also moved toward an emphasis on improvement, understanding, and effort. Teachers now share methods and techniques that encourage students to adopt learning goals across all classrooms.

School change, of course, is about more than just changing classrooms. Classrooms exist within schools and are affected by the policies and practices of the wider school culture. The efforts of an individual teacher to emphasize learning goals can be undermined by school policies that emphasize relative ability and comparative performance.

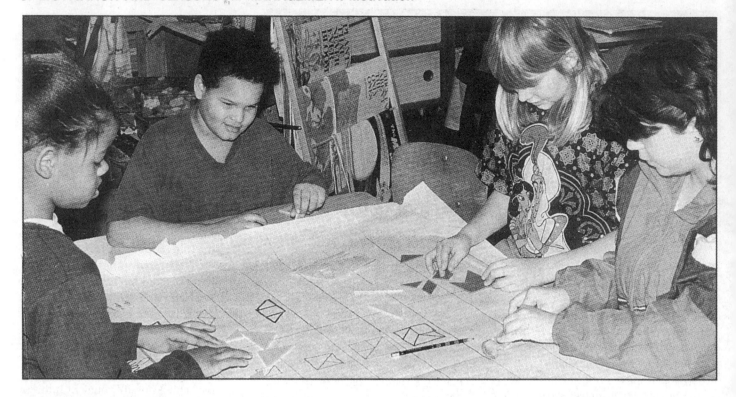

Abandoning the Honor Roll

As her understanding of achievement goal theory increased, Rawsonville's principal realized that the traditional honor roll defined the goal of learning as outperforming others, not improving regardless of relative performance. Each term, only a small group of students received honor roll certificates. In addition to serving as a disincentive for the children who never received the certificates, the honor roll also discouraged high-achieving children from trying challenging tasks.

The principal's decision to eliminate the honor roll started a firestorm of controversy. Many teachers felt that they had lost a carrot to urge students to try hard; they also pointed out that many parents took pride in the honor roll certificates. As they searched for ways to recognize children in a learning-focused manner, teachers came up with Rawsonville's Principles of Recognition. Instead of dictating uniform recognition policies and practices, these principles serve as guidelines that respect the professionalism, creativity, and personal style of teachers (see fig. 1).

Other schoolwide recognition policies were also guided by the new prin-

Peer tutoring, cooperative learning, and inter-age cooperation are hallmarks of the learning-focused classroom.

ciples. As an alternative to making the honor roll, every upper elementary student now receives a certificate recognizing him or her for an area of improvement, accomplishment, and effort. Similarly, at the 5th grade awards ceremony, every graduate is applauded for an accomplishment. In the past, only a handful of students were recognized for their achievements—and often these students received several awards. By the fifth or sixth time a student went up to collect an award, other students would groan instead of applaud.

The faculty at Rawsonville Elementary have also redesigned other schoolwide policies and practices in line with a more learning-focused environment. Rather than emphasizing rewards and punishments, discipline procedures now focus on teaching children to become problem solvers. The use of mini-lessons on conflict resolution and peer mediation, for

example, has lessened discipline problems more than rewarding the "good" and punishing the "bad" ever did.

After the three-year collaboration with the University of Michigan formally ended, Rawsonville sought out a second collaborative relationship with another nearby university with the goal of increasing students' computer literacy. Staff have implemented classroom computer use within the framework of achievement goal theory. Teachers now view computers as a way to help all children—not just slow learners or gifted students—learn problem-solving and reasoning skills.

Continuing the Effort

Rawsonville Elementary's approach is but one example of how to put achievement goal theory into practice. Other schools may decide to focus on other pressing issues or design solutions that are theoretically consistent

Rather than emphasizing rewards and punishments, discipline procedures now focus on teaching children to become problem solvers.

with, but superficially different from, Rawsonville's. What is important is the theoretical perspective, the philosophical underpinnings, that these changes in practice exemplify.

Today, because a large proportion of children entering Rawsonville is still considered at risk, the faculty's commitment to the course they have set has become more important than ever. At the beginning of each school year, the principal and teachers review the changes they made and discuss the rationale behind them. Teachers have taken over the researchers' role of questioning: Will every child benefit from this experience? What message will this give about the goal of learning? What does this say about what is valued at this school?

Now that we know that achievement goal theory can be put into practice, what difference has it made? Teachers have reported improved attendance, increased enthusiasm for learning, and decreased discipline problems. As one teacher said, "I could never go back to teaching the way I did before." Referring to students' improved attitude toward learning, a 20-year veteran wrote:

Some students became so interested in some aspect of classwork that they did correlating activities on their own at home. Children brought in books, magazines, newspapers, and artifacts that pertained to areas of study. They wrote plays, drew pictures, and made dioramas.... During our study of Japan, one little boy got so interested in haiku that he borrowed my books on it and began writing it—in school and at home. His mom reported that he was driving them "cuckoo" with his "haiku."

Parents are very supportive of these efforts to change. Through formal and informal feedback, they report that their children have become more confident, more willing to take on challenges, more excited about school, and better at working independently and with others. About her son, one parent wrote on a survey that she saw "great improvement in all areas—from a student who was failing and had low self-esteem to an interested, highly motivated *learner!*"

One clear example stands out of the extent to which the school community has embraced the changes brought about by achievement goal theory. At a recent PTO meeting, two parents suggested adding competitive rewards to an annual school event. Other parents told them that Rawsonville is not about winning and losing. It is about every child having access to the same enriching and educational experiences. It is about *learning*.

References

Ames, C. (1992). "Classrooms: Goals, Structures, and Student Motivation." *Journal of Educational Psychology* 84, 3: 261–271.

Covington, M. V. (1984). "The Self-Worth Theory of Achievement Motivation: Findings and Implications." *Elementary School Journal* 85: 5–20.

Elliott, E. S., and C. S. Dweck. (1988). "Goals: An Approach to Motivation and Achievement." *Journal of Personality and Social Psychology* 54: 5–12.

Maehr, M. L., and C. Midgley. (1991). "Enhancing Student Motivation: A Schoolwide Approach." *Educational Psychologist* 26, 3 & 4: 399–427.

Maehr, M. L., and P. R. Pintrich. (1991). *Advances in Motivation and Achievement, Vol. 7.* Greenwich, Conn.: JAI Press.

Authors' note: An earlier version of this paper was presented at the annual meeting of the American Educational Research Association, Atlanta, 1993. This work was supported in part by grants from the Office of Educational Research and Improvement. The opinions expressed, however, are those of the authors and do not represent OERI policy.

This collaboration would not have been possible without Carol Midgley and Martin Maehr of the University of Michigan and the teachers of Rawsonville Elementary School.

From Negation to Negotiation: Moving Away from the Management Metaphor

H. James McLaughlin

H. James McLaughlin formerly taught middle grades Social Studies and Mathematics. He conducts research about multiage grouping and issues related to caring and controlling, and collaborates with teachers to do team action research.

ABSTRACT

The purpose of this article is to critique the prevailing metaphor of classroom management. The article depicts three perspectives on classroom relationships that offer differing aims: obedience, responsibility, and solidarity. First, the purposes and uses of authority within an obedience perspective are examined. Then follows a description of recent efforts to widen the interpretation of the classroom management metaphor by shifting the focus from obedience to responsibility. Subsequently, the author discusses how teacher educators might perceive classrooms and schools as sites of negotiation between teachers and students. The purposes, realms, and limits of negotiating are examined, and ideas about how to enact negotiation are presented. A summary section explores the implications of a negotiatory perspective for teacher educators and researchers.

All metaphors about teaching and learning are legitimated within philosophical systems and corresponding political stances, and they serve the interests of certain people. "Classroom management" has long been the predominant metaphor for establishing relations of authority. In its most benign form (Brown, 1933; Sears, 1928), the classroom management of generations ago meant altering the environment to encourage learning, practicing democratic principles rather than relying on teacher autocracy, and balancing punishments with positive incentives. Alter the language, along with the dated cultural references, and Brown's open-ended, wide-ranging casebook of classroom management problems could be in print today. But alongside such accounts of the need for a democratic management, there have always been denunciations of student misbehavior and concomitant calls for greater obedience. At a societal level, the modern management metaphor mirrors a centuries-old movement to enact discipline and gain control over the individual. The term "management" accurately reflects a preoccupation with scientific efficiency and bureaucratic political control at the school level. Principals are no longer "lead teachers," but are middle-level managers.

At the classroom level, the management idea covers a lot of territory (Charles, 1989; Doyle, 1986; Duke & Meckel, 1984; and Emmer, Evertson, Sanford, Clements, & Worsham, 1989, offer extended explanations of approaches to classroom management). There is a broader definition that may entail organizing (keeping track of one's materials, establishing seating charts, and maintaining an accurate and up-to-date grading system), planning (utilizing a variety of instructional techniques), knowing students, evaluating oneself, and maintaining a positive attitude (Reed, 1991). But a significant segment of the education literature has described management in terms of rules, disciplinary actions, and other means of shaping students' actions.

The purpose of this article is to critique the prevailing metaphor of classroom management. The article depicts three perspectives on classroom relationships that encompass differing aims: obedience, responsibility, and solidarity. First, I examine the purposes and uses of authority within an "obedience perspective." Then I describe recent efforts to widen the interpretation of how to establish viable classroom relationships by shifting the focus from obedience to responsibility. Subsequently, there is a discussion of how we might perceive classrooms and schools as sites of negotiation between teachers and students. The purposes, realms, and limits of negotiating are described, and ideas about how to enact negotiation are presented. A summary section explores the implications of a negotiatory perspective for teacher educators and researchers.

From *Action in Teacher Education*, Spring 1994, pp. 75-85. © 1994 by the Association of Teacher Educators. Reprinted by permission.

THE OBEDIENCE PERSPECTIVE

A major purpose of authority—and the uses of power—in the obedience perspective is to maintain adult control over younger people. Teachers are to concern themselves with the most efficient means of control. The focus on efficiency is shown by an astonishing claim in the midst of a debate over the importance of student obedience:

> Without obedience and adult-formed structure, random forces will control student learning. This fosters inefficiency at best and, at worst, error. . . . Simply put, there *is* no task without clear and explicit teacher control, no matter how the control is manifest, and there is no "time on task" unless there is student obedience to that control (Zern, 1991, p. 7, author's emphasis).

In the preceding account, classroom management is a matter of *teacher behaviors* and not student actions. Learning tasks and structures are fashioned independent of student actions or concerns, and students are supposed to learn only what the teacher proposes. It is the professional version of 18th century aristocratic *noblesse oblige*: teachers should not share power with students because doing so constitutes legitimate authority in teaching; rather, students may learn something of interest to them or may offer a few suggestions about class rules because teachers are big-hearted and it fits their plans. Obedience is meant to result in greater time-on-task and efficiency.

Over the last decade "Assertive Discipline" has been the primary purveyor of the obedience perspective. Assertive Discipline places a strong emphasis on teachers taking charge, on being strong. Questions about its merits have swirled through the pages of leading educational journals. Has research proven this discipline program effective? How should we account for the views of practitioners in assessing program effectiveness? What are the unintended outcomes or hidden curriculum of Assertive Discipline? A recent exchange centered on such questions (McCormack, 1989; Render et al., 1989). The major research or anecdotal evidence for effectiveness included whether teachers, students and administrators perceived it as effective; whether disciplinary referrals of students decreased; and whether "off-task behavior" abated. Should teacher or administrator satisfaction with a program provide the sole evidence of its effectiveness? Is that sort of outcome related to greater student learning of important knowledge, or simply to stronger control by someone in assumed authority? Debates in journals will not resolve these issues.

There have been many criticisms of the obedience perspective on the grounds that it does not address the need for student input, it may exacerbate confrontations with students, it fails to teach students how to be responsible, it decreases teacher flexibility by pressuring teachers to publicly treat all students the same, and it is relatively ineffective anyway (Curwin & Mendler, 1988, 1989; Denscombe, 1985; Evans, Corsini, & Gazda, 1990; Jones, 1991; Lickona, 1991). Proponents of Assertive Discipline have denied the program's singular focus on obedience, and have asserted that the approach encourages students to be "self-managers" (Canter, 1989). But Assertive Discipline still embodies the supposition that self-control is born of unyielding obedience to adult domination, and that

student responsibility is engendered by the teacher's rules and consequences. The obedience perspective is flawed, but not because students should have the license to do whatever they wish in classrooms. There is no argument that some forms of social control are necessary for any classroom interaction to benefit the participants. The problem is that an obedience perspective incorporates a series of unexamined assumptions about the nature of power and control in classrooms and schools. The following five assumptions characterize certain myths of teacher control in classrooms.

Control is a classroom matter

Apple (1990), Foucault (1979), and Popkewitz (1987) painted with a broad brush the changing meanings of educational control from a societal standpoint. Denscombe (1985) has concentrated on the institutional contexts of control in schools. In Denscombe's analysis, teachers assume that classroom control is a prime duty because of prior experiences as students, the failure of teacher education to challenge assumptions, and their socialization as new teachers (p. 53). Control is also deemed necessary because of schools' social and physical organization, particularly the influence of classroom autonomy and isolation. The implicit demand for quiet, order and stillness in classrooms emanates from administrators, other teachers, and students themselves, and not just from classroom dynamics.

There exists a consensus about the aims of control, so we ought to concentrate on the means of control.

This assumed consensus is apparent in articles written by behavior management advocates (e.g., Schockley & Sevier, 1991). As I will point out shortly, the assumptions about aims are being challenged by those promoting education for responsibility and for solidarity.

Control is non-negotiated because power is assumed by the teacher's position and not conferred by students.

Glasser (1990) has articulated challenged this assumption. He talks of "boss-managers" who expect obedience and "lead-managers" who understand that real power is conferred by students when their basic needs are met. In traditional behavioral versions of classroom management, students may help to establish rules at the start of a school year, but the ongoing enforcement of those rules often is not cast as a series of negotiations over the exercise of power in the classroom—which I believe it is.

Control is basically non-curricular, and "classroom management" is differentiated from "instruction."

Denscombe (1985) posited that there are three kinds of teacher strategies which explicitly or implicitly aim to reduce teachers' reliance on personal charismatic authority and minimize uncertainty: domination, classwork management and co-optation. "Domination" strategies, which involve direct commands for compliance, fit neatly within the obedience perspective. The two other strategies assert control in less obtrusive ways. "Classwork management" relies on limited, teacher-led instructional strategies to maintain authority (such as recitation), and on group management strategies where the intention is to "keep 'em busy" and to utilize the threat of work or testing to control students' actions. "Co-optation" is achieved when students participate in sports, school committees and the like. "[T]he democratization tends to be illusory and is geared primarily to securing a certain commitment on the part of pupils to the existing social order" (p. 111). On a classroom level, teachers might use humor or a cultural identification with students to gain the students' personal commitment to class activities. Each of these strategies reflects how control is socially constructed in classrooms, even as school and societal contexts exert powerful effects. Denscombe's ideas about classwork management and co-optation relate instruction and management. McNeil (1987) and others have shown the workings of curricular control through the narrowing of content and the limiting of questioning. There is no sense in divorcing how one establishes and nurtures classroom relationships from how one teaches; the former is part-and-parcel of the latter.

Problems that threaten control are thought to reside in individual students, and so ought to be resolved through encounters with a student or a family.
There is a grievous lack of attention paid to the social nature of how one defines a "problem." Problems occur when individuals interact in a certain arena, and thus they reside within situated social systems (Purkey & Strahan, 1986, pp. 25–29). The contexts that Denscombe (1985) and others have described let us see that problems are socially and contextually defined, according to what is considered "normal" in a certain setting, and that the same actions could be labeled differently in another circumstance.

THE RESPONSIBILITY PERSPECTIVE

The responsibility perspective, which is often perceived by its proponents as a form of classroom management, offers a challenge to the behavior management metaphor that underlies an obedience perspective. Curwin and Mendler (1988) have aptly described the responsibility perspective. Its purpose is to teach students to take responsibility for their behavior. They can learn to be responsible if they are treated with dignity, if the teacher employs logical consequences, and if the teacher understands the relationship between good teaching and good discipline. The student learns that "I cause my own outcomes. I have more than one alternative behavior in any situation. I have the power to choose the best alternative" (p. 26). The authors are disdainful of a "packaged method" and supportive of a "caring classroom environment" (p. 31).

The promises and problems associated with the responsibility perspective can be found in many summaries: Evans, Corsini, & Gazda's "Individual Education" (1990); Glasser's "Control

Theory" (1990); Kohn's "Caring Schools" (1991); Lickona's "Educating for Character" (1991); Purkey & Strahan's "Positive Discipline" (1986); and Schaps & Solomon's "Developmental Discipline" (1990). Seldom do the writings on responsibility address the complex contexts of schooling and classrooms (Lickona, 1991, pp. 323–347 and 395–420, presents an exception, although the author does not account for culture, gender or social class as contexts of control and socialization). Discussions of the history and politics of control are rarely broached.

The purpose of classroom management within this perspective is most commonly to promote individual behavioral and attitudinal change—what could be labeled "self-discipline." Authors in this vein reject overt coercion, de-emphasize struggles over control, and emphasize individual choice-making and mutual respect (see examples in Curwin & Mendler, 1988, pp. 102–109). Lists of goals such as "responsibility, respect, resourcefulness, and responsiveness" (Evans, Corsini, & Gazda, 1990) or "trust, intentionality, respect, and optimism" (Purkey & Strahan, 1986) are promoted. Rewards and consequences are demoted in favor of efforts to intrinsically motivate students. Whatever consequences are enforced should be "natural" and "logical" (with hats off to Dreikurs Cassel, 1972).

In this perspective I applaud the emphasis on engendering students' self-discipline through teachers' caring acts. I also think that throughout this literature on responsibility there seems an uneasy peace between centering on responsibility for oneself (an emphasis that is quite pronounced in Evans, Corsini, & Gazda, 1990), and focusing more on group processes and responsibility for others (especially Kohn, 1991; Schaps & Solomon, 1990; and the numerous practical examples in Lickona, 1991). This is because in some cases there are *really two* potentially complementary purposes being discussed: responsibility and solidarity. Legitimate authority depends on establishing solidarity with and among students, through classroom negotiations. The next section of the article discusses the contexts, purposes, and practices of negotiation.

NEGOTIATION AND THE CREATION OF LEGITIMATE AUTHORITY

The tensions of establishing legitimate authority
For teachers today, issues of authority and control are dealt with through numerous inservice programs that purport to show them how to be better classroom "managers" and how to deal with discipline problems in a more efficient and positive manner. "Teacher as manager" is highlighted, and the idea of "teacher as negotiator" is generally ignored. Even so, good teachers are not simply well-meaning but unwitting institutional managers. Most teachers with whom I have taught and talked over the years wish to enact legitimate authority by encouraging varying levels of student participation. In doing so, they experience an important tension in teaching. *Tension* derives from the Latin "tendere," meaning "to stretch." Tension is the state of being stretched tight and made taut; or in another light, the

balance maintained in an artistic work between opposing forces or elements (Webster's). Frequently, tension is interpreted in negative terms. The teacher may feel stretched to the point of breaking because of an inability to control events in the classroom, or to maintain a caring approach to students. Such tensions are certainly present, but I want also to examine the positive form of tension, as a balance between differing (though not always opposing) forces.

In this case, I believe there are two sorts of tensions teachers feel. One is between the desire to care for students and the hope to control the environment and students' actions. The other tension is between a focus on individual responsibilities and a focus on group solidarity. Solidarity "involves the rapport established through social interaction or the feeling that the interaction is proceeding on the basis of some shared interest" (Bowers & Flinders, 1989, p. 141). Many teachers seek to legitimate their authority—and thus their uses of power—by balancing acts of caring and controlling, along with individual and shared interests (McLaughlin, 1991).

Facing up to these tensions compels teachers to understand and utilize various forms of *negotiation*, which is one aspect of caring for students. Negotiation is the basis for establishing "power with" students, rather than simply "power over" them (Kreisberg, 1992). It is built on a desire to determine shared interests, an ability to confer about decisions to be made and curricular ideas to be plumbed, and a willingness to face up to conflict and then shape a compromise. There are important questions to be asked about whose interests are shared in classrooms, and about how issues of gender, culture, and social class arise in these discussions. I will now pose a series of questions concerning the purposes, realms and limits of negotiation.

Purposes of negotiation: Why do we negotiate?

Kohn (1991) stated that two of the approaches to changing students' behaviors and attitudes are "encouraging commitment to values" ("to help that child see himself or herself as the kind of person who is responsible and caring") and "encouraging the group's commitment to values" (to help the child internalize the value of community) (p. 501). Schaps and Solomon (1990) noted how children are motivated by "belonging and contributing" (p. 39), and Glasser (1990) spoke of children's needs for "power and belonging" (p. 54). Those comments and others signal the need for schools to balance the goals of individual responsibility and group solidarity. Negotiation cannot work without an individual commitment which incorporates a sense of responsibility for oneself. Nor can negotiation work without a sense of social responsibility which enables shared interests to be sought and conflicts to be directly faced. Negotiatory acts are a form of power sharing that represents the teacher's caring commitment to democratic governance and an exploration of alternative forms of social control.

Realms of negotiation: What is negotiable? How do we negotiate?

Not everything in a classroom or school is negotiable. On a schoolwide level, such practices as grading, holding classes in scheduled 50-minute periods, responding to bells, doing fire drills, and the like are nearly inescapable aspects of much institutional work. There *are* numerous ways in which teachers might agitate for broad institutional changes, in addition to the common struggles over salary or working conditions. But the focus of this section lies on classroom interactions.

In the classroom a teacher can ignore students, encourage them, negotiate in one form or another, or try to directly control without negotiation. A common principle of classroom action is to ignore what appears to be peripheral and to control what seems seriously disruptive. All else could be deemed negotiable. Often, the realms of negotiation are perceived to encompass those times when students misbehave, when they reject one's "invitations" to participate in a positive manner (Purkey & Strahan, 1986, pp. 21–22). Another way to mark the boundaries is to conceive of "discipline" as "cooperative planning and problem solving" about matters of procedures, pedagogy and "housekeeping" (Kohn, 1991, p. 504). Matters of discipline and control are curricular and non-curricular, and the possible realms of negotiation are vast. I will now describe examples of how a teacher might negotiate in three classroom realms: setting rules and goals, developing curriculum, and organizing classroom activities.

Setting Rules and Goals

Much has been written on how to develop rules and procedures collaboratively. Curwin and Mendler (1988) talk of a "social contract" in classrooms (pp. 47–64), Lickona (1991) details a "cooperative approach to rule-setting" (pp. 112–134), and Glasser (1990) holds that "lead-managers have minimal rules" which are derived through discussion (pp. 122–127). Sarason (1971) thinks of rule-setting as a matter of governance, one among many "constitutional issues" (pp. 175–178).

The aforementioned authors nave offered numerous fine ideas to engage students in the negotiation of rules. There are also efforts to negotiate when conflicts arise between students, or between student and teacher. In Schaps and Solomon's "developmental discipline," the children "work collaboratively with the teacher to develop solutions to discipline problems" (1990, p. 39). Conflict resolution, a term referring to a range of formal negotiatory processes, is being enacted in scores of schools. Lickona (1991) gives examples of how teachers use "class meetings" to discuss classroom problems (pp. 143–147) and depicts several programs and information sources (286–299).

In addition to the teacher-directed approaches above, peer mediation has shown promise. The "Dispute Management in the Schools" project involved a cooperative venture between a university and school district (Araki & Takeshita, 1991). Researchers found that 95 percent of the disputes between students resulted in agreements that were still in effect a year later. "The project also revealed that all ethnic groups subscribe equally to the conflict management process, and that mediators need not be of the same ethnic group, sex, or position of influence as the disputants to be effective" (p. 36).

One more comment on this topic. Issues of gender, social status, and ethnicity should not be ignored during formal negotiations to resolve conflicts. Shook's descriptions of "ho'oponopono" (1985), a traditional Ḥawai'ian family problem-solving process, point out the cultural assumptions in mediation practices. There is more to be considered about the cultural and political assumptions of teacher- or peer-directed mediation.

In addition to rules and disputes, class goals can also be negotiated. Lickona (1991) detailed how some teachers have expanded students' roles in decision-making, which includes setting goals for the class. There needs to be more research and personal descriptions of the nature of teachers' and students' goals, and how the sometimes-conflicting goals might be negotiated.

Developing Curriculum

Teacher and students can cooperatively determine the topics for an upcoming curriculum unit. Beane (1990) has challenged the dominant subject-centered curriculum and proposed that an integrated curriculum center on students' personal concerns and vital social issues. Though Beane did not fully develop the planning process, in his scheme students' interests would be represented and a negotiatory process would be included in teachers' plans.

Curriculum is not a disembodied set of materials; it consists of the plans a teacher creates in advance and then continually re-creates in classroom interactions with students. A program called "Touchstones" encourages student leadership and participation in discussions by employing strategies to develop a group "where the students listen to and speak with one another, where every utterance is not mediated by the teacher" (Comber, Zeiderman, & Maistrellis, 1989, p. 40). Discussions are instances when students can negotiate with a teacher about the substance and the direction of the curriculum. Altering the forms and purposes of teacher questioning serves to further negotiation, if we will see it in that light.

Organizing Classroom Activities

The physical organization and appearance of classrooms can be subjected to negotiatory questions. What part can students play in establishing and maintaining the environment? Too many classrooms have no area in which to read, to draw, to put up student work. How can *they* be in the classroom, through a recognition of their accomplishments and their interests?

Organization also refers to the grouping of students. Regular whole-group seating arrangements or shifting arrangements for class activities can be negotiated. Grant and Sleeter (1989) made a good point that teachers may allow students to group themselves and think it participatory, when in fact it simply reproduces the social groupings stratified by gender, social class, and ethnic group. Perhaps we should seat students according to our notions of breaking down socially-sanctioned group stratifications. The widespread use of cooperative learning has been accompanied by just such an emphasis on controlled heterogeneous grouping to assure gender and ethnic balance in groups. Here is where control and caring collide: teachers must make

judgments whether it is more caring and educative to control the grouping of students, or to allow students to group themselves.

There is another aspect of cooperative learning that relates to negotiation. When students collaborate, they negotiate with each other in both obvious and subtle ways to determine leadership and to shape the outcomes of the activity. Why not include as part of the class's curriculum a clear focus on how groupwork operates as a form of negotiation, and then engage students in activities to learn how to negotiate with each other? This would constitute a kind of conflict resolution on an everyday basis. During small group work the teacher also negotiates with students regarding such matters as the goals of the group, the time limits of the activity, or the level of sound that is "allowable" before students are disturbed. These can be defined as teachers' unilateral decisions, or as matters that must be gauged by taking into account students' judgments.

The Limits and Risks of Negotiating

Creating a democratic, negotiatory classroom is a worthy aim, and there are many ways to do that. Kreisberg (1992) described how a teacher transformed his classroom into a place where community, shared decision making, cooperative learning, and individual and group problem solving were central themes of the year. Yet, teachers do not negotiate everything. There are times when control is enacted by the teacher in order to unilaterally establish order. The earlier discussion of who should compose classroom seating indicated a rationale for limiting negotiation, in that instance. There are numerous other situations where legitimate authority does not rule out unilateral, non-negotiated social control. Bowers (1987) warned us not to conceptualize emancipation as "the progressive stripping away of external forms of authority, responsibility, and embeddedness" (p. 77). Noblit's (1993) account of a teacher's ethical uses of power portrayed someone who projected moral authority. The teacher developed collective classroom rituals and routines (pp. 28–30) and engaged in "reciprocal negotiation" (p. 37), yet she did not abrogate her power to steer the curriculum and the interactions in ways that seemed to be right for children. Perhaps the central questions to ask oneself are "When will I *not* negotiate? Why not?" An exploration of the limits of negotiation would get at one's basic values and aims as a teacher.

Negotiation involves risks. Teachers who make their actions in any way accountable to students may risk maintaining control (Denscombe, 1985, p. 108). This is why "Don't smile until Christmas," "Start out tough and then you can always lighten up later," and other hackneyed phrases still have currency. These axioms are intended to scare new teachers away from idealistic notions of negotiating with students. Democracy will be discussed and not displayed. And the axiom-wielders are right, in one sense. If a teacher has no carefully considered plan for how to define and respond to students' interests, no serious scheme concerning when to ignore, encourage, negotiate or unilaterally control, then problems will multiply. Students have been socialized into restricted images of teachers, and they often rebel when asked to remake the images. Teachers must think deeply about how to establish legitimate authority and about the complexity of classroom negotiations.

IMPLICATIONS FOR TEACHER EDUCATORS

Learning how to negotiate with students—*to have power with*—is what caring teachers long have practiced. It is incumbent upon teachers at every level to think seriously about what constitutes our legitimate authority, to examine the purposes and realms of negotiation, and to consider also the institutional and personal limits and risks we face. Teacher educators are challenged to think about these matters on two levels: with regard to teaching prospective teachers, and with regard to their own practice. How will we address the ideas of authority and power, and the aims of obedience, responsibility, and solidarity, with our teacher education students? What concrete examples of classroom-level negotiations can we provide? Can we discuss these matters with practicing teachers and enlist their aid in helping prospective teachers to grapple with perplexing questions? And what about our own teaching? What are our purposes with regard to obedience, responsibility, and solidarity? What will we negotiate, and what are the limits and risks in doing so? Current efforts by teacher educators to engage in action research on their practice highlight some methodological paths to follow. By asking challenging questions about others' practice and our own, we can reconstitute the management metaphor of school relationships. By taking actions based on our tentative answers, we will move away from behavioral negation, toward enacting negotiation.

REFERENCES

Apple, M. W. (1990). *Ideology and curriculum.* New York: Routledge.
Araki, C. T., & Takeshita, C. (1991). Students helping students: Dispute management in the schools. *NASSP Bulletin,* November, 31–37.
Beane, J. (1990). *From rhetoric to reality.* Columbus, OH: National Middle School Association.
Bowers, C. A. (1987). *Elements of a post-liberal theory of education.* New York: Teachers College Press.
Bowers, C. A., & Flinders, D. J. (1990). *Responsive teaching.* New York: Teachers College Press.
Brown, E. J. (1933). *Everyday problems in classroom management.* Boston: Houghton Mifflin.
Canter, L. (1989). Assertive Discipline—More than names on the board and marbles in a jar. *Phi Delta Kappan, 71*(1), 57–61.
Charles, C. M. (1989). *Building classroom discipline.* New York: Longman.

Comber, G., Zeiderman, H., & Maistrellis, N. (1989). The Touchstones Project: Discussion classes for students of all abilities. *Educational Leadership, 46*(6), 39–42.
Curwin, R. L., & Mendler, A. N. (1988). *Discipline with dignity.* Alexandria, VA: Association for Supervision and Curriculum Development.
Curwin, R. L., & Mendler, A. N. (1989). We repeat, let the buyer beware: A response to Canter. *Educational Leadership, 46*(4), 83.
Denscombe, M. (1985). *Classroom control.* London: George Allen Unwin.
Doyle, W. (1986). Classroom organization and management. In M. C. Wittrock (Ed.), *Handbook of research on teaching* (3rd ed., pp. 392–431). New York: Macmillan.
Dreikurs, R., & Cassel, P. (1972). *Discipline without tears: What to do with children who misbehave.* New York: Hawthorne.
Duke, D. L., & Meckel, A. M. (1984). *Teacher's guide to classroom management.* New York: Random House.
Evans, T. D., Corsini, R. J., & Gazda, G. M. (1990). Individual education and the 4Rs. *Educational Leadership, 48*(1), 52–56.
Foucault, M. (1979). *Discipline and punish: The birth of the prison.* New York: Vintage.
Glasser, W. (1990). *The quality school.* New York: Harper Row.
Grant, G., & Sleeter, C. (1989). *After the school bell rings.* London: Falmer.
Jones, V. (1991). Resolved: That researchers and intellectuals grossly undervalue the importance of simple student obedience in the classroom (Con). *Curriculum Review, 31*(3), 6, 9–11, 12.
Kohn, A. (1991). Caring kids: The role of the schools. *Phi Delta Kappan, 72*(7), 496–506.
Kreisberg, S. (1992). *Educating for democracy and community: Toward the transformation of power in our schools.* Cambridge, MA: Educators for Social Responsibility.
Lickona, T. (1991). *Educating for character.* New York: Bantam.
McCormack, S. (1989). Response to Render, Padilla, and Krank: But practitioners say it works! *Educational Leadership, 46*(6), 77–79.
McLaughlin, H. J. (1991). Reconciling care and control: Authority in classroom relationships. *Journal of Teacher Education, 42*(3), 182–195.
McNeil, L. M. (1988). *Contradictions of control.* New York: Routledge.
Noblit, G. (1993). Power and caring. *American Educational Research Journal, 30*(1), 23–38.
Popkewitz, T. S. (1987). The formation of school subjects and the political contexts of schooling. In T. S. Popkewitz (Ed.), *The formation of the school subjects* (pp. 1–24). London: Falmer.
Purkey, W. W., & Strahan, D. B. (1986). *Positive discipline: A pocket of ideas.* Columbus, OH: National Middle School Association.
Reed, D. F. (1991). Effective classroom managers in the middle school. *Middle School Journal, 23*(1), 16–21.
Render, G. F., Padilla, J. M., & Krank, H. M. (1989). What research really shows about Assertive Discipline. *Educational Leadership, 46*(6), 72–75.
Sarason, S. B. (1971). *The culture of the school and the problem of change.* Boston: Allyn Bacon.
Schaps, E., & Solomon, D. (1990). Schools and classrooms as caring communities. *Educational Leadership, 48*(3), 38–42.
Schockley, R., & Sevier, L. (1991). Behavior management in the classroom: Guidelines for maintaining control. *Schools in the Middle, 1*(2), 14–18.
Sears, J. B. (1928). *Classroom organization and control.* Boston: Houghton Mifflin.
Shook, E. V. (1985). *Ho'oponopono: Contemporary uses of a Hawai'ian problem-solving process.* Honolulu, HI: University of Hawai'i Press.
Zern, D. (1991). Resolved: That researchers and intellectuals grossly undervalue the importance of simple student obedience in the classroom (Pro). *Curriculum Review, 31*(3), 6–9, 11–12.

Images of Management for Learner-Centered Classrooms

Catherine H. Randolph and Carolyn M. Evertson

Catherine Randolph is Research Assistant Professor, Department of Teaching and Learning, Peabody College, Vanderbilt University. Her interests include writing instruction and understanding classrooms as social and cultural settings.
Carolyn Evertson is chair of the Department of Teaching and Learning and Professor of Education, Peabody College, Vanderbilt University. She has authored numerous articles and books on classroom management and instruction.

ABSTRACT

This essay seeks to identify images of classroom management that are compatible with current images of learning, using scenes from one learner-centered classroom as examples. The increased complexity of classrooms with learning orientations demands more complex views of classroom management, and broader definitions of what "good management" entails. While many tasks of managing work-oriented settings and learning-oriented settings overlap, teachers in learning-centered classrooms must place additional emphasis on examining the social and academic task demands they create, and their implications for definitions of learning. Examples from a writing class illustrate how a model of learning may guide management decisions, and how management decisions may contribute to a definition of learning that is constructed in a classroom over time.

As teacher educators prepare preservice teachers for new models of learning, we must also provide new models of management that are compatible with these models of learning. We know that classroom management is the number one concern of practitioners, particularly new teachers (Veenman, 1984). However, we are lacking in images of management that match the images of learning communities we present. Most studies of classroom management have looked at classrooms where academic tasks and activities were fairly routinized and predictable. Relatively little research has examined different instructional contexts (e.g., whole language settings, inquiry-oriented mathematics, etc.) and what kinds of managerial decisions and teacher actions are required to enact academic tasks in these settings (Edelsky, Draper, & Smith, 1983). Therefore, prospective and novice teachers are likely to carry one set of images with them from their content methods courses (e.g., students working together, interacting freely, actively engaging in learning activities), and another set from their management coursework and textbooks (e.g., students in straight rows, guided step-by-step by teacher directions). In this paper, we seek to match images of learning and images of classroom management, arguing for a much closer conceptual link between content and instruction. In the process, it will become evident that the term "management" must take on a new set of meanings for all participants; in fact, it may be more useful to abandon the term altogether, in favor of one more reflective of teachers' roles in learning communities.

NEW IMAGES OF LEARNING

Management actions communicate information to students about the knowledge and participation that are valued in a particular setting. Our first task, then, must be to determine the kinds of messages about knowledge and participation we want to communicate. The messages sent by management actions must be consistent with the kinds of learning we want to encourage. In the current climate of school reform there are clear calls for teaching problem-solving and higher order thinking skills, integrating learning experiences within and across subject areas, and implementing multiple tasks (Resnick, 1987). The Council of Chief State School Officers (CCSSO, 1990) describes the movement: "Schools, previously asked to ensure the development of basic skills, are now required to teach all students a new, broad range of cognitive skills. . . . This new demand on schools is nothing less than a call for the democratization of thinking" (p. 2). Teachers' management decisions must facilitate such thinking and problem-solving.

The metaphors we use to conceptualize classrooms and classroom events shape our thinking, as they provide frameworks for what is possible in these settings. By far the most prevalent metaphor of the past, that of a workplace, has cast classrooms as settings similar to factories. The goal of a factory is production, and students are engaged in a "performance for grades exchange" (Becker, Geer, & Hughes, 1968). When operating within a factory metaphor, it is possible to conceptualize classroom management as the close supervision of laborers, with the intent of discouraging any divergence from plans that have been carefully structured to lead to predictable outcomes. However, if the contemporary calls for redesigning schools where learning for understanding and new models of the learner are paramount (e.g., Marshall, 1992), our images of classrooms and what occurs there must change from that of workplace or factory to that of learning place.

Marshall (1990) captures the argument by distinguishing between classrooms with work orientations and classrooms with learning orientations. While "the goal in a work setting is to produce a tangible, externally visible product or service for the benefit (profit) of the employer . . .the major goal in learning settings is . . .the acquisition or construction of knowledge or skills that are of benefit to the learner . . ." (p. 98). Thus, when we change our metaphor for classrooms, we refocus our thinking from the needs of "management" (for example, high productivity in terms of output of completed papers) to the needs of the "learner," which may imply more time for study, reflection, or discussion, and less paperwork. Instead of an agenda that is communicated from teacher/manager to student/worker, control over the classroom agenda is shared between teacher/facilitator and student/learner, as jointly negotiated goals are developed.

NEW IMAGES OF MANAGEMENT

To facilitate the activities of learning settings, teachers must operate with learning-oriented images of management. Such metaphors for management must replace the work-oriented models that have dominated past thinking. Learning-oriented settings are likely to be much more complex than work settings in terms of the variety and flexibility of activities that are offered. Some disagreement exists about how much direct teacher control is required to manage this complexity. One argument (Doyle, 1986) suggests that classrooms with complex organization will require more direct management and control than simpler settings. However, Marshall (1990) and Cohen and Lotan (1990) contend that, instead of *more* teacher control, settings where small groups of students use a variety of materials and procedures for high level conceptual learning will

Table 1
Possible Definitions of Management Terms in Different Classroom Settings

Management Concept	Work-Oriented Classroom	Learning-Oriented Classroom
Task	Listen, follow directions, generate correct responses, answer questions	Listen, follow directions, modify directions, explore, challenge answers, generate directions, generate questions, generate correct responses
On-Task	During a listening task: Sit quietly, ask questions During seatwork: Write independently (usually silently), remain in seat	During a listening task: Sit quietly, ask questions, propose alternatives During seatwork: Discuss with peers, share ideas, move to most appropriate location for gaining needed information (library, resource materials area, etc.)
Achievement	Emphasis is on accurately repeating/reconstructing information given by the teacher and/or text; standardized (mostly objective) tests	Emphasis is on using information from teacher, text, personal experience, research to generate creative or novel approaches, information, products. Individual (mostly subjective) measures
A "Well-Managed" Class	Quiet, cooperative, smoothly functioning, little ambiguity about tasks or expectations, little conflict, "a well-oiled machine"	Noisy, cooperative, smoothly functioning, more ambiguous tasks and expectations, high potential for conflict or disagreement, "a bee-hive of activity"
A "Good" Manager	Explicit, aware, reflective, directive, minimizes divergence from plan	Explicit, aware, reflective, less directive, recognizes/encourages divergence from plan

From Evertson, C. M., & Randolph, C. H. Classroom management in the learning-centered classroom. In Allan Ornstein (Ed.), *Teaching: Theory and Practice.* Copyright © 1995 by Allyn Bacon. Reprinted by permission.

require a different *kind* of teacher control. They argue that when complex instructional strategies are required, it is most efficacious for the teacher to delegate authority to students or groups of students, rather than attempting to supervise a multitude of overlapping tasks directly. According to Marshall (1990, p. 5), "Direct supervision is more appropriate to simpler routine tasks of the assembly-line variety."

Teachers in learner-oriented classrooms observed and identified by Marshall (1988) were more likely to use proactive, preventive management strategies; in the work-oriented setting, teachers were more likely to emphasize work completion. Another finding potentially important for understanding the management patterns in these classrooms was a difference in authority relationships, which were less hierarchical in the learning settings; Marshall (1990) described them as "authoritative rather than authoritarian" (p. 99).

Clearly the need for effective management exists in both work settings and learning settings. In both cases, smooth, well-running classrooms where time, space, and materials are used efficiently maximize the opportunities students have to engage material in a meaningful way. The difference can be identified by defining terms such as "efficient" and "well-running" in classrooms where "engaging material in a meaningful way" is also defined differently. Table 1 illustrates some possible differences between management in work-oriented classrooms and management in learning-oriented classrooms. As the table illustrates, when conceptions of learning and desired learning outcomes change, management must also change in order to be compatible with the new model.

Table 1 lists management concepts that recur in the literature on classroom management (task, on-task, etc.), along with possible definitions in work-oriented vs. learning-oriented classrooms. As the table shows, management demands in a learning-oriented classroom are significantly different from those in a work-oriented classroom. As long as curriculum is conceived of as something that is delivered from teacher to students, management must be conceived of as a tool for student control, a way of getting students quiet, in their seats, and ready to receive information. If, however, we believe curriculum is actively constructed by all of the participants in a setting, then the purpose of management becomes to facilitate active inquiry and collaboration among students. In a learning setting, the well-managed classroom will not necessarily be the quiet classroom, and on-task behavior is likely to look quite different than it does in a work setting. "Good" managers in both settings will be reflective. However, their reflections are likely to focus on different issues, about which they will come to different conclusions.

Thus far we have argued that, given current definitions of learning, new models of management will be necessary. This argument, however, does not in itself provide us with an understanding of what these new models of management will look like in operation. In the next section of this paper, we will present some images of management taken from one learning setting, and will discuss the kinds of management decisions and actions that are required in the creation of such images.

SEEING MANAGEMENT IN A LEARNER-CENTERED CLASSROOM

The following image comes from a classroom in which the teacher's explicit concern was to create a learner-centered environment. It is drawn from a year-long ethnographic study that examined interactions in an upper-elementary school writing class (Randolph, 1993). The study addressed questions about the nature of classroom interaction in the writers' workshop. The teacher, Ms. Cooper[1], taught writing to three groups of fifth and sixth grade students using a writers' workshop format. Over the course of a complete school year, Randolph observed and participated in Ms. Cooper's writing classes daily, documenting activities through field notes and audio tapes. Observations were supplemented by interviewing the teacher and students formally and informally, and by collecting documents such as student writing and class handouts provided by the teacher.

In general, a writers' workshop involves students working at their own paces, generating their own topics, sharing writing with each other at various stages of drafting and revision, and providing feedback to their peers. The approach claims to empower students by giving them ownership over their own work. Paralleling this claim of student power and ownership is a charge to teachers to redefine their roles in the classroom. Teachers are advised to "adopt more the role of a learner and less the role of a teacher" (Elbow, 1973, p. ix), and to function more as a "member or chair than as the sole source of knowledge and power" (Fulwiler, 1987, p. 143). These charges echo the characteristics of Marshall's metaphor of classrooms as "learning settings;" an example taken from such a setting, then, provides one image of what management could look like under these conditions.

This example comes from one of the last days of the school year, as students were sharing final drafts of writing projects they had been involved in during the previous six weeks.

It is early June, and students are sharing the products of the last writing unit, "Speechwriting." Jackson stands at the front of the room; Ms. Cooper sits in the back corner. Between them, groups of students seated at tables are facing Jackson, listening.

Jackson presents his speech on the Kennedy assassination, arguing that the assassin could not possibly have been working alone. At the end of the speech, Ms. Cooper comments on one of the conspiracy theories he has mentioned. Renee nods as Ms. Cooper speaks, then turns to Jackson with a questioning look: does Ms. Cooper's opinion agree with Jackson's research?

The discussion between Ms. Cooper and Jackson continues, with each contributing and modifying hypotheses about what really happened to JFK.

Ms. Cooper then asks the class for comments and questions. Students respond, directing their statements to Jackson. He leads the discussion, calling on and responding to his peers.

Jackson puts down the construction-paper map he has been using during his speech and turns to the chalkboard. Students follow his every move as he diagrams JFK's parade route, the grassy knoll, and the probable paths of the shots fired.

As the discussion continues, Ms. Cooper gets up and leaves the room to run an errand. There is no reaction from students; Jackson manages the discussion without interruption until she returns.

This picture of management may look like no management at all—management *in absentia*. When seen in the context of an entire year of writing class, however, the complexity of Ms. Cooper's long-term management activity becomes visible. The interaction pattern of the last day of class must be viewed as the product of a year's worth of messages about the social and academic expectations of writing class. Ms. Cooper's management across the year was a process of interacting with students, content, and tasks to build a set of shared beliefs about knowledge, teaching, learning, and studenting. Beliefs held in this setting included: knowledge comes from both students and teacher; the teacher is also a learner; learning involves drawing on past and present experiences; and studenting includes leading discussions as well as participating in them (Randolph, 1993). In this example, Ms. Cooper was able to delegate to students one aspect of management, guidance of a group discussion; this delegation reflected a year-long framework of definitions of knowledge and power that had been established through management and instructional decisions.

In this scene from the last day of writing class, students naturally turned to Jackson with their questions about the Kennedy assassination, just as he naturally acted as the knowledge expert. Jackson took on such typically teacher functions as managing the discussion by calling on the next speaker and answering questions. The reaction of the rest of the class demonstrated that his actions were within the accepted norms of the classroom. Students acknowledged the speaker's right to take on the teacher role by raising their hands and waiting to respond until called on by Jackson. Physically, they turned toward him, not toward Ms. Cooper.

Ms. Cooper was able to participate in the discussion as a learner, without taking back the authority Jackson had adopted; Renee turned to Jackson to question Ms. Cooper's contribution, rather than accepting Ms. Cooper's argument over Jackson's. Significantly, no change in the discussion occurred when Ms. Cooper left the room. The teaching and discussion management functions had been taken on by Jackson to the point that the class could operate smoothly without her, at least for a short period. Clearly Ms. Cooper taught more than writing to this class; the students also learned something about how to learn, with or without the teacher's presence.

Thus far, we have argued that models of learning must be used to define models of management in a given classroom. The converse is also true: a teacher's management decisions contribute to the definition of learning that is constructed in a particular classroom over time. Management behaviors carry messages about what "counts" as knowledge in this setting, about whose ideas are worth, and about where knowledge comes from. The next section of this paper will examine how this process occurred in Ms. Cooper's classroom.

DEVELOPING BELIEFS ABOUT LEARNING THROUGH MANAGEMENT

One area of study that has contributed to our understanding of classroom processes is research on classroom communication. This work focuses on both the student and the teacher as active mediators and constructors of the learning environment, identifying what students need to understand to participate in class lessons, how teachers orchestrate that participation, and how norms, rules, and expectations are signaled and resignaled across time. As students and teachers negotiate the social and academic demands of classroom tasks, beliefs about knowledge and learning are communicated and constructed. The social demands of a task (who can talk to whom, when, how, and for what purposes) and the academic demands (the cognitive requirements of the task) both contribute to a definition of learning. Thus, management of the social demands of classroom activities is interwoven with the academic demands of content. Management is not a precondition for content instruction; it carries messages about content, and must be considered along with content as plans and activities are developed.

As classroom interaction patterns are defined, they in turn define knowledge in the classroom. Consider, for example, typical discourse patterns in a traditional classroom (Mehan, 1979). The teacher initiates an interaction by asking a question (usually a question to which s/he already knows the answer) and nominating a student to respond. Following the student response, the teacher evaluates it as correct/acceptable or incorrect/unacceptable, either directly ("Yes, good answer") or indirectly (moving on to the next question or asking the class, "Is that right?"). The pattern is an efficient discussion management technique for teachers, allowing them to control pace and student involvement. As a management technique, however, it is not devoid of content. A particular view of knowledge and of the classroom is built through such interactions when they are repeated over time. In these interactions, knowledge (including knowledge of the right answer) is something the teacher has, and the teacher controls access to it. The emphasis in such interactions is on "right" answers, or the answers for which the teacher is looking, regardless of whether they seem "right" to students.

Another example from Ms. Cooper's class illustrates how her management decisions contributed to students' definitions of learning. The challenge for Ms. Cooper was how to manage this highly student-centered pedagogy. Her management decisions, as expressed through her management of classroom talk, had the potential to support or to hinder the construction of a definition of writing as a process, and of the writing class as a student-centered learning environment. The academic and social demands of one activity, which participants called *Generating Characteristics,* illustrate how management and curriculum intersect in the real world of the classroom, and how together they help to define the classroom as a learning community.

Generating Characteristics took place during the first week or two of every unit. The teacher announced a genre that would be the topic of study for the unit; for example, the first unit was Children's Story. Students' first task in the unit was to bring in a favorite children's story to share with the class. As stories were shared, the teacher led the group in generalizing from each story the characteristics that were representative of all children's stories. In the children's story, characteristics included "words are simple," "not too long," "predictable," "not a lot of print on a page." Students then used the characteristics derived from the models to begin writing their own children's stories.

The following example is taken from a *Generating Characteristics* discussion in the third unit, as students studied Myths and Fables.

Ms. Cooper: What can we say about the characteristics of the morals? . . . [several exchanges of talk are omitted]

Maybe we need to explain what a lesson or moral is—how to be a better person. I'm going to put that up, unless you all have objections.

Laurie: They're trying to prevent you from making mistakes.

Ms. Cooper writes on the chalkboard: STORIES ARE USED TO HELP YOU BECOME A BETTER PERSON AND NOT MAKE MISTAKES.

Tim: I disagree; sometimes some of the things are wrong.

Hillary: Can be [wrong].

Ms. Cooper: Yes. [She changes "ARE" to "CAN BE" in the sentence on the board; it now reads, STORIES CAN BE USED TO HELP YOU BECOME A BETTER PERSON AND NOT MAKE MISTAKES.]

Ms. Cooper initiated a discussion of morals, and after a few false starts, which have been omitted here, Laurie was able to supply an appropriate response. Ms. Cooper incorporated Laurie's contribution into the characteristic the teacher had contributed and was already writing on the chalkboard. So far, the discussion appears to be fairly traditionally teacher-centered. The nature of the interaction changed as Tim questioned the characteristic that was the joint construction of the teacher and Laurie. By disagreeing, Tim took on the evaluation of the characteristic that had been developed, moving Ms. Cooper into the role of co-collaborator with Laurie. Tim used as evidence for his position the models that had been provided and shared by his peers. The acceptance of his evaluation supported the validity of students' earlier contributions to the class's shared knowledge base, and indicated that the teacher's response was as open to evaluation as any other participant's.

The pattern of talk described here illustrates both management and instruction. The academic content of the task, defining morals, was presented within a particular set of understandings about the roles teacher and student may take as they participate in class discussion. While the teacher appeared at first to be acting in the traditional teacher role at the center of the interaction, by initiating and evaluating student contributions, Tim's comment contributed to a different understanding of typical interaction patterns in this classroom. His evaluative contribution, and the class's acceptance of it, highlighted the

way control over the creation and evaluation of knowledge was shared among teacher and students.

Together, the academic and social demands of the *Generating Characteristics* activity contributed to a definition of writing class as a place where students and teacher learn together, rather than a place where students memorize what the teacher tells them. What counts as knowledge in writing class is defined as what is jointly created there through class discussion, rather than what the teacher brings in to give to students. Because of the close match in messages between the academic and social demands of the *Generating Characteristics* activity, both contributed to a definition of writing as student-centered.

CONCLUSIONS AND IMPLICATIONS FOR TEACHER EDUCATION

Throughout this paper we have argued that the task for us as educators is to make sure that our images of classroom management support our images of learning. We have presented one set of images here, from a single learner-centered setting. Using the term "management" to describe these images seems inappropriate. The term management lends itself well to images of a teacher actively directing student activity; Ms. Cooper's activities described here seem to be of a different kind. The concept of management, as part of a work-place metaphor for classrooms, is essentially teacher-centered, while the classroom described above appears to be student-centered to the extent that it functions at times even without the teacher's presence. The term "orchestration" is one alternative that seems more compatible with such learner-oriented classrooms.

We realize that the argument that we can broaden our conception of management by thinking of it as orchestration does not provide us with practical steps for orchestrating learner-oriented classrooms. While we cannot provide a list of how-tos here, we would like to propose some ways of thinking as starting points. First, it is important to realize that changing our images of management does not mean forgetting all that we know about creating order. As we have already argued, many tasks of managing work-oriented settings and orchestrating learning-oriented settings overlap. The same needs exist for making expectations clear, for purposeful room arrangement, and for rules and procedures that are carefully constructed and taught. In the learner-centered classroom, however, special additional emphasis must be placed on explicit awareness of the social and academic task demands being created, and on their implications for learning. Specifically, we as teachers must ask ourselves: What is being learned in this classroom?

- What are the *social task demands*; for example, who can talk to whom, about what, when, where, in what ways and for what purposes? What self-management or group management skills will students need to have in order to accomplish these tasks? Are these skills they have already mastered, or are they new?
- What are the *academic task demands*; for example, what must be known, understood, and/or created to enhance learning?

- What is the match between the *social task demand* and the *academic task demand* of each planned event? Do both the social and the academic task demands facilitate and support the construction of desired definitions of learning?

Such thinking about management requires a conceptualization of management that goes beyond present practice and toward the realm of educational possibility. Teacher educators must facilitate such questioning and reflection as they discuss the orchestration of classroom events with their students. Most importantly, teacher education programs cannot divorce discussion of classroom management from discussion of content instruction, because any such split suggests that management and content are separate, rather than unavoidably interwoven. Instead, the task of teacher education must be to assist preservice teachers in constructing images and definitions of management that are compatible with and inseparable from the images and definitions of learning they will seek to encourage in their classrooms.

REFERENCES

Becker, H., Geer, B., & Hughes, E. (1968). *Making the grade: The academic side of college life.* New York: Wiley.

Cohen, E. G. & Lotan, R. A. (1990). Teacher as supervisor of complex technology. *Theory into Practice, 29*(2), 78–84.

Council of Chief State School Officers. (1990). *Restructuring learning for all students: A policy statement by the Council of Chief State School Officers on improved teaching of thinking.* Washington, DC: Author.

Doyle, W. (1986). Classroom organization and management. In M. C. Wittrock (Ed.), *Handbook of research on teaching* (3rd ed., pp. 392–431). New York: Macmillan.

Edelsky, C., Draper, K., & Smith, K. (1983). Hookin' 'em in at the start of school in a 'whole language' classroom. *Anthropology and Education Quarterly, 14*(4), 257–281.

Elbow, P. (1973). *Writing without teachers.* London: Oxford University Press.

Fulwiler, T. (1987). *Teaching with writing.* Upper Montclair, NJ: Boynton-Cook.

Marshall, H. H. (1988). Work or learning: implications of classroom metaphors. *Educational Researcher, 17*(9), 9–16.

Marshall, H. H. (1990). Beyond the workplace metaphor: Toward conceptualizing the classroom as a learning setting. *Theory into Practice, 29*(2), 94–101.

Marshall, H. H. (Ed.). (1992). *Redefining student learning: Roots of educational change.* Norwood, NJ: Ablex.

Mehan, H. (1979). *Learning lessons: Social organization and the classroom.* Cambridge, MA: Harvard University Press.

Randolph, C. H. (1993). *An ethnographic study of classroom interaction and literacy learning in a fifth/sixth grade writing class.* Unpublished doctoral dissertation, Vanderbilt University, Nashville, TN.

Resnick, L. (1987). *Education and learning to think.* Washington, DC: National Academy Press.

Veenman, S. (1984). Perceived needs of beginning teachers. *Review of Educational Research, 54*(2), 143–178.

NOTE

1. All names in examples are pseudonyms.

Why Violence Prevention Programs Don't Work—and What Does

David W. Johnson and Roger T. Johnson

David W. Johnson is Professor of Educational Psychology, and **Roger T. Johnson** is Professor of Curriculum and Instruction, University of Minnesota, Cooperative Learning Center, 202 Pattee Hall, 150 Pillsbury Drive, S.E., Minneapolis, MN 55455-0298.

The best school programs in conflict resolution tend to follow six key principles.

"Joshua was chasing Octavia. He pushed her down, and she kicked him."

"Danielle is going to beat up Amber after school. They were spitting in each other's faces and calling each other names."

"Tom shoved Cameron up against the lockers and threatened him. Cameron said he's going to bring a knife to school tomorrow to get even."

Schools are filled with conflicts. The frequency of clashes among students and the increasing severity of the ensuing violence make managing such incidents very costly in terms of time lost to instructional, administrative, and learning efforts.

If schools are to be orderly and peaceful places in which high-quality education can take place, students must learn to manage conflicts constructively without physical or verbal violence. The following six principles may be helpful to schools that are trying to accomplish this goal.

1. Go beyond violence prevention to conflict resolution training.

To curb violence among students, many schools have implemented violence prevention programs. Some schools focus on anger management and general social skills. Others invite guest speakers (for example, police officers) to school, employ metal detectors, or ask police to patrol the school. Still others show videotapes of violent encounters and structure discussions around how fights start and alternative ways to manage aggression.

The proliferation of such programs raises the question: Do they work? In a review of three popular violence prevention curriculums—Violence Prevention Curriculum for Adolescents, Washington [D.C.] Community Violence Prevention Program, and Positive Adolescent Choices Training—Webster (1993) found no evidence that they produce long-term changes in violent behavior or decrease the risk of victimization. The main function of such programs, Webster argues, is to provide political cover for school officials and politicians.

In their survey of 51 violence prevention programs, Wilson-Brewer and colleagues (1991) found that fewer than half of the programs even claimed to have reduced levels of violence, and few had any data to back up their claims. Tolan and Guerra (in press), after reviewing the existing research on violence prevention, concluded that (1) many schools are engaged in well-intentioned efforts without any evidence that the programs will work, and (2) some programs actually influence relatively nonviolent students to be more violence-prone.

Why don't violence prevention programs work? Here are a few possible reasons.

1. Many programs are poorly targeted. First, they lump together a broad range of violent behaviors and people, ignoring the fact that different people turn to violence for different reasons. Second, few programs focus on the relatively small group of children and adolescents who commit most of the acts of serious violence. In our studies of a peer mediation program in inner-city schools, for example, we found that less than 5 percent of students accounted for more than one-third of the violent incidents in the school (Johnson and Johnson 1994a).

2. The programs provide materials

Few violence prevention programs focus on the relatively small group of children and adolescents who commit most of the acts of serious violence.

but don't focus on program implementation. Many programs assume that (a) a few hours of an educational intervention can "fix" students who engage in violent behavior, (b) a few hours of training can prepare teachers to conduct the program, and (c) no follow-up is needed to maintain the quality of the program. In other words, the programs ignore the literature on successful innovation within schools (Johnson and Johnson, in press) and, therefore, are often poorly implemented.

3. Proponents of violence prevention programs confuse methods that work in neighborhoods with those that work in schools. Conflicts on the street often involve macho posturing, competition for status, access to drugs, significant amounts of money, and individuals who have short-term interactions with one another. The school, on the other hand, is a cooperative setting in which conflicts involve working together, sharing resources, making decisions, and solving problems among students who are in long-term relationships. Different conflict resolution procedures are required in each setting. Street tactics should not be brought into the school, and it is naive and dangerous to assume that school tactics should be used on the street.

4. Many programs are unrealistic about the strength of the social forces that impel children toward violence. To change the social norms controlling street behavior requires a broad-based effort that involves families, neighbors, the mass media, employers, health care officials, schools, and government. Schools do not have the resources to guarantee health care, housing, food, parental love, and hope for the future for each child. Educators cannot eliminate the availability of guns (especially semi-automatic handguns), change the economics of the

drug trade (and other types of crime), or even reduce the dangers of walking to and from school. Because there is a limit to what schools can do in reducing violence among children and adolescents outside of school, violence prevention programs should be realistic and not promise too much.

Initiating a violence prevention program will not reduce the frequency of violence in schools and in society as a whole. While violence does need to be prevented, programs that focus exclusively on violence prevention may generally be ineffective. Schools must go beyond violence prevention to conflict resolution training.

2. Don't attempt to eliminate all conflicts.

The elimination of violence does not mean the elimination of conflict. Some conflicts can have positive outcomes (Johnson and Johnson 1991, 1992). They can increase achievement, motivation to learn, higher-level reasoning, long-term retention, healthy social and cognitive development, and the fun students have in school. Conflicts can also enrich relationships, clarify personal identity, increase ego strength, promote resilience in the face of adversity, and clarify how one needs to change.

It is not the presence of conflict that is to be feared but, rather, its destructive management. Attempts to deny, suppress, repress, and ignore conflicts may, in fact, be a major contributor to the occurrence of violence in schools. Given the many positive outcomes of conflict, schools need to teach students how to manage conflicts constructively.

3. Create a cooperative context.

The best conflict resolution programs seek to do more than change individual students. Instead, they try to transform

the total school environment into a learning community in which students live by a credo of nonviolence.

Two contexts for conflict are possible: cooperative and competitive (Deutsch 1973, Johnson and Johnson 1989). In a competitive context, individuals strive to win while ensuring their opponents lose. Those few who perform the best receive the rewards. In this context, competitors often misperceive one another's positions and motivations, avoid communicating with one another, are suspicious of one another, and see the situation from only their own perspective.

In a cooperative context, conflicts tend to be resolved constructively. Students have clear perceptions of one another's positions and motivation, communicate accurately and completely, trust one another, and define conflicts as mutual problems to be solved. Cooperators typically have a long-term time orientation and focus their energies both on achieving mutual goals and on maintaining good working relationships with others.

Students cannot learn to manage conflicts constructively when their school experience is competitive and individualistic. In such a context, constructive conflict resolution procedures are often ineffective and, in fact, may make the students who use them vulnerable to exploitation. Instead, schools should seek to create a cooperative context for conflict management, which is easier to do when the majority of learning situations are cooperative (Johnson and Johnson 1989, Johnson et al. 1993).

4. Decrease in-school risk factors.

Three factors place children and adolescents at risk for violent behavior. The first is academic failure. One way that schools can promote higher achievement and greater competence in using higher-level reasoning by students is to emphasize cooperative learning more than competitive or individualistic learning (Johnson and Johnson 1989). The more students know and the greater their ability to analyze situations and think through decisions, the better able they will be to envision the consequences of their actions, respect differing viewpoints, conceive of a variety of strategies for dealing with conflict, and engage in creative problem solving.

A second factor that puts children and adolescents at risk for violent and destructive behavior is alienation from schoolmates. In order to create an infrastructure of personal and academic support, schools need to encourage long-term caring and committed relationships. Two procedures for doing so are (1) using cooperative base groups that last for a number of years (Johnson et al. 1992, 1993); and (2) assigning teams of teachers to follow cohorts of students through several grades, instead of changing teachers every year (Johnson and Johnson 1994a).

Third, children and adolescents who have high levels of psychological pathology are more at risk for violent and destructive behavior than students who are psychologically well adjusted. David Hamburg, the president of Carnegie Corporation, states that reversing the trend of violence among the young depends on teaching children how to share, work cooperatively with others, and help others. The more children and adolescents work in cooperative learning groups, the greater will be their psychological health, self-esteem, social competencies, and resilience in the face of adversity and stress (Johnson and Johnson 1989).

In summary, schools must not overlook the in-school factors that place students at risk for engaging in violence and other destructive ways of managing conflicts. Anything that allows students to fail, remain apart from classmates, and be socially inept and have low self-esteem, increases the probability that students will use destructive conflict strategies.

5. Use academic controversy to increase learning.

To show students that conflicts can have positive results, schools should make academic controversies an inherent and daily part of learning

situations. It is unclear whether cognitive, social, and moral development can take place in the absence of conflict. Academic *controversy* exists when one student's ideas, information, conclusions, theories, and opinions are incompatible with those of another, and the two seek to reach an agreement (Johnson and Johnson 1992).

For example, teachers can assign students to cooperative learning groups of four, divided into two pairs. One pair is assigned a pro position on an issue and the other pair, the con position. Each pair prepares a persuasive presentation (consisting of a thesis statement, rationale, and conclusion) to convince the other side of the position's validity. The two pairs then meet, and each side presents the best case possible for its position. Afterward, during an open discussion, students refute the opposing position (by discrediting the information and/or the inductive and deductive logic used) while rebutting criticisms of their position. At the same time, they try to persuade the other pair to change their minds. Next, a perspective reversal occurs in which each pair presents the best case possible for the opposing position. Finally, after trying to view the issue from both perspectives simultaneously, the students drop all advocacy and come to a consensus about their "best reasoned judgment" based on a synthesis of the two positions.

Over the past 25 years, we have conducted numerous studies on academic controversy. Similar to cooperative learning, academic controversy results in increased student achievement, critical thinking, higher-level reasoning, intrinsic motivation to learn, perspective-taking, and a number of other important educational outcomes (Johnson and Johnson 1979, 1992).

6. Teach all students how to resolve conflicts constructively.

Most of the diverse conflict resolution programs present in schools are either cadre or total student body programs. In the *cadre approach,* a small number of students are trained to serve as peer mediators for the entire school. While

this approach is relatively easy and inexpensive to implement, having a few peer mediators with limited training is not likely to decrease the severity and frequency of conflicts in a school.

In the *total student body approach,* every student learns how to manage conflicts constructively by negotiating agreements and mediating their schoolmates' conflicts. The responsibility for peer mediation is rotated throughout the entire student body (or class) so that every student gains experience as a mediator. A disadvantage of this approach is the time and commitment required by the faculty. The more students who are trained how to negotiate and mediate, however, the greater the number of conflicts that will be managed constructively in the school.

An example of the total student body approach is the *Teaching Students to Be Peacemakers Program,* which we have implemented in several countries (Johnson and Johnson 1991). We conceive the training as a 12-year spiral curriculum in which each year students learn increasingly sophisticated negotiation and mediation procedures.

The negotiation procedure consists of six steps. Students in conflict: (1) define what they want, (2) describe their feelings, and (3) explain the reasons underlying those wants and feelings. Then the students: (4) reverse perspectives in order to view the conflict from both sides, (5) generate at least three optional agreements with maximum benefits for both parties, and (6) agree on the wisest course of action.

The mediation procedure consists of four steps: (1) stop the hostilities, (2) ensure that the disputants are committed to the mediation process, (3) facilitate negotiations between the disputants, and (4) formalize the agreement.

Once the students complete negotiation and mediation training, the school (or teacher) implements the Peacemakers Program by selecting two students as mediators each day. It is the actual experience of being a mediator that best teaches students how to negotiate and resolve conflicts. In addition to using the procedures, students receive additional training twice a week for the rest of the school year to expand and refine their skills.

Until recently, very little research validating the effectiveness of conflict resolution training programs in schools has existed. Over the past five years, we have conducted seven studies in six different schools in both suburban and urban settings and in two different countries (Johnson and Johnson 1994b). Students in 1st through 9th grades were involved in the studies. We found that before training, most students had daily conflicts, used destructive strategies that tended to escalate the conflict, referred the majority of their conflicts to the teacher, and did not know how to negotiate. After training, students could apply the negotiation and mediation procedures to actual conflict situations, as well as transfer them to nonclassroom and nonschool settings, such as the playground, the lunchroom, and at home. Further, they maintained their knowledge and skills throughout the school year.

Given the choice of using a "win-lose" or a "problem-solving" negotiation strategy, virtually all untrained students used the former, while trained students primarily chose the problem-solving approach. In addition, students who were taught the negotiation procedure while studying a novel during an English literature unit not only learned how to negotiate, but performed higher on an achievement test on the novel than did students in a control group, who spent their entire time studying the novel. This study represents a model of how to integrate conflict resolution training into an academic class.

After their training, students generally managed their conflicts without involving adults. The frequency of student-student conflicts teachers had to manage dropped 80 percent, and the number of conflicts referred to the principal was reduced by 95 percent. Such a dramatic reduction of referrals of conflicts to adults changed the school discipline program from arbitrating conflicts to maintaining and supporting the peer mediation process.

Knowing how to negotiate agreements and mediate schoolmates' conflicts empowers students to regulate their own behavior. Self-regulation is a central and significant hallmark of cognitive and social development. Using competencies in resolving conflicts constructively also increases a child's ability to build and maintain high-quality relationships with peers and to cope with stress and adversity.

In short, training only a small cadre of students to manage conflicts constructively and to be peer mediators will not change the way other students manage their conflicts. For this reason, schools must teach all students skills in negotiation and mediation.

Making the Future a Better Place

Every student needs to learn how to manage conflicts constructively. Without training, many students may never learn how to do so. Teaching every student how to negotiate and mediate will ensure that future generations are prepared to manage conflicts constructively in career, family, community, national, and international settings.

There is no reason to expect, however, that the process will be easy or quick. It took 30 years to reduce smoking in America. It took 20 years to reduce drunk driving. It may take even longer to ensure that children and adolescents can manage conflicts constructively. The more years that students spend learning and practicing the skills of peer mediation and conflict resolution, the more likely they will be to actually use those skills both in the classroom and beyond the school door.

References

Deutsch, M. (1973). *The Resolution of Conflict.* New Haven, Conn.: Yale University Press.

Johnson, D. W., and R. Johnson. (1979). "Conflict in the Classroom: Controversy and Learning." *Review of Educational Research* 49, 1: 51–61.

Johnson, D. W., and R. Johnson. (1989). *Cooperation and Competition: Theory and Research.* Edina, Minn.: Interaction Book Company.

Johnson, D. W., and R. Johnson. (1991). *Teaching Students to Be Peacemakers.* Edina, Minn.: Interaction Book Company.

Johnson, D. W., and R. Johnson. (1992). *Creative Controversy: Intellectual Challenge in the Classroom.* Edina, Minn.: Interaction Book Company.

Johnson, D. W., and R. Johnson. (1994a). *Leading the Cooperative School.* 2nd ed. Edina, Minn.: Interaction Book Company.

Johnson, D. W., and R. Johnson. (1994b). *Teaching Students to Be Peacemakers: Results of Five Years of Research.* Minneapolis: University of Minnesota, Cooperative Learning Center.

Johnson, D. W., and R. Johnson. (In press). "Implementing Cooperative Learning: Training Sessions, Transfer to the Classroom, and Maintaining Long-Term Use." In *Staff Development for Cooperative Learning: Issues and Approaches*, edited by N. Davidson, C. Brody, and C. Cooper. New York: Teachers College Press.

Johnson, D. W., R. Johnson, and E. Holubec. (1992). *Advanced Cooperative Learning.* 2nd ed. Edina, Minn.: Interaction Book Company.

Johnson, D. W., R. Johnson, and E. Holubec. (1993). *Cooperation in the Classroom.* 6th ed. Edina, Minn.: Interaction Book Company.

Tolan, P., and N. Guerra. (In press). *What Works in Reducing Adolescent Violence: An Empirical Review of the Field.* Denver: Center for the Study of Prevention of Violence, University of Colorado.

Webster, D. (1993). "The Unconvincing Case for School-Based Conflict Resolution Programs for Adolescents." *Health Affairs* 12, 4: 126–140.

Wilson-Brewer, R., S. Cohen, L. O'Donnell, and I. Goodman. (1991). "Violence Prevention for Young Adolescents: A Survey of the State of the Art." Eric Clearinghouse, ED356442, 800-443-3742.

What Teachers Should Know

Elizabeth D. Evans ▪ *Rita C. Richardson*

"When I get the paddle, I feel I don't want to be in school." (6th grader)
"I got tired of getting hit; it made me feel bad." (school dropout)
"I had big bruises; I was embarrassed!" (8th grader)
"I hate the principal, the teacher. I hate school." (4th grader)
"I felt humiliated and violated." (11th grader)

Such reactions to corporal punishment echo in many schools throughout the United States. To date, 27 states have abolished this form of discipline either by state law or by regulation from State Departments of Education. In addition, 46 national associations, including The Council for Exceptional Children, have passed resolutions against corporal punishment.

Despite rising progress, 23 states have not enacted statewide legislation; and school districts within these states are entrusted to control punishment procedures.

According to a survey by the Office of Civil Rights, U.S. Department of Education, the states that reported the largest percentages of school corporal punishment were located in the South and Southwest regions of the United States (Hyman, 1990). The percentages of students paddled in the top 10 states during the 1989–1990 school year were: Mississippi (9.39), Arkansas (7.78),

The Council for Exceptional Children policy statement on corporal punishment:

The Council for Exceptional Children supports the prohibition of the use of corporal punishment in special education. Corporal punishment is here defined as a situation in which all of the following elements are present: an authority accuses a child of violating a rule and seeks from the child an explanation, whereupon a judgment of guilt is made, followed by physical contact and pain inflicted on the child. The Council finds no conditions under which corporal punishment so defined would be the treatment of choice in special education.

Alabama (7.32), Tennessee (6.52), Texas (3.9), Georgia (3.6), Louisiana (2.83), Oklahoma (2.61), South Carolina (2.25) and Kentucky (1.7) (Waters, 1993). Texas law does not prohibit teachers from using any means of punishment on schoolchildren except deadly force. While this state ranks fifth in percentages of reported cases, it leads the nation in the number of paddlings in schools. An estimated 166,003 paddlings were reported in 1 year for the Lone Star State (Loddeke, 1991). In 1992, Kentucky and Oklahoma attempted to pass regulations to ban corporal punishment in schools; however, reactions from ultraconservative groups killed the ban in Kentucky, while in Oklahoma the attorney general announced that the ban on corporal punishment was only advisory (Maurer, 1992–1993; Waters, 1993).

Support for Corporal Punishment

Corporal punishment is defined as chastisement inflicted on the body to modify behavior (Rich, 1989). Two significant cases have caused many school districts to support and maintain the use of corporal punishment in their discipline code. The U.S. Supreme Court affirmed that corporal punishment in school neither violates the Eighth Amendment protection against cruel and unusual punishment, nor does it breach the Fourteenth Amendment due process guarantees (*Baker v. Owen*, 1975; *Ingraham v. Wright*, 1977).

Public support for corporal punishment in schools varies in different regions of the country. The results of a national parent survey indicated that 55% disapproved, 38% approved, and 6% were not sure; however, in the South, the approval rate is 53% (Groller, 1989). In a survey of teachers, 75% of the respondents believed that corporal punishment was necessary to maintain discipline (Brown, 1988). The results of a study by Cotham, Strauss, Vargas-Moll, and Hyman (1987) revealed that 90% of parents disapproved of the use of physical discipline for students with disabilities; yet this practice was still being implemented in many schools (Rose, 1989).

Paddling Students with Disabilities

Students with behavioral or emotional disorders and learning and mental dis-

"When I get the paddle, I feel I don't want to be in school."

(6th grader)

"I got tired of getting hit; it made me feel bad."

(school dropout)

abilities are often at risk for physical abuse at home and in school because of the very nature of their disabilities (Zirpoli, 1990). The behaviors of these students do not fit the norm; they are frequently aggressive, disruptive, noncompliant, and antisocial. Management techniques for these students often involve intrusive and humiliating modes of punishment (Braaten, Simpson, Rosell, & Reilly, 1988).

In Tennessee, horror stories about punishment of students with disabilities led the antipaddling organization, Tennesseans Against Paddling (T.A.P.), to introduce a bill in the Tennessee legislature that would protect students with disabilities (Pride, 1992). Thus far, their efforts have been unsuccessful. In Texas, students with disabilities are subjected to physical discipline unless otherwise specified in the individualized educational program (IEP). Paddling is within the teachers' rights when the whipping is not excessive (Funkhouser, 1994). The Association for Retarded Citizens of Georgia is helping parents of children with disabilities to sue for damages in cases where teachers have physically punished students in special education classes (Maurer, 1992).

Paddling Students from Minority Groups

Other groups of students that are often subjected to physical abuse in schools are African American males and Hispanic males from low socioeconomic households (Cotham et al., 1987; Slate, Waldrop, & Justem, 1991). Nationally, black males in school are physically punished at a ratio of four to one, when compared to their white peers. Twelve percent of Hispanic males, compared to 8% of white males, receive corporal punishment (Hyman, 1990). In several Texas school districts, Hispanic males are more likely to receive corporal punishment than white or black students. An urban school district in Texas reported figures indicating that one paddling was administered for every 13 Hispanic students compared with one for every 30 white or black students (Eig, 1991).

Alternatives to Corporal Punishment

Many classroom teachers lack the training needed to discipline students without resorting to punishment. Paddling is a form of punishment that is momentarily effective; but violent acts teach very little, other than the countenance of violence. The use of corporal punishment in schools is not conducive to a healthy learning environment, and it is counterproductive.

Alternatives to corporal punishment should encompass both proactive and reactive strategies. Teaching prosocial skills is as important as a level system or the use of a token system to change behavior. In addition to using behavioral techniques, teachers can implement various strategies from the humanistic and ecological models.

Ecological interventions stress skills that enable students to operate independently across settings and situations. Students are taught self-regulation skills and discrimination training, which permit them to generalize and become self-sufficient.

Humanistic interventions emphasize self-worth. To become self-actualized, individuals need to be accepted and to develop self-esteem. Many students with disabilities operate under a self-fulfilling prophesy of defeat and learned helplessness. Teachers must become aware of their own interactions with students and the messages they convey through verbal and nonverbal forms of communication.

Awareness and knowledge are key elements for the successful implementation of change. When teachers are knowledgeable and aware of corporal punishment issues, they are empowered to become effective change agents. The acronym END, as in END corporal punishment, is a way to help teachers remember three strategies:

Educating self and others, saying **N**o to corporal punishment, and **D**eveloping alternatives to corporal punishment.

Educate:
Educate Self and Others

Teachers need to make a personal decision concerning their stand on the use of corporal punishment. They need to gain knowledge and share facts on the dangers of such disciplinary measures with colleagues, parents, and students. The following list of questions can serve as a catalyst for gaining knowledge.

1. Have you read articles or books on the effects of corporal punishment in school?

2. Are you familiar with the research on the use of corporal punishment in schools?

3. Does your local school district permit corporal punishment, and are policies and procedures for its administration clarified and periodically reviewed?

4. Do your students' parents support the use of corporal punishment in school?

5. What are your legal rights when dealing with the issues of corporal punishment in school?

6. Do you raise issues dealing with the use of corporal punishment with your colleagues?

7. Do you support efforts for a national, state, and local ban on corporal punishment in schools?

8. Do you search for alternatives to establish effective discipline in your classroom?

9. Do you share successful alternatives with colleagues and parents?

10. Do you model the use of nonviolent, logical solutions to solve problems?

"I had big bruises; I was embarrassed!"

(8th grader)

"I hate the principal, the teacher. I hate school."

(4th grader)

No:
Say No to Corporal Punishment

It's time to take a stand. By saying No, teachers become advocates for the abolition of corporal punishment in schools. The following questions can assist in developing advocacy.

1. Do you belong to a professional organization that has taken a stand against corporal punishment in schools?

2. Would you be willing to organize or participate in a local group to work toward the elimination of corporal punishment?

3. Are you aware of organizations that support the prevention of child abuse in schools and at home?

4. Do you know how to seek assistance from protective services, police, or professional counselors?

5. Do you know how to contact your state legislators, and would you be willing to communicate your knowledge on the effects of corporal punishment?

6. Have you organized resource information on national coalitions to abolish corporal punishment?

7. Do you know how to contact parents and/or civic organizations, and would you be willing to address such

groups on corporal punishment issues?

8. Do you know how to discuss your philosophy on corporal punishment rationally without alienating others?

9. Would you be willing to present a paper on corporal punishment at a local or national conference?

10. Would you be willing to write a brief article for your local paper or a letter to the editor on your opposition to corporal punishment?

Develop:
Develop Alternatives to Corporal Punishment

Abolishing school corporal punishment does not mean eliminating discipline. In fact, the teacher becomes more responsible and resourceful in behavior management strategies. There are no set solutions to socialize students, but the following questions can help in formulating alternatives.

1. Are you familiar with the various conceptual models of behavior management?

2. Do you hold class discussions on conflict resolution?

3. Do you involve students in developing discipline codes?

4. Are you consistent in enforcing school and classroom rules?

5. Are you flexible, and do you consider individual situations when enforcing discipline?

6. Do you use positive reinforcement and teach self-regulation?

7. Do you teach prosocial skills to develop character and moral reasoning?

8. Do you seek professional help when all your efforts are unsuccessful?

9. Do you involve parents in planning and implementing a behavior management program?

10. Do you encourage cooperative learning and teach students to mediate and to solve their problems?

Conclusion

Corporal punishment is harmful to all students. When children are paddled in school, it adds to the high violence in society; and it reinforces that violence is an effective way to solve problems (Hyman, 1990). Individuals who consistently receive corporal punishment rarely learn self-control, have a poor self-concept, and are less likely to be able to solve problems logically and peacefully (Parents and Teachers Against Violence in Education, PTVE, 1990). Often, corporal punishment is administered to students with disabilities who are already identified as having emotional or behavioral problems.

The use of corporal punishment is stressful for teachers and administrators. It often causes hard feelings, anger, and hostility. Its effects are short term, and it interferes with learning. In addition, it does not promote a caring relationship between student and teacher.

Alternatives to corporal punishment are not easy to implement. Teachers need training and support to discipline students with disruptive behaviors. The development and use of alternatives will occur when the paddle is taken away.

Teachers can teach effectively and schools can run peacefully without corporal punishment (Dunne, 1990). Students have fundamental rights to learn in a safe climate that is conducive to dignity. Education is the only profession that can legally hit its clients. If criminals are exempted from such measures, then let us also protect our children. It is time to end this violent practice in all our schools.

References

Baker v. Owen, 395 F. Supp. 294 (N.D. N.C. 1975), aff'd 403 907 (1975).

Braaten, S., Simpson, R., Rosell, J., & Reilly, T. (1988, Winter). Using punishment with exceptional children. *Teaching Exceptional Children, 21*(2), 79–81.

Brown, W. E. (1988). Policies/practices in public school discipline. *Academic Therapy, 23*(93), 298–301.

Cotham, D., Strauss, C., Vargas-Moll, I., & Hyman, I. (1987). *A study about attitudes toward corporal punishment in schools as it relates to race, sex, grade level and suspensions.* Paper presented at the 19th Annual Convention of the National Association of School Psychologists, New Orleans, LA.

Dunne, J. (1990, Spring). Clear Creek I.S.D. Trustee Margaret Snooks Speaks Out. *P.O.P.S. News: Newsletter of People Opposed to Paddling Students Inc.,* p. 4. (Available from P.O.P.S., P.O. Box 19045, Houston, TX 77224).

Eig, J. (1991, October 6). Hispanics punished more. *The Dallas Morning News,* p. 3.

Funkhouser, C. (1994). *Education in Texas: Policies, practices, and perspectives* (7th ed). Scottsdale, AR: Gorsuch Scarisbrick.

"I felt humiliated and violated."

(11th grader)

Groller, I. (1989, March). Spanking in schools: Americans are divided on corporal punishment in the classroom. *Parents,* p. 39.

Hyman, I. A. (1990). *Reading, writing and the hickory stick.* Lexington, MA: Lexington Books.

Ingraham v. Wright, 525 F. 2nd 248 (5 Cir. 1977).

Loddeke, L. (1991, October 22). Texas still #1 in paddling despite big drop in total. *Houston Post,* p. 21A.

Maurer, A. (Ed.). (1992, Spring). The handicapped. *The Last ? Resort: Newsletter of the Committee to End Violence Against the Next Generation, Inc.,* p. 9, (Available from End Violence Against the Next Generation, 977 Keeler Ave., Berkeley, CA 94708.)

Maurer, A. (Ed.). (1992–1993, Winter). Kentucky fails to keep its ban on paddles. *The Last ? Resort: Newsletter of the Committee to End Violence Against the Next Generation, Inc.,* p. 1.

Parents and Teachers Against Violence in Education (PTVE). (1990). *Understanding corporal punishment of school children.* Danville, CA: Author.

Pride, D. (1992, January 20). Tennessee No. 3 in use of paddling. *The Nashville Banner,* p. 6.

Rich, M. J. (1989, December). The use of corporal punishment. *The Clearing House, 63,* 142–152.

Rose, T. (1989). Corporal punishment with mildly handicapped students: Five years later. *Remedial and Special Education, 10*(1), 43–52.

Slate, J., Waldrop, P., & Justen, J. (1991). Corporal punishment used in a discriminatory manner. *The Clearing House, 64*(6), 361–364.

Waters, R. (1993, December). Mom, the teacher hit me. *Family Circle,* pp. 150–151, 192–196.

Zirpoli, T. J. (1990). Physical abuse: Are children with disabilities at greater risk? *Intervention, 25*(1), 6–11.

Elizabeth D. Evans *(CEC Chapter #846), Associate Professor, Department of Special Education, Southeastern Louisiana University, Hammond, Louisiana.* **Rita C. Richardson** *(CEC Chapter #1176), Associate Professor, Coordinator of Special Education, University of Texas at Brownsville, Brownsville, Texas.*

Assessment

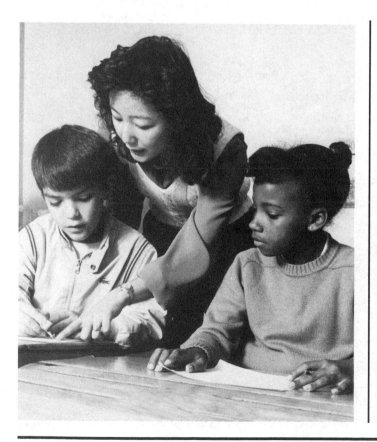

In which reading group does Jon belong? How do I construct tests? How do I know when my students have mastered the course objectives? How can I explain test results to Mary's parents? Teachers answer these questions, and many more, by applying principles of assessment. Assessment refers to procedures for measuring and recording student performance and constructing grades that communicate to other levels of proficiency or relative standing. Assessment principles constitute a set of concepts that are integral to the teaching-learning process. Indeed, a significant amount of teacher time is spent in assessment activities, and with more accountability has come a greater emphasis on assessment.

Assessment provides a foundation for making sound evaluative judgments about students' learning and achievement. Teachers need to use fair and unbiased criteria in order to assess student learning objectively and accurately and make appropriate decisions about student placement. For example, in assigning Jon to a reading group, the teacher will use his test scores as an indication of his skill level. Are the inferences from the test results valid for the school's reading program? Are his test scores consistent over several months or years? Are they consistent with his performance in class? The teacher should ask and then answer these questions so that he or she can make intelligent decisions about Jon. On the other hand, will knowledge of the test scores affect the teacher's perception of classroom performance and create a self-fulling prophecy? Teachers also evaluate students in order to assign grades, and the challenge is to balance "objective" test scores with more subjective, informally gathered information. Both kinds of evaluative information are necessary, but both can be inaccurate and are frequently misused.

The first article in this unit examines assessment principles in the context of large-scale and classroom assessment of young children. In "Making the Grade: What Benefits Students?" teachers' grading practices and procedures that benefit student learning and lead to accurate conclusions and reporting are reviewed. Teachers also need to differentiate between criterion-referenced grading for minimal objectives and using norms to evaluate achievement.

The next two essays discuss performance-based, "authentic" assessment. This form of assessment has great potential to integrate measurement procedures with instructional methods more effectively and to focus student learning on the application of thinking and problem-solving skills in real-life contexts. A related form of assessment, using portfolios, is described in "Planning for Classroom Portfolio Assessment."

In the last article, Blaine Worthen and Vicki Spandel review the characteristics and limitations of standardized aptitude tests. They provide suggestions for appropriate use of results from such tests.

Looking Ahead: Challenge Questions

What are some important principles for assessing young children? How is the purpose of the assessment related to these principles?

Many educators believe that schools should identify the brightest, most capable students. What are the assessment implications of this philosophy? How would low-achieving students be affected?

What is the essential difference between criterion-referenced and norm-referenced testing? What factors should be considered when deciding which approach to use?

What principles of assessment should teachers adopt for their own classroom testing? Is it necessary or feasible to develop a table of specifications for each test? How do we know if the tests teachers make are reliable and if valid inferences are drawn from the results?

How can teachers grade thinking skills such as analysis, application, and reasoning? How should objectives for student learning and grading be integrated? What are some grading practices to avoid? Why?

What are appropriate teacher uses of standardized test scores? What common mistakes do teachers make when interpreting these scores?

The Challenges of Assessing Young Children Appropriately

In the past decade, testing of 4-, 5-, and 6-year-olds has been excessive and inappropriate. Given this history of misuse, Ms. Shepard maintains, the burden of proof must rest with assessment advocates to demonstrate the usefulness of assessment and to ensure that abuses will not recur.

Lorrie A. Shepard

LORRIE A. SHEPARD is a professor of education at the University of Colorado, Boulder. She is past president of the National Council on Measurement in Education, past vice president of the American Educational Research Association, and a member of the National Academy of Education. She wishes to thank Sharon Lynn Kagan, M. Elizabeth Graue, and Scott F. Marion for their thoughtful suggestions on drafts of this article.

PROPOSALS to "assess" young children are likely to be met with outrage or enthusiasm, depending on one's prior experience and one's image of the testing involved. Will an inappropriate paper-and-pencil test be used to keep some 5-year-olds out of school? Or will the assessment, implemented as an ordinary part of good instruction, help children learn? A governor advocating a test for every preschooler in the nation may have in mind the charts depicting normal growth in the pediatrician's office. Why shouldn't parents have access to similar measures to monitor their child's cognitive and academic progress? Middle-class parents, sanguine about the use of test scores to make college-selection decisions, may be eager to have similar tests determine their child's entrance into preschool or kindergarten. Early childhood experts, however, are more likely to respond with alarm because they are more familiar with the complexities of defining and measuring

development and learning in young children and because they are more aware of the widespread abuses of readiness testing that occurred in the 1980s.

Given a history of misuse, it is impossible to make positive recommendations about how assessments could be used to monitor the progress of individual children or to evaluate the quality of educational programs without offering assurances that the abuses will not recur. In what follows, I summarize the negative history of standardized testing of young children in order to highlight the transformation needed in both the substance and purposes of early childhood assessment. Then I explain from a measurement perspective how the features of an assessment must be tailored to match the purpose of the assessment. Finally, I describe differences in what assessments might look like when they are used for purposes of screening for handicapping conditions, supporting instruction, or monitoring state and national trends.

Note that I use the term *test* when referring to traditional, standardized developmental and pre-academic measures and the term *assessment* when referring to more developmentally appropriate procedures for observing and evaluating young children. This is a semantic trick that plays on the different connotations of the two terms. Technically, they mean the same thing. Tests, as defined by the *Stan-*

dards for Educational and Psychological Testing, have always included systematic observations of behavior, but our experience is with tests as more formal, one-right-answer instruments used to rank and sort individuals. As we shall see, assessments might be standardized, involve paper-and-pencil responses, and so on, but in contrast to traditional testing, "assessment" implies a substantive focus on student learning for the purpose of effective intervention. While *test* and *assessment* cannot be reliably distinguished technically, the difference between these two terms as they have grown up in common parlance is of symbolic importance. Using the term *assessment* presents an opportunity to step away from past practices and ask why we should try to measure what young children know and can do. If there are legitimate purposes for gathering such data, then we can seek the appropriate content and form of assessment to align with those purposes.

Negative History of Testing Young Children

In order to understand the negative history of the standardized testing of young children in the past decade, we need to understand some larger shifts in curriculum and teaching practices. The distortion of the curriculum of the early grades dur-

From *Phi Delta Kappan*, November 1994, pp. 206-212. © 1994 by Phi Delta Kappa, Inc. Reprinted by permission.

ing the 1980s is now a familiar and well-documented story. Indeed, negative effects persist in many school districts today.

Although rarely the result of conscious policy decisions, a variety of indirect pressures — such as older kindergartners, extensive preschooling for children from affluent families, parental demands for the teaching of reading in kindergarten, and accountability testing in higher grades — produced a skill-driven kindergarten curriculum. Because what once were first-grade expectations were shoved down to kindergarten, these shifts in practice were referred to as the "escalation of curriculum" or "academic trickle-down." The result of these changes was an aversive learning environment inconsistent with the learning needs of young children. Developmentally inappropriate instructional practices, characterized by long periods of seatwork, high levels of stress, and a plethora of fill-in-the-blank worksheets, placed many children at risk by setting standards for attention span, social maturity, and academic productivity that could not be met by many normal 5-year-olds.

Teachers and school administrators responded to the problem of a kindergarten environment that was increasingly hostile to young children with several ill-considered policies: raising the entrance age for school, instituting readiness screening to hold some children out of school for a year, increasing retentions in kindergarten, and creating two-year programs with an extra grade either before or after kindergarten. These policies and practices had a benign intent: to protect children from stress and school failure. However, they were ill-considered because they were implemented without contemplating the possibility of negative side effects and without awareness that retaining some children and excluding others only exacerbated the problems by creating an older and older population of kindergartners.[1] The more reasonable corrective for a skill-driven curriculum at earlier and earlier ages would have been curriculum reform of the kind exemplified by the recommendations for developmentally appropriate practices issued by the National Association for the Education of Young Children (NAEYC), the nation's largest professional association of early childhood educators.[2]

The first response of many schools, however, was not to fix the problem of inappropriate curriculum but to exclude those children who could not keep up or who might be harmed. Readiness testing was the chief means of implementing policies aimed at removing young children from inappropriate instructional programs. Thus the use of readiness testing increased dramatically during the 1980s and continues today in many school districts.[3]

Two different kinds of tests are used: developmental screening measures, originally intended as the first step in the evaluation of children for potential handicaps; and pre-academic skills tests, intended for use in planning classroom instruction.[4] The technical and conceptual problems with these tests are numerous.[5] Tests are being used for purposes for which they were never designed or validated. Waiting a year or being placed in a two-year program represents a dramatic disruption in a child's life, yet not one of the existing readiness measures has sufficient reliability or predictive validity to warrant making such decisions.

Developmental and pre-academic skills tests are based on outmoded theories of aptitude and learning that originated in the 1930s. The excessive use of these tests and the negative consequences of being judged unready focused a spotlight on the tests' substantive inadequacies. The widely used Gesell Test is made up of items from old I.Q. tests and is indistinguishable statistically from a measure of I.Q.; the same is true for developmental measures that are really short-form I.Q. tests. Assigning children to different instructional opportunities on the basis of such tests carries forward nativist assumptions popular in the 1930s and

Illustration by Kay Salem

1940s. At that time, it was believed that I.Q. tests could accurately measure innate ability, unconfounded by prior learning experiences. Because these measured "capacities" were thought to be fixed and unalterable, those who scored poorly were given low-level training consistent with their supposedly limited potential. Tests of academic content might have the promise of being more instructionally relevant than disguised I.Q. tests, but, as Anne Stallman and David Pearson have shown, the decomposed and decontextualized prereading skills measured by traditional readiness tests are not compatible with current research on early literacy.[6]

Readiness testing also raises serious equity concerns. Because all the readiness measures in use are influenced by past opportunity to learn, a disproportionate number of poor and minority children are identified as unready and are excluded from school when they most need it. Thus children without preschool experience and without extensive literacy experiences at home are sent back to the very environments that caused them to score poorly on readiness measures in the first place. Or, if poor and minority children who do not pass the readiness tests are admitted to the school but made to spend an extra year in kindergarten, they suffer disproportionately the stigma and negative effects of retention.

The last straw in this negative account of testing young children is the evidence that fallible tests are often followed by ineffective programs. A review of controlled studies has shown no academic benefits from retention in kindergarten or from extra-year programs, whether developmental kindergartens or transitional first grades. When extra-year children finally get to first grade, they do not do better on average than equally "unready" children who go directly on to first grade.[7] However, a majority of children placed in these extra-year programs do experience some short- or long-term trauma, as reported by their parents.[8] Contrary to popular belief that kindergarten children are "too young to notice" retention, most of them know that they are not making "normal" progress, and many continue to make reference to the decision years later. "If I hadn't spent an extra year in kindergarten, I would be in __ grade now." In the face of such evidence, there is little wonder that many early childhood educators ask why we test young children at all.

Principles for Assessment And Testing

The NAEYC and the National Association of Early Childhood Specialists in State Departments of Education have played key roles in informing educators about the harm of developmentally inappropriate instructional practices and the misuse of tests. In 1991 NAEYC published "Guidelines for Appropriate Curriculum Content and Assessment in Programs Serving Children Ages 3 Through 8."[9] Although the detailed recommendations are too numerous to be repeated here, a guiding principle is that *assessments should bring about benefits for children, or data should not be collected at all.* Specifically, assessments "should not be used to recommend that children stay out of a program, be retained in grade, or be assigned to a segregated group based on ability or developmental maturity."[10] Instead, NAEYC acknowledges three legitimate purposes for assessment: 1) to plan instruction and communicate with parents, 2) to identify children with special needs, and 3) to evaluate programs.

Although NAEYC used *assessment* in its "Guidelines," as I do, to avoid associations with inappropriate uses of tests, both the general principle and the specific guidelines are equally applicable to formal testing. In other words, tests should not be used if they do not bring about benefits for children. In what follows I summarize some additional principles that can ensure that assessments (and tests) are beneficial and not harmful. Then, in later sections, I consider each of NAEYC's recommended uses for assessment, including national, state, and local needs for program evaluation and accountability data.

I propose a second guiding principle for assessment that is consistent with the NAEYC perspective. *The content of assessments should reflect and model progress toward important learning goals.* Conceptions of what is important to learn should take into account both physical and social/emotional development as well as cognitive learning. For most assessment purposes in the cognitive domain, content should be congruent with subject matter in emergent literacy and numeracy. In the past, developmental measures were made as "curriculum free" or "culture free" as possible in an effort to tap biology and avoid the confounding effects of past opportunity to learn. Of course, this was an impossible task because a child's ability to "draw a triangle"

or "point to the ball on top of the table" depends on prior experiences as well as on biological readiness. However, if the purpose of assessment is no longer to sort students into programs on the basis of a one-time measure of ability, then it is possible to have assessment content mirror what we want children to learn.

A third guiding principle can be inferred from several of the NAEYC guidelines. *The methods of assessment must be appropriate to the development and experiences of young children.* This means that — along with written products — observation, oral readings, and interviews should be used for purposes of assessment. Even for large-scale purposes, assessment should not be an artificial and decontextualized event; instead, the demands of data collection should be consistent with children's prior experiences in classrooms and at home. Assessment practices should recognize the diversity of learners and must be in accord with children's language development — both in English and in the native languages of those whose home language is not English.

A fourth guiding principle can be drawn from the psychometric literature on test validity. *Assessments should be tailored to a specific purpose.* Although not stated explicitly in the NAEYC document, this principle is implied by the recommendation of three sets of guidelines for three separate assessment purposes.

Matching the Why and How Of Assessment

The reason for any assessment — i.e., how the assessment information will be used — affects the substance and form of

> *The intended use of an assessment will determine the need for normative information or other means to support the interpretation of results.*

the assessment in several ways. First, the degree of technical accuracy required depends on use. For example, the identification of children for special education has critical implications for individuals. Failure to be identified could mean the denial of needed services, but being identified as in need of special services may also mean removal from normal classrooms (at least part of the time) and a potentially stigmatizing label. A great deal is at stake in such assessment, so the multifaceted evaluation employed must have a high degree of reliability and validity. Ordinary classroom assessments also affect individual children, but the consequences of these decisions are not nearly so great. An inaccurate assessment on a given day may lead a teacher to make a poor grouping or instructional decision, but such an error can be corrected as more information becomes available about what an individual child "really knows."

Group assessment refers to uses, such as program evaluation or school accountability, in which the focus is on group performance rather than on individual scores. Although group assessments may need to meet very high standards for technical accuracy, because of the high stakes associated with the results, the individual scores that contribute to the group information do not have to be so reliable and do not have to be directly comparable, so long as individual results are not reported. When only group results are desired, it is possible to use the technical advantages of matrix sampling — a technique in which each participant takes only a small portion of the assessment — to provide a rich, in-depth assessment of the intended content domain without overburdening any of the children sampled. When the "group" is very large, such as all the fourth-graders in a state or in the nation, then assessing a representative sample will produce essentially the same results for the group average as if every student had been assessed.

Purpose must also determine the content of assessment. When trying to diagnose potential learning handicaps, we still rely on aptitude-like measures designed to be as content-free as possible. We do so in order to avoid confusing lack of opportunity to learn with inability to learn. When the purpose of assessment is to measure actual learning, then content must naturally be tied to learning outcomes. However, even among achievement tests, there is considerable variability in the degree of alignment to a specif-

ic curriculum. Although to the lay person "math is math" and "reading is reading," measurement specialists are aware that tiny changes in test format can make a large difference in student performance. For example, a high proportion of students may be able to add numbers when they are presented in vertical format, but many will be unable to do the same problems presented horizontally. If manipulatives are used in some elementary classrooms but not in all, including the use of manipulatives in a mathematics assessment will disadvantage some children, while excluding their use will disadvantage others.

Assessments that are used to guide instruction in a given classroom should be integrally tied to the curriculum of that classroom. However, for large-scale assessments at the state and national level, the issues of curriculum match and the effect of assessment content on future instruction become much more problematic. For example, in a state with an agreed-upon curriculum, including geometry assessment in the early grades may be appropriate, but it would be problematic in states with strong local control of curriculum and so with much more curricular diversity.

Large-scale assessments, such as the National Assessment of Educational Progress, must include instructionally relevant content, but they must do so without conforming too closely to any single curriculum. In the past, this requirement has led to the problem of achievement tests that are limited to the "lowest common denominator." Should the instrument used for program evaluation include only the content that is common to all curricula? Or should it include everything that is in any program's goals? Although the common core approach can lead to a narrowing of curriculum when assessment results are associated with high stakes, including everything can be equally troublesome if it leads to superficial teaching in pursuit of too many different goals.

Finally, the intended use of an assessment will determine the need for normative information or other means to support the interpretation of assessment results. Identifying children with special needs requires normative data to distinguish serious physical, emotional, or learning problems from the wide range of normal development. When reporting to parents, teachers also need some idea of what constitutes grade-level performance, but such "norms" can be in the form

of benchmark performances — evidence that children are working at grade level — rather than statistical percentiles.

To prevent the abuses of the past, the purposes and substance of early childhood assessments must be transformed. Assessments should be conducted only if they serve a beneficial purpose: to gain services for children with special needs, to inform instruction by building on what students already know, to improve programs, or to provide evidence nationally or in the states about programmatic needs. The form, substance, and technical features of assessment should be appropriate for the use intended for assessment data. Moreover, the methods of assessment must be compatible with the developmental level and experiences of young children. Below, I consider the implications of these principles for three different categories of assessment purposes.

Identifying Children with Special Needs

I discuss identification for special education first because this is the type of assessment that most resembles past uses of developmental screening measures. However, there is no need for wholesale administration of such tests to all incoming kindergartners. If we take the precepts of developmentally appropriate practices seriously, then at each age level a very broad range of abilities and performance levels is to be expected and tolerated. If potential handicaps are understood to be relatively rare and extreme, then it is not necessary to screen all children for "hidden" disabilities. By definition, serious learning problems should be apparent. Although it is possible to miss hearing or vision problems (at least mild ones) without systematic screening, referral for evaluation of a possible learning handicap should occur only when parents or teachers notice that a child is not progressing normally in comparison to age-appropriate expectations. In-depth assessments should then be conducted to verify the severity of the problem and to rule out a variety of other explanations for poor performance.

For this type of assessment, developmental measures, including I.Q. tests, continue to be useful. Clinicians attempt to make normative evaluations using relatively curriculum-free tasks, but today they are more likely to acknowledge the fallibility of such efforts. For such difficult assessments, clinicians must have specialized training in both diagnostic assessment and child development.

When identifying children with special needs, evaluators should use two general strategies in order to avoid confounding the ability to learn with past opportunity to learn. First, as recommended by the National Academy Panel on Selection and Placement of Students in Programs for the Mentally Retarded,[11] a child's learning environment should be evaluated to rule out poor instruction as the possible cause of a child's lack of learning. Although seldom carried out in practice, this evaluation should include trying out other methods to support learning and possibly trying a different teacher before concluding that a child can't learn from ordinary classroom instruction. A second important strategy is to observe a child's functioning in multiple contexts. Often children who appear to be impaired in school function well at home or with peers. Observation outside of school is critical for children from diverse cultural backgrounds and for those whose home language is not English. The NAEYC stresses that "screening should never be used to identify second language learners as 'handicapped,' solely on the basis of their limited abilities in English."[12]

In-depth developmental assessments are needed to ensure that children with disabilities receive appropriate services. However, the diagnostic model of special education should not be generalized to a larger population of below-average learners, or the result will be the reinstitution of tracking. Elizabeth Graue and I analyzed recent efforts to create "at-risk" kindergartens and found that these practices are especially likely to occur when resources for extended-day programs are available only for the children most in need.[13] The result of such programs is often to segregate children from low socioeconomic backgrounds into classrooms where time is spent drilling on low-level prereading skills like those found on readiness tests. The consequences of dumbed-down instruction in kindergarten are just as pernicious as the effects of tracking at higher grade levels, especially when the at-risk kindergarten group is kept together for first grade. If resources for extended-day kindergarten are scarce, one alternative would be to group children heterogeneously for half the day and then, for the other half, to provide extra enrichment activities for children with limited literacy experiences.

Classroom Assessments

Unlike traditional readiness tests that are intended to predict learning, classroom assessments should support instruction by modeling the dimensions of learning. Although we must allow considerable latitude for children to construct their own understandings, teachers must nonetheless have knowledge of normal development if they are to support children's extensions and next steps. Ordinary classroom tasks can then be used to assess a child's progress in relation to a developmental continuum. An example of a developmental continuum would be that of emergent writing, beginning with scribbles, then moving on to pictures and random letters, and then proceeding to some letter/word correspondences. These continua are not rigid, however, and several dimensions running in parallel may be necessary to describe growth in a single content area. For example, a second dimension of early writing — a child's ability to invent increasingly elaborated stories when dictating to an adult — is not dependent on mastery of writing letters, just as listening comprehension, making predictions about books, and story retellings should be developed in parallel to, not after, mastery of letter sounds.

Although there is a rich research literature documenting patterns of emergent literacy and numeracy, corresponding assessment materials are not so readily available. In the next few years, national interest in developing alternative, performance-based measures should generate more materials and resources. Specifically, new Chapter 1 legislation is likely to support the development of reading assessments that are more authentic and instructionally relevant.

For example, classroom-embedded reading assessments were created from ordinary instructional materials by a group of third-grade teachers in conjunction with researchers at the Center for Research on Evaluation, Standards, and Student Testing.[14] The teachers elected to focus on fluency and making meaning as reading goals; running records and story summaries were selected as the methods of assessment.

But how should student progress be evaluated? In keeping with the idea of representing a continuum of proficiency, third-grade teachers took all the chapter books in their classrooms and sorted them into grade-level stacks, 1-1 (first grade, first semester), 1-2, 2-1, and so on up to

fifth grade. Then they identified representative or marker books in each category to use for assessment. Once the books had been sorted by difficulty, it became possible to document that children were reading increasingly difficult texts with understanding. Photocopied pages from the marker books also helped parents see what teachers considered to be grade-level materials and provided them with concrete evidence of their child's progress. Given mandates for student-level reporting under Chapter 1, state departments of education or test publishers could help develop similar systems of this type with sufficient standardization to ensure comparability across districts.

In the meantime, classroom teachers — or preferably teams of teachers — are left to invent their own assessments for classroom use. In many schools, teachers are already working with portfolios and developing scoring criteria. The best procedure appears to be having grade-level teams and then cross-grade teams meet to discuss expectations and evaluation criteria. These conversations will be more productive if, for each dimension to be assessed, teachers collect student work and use marker papers to illustrate continua of performance. Several papers might be used at each stage to reflect the tremendous variety in children's responses, even when following the same general progression.

Benchmark papers can also be an effective means of communicating with parents. For example, imagine using sample papers from grades K-3 to illustrate expectations regarding "invented spelling." Invented spelling or "temporary spelling" is the source of a great deal of parental dissatisfaction with reform curricula. Yet most parents who attack invented spelling have never been given a rationale for its use. That is, no one has explained it in such a way that the explanation builds on the parents' own willingness to allow successive approximations in their child's early language development. They have never been shown a connection between writing expectations and grade-level spelling lists or been informed about differences in rules for first drafts and final drafts. Sample papers could be selected to illustrate the increasing mastery of grade-appropriate words, while allowing for misspellings of advanced words on first drafts. Communicating criteria is helpful to parents, and, as we have seen in the literature on performance assessment, it also helps children to understand what is expected and to become better at assessing their own work.

Monitoring National and State Trends

In 1989, when the President and the nation's governors announced "readiness for school" as the first education goal, many early childhood experts feared the creation of a national test for school entry. Indeed, given the negative history of readiness testing, the first thing the Goal 1 Technical Planning Subgroup did was to issue caveats about what an early childhood assessment must *not* be. It should not be a one-dimensional, reductionist measure of a child's knowledge and abilities; it should not be called a measure of "readiness" as if some children were not ready to learn; and it should not be used to "label, stigmatize, or classify any individual child or group of children."[15]

However, with this fearsome idea set aside, the Technical Planning Subgroup endorsed the idea of an early childhood assessment system that would periodically gather data on the condition of young children as they enter school. The purpose of the assessment would be to inform public policy and especially to help "in charting progress toward achievement of the National Education Goals,

Beginning in 1998-99, a representative sample of 23,000 kindergarten students will be assessed and then followed through grade 5.

and for informing the development, expansion, and/or modification of policies and programs that affect young children and their families."[16] Assuming that certain safeguards are built in, such data could be a powerful force in focusing national attention and resources on the needs of young children.

Unlike past testing practices aimed at evaluating individual children in comparison with normative expectations, a large-scale, nationally representative assessment would be used to monitor national trends. The purpose of such an assessment would be analogous to the use of the National Assessment of Educational Progress (NAEP) to measure major shifts in achievement patterns. For example, NAEP results have demonstrated gains in the achievement of black students in the South as a result of desegregation, and NAEP achievement measures showed gains during the 1980s in basic skills and declines in higher-order thinking skills and problem solving. Similar data are not now available for preschoolers or for children in the primary grades. If an early childhood assessment were conducted periodically, it would be possible to demonstrate the relationship between health services and early learning and to evaluate the impact of such programs as Head Start.

In keeping with the precept that methods of assessment should follow from the purpose of assessment, the Technical Planning Subgroup recommended that sampling of both children and assessment items be used to collect national data. Sampling would allow a broad assessment of a more multifaceted content domain and would preclude the misuse of individual scores to place or stigmatize individual children. A national early childhood assessment should also serve as a model of important content. As a means to shape public understanding of the full range of abilities and experiences that influence early learning and development, the Technical Planning Subgroup identified five dimensions to be assessed: 1) physical well-being and motor development, 2) social and emotional development, 3) approaches toward learning, 4) language usage, and 5) cognition and general knowledge.

Responding to the need for national data to document the condition of children as they enter school and to measure progress on Goal 1, the U.S. Department of Education has commissioned the Early Childhood Longitudinal Study: Kindergarten Cohort. Beginning in the 1998-99 school year, a representative sample of 23,000 kindergarten students will be assessed and then followed through grade 5. The content of the assessments used will correspond closely to the dimensions recommended by the Technical Planning Subgroup. In addition, data will be collected on each child's family, communi-

ty, and school/program. Large-scale studies of this type serve both program evaluation purposes (How effective are preschool services for children?) and research purposes (What is the relationship between children's kindergarten experiences and their academic success throughout elementary school?).

National needs for early childhood data and local needs for program evaluation information are similar in some respects and dissimilar in others. Both uses require group data. However, a critical distinction that affects the methods of evaluation is whether or not local programs share a

Fearing that "assessment" is just a euphemism for more bad testing, many early childhood professionals have asked, Why test at all?

common curriculum. If local programs, such as all the kindergartens in a school district, have agreed on the same curriculum, it is possible to build program evaluation assessments from an aggregation of the measures used for classroom purposes. Note that the entire state of Kentucky is attempting to develop such a system by scoring classroom portfolios for state reporting.

If programs being evaluated do not have the same specific curricula, as is the case with a national assessment and with some state assessments, then the assessment measures must reflect broad, agreed-upon goals without privileging any specific curriculum. This is a tall order, more easily said than done. For this reason, the Technical Planning Subgroup recommended that validity studies be built into the procedures for data collection. For example, pilot studies should verify that what children can do in one-on-one assessment settings is consistent with what they can do in their classrooms, and assessment methods should always allow children more than one way to show what they know.

Conclusion

In the past decade, testing of 4-, 5-, and 6-year-olds has been excessive and inappropriate. Under a variety of different names, leftover I.Q. tests have been used to track children into ineffective programs or to deny them school entry. Prereading tests held over from the 1930s have encouraged the teaching of decontextualized skills. In response, fearing that "assessment" is just a euphemism for more bad testing, many early childhood professionals have asked, Why test at all? Indeed, given a history of misuse, the burden of proof must rest with assessment advocates to demonstrate the usefulness of assessment and to ensure that abuses will not recur. Key principles that support responsible use of assessment information follow.

• No testing of young children should occur unless it can be shown to lead to beneficial results.

• Methods of assessment, especially the language used, must be appropriate to the development and experiences of young children.

• Features of assessment — content, form, evidence of validity, and standards for interpretation — must be tailored to the specific purpose of an assessment.

• Identifying children for special education is a legitimate purpose for assessment and still requires the use of curriculum-free, aptitude-like measures and normative comparisons. However, handicapping conditions are rare; the diagnostic model used by special education should not be generalized to a larger population of below-average learners.

• For both classroom instructional purposes and purposes of public policy making, the content of assessments should embody the important dimensions of early learning and development. The tasks and skills children are asked to perform should reflect and model progress toward important learning goals.

In the past, local newspapers have published readiness checklists that suggested that children should stay home from kindergarten if they couldn't cut with scissors. In the future, national and local assessments should demonstrate the richness of what children do know and should foster instruction that builds on their strengths. Telling a story in conjunction with scribbles is a meaningful stage in literacy development. Reading a story in English and retelling it in Spanish is evidence of reading comprehension. Evidence of important learning in beginning mathematics should not be counting to 100 instead of to 10. It should be extending patterns; solving arithmetic problems with blocks and explaining how you got your answer; constructing graphs to show how many children come to school by bus, by walking, by car; and demonstrating understanding of patterns and quantities in a variety of ways.

In classrooms, we need new forms of assessment so that teachers can support children's physical, social, and cognitive development. And at the level of public policy, we need new forms of assessment so that programs will be judged on the basis of worthwhile educational goals.

1. Lorrie A. Shepard and Mary Lee Smith, "Escalating Academic Demand in Kindergarten: Counterproductive Policies," *Elementary School Journal*, vol. 89, 1988, pp. 135-45.

2. Sue Bredekamp, ed., *Developmentally Appropriate Practice in Early Childhood Programs Serving Children from Birth Through Age 8,* exp. ed. (Washington, D.C.: National Association for the Education of Young Children, 1987).

3. M. Therese Gnezda and Rosemary Bolig, *A National Survey of Public School Testing of Pre-Kindergarten and Kindergarten Children* (Washington, D.C.: National Forum on the Future of Children and Families, National Research Council, 1988).

4. Samuel J. Meisels, "Uses and Abuses of Developmental Screening and School Readiness Testing," *Young Children,* vol. 42, 1987, pp. 4-6, 68-73.

5. Lorrie A. Shepard and M. Elizabeth Graue, "The Morass of School Readiness Screening: Research on Test Use and Test Validity," in Bernard Spodek, ed., *Handbook of Research on the Education of Young Children* (New York: Macmillan, 1993), pp. 293-305.

6. Anne C. Stallman and P. David Pearson, "Formal Measures of Early Literacy," in Lesley Mandel Morrow and Jeffrey K. Smith, eds., *Assessment for Instruction in Early Literacy* (Englewood Cliffs, N.J.: Prentice-Hall, 1990), pp. 7-44.

7. Lorrie A. Shepard, "A Review of Research on Kindergarten Retention," in Lorrie A. Shepard and Mary Lee Smith, eds., *Flunking Grades: Research and Policies on Retention* (London: Falmer Press, 1989), pp. 64-78.

8. Lorrie A. Shepard and Mary Lee Smith, "Academic and Emotional Effects of Kindergarten Retention in One School District," in idem, pp. 79-107.

9. "Guidelines for Appropriate Curriculum Content and Assessment in Programs Serving Children Ages 3 Through 8," *Young Children*, vol. 46, 1991, pp. 21-38.

10. Ibid., p. 32.

11. Kirby A. Heller, Wayne H. Holtzman, and Samuel Messick, eds., *Placing Children in Special Education* (Washington, D.C.: National Academy Press, 1982).

12. "Guidelines," p. 33.

13. Shepard and Graue, op. cit.

14. The Center for Research on Evaluation, Standards, and Student Testing is located on the campuses of the University of California, Los Angeles, and the University of Colorado, Boulder.

15. *Goal 1: Technical Planning Subgroup Report on School Readiness* (Washington, D.C.: National Education Goals Panel, September 1991).

16. Ibid., p. 6.

Making the Grade:
What Benefits Students?

Thomas R. Guskey

Thomas R. Guskey is Professor of Education Policy Studies and Evaluation, College of Education, University of Kentucky, Lexington, KY 40506.

Although the debate over grading and reporting practices continues, today we know which practices benefit students and encourage learning.

Charged with leading a committee that would revise his school's grading and reporting system, Warren Middleton described his work this way:

> The Committee On Grading was called upon to study grading procedures. At first, the task of investigating the literature seemed to be a rather hopeless one. What a mass and a mess it all was! Could order be brought out of such chaos? Could points of agreement among American educators concerning the perplexing grading problem actually be discovered? It was with considerable misgiving and trepidation that the work was finally begun.

Few educators today would consider the difficulties encountered by Middleton and his colleagues to be particularly surprising. In fact, most probably would sympathize with his lament. What they might find surprising, however, is that this report from the Committee on Grading was published in 1933!

The issues of grading and reporting on student learning have perplexed educators for the better part of this century. Yet despite all the debate and the multitude of studies, coming up with prescriptions for best practice seems as challenging today as it was for Middleton and his colleagues more than 60 years ago.

Points of Agreement

Although the debate over grading and reporting continues, today we know better which practices benefit students and encourage learning. Given the multitude of studies—and their often incongruous results—researchers do appear to agree on the following points:

1. Grading and reporting aren't essential to instruction. Teachers don't need grades or reporting forms to teach well. Further, students don't need them to learn (Frisbie and Waltman 1992).

Teachers do need to check regularly on how students are doing, what they've learned, and what problems or difficulties they've experienced. But grading and reporting are different from checking; they involve judging the adequacy of students' performance at a specific time. Typically, teachers use checking to diagnose and prescribe and use grading to evaluate and describe (Bloom et al. 1981).

When teachers do both checking and grading, they become advocates as well as judges—roles that aren't necessarily compatible (Bishop 1992). Finding a meaningful compromise

between these dual roles makes many teachers uncomfortable, especially those with a child-centered orientation (Barnes 1985).

2. No one method of grading and reporting serves all purposes well. Grading enables teachers to communicate the achievements of students to parents and others, provide incentives to learn, and provide information that students can use for self-evaluation. In addition, schools use grades to identify or group students for particular educational paths or programs and to evaluate a program's effectiveness (Feldmesser 1971, Frisbie and Waltman 1992). Unfortunately, many schools attempt to address all of these purposes with a single method and end up achieving none very well (Austin and McCann 1992).

Letter grades, for example, briefly describe learning progress and give some idea of its adequacy (Payne 1974). Their use, however, requires abstracting a great deal of information into a single symbol (Stiggins 1994). In addition, the cut-off between grade categories is always arbitrary and difficult to justify. If scores for a grade of *B* range from 80 to 89, students at both ends of that range receive the same grade, even though their scores differ by nine points. But the student with a score of 79—a one-point difference—receives a grade of *C*.

The more detailed methods also have their drawbacks. Narratives and checklists of learning outcomes offer specific information for documenting progress, but good narratives take time to prepare, and—not surprisingly—as

Teachers don't need grades or reporting forms to teach well. Further, students don't need them to learn.

teachers complete more narratives, their comments become increasingly standardized. From the parents' standpoint, checklists of learning outcomes often appear too complicated to understand. In addition, checklists seldom communicate the appropriateness of students' progress in relation to expectations for their level (Afflerbach and Sammons 1991).

Because one method won't adequately serve all purposes, schools must identify their primary purpose for grading and select or develop the most appropriate approach (Cangelosi 1990). This process often involves the difficult task of seeking consensus among several constituencies.

3. Regardless of the method used, grading and reporting remain inherently subjective. In fact, the more detailed the reporting method and the more analytic the process, the more likely subjectivity will influence results (Ornstein 1994). That's why, for example, holistic scoring procedures tend to have greater reliability than analytic procedures.

Subjectivity in this process, however, isn't always bad. Because teachers know their students, understand various dimensions of students' work, and have clear notions of the progress made, their subjective perceptions may yield very accurate descriptions of what students have learned (Brookhart 1993, O'Donnell and Woolfolk 1991).

When subjectivity translates into bias, however, negative consequences can result. Teachers' perceptions of students' behavior can significantly influence their judgments of scholastic performance (Hills 1991). Students with behavior problems often have no chance to receive a high grade because their infractions overshadow their

performance. These effects are especially pronounced in judgments of boys (Bennett et al. 1993). Even the neatness of students' handwriting can significantly affect a teacher's judgment (Sweedler-Brown 1992).

Training programs can help teachers identify and reduce these negative effects and lead to greater consistency in judgments (Afflerbach and Sammons 1991). Unfortunately, few teachers receive adequate training in grading or reporting as part of their preservice experiences (Boothroyd and McMorris 1992). Also, few school districts provide adequate guidance to ensure consistency in teachers' grading or reporting practices (Austin and McCann 1992).

4. Grades have some value as rewards, but no value as punishments. Although educators would undoubtedly prefer that motivation to learn be entirely intrinsic, the existence of grades and other reporting methods are important factors in determining how much effort students put forth (Chastain 1990, Ebel 1979). Most students view high grades as positive recognition of their success, and some work hard to avoid the consequences of low grades (Feldmesser 1971).

At the same time, no studies support the use of low grades as punishments. Instead of prompting greater effort, low grades usually cause students to withdraw from learning. To protect their self-image, many students regard the low grade as irrelevant and meaningless. Other students may blame themselves for the low mark, but feel helpless to improve (Selby and Murphy 1992).

Sadly, some teachers consider grades or reporting forms their "weapon of last resort." In their view, students who don't comply with

requests suffer the consequences of the greatest punishment a teacher can bestow: a failing grade. Such practices have no educational value and, in the long run, adversely affect students, teachers, and the relationship they share. Rather than attempting to punish students with a low mark, teachers can better motivate students by regarding their work as incomplete and requiring additional effort.

5. Grading and reporting should always be done in reference to learning criteria, never on the curve. Using the normal probability curve as a basis for assigning grades typically yields greater consistency in grade distributions from one teacher to the next. The practice, however, is detrimental to teaching and learning.

Grading on the curve pits students against one another in a competition for the few rewards (high grades) distributed by the teacher. Under these conditions, students readily see that helping others will threaten their own chances for success (Johnson et al. 1979, Johnson et al. 1980). Learning becomes a game of winners and losers—with most students falling into the latter category (Johnson and Johnson 1989). In addition, modern research has shown that the seemingly direct relationship between aptitude or intelligence and school achievement depends upon instructional conditions, not a probability curve.

When the instructional quality is high and well matched to students' learning needs, the magnitude of this relationship diminishes drastically and approaches zero (Bloom 1976). Moreover, the fairness and equity of grading on the curve is a myth.

Learning Criteria

When grading and reporting relate to learning criteria, teachers have a clearer picture of what students have learned. Students and teachers alike generally prefer this approach because it seems fairer (Kovas 1993). The types of learning criteria usually used for grading and reporting fall into three categories:

■ *Product criteria* are favored by advocates of performance-based

A Look Back at Grading Practices

Although student assessment has been a part of teaching and learning for centuries, grading is a relatively recent phenomenon. The ancient Greeks used assessments as formative, not evaluative, tools. Students demonstrated, usually orally, what they had learned, giving teachers a clear indication of which topics required more work or instruction.

In the United States, grading and reporting were virtually unknown before 1850. Back then, most schools grouped students of all ages and backgrounds together with one teacher. Few students went beyond the elementary education offered in these one-room school-houses. As the country grew—and as legislators passed compulsory attendance laws—the number and diversity of students increased. Schools began to group students in grades according to their age, and to try new ideas about curriculum and teaching methods. Here's a brief timeline of significant dates in the history of grading:

Late 1800s: Schools begin to issue progress evaluations. Teachers simply write down the skills that students have mastered; once students complete the requirements for one level, they can move to the next level.

Early 1900s: The number of public high schools in the United States increases dramatically. While elementary teachers continue using written descriptions to document student learning, high school teachers introduce percentages as a way to certify students' accomplishments in specific subject areas. Few educators question the gradual shift to percentage grading, which seems a natural by-product of the increased demands on high school teachers.

1912: Starch and Elliott publish a study that challenges percentage grades as reliable measures of student achievement. They base their findings on grades assigned to two papers

written for a first-year English class in high school. Of the 142 teachers grading on a 0 to 100 scale, 15 percent give one paper a failing mark; 12 percent give the same paper a score of 90 or more. The other paper receives scores ranging from 50 to 97. Neatness, spelling, and punctuation influenced the scoring of many teachers, while others considered how well the paper communicated its message.

1913: Responding to critics—who argue that good writing is, by nature, a highly subjective judgment—Starch and Elliott repeat their study but use geometry papers. Even greater variations occur, with scores on one paper ranging from 28 to 95. Some teachers deducted points only for wrong answers, but others took neatness, form, and spelling into account.

1918: Teachers turn to grading scales with fewer and larger categories. One three-point scale, for example, uses the categories of Excellent, Average, and Poor. Another has five categories (Excellent, Good, Average, Poor, and Failing) with the corresponding letters of A, B, C, D, and F (Johnson 1918, Rugg 1918).

1930s: Grading on the curve becomes increasingly popular as educators seek to minimize the subjective nature of scoring. This method rank orders students according to some measure of their performance or proficiency. The top percentage receives an A, the next percentage receives a B, and so on (Corey 1930). Some advocates (Davis 1930) even specify the precise percentage of students to be assigned each grade, such as 6–22–44–22–6.

Grading on the curve seems fair and equitable, given research suggesting that students' scores on tests of innate intelligence approximate a normal probability curve (Middleton 1933).

As the debate over grading and reporting intensifies, a number of

schools abolish formal grades altogether (Chapman and Ashbaugh 1925) and return to using verbal descriptions of student achievement. Others advocate pass-fail systems that distinguish only between acceptable and failing work (Good 1937). Still others advocate a "mastery approach": Once students have mastered a skill or content, they move to other areas of study (Heck 1938, Hill 1935).

1958: Ellis Page investigates how student learning is affected by grades and teachers' comments. In a now classic study, 74 secondary school teachers administer a test, and assign a numerical score and letter grade of A, B, C, D, or F to each student's paper. Next, teachers randomly divide the tests into three groups. Papers in the first group receive only the numerical score and letter grade. The second group, in addition to the score and grade, receive these standard comments: *A—Excellent! B—Good work. Keep at it. C—Perhaps try to do still better? D—Let's bring this up. F—Let's raise this grade!* For the third group, teachers mark the score and letter grade, and write individualized comments.

Page evaluates the effects of the comments by considering students' scores on the next test they take. Results show that students in the second group achieved significantly higher scores than those who received only a score and grade. The students who received individualized comments did even better. Page concludes that grades can have a beneficial effect on student learning, but only when accompanied by specific or individualized comments from the teacher.

—*Thomas R. Guskey*

Source: H. Kirschenbaum, S. B. Simon, and R. W. Napier, (1971), *Wad-ja-get? The Grading Game in American Education*, (New York: Hart).

approaches to teaching and learning. These educators believe grading and reporting should communicate a summative evaluation of student achievement (Cangelosi 1990). In other words, they focus on what students know and are able to do at that time. Teachers who use product criteria often base their grades or reports exclusively on final examination scores, overall assessments, or other culminating demonstrations of learning.

■ *Process criteria* are emphasized by educators who believe product criteria don't provide a complete picture of student learning. From their perspective, grading and reporting should reflect not just the final results but also *how* students got there. Teachers who consider effort or work habits when reporting on student learning are using process criteria. So are teachers who take into consideration classroom quizzes, homework, class participation, or attendance.

■ *Progress criteria*, often referred to as "improvement scoring" and "learning gain," consider how much students have gained from their learning experiences. Teachers who use progress criteria look at *how far* students have come rather than where they are. As a result, scoring criteria may become highly individualized.

Teachers who base their grading and reporting procedures on learning criteria typically use some combination of the three types (Frary et al. 1993; Nava and Loyd 1992; Stiggins et al. 1989). Most researchers and measurement specialists, on the other hand, recommend using product criteria exclusively. They point out that the more process and progress criteria come into play, the more subjective and biased grades become (Ornstein 1994). How can a teacher know, for example, how difficult a task was for students or how hard they worked to complete it? If these criteria are included at all, most experts recommend they be reported separately (Stiggins 1994).

Practical Guidelines
Despite years of research, there's no evidence to indicate that one grading or reporting method works best under all conditions, in all circumstances. But in developing practices that seek to be fair, equitable, and useful to students, parents, and teachers, educators can rely on two guidelines:

■ *Provide accurate and understandable descriptions of learning.* Regardless of the method or form used, grading and reporting should communicate effectively what students have learned, what they can do, and whether their learning status is in line with expectations for that level. More

than an exercise in quantifying achievement, grading and reporting must be seen as a challenge in clear thinking and effective communication (Stiggins 1994).

■ *Use grading and reporting methods to enhance, not hinder, teaching and learning.* A clear, easily understood reporting form facilitates communication between teachers and parents. When both parties speak the same language, joint efforts to help students are likely to succeed. But developing such an equitable and understandable system will require the elimination of long-time practices such as averaging and assigning a zero to work that's late, missed, or neglected.

Averaging falls far short of providing an accurate description of what students have learned. For example, students often say, "I have to get a *B* on the final to pass this course." Such a comment illustrates the inappropriateness of averaging. If a final examination is truly comprehensive and students' scores accurately reflect what they've learned, why should a *B* level of performance translate to a *D* for the course grade?

Any single measure of learning can be unreliable. Consequently, most researchers recommend using several indicators in determining students' grades or marks—and most teachers concur (Natriello 1987). Nevertheless, the key question remains, "What information provides the most accurate depiction of students' learning at this time?" In nearly all cases, the answer is "the most current information." If students demonstrate that past assessment information doesn't accurately reflect their learning, new information must take its place. By continuing to rely on past assessment data, the grades can be misleading about a student's learning (Stiggins 1994).

Similarly, assigning a score of zero to work that is late, missed, or neglected doesn't accurately depict learning. Is the teacher certain the student has learned absolutely nothing, or is the zero assigned to punish students for not displaying appropriate responsibility (Canady and Hotchkiss

1989, Stiggins and Duke 1991)?

Further, a zero has a profound effect when combined with the practice of averaging. Students who receive a single zero have little chance of success because such an extreme score skews the average. That is why, for example, Olympic events such as gymnastics and ice skating eliminate the highest and lowest scores; otherwise, one judge could control the entire competition simply by giving extreme scores. An alternative is to use the median score rather than the average (Wright 1994), but use of the most current information remains the most defensible option.

Meeting the Challenge
The issues of grading and reporting on student learning continue to challenge educators today, just as they challenged Middleton and his colleagues in 1933. But today we know more than ever before about the complexities involved and how certain practices can influence teaching and learning.

What do educators need to develop grading and reporting practices that provide quality information about student learning? Nothing less than clear thinking, careful planning, excellent communication skills, and an overriding concern for the well being of students. Combining these skills with our current knowledge on effective practice will surely result in more efficient and more effective reporting.

References
Afflerbach, P., and R. B. Sammons. (1991). "Report Cards in Literacy Evaluation: Teachers' Training, Practices, and Values." Paper presented at the annual meeting of the National Reading Conference, Palm Springs, Calif.
Austin, S., and R. McCann. (1992). "'Here's Another Arbitrary Grade for your Collection': A Statewide Study of Grading Policies." Paper presented at the annual meeting of the American Educational Research Association, San Francisco.
Barnes, S. (1985). "A Study of Classroom Pupil Evaluation: The Missing Link in Teacher Education." *Journal of Teacher Education* 36, 4: 46–49.
Bennett, R. E., R. L. Gottesman, D. A. Rock, and F. Cerullo. (1993). "Influence of Behavior Perceptions and Gender on

Teachers' Judgments of Students' Academic Skill." *Journal of Educational Psychology*, 85: 347–356.

Bishop, J. H. (1992). "Why U.S. Students Need Incentives to Learn." *Educational Leadership* 49, 6: 15–18.

Bloom, B. S. (1976). *Human Characteristics and School Learning*. New York: McGraw-Hill.

Bloom, B. S., G. F. Madaus, and J. T. Hastings. (1981). *Evaluation to Improve Learning*. New York: McGraw-Hill.

Boothroyd, R. A., and R. F. McMorris. (1992). "What Do Teachers Know About Testing and How Did They Find Out?" Paper presented at the annual meeting of the National Council on Measurement in Education, San Francisco.

Brookhart, S. M. (1993). "Teachers' Grading Practices: Meaning and Values." *Journal of Educational Measurement* 30, 2: 123–142.

Canady, R. L., and P. R. Hotchkiss. (1989). "It's a Good Score! Just a Bad Grade." *Phi Delta Kappan* 71: 68–71.

Cangelosi, J. S. (1990). "Grading and Reporting Student Achievement." In *Designing Tests for Evaluating Student Achievement*, pp. 196–213. New York: Longman.

Chapman, H. B., and E. J. Ashbaugh. (October 7, 1925). "Report Cards in American Cities." *Educational Research Bulletin* 4: 289–310.

Chastain, K. (1990). Characteristics of Graded and Ungraded Compositions." *Modern Language Journal*, 74, 1: 10–14.

Corey, S. M. (1930). "Use of the Normal Curve as a Basis for Assigning Grades in Small Classes." *School and Society* 31: 514–516.

Davis, J. D. W. (1930). "Effect of the 6-22-44-22-6 Normal Curve System on Failures and Grade Values." *Journal of Educational Psychology* 22: 636–640.

Ebel, R. L. (1979). *Essentials of Educational Measurement* (3rd ed.). Englewood Cliffs, N.J.: Prentice Hall.

Feldmesser, R. A. (1971). "The Positive Functions of Grades." Paper presented at the annual meeting of the American Educational Research Association, New York.

Frary, R. B., L. H. Cross, and L. J. Weber. (1993). "Testing and Grading Practices and Opinions of Secondary Teachers of Academic Subjects: Implications for Instruction in Measurement." *Educational Measurement: Issues and Practices* 12, 3: 23–30.

Frisbie, D. A., and K. K. Waltman. (1992). "Developing a Personal Grading Plan." *Educational Measurement: Issues and Practices* 11, 3: 35–42.

Good, W. (1937). "Should Grades Be Abolished?" *Education Digest* 2, 4: 7–9.

Heck, A. O. (1938). "Contributions of Research to Classification, Promotion, Marking and Certification." Reported in *The Science Movement in Education (Part II), Twenty-Seventh Yearbook of the National Society for the Study of Education*. Chicago: University of Chicago Press.

Hill, G. E. (1935). "The Report Card in Present Practice." *Education Methods* 15, 3: 115–131.

Hills, J. R. (1991). "Apathy Concerning Grading and Testing." *Phi Delta Kappan* 72, 2: 540–545.

Johnson, D. W., and R. T. Johnson. (1989). *Cooperation and Competition: Theory and Research*. Endina, Minn.: Interaction.

Johnson, D. W., L. Skon, and R. T. Johnson. (1980). "Effects of Cooperative, Competitive, and Individualistic Conditions on Children's Problem-Solving Performance." *American Educational Research Journal* 17, 1: 83–93.

Johnson, R. H. (1918). "Educational Research and Statistics: The Coefficient Marking System." *School and Society* 7, 181: 714–116.

Johnson, R. T., D. W. Johnson, and M. Tauer. (1979). "The Effects of Cooperative, Competitive, and Individualistic Goal Structures on Students' Attitudes and Achievement." *Journal of Psychology* 102: 191–198.

Kovas, M. A. (1993). "Make Your Grading Motivating: Keys to Performance-Based Evaluation." *Quill and Scroll* 68, 1: 10–11.

Middleton, W. (1933). "Some General Trends in Grading Procedure." *Education* 54, 1: 5–10.

Natriello, G. (1987). "The Impact of Evaluation Processes On Students." *Educational Psychologists* 22: 155–175.

Nava, F. J. G., and B. H. Loyd. (1992). "An Investigation of Achievement and Nonachievement Criteria in Elementary and Secondary School Grading." Paper presented at the annual meeting of the American Educational Research Association, San Francisco.

O'Donnell, A., and A. E. Woolfolk. (1991). "Elementary and Secondary Teachers' Beliefs About Testing and Grading."

Paper presented at the annual meeting of the American Psychological Association, San Francisco.

Ornstein, A. C. (1994). "Grading Practices and Policies: An Overview and Some Suggestions." *NASSP Bulletin* 78, 559: 55–64.

Page, E. B. (1958). "Teacher Comments and Student Performance: A Seventy-Four Classroom Experiment in School Motivation." *Journal of Educational Psychology* 49: 173–181.

Payne, D. A. (1974). *The Assessment of Learning*. Lexington, Mass.: Heath.

Rugg, H. O. (1918). "Teachers' Marks and the Reconstruction of the Marking System." *Elementary School Journal* 18, 9: 701–719.

Selby, D., and S. Murphy. (1992). "Graded or Degraded: Perceptions of Letter-Grading for Mainstreamed Learning-Disabled Students." *British Columbia Journal of Special Education* 16, 1: 92–104.

Starch, D., and E. C. Elliott. (1912). "Reliability of the Grading of High School Work in English." *School Review* 20: 442–457.

Starch, D., and E. C. Elliott. (1913). "Reliability of the Grading of High School Work in Mathematics." *School Review* 21: 254–259.

Stewart, L. G., and M. A. White. (1976). "Teacher Comments, Letter Grades, and Student Performance." *Journal of Educational Psychology* 68, 4: 488–500.

Stiggins, R. J. (1994). "Communicating with Report Card Grades." In *Student-Centered Classroom Assessment*, pp. 363–396. New York: Macmillan.

Stiggins, R. J., and D. L. Duke. (1991). "District Grading Policies and Their Potential Impact on At-risk Students." Paper presented at the annual meeting of the American Educational Research Association, Chicago.

Stiggins, R. J., D. A. Frisbie, and P. A. Griswold. (1989). "Inside High School Grading Practices: Building a Research Agenda." *Educational Measurement: Issues and Practice* 8, 2: 5–14.

Sweedler-Brown, C. O. (1992). "The Effect of Training on the Appearance Bias of Holistic Essay Graders." *Journal of Research and Development in Education* 26, 1: 24–29.

Wright, R. G. (1994). "Success for All: The Median Is the Key." *Phi Delta Kappan* 75, 9: 723–725.

Creating Tests Worth Taking

The Director of Research at CLASS provides questions, criteria, and suggestions for test designers who want to engage students as well as evaluate their performance.

GRANT WIGGINS

Grant Wiggins is the Director of Research and Programs for the Center on Learning, Assessment, and School Structure (CLASS), 39 Main St., Geneseo, NY 14454. These design ideas derive from the work of CLASS in Frederick County, Md.; South Orange-Maplewood, N.J.; Urbandale, Iowa.; and with faculties in Monroe, Orange, Suffolk, Ulster, and Wayne counties, N.Y.

Should a test be enticing? I think so. And should tests more often be authentic simulations of how knowledge is tested in adult work and civic settings? Many of us believe so. "Performance assessment" calls upon test makers to be creative designers then, not just technicians.

In performance assessment the design issues resemble those facing the architect. There is ground to be covered (the syllabus), there are the logistics of making the design fit the site (making large-scale assessment work in the school), and there are building codes (psychometric norms) and town elders (school board members and district testing directors) to worry about. But designers have typically avoided another, more basic obligation: the need to serve the users — in this case, students and teachers. The clients must "own" the design; form must follow function. The more the tasks (like the house) fit seamlessly with both the environment and the client's aspirations, the better the design and the result.

In this article I offer some proven design tips, tools, and criteria for fashioning assessment tasks that are more enticing, feasible, and defensible — tests worth taking.

Questions and Criteria

Designers of performance assessments should use the following key questions as a tool to guide the design process:

• What kinds of essential tasks, achievements, habits of mind, or other valued "masteries" are falling through the cracks of conventional tests?

• What are the core performances, roles, or situations that all students should encounter and be expected to master?

• What are the most salient and insightful discriminators in judging actual performances?

• What does genuine mastery of each proposed assessment task look like? Do we have credible and appropriate exemplars to anchor our scoring system? Have we justified standards so they are more than local norms?

• Are the test's necessary constraints — imposed on help available from others, access to resources, time to revise, test secrecy, prior knowledge of standards —authentic?

• Do our assessment tasks have sufficient depth and breadth to allow valid generalizations about overall student competence?

• Have we ensured that the test will not be corrupted by well-intentioned judges of student work?

• Who are the audiences for assessment information, and how should assessment be designed, conducted, and reported to accommodate the needs of each audience? When are audit-tests appropriate and inappropriate?

These questions can be summarized and reframed to produce eight basic design criteria:

1. Assessment tasks should be, whenever possible, authentic and meaningful — worth mastering.

2. The set of tasks should be a valid sample from which apt generalizations about overall performance of complex capacities can be made.

3. The scoring criteria should be authentic, with points awarded or taken off for essential successes and errors, not for what is easy to count or observe.

4. The performance standards that anchor the scoring should be genuine benchmarks, not arbitrary cut scores or provincial school norms.

5. The context of the problems should be rich, realistic, and enticing — with the inevitable constraints on access to time, resources, and advance knowledge of the tasks and standards appropriately minimized.

6. The tasks should be validated.

7. The scoring should be feasible and reliable.

8. Assessment results should be reported and used so that *all* customers for the data are satisfied.

The suggestions and observations that follow offer further assistance to would-be designers.

Choosing What to Test

Choose exit outcomes or areas of the curriculum that now tend to fall through the cracks of conventional testing. Typical tests, even demanding ones, tend to overassess student "knowledge" and underassess student "know-how with knowledge" — that is, intellectual performance. Auditing local tests with Bloom's taxonomy as criteria, for example, shows that synthesis is infrequently assessed at present, and is *inherently resistant* to assessment by multiple-choice tests because it requires "production of a unique communication" that bears the stamp of the student.[1]

Faculties should also consider their institutional "customers." What kinds of tasks must our *former* students master? Here, for example, is a question from a freshman final exam in European history at a prestigious college; it suggests how even our better students are often ill-prepared for real intellectual tasks:

> Imagine yourself Karl Marx, living half a century later. Write a brief evaluation of the programs of the Fabian socialists and the American reformers such as T. Roosevelt to present to the Socialist International.

Think of the knowledge to be tested as a tool for fashioning a performance or product. Successful task design requires making the essential material

of a course a *necessary means* to a successful performance *end*. Example: a 5th grade teacher assesses geography knowledge by having his students devise a complete itinerary, map, and travel packet for their favorite rock group's world tour, within certain budget, logistical, cultural, and demographic restrictions.

Another example: students are asked to design a museum exhibit around a theme studied in a history course, selecting from many real or facsimile artifacts; required to justify what is both included and excluded in the exhibit; and must seek funding from a "foundation" of teachers and peers for the exhibit.

We want to know: Can the student use knowledge and resources effectively, *to achieve a desired effect*? This is the question Bloom and his colleagues argued was at the heart of synthesis. These tasks should only be judged well done to the extent that the content is well used.

Designing the Tasks

Contextualize the task. The aim is to invent an authentic simulation, and like all simulations, case studies, or experiential exercises, the task must be rich in contextual detail. A context is rich if it supports multiple approaches, styles, and solutions and requires good judgments in achieving an effective result. One must please a real audience, make a design actually work, or achieve an aesthetic effect that causes pride or dismay in the result.

The test may be a contrivance, but it needn't *feel* like one.[2] Consider professional training and testing. Doctors and pilots in training confront situations that replicate the challenges to be later faced. Business and law students learn by the case method, fully immersed in the facts of real past cases. A context is realistic to the extent that we so accept the premises, constraints, and "feel" of the challenge that our desire to master it makes us lose sight of the extrinsic factors and motives at stake — namely that someone is evaluating us. In just this way, for example, putting out a school newspaper for a journalism course doesn't feel contrived.

Here's an example of how a teacher's attempt to design a performance task evolved as a concern for context was introduced. The original task, in a global studies course, required students to design a trip to China or Japan. But what kind of trip? For what customers? With what constraints of budget or time? The teacher then refined the task so that each student had a $10,000 budget for **designing a month-long, cultural-exchange trip for students their age. Still, the purpose is too abstract.** What must the tour designers accomplish? Are they trying to design a tour in the abstract or really attract tour-takers? The students were finally charged to be travel agents who develop an extensive brochure and research the cost and logistical information using a computer reservations system.

There is no such thing as performance-in-general. To understand what *kind* and *precision* of answer fits the problem at hand, the student needs contextual detail: it clarifies the desired result, hence the criteria and standards. Too many measurement tasks have an acceptable margin of error that is arbitrary. Are we measuring body temperature or roasts in the oven? It matters. The task's standard of performance (desired precision or quality of product) should be apparent. In fact, an important oversight by the global studies teacher was her failure to give the students model tour brochures.[3]

Aim to design "meaningful" tasks — not the same as "immediately relevant or practical" tasks. An assessment task will be meaningful to the extent that it provokes thought and thus engages the student's interest. But a task can be engaging without being of apparent, immediate usefulness. Whether it be mysteries, debates, mock trials, putting on plays — or, for that matter, Nintendo — students clearly respond to "irrelevant" but real challenges. What do such tasks have in common? Designers need to conduct better

empirical studies to discover the tasks that tap those twin intellectual needs: *our urge for efficacy and our need for meaningful connections.*

This caution about meaning vs. relevance is particularly warranted to avoid turning important theoretical problems into crude utilitarian ones. Many genuine problems do not have obvious practical value, but they nonetheless evoke interest and provide insight into student abilities. Consider two such problems, one in geometry and one in history/English:

We all know the Pythagorean theorem: $A^2 + B^2 = C^2$; but does it have to be a square that we draw on each leg? Suppose we drew the same shape on each leg; would the areas on A and B add up to the area on C? Find other shapes that make the equation work, too, and try to derive a more general formula of the theorem.[4]

You and your colleagues (groups of 3 or 4) have been asked to submit a proposal to write a U.S. history textbook for middle school students. The publishers demand two things: that the book hit the most important things, and that it be interesting to students. Because of your expertise in 18th-century American history, you will provide them a draft chapter on the 18th century, up to but not including the Revolution, and "field tested" on some middle school students. They also ask that you fill in an "importance" chart with your response to these questions: (1) Which event, person, or idea is most important in this time period, and why? (2) Which of three sources of history — ideas, people, events — is most important? You will be expected to justify your choices of "most important" and to demonstrate that the target population will likely be interested in your book.

Design performances, not drills. A test of many items (a drill) is not a test of knowledge in use. "Performance" is not just doing simplistic tasks that cue us for the desired bit of knowledge. It entails "putting it all together" with good judgment; good judgment cannot be tested through isolated, pat drills. As one teacher put it to me a few years ago: "The

trouble with kids today is that they don't know what to do when they don't know what to do." She is right — and a prime reason is that tests rarely put students in an authentic performance situation, where *thinking,* not just an obvious bit of knowledge, is required.

The designer's aim, then, is to avoid inventing a new round of (this time, hands-on) isolated items. Rather, we should consider the difference between drilled ability vs. performance ability and ask: *What is the equivalent of the game or recital in each subject matter?* What does the "doing" of mathematics, history, science, art, language use, and so forth, look and feel like in context? What are the projects and other kinds of synthesizing tasks performed all the time by professionals, consumers, or citizens that can be adapted to school use?

Such tasks are always "higher-order," and we would do well to use Lauren Resnick's criteria in our search for better-designed assessments. Higher-order thinking

• is *nonalgorithmic* — that is, the path of action is not fully specified in advance;

• is *complex*, with the total path not visible from any single vantage point;

• often yields *multiple solutions,* each with costs and benefits;

• involves *nuanced judgment* and interpretation;

• involves the *application of multiple criteria*, which sometimes conflict with one another;

• often involves *uncertainty*, because not everything that bears on the task is known;

• involves *self-regulation* of the thinking process, rather than coaching at each step;

• involves *imposing meaning*, finding structure in apparent disorder;

• is *effortful*, with considerable mental work involved.[5]

It may help to think of this problem as the search for larger, more interrelated but complex chunks of content to build tasks around. What, for example, might be 8 to 10 important performance tasks in a subject that effectively and efficiently "map" the essential content? Vocational programs usually grapple well with this problem by casting the course objectives as a set of increasingly complex tasks to be mastered, in which the student in the last task(s) must literally put it all together, for example, build a house in carpentry.

Refine the tasks you design by building them backwards from the models and scoring criteria. A complex task is not a vague task, with the objective or specifications unknown. All real-world performers know the target and the standards, not just their task in advance; such knowledge guides their training and

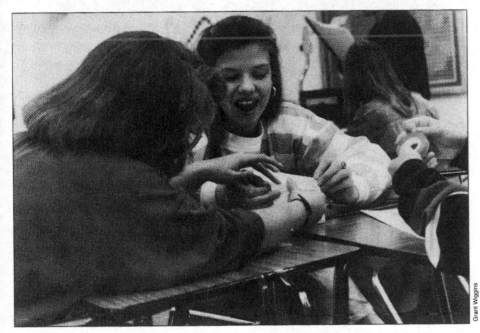

Grant Wiggins

rehearsals. Students should never have to wonder "Is this right?" "Am I finished?" "How am I doing?" "Is this what you want?" In a "real" problem the task is ill-structured but well-defined: the goal, specifications, or desired effect is known, but it is not obvious how to meet it. Knowing the *requirements of task mastery* — the "specs" — means the student must be habituated by testing to think of mastery as control over the *knowable* essentials, not as calculated cramming and good guesses. This requires providing the student with scoring criteria and models of excellent performance or production as part of instruction. (Think of diving and

debate.) Such practice is the norm throughout Carleton, Ontario, where students work from "exemplar booklets" to practice grading student work — in the same way now reserved for judges in our assessments.

"What does mastery at the task look like? What will we be able to properly infer from the collected student work?" These become the *key* questions to ask in the challenge of taking a basic idea and making a valid performance-assessment task out of it (as opposed to an instructional task). The questions properly focus on judging anticipated results and move away from design that produces merely pleasant or interesting work.

Scoring Considerations

Score what is most important for doing an effective job, not what is easiest to score. The scoring rubrics should represent generalizations about the traits found in an array of actual performances. But too often we resort to scoring what is easiest — or least controversial — to observe. A fine task can be rendered inauthentic by such bogus criteria.

Two key questions for setting up a scoring system therefore are: "What are the most salient characteristics of each level or quality of response?" and "What are the errors that are

most *justifiable* for use in lowering a score?" Obvious successes and errors (such as those that relate to spelling or computation) are not necessarily the most accurate indicators of mastery or its absence.[6] Too many essay scoring systems reward students for including merely *more* arguments or examples; quantity is not quality, and we teach a bad lesson by such scoring practices.

When possible, scoring criteria should rely on descriptive language, not evaluative and/or comparative language such as "excellent" or "fair." Judges should know specifically where in performance to look and what to look for. The ACTFL foreign language proficiency guidelines and the Victoria, Australia, "Literacy Profiles" are perhaps the best examples available of such empirically grounded criteria.[7] Teachers may also want to have students analyze a task and help devise the scoring system. This builds ownership of the evaluation, makes it clear that judgments need not be arbitrary, and makes it possible to hold students to higher standards because criteria are clear and reasonable.

"Benchmark" the standards for performance to ensure that your scoring standards are wisely chosen and suited to wider-world or next-level demands. Standard-setting for performance involves selecting exemplary samples of performance or production. The challenge is to avoid using local age-grade norms; the solution is to equate our exit-level standards at desirable colleges or professions. That advice, of course, begs a more fundamental question: Whose view of excellence should count? It is at least prudent to equate local standards of scoring to some credible wider-world or next-level standard—something routinely done in the performing arts, athletics, and vocational education.[8] *And, every so often, refer to next-level standards when scoring the work of younger students.* (I believe Illinois was the first state to assess both 6th and 8th grade writing samples against 8th grade exemplars, for instance.)

6. ASSESSMENT

Administering the Assessments

Since constraints always exist in testing, make them as authentic as possible. The question is not "Should there be constraints in testing?" but rather "When are constraints authentic, and when are they inauthentic?" It is often a matter of degree, but the principle needs to be maintained and defended.

Constraints facing the designer of authentic assessment tasks typically involve access or restrictions to the following resources: (1) time (including time to prepare, rethink, and revise), (2) reference material, (3) other people (including access to peers, experts, the test designer, and/or the judge), and (4) prior knowledge of the tasks and how they will be assessed (the issue of test security). The question then becomes: What are *appropriate* limits on the availability of these resources?

Traditional testing, because it involves indirect proxies for performance, requires numerous inauthentic constraints to preserve validity. The validity of most multiple-choice tests, for example, is compromised if questions are known in advance or if reference material can be consulted during the test. These habits of administration run deep; they seem obviously required. But what of the validity issues raised by denying students access to basic resources? Just what is being tested when the student cannot predict the historical periods or books that will be assessed, or cannot consult resources while writing?

We need not keep textbooks and other materials from students if the task is genuinely authentic. For example, in many of Connecticut's performance tasks in mathematics, the key formulas are given to the student as background to the problem. And why not allow the student to bring notes to the exam? A physics teacher I know allows students to bring an index card to the exam with anything on it; the card often reveals more about the student's knowledge than the exam answers!

Too little time for performing is not always the key issue either. Is the

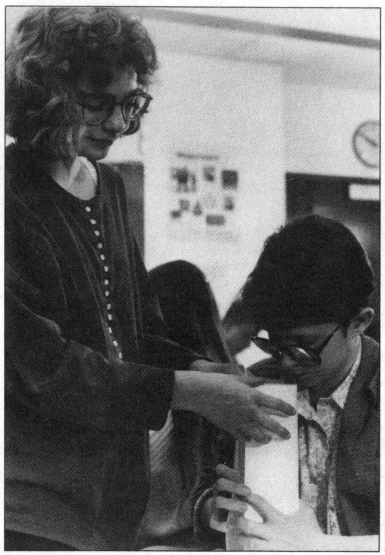

Grant Wiggins

limiting of the test to *one sitting* authentic? If writing is indeed revision, for example, why not allow writing assessment to occur over three days, with each draft graded? Many districts now do so, including Jefferson County, Kentucky, and Cherry Creek, Colorado.[9]

I am not arguing that the student should have unlimited time and access in testing.[10] Let us ask: What kinds of constraints authentically simulate or replicate the constraints and opportunities facing the performer in context? What kinds of constraints tend to bring out the best in apprentice performers and producers?

Develop a written, thorough protocol that details how the task should be administered — especially so judges will know the proper limits of their interventions to student acts, comments, or questions. It is incred-

ibly easy to invalidate performance assessment by varying the instructions, the amount of assistance provided, and the depth of responses given to inevitable student questions. Determining beforehand what is acceptable response and intervention by adults is essential; test administrators must receive standard verbal responses for delicate situations, confusions, or problems that arise.

And don't forget that kids can do the darndest things with directions that aren't thought through. In a hands-on science experiment that asked whether "the sun" heated up different colored liquids at different rates, a student did not use the heat lamp provided, moved all his equipment to the window, saw it was a cloudy day, and wrote "no."

Make the tasks maximally self-sustaining and the record-keeping obligation mostly the student's. Many educators who have never seen large-scale performance assessment cannot fathom how all students can be efficiently and effectively assessed. But they assume that the teacher will have to guide activity every step of the way and record massive amounts of information simultaneously. Thoughtful preparation, designed to make the assessment self-running, frees the teacher to be a perceptive judge.

Creating a Tool Kit

Develop a districtwide "tool kit" of exemplary tasks, task templates, and design criteria for assessment tasks. Not all of us are good designers, but why should we have to be? Teachers can help their colleagues by providing a sampler of tasks and task templates. Kentucky has done this at the statewide level, providing dozens of tasks and task ideas to teachers as part of the new state performance-based assessment system. We should consider including not only current examples of model assessment tasks, but traditional performance-based challenges such as debates, treasure hunts, mysteries, design competitions, historical reenactments, science fairs, Odyssey of the Mind tasks, Scout Merit Badges, student-run banks and stores, and so forth.

The mathematics performance assessment team of the Connecticut Department of Education has identified the following types of problems as central to its work:

- Given data on graphs, write a story that represents the data or graph.
- Given headlines or claims with background data, explain whether or not the claims are reasonable.
- Given student work containing common errors, write a response to the student.
- Given equations or number facts, write a problem that the equations or facts could solve.
- Given trends or sample data, make and justify predictions.
- Given consumer- or job-related buying, selling, or measuring situations, solve a problem.

- Given multiple or competing interpretations of given data, justify each interpretation.

Job roles provide ample opportunities for task designers to create simulations. Here are some suggestions.

- Museum curator: design museum exhibits; compete for "grant" money.
- Engineer or surveyor: bid and meet specs for largest-volume oil container; build a working roller coaster; map or survey a region around school or in the building.
- Ad agency director: design advertising campaigns, book jackets, or blurbs for books read in class.
- Psychologist/sociologist: conduct surveys, perform statistical analyses, graph results, write newspaper articles on the meaning of results.
- Archaeologist: determine the culture or time frame of a mystery artifact or person.
- Newspaper editor and writer: write articles and editorials set in the studied historical time.
- Policy analyst: predict the future in a country being studied.
- Product designer: conduct research, design ad campaign, present proposal to panel.
- Job interviewee: present portfolio and try to get "hired" for a specific job related to skills of current course (interview conducted by other students or teacher).
- Expert witness to Congress: testify on behalf of or against advertising claims, regulation of children's TV, or current policy issue.
- Commercial designer: Propose artwork for public buildings.

Piloting and Reporting

Always pilot some or all of the test. Assessment design is like software design: one can *never* accurately and fully anticipate the naive user's response. A first design may not fit the purpose or maximally evoke the desired knowledge; a prompt might result in irrelevant responses that are nonetheless appropriate or reasonable to the student; the logistical constraints of a context can turn out to be more daunting than anticipated; the judges may be too self-interested in

the results or insufficiently trained. A pilot is the only way to find out, even if it involves only a tiny sample of performers. And the de-bugging requires a *naive* "guinea pig" — a teacher from a different subject or a few students — if the hidden problems in the goal, directions, or procedures are to be found.

You are what you report: Make sure that your report cards, transcripts, and district accountability reports relate achievement and progress to essential performance tasks and exit-level standards. Few transcripts reflect achievement in reference to outcomes. They tend to certify that tests were passed on each isolated packet of content instead of documenting what the student can do and to what level of performance. Further, a one-shot test cannot validly assess many important capacities, as the phrases "habits of mind" or "consistency of performance" suggest. Grading and reporting thus need to move toward scoring that provides a "progress" measure — that is, work scored against exit-level performance standards. And no worthy performance is reducible to one aggregate score. Every student ought to have the equivalent of a baseball card — many different kinds of abilities measured and a brief narrative report — if we are seriously interested in accurately documenting and improving complex performance.

Assessment's Role in School Reform

An underlying premise of this kind of assessment reveals why I believe that assessment reform is the Trojan horse of real school reform. We badly need better definitions of mastery or *understanding* to guide assessment design, curriculum design, and teacher job descriptions and performance appraisal. Circling "correct" answers to problems only test makers care about is not "knowing," nor is it the aim of teaching. Authentic tests provide a stimulating challenge instead of an onerous obligation.

Perhaps more important for school restructuring is the need to build local

Horace's School: Redesigning the American High School

Theodore R. Sizer
Boston:
Houghton Mifflin Company, 1992

This book is a valuable tool for a school in the midst of a major assessment/restructuring process. Presented as an extended case study centering around the fictional teacher, Horace Smith, the book follows Horace through a series of restructuring committee meetings he is chairing at Franklin High School.

The meetings accurately capture the blend of tedium and excitement characteristic of the committee process. Flowing from the discussions of what it means to be well educated and how to best provide this education are several examples of "exhibitions." These are the means whereby students demonstrate their understanding of ideas and skills underlying the school's newly devised program. The exhibitions provide readers Sizer's best examples of performance assessments for high school students.

Interspersed with Sizer's commentary is his narrative. It is here I found him at his best. The chapter "Policy and Power" is as cogent and heartfelt a statement about reform as I have read.

The book draws from years of research and the author's work with the Coalition of Essential Schools. Sizer delineates the Coalition's "nine common principles," which recognize there is no one way for a good school to look or proceed. Likewise, there are no shortcuts in the restructuring process, especially as it seeks to challenge the underlying principles of our current schools. This book sheds light on the reform process and helps clarify the challenge. The rest is up to us.

Available from Houghton Mifflin Company, Two Park St., Boston, MA 02108, for $19.95 (paperback).

— *Reviewed by Stephen Garger, University of Portland, Portland, Oregon.*

educator capacity and interest in quality assessment.[11] Genuine faculty empowerment is impossible without deep ownership of local standards and measures. Farming all these problems out to distant "experts" is a grave mistake — one rarely made in any other country. Good teaching is inseparable from good assessing. It may well be that experts can design more rigorous tests, and that correlational/predictive validities exist in standardized tests. But schooling we can be proud of and held genuinely accountable for demands more locally useful, authentic, and enticing assessments.

---

[1]Bloom, (1954), pp. 163, 175. Serious would-be test designers would do well to reread the *text* of the taxonomy, not just the Appendix/list, as well as the follow-up handbook developed by Bloom, Madaus, and Hastings, (1981).

[2]"The student should [have] freedom from excessive tension . . . be made to feel that the product of his efforts need not conform to the views of the instructor . . . [and] have considerable freedom of activity . . . [including] freedom to determine the materials or other elements that go into the final product." In Bloom, (1954), p. 173.

[3]See Linn, Baker, and Dunbar, (1991), for further discussion of validity design issues.

[4]I have watched half a dozen classes immerse themselves in this problem and beg to continue when time ran out.

[5]From Resnick (1987).

[6]Describing key errors and using them in the rubric is a *very different* matter than building them into test answers as "distractors."

[7]A related issue that emerges in designing rubrics (and thus far unaddressed by measurement experts) is the difference between the degree of difficulty of the task and the desired quality of the performance — a distinction made in New York's music performance assessments.

[8]See Wiggins (1991).

[9]Yes, yes, I know the issue is *really* one of cheating. Let the teacher "sign off" on the papers, then, certify authorship, as they do in Australia and now in Vermont.

[10]Though many New York State tests do allow the student what amounts to unlimited time — all day — given the shortness of the test. And certifiably learning disabled students are allowed unlimited time on the SATs as well as many state achievement tests.

[11]See Stiggins (1991).

References and Readings

Bloom, B. S., ed. (1954). *Taxonomy of Educational Objectives: The Classification of Educational Goals; Handbook I: The Cognitive Domain.* New York: Longman Publishers.

Bloom, B. S., G. F. Madaus, and J. T. Hastings. (1981). *Evaluation to Improve Learning.* New York: McGraw-Hill. [A major revision of *Handbook on Formative and Summative Evaluation of Student Learning.* (1971). McGraw-Hill].

Linn, R. L., E. L. Baker, and S. B. Dunbar. (November 1991). "Complex, Performance-Based Assessment: Expectations and Validation Criteria." *Educational Researcher* 20, 8: 15-21.

Mitchell, R. (1992). *Testing for Learning: How New Approaches to Evaluation Can Improve American Schools.* New York: The Free Press.

National Council of Teachers of Mathematics. (Forthcoming). *Mathematics Assessment: Myths, Models, Good Questions, and Practical Suggestions.* Reston, Va.: NCTM.

Resnick, L. (1987). *Education and Learning to Think.* Washington, D.C.: National Academy Press.

Schwartz, J. L., and K. A. Viator, eds. (1990). "The Prices of Secrecy: The Social, Intellectual, and Psychological Costs of Testing in America." A Report to the Ford Foundation. Education Technology Center, Cambridge, Mass.: Harvard Graduate School of Education.

Stiggins, R. (March 1991). "Assessment Literacy." *Phi Delta Kappan* 72, 7: 534-539.

Victoria Ministry of Education. (1990). *Literacy Profiles: Handbook.* Victoria, Australia. [Distributed in the U. S. by TASA, Brewster, N.Y.]

Wiggins, G. (February 1991). "Standards, Not Standardization: Evoking Quality Student Work." *Educational Leadership* 48, 5:18-25.

Wiggins, G. (June 1990). "Finding Time." *Basic Education* 34, 10.

Wiggins, G. (May 1989). "A True Test: Toward More Authentic and Equitable Assessment." *Phi Delta Kappan* 70, 9: 703-713.

Wiggins, G. (April 1989). "Teaching to the (Authentic) Test." *Educational Leadership* 46, 7: 41-47.

Performance Assessment

The Realities That Will Influence the Rewards

Carol Anne Pierson
and Shirley S. Beck

Carol Anne Pierson is Associate Professor and Assistant Dean of Education, University of Central Arkansas, Conway. Shirley S. Beck is Assistant Professor, Department of Curriculum and Instruction, Southwest Texas State University, San Marcos.

As educators continually strive to improve evaluation methods, performance assessment has grown in popularity and use. Performance assessment is an authentic way to acquire accurate information about students' performance and comprehension (Perrone, 1991). Its appeal may be related to the growing need for local decision-making about student progress and instructional programs, as well to the interest in outcome-based education. Extensive debate about this type of assessment is carried on in education journals, professional meetings and education policy discussions. "Expert" perceptions of the "movement" range from skepticism to a belief that it is the solution to all of education's ills (Arter, 1991; Cizek, 1991).

At best, performance assessment could be the key to restructuring schools for higher standards and improved accountability. At the very least, it adds an expanded dimension to education assessment. At worst, performance assessment could become another promising idea tossed on the junk heap of discarded innovations if care is not taken to really understand its nature and limitations. As more schools move toward performance assessment for student evaluations, teachers and particularly administrators must become knowledgeable users.

Performance assessment is not a totally new idea. It is a common form of assessment in fields such as medicine and law. Industry uses performance assessment to make promotion decisions. Performance assessment was once the most common form of assessment in education, prior to the widespread use of standardized tests (Perrone, 1991). And it has been used regularly in such subjects as physical education, music and art.

> *At best, performance assessment could be the key to restructuring schools for higher standards and improved accountability.*

Language arts teachers, in particular, have embraced the concept of performance assessment, perhaps because they have been using performance testing to varying degrees for many years (i.e., to evaluate essays, speeches, book reports and various forms of oral reading). Their cry to legitimize teacher observations of students engaged in actual literacy tasks is being heard and supported by other teachers, administrators, governors and legislators. Performance assessment of reading and writing is becoming a reality in many classrooms across the United States.

As the "movement" generates increased enthusiasm and optimism, more and more administrators are seeking help to establish performance assessment procedures not only for reading and English programs, but also for other content areas, such as math and science. The authors, as assessment consultants, have discovered that enthusiasm for and acceptance of performance assessment often exceed knowledge about its nature and complexity. As they wrestle with the task of helping administrators develop environments and structures for moving toward performance assessment, the authors have identified three basic and critical questions that often go unanswered when schools rush to jump on the performance assessment bandwagon:

- What exactly is performance assessment?

- What advice is available from experts and the research?
- What issues and concerns must be addressed?

What Exactly Is Performance Assessment?

Few discussions of performance assessment clearly define the phrase. The authors found Berk's (1986) operational definition to be a fair and concise representation of current beliefs about performance assessment. He defines performance assessment as "the process of gathering data by systematic observation for making decisions about an individual" (p. ix). Stiggins and Bridgeford (1986) establish three criteria for a performance assessment. First, students must apply knowledge they have acquired. Second, students must complete a clearly specified task within the context of either a real or simulated exercise. Third, the task or completed product must be observed

Spontaneous assessment grows out of teachers' day-to-day intuitive observations and judgments . . .

and rated with respect to specified criteria in accordance with specified procedures, requiring students to actually demonstrate proficiency.

Stiggins and Bridgeford make a very important distinction between spontaneous and structured performance assessments. Spontaneous assessment grows out of teachers' day-to-day intuitive observations and judgments in the classroom. On the other hand, structured performance assessment must meet standards for reliability and validity and is systematically designed and planned for specific purposes. It uses clearly designed and specified scoring criteria and assesses very well-defined behaviors. Structured performance assessment is

the type most performance assessment experts want us to understand.

An example of the critical distinction between structured and unstructured assessments can be found in portfolio assessment. Many articles about portfolio assessment of writing, in particular, do not suggest rigorous criteria for the selection and analysis of portfolio entries. Gathering a collection of student products is certainly a legitimate task for a teacher or school. It must be understood, however, that an unstructured collection provides no data for analysis or comparison. If performance assessment is to become a viable alternative to conventional testing, it must be rigorous. Standards for selection and analysis must be a part of every performance assessment.

Cizek (1991) makes a distinction between indirect and direct measures of student assessment. He suggests that conventional paper-and-pencil tests are indirect measures of what students know about a topic, whereas performance tests are direct measures of students' ability to employ that knowledge during an actual task. Performance assessment goes beyond measuring what students *know* to measuring what students can *do* or *apply*.

What Advice Is Available from Experts and the Research?

Structured performance assessment has been used for decades in business, industry, fine arts and sports. The actual sales record, product, play and game are recognized as legitimate means of assessing knowledge and ability to perform. Managing, supervising, directing and coaching focus on end products or performances. Structured performance assessment is not new to academic subjects, but it has not always been considered as "legitimate" a form of assessment as so-called objective or norm-referenced tests. Performance assessment is more likely to develop into a long-lived innovation if we pay heed to the following five sug-

gestions offered by assessment experts and researchers.

- First, the use of performance assessment in other fields alerts us to the necessity of carefully and clearly describing and analyzing the tasks students will be expected to perform. Commenting on the business sector, Nathan and Cascio (1986) state, "A job analysis is necessary for showing the job-relatedness of all performance appraisal methods and is the basis for the performance standards fed back to employees" (p. 33). This same process must be applied to education. Analysis of the task that the student is to perform is a critical factor in making performance assessment a viable measurement. We cannot construct a list of criteria or a means of rating that criteria if we have not first determined what we expect students to produce.

- Second, all reliability, validity, administration and scoring standards relevant to conventional forms of assessment must also be applied to performance assessment (Brandt, 1992). Unless performance assessment is rigorous, its usefulness will be questioned. We must be wary of the misconception that any alternative assessment will automatically be a better assessment (Arter, 1991). Articles advocating portfolio assessment, for example,

Unless performance assessment is rigorous, its usefulness will be questioned.

often do not include detailed criteria for selecting and evaluating portfolio entries (Rief, 1990) and may lead practitioners to believe that evaluation can be accomplished simply by collecting and describing samples of student work.

■ Third, Grant Wiggins suggests that in order for structured performance assessment to be useful, models must be created and criteria and standards must be set (Brandt, 1992). Education does not have to invent this wheel. Established models in art, music, drama, speech and athletics may help educators develop new models appropriate for academic subjects. A significant step was taken in 1985 when a joint committee composed of representatives from American Educational Research Association, American Psychological Association and National Council on Measurement in Education established a set of standards for educational and psychological measurement that included performance assessment standards (AERA/APA/NCME Joint Committee, 1985). These standards are an excellent place for schools to begin their search for appropriate models. States such as Colorado have taken the lead in establishing

... evidence gathered from other professions . . . indicates performance assessment is much more transferable to real world tasks.

models that can be tested and revised to meet local needs (Gilbert, 1990).

■ Fourth, education professionals need to recognize and respond to factors that may impede further development and use of performance assessment. Developing strategies and structures for dealing with these factors may be as important as developing the new assessment instruments themselves. Speed and low cost were two attractive features of conventional tests.

Performance tests, however, are much more time-consuming to construct and administer (Maeroff, 1991). Developing, administering and scoring performance assessments are labor-intensive tasks, and the teachers who develop these new instruments will require released time. The cost of performance assessments will necessarily be weighed against their usefulness. Widespread support, as well as funding, will be the essentials that keep performance assessment from being discarded as a nonviable innovation.

■ Finally, we must be aware that the performance assessment movement in education is really still in its infancy and the body of definitive research is very small. Nor do we have clear research evidence to determine if students who do poorly on conventional tests will do appreciably better on performance tests. Furthermore, there is insufficient research evidence to establish a clear link between re-

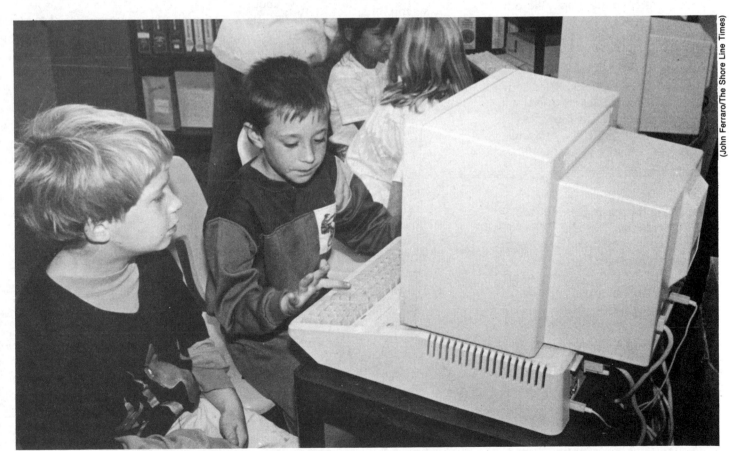

(John Ferraro/The Shore Line Times)

As a method for extending performance assessment, proper use of the computer in a learning situation provides another tool for tracking, in a very individualized way, the progress of a student.

sults of performance assessment and effective functioning in college or on the job. We can, however, use evidence gathered from other professions that indicates performance assessment is much more transferable to real world tasks. Educators must continue to share what they know about the state of performance assessment if this form of evaluation is to become increasingly useful.

What Issues and Concerns Must Be Addressed?

Issues and concerns specific to the unique applications of performance assessment in education must be addressed carefully and systematically. As more and more districts move toward performance assessment, more and more issues and concerns about the design and use of the new tests will be raised. The questions generated by the following issues do not yet have "right" answers, or even general agreement on possible answers. Performance assessment cannot move ahead, however, until education planners at least come up with answers that are appropriate to their local situations.

The authors have identified four major issues and related questions that are most frequently discussed in the literature and must be answered before performance assessment can be implemented.

ISSUE 1: Establishing Standards for Performance Testing

- Is the assigned task worthy of being assessed?
- Is the end product clearly defined through models of acceptable products?
- Are the criteria for administering and scoring the test precise and clear?
- Do the scoring rubrics, or guidelines and procedures, accurately represent the agreed-upon criteria?
- Who will decide on the criteria? Will parents and students be a part of these decisions?

- How will criteria and standards be conveyed to all stakeholders (teachers, administrators, students, parents, the political community, others)?

ISSUE 2: Assuring Precision of Performance Assessment Instruments

- Is a performance test the best way to assess the behavior under consideration?
- Are uniform operational definitions available for all terms used? For example, the term "composite portfolio" has several definitions in the literature and in practice. One definition must be agreed upon if this term is to be used in a local proposal.
- How carefully structured is the relationship between the performance assessment and other tests in use (predictive validity)? For example, if college admission is a concern for a school district, will its high school writing test predict success on SATs?
- How do the criteria to be judged match the rating items, the prompt and the end product (content validity for observable behavior, construct validity for abstract concepts)? For example, if the end product and the criteria of a speech test were focused on persuasive ability while the prompt required the student to give an informational speech, the content validity of the assessment would be questionable.
- Are the performance assessment tasks related to and transferable to real world tasks (ecological validity)? For example, reading assessment tasks that involve narrative text may not be related to technical types of reading demanded in the workplace (Quellmalz, 1986).
- Will all raters who administer the performance tests achieve a reasonable degree of concur-

rence or inter-rater reliability?
- Will multiple samples be assessed to achieve a more reliable view of performance?
- Will the performance instrument be systematically critiqued and revised as needed?

ISSUE 3: Using Performance Assessment Scores and Results

- How will performance assessment results be translated into grades for report cards, etc. (Jongsma, 1991)?
- How will performance assessment results be used to affect classroom decisions and instructional practices?
- Will performance assessment results be used to describe individual achievement, group performance or both?
- Will performance assessment results be used in concurrence with conventional test results?
- Will the performance assessment become the new high-stakes test?

ISSUE 4: Training Personnel To Use Performance Assessments

- Are personnel who will design, administer and interpret the performance instruments knowledgeable about assessment—are they assessment literate (Stiggins, 1991)?
- Who will train personnel to administer the assessments?
- How will quality training programs be guaranteed?
- Who will train students to interpret performance assessment feedback or participate in self-assessment?

Some Final Thoughts

As knowledge and understanding of learning continue to grow, the need for more flexible and diverse measurements will only increase. Performance assessment is a promising addition to the traditional tools. If this new tool is to fulfill its promise, performance assessment must be understood and used responsibly. Educators' professional judgments may finally achieve the legitimacy and worth they deserve, provided their assessment expertise grows as well. It is the authors' hope that educators will not leave the development of this new assessment tool solely to testing companies or so-called experts, but will strive to become experts themselves.

References

AERA/APA/NCME Joint Committee. (1985). *Standards for educational and psychological testing*. Washington, DC: American Psychological Association.

Arter, J. (1991). *Performance assessment: What's out there and how useful is it really?* Portland, OR: Northwest Regional Educational Lab. (ERIC Document Reproduction Service No. ED 333 051)

Berk, R. A. (Ed.). (1986). *Performance assessment*. Baltimore, MD: The Johns Hopkins University Press.

Brandt, R. (1992). On performance assessment: A conversation with Grant Wiggins. *Educational Leadership, 49*, 35-41.

Cizek, G. J. (1991). Innovation or enervation? Performance assessment in perspective. *Phi Delta Kappan, 72*, 695-699.

Gilbert, J. C. (1990). *Performance-based assessment resource guide*. Denver, CO: Colorado Department of Education. (ERIC Document Reproduction Service No. ED 327 304)

Jongsma, K. S. (1991). Rethinking grading practices. *The Reading Teacher, 45*, 318-320.

Maeroff, G. I. (1991). Assessing alternative assessment. *Phi Delta Kappan, 73*, 272-281.

Nathan, B. R., & Cascio, W. F. (1986). Technical and legal standards. In R. A. Berk (Ed.), *Performance assessment* (pp. 1-50). Baltimore, MD: The John Hopkins University Press.

Perrone, V. (Ed.). (1991). *Expanding student assessment*. Alexandria, VA: Association for Supervision and Curriculum Development.

Quellmalz, E. S. (1986). Writing skills assessment. In R. A. Berk (Ed.), *Performance assessment* (pp. 492-509). Baltimore, MD: The John Hopkins University Press.

Reif, L. (1990). Finding the value in evaluation: Self-assessment in a middle school classroom. *Educational Leadership, 47*, 24-29.

Stiggins, R. J. (1991). Assessment literacy. *Phi Delta Kappan, 72*, 534-539.

Stiggins, R. J., & Bridgeford, N. J. (1986). In R. A. Berk (Ed.), *Performance assessment* (pp. 469-492). Baltimore, MD: The Johns Hopkins University Press.

PLANNING FOR CLASSROOM
PORTFOLIO
ASSESSMENT

Diana V. Lambdin
and Vicki L. Walker

Diana Lambdin teaches at Indiana University in Bloomington, IN 47405-1006. Her special interests include problem solving, curriculum development, assessment and evaluation, and writing to learn mathematics. Vicki Walker teaches middle school mathematics at Louisville Collegiate School, Louisville, KY 40207. She is interested in alternative methods of assessment, particularly portfolio assessment.

Three years ago, the mathematics teachers from grades 4–12 in our school met for two weeks during the summer for an in-service program related to assessment and decided to begin using portfolios with our students in the fall. I was enthusiastic, although I had no idea at that time how drastically my approach to assessment—and to teaching in general—would change as a result of the portfolio decision.

In the three years since that assessment meeting, I've struggled with learning how to use portfolios for classroom assessment and discovered many tips toward planning for their use. Among the most important things that I've learned are (*a*) the importance of having a clear

This article, although written in the first person singular, is actually a collaborative effort of the two authors, who shared equally in its conceptualization and writing. The authors became acquainted in 1990 when Louisville Collegiate School requested that mathematics educators at Indiana University give them some advice about bringing their mathematics teaching more in line with the NCTM's curriculum and evaluation standards. Frank Lester suggested the use of portfolio assessment as a catalyst for change. He and Diana Lambdin consulted with the Collegiate teachers for several years as they worked through the process of establishing the use of portfolio assessment in all their mathematics classes, grades 4–12. In 1992, the state of Kentucky began mandating the use of portfolios in mathematics assessment. For a related article see "Implementing the K–4 Mathematics Standards in Kentucky" in the November 1993 issue.

idea of the reason for assigning students to compile portfolios; (*b*) the importance of establishing workable routines for managing the production, organization, and storage of the portfolios; and (*c*) the importance of giving students clear guidance about expectations for their portfolios.

> Portfolios are
> more than
> student folders.

Why Use Portfolios?

The mathematics teachers in my school established certain goals for our use of students' portfolios. First, we were looking for a better way to assess the whole

child than just relying on test scores. Second, and perhaps most important, we wanted to help students develop better self-assessment skills and become less reliant on the grades we assign to their work. Third, we wanted to establish a better means of communication among students, parents, and teachers about the kinds of mathematical learning taking place in our classrooms.

These were lofty goals. Although it seemed that portfolios could help us attain them, early on it was not clear exactly how. In retrospect, I realize that I really had very little idea at first what good portfolios should look like, much less how I intended to manage or evaluate them. I discussed the portfolio project with my students during the first weeks of school and sent home a letter informing their parents, but for quite a while, I was actually just feeling my way along. As the year went on, the students and I all raised questions about portfolios, shared thoughts, and communicated about mathematics (and about what we thought demonstrated mathematical learning), and gradually a clearer picture developed. **Table 1,** taken from guidelines distributed in 1992 by the Kentucky Department of Education as part of an Educational Reform Act mandating the use of portfolios in mathematics assessment, furnishes an overview of the philosophy of portfolio assessment that I have gradually come to espouse. Although the process of searching for meaning has been important to my own growth as a professional, I might have been able to grow more quickly and efficiently had I realized certain things. In this article, I share some of the insights I've gained about portfolio assessment. (Resources I've found especially useful are listed in the **Bibliography.**)

PLANNING

FOR INSTRUCTION

From *Arithmetic Teacher,* February 1994, pp. 318-324. © 1994 by the National Council of Teachers of Mathematics. Reprinted by permission.

TABLE 1

Mathematics-portfolio philosophy

A workable mathematics-portfolio philosophy—

- supports a method of evaluation that allows students to demonstrate their strengths rather than their weaknesses;
- values a variety of learning styles;
- values mathematics as a subject that requires careful and thoughtful investigation;
- promotes self-assessment and students' confidence in mathematics;
- encourages students to communicate their understandings of mathematics with a high level of proficiency;
- promotes a vision of mathematics that goes beyond correct answers; and
- emphasizes the role of the student as the active mathematician and the teacher as the guide.

(Adapted from Kentucky Department of Education [1992, 1–4])

Portfolios Are Not the Same as Folders

In the beginning, I tended to equate portfolios with student folders in my mind. I'd often kept folders containing examples of students' work and conference comments, and I initially thought that was more or less what the portfolios would be like. I now realize that a very important element was missing in that conception of the portfolio process—the element of self-evaluation. In the portfolio process that has evolved in my classroom, students are much more in control when putting together their portfolios than they ever were with my old folders. Developing a portfolio involves reflection, writing, and self-critiquing in an effort to present a composite picture of oneself. This approach makes a portfolio much different from simply being a collection of sample pieces of a student's work.

Deciding what kind of envelopes or folders to use as portfolios and where to store them seemed at first to be relatively minor details, but I later realized that such routine decisions can have important implications. The department had decided that students would keep a *working portfolio* (a manila file folder) and a *permanent portfolio* (a dark blue, card-stock accordion-style folder). Throughout the grading period, students placed those papers they were considering as possible portfolio entries in their working portfolio, which served as a sort of holding tank for their selections. At the end of each grading period, students reevaluated their work and made the final selections to transfer to their permanent portfolio. During the first year, all the portfolios were kept in storage boxes that tended to float around my classroom, depending on where space was available at any given moment. When it came time for a class period devoted to working on portfolios, the storage boxes were pulled out usually from underneath a mass of papers, books, and dust.

Portfolios can improve communication with students and parents.

Looking back, I can see that something was fundamentally wrong with my whole approach toward the management of the portfolios. The idea of having a working portfolio and a permanent portfolio was, and remains, an essential part of my portfolio procedures. Yet my early method of managing the working portfolios meant that portfolio selection was just one more thing to fit into all the many instructional activities I must orchestrate. In that first year, whenever the end of a grading period approached, I scrambled to squeeze in class time for portfolio work and processing. As the portfolios were dug out, I proclaimed to my classes that we all needed to value this process of compiling portfolios. Students were instructed to choose papers that would demonstrate their competencies and their insights. After the first grading period, when many portfolios appeared to be random selections of papers, I required students to attach a comment to each piece telling why they had chosen it for their portfolio. I pleaded that they reflect thoughtfully about their mathematical endeavors and hoped they would turn in masterpieces of mathematical revelation. Then I was extremely disappointed when many portfolios consisted primarily of computational work with comments such as "I chose this because it is neat" or "I chose this because I got all the right answers." Because I had talked about demonstrating good problem solving and displaying mathematical thinking and because I had set aside what I felt to be very valuable instructional time for students to select portfolio pieces and to write comments about them, I had naively assumed that my students would share my expectations about what constituted thoughtful reflection. That first year I sat at my desk facing a huge mound of blue folders, upset not only because most of my students' choices seemed to be off target and their reflections rather shallow but also because I had no earthly idea what I should do to evaluate the portfolios.

Tips for Getting Started with Portfolio Assessment

What seems obvious to me now is that by keeping portfolios in storage boxes and only pulling them out occasionally, I was inadvertently conveying a message to my students about the value of the portfolios that was quite contrary to my preachings. By stressing portfolio work only at the end of each grading period, I was defeating my own goal of having my students invest themselves in a process of self-reflection that would culminate in a product called a portfolio. I never imagined that I was instilling anything but positive ideas about maintaining portfolios in my students. Yet, little by little, I began to realize some important adjustments that needed to be made.

Portfolios need to be accessible

First of all, I rearranged things in my room, purchased some inexpensive shelves, and made a permanent home for the portfolios. At present the shelves are located in the front of my room, the area is clearly labeled "Portfolios," and student samples and selection guidelines are posted on the wall directly above the shelves. Since the portfolios are visible and accessible every day, they are tended to more consistently. They are now an integral part of my classroom and of its activities.

Students need guidance in labeling and choosing

Getting my students to label their portfolio selections clearly is a challenge. I expect not just names and page numbers but also dates, assignment titles, and descriptions that clarify what the work is all about. I did not ask for this information initially, and consequently, I did not get it. As I began to give students more specific guidelines about how to label their entries, I began to see marked improvements in their portfolio work. Moreover, I believe my students began to be much more aware of the range of activities in which we were involved and the reasons we were doing these different types of work.

Initially I gave students key phrases for the types of items I expected to go into their portfolios: for example, *favorite piece, best effort, most improved, awesome problem-solving work.* I supplied self-stick notes on which they were to indicate the reasons for their selections; the notes were to be attached to the corresponding pieces. Some students spent considerable time thinking about which pieces of their work might qualify for inclusion in their portfolio and why. Most students, however, just raced through their notebooks and their working portfolios grabbing things they thought might fit the bill. Those who just wanted to get finished fast tended to focus primarily on superficial aspects like neatness and correctness and on computational tasks, rather than reflecting on the thinking they had done in solving nonroutine problems.

The many changes I have made in my guidelines for portfolio selections and portfolio writings have convinced me that I will probably continue to make adjustments with each passing year, but I can share some ideas about what I do currently. I give my students written guidelines about the different types of work to include in their portfolios (see **tables 2** and **3**). I also supply a handout of "thinking questions" for them to work through before preparing the written reflections that I now require to accompany each entry (see **table 4**). (These written reflections have replaced the self-stick notes, which I decided were too small and informal for my purposes.) In general, my goal is to guide students through a process of reflecting, and then writing, about why they've chosen specific pieces—in particular, what they've learned from the activities or work that they select and what kind of connections they can make between this work and other school topics or other aspects of

---

TABLE 2

Mathematics-portfolio entries

A complete portfolio will include—

- a completed table of contents;
- a letter to the reviewer written by the student that describes the portfolio;
- five best entries reflective of the topics studied and the activities completed in the course.

Each entry must include the original question, task, or problem posed; a title; the date; and the student's name. Entries must be in the same order as listed in the Table of Contents and must be numbered accordingly. If an entry is in the category of photographs, audiotapes, videotapes, or computer disks, then the entry must be accompanied by a brief paragraph describing the activity and its rationale.

(Adapted from Kentucky Department of Education [1992, 1–4])

TABLE 3

Mathematics-portfolio entry types

Writing
This type of entry includes journal entries, mathematics autobiographies, explanations, reflections, justifications, and so on.

Investigations or Discovery
This type of entry can be described as an exploration that leads to understanding of mathematical ideas or to the formulation of mathematical generalizations. Examples include gathering data, examining models, constructing arguments, and performing simulations.

Application
This type of entry is to include the selection and use of concepts, principles, and procedures to solve problems in a well-grounded, real-world context.

Interdisciplinary
This type of entry demonstrates the use of mathematics within other disciplines.

Nonroutine Problems
This type of entry includes problems for which the solution or strategies are not immediately evident. This category may include mathematical recreations such as puzzles and logic problems.

Projects
This type of entry includes activities that extend over a period of days and requires a formal presentation of the material learned. This category may include research projects, designs, constructions, and original computer programs.

Note: A portfolio entry may fall into more than one of the foregoing types.

(Adapted from Kentucky Department of Education [1992, 1–4])

TABLE 4

Portfolio "thinking questions"

Please think through these questions carefully as you begin finalizing your portfolio selections and preparing your written summaries.

- What activity or mathematical topic was involved?
- How did the activity help you learn something new?
- What did you learn from this experience?
- Can you describe any connections between the activity and other subject areas or real-life situations?
- Would you do anything differently if you had more time?
- What strategies did you use? (What did you *think* as you worked through the task?)
- What mathematical skills were used in your solution process?
- How would you rate your overall performance related to the activity?
- What are your areas of strength in mathematics?
- What goals have you set for yourself in mathematics?

Students Need Guidance in Being Reflective

I never realized before I began using portfolios the importance of giving students opportunities to categorize, edit, critique, and analyze their own work and the work of other students, so that they can develop an intuitive sense of what constitutes quality. Projecting transparencies of students' work for whole-class discussion about mathematical content and quality of work has now become a common instructional activity in my class. My students seem to benefit considerably from these whole-class discussions. Similarly, I have learned a lot about which areas of my instruction have made sense to them and on which topics they have remained confused. As we have begun to spend more time analyzing and processing material in class, my students and I have both become more engaged in reflecting on the value of various activities. Even though I had included problem-solving activities, writing tasks, group work, and special project work in

their lives. (See **fig. 1** for an example of one student's work on an assignment involving estimation and her rationale for including that work in her portfolio.)

lio now has a definite beginning and end and a clearer vision-at-a-glance of what it contains and what message it is meant to convey. Furthermore, the table of contents allows for easier perusal on my part and has saved me a great deal of time during my evaluation process.

> At first I did not know how to evaluate portfolios.

A table of contents is essential

I now require students to have a table of contents for their portfolios, and I have seen remarkable improvement in their portfolios since doing so. Offering students help in preparing a table of contents is fairly easy, yet extremely critical. I generally display a sample table of contents on the overhead projector (see **fig. 2**) so that students can take notes on the format. Since I've required a table of contents, I get far fewer portfolios that are just piles of papers with fragmented thoughts attached. Students seem to be more thorough regarding the layout of their work and the overall appearance of their portfolio, perhaps because they have more of a sense of a completed project. Each portfo-

---

TABLE 5

Selected peer-evaluation portfolio reflections

Activity: Students engaged in partner conferences to discuss their portfolio selections, give advice to one another, and comment on stand-out selections

1. When I looked at the portfolio selections with Shawn, I noticed a lot of things I could have done better on. For instance, on my problem-solving section I did not do so good because it was the beginning of the year and I had not really gotten into school yet.

2. I worked with Jeff today. He helped me see many things about my papers but most of all he helped pick my best work. This is "How many books are in the library?" This work shows reasoning, estimation, observations, and many others things. This is why this work stands out so well. It shows what my work was. This was also challenging and exciting to me. Even though my estimation was 5600 and the actual was 19,000, I still think my reasoning and attitude towards this project was very good.

3. Today I worked with Andrew. He helped me see the things I was doing wrong. I had a codecracker which didn't show a lot but he helped me see how to make it work. He told me to add an explanation about it for it to fit. I think a standout piece is my million's project. It shows everything I need. It has the original problem plus it shows all my work. It has an explanation about the problem and what we did.

4. One piece of work I think I did super was the "Buckets of Trouble." Even though the explanation wasn't perfect, it showed what our group had done and had pictures to show strategies and the solution. This was a standout piece, and was a fun experiment too. Our group had to work with cups to visualize what we were doing and if it would work.

5. Today I conferenced with Jenny. She pointed out that some of my work needed explanation and helped me choose another piece of work that helps make my portfolio stand out. We chose the Library Book project. The piece was neat, colorful, and had a wonderful explanation!

FIGURE 1

Student work with portfolio reflection

Portfolio paragraph

Anne
5-25-93

I chose my "books in the library" project for an entry because it shows my work and has a clear explanation of the process I used. I enjoyed this project because we got to work our own way and find the answer alone. This project taught me to collect data, organize it, and to understand what I did enough to put it in words. Even though my answer wasn't very exact I feel that for the beginning of the year it is pretty good.

Anne
9/16/92

Books in the
Library

When I began the Library Books project I thought there might be 400 books. First of all I counted 3 shelves—1 full, 1 medium, and 1 with barely any. Next I averaged them. After that I counted the number of shelves upstairs and multiplied the average amount of books per shelf by the number of shelves. Then I went downstairs and counted the books on the spinners, counted the books in the Kiddie Library, and counted all the books on the downstairs shelves. The total amount of books in the library is ...

26,057

This is how I got my answer:

Upstairs : 51 per shelf
x 198 shelves
10,098 on the shelves
+ 97 countertop
10,195

Downstairs:
961 Kiddie Room
14,770 all shelves
9 atlases
+ 122 spinners
15,862

Downstairs 10,195
+ 15,862
26,057 total

Upstairs

my classes for years, I was surprised to discover that many of my students had never thought about the distinctions among these types of learning activities. A case in point is one student who chose only computational selections for his portfolio and justified his selections with the statement that he had spent a lot of time working the "problems." Time spent was what made them problem *solving* for him.

Whole-class discussions prompt reflection.

In addition to having the whole class share and discuss examples presented on the overhead projector, I frequently engage students in peer-evaluation activities. I pair students or have them work in small groups to make portfolio selections and record comments about their selections. This type of activity may involve having students respond to some important questions I've placed on the overhead projector or may occur at the end of a particular unit when I ask students to summarize the main ideas related to the unit. (See **table 5** for some examples of students' writing from a peer-evaluation activity.)

I involve students in peer-evaluation activities a couple of times a month. During such activities, I am able to circulate around the room, take note of valuable comments I hear, make informal assessments of students, and exchange thoughts with small groups or individuals about the type or quality of work they've completed. In this manner, my instructional style and my assessment procedures have become more unified, and portfolio selection is no longer a one-day activity at the end of each marking period. The primary goal of my peer-evaluation activities is that the students spend time thinking about, and sharing their ideas related to, mathematics. The additional benefits of such activities are that students become more aware of what they have studied and what they have learned, I gain valuable insights

I place on reflection and on written expression.

FIGURE 2

Sample portfolio table of contents

NAME_____

GRADE_____

DATE_____

TABLE OF CONTENTS

Title of Entry	Date Completed	Page
1. Will All Quadrilaterals Tessellate?	15 Nov. 1991	1
2. Buckets of Trouble	27 Oct. 1991	3
3. M&M Probability	16–18 Mar. 1992	5
4. Statistical Project on Immigration	2–12 Feb. 1992	8
5. My Sixth-Grade Mathematics Experience	19 Apr. 1992	10

---

about my instruction, and the entire portfolio-assessment process becomes an integral part of all that we do.

Portfolio Evaluation

Evaluating student portfolios is very time consuming. I have found it easier to handle if I evaluate one class of portfolios at a time rather than try to grade all classes at once. The letter grade that I assign to each portfolio is included as part of the overall grade for the marking period and is based on three things: the diversity of selections, written reflections about selections, and the organization of the portfolio. Note that I do not grade portfolios on the quality of the selections included (homework, group work, writing assignments, tests, etc.) because many of these have already been graded. Thus, it is possible for a student who gets below-average grades on the mathematics work to receive a better portfolio grade than a student with very high grades on her or his work if the former portfolio is more thoughtfully chosen and carefully documented than the latter.

I use a two-step procedure for portfolio assessment. First I read through all the portfolios and sort them into three piles: *excellent, satisfactory,* and *needs improvement.* Then I go back through each pile and assign a score to each portfolio by using a five-point scale (1–5) for each of my three categories (selection, reflection, and organization). Assigning these points is a difficult, fairly

subjective, process. But I try to set general guidelines ahead of time.

When assigning points for the selection category, I consider the diversity of the entries, the time periods represented (work should be represented from throughout the school year thus far), and the overall appropriateness of the selections. Points assigned for reflection are based on the students' written reflections about their choices. I consider clarity of thought, analysis of the problem or the mathematical concepts being displayed, use of complete sentences, legibility, and overall quality of the reflections. The category for organization involves the more technical aspects of the portfolio, such as whether it contains a table of contents, has all its pieces correctly ordered and labeled, and includes the required parental signature. I generally assign five points per category for those portfolios that show excellent work, three points for those that are satisfactory, and one point for those needing improvement. (Four points and two points are assigned, as needed, for work that seems to fall in between.) For example, a student might receive four points for diversity of selection, three points for written reflections, and five points for organization, for a total of twelve points (of fifteen possible) for the portfolio.

The final step of the evaluation process involves writing personal comments to each student about the strengths and weaknesses of his or her portfolio. Although this writing takes a great deal of my time, it greatly enhances my communication with my students and reinforces the value

Portfolios Facilitate Communication

Using portfolios has changed my communication with students and their parents in ways I had never considered before. For example, portfolios now serve as a powerful tool in parent-teacher or student-teacher conferences. As we examine together examples of such things as group work, problem solving, or written reflections, I can clarify my goals for such assignments, we can compare this type of work with more traditional textbook assignments, and students can ask questions or try to clarify thoughts that they might not have expressed well on paper. Valuable student-teacher communication also takes place through portfolio writings in which students are

> **Portfolios have to be accessible all the time.**

assigned to share their reactions to class activities or assignments and to reflect on their personal goals for mathematics learning. (**Fig. 3** presents an example of a student's reflection on his personal strengths and weaknesses in mathematics.)

Student-parent communication has also benefited from my use of portfolios, especially since I began requiring parental signatures on the portfolios and encouraging input from parents on students' selections. During my second year of using portfolios I began sending home a newsletter at the end of each grading period to summarize the major topics and ideas that had been covered in class. The newsletter not only has helped me review important ideas with my students as they prepare their portfolios but has facilitated student-parent communication about what has been stressed in class and why.

FIGURE 3

Student self-reflection

> On long complex problem solving I have a hard time comprending the info. I'm very good at organizing me thinking. I have a hard time going about the problem and deciding which mathematical method to use. Sometime I don't know how far to carry out the problem

> I enjoy finding patterns in a group of numbers. Sometimes it takes a long time I'm not very good at making predictions or estimations. I'm not a very logical thinker. I like to plot & draw graphs. And I like to analyze data + graphs.

> I have a hard time expressing my thoughts with #'s + problems. But I express my ideas well in pictures + graphs. That is why I put 10 in each box

> I guess you could say Integration connections is not on my good side. To me math is a by it's self. Now I never use math outside of school. even though I know that will change I also have a hard time relating #'s. #'s don't really have that much meaning to me.

Some Final Thoughts

Portfolio assessment has helped me and my students make progress toward a number of the goals recommended by the NCTM's *Curriculum and Evaluation Standards for School Mathematics* (1989).

My students are more thoughtful about what mathematics they are studying and why. They seem to be developing a better understanding of what is meant by problem solving and mathematical reasoning, less often resorting to the blind application of computational algorithms when confronted with problems. In making portfolio selections, my students are learning to look for connections among mathematics topics (and between mathematics and other aspects of their lives), and they are learning to take personal responsibility for self-assessment. In writing their portfolio reflections, they are improving their abilities to communicate about mathematical ideas and about their own personal strengths and weaknesses.

I must admit, quite honestly, that portfolio assessment is time-consuming and labor-intensive for teachers, especially those who have many students. But careful planning and establishment of routines can eliminate much wasted effort and will make the job easier to do. I have found the results well worth it. Since using portfolios with my classes, I have no doubt that my students are learning more mathematics, and that has always been my ultimate goal.

Bibliography

Kentucky Department of Education. *Kentucky Mathematics Portfolio: Teacher's Guide.* Frankfort, Ky.: The Department, 1992.

Mumme, Judith. *Portfolio Assessment in Mathematics.* Santa Barbara, Calif.: University of California, 1990. (A publication from the California Mathematics Project.)

National Council of Teachers of Mathematics. *Curriculum and Evaluation Standards for School Mathematics.* Reston, Va.: The Council, 1989.

Petit, Marge. *Getting Started: Vermont Mathematics Portfolio—Learning How to Show Your Best!* Cabot, Vt.: Cabot School, 1992.

Stenmark, Jean Kerr, ed. *Assessment Alternatives in Mathematics: An Overview of Assessment Techniques That Promote Learning.* Berkeley: University of California, 1989.

———. *Mathematics Assessment: Myths, Models, Good Questions, and Practical Suggestions.* Reston Va.: National Council of Teachers of Mathematics, 1991.

Vermont Portfolio Committee. *The Vermont Mathematics Portfolio: What It Is, How To Use It.* Montpelier, Vt.: Vermont Department of Education, 1991.

Putting the Standardized Test Debate in Perspective

When used correctly, standardized tests *do* have value, but they provide only part of the picture and have limits—which we must understand and work to improve.

BLAINE R. WORTHEN AND VICKI SPANDEL

Blaine R. Worthen is Professor and Chair, Research and Evaluation Methodology Program, Utah State University, Psychology Department, Logan, UT 84322. **Vicki Spandel** is Senior Research Associate, Evaluation and Assessment Program, Northwest Regional Educational Laboratory, 101 S.W. Main St., Portland, OR 97204.

Are the criticisms of educational testing valid, or do most of the objections stem from the fact that such tests are often misused? By far the most common type of standardized test is the norm-referenced test—that in which a student's performance is systematically compared with the performance of other (presumably) similar students. Minimum competency and criterion-referenced tests—those that measure student performance against established criteria—can also be standardized. However, not coincidentally, most criticism has been leveled at standardized, norm-referenced tests.

Criticisms of Standardized Tests

Among the current criticisms, a few stand out as most pervasive and most bothersome to those who worry over whether to support or oppose standardized testing. In this article, we'll look at seven of the most common criticisms.

Criticism #1: Standardized achievement tests do not promote student learning. Critics charge that standardized achievement tests provide little direct support for the "real stuff" of education, namely, what goes on in the classroom. They do nothing, critics contend, to enhance the learning process, diagnose learning problems, or provide students rapid feedback.

True, standardized tests do paint student performance in broad brush strokes. They provide general performance information in content areas like math or reading—as the test developers have defined these areas. They do not, nor are they *meant* to, pick up the nuances of performance that characterize the full range of a student's skill, ability, and learning style. Of course, we hope that standardized test results are only a small portion of the assessment information a teacher relies on in making academic decisions about students or curriculum. Good classroom assessment begins with a teacher's own observations and measurement of what students are gaining from instruction every day. Standardized testing can never replace that teacher-centered assessment. But it *can* supplement it with additional information that may help clarify a larger picture of student performance.

Criticism #2: Standardized achievement and aptitude tests are poor predictors of individual students' performance. While some tests may accurately predict future performances of *groups*, critics of testing argue that they are often inaccurate predictors of *individual* performance. Remember Einstein flunked 6th grade math, the critics point out eagerly. Clearly, no test can tell everything. If standardized tests were thousands of items long and took days to administer, they'd probably be better predictors than they are now. But remember—there are predictions and predictions. When a person passes a driver's test, we can't say she'll never speed or run a red light. Similarly, when a child scores well on a standardized reading test, that doesn't mean we can kick back and say, "Well, he's a terrific reader, all right. That's how it will always be." Ridiculous. Maybe he felt extra confident. Maybe the test just happened to touch on those things he knew well. But if we look at *all* the students with high scores and *all* those with low scores, we can safely predict more reading difficulties among students with low scores.

What all this means is that in a standardized test we have the best of one world—a measure that is relatively accurate, pretty good at what it does, but necessarily limited in scope.

Because there are so many drivers to be tested and only a finite amount of time, we cannot test each driver in every conceivable driving situation; and, similarly, we cannot measure all we might like to measure about a child's reading skills without creating a standardized test so cumbersome and complex no one would want to use it. The world of testing is, to a large extent, a world of compromise.

Criticism #3: The content of standardized achievement tests is often mismatched with the content emphasized in a school's curriculum and classrooms. Because standardized tests are intended for broad use, they make no pretense of fitting precisely and equally well the specific content being taught to 3rd graders in Salt Lake City's public schools and their counterparts at the Tickapoo School downstate. Instead, they attempt to sample what is typically taught to *most* 3rd graders in *most* school districts. The result is a test that reflects most curriculums a little, but reflects none precisely. For most users, there are big gaps—whole lessons and units and months of instruction skimmed over or left out altogether. Or the emphasis may seem wrong—too much attention to phonics, not enough on reading for meaning, perhaps. Again, the problem is the size of the test. We simply cannot cover in 10 or 20 test items the richness and diversity that characterize many current curriculums.

Criticism #4: Standardized tests dictate or restrict what is taught. Claims that standardized tests dominate school curriculums and result in "teaching to the test" are familiar and can be leveled at any type of standardized testing that has serious consequences for the schools in which it is used. On the surface it may seem inconsistent to claim that standardized tests are mismatched with what is taught in the schools and at the same time to complain that the tests "drive the curriculum." But those two allegations are not necessarily at odds. The first is grounded in a fear that in trying to represent everyone somewhat, standardized tests will wind up representing no one really well; the second arises from the consequent fear that everyone will try to emulate the ge-

neric curriculum suggested by the test content. This doesn't have to happen, of course.

Further, to the extent it does happen, it seems absurd to blame the test. The question we really need to be asking is "How are decisions about curriculum content being made?" There's often considerable fuzziness on that issue. Here's one sobering note:

Achievement test batteries are designed around what is thought to be the content of the school curriculum as determined by surveys of textbooks, teachers, and other tests. Textbooks and curriculums are designed, on the other hand, in part around the content of tests. One cannot discern which side leads and which follows; each side influences the other, yet nothing assures us that both are tied to an intelligent conceptualization of what an educated person ought to be.[1]

Criticism #5: Standardized achievement and aptitude tests categorize and label students in ways that cause damage to individuals. One of the most serious allegations against published tests is that their use harms students who are relentlessly trailed by low test scores. Call it categorizing, classifying, labeling (or mislabeling), or whatever, the result is the same, critics argue: individual children are subjected to demeaning and insulting placement into categories. The issue is really twofold: (1) tests are not infallible (students can and do change and can also be misclassified); and (2) even when tests *are* accurate, categorization of students into groups that carry a negative connotation may cause more harm than any gain that could possibly come from such classification.

Published tests, critics claim, have far too significant an effect on the life choices of young people. Some believe that achievement and intelligence tests are merely convenient and expedient means of classifying children and, in some cases, excluding them from regular education. But here again, it's important to raise the question of appropriate use. Even if we agree that it's okay to classify some children in some cases for some purposes, we must still ask whether standardized tests provide sufficient information to allow for intelligent decisions. We must also ask whether such tests provide any really useful information not already available from other sources.

Here's something to keep in mind, too. Some test results rank students along a percentile range. For instance, a student with a percentile ranking of 75 on a reading test may be said to have performed better than 75 percent of the other students who took the same test. But a difference in performance on even *one test item* could significantly raise or lower that percentile ranking. Knowing this, should we classify students on the basis of standardized tests? That probably depends on the consequences, on whether the information is appropriate and sufficient for the decision at hand, and on whether there is any corroborating evidence. Suppose we identify talented and gifted students on the basis of standardized math and reading tests. We ought, then, to at least be able to show that high performance on those tests is correlated directly with high probability of success in the talented and gifted program.

Criticism #6: Standardized achievement and aptitude measures are racially, culturally, and socially biased. Perhaps the most serious indictment aimed at both norm-referenced and minimum competency tests is that they are biased against ethnic and cultural minority children. Most published tests, critics claim, favor economically and socially advantaged children over their counterparts from lower socioeconomic families. Minority group members note that many tests have disproportionately negative impact on their chances for equal opportunities in education and employment. We must acknowledge that even well-intentioned uses of tests can disadvantage those unfamiliar with the concepts and language of the majority culture producing the tests. The predictable result is cultural and social bias—failure of the test to reflect or take into account the full range of the student's cultural and social background.

A conviction that testing is biased against minorities has led some critics to call for a moratorium on testing and has also prompted most of the legal challenges issued against minimum competency tests or the use of norm-referenced standardized tests to classify students. It is tempting, in the face of abuses, to outlaw testing. But simplistic solutions rarely work well. A more conservative, and far more challenging, solution is to improve our tests, to build in the sensitivity to cultural differences that would make them fair for all—and to interpret results with an honest awareness of any bias not yet weeded out.

Making such an effort is crucial, if one stops to consider one sobering thought. Assume for the moment that there *is* a bit of cultural bias in college entrance tests. Do away with them, right? Not unless you want to see college admission decisions revert to the still more biased "Good Old Boy" who-knows-whom type of system that excluded minorities effectively for decades before admissions tests, though admittedly imperfect, provided a less biased alternative.

Criticism #7: Standardized achievement and aptitude tests measure only limited and superficial student knowledge and behaviors. While test critics and supporters agree that tests only sample whatever is being tested, critics go on to argue that even what is measured may be trivial or irrelevant. No test items really ask "Who was buried in Grant's Tomb?" but some are nearly that bad.

They don't have to be. The notion that multiple choice tests can tap only recall is a myth. In fact, the best multiple choice items can—and do—measure students' ability to analyze, synthesize information, make comparisons, draw inferences, and evaluate ideas, products, or performances. In many cases, tests are improving, thanks in large part to critics who never give up.

Better Than the Alternatives
No test is perfect, and taken as a whole, educational and psychological measurement is still (and may always be) an imperfect science. Proponents of standardized tests may point to psychometric theory, statistical evidence, the merits of standardization, the predictive validity of many specific tests, and objective scoring procedures as arguments that tests are the most fair and bias-free of any procedures for assessing learning and other mental abilities. But no well-grounded psychometrician will claim that tests are flawless, only that they are enormously useful.

What do they offer us that we couldn't get without them? Comparability, for one thing. Comparability in the context of the "big picture," that is. It isn't very useful, usually, for one

teacher to compare his or her students' performance with that of the students one room down and then to make decisions about instruction based on that comparison. It's too limited. We have to back away to get perspective. This is what standardized test results enable us to do—to back off a bit and get the big, overall view on how we can answer global questions: In *general*, are 3rd graders learning basic math? Can 6th graders read at the predefined level of competency?

Thus, such tests will be useful to us if we use them as they were intended and do not ask them to do things they were never meant to do, such as giving us a microscopic view of an individual student's range of skills.

Appropriate Use Is the Key
On their own, tests are incapable of harming students. It is the way in which their results can be misused that is potentially harmful. Critics of testing often overlook this important distinction, preferring to target the instruments themselves, as if they were the real culprits. That is rather like blaming the hemlock for Socrates' fate. It is palpable nonsense to blame all testing problems on tests, no matter how poorly constructed, while absolving users of all responsibility—not that bad tests should be condoned, of course. But even the best tests can create problems if they're misused. Here are some important pitfalls to avoid.

1. *Using the wrong tests.* Schools often devise new goals and curriculum plans only to find their success being judged by tests that are not relevant to those goals or plans yet are imposed by those at higher administrative levels. Even if district or state level administrators, for example, have sound reasons for using such tests at *their* level, that does not excuse any school for allowing such tests to be the *only* measures of their programs. Teachers and local administrators should exert all the influence they can to see that any measures used are appropriate to the task at hand. They can either (1) persuade higher administrators to select new standardized achievement or minimum competency measures that better match the local curriculum or (2) supplement those tests with measures selected or constructed specifically to measure what the school is attempting to accomplish.

Subtle but absurd mismatches of purpose and test abound in education. Consider, for instance, use of statewide minimum competency tests to make interschool comparisons, without regard for differences in student ability. Misuse of tests would be largely eliminated if every test were carefully linked with the decision at hand. And if no decision is in the offing, one should question why *any* testing is proposed.

2. *Assuming test scores are infallible.* Every test score contains possible error; a student's *observed* score is rarely identical to that student's *true* score (the score he or she would have obtained had there been no distractions during testing, no fatigue or illness, no "lucky guesses," and no other factors that either helped or hindered that score). Measurement experts can calculate the probability that an individual's *true* score will fall within a certain number of score points of the *obtained* score. Yet many educators ignore measurement error and use test scores as if they were highly precise measures.

3. *Using a single test score to make an important decision.* Given the possibility of error that exists for every test score, how wise is it to allow crucial decisions for individuals (or programs) to hinge on the single administration of a test? A single test score is too suspect—in the absence of supporting evidence of some type—to serve as the sole criterion for *any* crucial decision.

4. *Failing to supplement test scores with other information.* Doesn't the teacher's knowledge of the student's ability count for anything? It should. Though our individual perceptions as teachers and administrators may be subjective, they are not irrelevant. Private observations and practical awareness of students' abilities can and should supplement more objective test scores.

5. *Setting arbitrary minimums for performance on tests.* When minimum test scores are established as critical hurdles for selection and admissions, as dividing lines for placing students, or as the determining factor in awarding certificates, several issues become acute. Test validity, always important, becomes crucial; and the minimum standard itself must be carefully scrutinized. Is there any empirical evidence that the minimum standard is

set correctly, that those who score higher than the cutoff can be predicted to do better in subsequent academic or career pursuits? Or has the standard been set through some arbitrary or capricious process? Using arbitrary minimum scores to make critical decisions is potentially one of the most damaging misuses of educational tests.

6. *Assuming tests measure all the content, skills, or behaviors of interest.* Every test is limited in what it covers. Seldom is it feasible to test more than a sample of the relevant content, skills, or traits the test is designed to assess. Sometimes students do well on a test just because they happen to have read the *particular* chapters or studied the *particular* content sampled by that test. Given another test, with a different sampling of content from the same book, the students might fare less well.

7. *Accepting uncritically all claims made by test authors and publishers.* Most test authors or publishers are enthusiastic about their products, and excessive zeal can lead to risky and misleading promises. A so-called "creativity test" may really measure only verbal fluency. A math "achievement" test administered in English to a group of Inuit Eskimo children (for whom English is a second language) may test understanding of English much more than understanding of math.

8. *Interpreting test scores inappropriately.* The test score *per se* tells us nothing about *why* an individual obtained that score. We watched the SAT scores fall year after year, but there was nothing in the scores themselves to tell us *why* that trend was downward. There turned out, in fact, to be nearly as many interpretations of the trend as there were interpreters.

A student's test *score* is not a qualitative evaluation of performance, but rather, a mere numeric indicator that lacks meaning in the absence of some criteria defining what constitutes "good" or "bad" performance.

9. *Using test scores to draw inappropriate comparisons.* Unprofessional or careless comparisons of achievement test results can foster unhealthy competition among classmates, siblings, or even schools because of ready-made bases for comparisons, such as grade-level achievement. Such misuses of tests not only potentially harm both the schools and the children involved, but also create an understandable backlash toward the tests, which should have been directed toward those who misused them in this way.

10. *Allowing tests to drive the curriculum.* Remember that *some* individual or group has selected those tests, for whatever reason. If a test unduly influences what goes on in a school's curriculum, then someone has allowed it to override priorities that educators, parents, and the school board have established.

11. *Using poor tests.* Why go to the effort of testing, then employ a poorly constructed or unreliable measure—especially if a better one is at hand? Tests can be flawed in a multitude of ways, from measuring the wrong content or skills (but doing it well) to measuring the correct content or skills (but doing it poorly). Every effort should be made to obtain or construct the best possible measures.

12. *Using tests unprofessionally.* When educational tests are used in misleading or harmful ways, inadequate training of educators is often at fault. When test scores are used to label children in harmful ways, the fault generally lies with those who affix the labels—not with the test. When scores are not kept confidential, that is the fault of the person who violated the confidence, not the test maker. In short, as educators, we have a serious ethical obligation to use tests *well*, if we use them at all.

In Search of a Balanced View

Not all criticisms of tests can be deflected by claiming that they merely reflect misuses of tests. There are also apparent weaknesses in many tests, partly because we have yet a good deal to learn about measurement. We know enough already, however, to state unequivocally that uncertainty and error will always be with us, and no test of learning or mental ability or other characteristics can ever be presumed absolutely precise in its measurements. The professional judgments of teachers and other educators will continue to be essential in sound educational decision making. But we also assert—as do test advocates—that tests are often a great deal better than the alternatives. Thus, we find ourselves caught in the middle of the debate between testing critics and enthusiasts.

The stridency of that debate occasionally calls to mind the old rhyme, "When in danger or in doubt, run in circles, scream, and shout!" In more recent years, however, there has been some softening on both sides. Measurement experts spend less time defending tests and deriding their detractors and more time working to improve the science of measurement. At the same time, they have become more comfortable in acknowledging that test scores are approximations and less obsessed with claiming unflinching scientific support for every test they devise.

Meanwhile, critics seem less intent on diagnosing psychometric pimples as terminal acne. They seem more aware that many testing problems stem from misuse, and their calls for "testing reform" have quieted somewhat as they have recognized that even the best tests, if subjected to the same sorts of misuse, would prove no more helpful. Further, most critics are beginning to acknowledge that abolishing testing would leave us with many decisions still to make—and even less defensible bases on which to make them.

But even if there are no quick-fix answers to the testing dilemma, there are things we can do. We can: (1) scrupulously avoid any misuses of tests or test results; (2) educate ourselves and our colleagues about tests so that we understand their capabilities and limitations and do not ask them to tell us more than they can; (3) stretch to the limit our creative talents in test design, teaching ourselves to develop test items that not only resound with our own thoughtful understanding of critical content but that encourage students to think; and (4) recall, even when pressed for hasty or expedient decisions, that no matter how much any test may tell us, there is always so much more to be known.

---

[1]G. V. Glass, (1986), "Testing Old, Testing New: Schoolboy Psychology and the Allocation of Intellectual Resources," in *The Future of Testing*, Buros-Nebraska Symposium on Measurement and Testing, Vol. 2, p. 14, edited by B. S. Plake, J. C. Witt, and J. V. Mitchell, (Hillsdale, N.J.: Lawrence Erlbaum Associates).

Credits/Acknowledgments

Cover design by Charles Vitelli

1. Perspectives on Teaching
Facing overview—United Nations photo by John Isaac.

2. Development
Facing overview—Photo by Cheryl Greenleaf.

3. Exceptional and Culturally Diverse Children
Facing overview—Digital Stock photo.

4. Learning and Instruction
Facing overview—Dushkin Publishing Group/Brown & Benchmark Publishers photo.

5. Motivation and Classroom Management
Facing overview—Photo by Pamela Carley.

6. Assessment
Facing overview—Photo by Steve Takatsuno.

PHOTOCOPY THIS PAGE!!!*

ANNUAL EDITIONS ARTICLE REVIEW FORM

■ NAME: _____ DATE: _____

■ TITLE AND NUMBER OF ARTICLE: _____

■ BRIEFLY STATE THE MAIN IDEA OF THIS ARTICLE: _____

_____

■ LIST THREE IMPORTANT FACTS THAT THE AUTHOR USES TO SUPPORT THE MAIN IDEA:

_____

_____

_____

_____

_____

_____

■ WHAT INFORMATION OR IDEAS DISCUSSED IN THIS ARTICLE ARE ALSO DISCUSSED IN YOUR TEXTBOOK OR OTHER READING YOU HAVE DONE? LIST THE TEXTBOOK CHAPTERS AND PAGE NUMBERS:

_____

_____

_____

_____

_____

_____

_____

■ LIST ANY EXAMPLES OF BIAS OR FAULTY REASONING THAT YOU FOUND IN THE ARTICLE:

_____

_____

_____

_____

_____

■ LIST ANY NEW TERMS/CONCEPTS THAT WERE DISCUSSED IN THE ARTICLE AND WRITE A SHORT DEFINITION:

_____

_____

_____

_____

_____

_____

*Your instructor may require you to use this Annual Editions Article Review Form in any number of ways: for articles that are assigned, for extra credit, as a tool to assist in developing assigned papers, or simply for your own reference. Even if it is not required, we encourage you to photocopy and use this page; you'll find that reflecting on the articles will greatly enhance the information from your text.

ANNUAL EDITIONS: EDUCATIONAL PSYCHOLOGY 96/97
Article Rating Form

We Want Your Advice

Here is an opportunity for you to have direct input into the next revision of this volume. We would like you to rate each of the 40 articles listed below, using the following scale:

1. **Excellent: should definitely be retained**
2. **Above average: should probably be retained**
3. **Below average: should probably be deleted**
4. **Poor: should definitely be deleted**

Your ratings will play a vital part in the next revision. So please mail this prepaid form to us just as soon as you complete it.
Thanks for your help!

Annual Editions revisions depend on two major opinion sources: one is our Advisory Board, listed in the front of this volume, which works with us in scanning the thousands of articles published in the public press each year; the other is you—the person actually using the book. Please help us and the users of the next edition by completing the prepaid article rating form on this page and returning it to us. Thank you.

Rating	Article	Rating	Article
	1. A Piece of Cake		22. The Tyranny of Self-Oriented Self-Esteem
	2. The Six National Goals: A Road to Disappointment		23. Beyond the Pendulum: Creating Challenging and Caring Schools
	3. Using Action Research to Assess Instruction		24. About Instruction: Powerful New Strategies Worth Knowing
	4. Learning through "Play" as Well as "Work" in the Primary Grades		25. Problem Based Learning: An Instructional Model and Its Constructivist Framework
	5. Helping Children Develop Self-Control		26. Allowing for Thinking Styles
	6. Young Children's Understanding of Everyday Emotions		27. How K–12 Teachers Are Using Computer Networks
	7. Encouraging Positive Social Development in Young Children		28. Choices for Children: Why and How to Let Students Decide
	8. Caring for Others and Being Cared For: Students Talk Caring in School		29. Motivating Underachievers: Make Them *Want* to Try
	9. At-Risk Students and Resiliency: Factors Contributing to Academic Success		30. Using Motivational Theory with At-Risk Children
	10. When Your Child Is Special		31. From Negation to Negotiation: Moving Away from the Management Metaphor
	11. Courtside: W(h)ither Full Inclusion?		32. Images of Management for Learner-Centered Classrooms
	12. Ability Grouping: Geared for the Gifted		33. Why Violence Prevention Programs Don't Work—and What Does
	13. Meeting the Needs of Your High-Ability Students		34. Corporal Punishment: What Teachers Should Know
	14. What We Can Learn from Multicultural Education Research		35. The Challenges of Assessing Young Children Appropriately
	15. "All Kids Can Learn": Masking Diversity in Middle School		36. Making the Grade: What Benefits Students?
	16. Student Diversity: Implications for Classroom Teachers		37. Creating Tests Worth Taking
	17. Remembering the Forgotten Art of Memory		38. Performance Assessment: The Realities That Will Influence the Rewards
	18. The Mind's Journey from Novice to Expert		39. Planning for Classroom Portfolio Assessment
	19. The Rewards of Learning		40. Putting the Standardized Test Debate in Perspective
	20. Rewards versus Learning: A Response to Paul Chance		
	21. Sticking Up for Rewards		

(Continued on next page)

ABOUT YOU

Name _____ Date _____
Are you a teacher? ❑ Or student? ❑
Your School Name _____
Department _____
Address _____
City _____ State _____ Zip _____
School Telephone # _____

YOUR COMMENTS ARE IMPORTANT TO US!

Please fill in the following information:

For which course did you use this book? _____
Did you use a text with this Annual Edition? ❑ yes ❑ no
The title of the text? _____
What are your general reactions to the Annual Editions concept?

Have you read any particular articles recently that you think should be included in the next edition?

Are there any articles you feel should be replaced in the next edition? Why?

Are there other areas that you feel would utilize an Annual Edition?

May we contact you for editorial input?

May we quote you from above?

ANNUAL EDITIONS: EDUCATIONAL PSYCHOLOGY 96/97

BUSINESS REPLY MAIL

First Class   Permit No. 84   Guilford, CT

Postage will be paid by addressee

**Dushkin Publishing Group/
Brown & Benchmark Publishers**
Sluice Dock
Guilford, Connecticut 06437